PUBLIC SCHOOL FINANCE

KERN ALEXANDER

Murray State University

RICHARD G. SALMON

Virginia Tech

ALLYN AND BACON

Boston   London   Toronto   Sydney   Tokyo   Singapore

Series Editor: Ray Short
Editorial Assistant: Christine M. Shaw
Marketing Manager: Ellen Mann
Production Administrator: Annette Joseph
Production Coordinator: Holly Crawford
Editorial-Production Service: Connie Leavitt, Camden Type 'n Graphics
Composition Buyer: Linda Cox
Manufacturing Buyer: Megan Cochran
Cover Administrator: Suzanne Harbison
Cover Designer: Jennifer Burns

Portions of this material appeared as *The Economics and Financing of Education*, by Roe L. Johns, Edgar L. Morphet, and Kern Alexander. © 1983, 1975, 1969, 1960 by Allyn and Bacon.

This book is printed on
recycled, acid-free paper.

Library of Congress Cataloging-in-Publication Data

Alexander, Kern
    Public school finance / Kern Alexander, Richard G. Salmon.
        p.   cm.
    Includes bibliographical references and index.
    ISBN 0–205–16631–8
    1. Education—United States—Finance.   I. Salmon, Richard G.
    II. Title.
    LB2825.A63   1995
    379.1'1'0973—dc20   94–35294
                                                                   CIP

Printed in the United States of America

10   9   8   7   6   5   4   3   2   00   99   98   97

CONTENTS

**CHAPTER 9   STRUCTURE OF STATE SYSTEMS OF
                 SCHOOL FINANCE   191**

CHAPTER 11   THE POLITICS OF SCHOOL FINANCE   246

**CHAPTER 12   THE FEDERAL ROLE IN
FINANCING EDUCATION   272**

PREFACE

The English social philosopher R. H. Tawney once said that "an institution which possesses no philosophy of its own inevitably accepts that which happens to be fashionable."[1] The institution about which this book is written is the public common school system of the United States. The study of the financing of public schools should not merely reflect the floating whim of current popular opinion, but rather it should be couched in principles that justify the expenditure of public resources for education. While this book is by no stretch of the imagination a deep philosophical treatment of public institutions, it does present certain rationales, both implicitly and explicitly, that support the creation and maintenance of the public common school as an essential organ of American society. Undergirding virtually every paragraph is the conviction that the institution of public schools is undoubtedly the unique, most highly desirable, and effective vehicle for the well-being and progress of society. As Galbraith notes, it is only by universal public education that individuals can slip from the bonds of poverty and "access the world outside."[2]

In the study of public school finance it is not sufficient to teach only formulas, indexes and ratios, tax collections and distributions without reference to the basis of the public school as a social institution. Numbers and formulas alone cannot convey what is good or bad, right or wrong, moral or immoral, equitable or inequitable. A correlational analysis or a Gini coefficient standing alone is of little worth. In a public school finance course the student should learn the considerations that underpin the deployment of societal resources for public schools as well as become well versed in the technical aspects of public finance. The student of school finance should know the consequences of finance decisions and be able to understand the far-reaching implications for advancement of learning. The ideal of the public common school itself is based on a set of values emanating from the era of the Enlightenment. To know and to understand these are prerequisites to evaluating public finance distributions.

It should not escape us that the primary basis for public schools is to advance the democratic form of government; we are not simply paying for the teaching and testing of substantive knowledge in the abstract, unrelated to ideals of our social existence. We should know that public schools were in fact created not merely to convey value-free knowledge geared to the pursuit of jobs and constancy of employment, but were founded in great part for the inculcation of the desire for and understanding of the principles of a virtuous government.

We educate our children with the goal of creating citizens who will value democracy, because that particular form of government is best able to assure that the affairs of state will be conducted in the most virtuous manner possible. If more virtue could be assured with any other type of government, then the democratic form should give way. A better alternative form, however, has not yet been discovered. Montesquieu early observed that all forms of government require education, that monarchies require education to instill deference and politeness, that despotisms require education to teach excessive obedience, and that the republican form of government requires education to instill a desire for freedom and equality, a preference for public over private interests, and an appreciation of the expansion of knowledge.[3] Montesquieu therein captures the essential nature of the republic and the key ingredients of the public common school system: liberty, equality, and community purpose buttressed by the limitless expansion of knowledge.

Today, throughout the world in sites too numerous to mention we see the bitter fruit of educational systems that have failed to instill the importance of virtue in government: conflicts of extreme nationalism, ethnic strife, and racial and religious intolerance. We can clearly see in most of these strife-torn areas the triumph of self-interest over selflessness and commonality. The schools and our finance systems must address the component content of virtue in government, and we should be made cognizant of any movement in our political decision-making process that would take us away from the basic virtues of liberty and equality. Modern democracy is founded on these twin principles.[4] Each is dependent upon the other,[5] not mutually exclusive, and when one is eroded the other is sure to follow.

Few could rationally contend that the children of American core cities, of Appalachia, and of the rural South have the same liberties and opportunities afforded to children in affluent suburban school districts. Some have even concluded that the public schools, rather than expanding equality of opportunity and fostering commonality, do in fact tend to reinforce inequality and self-interest in derogation of the common good. While this is surely an overstatement, the original intent of public schools as the primary engine of society to smooth out class differences and to provide for equality of opportunity has in some instances been severely compromised by the forces of factionalism that would use public resources to advance self-interest and particularism.

We can observe today the forces of particularism and intolerance that are endemic to any society, more severe at certain times than at others, that appear bent on destroying the public school ideal under the banners of pluralism and private school choice. Pluralism is, of course, essential to a free society. The right to remain distinctive and different in ethnic origin, religion, culture, or the like, in a nation or society is highly desirable and, indeed, essential to a free people. Yet one can easily confuse the virtue of individual liberty with the inequity of group pluralism to the detriment of the community interest and commonality of purpose of a democratic state. Many of today's arguments for pluralism are masked attempts to preserve some economic or social advantage or to use public funds to advance a special sectarian interest. John Dunn in his memorable work *Western Political Theory in the Face of the Future* observed, "Most recent pluralist political theory rests fairly banally at the level of vulgar politics and offers no intellectually coherent conception of human value at all."[6] Clearly, special interest groups in the United States appeal to pluralism in order to preserve educational privilege in enclaves of wealth in suburbs, or to cloak fundamentalist Protestant and Catholic quests for the use of public funds for religious purposes. These are examples of intolerance masquerading as virtue.

As with pluralism, choice is invoked as a moral justification to support vouchers as a method of distributing public funds to support private schools. Individualism, liberty, and choice are principles without which no virtuous government can be maintained. We should always be mindful of a Rousseau aphorism wherein he drew the vital connections among liberty, virtue, and citizen modeling through education. He said, "There can be no patriotism without liberty, no liberty without virtue, no virtue without citizens: create citizens (by means of education), and you have everything you need."[7] Yet the right to be individual and distinctive must have some boundaries. To exercise individualism may move a long way toward disregarding the interests of others or destroying community interests that are beneficial to all. Being individualistic, exercising various liberties, and asserting the right of choice must be subject to some definition. Choice exercised in self-interest can easily veer toward a negative and immoral end. Choice as a manifestation of liberty holds the imprimatur of morality and cannot be directly contradicted. Choice then becomes a safe haven for those who desire to practice the politics of exclusion by capturing public resources and turning them to their direct advantage. Reinhold Niebuhr effectively identified the real purposes of the choice and voucher movement when he pointed out, "The moral attitudes of privileged groups are characterized by universal self-deception and hypocrisy."[8] They seek to clothe inequality and sectarian interests in the respectable coat of morality. Those who try to capture public funds for their own special and exclusive purposes invent "specious proofs for the theory that universal values spring from,"[9] and they maintain and attempt to convince others that the general interests of society are best served by affording such special privileges. Those special privileges may be for economic advantage, educational hegemony, or for racial, religious, ethnic, or cultural separatism. The public common school stands as a bulwark against such incursions and is therefore subject to attack by those groups that seek special privilege at public expense.

Allowing special interests to capture public resources for their own private purposes works to erode the liberties of the majority who are relegated to a position of relative disadvantage by the reduction in the residual resources available for public common interests. There is therefore good logic to support those who contend that if public funds are siphoned off by the private schools, the remaining public school children will be denied not only equal opportunity but also those liberties that are dependent on such opportunities. Thus the cant about pluralism and choice serves most efficiently as a cover for the conversion of public school resources to private advantage, clearly inhibiting liberty rather than enhancing it. An understanding of public school finance presupposes an ability to detect the true purposes and intentions for diversions of the public's financial resources.

Much is said in this book about equality because the authors believe that equality is the cornerstone of virtuous government. Equality is desirable not only because it is moral and just but also because inequality is economically inefficient. Equality fuels economic growth.[10] Fukuyama has pointed out that the mixture of liberal trade policies coupled with decreased income inequality has catapulted the Taiwanese, South Korean, and Japanese economies into competitive world economic status in a relatively short time. There is no conflict between equality and efficiency. The most efficient economic systems are those that are supported by wide-ranging equality of opportunity. Equality of education is economically efficient because it systematically develops intellectual capacities throughout society and the wastage attributable to underdeveloped human capabilities is kept to a minimum. Even the most conservative philosophers of political economy acknowledge the importance of educational opportunity as a public enterprise to undergird economic growth.[11] John Stuart Mill, the archetypal champion of private values, singled out education as one of the few exceptions that should be publicly governed to assure that imperfections in private demand and lack of aspiration would not be permitted to stifle individual intellectual development and thereby reduce economic capability of the nation as a whole. According to Mill, equality of educational opportunity is essential to a utilitarian government because without it members of the community would "suffer seriously from the consequences of ignorance and want of education in their fellow-citizens."[12]

It is a false antithesis that postulates that equality is injurious to efficiency or that equality is detrimental to quality of social utility. In fact current thinking regarding economic development strongly supports the theory that greater income equality is compatible with economic growth and that heavy emphasis on universal education results in higher growth and lower inequality.[13] If equality is both economically productive and utilitarian, it can hardly be rationally maintained that equality is subversive to quality or that U.S. schools cannot be both equal and excellent. Thus, decisions with regard to school financing that deprive some of equal opportunity in the name of quality education for a few are sustained on assumptions that are erroneous and socially and economically injurious. The discussions throughout this book implicitly assume that equality and quality education are complementary and mutually supportive.

This book then pays attention to these foundational issues supporting public schools and expresses evaluative opinions in keeping with the principles enunciated herein.

Regardless of the technical discussions undertaken in this book, the underlying values of public common school ideals will emerge as evaluative criteria. Whether taxpayers are treated equitably, whether tax burdens are properly apportioned, whether equal distributions are achieved, whether the finance system supports the common good and deters privilege and separatism, and whether the educational needs of all children are addressed equally are all relevant to our determinations of how public funds should be distributed.

ENDNOTES

1. R. H. Tawney, *Religion and the Rise of Capitalism*, first published in 1922 (London: Penguin Books, 1990), p. 192.

2. John Kenneth Galbraith, *The Nature of Mass Poverty* (London: Penguin Books, 1979), p. 84.

3. Montesquieu, *The Spirit of Laws, 1748*, ed. David Wallace Carrithers (Berkeley: University of California Press, 1977), pp. 126–130.

4. Francis Fukuyama, *The End of History and the Last Man* (New York: Avon Books, 1992), p. ix.

5. Rousseau called this natural tendency to take advantage of others *amour-propre* (self-love). Since everyone has this same self-love, all human interaction is pervaded by relentless competition and striving to gain dominance. See N. J. H. Dent, *A Rousseau Dictionary* (Oxford: Blackwell Publishers, 1992), p. 108.

6. John Dunn, *Western Political Theory in the Face of the Future* (Cambridge: Cambridge University Press, 1990), p. 51.

7. Jean Jacques Rousseau, *A Discourse on Political Economy*, as cited in N. J. H. Dent, *A Rousseau Dictionary*, op. cit., p. 69.

8. Reinhold Niebuhr, *Moral Man and Immoral Society* (New York: Charles Scribner's Sons, 1932), p. 117.

9. Ibid.

10. Fukuyama, op. cit., p. 102.

11. John Stuart Mill, *Political Economy*, vol. II (London: Colonial Press, 1900), pp. 454–456.

12. Ibid., p. 455.

13. Sylvia Nasar, "Economics of Equality: A New View," *New York Times*, January 8, 1994.

CHAPTER 1

THE NATURE OF THE PUBLIC SCHOOL SYSTEM

TOPICAL OUTLINE OF CHAPTER

Common Schools • A System of Schools • Equality of Opportunity • The Public School Ideal • Historical Basis • Ye Olde Deluder Satan • Parochial Schools • Rate Bills • Evolution of Tax Support for Public Schools • Advocates for Public Schools • Public School Expansion • The Forgotten Man • Structural Issues Today • Free Common Schools • Public School Precepts

INTRODUCTION

The understanding of public school finance requires at least a rudimentary knowledge of what public schools are and how they developed in both their philosophical and historical contexts. To know merely the mechanisms of how public tax dollars are distributed by governments for the purpose of education without knowing the purpose for which they are distributed is to know the means but to ignore the ends. This book will go into substantial detail about the technicalities of the allocation of funds for public schools, but first it is appropriate that a few words in this chapter be devoted to the end to be achieved by public schools.

As a nation we did not create public schools merely to teach persons to read and write, but rather and more fundamentally, to provide universal education for the purpose of maintaining a republican form of government. It was believed of course that knowledgeable people would reject the restraints of tyranny, and if they understood their options would always recognize and revere liberty and equality. Yet learned people do not choose a republican form of government in the abstract; rather, they adopt a republican form of government to acquire and maintain a government of virtue. A virtuous government holds freedom, liberty, and equality in the highest regard and dispenses social justice to achieve that end (for a government without virtue is not worth preserving). The underlying objective is to achieve virtue in government and it is believed that this end can best be achieved by an educated citizenry.

Sustaining a virtuous government requires a people of sensitivity and compassion willing to act for the common weal. Persons with little education may be easily oppressed because they are not aware of the options that knowledge bestows. Knowledge removes each person further from the state of nature of Hobbes's *Leviathan*, a state in which passions and avarice reign instead of harmony and accord. Knowledge thus empowers citizens to discern the legitimacy of government and to balance the preservation of individual liberties against the necessary subordination of self-interest to the mutual benefit of society.

1

If government is virtuous then all people should be exposed to an educational system that instills the appropriate ideals reflecting the social justice to be fostered by the society at large. A system of education that exhibits social injustice and inequity will help destroy republicanism and the virtue in government that it was designed to sustain. The system of public common schools as envisaged by our forefathers and circumscribed in each state constitution represents society's best effort to broadly diffuse knowledge to effectuate the end of a desirable government. The United States is still involved in the public common school experiment, started little more than a century ago, that seeks to achieve these ideals.

Certain terms of art are included in state constitutions that circumscribe the intent and purpose of public schools. Terms of art are descriptive words or phrases that by virtue of long and continuous use have gained nearly universal acceptance of their meaning. Three of these, *common*, *system*, and *equality of opportunity* lay the foundation for our public schools.

Common Schools

The use of the word *common* invokes special meaning in both the historical and constitutional contexts. Common schools were created as institutions where all children, regardless of economic or social condition, could obtain public instruction free of charge. The costs were to be shouldered by the public through taxation. The instruction was to benefit all in common and the costs were to be shared by all in common. Use of the term *common* as an adjective implies that the schools are free. The great educational debate of the nineteenth century was whether schools should be free to the students. The costs are borne by the citizenry from revenues gained from taxation.

The framers of the various state constitutions in using the term *common* evidenced an unmistakable state role for the general diffusion of knowledge. Importantly, the intent was to create

state-operated schools that were free to all. Early on, as it became clear that private schools had failed to meet the general educational needs of the people, some states experimented with public academies, but it soon became apparent that they were ineffectual in educating the masses. Though academies and pauper schools proliferated, they failed to enroll a significant segment of the youth and soon disappeared; thus public schools became dominant.

As the private and quasi-private forms of schooling foundered and failed to meet the needs of an expanding nation, an awakening educational consciousness called for a government-maintained system of schools for all children. This enlightened philosophy generally followed the ideas of eminent thinkers of the time who sought to build a republican government on the foundation of a more literate and homogeneous mass of people. Unifying the people through education was recognized as a precedent to a strong and viable democracy.

The creation of the common school system was a public response to the inadequacies of private education. Specifically, the common schools were designed to remedy three major shortcomings: (1) The private schools did not constitute a system but were created and funded by different means by various initiatives for private objectives. There was no state system. (2)

Box 1.1 _____

The Melting Pot

You know that the great melting-pot of America, the place where we are all made Americans of, is the public school, where men of every race and of every origin and of every station in life send their children, or ought to send their children, and where, being mixed together, the youngsters are all infused with the American spirit and developed into American men and American women.

Source: Woodrow Wilson, *The New Freedom*, cited in Harold J. Carter, *Intellectual Foundations of American Education* (New York: Pitman, 1965), p. 82.

The private and parochial schools were not normally free. Poor families struggled financially in order to enroll their children. (3) The private and parochial schools had special motivations of religious, social, ethnic, economic, and sometimes racial separation.

Observations of the inadequacies of private and quasi-private schools led to the conclusion that there was a great need for common schools. In one example that demonstrated the need for common schools, the governor of Kentucky in 1816 conveyed the common school rationale: "Every child born in the state should be considered a child of the republic, and educated at public expense."[1] Later, in 1820, the same governor exhorted the legislature to provide funds for education, maintaining the importance of commonality of purpose in providing education to all, saying,

> Education is more vitally important in a republican than in any other form of government; for there the right to administer the government is common to all, and when they have the opportunity of administration it should be accessible to all.[2]

When the common school system was finally established in the United States, the recurrent theme enunciated by the earlier proponents encompassed certain elements that distinguished public common schools from their forerunners. These common schools were based on certain *a priori* considerations:

1. Each child was equally important to the republic.
2. Education benefitted all, not just the person being educated.
3. All should pay in common.
4. All should receive the educational benefits in common.

The word *common* as it relates to schools has special and significant meaning. The common school system as envisioned by the policymakers during its formative years is a stark contrast with its educational antecedents. The common school was unique because it was:

Box 1.2 _____

The Bosom of Equality

Public education, therefore, under regulations prescribed by the government, and under magistrates established by the Sovereign, is one of the fundamental rules of popular or legitimate government. If children are brought up in common in the bosom of equality; if they are imbued with the laws of the State and the precepts of the general will; if they are taught to respect these above all things; if they are surrounded by examples and objects which constantly remind them of the tender mother who nourishes them, of the loves she bears them, of the inestimable benefits they receive from her, and of the return they owe her, we cannot doubt that they will learn to cherish one another mutually as brothers, to will nothing contrary to the will of society, to substitute the actions of men and citizens for the futile and vain babbling of sophists, and to become in time defenders and fathers of the country of which they will have been so long the children.

Source: Jean Jacques Rousseau, *A Discourse of Political Economy, 1758*, translation and introduction by G.D.H. Cole, in *The Social Contract and Discourses* (London: J. M. Dent & Sons, 1973), p. 149.

---

1. A free school, where the levy of tuition or fees could not impose a burden on poor children.
2. A school open to all, not just the poor but a cross-section of the population where all classes could mingle and learn together.
3. A school supported by taxation of all the people of the state.
4. A school operated and governed as a public secular entity, free from sectarian or special interest control.
5. A school that was part of a system where a high degree of uniformity existed throughout the state.

A System of Schools

In the late eighteenth and early nineteenth centuries the word *system* in state constitutions held a special connotation emanating from revolu-

Box 1.3

Public School System

What was fresh in the republican style (though scarcely fresh in the history of Western thought) was the emphasis on system, on a functional organization of individual schools and colleges that put them into regular relationship with one another and with the polity. The very novelty of the idea bespoke a variety of approaches, and indeed one leading theme in the history of American education during the first century of the Republic is the remarkable multiplicity of instructional ways and means by which states and localities moved to the creation of public school systems.

Source: Lawrence A. Cremin, *American Education: The National Experience, 1783–1876* (New York: Harper & Row, 1980), p. 148.

tionary enlightenment republicanism. Public common schools were to be considered a system. The idea that public education of the masses was the key to the formation of the new political order and general happiness of the people was a pervasive theme as it became clear that tutorials, home instruction, private schools, and other limited devices such as the pauper schools, were inadequate to support a new and thriving nation.

The new concept of mass public education was premised on four beliefs: (1) that education was vital to the republic; (2) that a proper education consisted of the general diffusion of knowledge; (3) that virtue and civic responsibility were essential; and (4) that public schools and colleges were the best means of providing mass education on the scale required.[3] Two important and distinguishing characteristics of this new concept of education were that it was a system and that it was of the polity. Cremin observed, "What was fresh in the republican style was the emphasis on 'system,' on a functional organization of individual schools and colleges that put them in regular relationship with one another and with the polity."[4] Earlier forms of education were not publicly supported and were not systems.

The historical discussion of *system* usually employed terms such as *machine* as well as *harmony* and *uniformity*. The educational system was to be likened to a machine, which would function smoothly and efficiently in the general diffusion of knowledge. The efficient machine was a natural metaphor of the era of the industrial revolution in which the early state constitutions were promulgated. An efficient system demanded the balance and harmony of its working parts.

The term *system* was used in at least four different but related senses.

1. A vertical incremental pattern of institutions which permitted progress from one level of educational attainment to another (primary, secondary, and college).
2. A related curriculum of standard subjects which would provide a firm knowledge base for all persons.
3. A uniformity of offerings which would assure that all persons received the education necessary to carry out civic responsibilities.
4. An aspect of the polity, or extra-familial, as opposed to familial. It was necessary to fashion a system in which education was not dependent on the private sector or the family, but instead was dependent on the public.

Thus the term *system* assumes a coordinated curriculum and allows for a progression of educational achievement. Uniformity, equality, and harmony of function are implicit features of a system, and are essential to the efficient diffusion of knowledge throughout the population.

Equality of Opportunity

A tenet of public common schools is equality of educational opportunity. Society may rationally classify children in many ways in order to effectuate reasonable educational objectives. However, to create a system that classifies and confines children to educational disadvantage due solely to location and financial capability of the local school district is immoral, and in a growing number of states has been held to be illegal. The method by which the public schools are financed today in the United States, with significant reliance upon local tax sources, is marked by inequality of opportunity that results from attendant disparities in funding.

Inequality of educational opportunity is a term much confused by inaccurate discourse and poor definition. Many times inequality of funding is defended by oblique arguments that interject discussions of outputs, measures of efficiency, production functions, and achievement tests. We will say more about these later, but here it is important to note that the question of inequality of opportunity must be clarified and must not be confused with complex and imprecise econometric analyses of outputs and outcomes. The state is responsible for the provision of substantial uniformity in courses, programs, facilities, and personnel, and above all it must not create inequalities by state action that favors some children over others. In this regard it is helpful to speak in terms of equal prospects and equal resources rather than equal gain[5] or equal ends. The state is responsible to provide for equal prospects, but it cannot assure equal outcomes.

Types of Inequality. For our purposes, in school finance, inequality of funding can best be explained by reference to four types of inequality.

1. *Luck.* The secret workings of providence: Some people are lucky and some just happen to be in the wrong place at the wrong time.
2. *Natural inequality.* Nature creates differences among all individuals: No two have the same native intelligence, height, weight, or other characteristics.
3. *Environmental inequality.* The social and economic environment permits or creates inequalities, results of human interaction.
4. *State-created inequality.* The state itself by its own laws causes inequality of treatment.

The first three types of inequality are undesirable and damaging to a person's prospects in life, but they cannot always be avoided. The last of the types, state-created inequality, is invidious be-

cause it is caused by the state itself, and therefore must be corrected. This last type of inequality was the essence of state-created racial segregation of schools. Present state allocations create similar advantages or disadvantages based on economic condition. It is this state-created inequality of resources to which much of the discussion of this book is directed.

Presently, widely disparate local tax bases cause substantial variations in per pupil revenue available to school districts in most states. Such disparities are state-created; all state and local taxes are either levied or authorized by state legislatures.[6] Historically, the public schools have been tied primarily to local property taxes with the potential availability of several smaller taxes for supplemental revenue. For most of the less fiscally able school districts, supplemental property tax revenues have remained either unavailable or negligible in yield. Where nonproperty tax resources are available, the disparities in tax bases and yields usually do little to create greater equality. Therefore, reliance on local taxation to support the schools has usually had a detrimental effect on the equality of school funding. This reliance has contributed to the problems of a system that has both inadequate resources and an unequal distribution of those limited resources. Because of these disparities in fiscal capacity, most school finance systems require taxpayers in the less fiscally able school districts to exert several times more tax effort than that of the more fiscally able districts if they are to provide equal resources for their children. Reform has been glacial, and students in the poor school districts remain at a substantial educational disadvantage because of underfinanced educational programs and services.

This common variety of inequality emanating from unequal local capacity is the result of state action. States have created these inequalities by

1. Significant reliance on local taxation
2. Use of distribution formulas that do not fully compensate for deficiencies in local wealth or tax effort

3. Limited use of the fiscal equalization of school finance systems

The result is a system of school financing in virtually all of the states that creates educational disadvantages for students in school districts of low fiscal capacity. In essence, the quality of a child's public education is largely dependent upon the fiscal capacities of school districts. The range of curriculum offerings, counseling services, and extracurricular activities are primarily a function of the location of school districts and their accompanying economic circumstances.

The Public School Ideal

The public schools of the United States were formed from a philosophical reasoning that sought virtue in government through commonality, mutuality, and harmony of interests. The common school followed the idea of community as opposed to that of "predatory self-interest" and elevation of self over the interests of the state. The public school's philosophical foundation is found in no less early an authority than Aristotle in his *Politics*,[7] in which each citizen is pledged in allegiance to the state to place the interests and common good of all above those of self and separate interests. Aristotle maintained that a natural impulse of man, a "political animal," is to increase individual pleasure and reduce personal pain by the elevation of the condition of the entire community. The state, according to Aristotle, "has a natural priority over the household and over the individual among us. For the whole must be prior to the part."[8] This pursuit of the common good through political association enables liberty and justice for the individual to prevail.

The Aristotelian argument simply maintains that all are better served by the "wisdom of collective judgments" than determinations of individuals.[9] In Aristotle's view, popular judgment was also more efficient simply because in the long run decisions made in consideration of self-interest will only consider a part and not the whole. The vagaries of decision by many parts without considering the common good will inevitably result in an inefficient government. Public schools are no different. Decisions to advance the conditions of all people are more likely to be good ones if made by the many rather than the few. It is said that Canning, the prime minister of England, once pithily commented, "The House of Commons as a body had better taste than the man of best taste in it. . . ." This view was very much prevalent in the mid-nineteenth century when the public schools were formed in the United States. That the common will was a more reliable standard for social conduct than individual caprice was an underlying assumption of both democratic government and public schools.

This was the view of the philosopher Condorcet who, in his 1792 *Report on the General Organization of Public Instruction* to the National Assembly of France, argued that "only through universal education could citizens be taught effectively to enjoy their rights and fulfill their responsibilities."[10] This quest for the general will was enunciated earlier by Rousseau as the "most important rule of legitimate and popular government,"[11] the general will being of the collective spirit as opposed to the particular will.

This philosophy translated into the need for an educated citizenry to preserve the republican form of government. The view was best expressed by Madison when he concisely explained, "A people who mean to be their own Governors, must arm themselves with the power which knowledge gives."[12] This view, as Butts and Cremin point out, held simply "that if an individual failed to receive an education, it was not he alone who suffered the consequences. Society too would suffer, for in his subsequent limitation in knowledge and the skills of getting knowledge, he would not be helping the electorate to make the best possible decisions."[13]

Thus the state has an interest in educating the masses that transcends the individual's right to an education. The right of an individual to an education should be denominated as constitutionally fundamental because without equal opportunity for education a person's prospects for life are substantially diminished. As individual prospects are diminished, the prospects of the state will closely follow. By assuring a fundamental right, the state is in reality protecting itself against ignorance of the citizenry and all the liabilities—political, social, and economic—that a lack of knowledge imposes.

HISTORICAL BASIS FOR PUBLIC SCHOOLS

State concern for public education and tax support for the public schools can be traced to actions of the colonial legislature of Massachusetts. The Massachusetts law of 1642 directed "certain chosen men of each town to ascertain from time to time, if parents and masters were attending to their educational duties; if the children were being trained in learning and labor and other employments . . . profitable to the state; and if children were being taught to read and understand the principles of religion and the capital laws of the country they were empowered to impose fines on those who refuse to render such accounts to them when required."[14] Cubberley observed that this was the first time in the English-speaking world that a legislative body enacted legislation requiring that children be taught to read.[15]

Ye Olde Deluder Satan

The 1642 law was tried for five years and found to be unsatisfactory. In 1647, the General Court (the legislative body of the Massachusetts colony) enacted the famous "ye old deluder law." The preamble of the law stated that one of the chief projects of "ye olde deluder Satan" was to keep people in ignorance of the Scriptures. Accordingly, the obvious way to defeat Satan's purposes was to teach the people to read and write. To that end, the legislative body, under the provisions of the 1647 law, ordered

1. that every town having fifty householders shall at once appoint a teacher of reading and writ-

ing, and provide for his wages in such manner as the town might determine; and
2. that every town having one hundred householders must provide a grammar school to fit youths for the university, under a penalty of 5 pounds [afterward increased to 20 pounds] for failure to do so.[16]

This act is remarkable for the following reasons:

1. It set the precedent for the authority of the state to establish educational requirements.
2. It gave local governmental bodies authority to levy taxes to assist in financing both elementary and secondary schools.
3. It demonstrated that if the state requires an educational program to be provided, it must also provide a means for financing that program if it is to become available.

The Massachusetts laws of 1642 and 1647 influenced other New England colonies. Connecticut, Maine, New Hampshire, and Vermont all enacted legislation establishing public schools by 1720. The acts passed by those colonies closely resembled the Massachusetts laws of 1642 and 1647.

Church Schools and Rate Bills

In the central colonies of New York, Pennsylvania, and New Jersey, various church denominations established parochial schools. These were financed by the respective churches and from fees or rate bills. A rate bill is a special tax levied on parents, assessed in proportion to the number of children sent to school. The teaching of religion, in addition to reading, writing, and arithmetic, was a central purpose of both the New England and the central colonies.

It is interesting to note that the New England colonies did not establish a school system similar to that of England. The early settlers of New England were almost all religious dissenters who came to America to establish a society different from that in England. On the other hand, the early settlers of Virginia and the other Southern colonies were not church dissenters. They came to America primarily to improve their fortunes. They supported the Church of England, and as a result the Southern colonies provided for education by much the same means as that used in England at the time. Under that system the schools were under either church or private control. Private schools were financed by tuition charges and were patronized primarily by the well-to-do. The Southern colonies did provide a limited amount of schooling for orphans and the children of paupers. Cubberley, commenting on education in colonial Virginia, stated:

> The tutor in the home, education in small private pay schools, or education in the mother country were the prevailing methods adopted among well-to-do planters, while the poorer classes were left with only such advantages as apprenticeship training or charity schools might provide.[17]

Thus in the colonial period of America, public education was available in only a few New England colonies, and even in those education was not entirely free. Outside of New England, education was provided by parochial or private schools financed primarily by parents of the children attending them. Under this system, educational opportunity was basically a function of the wealth of a child's parents and few children were educated who did not come from the more well-to-do ranks of society.

EVOLUTION OF TAX SUPPORT FOR PUBLIC SCHOOLS

The general public's attitude toward education in the national period of American history, from about 1783 to 1876, is perhaps best reflected in the prefix of the Ordinance of 1787, enacted by the Congress of the Confederation. It reads as follows: "Religion, morality, and knowledge being necessary to good government and the happiness of mankind, schools, and the means of education shall forever be encouraged."[18] This ordinance, which applied only to the states carved from the Northwest Territory, implied that education was a state responsibility and a vi-

tal aspect of a democratic form of government. The words of this ordinance encapsulate the political and educational philosophies of the nation's founders.

The beliefs of persons of advanced knowledge and forward-looking perspectives have a profound influence on subsequent events even though the policies advocated may not have been accepted at the time. Current problems of school financing can be better understood by contemplating the issues faced by the early leaders of public education. More discussion of these ordinances and on the federal role in education is given in Chapter 12, but of primary importance here is the philosophical belief in liberty, equality, and commonality of purpose in establishing a virtuous government.

Public Education for Liberty

Public education developed slowly in the early national period. The best known of the early advocates was Thomas Jefferson. In 1787 he wrote in a letter to James Madison: "Above all things I hope the education of the common people will be attended to; convinced that on this good sense we may rely with the most security for the preservation of a due sense of liberty." In 1816, after his retirement from the presidency, he wrote to Yancy: "If a nation expects to be ignorant and free in a state of civilization it expects what never was and never will be. . . . There is no safe deposit [for the foundations of government] but with the people themselves; nor can they be safe with them without information."[19]

Despite the advocacy of Jefferson and many others, tax-supported public education did not generally become available in the Middle Atlantic and Midwestern states until after 1830, and in the Southern states not until the last quarter of the nineteenth century. Although some progress had been made, free public education was not generally available in the United States by the middle of the nineteenth century. According to the Seventh Census of the United States, in 1850 only about one-half of the children of

New England were provided free education, one-sixth in the West, and one-seventh in the Middle states.[20] As late as 1870 only 57 percent of the population 5–17 years of age was enrolled in the public schools and the average length of the school term was only 78 days.[21] Commentary by leading advocates for public schools during the nineteenth century remains instructive today.

Advocates for Public Schools

The most influential advocates of tax-supported public schools in the United States were laypeople and organizations. Professionally trained educators offered very little leadership in the nineteenth century for the establishment of free public education. Actually very little professional training was provided for teachers or educational leaders prior to 1900. Horace Mann, who became secretary of the State Board of Education of Massachusetts in 1837, and his contemporary, Henry Barnard, who served as chief state school officer of both Rhode Island and Connecticut, had a powerful influence on the establishment of tax-supported public schools.[22]

Horace Mann is particularly worthy of special mention because he not only revitalized public schools in Massachusetts, but also had a powerful influence throughout the nation. Many states called on him for advice and counsel and his twelve annual reports to the State Board of Education remain memorable documents.[23] Mann was particularly effective in convincing the public to sustain tax-supported public schools. A part of this support came from organized labor, which historically bolstered free public schools. Organized labor had gained some strength in the United States by the end of the first quarter of the nineteenth century and had begun to advocate tax-supported public schools. An example of such support can be found in an 1830 report by an association of working men in Philadelphia. The report stated,

> When the committees contemplate their own condition, and that of the great mass of their fellow la-

borers; when they look around on the glaring inequality of society, they are constrained to believe, that, until the means of equal instruction shall be equally secured to all, liberty is but an unmeaning word, and equality an empty shadow, whose substance to be realized must first be planted by an equal education and proper training in the minds, in the habits and in the feelings of the community.[24]

Similar pronouncements came from individuals as well. One outspoken advocate, the great legislator Thaddeus Stevens, in an eloquent plea to the Pennsylvania House of Representatives in 1835, called for the continuance of tax supported public schools.

> If an elective republic is to endure for any great length of time, every elector must have sufficient information, not only to accumulate wealth, and take care of his pecuniary concerns, but to direct wisely the legislatures, the ambassadors, and the executive of the nation—for some part of all these things, some agency in approving or disapproving of them, falls to every freeman. If then, the permanency of our government depends upon such knowledge, it is the duty of government to see that the means of information be diffused to every citizen. This is a sufficient answer to those who deem education a private and not a public duty—who argue that they are willing to educate their own children, but not their neighbor's children.[25]

Such advocacy not only influenced public opinion to support free public schools, but created a philosophical foundation that would justify the creation of public schools throughout the country.

Public School Expansion

Tax support for the public schools was largely confined to the elementary grades until the latter part of the nineteenth century. Cubberley noted that up until 1840, not many more than a dozen high schools had been established in Massachusetts and not more than an equal number in all the other states combined.[26] Private academies and parochial schools provided most of the secondary education available. Throughout this period, legislation providing for the establishment of high schools was attacked in the courts of many states. One such challenge, the famous Kalamazoo case, was to become a resounding justification for the creation of public high schools nationwide. In this case, the Supreme Court of the state of Michigan rendered, in 1875, an opinion so favorable and so positive in support of taxes for high schools that it greatly influenced the development of high schools in many other states. Yet high school education was not universally available by the close of the nineteenth century. Only 8 percent of the population 14–17 years of age was enrolled in grades 9 through 12 in public high schools by 1900.[27] In fact, public high schools did not become available in many of the rural areas of the United States until after World War I.

Free public education developed very slowly in the United States during the first quarter of the nineteenth century. However, between 1830 and 1860, constitutional and statutory authorization for tax-supported public schools was general in the Middle Atlantic and Midwestern states. All of the New England states had authorized tax support of the public schools prior to 1830. Legal provision for tax support of the public schools in the South was not generally authorized by state legislatures until the last quarter of the nineteenth century. But even after tax levies for public schools were authorized, supporters of public schools, not only in the South but also in other states, frequently faced bitter opposition to such levies. The colonial belief that church and parents were solely responsible for the education of children was an obstacle that was to give ground only grudgingly and remains very much in evidence today.

Although taxes for public schools were generally authorized during the nineteenth century, they were frequently supplemented by tuition charges and/or rate bills. Rate bills were abolished in most of the Northern and Midwestern states between 1834 and 1871.[28] However, the practice of charging tuition, especially for public high schools, continued well into the twentieth century. Tuition was frequently disguised by calling it an "incidental fee." Such fees made education still largely the province of the more affluent, with the poor in many cases unable to participate.

The Forgotten Man

The difficulties faced by those advocating tax-supported public schools in the South was well described by Walter Hines Page in his famous lecture, "The Forgotten Man," delivered at the State Normal and Industrial School for Women at Greensboro, North Carolina, in June 1897. In that address he discussed the educational conditions in North Carolina, his native state.

> In 1890, twenty-six percent of the white persons of the State were unable even to read and write. One in every four was wholly forgotten. But illiteracy was not the worst of it; the worst of it was that the stationary social condition indicated by generations of illiteracy had long been the general condition. The Forgotten Man was content to be forgotten. He became not only a dead weight, but a definite opponent of social progress. He faithfully heard the politicians on the stump praise him for virtues that he did not have. The politicians told him that he had lived in the best state in the Union, told him that the other politician had some harebrained plan to increase his taxes, . . . told him to distrust anybody who wished to change anything. What was good enough for his fathers was good enough for him. Thus the Forgotten Man became a dupe, became thankful for being neglected.[29]

Page, through his writings and lectures, had a significant influence on the development of public education in the United States. He stated his creed as follows:

> I believe in the free public training of both the hands and the mind of every child born of woman. I believe that by the right training of men we add to the wealth of the world. All wealth is the creation of man, and he creates it only in proportion to the trained uses of the community; and, the more men we train, the more wealth everyone may create. I believe in the perpetual regeneration of society, in the immortality of democracy, and in growth everlasting.[30]

In Page's statements are found the realities of political opportunism and intellectual incapacity that have prevented the expansion of universal public education in America since its inception. Such conditions, though deleterious to equality of opportunity, remain often heard in public forums today. The counter arguments, moral, social and economical, expressed by Page as the need for intellectual growth are necessary for betterment of the nation.

STRUCTURAL ISSUES TODAY

The issues that confronted the founders of public schools in the 1830s remain in contention today. Two major structural issues are foremost at present. The first is the omnipresent problem of an absence of equal opportunity within the present public school system. This inequality is caused primarily by variations in local financial ability among school districts. Incapacities in taxpaying ability create an ongoing dilemma of how to best equalize the states' tax resources, thereby providing each child with equal prospects in life from exposure to quality educational programs.

The second major issue is whether the institution of public common schools, as now constituted, will continue to exist or whether it will be replaced by another type of system or entity. Allegations that public schools are inefficient and wasteful of public resources, that they are great gluttons of public funds, that more money will not produce better results, that they are ineffective in raising achievement test scores, that they are stultified and immobilized by bureaucracy, that they are vast monopolies unaffected by life-giving competition, that they are godless, that they unfairly entice students away from private and parochial schools, are all complaints launched regularly by conservative economists, fundamentalist preachers, parochial school advocates, and others who profess political viewpoints that seek restriction and reduction of government activities that do not conform to their dogma. Similar groups have opposed the idea of public schools since their creation in the 1830s.

In 1992, the Bush administration called for a "refounding" and a "redefinition" of public schools. President Bush called for a new structure with public and private schools enmeshed together, both receiving public tax funds. Under the Bush plan all schools would compete for public funds. Parents could exercise choice and public funds would follow to the school of their choosing. Regardless of parental motivation, or whether the schools were chosen for academic, religious, racial, ethnic, or nationalistic reasons, the results would be the same: The schools would receive public tax money.

If the institution of public common schools as we know it is to survive there must remain a constancy of purpose as reflected in certain basic precepts emanating from both its philosophical and historical traditions. These precepts undergird a system of common interest and commonality of purpose enhancing personal freedom by strengthening the common good. Modern restate-

---

Box 1.4 _____

Free Public Schools

Education stimulates an interest in the political process and provides the intellectual and practical tools necessary for political action. Indeed, education may well be "the dominant factor in influencing political participation and awareness." . . . Without high quality education, the populace will lack the knowledge, self-confidence, and critical skills to evaluate independently the pronouncements of pundits and political leaders. . . .

The public schools bring together members of different racial and cultural groups and, hopefully, help them to live together "in harmony and mutual respect." . . .

The free school guarantee lifts budgetary decisions concerning public education out of the individual family setting and requires that such decisions be made by the community as a whole. . . .

Source: Supreme Court of California in *Hartzell* v. *Connell,* 201 Cal.Rptr. 601, 679 P.2d 35 (1984).

ments of these ideals may be found in many sources, but two such enunciations emerged from the school litigation in California in 1984, and from the Kentucky school finance case in 1989. The California court gave one of the clearest and most complete justifications for public schools, and the Kentucky court set out in summary fashion the prevailing precepts for common schools.

In the California case, *Hartzell* v. *Connell*,[31] the Supreme Court of California rejected the levy of fees in public schools as a manifest violation of a fundamental principle of the public school concept, that the schools be free to all. A short excerpt from the California case is given in Box 1.4.

PUBLIC SCHOOL PRECEPTS*

The discussion of the philosophical and historical bases for public schools may be summarized in a list of precepts or principles that form the rationale for the creation and maintenance of public schools in the United States. The principles given were adapted from a statement provided by a select committee appointed by Kentucky Circuit Judge Ray Corns as a part of his landmark decision in 1988 that held the system of public school education in Kentucky unconstitutional. The principles were accepted and were reflected in the standards adopted by the Kentucky Supreme Court.

1. *The schools are to be public, of the body politic, and are to be governed and controlled by the people.* Early experimentation showed that

*Adapted from select committee members: Report by the Select Committee to Judge Ray Corns, Franklin Circuit Court, Kentucky, September 15, 1988. *Committee for Better Education, Inc.* v. *Wilkinson*, members of select committee appointed by Judge Ray Corns, Franklin Circuit Court. Kern Alexander, chairman, Select Committee; John Brock, Superintendent of Public Instruction; Larry Forgy, attorney, Lexington, and former Kentucky State Budget Director; Sylvia Watson, director of development, Georgetown College and former city commissioner, Louisville. Published with permission of *Journal of Education Finance*, vol. 15, Fall 1989, no. 2, pp. 142–144.

quasi-private and semi-public schools would not suffice to educate the masses. Control by private interest groups, regardless of their nature, always placed limitations that reduced public participation and prevented full access of the people. To assure openness to all, the system must be controlled by the polity.

2. *The schools are to be established as a system, an organic whole, arranged with interdependent parts.* The word *system*, though, requires a measure of orderliness and uniformity regardless of the number of school districts. The state system must form a cohesive whole and cannot be merely a conglomeration of local independent initiatives.

3. *The schools are to be free and common to all with no charges to limit access.* Reluctance on the part of the people to finance schools from the public treasury was a primary hindrance to the establishment of a viable common school system. Early attempts to create an educational system failed partially because of user charges, usually in the nature of tuition and fees, which limited attendance to those who could afford to pay the requisite costs of operating the schools. The public schools are to benefit all the people, and all of the people must pay for them.

4. *The schools are to be secular and free from sectarian religious control, and public funds should not be expended for religious or parochial schools.* Public schools should exemplify toleration, and the power of the state should not be used to promote or inhibit the free exercise of religion. A strict religious neutrality should be maintained in the public schools. Public tax monies should not be used to establish religion by preferring one religion over another nor by aiding a "multiple establishment" of more than one religion.

5. *The schools are to be financed by tax resources which are distributed in such a manner as to ensure that the quality of a child's education will not be dependent on the fiscal ability of the local school district.* The quality of a child's education in virtually all the states is determined by the financial ability of the community in which the child attends school. A system of schools cannot be efficient if some children are denied educational programs and services because their local communities do not happen to have wealth or income to sustain school revenues through larger and more lucrative local tax bases.

6. *The schools are to provide equitable educational treatment to all children in the accommodation of their educational needs.* All educational programs and services cannot be precisely uniform. School districts in different areas of a state may have children with varying educational needs. For example, every school district will not have precisely the same percentage of handicapped or culturally deprived children. Children having such special needs may require particular educational programs which cost more than regular programs. Equity requires that additional funds be expended if the state's moral and legal obligation of an efficient system is to be met.

7. *The schools shall be financed in a manner which will prevent the quality of a child's education from being dependent on the vagaries of local tax effort.* Whether a local school district has high or low tax effort to support the schools may be determined by conditions quite unrelated to education. The social, political, and economic structure of each community is different and each community, for various reasons, may respond differently to entreaties to support the schools. This may be true even if the people, from community to community, have the same desire and aspiration for the education of their children. Because the schools of a state exist as a unified system, the caprice of local political conditions cannot be permitted to harm the educational opportunity of a child. No community has a right to impose an inferior education on its children.

8. *The schools shall be properly managed to ensure the most effective and productive use of tax funds.* The Constitution contemplates the utilitarian use of public school funds and in so doing the schools are accountable to the people. In creating a state school system, the framers of the Constitution sought to capture the advantages and utility of educating the masses in the most efficient

manner possible. If aspects of the school system's management hinder efficiency of operation, they must be revised and more acceptable alternatives must be incorporated and enforced.

9. *The General Assembly of each state is to bear the responsibility for the enactment of laws to govern the common schools.* The establishment and maintenance of the common schools is not a matter of local discretion. Neither is it primarily a federal function. While the time-honored concept of local control is desirable and should be assured and safeguarded, the ultimate discretion over the schools, within the bounds of the state and federal constitutions, rests with the legislature. Responsibility for taxation in support of public schools falls upon the state legislature and cannot be delegated away.

SUMMARY AND CONCLUSIONS

In summarizing and concluding this chapter, it should be noted that, although great progress has been made, we have not yet developed satisfactory systems of tax support for the public schools in many states, and that the struggle for a satisfactory level of financial support continues in all states. As will be shown later in this book, the public schools are still involved in what Huxley called a "struggle for existence,"[32] and the battle for tax-supported public schools is a continuing struggle for survival and growth beyond survival. In a rapidly changing world, there must be improvement in the public schools or the public school as an institution fundamental to democracy may be harmed or permanently impaired. This in turn will threaten liberty, equality of opportunity, and ultimately the republican form of government.

The public common school concept rests on the belief that a knowledgeable people will be better able to perpetuate a republican form of government than will persons of little or marginal knowledge. The object and interest of the people is to have a virtuous government that will protect liberty and advance equality. This may best be accomplished in a democratic form of government that rests on the foundation of an informed citizenry. Public common schools are the vehicle fashioned by the people to maintain a knowledgeable electorate.

The term *common schools* envisages free schools which all persons rich and poor attend and from which all benefit in common. The common school concept further requires that all persons pay in common through general taxation to support the schools.

The creation of public common schools was a response to the recognized limitation and inadequacies of private schools to meet the needs of a modern nation. In creating public schools, the people of the states implicitly decided that all children were children of the republic with equal rights and opportunities. The meaning of the word *common* encompasses all the presumptions necessary to provide mass universal education.

The term *system* is an important aspect of public common schools. Early in this country, states employed piecemeal approaches to the provision of education, utilizing inadequate devices such as rate bills, pauper schools, and quasi-public academies in endeavoring to redress a prevailing cognizance of the need for universal education. These methods failed because they were not systems of incremental education. Moreover, they failed to provide uniformity or thoroughness across the state.

As envisaged by the founders, a system of public schools has the attributes of uniformity, thoroughness, and equality. Moreover, the founders saw universal public education as a great machine which operates with harmony and efficiency in the conveyance of knowledge and prosperity.

Public schools were seen as a vehicle to reduce inequalities in society and to make the foundations of the social system rest on merit instead of privilege.

Much in evidence in the notion of the common school is that a reliable standard of social conduct can better be determined by the common considerations of all rather than by individual interest and caprice. In this regard, Rousseau maintained that public education is the most important role of legitimate and popular government.

The historical foundations of public schools were laid by the ordinances of 1785 and 1787, but viable systems of public schools did not develop until the mid- and late-nineteenth century.

Expansion of public schools was usually in opposition to some taxpayers or private school proponents who had a limited view of the common interest or saw the public schools as encroaching on their own self-interest.

Public school precepts may be summarized as follows: To be of the public; to be a system, an organic whole; to be free and common to all; to be secular; to be financed from general taxation; to be equitable; to be equal regardless of location; to be efficient; and to be the responsibility of the state.

KEY TERMS

Common schools	General diffusion of knowledge	Pauper schools
Public schools	Ye olde deluder Satan	Kalamazoo case
Free schools	Rate bills	The Forgotten Man
System of schools		

ENDNOTES

1. Moses Edward Ligon, *A History of Public Education in Kentucky* (Lexington, KY: University of Kentucky, 1942), vol. XIV, no. 4, p. 56.
2. Ibid., p. 57.

3. Lawrence A. Cremin, *American Education, The National Experience, 1783–1876* (New York: Harper & Row, 1980), p. 148.
4. Ibid., p. 118.

5. Brian Barry, *Theories of Justice* (Berkeley: University of California Press, 1989), p. 109.

6. Local taxes authorized in state constitutions are not subject to state legislation in only a few instances.

7. Aristotle, *Politics*, translated by T. A. Sinclair, revised and re-presented by Trevor J. Saunders (London: Penguin Books, 1981), p. 60.

8. Ibid.

9. Ibid., p. 201.

10. R. Freeman Butts and Lawrence A. Cremin, *A History of Education in American Culture* (New York: Henry Holt and Company, 1953), p. 190.

11. Jean Jacques Rousseau, *A Discourse on Political Economy*, 1758, in *The Social Contract and Discourses*, translation and introduction by G. D. H. Cole (London: J. M. Dent & Sons, 1973), p. 135.

12. James Madison to W. T. Barry, August 4, 1822, *The Writings of James Madison Comprising His Public Papers and His Private Correspondence, Including Numerous Letters and Documents Now for the First Time Printed* ed. Gaillard Hunt (New York: Putman, 1910), vol. IX, p. 103.

13. Butts and Cremin, op. cit., p. 202.

14. Ellwood P. Cubberley, *The History of Education* (Boston: Houghton Mifflin, 1920), p. 364.

15. Ibid., p. 364.

16. Ibid., p. 365.

17. Ibid., p. 372.

18. Cremin, op. cit., p. 148.

19. Cubberley, op cit., p. 526.

20. Newton Edwards and Herman G. Richey, *The School in the American Social Order* (Boston: Houghton Mifflin, 1963), p. 292.

21. U.S. Department of Commerce, Bureau of the Census, *Historical Statistics of the United States: Colonial Times to 1957* (Washington, DC: U.S. Government Printing Office, 1960), p. 207.

22. See Edith Nye MacMillan, *Henry Barnard and Nineteenth-Century School Reform* (New Haven, CT: Yale University Press, 1991).

23. Cubberley, op. cit., p. 689.

24. Edwards and Richey, op. cit., p. 281.

25. *Hazards Register of Pennsylvania* 15, no. 18 (May 2, 1835).

26. Cubberley, op. cit., p. 700.

27. Computed from U.S. Department of Commerce, Bureau of the Census, *Statistical Abstracts of the United States: 1900 and 1980* (Washington, DC: U.S. Government Printing Office: Various Years).

28. Cubberley, op. cit., p. 686.

29. Walter Hines Page, *The School that Built a Town* (New York: Harper & Row, 1952), p. 31. This series of lectures by Page was delivered in the latter part of the nineteenth century and the first part of the twentieth century.

30. Ibid., p. 3.

31. *Hartzell* v. *Connell*, 35 Cal. 3d 899, 201 Cal.Rptr. 601, 679 P.2d 35 (1984).

32. Aldous Huxley, *Brave New World*. (New York: Perennial Library, 1989).

CHAPTER 2

LEGAL ASPECTS OF
EDUCATIONAL FINANCE

TOPICAL OUTLINE OF CHAPTER

*Power to Tax • Federal Legislation • Religion • Dismantling the
Wall of Separation • Equality and Uniformity of Taxation • School
Finance Cases • Federal Equal Protection • The Rodriguez Case
• State Equal Protection • Fundamentality • Education Clauses
State Constitutional Terminology*

INTRODUCTION

When the United States was formed, the function of education was not specifically delegated to the federal government; because of this omission from the Constitution, education was reserved to the states and/or to the people. At that time education was considered primarily a private responsibility, and where governmental schools did exist they were considered to be an activity of local government. However, the federal government has historically influenced and regulated certain aspects of educational development. The authority for this, though it has not yet been fully defined or clarified, is found in the powers delegated to the federal government in one or more clauses of the Constitution. Although most of these clauses state general principles, in some instances the powers have been more clearly defined by decisions of the U.S. Supreme Court embellishing and providing a gloss for the actual constitutional provisions themselves.

Since education is primarily a function of the respective states, it ultimately becomes a responsibility of the people of each state. The beliefs and attitudes of the people about public educa-tion are usually incorporated, in general terms, into the constitutions and statutes of the states. If constitutional provisions are restrictive, they are likely to handicap at least some school systems or certain aspects of education. Such restrictions cannot be removed by the legislature or in any other manner except by amendment of the constitution or perhaps a decision by the courts.

The legislature of each state has what is commonly called *plenary power*; that is, it may pass any laws it considers desirable, and these laws must be observed unless they are later found to be inconsistent with provisions of the state constitution or in conflict with federal constitutional provisions. Such a finding, however, must be made by the courts on the basis of a controversy. Recent school finance cases have substantially reduced the inviolate nature of the legislative prerogative and have rendered legislative power less plenary.

Laws constitute an expression of state policy. If in any state a serious attempt has been made to agree upon long-range policies, and if the policies relating to finance or to other aspects of the educational program have been wisely and carefully developed, the laws are likely to be much more defensible than those in a state in which such foresight and vision have not been exercised. Ideas for laws come from many sources. However, if they come from special-interest groups that are primarily concerned with legislation designed to promote their own goals, they are not as likely to be consistent with a sound overall conceptual design as those ideas developed on the basis of careful study and through the cooperative efforts of groups concerned with all aspects of education and the common interest. Some of the difficulties in many states arise because much legislation relating to education or finance is of a patchwork nature and is sponsored by groups that have not had an opportunity or been willing to consider proposals in relationship to bona fide statewide needs.

As explained more fully in other chapters, there are some major inequities in educational opportunities and in most states' abilities and efforts to support schools. Some of these inequities result from differences in local aspirations, leadership, or management, but many of the most significant inequities have been created or perpetuated by indefensible state laws. Fortunately, inequities in several states relating especially to educational opportunities and financial support have been or are being lessened or eliminated by court decisions, as discussed later in this chapter.

The most significant judicial decisions regarding education are made by the federal courts, especially by the U.S. Supreme Court. Decisions rendered by the supreme court of a state have direct implications only for policies and practices within that state, with some indirect implications for other states in which they may be cited as legal precedents.

The courts do not undertake to establish policies or to resolve controversies on their own initiative. They accept cases only after a formal request or appeal has been filed for a decision on some important constitutional question or other legal issue. Most of these questions relate rather directly to, or require interpretations of, some provision in the federal Constitution or in a state constitution. Court decisions thus become precedents for later decisions unless or until they are modified or reversed.

The law governing educational finance derives from issues concerning taxation, distribution, or the appropriate management of public funds. Legal questions of taxation bear on equity and justice to taxpayers with regard to the state or school district's discretion to tax, procedures for the levying of taxes, and the nature of the burden the taxpayer must sustain. Historically, the distribution of state funds has been of little concern to the courts until the last decade, when litigation emerged from many states challenging state aid formulas under both the state and federal constitutions. This litigation, which has been gaining momentum lately, will almost certainly continue. As may be expected, issues pertaining to the stewardship of school funds have been a major subject of litigation. Accountability for public funds is always a concern for the watchful public eye.

Power to Tax

The power to tax is vested in the state by virtue of its sovereign and inherent responsibility to provide for the welfare of the people. The U.S. Supreme Court has explained the general taxing authority of the states in the following way:

> In our system of government the states have general dominion, and, saving as restricted by particular provisions of the Federal Constitution, complete dominion over all persons, property, and business transactions within their borders; they assume and perform the duty of preserving and protecting all such persons, property, and business, and in consequence, have the power normally pertaining to governments to resort to all reasonable forms of taxation in order to defray the governmental expenses.[1]

The power of taxation is exercised through legislative acts and is limited only by state and federal constitutions. The Supreme Court of the United States has said, "Unless restrained by provisions of the Federal Constitution, the power of the state as to the mode, form, and extent of taxation is unlimited, where the subjects to which it applies are within her jurisdiction."[2] The federal Constitution restrains state taxation only when it is imposed in such a way as to deny an individual right or freedom.

A State Function.   Taxing authority must be derived from state constitutions or state statutes and is never considered to be inherent in local school districts. State constitutions may be general or quite specific with regard to state taxation, but some constitutions specifically prohibit certain types of taxes, such as Florida's constitutional prohibition of the personal income tax. State constitutions may also severely restrict the authority of state agencies to tax by means such as the Indiana and Kentucky debt limitations based on a percentage of the assessed valuation of property. Generally, though, the legislation governing taxing prerogative is quite broad and has been described by some courts as plenary in nature.[3]

Taxation philosophy has become a judicial consideration in those cases in which the courts have adopted the sacrifice theory rather than the benefit theory as a justification for taxation. As pointed out in Chapter 5, controversy has existed for centuries over whether a tax should be justified merely on the *quid pro quo* rationale—that the taxpayer should receive a benefit commensurate with the value of the tax. The courts have rejected this benefit theory of taxation with regard to public schools.

> It is no defense to the collection of a tax for school or other purposes that the person or property taxed is not actually benefitted by the expenditure of the proceeds of the tax nor as much benefitted as others. Accordingly, a childless, nonresident or corporate owner of property may be taxed for school purposes.[4]

In the same vein, other courts have said that the taxes do not need to bear a relationship to the benefits received. One court observed that the benefits may be "intangible and incapable of pecuniary ascertainment,"[5] thus no direct benefits

can be determined, especially in the area of public education.

School taxes are state taxes even though they may be levied at the local level, and the decision to levy is vested in local district education authorities.[6] When public schools were first organized, the state legislatures usually authorized localities to tax for education by levying rates on the assessed valuation of property. This led to a presumption on the part of many that school taxes were local taxes. This is not the case, however, and the state legislature may, in the exercise of its legitimate discretion, arrange to support the schools by taxes levied at the state or local level, or by a combination of the two. In nearly all states legislatures have used a combination of state and local revenues, but regardless of where the tax is levied, public school taxes are considered by law to be state taxes.

Delegation of Taxing Power.   As a general rule, legislatures cannot delegate their legislative authority; however, with proper authorization specifying what is to be taxed and how, the legislature can delegate the power to levy a tax to local school districts. Not only can the legislature delegate the power to tax at the local level, but it can also compel local school districts to levy particular rates.[7] Legislation which is vague or permissive, however, will not be upheld by the courts as a proper legislative delegation of taxing authority. The power to tax must be either expressly granted or derived from necessary implication of powers which have been expressly granted.[8] Courts look on the power to tax with particular circumspection and will not easily grant taxing power on mere implication. The power to tax goes to the heart of the governmental process; where taxes are concerned, the courts are careful not to interpret implied powers too broadly. The Supreme Court of Kansas has said:

> The authority to levy taxes is an extraordinary one. It is never left to implication, unless it is a necessary implication. Its warrant must be clearly found in the act of the legislature. Any other rule might

lead to great wrong and oppression, and when there is a reasonable doubt as to its existence the right must be denied. Therefore, to say that the right is in doubt is to deny its existence.[9]

Thus a school district cannot levy a tax unless the power is conferred by statute. The precise limits of implication are not easy to define. In one of the historic cases in education, the *Kalamazoo* decision, the Supreme Court of Michigan drew very broad implications from a statute allowing taxation for secondary grades when the statute only explicitly conferred authority to tax for primary education.[10] The court reasoned that the grades and branches of knowledge should not be limited if the voters consented to raise taxes for an expansion of educational services.

Types of Taxes to Be Levied

Whether a tax may be levied for school purposes depends on the individual state's constitution and statutes. Although states have traditionally relied on local property taxes for the basic support of public schools, there is no reason that a state cannot also provide for the levy of local sales, income, or other taxes. Some states have used poll taxes, bank share taxes, liquor license taxes, occupational taxes, and business taxes at the local level. The imposition of a tax on the wages of residents and on the net profits of businesses and professions by school districts in Pennsylvania has been upheld. Pennsylvania, though, has a relatively unique situation by virtue of the legislature's so-called "Tax Anything Act," which by its nature allows local taxing prerogatives not typical of most other states.

The importance of the property tax as a local source of school revenue is evidenced by the substantial amount of litigation which has arisen about it over the years. The general rule is that the governmental unit in which the property is located has the prerogative of levying the tax. Situs of real property is determined by the place where it is located or personal property of the domicile of the owner. Real estate may be taxed only in the state or school district in which it is located. Thus, when a piece of real property lies in two school districts, each district can tax only that portion within its geographical boundary.

Tangible personal property, because it can be easily moved, creates problems of taxation not present with real estate. Such property may be taxed at either the domicile of the owner or at the place of its location, but not at both. The U.S. Supreme Court held in 1905 that if tangible personal property has acquired taxable situs in one state it cannot be taxed at the owner's domicile in another state without violating the due process clause of the Fourteenth Amendment.[11] Within one state, the legislature may establish the taxable situs of personal property, whether tangible or intangible, at either the situs of the property or the domicile of the owner.

Sales and use taxes have in recent years come into the forefront of school financing, having been levied at both state and local levels. A Washington state use tax of 2 percent, placed on the privilege of using products from neighboring states, was upheld by the U.S. Supreme Court in 1937.[12] The tax was levied generally, except on property which had already been subjected to an equal or greater sale or use tax in Washington or any other state. This exception, the Supreme Court observed, was within the standard of equality required by the Interstate Commerce clause in that the tax did not impose greater burdens on the stranger than on the dweller within the state; therefore, in-state and out-of-state products were treated in the same way.

Sales of goods brought in from other states are subject to nondiscriminatory taxation by the recipient state. Thus, a tax confined to the sale of goods manufactured outside of the state, and not applied to the same products manufactured within the state, was set aside as unconstitutional.[13] According to Justice Reed, "The Commerce Clause forbids discrimination, whether forthright or ingenious."[14]

Besides property taxes, sales taxes, and use taxes, the states rely on both personal and corporate income taxes for educational financing. A state has the authority to tax the income from the property owned by a person who is a resident of another state. Similarly, the income from a business conducted or located in a state can be taxed regardless of where the person who owns the business resides. The U.S. Supreme Court has said

> that the State, from whose laws property and business and industry derive the protection and security without which production and gainful occupation would be impossible, is debarred from exacting a share of those gains in the form of income taxes for the support of the government, is a proposition so wholly inconsistent with fundamental principles as to be refuted by its mere statement. That it may tax the land but not the crop, the tree but not the fruit, the mine or well but not the product, the business but not the profit derived from it, is wholly inadmissible.[15]

The cardinal rule, though, is that a state cannot impede trade and the normal flow of commerce beyond state boundaries. Overall, when the sovereign power of taxation is viewed in its broadest context, the state has great legal latitude for deriving revenues to support the public schools.

FEDERAL FUNDS AND CONTROL

The limits of federal prerogative are not clearly defined by the interpretation of the power of the federal government to enact laws pursuant to the Commerce[16] and General Welfare clauses.[17] The Supreme Court has held that, in effect, the Commerce clause places few limitations on the central government. In creating this substantial if not unlimited federal discretion, the Court refused to attempt to specify limitations on potential areas of federal encroachment on state sovereignty. Nor would the Court define or dictate the parameters of the "sacred province of state autonomy."[18]

The General Welfare clause provides that the federal government can tax and spend for the general welfare subject only to Congress's own interpretation of the scope of "general welfare."

The provision, according to the Supreme Court, is elastic and changes with the times. (See Chapter 12 for further elaboration on the General Welfare clause.) Congressional actions on behalf of education may therefore be legitimized under either the Commerce or General Welfare clauses.[19]

Legal controversies have arisen in greater number as the federal government has become increasingly active in the aid and regulation of education. Federal funds are granted through categorical programs which support state efforts to provide specific educational programs such as vocational education, compensatory education, and education for the disabled.

Federal-State Powers

One case important to federal-state relations resulted from a conflict between state and federal interests in the implementation of Title I of the Elementary and Secondary Education Act of 1965, the compensatory education legislation. Provisions in the act for programs in private schools comparable to public schools offended the constitution of Missouri's church-state provision, and local education agencies in that state refused to implement the program as desired by the parochial schools.[20] The plaintiffs for the parochial schools sought to compel the state to implement Title I in spite of the Missouri Constitution, maintaining that the federal statute should prevail over the state constitutional prohibition. The Supreme Court held that Congress clearly did not intend for Title I to preempt state constitutional spending proscriptions as a condition of accepting federal funds. Thus, Title I should not be interpreted as overriding state constitutional law, and if a conflict exists between the two, a solution must be sought that would not subordinate the state constitution to federal statute. The Court suggested that the state seek ways of implementing the Title I "comparability" requirement which would not offend the state constitution and that the parochial schools agree to alternatives that would define "comparability" in broader terms without requiring that the funds be used for on-the-premises instruction in parochial schools.

Disabled Children

The emergence of greatly increased aid for disabled children from both state and federal levels has been a most apparent innovation in public school finance in recent years. The legal impetus came from two federal district court cases, one in Pennsylvania and the other in Washington, DC. In the Pennsylvania case, the state was enjoined from denying equal educational opportunity to disabled children, and shortly thereafter the court in the District of Columbia required that disabled children be provided publicly supported educational programs suitable to their needs. To the argument that such special programs were too expensive and could not be afforded, the federal district court in the Washington, D.C. case responded:

> If insufficient funds are available to finance all of the services and programs that are needed and desirable in the system, then the available funds must be expended equitably in such a manner that no child is entirely excluded from a publicly supported education. . . . The inadequacies of the District of Columbia Public School System, whether occasioned by insufficient funding or administrative inefficiency, certainly cannot be permitted to bear more heavily on the "exceptional" or handicapped child than on the normal child . . .[21]

These cases played a major role in creating a public awareness of problems associated with funding programs for disabled children and were instrumental in the federal government's ultimate response, the enactment of Public Law 94-142, later to become the Individual Disabilities Education Act (IDEA).

Supremacy of Federal Law

Federal legislation can have a direct effect on the distribution of state funds to local school districts. When a state statute directly conflicts with a federal statute, and no extenuating constitutional questions are involved, the federal statute takes precedence. One such conflict occurred in a Virginia case in 1968 in which the state foundation program law was challenged by a taxpayer because it charged back Public Law 874 funds against the state foundation program allocation.[22] In order to bring about greater fiscal equalization among school districts, the state of Virginia had decided to count P.L. 874 funds as local funds contributing to the local school district's fiscal ability. The effect of the chargeback was to effectively redirect state funds to financially needy school districts. The federal district court ignored the equalization question and ruled that the Supremacy Clause of the federal Constitution requires that when federal law conflicts with state law the federal intent must be upheld. This case resulted in some fifteen states revising their state-aid laws to delete provisions which counted P.L. 874—Impact Aid—funds as local fiscal ability.

ESTABLISHMENT OF RELIGION

According to the U.S. Supreme Court, the Establishment of Religion Clause of the First Amendment means that "no tax in any amount, large or small, can be levied to support any religious activities or institutions, whatever they may be called, or whatever form they may adopt to teach or practice religion."[23] Despite this rather clear proscription, state legislatures and the Congress have time and again enacted laws which aid parochial schools, such as Title I of the Elementary and Secondary Education Act of 1965 which is the largest and most influential. Also, state legislatures, particularly in New York, Pennsylvania, Ohio, and Rhode Island, have through various schemes sought to aid parochial schools and in each instance they have met with judicial disapproval.

Prior to 1970, the Supreme Court applied two constitutional tests to parochial school legislation, the secular legislative purpose test and the primary effect test. The former required that there be some purpose for the legislation other than aiding religion. Under the second test, the Court sought to determine whether the primary effect of the legislation was either to advance or inhibit religion. These two tests were used in the famous *Everson* case, in which a New Jersey law providing public funds for transportation of school children to parochial schools was held to be constitutional and in the later *Allen* case, in which the loan of textbooks to parochial schools was also upheld.[24] Neither of these tests proved to be very restrictive, and after *Allen* in 1968 many states moved to enact funding programs which would more directly aid parochial schools.

The first two of these new laws were almost immediately challenged in Pennsylvania and Rhode Island, and a decision by the Supreme Court invalidated them in 1971.[25] Under Pennsylvania law, the state superintendent was authorized to "purchase" specified secular education from parochial schools, and in Rhode Island the state law gave a salary supplement to parochial school teachers. In reaching a decision in these cases, the Supreme Court relied on a new, third test of establishment: excessive entanglement.[26] Thus, the precedents combined to provide a new three-part standard that (1) required a secular purpose, (2) neither enhanced nor inhibited religion, and (3) prohibited excessive entanglement. The third test holds invalid any legislation which tends to introduce state regulation into church affairs or to allow church encroachment on public policy decisions. In applying all three tests, the Court held that the Pennsylvania and Rhode Island aid provisions did not evince a legislative purpose to aid religion nor did they have the effect of advancing religion; nevertheless, both laws violated the excessive entanglement test, because both would have required such a degree of state scrutiny into the parochial school programs as to excessively entangle church and state.

Other methods of distributing state funds to aid parochial schools have been similarly stricken in recent years. A comprehensive law in New York provided for three methods of aiding parochial schools:

1. Maintenance and repair of school facilities
2. A tuition grant program
3. A tax benefit provision

The Court held that all three programs had the effect of aiding and advancing religion.[27] The Court observed that the provision to maintain and repair facilities could actually lead to the use of state funds to renovate classrooms in which religion was taught or to maintain a school chapel. The tuition grant, which provided reimbursement to low-income families who sent their children to private schools, had a sectarian orientation and effectively aided religion.[28] The third program, a plan to give tax benefits, was most innovative in seeking to bypass the excessive entanglement test by allowing parents with less than $25,000 in annual income to deduct specified amounts from their adjusted gross incomes for state income tax purposes. The Court held that such tax benefits were little different from tuition grants, since both fundamentally advance religion. That the tax benefits were directed to the parents rather than the parochial schools was irrelevant, since the net effect of the legislation was to strengthen the parochial schools by giving parents financial incentives to enroll their children in such schools. This case appeared to foreclose the possibility of other states or the federal government fashioning a constitutionally acceptable scheme for tuition tax credits to aid parochial schools.

Loans of instructional materials and equipment were held unconstitutional by the Supreme Court in another Pennsylvania case, *Meek* v. *Pittenger*.[29] The Court declared that one cannot separate the secular from the sectarian purposes of church-related elementary and secondary schools, and that aid to what may seemingly be a secular aspect of such school programs will undoubtedly result in spillover aid to the sectarian part of the schools' programs. The Court in *Meek* said:

> The very purpose of many of those schools is to provide an integrated secular and religious education; the teaching process is, to a large extent, de-

Box 2.1 _____

Separation Strengthens Both Church and State

Most Britons (including members of the royal family itself) pay scant heed to the rules of observance laid down by the church of which the monarch is Supreme Governor. For the first time in years, politicians and newspapers of all stripes are discussing whether disestablishment of the Church of England might benefit monarchy, church and nation. . . .

The Church of England has become a minority sect whose formal tie to the state does little to invigorate it. Britain has not been a Christian society for years but refuses to admit to agnosticism, largely out of nostalgia. Of the fewer than 4m (million) English in the pews on a typical Sunday, 1.3m are Roman Catholics, 1.2m attend the independent Protestant churches and a measly 1.1m—barely 2% of the populace—are Anglican. Less than a tenth of the English people are zealous Christians. . . .

The contrast with the United States is irresistible. . . . Between 40% and 50% of Americans are in church on a typical Sunday. President-elect Bill Clinton sings in a Baptist choir. Nearly two-thirds of Americans say a strong religious commitment is "absolutely essential" or "very important."

The paradox, of course, is that disestablishment of the American churches is ferociously enforced. . . . (In England there is no separation of church and state.)

Source: "The Worst of Worlds," *The Economist*, December 6, 1992–January 8, 1993, p. 80.

secondary education has remained rather firm. The *Wolman* v. *Walter* case, however, proved to be an exception because in it the Supreme Court upheld certain aspects of a complicated Ohio statute providing parochial school children not only with textbooks, but also with testing and scoring services, diagnostic services, therapeutic services, instructional materials and equipment, and field trips.[31] The Court disallowed state funding of instructional materials, equipment, and field trip provisions for parochial schools as effectively aiding and enhancing religion and violating the excessive entanglement test. On the other hand, testing and scoring services designed to measure the progress of parochial school students in secular subjects were upheld. Aid for diagnostic services for speech, hearing, and psychological disorders were upheld as constitutional. The Court found that diagnostic services were unlike teaching and counseling, and thus more remotely associated with the mission of the nonpublic school. Potential intrusion of sectarian views was believed to be minimal. The third element, therapeutic services for nonpublic school students, was upheld because the services were provided in public facilities, and were supervised by public employees. The Court did not seem to think that the state was enhancing religion by providing therapeutic services, although the services were exclusively for nonpublic school students and were held in mobile units used as annexes to the parochial school.

Dismantling the Wall

The influence of the Reagan administration's efforts to lower the wall of separation between church and state was first evidenced in a school funding case in 1983, *Mueller* v. *Allen*.[32] In this case, Van Mueller, a professor of educational administration at the University of Minnesota, and others contested the constitutionality of a Minnesota state statute allowing state income tax deductions for "tuition, textbooks, and transportation" for students attending public, private, and parochial schools. Because such costs are

voted to the inculcation of religious values and belief. . . . Substantial aid to the educational function of such schools, accordingly, necessarily results in aid to the sectarian school enterprise as a whole. . . . "[T]he secular education those schools provide goes hand in hand with the religious mission that is the only reason for the schools' existence. Within the institution, the two are inextricably intertwined.[30]

Beyond allowing for state aid for transportation and textbooks, the wall of separation between church and state in elementary and normally free to public school students, the statute in actuality constituted a subsidy to parents of children attending private and parochial schools. In this case the U.S. Supreme Court, with Justice Rehnquist writing for the majority, upheld the statute aiding parochial schools. The Court reasoned that because the subsidy theoretically went to public school parents as well as parents of children in private and parochial schools, the law neither enhanced nor inhibited religion. The Court further found that the state's efforts to defray education costs had a secular purpose and that the deduction from gross income of parents did not create an excessive entanglement between church and state.

The direction taken by the Supreme Court in the *Wolman* and *Mueller* cases indicated that the traditional wall of separation between church and state may be largely dismantled by the appointees of the Reagan-Bush administrations when the opportunity arises. Chief Justice Rehnquist in *Wallace* v. *Jaffree*[33] in 1985 provided the new philosophical rationale that would allow public tax monies to be used for parochial schools. He explained that the Establishment clause of the First Amendment was intended merely to prohibit a "national religion" or the "official designation of any church as a national one" as well as to discourage the preference of one religion over another. According to Rehnquist, a state or the federal government could aid all religious schools and not violate the principle of separation.

Should Rehnquist's interpretation prevail, the First Amendment prohibitions of vouchers, tuition tax credits, or tax deductions for aid to parochial schools will be negated. In such an event, the judicial interpretations of state constitutions by state courts will be the only barrier to a free flow of public tax funds to religious schools.

Such an interpretation by the appointees of the Reagan-Bush administrations would sweep away the three-part standard used by the Court since 1971 and run flatly counter to the Madison and Jefferson[34] concept of separation of church

and state. Madison specifically rejected early attempts in Virginia to provide tax funds to aid all churches, and his reasoning was clearly elucidated in his famous *Memorial Remonstrance Against Religious Assessments*. In *Everson* v. *Board of Education*[35] in 1947 the Supreme Court, following Madison, said clearly, "Neither a state nor the Federal Government can set up a church, aid all religions, or prefer one religion over another." The historical prohibition of "establishment of religion"[36] applied to "not just one preferred church" over another, but "to *all* churches that had legal and financial connections with the state."[37]

If the strength of the Establishment Clause of the U.S. Constitution is weakened by the Supreme Court one may look to state courts and state constitutions for renewed activity regarding state aid to church schools. Bills for state aid to parochial schools were introduced in well over one-half of state legislatures from 1991 to 1993. In several of the states, the state constitutions have church-state provisions at least as strong as the federal First Amendment's Establishment and Free Exercise clauses. Because of the strength of these constitutional provisions, proponents of state aid to parochial schools have launched a series of initiatives to gain favorable precedents in state courts or, in the alternative, to amend the state constitutions to allow tax support for parochial schools.

In November 1993, the California voters resoundingly defeated a voucher initiative, Proposition 174, to amend the California Constitution to allow aid to parochial schools. This amendment would have given tax-funded vouchers of $2,600 per pupil to children attending religious and private schools. In 1992, Colorado voters defeated by a vote of 67 percent to 33 percent an amendment to the Colorado Constitution that would have provided an estimated $85 million per year for sectarian private schools and for homeschooling through a voucher program. Earlier, in 1990, a similar initiative was defeated in Oregon by a two-to-one margin. Efforts to gain state tax support for parochial schools will probably intensify during the decade of the 1990s. The battlegrounds will undoubtedly shift from the federal courts to the state courts, and state legislatures will come under new and increased pressure to use tax monies to aid private and parochial schools.

Equality and Uniformity of Taxation

As a general rule, courts will not hold an act of the legislature unconstitutional unless it can be clearly demonstrated that the legislature exercised its authority in an arbitrary or capricious manner. State courts have rarely overthrown their own legislatures' taxing provisions. For an act to be arbitrary or capricious in the uniformity or equality sense, it must be shown that the state unreasonably classified a particular group of persons or in some way discriminated against them through the tax system. If such discrimination did exist, then state as well as federal guarantees against unconstitutional classifications would be violated. The equality question, with regard to taxation, is clearly enunciated by the U.S. Supreme Court *in dictum* in the *Bell's Gap* Case, where Justice Bradley explained:

> [The Equal Protection Clause] was not intended to prevent a state from adjusting its system of taxation in all proper and reasonable ways. . . . We think we are safe in saying, that the Fourteenth Amendment was not intended to compel the state to adopt an iron rule of equal taxation. If that were its proper construction it would not only supersede all those constitutional provisions and laws of some of the states, whose object is to secure equality of taxation, and which are usually accompanied with qualifications deemed material; but it would render negatory those discriminations which the best interests of society require.[38]

The state legislature may therefore utilize the taxing system to equalize the rich and poor, as is done, for instance, through the redistributional effects of a graduated income tax. Also, if it wishes, the state may collect tax funds from wealthy school districts and redistribute them to poorer districts in other parts of the state. In this context, neither state uniformity and equality of taxation provisions nor the federal Equal Protection clause require that proceeds from taxes be distributed in any particular manner or method. In *Sawyer* v. *Gilmore*, a 1912 case, the Supreme Court of Maine reasoned:

> The method of distributing the proceeds of such a tax rests in the wise discretion and sound judgment of the Legislature. If this discretion is unwisely exercised, the remedy is with the people, and not with the court. . . . In order that taxation may be equal and uniform in the constitutional sense, it is not necessary that the benefits arising therefrom should be enjoyed by all the people in equal degree, nor that each one of the people should participate in each particular benefit.[39]

Uniformity and equality of taxation provisions of state constitutions cannot be invoked by the taxpayer to challenge the distribution of state school funds among school districts. While state and local taxation must be uniform and equal, the distribution of the revenues can be unequal in order to achieve a valid state objective. The law may be summarized thus:

> In the absence of constitutional regulation the method of apportioning and distributing a school fund, accruing from taxes or other revenue, rests in the wise discretion of the state legislature, which method, in the absence of abuse of discretion or violation of some constitutional provision, cannot be interfered with by the courts. . . . The fact that the fund is distributed unequally among the different districts or political subdivisions does not render it invalid.[40]

Such precedents make it quite clear that courts are hesitant to interfere with legislative discretion in the realm of taxation, and that the methods used by legislatures to distribute state aid to their school districts[41] will not come under judicial regulation. Similarly, the federal courts will tend to exercise a high degree of judicial restraint when the Equal Protection clause of the Fourteenth Amendment is invoked in challenging state systems of taxation.

The School Finance Cases

Methods of apportioning state funds for public schools have been challenged under both federal and state constitutions. These actions have been brought either by those who claim that the tax system used for raising school revenues does not treat taxpayers uniformly and equally, or by parents who maintain that their children are denied equal educational opportunity because of an unequal distribution of tax revenues among school districts. As noted above, taxpayer plaintiffs have frequently couched their claims in the following basic contentions:

1. The Equal Protection clause of the U.S. Constitution
2. Education provisions in state constitutions that usually require the state to provide a uniform, thorough, efficient, or equal system of education for all children of the state
3. The equal protection clauses found in state constitutions

Recently, state courts have become more active and less likely to defer to legislative prerogative regarding the structure of school finance systems and the distribution of public school funds. In 1968 a wave of school finance litigation began that has touched virtually all states and has not abated. These cases have created a major change in the way we think about state school financing. Not only do such cases bring into play the third branch of government, but the legal logic that supports them has caused reconsideration of the methods we use to fund public schools. These cases are a forthright challenge to the fairness of legislative allocations of funds favoring children who attend school in more affluent school districts. The legal logic of these cases is not unlike the rationale of the desegregation cases that had successfully asserted that the government cannot treat equally situated persons unequally.

A Child of the State.   The underlying philosophical and legal rationale is that (1) public education is a state function not a local one, (2) a child is a child of the state and not of the locality, (3) all school revenues are state revenues regardless of whether they are collected at state or local levels, and (4) all school children are equal under the law of the state. Therefore, the state cannot combine its state and local tax resources in such a manner as to advantage some children and disadvantage others.

Logic Flow of School Finance Cases
1. All persons are entitled to equal treatment under the law.
2. Education is a state function.
3. The state legislature is responsible for education.
4. Public schools are created as an exercise of legislative responsibility.
5. Every child is a child of the state, not of the local district.
6. All taxes are state taxes, whether collected at the state or local level.
7. The legislature cannot create educational disadvantage by disparate distribution of tax resources.

This reasoning leads to the conclusion that in a sovereign state system children of the state cannot be treated differently for purposes of their education merely because some children are less fortunate than others and must attend school in poor districts. These school finance cases caused a reexamination of the older justifications for inequality of funding which basically held that (1) legislatures had plenary power over taxation and allocation and were unrestrained in their judgment, (2) public schools were for all intents and purposes local institutions, and (3) state funds were merely supplements to local tax dollars. These assumptions had led to the understanding in virtually all states that the legislative responsibility was fulfilled if children in poor school districts were given only a foundation of support while children in more affluent school districts received funding above and beyond that foundation.

State-Created Privilege.   As indicated above, the plaintiffs in the school finance cases borrowed logic from the desegregation cases that challenged state-created disparities based on race. In state school funding statutes, legislatures had combined state and local fiscal resources to create bright education prospects for some children while allowing only dismal prospects for others. Plaintiffs claimed that when legitimate differences existed among children, the state was justified in dispensing its resources to help the less advantaged, but there was no justification for the state to create disparities in fiscal resources to favor the more advantaged. By launching these court actions the plaintiffs sought to compel legislatures to defend their allocation decisions in terms of fairness and equity. Prior to these school finance cases the legislative enactments had been treated as though they were infallible. The courts had always deferred to legislative discretion, and the children attending schools in districts with low fiscal capacity suffered the consequences without hope of redress. The school finance litigation provided the aggrieved children in poor school districts a means to alleviate their plight.

Two Types of Cases. The school finance cases are of two basic substantive types. The first type reasons that equality is preemptory in societal consideration and wide inequalities created or condoned by the state may be challenged. Presumably all who have thought seriously and objectively about the question agree that government should treat all people in like circumstances equally. Dworkin, a leading modern legal philosopher, says, "I assume that we . . . accept, as fundamental, the principle that people should be treated *as equals* in the matter of distribution. That is to say that they should be treated as equals unless they are, in fact, not equal in some relevant way."[42]

The second type approaches the issue with an awareness that all persons do not enter life and/or school at equal levels of ability, or social or economic circumstance, and because of these initial differences, more resources for some than for others may be justified. Justice requires that

some have greater resources for their education because they have come into the arena with greater deficiencies. Equity may thus emerge from both assumptions—equal treatment of equals and unequal treatment of unequals.

Equal Treatment of Equals. The first assumption, equal treatment of equals, is a natural and basic element in the general theory of justice. Government must treat all persons in like circumstances equally. If government does not treat equals in an equal manner it must provide "sufficient reason not to do so."[43] The happenstance of geographical location or the fact that a child is born to poor parents or resides in a property-poor school district is not sufficient reason to justify such a disparity in school revenues as to create an educational disadvantage for that child.

Unequal Treatment of Unequals. Unequal treatment of unequals may well be necessary when equality of opportunity is impeded by circumstances that deprive some of equal prospects in life. This brings into consideration the "educational needs" arguments. If some children come to school with learning disadvantages, whether caused by natural, social, or economical conditions, the state may be justified in providing them with relatively greater financial resources. Concentrating more resources on the less advantaged children who have greater educational needs may be both socially desirable and morally defensible. Equality of opportunity may require substantially more funds for those with the greatest educational deficiencies. Educational need is sufficient reason to give more to some than to others.

Constitutional Logic. These two types of cases have been argued in both federal and state courts. The constitutional bases are found under equal protection and education clauses in state constitutions. The federal Constitution and most state constitutions have equal protection clauses. The federal Equal Protection clause in the Fourteenth Amendment was understandably the first constitutional rationale seized upon by school finance reformers because it had been the constitutional vehicle to end state-enforced segregation of public schools during the 1950s and 1960s. Invidious racial discrimination in provision of school facilities and educational opportunities was similar to the type of financial discrimination suffered by poor children living in poor school districts. In fact some of the same arguments made to defend segregation are now being used to defend disparities in school revenues among school districts.

In current school finance litigation the state often defends inequality of school funding by asserting that rich districts already give more to the state treasury than they receive back in school funding. Richard Kluger observes that this same logic was used to defend less money for black schools[44] in the segregation era before 1954. Kluger points out that Prince Edward County, Virginia, defended giving more money to schools for whites than for blacks, by asserting that ". . . the whites were doing far more already for the colored people than their (colored people) tax contributions warranted."[45] In other words, the poor blacks paid less into the system and were therefore entitled to receive less benefits back from it. The same arguments of course have been used throughout history to justify inequality. Niebuhr has best summarized the justification of discrimination against the less fortunate.

> It has always been the habit of privileged groups to deny the oppressed classes every opportunity for the cultivation of innate capacities and then to accuse them of lacking what they have been denied the right to acquire.[46]

In the school finance cases the plaintiffs have shown that the states' intentional denial of educational opportunity has a generational impact resulting in lower income and wealth for those who in earlier years were denied educational opportunity. They therefore cannot contribute sufficient tax funds to support schools for their own children. The downward spiral of less money contributing to even lower levels of opportunity

is prevalent in most state systems today, and perversely many state legislatures and affluent school systems vigorously defend systems that foster such inequities. The constitutional logic of these cases was designed to counteract the various justifications for educational privilege in public schools based on the fortuitous circumstances of wealth.

Federal Equal Protection

Smoldering discontent with legislative inaction in remediating fiscal inequalities among school districts was given legal foundation in a book entitled *Rich Schools, Poor Schools*, written by Wise in 1968.[47] Wise's basic thesis was that since education was a state responsibility, the wide disparities created by state funding schemes that classified children according to the fiscal ability or inability of their respective school districts could not withstand constitutional challenge.

The first case to follow this rationale and to challenge the constitutionality of a state school finance program was *Burruss* v. *Wilkerson*, decided in Virginia in 1968.[48] Shortly thereafter, in *McInnis* v. *Shapiro*, filed in Illinois, plaintiffs made similar claims, alleging that the method of financing used by the state of Illinois denied plaintiff children equal protection of the 14th Amendment by depriving those children from low-income families in poor school districts access to equitable resources for their educations.[49] Plaintiffs in both *Burruss* and *McInnis* alleged that a state school finance program violates equal protection if it does not correct for financial inabilities among local school districts and if it does not take into account the educational needs of the children. In other words, the state must fiscally equalize among school districts to erase revenue disparities and to provide funds on the basis of educational need, taking into account social, economic, cultural, physical, or mental deficiencies that detract from educational opportunity.

The federal district courts in both cases held against the plaintiffs, and on appeal the U.S.

Supreme Court summarily affirmed the lower courts' decisions. The position of the courts with regard to equalization of local tax resources is well encapsulated by the federal district court in *McInnis*.

> Unequal educational expenditures per student, based upon the variable property values and tax rates of local school districts, do not amount to an invidious discrimination. Moreover, the statutes which permit these unequal expenditu\res on a district to district basis are neither arbitrary nor unreasonable.[50]

Thus, plaintiffs were required to show not only that the expenditure disparities existed, but also that the disparities resulted in invidious discrimination against a particular class of persons. According to the court, although substantial differences existed, there was a rational relationship between the state's funding scheme and the results it was designed to achieve.

With regard to the educational needs aspect of the plaintiff's argument, the *McInnis* court refused to intervene and substitute its judgment for legislative prescription, saying, "The courts have neither the knowledge, nor the means, nor the power to tailor the public moneys to fit the varying needs of these students throughout the state."[51] Further, the *McInnis* court concluded that there were no "judicially manageable standards" by which it could accurately determine the extent to which educational needs were being met. Both *Burruss* and *McInnis* were affirmed by the U.S. Supreme Court, but without an opinion. It was therefore impossible to know exactly what the Court's rationale was for the summary affirmations in either case.

The Rodriguez Case. The position of the U.S. Supreme Court was not to be known until 1973, when, in the now famous case of *San Antonio Independent School District* v. *Rodriguez*, the high Court held in a 5-to-4 decision that the state foundation program in Texas did not violate the federal Equal Protection clause.[52] Plaintiffs maintained that education was a fundamental right and that children attending school in poor school districts constituted a suspect classification and thus the Supreme Court must strictly scrutinize the Texas system, forcing the burden of proof on the state to show that it had a "compelling interest" rather than mere "rationality" in maintaining the state school finance program. If invoked, the strict scrutiny test means that the state's system is not entitled to the usual presumption of validity; rather, the state must sustain a heavy burden of justification.

Texas virtually conceded that its school finance legislation could not withstand the strict scrutiny burden, but it could show that its system was at least not irrational. The decision then rested on which constitutional test the U.S. Supreme Court used. Taking the issues one by one, the Court first found that education is not a fundamental right under the Equal Protection clause. Secondly, it determined that the plaintiffs had not clearly delineated a suspect class of poor at which the alleged state discrimination was directed. In so finding, the Court concluded that the appropriate test to be applied was not "strict scrutiny" but "rational relationship." In summation, the Court found that the extent to which

> . . . the Texas system of school financing results in unequal expenditures between children who happen to reside in different districts, we cannot say that such disparities are the product of a system that is so irrational as to be invidiously discriminatory.[53]

The Court went on to say that education presents a myriad of intractable economic, social, and philosophical problems the complexity of which suggests that the legislatures of the states should be given wide discretion within the limits of rationality.

State Equal Protection

After the *Rodriguez* decision, school finance litigation turned almost exclusively to state constitutions and state courts. In the absence of federal constitutional redress, the avenues of relief for plaintiffs centered on the equal protection and

Box 2.2

Three Standards of Equal Protection

Three standards of review may be employed in equal protection decisions.

The Rational Relationship Test. The first standard of review is the rational relationship test . . . developed for use in both equal protection and substantive due process issues in the post-1937 decisions in Court. The court will not grant any significant review of legislative decisions to classify persons in terms of general economic legislation. In this area the justices have determined that they have no unique function to perform; they have no institutional capability to assess the scope of legitimate governmental ends in these areas or the reasonableness of classifications that is in any way superior to that of the legislature. Thus, if a classification is of this type the Court will ask only whether it is conceivable that the classification bears a rational relationship to an end of government which is not prohibited by the Constitution. So long as it is arguable that the other branch of government had such a basis for creating the classification a court should not invalidate the law.

The Strict Scrutiny Test. The second type of review under the equal protection guarantee is generally referred to as "strict scrutiny." This test means that the justices will not defer to the decision of the other branches of government but will instead independently determine the degree of relationship which the classification bears to a constitutionally compelling end. . . . The Court will not accept every permissible government purpose as sufficient to support a classification under this test, but will instead require the government to show that it is pursuing a "com-pelling" or "overriding" end—one whose value is so great that it justifies the limitation of fundamental constitutional values.

Even if the government can demonstrate such an end, the Court will not uphold the classification unless the justices have independently reached the conclusion that the classification is necessary to promote that compelling interest. . . .

The Intermediate Test. [The third standard] [I]n more recent years there have appeared a number of cases in which the Court has given very little deference to legislative judgements when reviewing legislation classifications but in which the Court has not employed either the traditional rational basis or compelling interest standard. This form of independent, but not technically "strict scrutiny," review has appeared in a variety of modern cases. . . .

The standard of review of these cases eliminates the strong presumption of constitutionality that exists under the rational bases standard of review but it allows the government to employ a . . . classification so long as it is a reasonable means of achieving substantial government ends and not merely the arbitrary classifying of people. . . .

The most recent decisions demonstrate that the Court will review classifications based on illegitimacy in a meaningful way: the Court now requires that the use of such classifications be substantially related to a legitimate governmental interest. While the precise nature of this test is unclear, what is clear is that a majority of the justices now require some demonstration that the classification is not an arbitrary burden on illegitimates or their parents due to moral approbation or stereotypes. . . .

Source: Reprinted from *Constitutional Law,* John E. Nowak, Ronald D. Rotunda, and J. Nelson Young (St. Paul, MN: West Publishing Company, 1986) pp. 530–552 with permission of the West Publishing Corporation.

---

education clauses of state constitutions (see Appendixes A and B).

As noted earlier, virtually all states have an equal protection clause or its equivalent.[54] Equal protection clauses, whether federal or state, are designed to protect individuals so that "all governmental actions [equitably] classify individuals for different benefits or burdens under the law."[55] Equal protection mandates that "similar individuals be dealt with in a similar manner by the law."[56] Justice Black once referred to these prohibitions against governmental infringement on individual rights or liberties as "a remarkable collection of 'thou shalt nots'"[57] Prohibitions of this type have their roots in the theory of natural rights advanced by Locke and later espoused by Jefferson. When these rights have been expressed or implied by the language of state constitutions, the courts have held that they establish a fundamental right.[58]

Thus, the state equal protection provision—in effect, as a negative, "thou shalt not"—may, on its own, constitute a viable approach to challenge the unequal distribution of school funds.[59] However, while it does not prohibit government from "drawing lines" to classify persons, it does guarantee that those classifications will not be based on arbitrary or impermissible criteria.[60]

In *Rodriguez* the U.S. Supreme Court said that the state of Texas could "draw lines" around school districts, thereby classifying children, and that such classification was not impermissibly discriminatory or irrational. Further, in *Rodriguez* the Court reasoned that differences in school revenues created by the state based on local school district wealth were not an arbitrary state creation of benefits and burdens. The constitutional rationale that has thus developed governing equal protection litigation may be summarized in three parts.

1. There must be a suspect discrete class of deprived persons.
2. These deprived persons must be denied benefits available to others.
3. This denial adversely affects a fundamental right.

The Court held that such conditions were not present in the factual situation in *Rodriguez*. These were of course precisely the issues that reemerged as the plaintiffs in poor school districts turned away from federal courts and began to seek their fortunes in state courts under state constitutions. It is precisely this type of case that is being pursued so actively in many state courts today.

Independent Vitality.   During the 1970s and 1980s, as federal courts became less active in ex-

panding federal constitutional protection, many state courts began to show a revival of their own authority and influence. While most state supreme courts had earlier interpreted their respective state equal protection clauses to be consistent with and limited to the scope of the federal Equal Protection clause, several recent state court decisions have given their own equal protection clauses an "independent vitality" that exceeds the protection guaranteed by the federal Constitution. The Supreme Court of California in the 1976 *Serrano* v. *Priest*,[61] following the U.S. Supreme Court's 1973 *Rodriguez* decision, ruled that the equal protection clause of the California Constitution need not be confined to the more limited scope of the federal equal protection guarantee, but can exceed it in breadth of application to state legislation. The *Serrano* Court said:

> Our state equal protection provisions, while substantially equivalent of the guarantees contained in the Fourteenth Amendment to the United States Constitution, are possessed of an independent vitality which, in a given case, may demand an analysis different from that which [it] would obtain if only the federal standard were applicable.[62]

This "independent vitality," a newfound strength in state equal protection clauses, has been the frame of constitutional reference used by several other state supreme courts in ruling for the plaintiffs in school finance litigation. The Wyoming Supreme Court expanded the meaning of equal protection said, "The right to an education cannot constitutionally be conditioned on wealth in that such a measure does not afford equal protection."[63]

Suspect Classification.   The Wyoming Supreme Court also rejected the narrower view of the U.S. Supreme Court in *Rodriguez* that found that school district wealth did not create a suspect classification.

> A classification on the basis of wealth is considered suspect, especially when applied to fundamental interests. . . . The respective tax bases of the

school districts of this state and their per-student resources reflect discordant correlations which plainly demonstrate the failure of the current system to provide equal educational opportunity.[64]

The independent vitality of state constitutions was further demonstrated in the Connecticut case, *Horton 1*,[65] in which that state's supreme court found that free public education was so important and so basic that the law of equal protection was implicated "in significant aspects *sui generis* [the only one of its kind] and hence could not be measured by accepted conventional tests."[66] Nor, the court said, could the application of mechanical standards normally ascribed to the evaluation of equal protection be applied where inequalities in school funding blatantly existed.[67]

Fundamentality.   A basic requirement to obtain redress under the equal protection clauses of the state constitutions is that the alleged denial or discrimination affect a fundamental right. Government may legitimately create all sorts of classifications of persons and bestow benefits and detriments without offending equal protection, but equal protection is offended if governmental action adversely affects a fundamental right. It came as a surprise to many that the U.S. Supreme Court in 1973 in *Rodriguez* found that education is not a fundamental right protected by the Equal Protection clause of the Fourteenth Amendment. After *Rodriguez*, as litigation reverted to state constitutions, state court decisions have gone both ways, some have agreed with *Rodriguez*[68] and others have held that education is a fundamental right.[69] In *Pauley* v. *Kelly*, the Supreme Court of West Virginia concluded that the mandatory nature of the education clause in that state's constitution made education "a fundamental, constitutional right."[70] The Supreme Court of Kentucky too found that the animus— the intent, design, and disposition of the framers of the Kentucky Constitution—was to make education a fundamental right in that state. These courts hold that education is so important to the individual and to good government that any

---

Box 2.3 _____

Wealth

Wealth is not without its advantages and the case to the contrary, although it has often been made, has never proved widely persuasive.

Source: John Kenneth Galbraith, in A. B. Atkinson, *Unequal Shares* (Harmondsworth, England: Penguin Books, 1974), p. 25.

---

thoughtful consideration of the question can lead to but one conclusion, that education is indeed fundamental (see Appendixes A and B).

Some state courts, though, do not agree with this conclusion. It is their view that while education is important it does not rise to the level of constitutional fundamentality. The Maryland Supreme Court sees education as merely another type of ordinary governmental service: "The right to adequate education in Maryland is no more fundamental than the right to personal security, to fire protection, to welfare subsidies, to health care or like vital governmental services."[71] The Oklahoma Supreme Court took a similar position, maintaining that the mere fact that education is provided for in the Oklahoma constitution does not make it a fundamental right and such provisions do not guarantee equality of educational opportunity.[72] The reasoning of the Supreme Court of Georgia was very close to that of the courts in Maryland and Oklahoma. The Georgia court acknowledged that even though education may be vital, it is not fundamental and is of no more constitutional importance than food, lodging, police and fire protection, water, and health services.[73]

The state courts that refuse to give education the status of a fundamental right for equal protection purposes always cite *Rodriguez* as the legal authority for their conclusions. They do not attribute an "independent vitality" or more expansive definition to their own state equal protection clauses than the U.S. Supreme Court gives to protection under the Fourteenth Amendment. In virtually all cases when a state court declares education a fundamental right, it is a sign of some certitude that the court is prepared to hold for the plaintiffs. As noted earlier, to declare that education is a fundamental right provides the critical legal step that is normally taken in order to invoke strict judicial scrutiny, thereby forcing the state government to show a compelling reason for its creation of funding disparities among local school districts. Few states are able to show that there is a compelling need to give more resources to wealthy school districts than to poor school districts.

Yet the invoking of fundamentality does not always lead to a decision for the plaintiffs. For example, the Arizona Supreme Court found that education is a fundamental right under the Arizona Constitution but did not apply the "strict scrutiny" burden of proof to the state to show a "compelling reason" for the creation of funding disparities.[74] Instead, the court required only that the state show that the funding program was "rational, reasonable, and neither discriminatory nor capricious" to meet state equal protection requirements.[75] The legal effect was to make the declaration of fundamentality relatively meaningless.

In still another deviation, the Supreme Court of Arkansas held that it was unnecessary to address the fundamentality question because the state system of funding would not even meet the lesser rational relationship test.[76] In holding for the plaintiff—children in poor school districts—this court said, "We find no constitutional basis for the present system, as it has no rational bearing on the educational needs of the districts."[77]

Thus, equal protection provisions in state constitutions may be an effective legal tool to force legislatures to create greater equity in school funding; however, the precedents indicate that the courts can take widely differing views as to the scope of equal protection and the extent of its surety of equality of educational opportunity. As an avenue of constitutional redress for disparate funding, equal protection is probably less reliable than the education clauses of state constitutions.

EDUCATION CLAUSES IN STATE CONSTITUTIONS*

The education clause (in a state constitution) is normally a positive requirement that the legislature provide for education, while the state equal protection clause, or its equivalent, is a negative prohibition forbidding the state from taking away an individual's right. (See Figure 2.1 and Appendixes A and B for examples of state constitutional provisions relating to and establishing public schools.) Three positive education clauses, usually found in the body of the constitution, are: virtue provision, systems without adjectives, and requirements with emphasis or adjectives.

Virtue.   Some state provisions broadly affirm the value of education, extolling education as the surety of a virtuous government.[78] Such provisions call on the government to "cherish"[79] education as in the New England clause because it emanated from early consideration of public education in that region.[80] Virtue emanates from the Enlightenment as the end that good government should seek to achieve. Such language employs terminology used by Jefferson in his "Bill For the More General Diffusion of Knowledge" in 1779.[81] This provision, while appearing to be of less force than other types of provisions, in actuality has substantial historical and constitutional strength in enforcing equality of educational opportunity.[82]

System without Adjective.   The second type of positive provision requires that the legislature establish and maintain a system of public schools. Although the word *system* is replete with historical meaning, the term alone does not have the strength of more specific wording to define the type of system required. For example,

*This section is quoted in part from Kern Alexander, "The Common School Ideal and the Limits of Legislative Authority: The Kentucky Case," *Harvard Journal on Legislation*, vol. 28, no. 2 (Summer 1991), pp. 351–356. Permission granted by the Harvard Journal on Legislation. Copyright © 1991 by the President and Fellows of Harvard College.

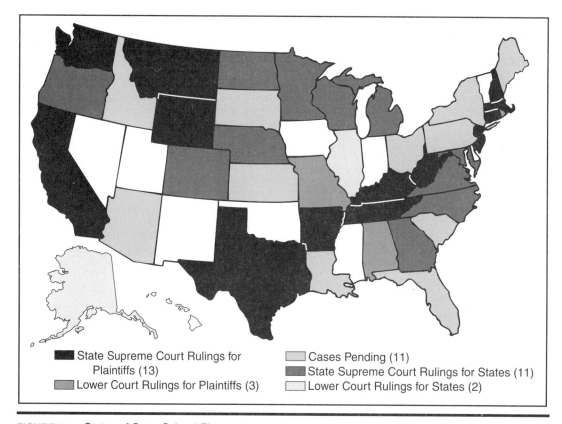

State Supreme Court Rulings for Plaintiffs (13)

Lower Court Rulings for Plaintiffs (3)

Cases Pending (11)

State Supreme Court Rulings for States (11)

Lower Court Rulings for States (2)

FIGURE 2.1   Status of State School-Finance Lawsuits

Source: Center for the Study of Educational Finance, Illinois State University.

the Supreme Court of California held that the undefined term *system* in the clause, "The legislature shall provide for a system of common schools . . . ,"[83] could not be interpreted to require uniform expenditures among the school districts.[84] The California court had earlier held that the word *system* as used in Article IX, Section 5 of the state's constitution, implies a "unity of purpose, as well as an entirety of operation," requiring the legislature to provide "one system which shall be applicable to all the common schools within the state,"[85] but the word *system*, used without a modifier, could not be interpreted to require equality of expenditures.[86]

Tennessee is another state whose constitution uses the word *system* without an adjective or modifier. Article IX, Section 12 of the Tennessee

Constitution requires that the "General Assembly shall provide for the maintenance, support and eligibility standards of a system of free public schools."[87] Here the system must be "maintained and supported," implying that an inadequately funded system may be constitutionally deficient, but the lack of a modifier for *system* tends to weaken the requirement.

Adjectives as Terms of Art.   The third type of positive constitutional provision includes one or more adjectives or terms of art to define the kind of system required. Words and phrases such as *general and uniform,*[88] *efficient,*[89] *thorough and efficient,*[90] *adequate,*[91] *thorough and uniform,*[92] and other combinations tend to give more substantive meaning to the constitutional mandate.

The education provision of a state constitution may, without support or complement from any other constitutional source, require substantial uniformity in the allocation of school funds. The New Jersey Supreme Court in *Robinson* v. *Cahill* first expressed this view by indicating that the system of school financing could be held unconstitutional solely on the basis of the positive mandate of the education provision of the state constitution.[93] Unlike the Kentucky case, *Robinson* did not find that education was fundamental, nor did it need to. Rather, the New Jersey court found that unconstitutionality could be determined even though education is *not* fundamental for equal protection purposes. The court in *Robinson* held simply that the affirmative mandate of the education provision of the New Jersey Constitution had not been fulfilled by the legislature, and that "a system of instruction in any district of the state which is not thorough and efficient falls short of the constitutional command."[94]

Another application of both the education provision and the state equal protection clause, slightly different from either Kentucky's or New Jersey's, is expressed in West Virginia's *Pauley* v. *Kelly*.[95] The West Virginia Supreme Court found the positive mandate of the education provision sufficient to establish fundamentality, and that this fundamentality could be applied to invoke that state's equal protection clause.[96] In *Pauley*, the court saw the equal protection clause and the "thorough and efficient" education provision to be harmonious and complementary. The court wrote, "Certainly, the mandate requirement of a 'thorough and efficient system of free schools,' . . . demonstrates that education is a fundamental constitutional right in the state."[97]

Harmony of Provisions.   The Kentucky case, in tandem with *Serrano*, *Robinson*, and *Pauley*, suggests substantial judicial flexibility in the application of both the negative constitutional prohibitions of equal protection and the positive constitutional requirements of the education provisions in redressing the unequal apportionment of school funds. This flexible view may allow a separate application of either the equal protection or the education provision, or rather it may permit some "harmonious" combination of the two to strike down an unequal allocation of school funds. In a vein of even greater flexibility, the Kentucky court appeared to suggest that education is by its very nature an inherent right, obligating the court to give it special consideration when carefully scrutinizing any legislation which may deny its equal exercise and benefits.

Infirmity of Precedent.   The courts, though, have been rather inconsistent in their interpretations, regardless of wording. Thus there are no commonly accepted judicial definitions for the words that are frequently found in state constitutions prescribing the kind of public school systems that are required by the people. Some of these terms—efficient, equal, thorough, uniform, general quality, and general diffusion of knowledge—have been given great weight and substance by some state courts and are said to mean very little by others. For example, the word *efficient* as an adjective to *system* has been given substantial import and expansive content by courts in Kentucky,[98] Texas,[99] New Jersey,[100] and West Virginia,[101] but the same term in the Maryland[102] and Illinois[103] constitutions was viewed more narrowly by the courts. (See Appendix A).

The term *efficient* was the operative term in the Kentucky Constitution that the Kentucky Supreme Court found to be of such intent and strength to hold Kentucky's entire system of public schools unconstitutional. The Kentucky court found that the essential, and minimal, characteristics of an efficient system of common schools included requirements of substantial uniformity, equality of access to the financial resources of the state and the implicit mandate of adequacy of funding.

Both the New Jersey[104] and West Virginia Constitutions require the legislature to establish and maintain "thorough and efficient" systems of public schools. The New Jersey court in

Robinson in 1973 found that the "thorough and efficient" requirement meant that equality of educational opportunity must be provided:

> The Constitution's guarantee must be understood to embrace that educational opportunity which is needed in the contemporary setting to equip a child for his role as a citizen and as a competitor in the labor market.[105]

Further, as noted earlier, the West Virginia court[106] ruled that the "thorough and efficient" provision of the education clause elevated education to a position of a fundamental right for equal protection purposes.[107]

However, other courts have not found the term *efficient* to convey such a pervasive meaning. The words of the Ohio Constitution requiring the legislature to "secure a thorough and efficient system"[108] were given scant importance by the Ohio Supreme Court in 1979, and the same words, "thorough and efficient" in the Colorado Constitution were not weighty enough to invalidate the disparities in that state's system of school finance. The word *efficient* even when combined with a requirement to obtain a high quality of public education, was left without significant substance by the Illinois Supreme Court.[109]

Court decisions fall on both sides of other terminology as well. The Jeffersonian language requiring "general diffusion of knowledge"[110] was given great weight by the Texas Supreme Court in *Edgewood*,[111] and an even stronger and more definitive interpretation by a lower court in Missouri in 1993.[112] However, a lower court in Virginia—Jefferson's own state—indicated in 1992 that these historical terms of art meant nothing as a substantive guide to the state's legislature.

In interpreting the meaning of *efficient* in tandem with the Texas Constitution's requirement that there be a general diffusion of knowledge, the Texas Supreme Court said:

> Children who live in poor districts and children who live in rich districts must be afforded a substantially equal opportunity to have access to educational funds. Certainly, this much is required if the state is to educate its populace efficiently and provide for a general diffusion of knowledge statewide.[113]

Contradictions as to the intent and meaning of education clauses of state constitutions evidence the fluid state of the litigation as late as 1993. State courts continue to hand down cases both approving and disapproving of state school finance formulas. The most important and significant aspect of these decisions is perhaps not that there is agreement among the courts, or whether a clear pattern of precedent is emerging, but rather that the state courts are no longer blindly deferential to state legislatures. The rulings of the earlier courts that avowed noninterference with legislative prerogative, or judicial assertions that guaranteed plenary power to the legislature in the distribution of funds for public schools are now precedents of another era. The new era is one in which state courts will increasingly be called upon to correct inequities created by state legislation, and many of these courts will cast aside judicial deference and impose their own interpretations of state constitutional intent.

SUMMARY AND CONCLUSIONS

This chapter provides a brief overview of the law as it affects public school finance. References are made to pertinent federal constitutional and statutory provisions that have a bearing on the flow of educational funds. Most importantly, though, this chapter discusses the legal issues that pertain to the whole series of school finance equity cases that have now touched nearly every state.

Because education is not a delegated function of the central government, some of the most relevant and revealing foundational statements regarding public schools are found in state constitutions as enunciations of the will of the people.

State constitutional provisions both empower and restrict state legislatures. Empowerment is usually coupled with corresponding responsibilities that legislatures are obliged to fulfill. Restraints usually flow from the protection of individual freedoms or rights that the legislature cannot transgress.

Some of the most common constitutional restrictions are imposed on the legislative power to levy taxes. This power to tax is jealously guarded by the people, and legislatures are frequently restricted in its use. Moreover, legislatures are not permitted to share or delegate their taxing powers to subordinate agencies except through specific authorization.

Federal funds allocated to states for educational purposes cannot be used to coerce from states constitutional prerogatives that the U.S. Constitution does not otherwise delegate to the federal government.

Provisions for federal funding of education are volitional on the part of the states, and arrangements to receive federal funds are viewed as contracts by the courts.

The First Amendment of the U.S. Constitution has been a major deterrent to states that have sought to provide tax funds for religious schools. The "wall of separation" between church and state has been protected by a three-part test and has been employed numerous times by the federal courts during the last 20 years. Today, this wall appears to be in danger of dismantlement by the sitting members of the U.S. Supreme Court, the majority of whom appear to be less than enthusiastic about preventing public tax moneys from flowing as aid to religious groups.

State constitutions usually have provisions that require equity and uniformity of taxation. Such provisions, however, have found few applications to state tax legislation. State courts rarely will utilize such measures to invalidate state taxing provisions unless those provisions are clearly arbitrary or capricious.

School finance equity cases have now been filed in virtually every state. In these cases, parents of children in property-poor school districts have challenged the methods that state legislatures use to distribute tax funds among school districts. Courts in numerous states have held the systems of state school finance unconstitutional under state education or equal protection clauses in state constitutions. When plaintiffs have prevailed, the courts have reasoned that (1) education is a state function and the legislature is responsible for its equitable provision; (2) all children are children of the state and not the locality; and (3) all taxes are state taxes regardless of where they are actually levied.

When there are wide differences in per-pupil funding, the courts, where plaintiffs have prevailed, have ruled that the legislature violates the state constitution when it statutorily creates educational privilege for some and disadvantage for others.

Such challenges have not been successful in federal courts due to the U.S. Supreme Court precedent in *San Antonio Independent School District* v. *Rodriguez* in 1973. In this case the Supreme Court refused to extend the federal Equal Protection clause to redress disparities in state school funding schemes.

An important aspect of such cases is whether the courts believe that the constitutional provision under litigation views education as a fundamental right. In *Rodriguez* the U.S. Supreme Court held that education was not a fundamental right under the Fourteenth Amendment. This view has not been accepted by many state courts, the more assertative of which claim that their own state constitutions have "independent vitality" providing protections that exceed those of the federal Constitution.

Education clauses in state constitutions are independent and separate of state equal protection provisions. Such education clauses have been interpreted by state courts to have pervasive and important meaning regarding the kind and nature of relevant legislative enactments. Such positive constitutional provisions in fact prescribe the boundaries within which the legislatures must operate in providing for public education.

KEY TERMS

Sacrifice theory of taxation	Establishment clause	Independent vitality
Benefit theory of taxation	Uniformity of taxation	Suspect classification
Situs of property	Rational relationship test	Fundamentality of education
Commerce clause	Strict scrutiny test	Virtue provisions
General welfare clause	Intermediate test	

ENDNOTES

1. *Shaffer* v. *Carter*, 252 U.S. 37 (1970).

2. Ibid.

3. *Miller* v. *Childers*, 107 Okla. 57, 238 P. 204 (1924).

4. *Dickman* v. *Porter*, 35 N.S. 2d 66 (Iowa 1948).

5. *Morton Salt Co.* v. *City of South Hutchinson*, 177 F.2d 889 (10th Cir. 1949).

6. Newton Edwards, *The Courts and the Public Schools* (Chicago: University of Chicago Press, 1971), p. 256.

7. *State* v. *Board of Commissioners of ELR County*, 58 P. 959 (Kan. 1899).

8. Leroy J. Peterson, Richard A. Rossmiller, and Marlin M. Volz, *The Law and Public School Operation* (New York: Harper & Row, 1978), p. 150.

9. *Marion & McPherson Railway Co.* v. *Alexander*, 64 P. 978 (Kan. 1901).

10. *Stuart* v. *School District No. 1 of Village of Kalamazoo*, 30 Mich. 69 (1874).

11. *Union Refrigerator Transit Co.* v. *Kentucky*, 199 U.S. 194 (1905).

12. *Henneford* v. *Silas Mason Co.*, 300 U.S. 577 (1937).

13. *Welton* v. *Missouri*, 91 U.S. 275 (1876).

14. *Best & Co.* v. *Maxwell*, 311 U.S. 454 (1940).

15. *Shaffer* v. *Carter*, op. cit.

16. *Constitution of the United States*, Article I, Section 8, Clause 3.

17. *Constitution of the United States*, Article I, Section 8.

18. *Garcia* v. *San Antonio Metropolitan Transit Authority*, 469 U.S. 529, 105 S.Ct. 1005 (1985).

19. *United States* v. *Butler*, 297 U.S. 1, 56 S.Ct. 312 (1936).

20. *Wheeler* v. *Barrera*, 714 U.S. 402 (1974).

21. *Pennsylvania Association for Retarded Children* v. *Pennsylvania*, 334 F.Supp. 1257 (Pa. 1971); *Mills* v. *Board of Education of the District of Columbia*, 348 F.Supp. 866 (D.C. 1972).

22. *Shepheard* v. *Godwin*, 280 F.Supp. 869 (1968).

23. *Everson* v. *Board of Education*, 330 U.S. 1 (1947).

24. Ibid.; *Board of Education* v. *Allen*, 392 U.S. 236 (1968).

25. *Lemon* v. *Kurtzman*, 403 U.S. 602 (1971).

26. *Walz* v. *Tax Commission*, 397 U.S. 664 (1970).

27. *Committee for Public Education and Religious Liberty* v. *Nyquist*, 413 U.S. 756 (1973).

28. See also *Sloan* v. *Lemon*, 413 U.S. 825 (1973).

29. *Meek* v. *Pittenger*, 421 U.S. 349, (1975).

30. Ibid., p. 366.

31. *Wolman* v. *Walter*, 433 U.S. 229 (1977).

32. *Mueller* v. *Allen*, 463 U.S. 388, 103 S.Ct. 3062 (1983).

33. *Wallace* v. *Jaffree*, 472 U.S. 38, 105 S.Ct. 2479 (1985).

34. Thomas Jefferson, *An Act For Establishment of Religious Freedom*, introduced in Virginia House of Delegates in 1779 and enacted in 1786.

35. *Everson* v. *Board of Education*, 330 U.S. 1, 67 S.Ct. 504 (1947).

36. R. Freeman Butts and Lawrence A. Cremin, *A History of Education in American Culture* (New York: Henry Holt and Company, 1953), p. 22.

37. Ibid.

38. *Bell's Gap Railroad Co.* v. *Pennsylvania*, 134 U.S. 232 (1890).

39. *Sawyer* v. *Gilmore*, 109 Me. 169, 83 A. 673 (1912).

40. 79 Corpus Juris Secundum sec. 411.

41. See also *Board of Trustees* v. *Board of County Commissioners of Cassia County*, 83 Idaho 172, 359 P. 2d 635 (1961) and *Rice* v. *Cook*, 22 Ga. 499, 150 S.E. 2d 822 (1966).

42. Ronald Dworkin, *A Matter of Principle* (Oxford: Clarendon Press, 1986), p. 269.

43. Isaiah Berlin, "Equality," in *Concepts and Categories, Philosophical Essays* (New York: The Viking Press, 1978), p. 82.

44. Richard Kluger, *Simple Justice* (New York: Vintage Books/A Division of Random House, 1977).

45. Ibid., p. 459.

46. Reinhold Niebuhr, *Moral Man and Immoral Society* (New York: Charles Scribner's Sons, 1932), p. 118.

47. Arthur Wise, *Rich Schools, Poor Schools* (Chicago: University of Chicago Press, 1968).

48. *Burruss* v. *Wilkerson*, 310 F.Supp. 572 *affirmed mem.*, 397 U.S. 44 (1970).

49. *McInnis* v. *Shapiro*, 293 F.Supp. 327 *affirmed mem.*, 394 U.S. 322 (1969).

50. Ibid.

51. Ibid.

52. *San Antonio Independent School District* v. *Rodriguez*, 411 U.S. 1 *rehearing denied* 411 U.S. 959 (1973).

53. Ibid.

54. For example, Alabama and Virginia do not have what may be fully interpretable as equal protection clauses. Alabama's Declaration of Rights states that all persons are "equally free and independent," but it does not indicate that all persons are entitled to equal protection of the laws. Alabama Constitution, Article I, Section 1.

55. John E. Nowak, Ronald D. Rotunda, and J. Nelson Young, *Constitutional Law* (St. Paul: West Publishing Company, 1986), pp. 523–524.

56. Ibid., p. 525.

57. *Reid* v. *Covert*, 354 U.S. 1, 9 (1956).

58. Cal. Const. Art. I, § 7(a).

59. *Serrano* v. *Priest*, 18 Cal. 3d 728, 764, 557 P.2d 929, 950, 135 Cal. Rptr. 345, 366 (1977).

60. Ibid.

61. *Serrano* v. *Priest*, 18 Cal. 3rd 728, 557 P. 2d 929 (1976).

62. Ibid.

63. *Washakie County School District No. One* v. *Herschler*, 606 P.2d 310, *cert. denied sub nom.*, *Hot Springs County School District No. One* v. *Washakie County School District No. One*, 449 U.S. 824, 101 S.Ct. 86 (1980).

64. Ibid., pp. 333–334.

65. *Horton* v. *Meskill*, 31 Conn. Supp. 377, 332 A.2d 813 (1974).

66. *Horton* v. *Meskill*, 195 Conn. 24, 486 A.2d 1099 (1985).

67. Ibid., p. 1105.

68. Other cases finding that education is not a fundamental right, justifying the courts' strict scrutiny of school finance legislation, include: *Milliken* v. *Green*, 390 Mich. 389, 212 N.W.2d 711 (1973); *Thompson* v. *Engelking*, 96 Idaho 793, 537 P.2d 635 (1975); *Olsen* v. *State*, 276 Or. 9, 554 P.2d 139 (1976); *Danson* v. *Casey*, 484 Pa. 415, 58 Ohio St. 2d 368, 399 A.2d 360 (1979); and *Bensalem Township School District* v. *Commonwealth of Pennsylvania*, 105 Pa. Cmwlth. 388, 524 A.2d 1027 (1987); *Board of Education of the City School Dist. of Cincinnati* v. *Walter*, 390 N.E.2d 813 (1979), *cert. denied*, 444 U.S. 1015, 100 S.Ct. 665 (1980); *Britt* v. *North Carolina State Board of Education*, 357 S.E.2d 432 (1987); *School Board of the Parish of Livingston* v. *Louisiana State Board of Elementary and Secondary Education*, 830 F.2d 563 (5th Cir. 1987), *cert. denied* 487 U.S. 1223, 108 S.Ct. 2884 (1988); *Richland County* v. *Campbell*, 294 S.Ct. 346, 364 S.E.2d 470 (1988).

69. Other court decisions declaring that education is fundamental include *Knowles* v. *State Board of Education*, 219 Kan. 271, 547 P.2d 699 (1976); *Buse* v. *Smith*, 74 Wis. 2d 550, 247 N.W.2d 141 (1976), and *Kukor* v. *Grover*, 436 N.W.2d 568 (1989); *Serrano* v. *Priest*, 5 Cal. 3d 584, 96 Cal. Rptr. 601, 487 P.2d 1241 (1971), and *Serrano* v. *Priest*, 18 Cal. 3d 728, 135 Cal. Rptr. 345, 557 P.2d 929 (1976), *cert. denied*, 432 U.S. 907, 97 S.Ct. 2951 (1977), and *Serrano* v. *Priest*, 200 Cal. App. 3d 897, 226 Cal Rptr. 584 (1986); *Horton* v. *Meskill*, 172 Conn. 615, 376 A.2d 359 (1977); *State ex rel. Board of Education for Grant County of Grant* v. *Manchin*, 366 S.E.2nd 743 (1988); *Washakie County School District No. One* v. *Herschler*, 606 P.2d 310 (Wyo. 1980), *cert. denied sub nom.*; *Hot Springs County School District Number One* v. *Washakie County School District Number One*, 449 U.S. 824, 101 S.Ct. 86 (1980); *Edgewood Independent School District* v. *Kirby*, 777 S.W.2d 391 (Tex. 1989).

70. *Pauley* v. *Kelly*, 225 S.E.2d 859 (1979).

71. *Hornbeck* v. *Somerset County Board of Education*, 295 Md. 597, 458 A.2d 758 (Md. 1983).

72. *Fair School Finance Council of Oklahoma, Inc.* v. *State of Oklahoma*, 746 P.2d 1135 (Okl. 1987).

73. *McDaniel* v. *Thomas*, 248 Ga. 632, 285 S.E.2d 156 (1981).

74. *Shofstall* v. *Hollins*, 110 Ariz. 88, 515 P.2d 590 (1973).

75. Ibid.

76. *Dupree* v. *Alma School District No. 30 of Crawford County*, 279 Ark. 340, 651 S.W.2d 90 (1983).

77. Ibid.

78. A. E. D. Howard, *Commentaries on the Constitution of Virginia*, vol. I (1974), p. 282. Charlottesville, Va.: University of Virginia Press.

79. Mize, *San Antonio Independent School District* v. *Rodriguez: A Study of Alternatives Open to State Courts*, 8 U.S.F.L. Rev. 90 (1973–74), pp. 110–111.

80. See, for example, Mass. Const. Pt. 2, Ch. V, Subsection 11: The Encouragement of Literature, Etc.

Duty of legislatures and magistrates in all future periods:

Wisdom, and knowledge, as well as virtue, diffused generally among the body of the people, being necessary for the preservation of their rights and liberties; and as these depend on spreading the opportunities and advantages of education in the various parts of the country, and among the different orders of the people, it shall be the duty of legislatures and magistrates, in all future periods of this commonwealth, to cherish the interests of literature and the sciences, and all seminaries of them; especially the university of Cambridge, public schools and grammar schools in the towns; to encourage private societies and public institutions. . . .

81. *The Works of Thomas Jefferson*, ed. P. Ford (New York: Putnam, 1904), pp. 414–426.

82. See *McDuffy et al.* v *Secretary of Executive Office of Education et al.*, Number SJC-6128, Supreme Judicial Court for the Commonwealth of Massachusetts, June 15, 1993. See also Mary Jane Guy, *Common, System, Uniform and Efficient as Terms of Art in the Education Article of State Constitutions: A Philosophical Foundation for the American Common School* (Blacksburg, VA: Ph.D. Dissertation, 1992).

83. Cal. Const. Art., IX, § 5.

84. *Serrano* v. *Priest*, 5 Cal. 3d 584, 595, 487 P.2d 1241, 1249 (1971). The court instead relied on the Equal Protection clause of the California Constitution to invalidate the state school finance program.

85. Ibid. (citing *Kennedy* v. *Miller*, 97 Cal. 429, 432, 32 P. 558 (1893)).

86. Ibid. at 596. The California Supreme Court has subsequently held that the words of the California Constitution requiring that the legislature "provide for a system of common schools by which a *free school* shall be kept up and supported in each district . . ." mean that "public education is a right enjoyed by all—not a commodity for sale. Educational opportunities must be provided to all students without regard to their families' ability or willingness to pay. . . . This fundamental feature of public education is not contingent upon the inevitably fluctuating financial health of local school districts." *Hartzell* v. *Connell*, 35 Cal. 3d 899, 904, 913, 679 P.2d 35, 201 Cal. Rptr. 601, 604, 610 (1984). It seems that the California court's view is that fundamentality can be found in the state's positive education provision even though only *system* is used because "[p]ublic education forms the basis of self-government and constitutes the very cornerstone of republican institutions." *Hartzell*, 35 Cal. 3d at 906, 679 P.2d at 40, 201 Cal. Rptr. at 606 (citing Winans, Chairman, Committee on Education in Cal. Const. Convention, Debates and Proceedings 1878–1879, at 1087). The court seems to say that education is, by its very nature, fundamental.

87. Tenn. Const. Art. XI, Sec. 12 (providing for "the maintenance, support and eligibility standards of a system of free public schools"); *Tennessee Small School Systems et al.* v. *McWherter, et al.,* 1993 (Tenn. App.) No. 01-A-01-9211-CH00447.

88. Ariz. Const. Art. XI, Sec. 1 (providing for "the establishment and maintenance of a general and uniform public school system, which system shall include kindergarten schools, and a university"); see *Shofstall* v. *Hollins*, 110 Ariz. 88, 515 P.2d 590 (1973).

89. Ky. Const. § 183 (providing for "an efficient system of common schools throughout the state"); see also Tex. Const. Art. VII, § 1 ("[I]t shall be the duty of the legislature of the state to establish and make suitable provision for the support and maintenance of an efficient system of public free schools.")

90. Ohio Const. Art. 6, § 2 (providing for "a thorough and efficient system of common schools throughout the state"); See *Board of Educ. of City School Dist. of the City of Cincinnati* v. *Walter*, 58 Ohio St. 2d 368, 390 N.E.2d 813 (1979). W.VA. Const. Art. XII, § 1 (providing for a "thorough and efficient system of free schools. . . ."); see *Pauley* v. *Kelly*, 162 W.Va. 672, 255 S.E.2d 859 (1979).

91. Ga. Const. Art. VIII, § I, Para. I ("The provision of an adequate education for all citizens shall be a primary obligation of the State of Georgia, the expense of which shall be provided for by taxation."); see *McDaniel* v. *Thomas*, 248 Ga. 632,285 S.E.2d 156 (1981). The Georgia Constitution is the only state constitution which uses the term "adequate" in its education provision.

92. Colo. Const. Art. IX, § 2; see *Lujan* v. *Colorado State Bd. of Educ.*, 649 P.2d 1005 (Colo. 1982).

93. *Robinson* v. *Cahill*, 303 A.2d 273, *cert. denied*, 414 U.S. 976 (1973).

94. Ibid. at 294.

95. *Pauley* v. *Kelly*, op. cit.
96. Ibid. at 859.
97. Ibid. at 878.
98. *Rose* v. *Council for Better Education, Inc.*, 790 S.W.2d 186 (Ky. 1989).
99. *Edgewood* v. *Kirby*, 777 S.W.2d 391 (1989).
100. *Robinson* v. *Cahill*, 62 N.J. 473, 303 A.2d 273 (1973); *Abbott* v. *Burke*, 119 N.J. 287, 575 A.2d 359 (1990).
101. *Pauley* v. *Burke*, 255 S.E. 2d 859 (1979).
102. *Hornbeck* v. *Somerset Co. Sch. Bd.*, 295 Md. 597, 458 A.2d 758 (Md. 1983).
103. *Blase* v. *Illinois*, 302 N.E. 2d 46 (1973).

104. *Robinson* v. *Cahill*, op. cit.
105. Ibid.
106. *Pauley* v. *Kelly*, op. cit.
107. *Pauley* v. *Kelly*, 255 S.E.2d 859 (W.VA. 1979); *Pauley* v. *Bailey*, 324 S.E.2d 128 (1984).
108. Ohio Const., Art. VI, Sec. 2, op. cit.
109. *Blase* v. *Illinois*, 302 N.E.2d 46 (1972).
110. Language taken from Jefferson's bill to establish a public school system in Virginia in 1779.
111. *Edgewood* v. *Kirby*, 777 S.W.2d 391 (1989).
112. *Halifax County School Board* v. *Commonwealth of Virginia*, Circuit Court of City of Richmond (1992).
113. *Edgewood* v. *Kirby*, op. cit.

APPENDIX A

Status of State School Finance Constitutional Litigation

I. Plaintiffs won at state supreme court level: (9)

Arkansas	*Dupree* v. *Alma School District*, 1983
Kentucky	*Rose* v. *The Council*, 1992
Texas	*Edgewood* v. *Kirby*, 1989
Tennessee	*Tennessee Small School Systems* v. *McWherter*, 1993
Massachusetts	*McDuffie* v. *Secretary of Education*, 1993
Washington	*Seattle* v. *Washington*, 1978
Connecticut	*Horton* v. *Meskill*, 1977
Missouri*	*The Committee* v. *Missouri and Lee's Summit P.S.U.* v. *Missouri*, 1994
Arizona	*Roosevelt Elem. School Dist. 66* v. *Bishop*, 1994

II. Plaintiffs won at the state supreme court level, but further compliance litigation was also filed: (5)

Wyoming	*Washakie* v. *Hershler*, 1980
California	*Serrano* v. *Priest*, 1971, 1977
West Virginia	*Pauley* v. *Kelly*, 1979; 1988
New Jersey	*Robinson* v. *Cahill*, 1973; *Abbott* v. *Burke*, 1985, 1990, 1994
Montana	*Helena School District* v. *Montana*, 1989, 1993
	Montana Rural Ed Assoc v. *Montana*, 1993

III. Plaintiffs lost at supreme court level and there have been no further complaints filed or further complaint lost also: (10)

Michigan	*Milliken* v. *Green*, 1973
Georgia	*McDaniels* v. *Thomas*, 1981
Colorado	*Lujan* v. *State Board of Education*, 1982
Maryland	*Hornbeck* v. *Somerset County*, 1983
Wisconsin	*Kukor* v. *Grover*, 1989
Oregon	*Olsen* v. *Oregon*, 1979; *Coalition for Ed. Equity* v. *Oregon*, 1991
Minnesota	*Skeen* v. *Minnesota*, 1993
North Dakota[1]	*Bismarck Public Schools* v. *North Dakota*, 1993
Nebraska[8]	*Gould* v. *Orr*, 1993
Virginia[8]	*Allegheny Highlands* v. *Virginia*, 1991 (Case withdrawn 8/91)
	Scott v. *Virginia*, 1994

(continued)

APPENDIX A   continued

IV. Plaintiffs lost at supreme court level, but there have been further complaints filed: (7)

Pennsylvania[3]	*Dansen* v. *Casey,* 1979; 1987
	Pennsylvania Association of Rural and Small Schools v. *Casey,* 1991
Ohio[3,5]	*Board of Education* v. *Walter,* 1979; *Howard* v. *Walter,* 1979
	Thompson v. *State of Ohio,* 1991; *DeRolph* v. *State,* 1992
New York[4]	*Board of Education* v. *Nyquist,* 1982; 1987
	Reform Educational Financing Inequities Today (R.E.F.I.T.) v. *Cuomo,* 1991
Idaho[3]	*Thompson* v. *Engleking,* 1975; *Frazier et al.* v. *Idaho,* 1990
Louisiana[3]	*School Board* v. *Louisiana,* 1987; 1988
	Charlet v. *Legislature of State of Louisiana,* 1992
South Carolina	*Richland* v. *Campbell,* 1988; *Lee County* v. *Carolina,* 1993
North Carolina	*Britt* v. *State Board,* 1987; *Leandro v. State,* 1994

V. Litigation is present and/or a lower court ruling has been issued, but no supreme
    court decision has been rendered: (8)

Illinois[4]	*The Committee* v. *Edgar,* 1990
Alabama[5]	*Alabama Coalition for Equity* v. *Hunt,* 1990; *Harper* v. *Hunt,* 1991
Alaska[6]	*Matanuska-Susitna Borough* v. *Alaska,* 1989
South Dakota	*Bezdichek* v. *South Dakota,* 1991
New Hampshire[6]	*Claremont, New Hampshire* v. *Gregg,* 1991
Rhode Island[5]	*City of Pawtucket* v. *Sundlun,* 1992
Kansas	(Consolidated)
	Newton Unified School District 373, et al. v. *Kansas,* 1993
	Unified School District 229, et al. v. *Kansas,* 1991
	Unified School District 244, Coffey County, et al. v. *State*
	Unified School District 217, Rolla, et al. v. *State*
	M.S.A.D. #1 v. *Leo Martin* (1992)

VI. No litigation is present or case is dormant: (11)

Delaware		Mississippi
Hawaii		Nevada
Iowa		New Mexico
Florida	*Christiensen* v. *Graham*	Utah
Oklahoma	*Fair School* v. *State,* 1987	Vermont
Indiana	*Lake Central* v. *Indiana,* 1987	

Category A: States in which the State Supreme Court has declared that education is
             a fundamental constitutional right   (14)

Arizona	*Shofstall* v. *Hollins,* 1973
Wisconsin	*Busse* v. *Smith,* 1976
California	*Serrano* v. *Priest,* 1977
Connecticut	*Horton* v. *Meskill,* 1977
Wyoming	*Washakie* v. *Hershler,* 1980
West Virginia	*Pauley* v. *Bailey,* 1984
Montana	*Helena* v. *State,* 1989
Kentucky	*Rose* v. *The Council,* 1989
Tennessee	*Tennessee Small School Systems* v. *McWherter,* 1993
Washington	*Seattle* v. *Washington,* 1978
Massachusetts	*McDuffie* v. *Secretary of Education,* 1993

APPENDIX A   continued

Minnesota	*Skeen* v. *Minnesota*, 1993
New Hampshire	*Claremont, New Hampshire* v. *Gregg*, 1991
Virginia	*Scott* v. *Virginia*, 1994

Category B: States in which the State Supreme Court has declared that education is NOT
 a fundamental constitutional right   (10)

New Jersey	*Robinson* v. *Cahill*, 1973
Michigan	*Milliken* v. *Green*, 1973
Idaho	*Thompson* v. *Engelking*, 1975
Oregon	*Olsen* v. *State*, 1976
Pennsylvania	*Dansen* v. *Casey*, 1979
Ohio	*Board* v. *Walter*, 1979
New York	*Levittown* v. *Nyquist*, 1982
Colorado	*Lugan* v. *Colorado*, 1982
Georgia	*McDaniel* v. *Thomas*, 1982
Arkansas[7]	*Dupree* v. *Alma*, 1983

Category C: Lower court decision on education as a fundamental right

1. States in which a circuit or appellate court has declared that education IS a fundamental right   (5)

Alabama	*Alabama Coalition for Equity* v. *Hunt*, 1993
Missouri	*Committee* v. *Missouri*, 1993
Minnesota	*Skeen* v. *Minnesota*, 1992
North Dakota	*Bismarck Public Schools* v. *North Dakota*, 1993
Ohio	*DeRolph* v. *State*, 1994

2. States in which a circuit or appellate court has declared that education is NOT a fundamental right   (2)

Illinois	*Committee* v. *Edgar*, 1992
New Hampshire	*Claremont, New Hampshire* v. *Gregg*, 1991

Source: Compiled by G. Alan Hickrod and Gregory Anthony, Center for the Study of Educational
Finance, Illinois State University, Normal, IL, August 1994.

[1]Majority (3) ruled in favor of plaintiff but North Dakota requires four justices to declare a statutory law unconstitutional

[2]Hearing completed at Supreme Court level

[3]Defeated Motion to Dismiss

[4]Litigation of Motion to Dismiss

[5]Circuit Court decision in favor of the plaintiffs, no appeal in Alabama

[6]Circuit Court decision in favor of the defendants, reversed in New Hampshire

[7]States in which the funding system failed to pass the "rational basis" test of the equal protection
 clause

[8]Lost on Motion to Dismiss or Motion for Summary Judgment

*Partial win only: Dismissed State's appeal on technical grounds.

APPENDIX B

School Finance Case Citations by State

ALABAMA	*Alabama Coalition for Equity, Inc.* v. *Hunt, Circuit Court of Montgomery County,* Alabama, Civil Action No. CV-90-883-R, CV-91-0117-R (1993)
ARIZONA	*Shofstall* v. *Hollins*, 110 Ariz. 88, 515 P. 2d 590 (1973)
	Roosevelt Elem. School Dist. v. *Bishop*, WL 378649, 1994
ARKANSAS	*Dupree* v. *Alma School District No. 30 of Crawford County*, 279 Ark. 340, 651 S.W. 2d 90 (1983)
CALIFORNIA	*Serrano* v. *Priest*, 487 P. 2d 1241 (1971) (Serrano I)
	Serrano v. *Priest*, 557 P. 2d 929 (1976) (Serrano II), *reh. denied*, Jan. 27, 1977; as modified Feb. 1, 1977 *cert. denied*, 432 U.S. 907 (1977)
COLORADO	*Lujan* v. *State Board of Education*, 649 P. 2d 1005 (Colo. 1982)
CONNECTICUT	*Horton* v. *Meskill*, 172 Conn. 615, 376 A. 2d 359 (1976)
FLORIDA	*Florida Dept. of Ed.* v. *Glasser*, No. 80288 (Supreme Court of Florida) 622 So. 2d 944 (1993)
GEORGIA	*Thomas* v. *Stewart*, No. 8375 (Sup. Ct. of Polk Cty.), revd. in part and affd. in part *sub. nom. McDaniel* v. *Thomas*, 243 Ga. 632, 285 S.E. 2d 156 (1981)
IDAHO	*Thompson* v. *Engleking*, 537 P. 2d 635 (id 1975)
ILLINOIS	*Blase* v. *Illinois*, 302 N.E. 2d 46 (1973)
KANSAS	*Knowles* v. *State Board of Educ.*, 547 P. 2d 699 (1976)
KENTUCKY	*Rose* v. *Council for Better Education, Inc.*, 790 S.W. 2d 186 (Ky. 1989)
LOUISIANA	*Louisiana Association of Educators* v. *Edwards*, 521 So. 2d 390 (1988)
MARYLAND	*Hornbeck* v. *Somerset County Board of Education*, 295 Md. 597, 458 P. 2d 758 (Md. 1983)
MASSACHUSETTS	*McDuffy* v. *Secretary of Exec. Office of Educ.*, 415 Mass. 545 (1993)
MICHIGAN	*Milliken* v. *Green*, 203 N.W. 457 (Mich. 1972), *vacated mem.*, 212 N.W. 2d 711 (Mich. 1973)
MINNESOTA	*Skeen et al.*, v. *State of Minnesota et al.*, File Nos. C5-92-677, C7-92-678 (1992)
MISSOURI	*Committee for Educational Equality, et al.*, v. *State of Missouri and Lee's Summit School District R-VIII, et al.* v. *State of Missouri*, Circuit Court of Cole County, Mo. Civil Action No. CV190-1371CC and No. CV 190-510CC (1993)
MONTANA	*Helena Elementary School District No. 1 et al.* v. *State*, 236 Mont. 44, 769 P. 2d 684 (1989) opinion amended by 236 Mont. 44, 784 P. 2d 412 (1990)
NEBRASKA	*Gould* v. *Orr*, 244 Neb. 163, 506 N.W. 2d 349 (1993)
NEW JERSEY	*Robinson* v. *Cahill*, 62 N.J. 473, 303 A. 2d 273, *cert. denied sub. nom. Dickey* v. *Robinson*, 414 U.S. 976, (1973) (Robinson I); after remand, 355 A. 2d 129 (1976) (Robinson II)
	Abbott v. *Burke*, No. C-1983-80 (Sup. Ct. N.J., Chancery Div. Mercer Cty. 1982)
	Abbott v. *Burke*, 119 N.J. 287, 575 A. 2d 359 (1990)
	Abbott v. *Burke*, WL 376417, A. 2d, (N.J. 1994)
NEW YORK	*Board of Education, Levittown* v. *Nyquist*, 408 N.Y.S. 2d 606 (Nassau Cty. Sup. Ct. 1978); *affd.* 443 N.Y.S. 2d 843 (1982); *revd.* 57 N.Y. 2d 27, 453 N.Y.S. 2d 643,

APPENDIX B continued

	439 N.E. 2d 359, (N.Y. 1982) *petition for cert. filed sub. nom.*
	R.E.F.I.T. v. *Cuomo*, 578 N.Y.S. 2d 969 (1991)
NORTH CAROLINA	*Britt* v. *North Carolina State Board of Education*, 361 S.E. 2d 71 (1987)
NORTH DAKOTA	*Bismarck Public School District No. 1, et al.* v. *The State of North Dakota*, Civil No. 41554 (1993)
OHIO	*Board of Education of the City School Dist. of Cincinnati* v. *Walter*, 390 N.E. 2d 813 (1979), *cert. denied*, 444 U.S. 1015 (1980)
	DeRolph v. *State of Ohio*, Common Pleas, Perry County, Ohio, Case No. 22043 (1994)
OKLAHOMA	*Fair School Finance Council of Okla.* v. *State of Oklahoma*, 746 P. 2d 1135 (Okla. 1987)
OREGON	*Olsen* v. *State*, 554 P. 2d 139 (Or. 1976)
	Coalition for Equitable School Funding v. *State of Oregon*, 811 P.2d 116
PENNSYLVANIA	*Dansen* v. *Casey*, 484 A. 2D 415 (Pa, 1979)
	Ben Salem Township School District v. *Commonwealth of Pennsylvania*, 105 Pa. Cmwlth. 388, 524 A. 2d 1027 (1987)
SOUTH CAROLINA	*Richland County* v. *Campbell*, 294 S.C. 364 S.E. 2d 470 (1988)
SOUTH DAKOTA	*Oster* v. *Kneip*, (S.D. Hughes Cty. Cir. Court)
TENNESSEE	*Tennessee Small School Systems, et al.* v. *McWherter, et al.*, 1993 WL 295006
TEXAS	*Edgewood Independent School Dist.* v. *Kirby*, 777 S.W. 2d 391 (1989)
	Carrolton-Farmers Branch Independent School District, et al. v. *Edgewood Independent School District, et al.*, 826 S.W. 2d 489 (1992)
WASHINGTON	*Northshore* v. *Kinnear*, 530 P. 2d 178 (Wash. 1974)
	Seattle Sch. Dist. No. 1 of King County v. *State*, 90 Wash. 2d 476 585 p. 2d 71 (1978), No. 81-2-1713-1 (Thurston Cty. Superior Ct. 1981)
WEST VIRGINIA	*Pauley* v. *Kelly*, 255 S.E. 2d 859 (W.Va. 1979) *on remand sub. nom.*
	Pauley v. *Bailey*, 324 S.E. 2d 128 (1984)
WISCONSIN	*Buse* v. *Smith*, 74 Wisc. 2d 650, 247 N.W. 2d 141 (1976)
	Kukor v. *Grover*, 436 N.W. 2d 568 (1989)
WYOMING	*Washakie Co., Sch. Dist. No. One* v. *Herschler*, 606 P. 2d 310 (Wyo. 1980) *cert. denied*, 449 U.S. 824, 101 S. Ct. 86, 66 L. Ed. 2d 28 (1980)

CHAPTER 3

EDUCATION AS AN INVESTMENT IN HUMAN CAPITAL

TOPICAL OUTLINE OF CHAPTER

*Education and Economic Growth • The Classical View
• Investment in Human Capital • Wealth of Nations • Cash Value of
Education • Earnings Profiles • Private Costs • Social Costs
• Rates of Return • External Benefits • Educated Workforce
• Health Benefits of Education • Crime Prevention
• Overpopulation Deterrent • Household Benefits*

INTRODUCTION

Historically, human beings have been valued for their physical rather than mental capabilities, as soldiers or slaves, for example. Throughout the centuries, the labor of individuals has shaped markets, whether that labor was provided by freemen, serfs, or slaves.[1] The market value of the human, however, changes dramatically with fluctuations in the supply of workers. As Tuchman observed, a decline in population caused by the bubonic plague of the fourteenth century placed such a premium on labor that the value of the individual was reflected in wage reforms which swept western Europe and affected commerce for centuries.[2]

Throughout these earlier eras, valuation of people was based on their physical productivity as hewers of wood and drawers of water, not as philosophers, scientists, teachers, or physicians. According to this method of valuing the individual, the nation with the greatest population had the greatest human capital value. However, the fallacy in this approach became apparent in the nineteenth and twentieth centuries, as the world's work force became less "labor intensive" and more "brain intensive." The country with the greatest population was not necessarily the most productive or influential. If sheer numbers had been the measure of human value, England would have been a dependent of India rather than vice versa.

It was not until the 1960s that an awakening to the real value of human capital actually occurred. Guided by Theodore W. Schultz, later to win the Nobel Prize for Economic Science, economists and educators began to recognize the economic importance of the human being in the production process, and to begin to seek ways to measure the magnitude of human capital.[3] This is not to say that human knowledge and skill were never observed before, but it is certainly true that no attempts were made in an economic sense to quantify the value of human capital. The economist Petty had earlier observed "that the value of mankind is worth twenty times the present annual earning of labor,"[4] but Petty's estimates were without empirical base. Although he recognized the value of human capital, his imprecision of measurement tended to create problems of academic credibility.

EDUCATION AND ECONOMIC GROWTH

The situation is much different today. A plethora of empirical research by scholars throughout the world working for major universities, governments, the Organization for Economic Growth and Cooperative Development (OECD), and the World Bank has shown the primacy of human capital investment for economic development. The 1991 World Development Report of the World Bank relied on five large multi-country studies covering approximately 60 countries and concluded that

> . . . sustained development in many countries, notably the Scandinavian countries after 1870 and the East Asian economies after World War II, can be largely explained by education. . . .[5]

In a 1991 analysis entitled "Where Tigers Breed, A Survey of Asia's Emerging Economies," *The Economist* discussed reasons for the unprecedented recent economic growth of the countries of the Pacific Rim—referred to as the economic tigers—that include China, South Korea, Taiwan, Hong Kong, Singapore, Indonesia, and Malaysia. The article noted several lessons to be learned from them, but concluded:

> The last lesson is probably the most important: investing in education pays in spades. The tigers' single biggest source of comparative advantage is their well-educated workers.[6]

Later, in a special edition in November of 1992, *The Economist* made several observations regarding investment in education in most developed and developing nations. "Education reform is in the air everywhere, from France to South Korea, from Australia to Germany."[7] In an article that cites significant data and provides lucid commentary on the elevation of education to the top of national political agendas, Wooldridge, writing for *The Economist*, observed that politicians in the three powerhouse economic systems of the world—America, Europe, and Asia—to a large extent see their futures determined by their ability to educate their workforces and to create "high value-adding" jobs.[8] Pointedly, *The Econ-*

omist maintains that, "governments now treat education not as a consumer good but as a productive asset."[9] It has become clear that education, more than most other governmental expenditures, is not simply consumed but rather is a well-documented investment.

Importantly, the debate over how to best stimulate economic growth has reached a new plane. In earlier generations it was obliquely recognized that human capital investment led the way to more productive economies. Today, however, the issue tops national agendas because it has become vastly more apparent that the new technological demands of the age require a much higher level of knowledge of the people. "There is nothing new in the triumph of brain over brawn. The richer countries have long found that ever larger proportions of their populations are employed in jobs that require mental power rather than muscle power."[10] What is new is that the unremitting progress of innovation and technology has created an even greater premium on education and a highly skilled work force. The shift toward the "smarter jobs"[11] of the information age has placed requirements on all economies to educate and train the masses for advanced learning.

CLASSICAL ECONOMIC VIEW

Early economists differed on the issue of whether or not to recognize people in their overall definition of wealth or capital. John Stuart Mill, for example, did not define wealth as including human capital. He said, "In propriety of classification, however, the people of a country are not to be counted in its wealth. . . . They are not wealth themselves, though they are means of acquiring it."[12] On the other hand, Adam Smith in 1776 did include human capital in his definition of fixed capital, saying it consisted "of the acquired and useful abilities of all the inhabitants or members of society. The acquisition of such talents by the maintenance of the acquirer during his education, study or apprenticeship, always costs a real expense, which is a capital fixed and realized, as it were, in his person."[13] Yet Smith never really related the educational function of government to the development of human potential nor did he attempt to measure it. Basically, Smith was unable to perceive of a man in any terms other than that of an "expensive machine," a position fundamentally adhered to by the Cambridge economist Alfred Marshall.[14] Marshall, an economist of great prestige, maintained that while humans were certainly capital from an abstract point of view, it was impractical to include them as an element when analyzing national investment and development.[15]

Interestingly, some antecedents in both education and economics do exist for the work of Schultz and others of the 1960s beyond the political economy of Smith and Marshall. Smith and Marshall both recognized that more training and experience increased the productivity of the worker, but neither apparently realized that overall increases in human knowledge, aside from skills directly related to production, could have a profound effect on a nation's economy.

The limitations of this narrow view were recognized by a few educators and economists over 100 years ago at a time when the public schools of this country were yet in infancy. In fact, Horace Mann in his 1848 education report said,

> Our means of education is the grand machinery by which "raw material" of human nature can be worked into inventors and discoverers, into skilled artisans and scientific farmers, into scholars and jurists, into the founders of benevolent institutions, and the great expounders of ethical and theological

---

Box 3.1

Meiji Japan's Penchant for Education

Countries with a longstanding commitment to educating their populations have the most advanced economies today. The policy changes associated with the restoration of the Meiji emperor in Japan in 1868 are a case in point. Japan had been isolated from global technological developments for more than two centuries, and was agricultural and largely feudal. In the mid 1800s, it came under intense pressure from European and U.S. traders to open its ports and, more generally, to match the economic and military prowess of the West. A revolution brought a new, technocratic government to power. The government's initiatives to import technology are by now legendary: missions were sent abroad to learn about science, technology, and administration; machinery was imported; legions of foreign advisers were hired; and model factories were established in textiles, glass, cement making, and machine tools. The salaries hired foreigners who accompanied imported new machinery between 1870 and 1885 averaged 42 percent of total annual expenditures of the Ministry of Industrial Affairs. Engineers and technicians accounted for 40 percent of all foreigners employed by the government and private firms.

What is less well-known, but probably more important for Japan's sustained success, is that extraordinary changes were made in the educational system. At the beginning of the Meiji era, literacy was only 15 percent, but by 1872 a universal and compulsory system of elementary education had been introduced and the foundations for secondary education had been laid. On the basis of careful investigation, the education system was patterned on the French system of school districts; the university system was patterned on that of the United States. Primary school attendance rates grew from less than 30 percent in 1873 to more than 90 percent in 1907. The number of secondary schools expanded tenfold during the period 1885–1915. Japan became one of the world's most educated and most education-conscious nations. Achieving this required a strong commitment. Japan consistently expended a greater share of its real domestic product on education than any European or other Asian nation.

Source: World Bank, *World Development Report 1991, The Challenge of Development* (Oxford: The World Bank and Oxford University Press, 1991), p. 58. Reprinted with permission.

science. By means of early education, these embryos of talent may be quickened, which will solve the difficult problems of political and economical law.[16]

Mann attacked the philosophy of Adam Smith and others whose views of political economy failed to recognize the condition of the poor uneducated workers of the industrial revolution, and asserted that the true wealth of a nation lay largely in the intelligence of its people. In this regard Mann said,

> For creation of wealth, then—for the existence of a wealthy people and a wealthy nation—intelligence is the grand condition. The number of improvers will increase, as the intellectual constituency, if I may so call it, increases. In former times, and in most parts of the world even at the present day, not one man in a million has ever had such a development of mind, as made it possible for him to become a contributor to art or science. Let this development proceed, and contributions, numberless, and of inestimable value, will be sure to follow. That Political Economy, therefore, which busies itself about capital and labor, supply and demand, interest and rents, favorable and unfavorable balances of trade; but leaves out of account the element of a wide-spread mental development, is nought but stupendous folly. The greatest of all the arts in political economy is to change a consumer into a producer—an end to be directly attained, by increasing his intelligence.[17]

With few exceptions, Mann's perception of the thinking of political economists of the nineteenth century was accurate: their efforts were spent almost entirely on matters of physical capital and little if any concern was directed toward human capital. The balance sheet of political economy did not include entries for the store of human potential or lack of it.

An exception to the general trend of economic thought was reflected by the economist Von Thunen, who, a decade after Mann's report, pointed out the importance of including humans as part of a nation's capital. He said,

> There is no doubt about the answer to the very controversial question of whether the immaterial goods [services] of mankind form a part of national wealth or not. Since a more highly schooled nation, equipped with the same material goods, creates a much larger income than an uneducated people, and since this higher schooling can only be obtained through an educational process which requires a larger consumption of material goods, the more educated nation also possesses a larger capital, the returns of which are expressed in the larger product of its labor.[18]

Despite the efforts of Mann and Von Thunen, however, only sporadic recognition of their views was given in the literature until Schultz measured the value of human capital in 1961.[19]

HUMAN CAPITAL APPROACH

Schultz observed that the classical economists had "put us on the wrong road" of economic thought. Adam Smith, David Ricardo, and others viewed economic growth in terms of land and labor, with land fixed by nature and labor homogeneous. That is, Smith, in spite of his acknowledgement of the importance of labor skills, basically assumed labor to be of a given quality regardless of technological change. His equations did not allow for an expanded view of capital which would account for increasing knowledge and advancement of technology.[20] What Schultz observed was the heterogeneity of capital, and he saw that the individual human was a form of capital that could be developed. Schultz's important contribution was the assertion that skills and knowledge are a form of capital.

> Although it is obvious that people acquire useful skills and knowledge, it is not obvious that these skills and knowledge are a form of capital, that this capital is in substantial part a product of deliberate investment that has grown in Western societies at a much faster rate than conventional [nonhuman] capital, and that its growth may well be the most distinctive feature of the economic system.[21]

Schultz and others noted that the income of the United States and other countries had been increasing at a vastly higher rate than could be accounted for by combining the amount of land, number of hours worked, and stock of reproducible goods used to produce this income. As the discrepancy between the two amounts became larger, economists, without knowing its nature, called the difference "resource productivity." Schultz said that to call this discrepancy "a measure of 'resource productivity' gives a name to our ignorance but does not dispel it."[22]

With Schultz's work as an impetus, a rejuvenation of thinking occurred in the 1960s, with many economists attempting to measure the effects of human capital on the economy. Educators eagerly sought evidence to support their assertions that greater investment in the public schools would yield higher economic returns. Within a few years the volume of research was so great that the question of the value of human capital became an important subspecialty of both economic and social science. The ultimate acknowledgment of the importance of human capital research was given in 1978 when the Nobel Prize for Economic Science was awarded to Theodore W. Schultz and Sir W. Arthur Lewis for their efforts in this area.

HUMAN RESOURCES AND THE WEALTH OF NATIONS

The importance of human resources to economic development is richly illustrated in a book by Frederick H. Harbison, in which he maintained "that human resources—not capital, nor income, nor material resources—constitute the ultimate basis for the wealth of nations."[23] As this quotation indicates, Harbison took to task those economists of the Adam Smith school who largely ignored human resources in their theories of political economy. Harbison pointed out that capital and material resources are passive factors of production which can only be activated by the catalyst of human resources.

> Human beings are the active agents who accumulate capital, exploit natural resources, build social, economic, and political organizations, and carry

forward national development. Clearly, a country which is unable to develop the skills and knowledge of its people and to utilize them effectively in the national economy will be unable to develop anything else.[24]

Accordingly, Harbison maintained that the wealth of nations should not only be measured in terms of gross national product, national income, and gross domestic product, but should also reflect what ought to be the primary objective of national economic policy, the stock and condition of human capital. The strength of national economies would therefore be more accurately judged by whether human resources were adequately developed and appropriately used. Education, he noted, is a primary instrument for resolving economic problems related to both underdevelopment and underutilization of human resources.

Absorption Effect

Research and writing in the area of human capital and economic development ranged from the broad sociological aspects to precise mathematical measurements. Much work was conducted internationally to analyze the importance of education and new knowledge acquisition in underdeveloped countries. W. Arthur Lewis, working extensively in nonindustrialized countries, observed that the level of literacy and the type of social conditions combined to either enhance or retard technological development. Societies with rigid class systems tended to withhold education from the masses, thereby retarding economic growth.[25] Also, it was observed that a certain "absorption effect" was at work wherein the masses had to have a minimum level of education in order to become intelligent consumers.[26] An illiterate populace could not appreciate or take advantage of technological advances.

Because the knowledge of the people must be of such quality to allow absorption of technological advances, the educational underpinnings of a national system of education must be firmly established. Investment in elementary and secondary schools provide this foundation. A government that invests too lavishly in higher education while denying resources to lower levels of education builds its house upon the proverbial sand. In a 1992 report for the World Bank, Tan and Mingat show that the malapportionment of fiscal resources—giving inordinately greater amounts to higher education to the detriment of primary education—is an earmark of poorer countries.[27] Moreover, such an imbalance in educational investment harms the equity of a nation. The authors note, "If a government allocates most of its spending on education to the higher levels to benefit a few people, leaving few resources for primary school pupils, it achieves a lower level of structural equity in the education system than a government that pursues the opposite policies."[28] Education is important not only as a direct investment in output but also as a consumer good, to enable people to enjoy life and to understand their environment better.[29]

Skill Acquisition

Beyond the absorption or consumption aspect, a nation's economic output "is a function of the infrastructure it has developed and the skill of its people."[30] Skills and competence in the workforce are acquired primarily through formal educational systems designed to transmit acquired knowledge, skills, and techniques. Ginsberg observed that formal education is the primary source of the skill acquisition necessary for economic development.

> [M]any years of exposure to didactic instruction in the classroom, supplemented by reading assignments on the outside, result in young people's acquiring a considerable stock of knowledge that helps inform their judgments about private and public issues on which they must act. . . . The schools are not solely responsible for these horizon-stretching, comprehension-deepening efforts, for the media play important complementary roles. But the contribution of the formal education system is primary.[31]

Of course, it would be inaccurate to attribute all acquisition of knowledge and skill to formal school processes. Knowledge and skill formation actually come about through three modes:

1. General formal schooling
2. Formal vocational education which extends from early high school through graduate professional schools
3. Learning opportunities provided by employers through on-the-job training or in special industry-financed programs, which usually take the form of short intensive seminars and institutes for management and white-collar workers

All of these combine to constitute the total of a nation's educational investment. More broadly, investment in human resources should not be viewed as limited to knowledge and skill acquisition, but must also include the health of the nation. It goes without saying that a nation of people suffering from hunger and poor health will not be economically productive. Politics—and indeed the political economy of any society—is first and foremost "bread politics," a set of measures founded on a nutritional determinant.[32] When basic nutritional needs are met, the individual can then turn thoughts and actions to higher levels of economic considerations that ultimately enhance overall productivity. Advancements in health generally extend the productivity of individuals and make any investment in education longer lived and more rewarding.[33]

MEASURING THE BENEFITS OF EDUCATION

The benefits of education may be broadly defined as anything that

1. Increases production through enhancement of the capacity of the labor force
2. Increases efficiency by reducing costs, thus reserving or releasing resources for other productive pursuits

3. Increases the social consciousness of the community so that the standard of living is enhanced[34]

Beyond these generalizations, though, the actual measurement of the benefits of education becomes more difficult. Since the early 1960s literally hundreds of research projects have been undertaken which have sought to quantify the benefits of education, all supplying pieces to a complex puzzle but none truly achieving the desired precision of measurement. Most of the analyses can be categorized into four basic approaches:

1. Simple relationship analysis
2. Residual
3. Cash-value or direct-monetary-return
4. Cost–benefit or rate-of-return[35]

Relationship Analysis Approach

One approach to measuring the benefits of education is simply to compare levels of educational attainment with other socioeconomic indicators. For example, the number of years of schooling for persons in certain age groups can be compared to their annual incomes.[36] In 1992 *The Economist* pithily stated: "The educated are different: they earn more."[37] One may also statistically compare the relationship between the income of certain wage earners and their education level, between the amount of their retail sales and their years of schooling, between their economic attitudes and their education levels, or the number of high-school dropouts and their annual loss in dollars.[38]

On a macroeconomic scale, such studies may relate an index of educational attainment to the GNP per capita, national income per capita, or any other broad economic measure. For example, enrollment ratios have been found to have a positive correlation with GNP per capita.[39]

While helpful, these studies are far from definitive because they are unable to show cause-and-effect relationships between education and economic growth. Other important factors which relate to both may be present, influencing the positive relationships.

Residual Approach

This approach is also known as the growth accounting method and is based on the concept of an aggregate production function using multiple regression analyses that links outputs (growth) to inputs of physical capital and labor.[40] Recognition that the classical inputs of land, labor, and capital were not the sole determinants of a nation's economic advancement is the basis for other macroeconomic analyses which have sought to ferret out the various contributors to economic growth. As indicated earlier, economists found that even after all physical inputs were considered, a persistent and unidentified residual remained. Kendrick examined this phenomenon in 1961 and estimated that for the period between 1889 and 1957 a combined index of inputs increased 1.9 percent annually while the nation's output index increased 3.5 percent annually, leaving an unexplained discrepancy of 1.6 percent.[41] He found that about 80 percent of the increased output per unit of labor input was attributable to a residual—something other than land, labor, and capital. Massell employed different procedures, but also found a residual to equal roughly 90 percent of the increase in output per worker-hour in the United States economy from 1915 to 1955.[42] Fabricant found that only 1.0 percent of the annual increase in GNP of 3.1 percent could be attributed to land, labor, and capital. He suggested, but did not substantiate, that the residual may be largely explained by investments in education, research and development, and other intangible capital.[43]

More recent advancements in economic analysis have sought to more clearly identify the contents of the residual, and have developed new terminology describing the reasons for economic growth. A new measure entitled *total factor productivity* (TFP) quantifies the relationship between output per unit of all inputs combined (see Box 3.2 for a more complete explanation). Early calculations estimated that about one-half of the growth output could be attributed to technology.[44] But technology has component parts that entail a mix of capital and labor—that is, physical capital and human capital. Then what actually makes up the residual? It has been concluded by the World Bank studies that technological innovations do play an important part in TFP, but "the main additional element is in the quality of labor." Thus, a better educated and more skilled labor force increases the portion of the residual growth that is attributable to labor.[45]

Schultz in 1961 and Denison in 1962 set out to explain this residual and to determine what portion of it was attributable to education.[46] Schultz estimated that 44 percent of the increase in earnings of labor could be attributed to additional education from 1929 to 1957.[47] Schultz's method-

---

Box 3.2

Total Factor Productivity in Economic Growth

An important advance in economics of the past fifty years has been to identify and measure total factor productivity, which measures changes in output per unit of all inputs combined. Before, most analyses of productivity focused on the growth of labor productivity, and to a lesser degree, on the growth of the average productivity of capital.

Observe the following differences. The total output of the United States in the first part of the twentieth century grew at about 3 percent a year. Its capital stock also grew at about 3 percent, whereas the labor input (measured in worker-hours) grew at only about 1 percent a year. In the capital-labor mix, capital accounted for about one-third, and labor, two-thirds. So inputs were rising about 1.7 percent a year: two-thirds times 1 percent plus one-third times 3 percent. Total factor productivity, or the residual, thus accounted for 1.3 percent in output growth: 3 percent (the rate of growth of output) minus 1.7 percent (the growth rate of inputs).

The early calculations of total factor productivity for different countries led to the conclusion—surprising at the time—that about half of growth in output was due to the residual, which was quickly baptized as technical change. What makes up the residual? Technological innovations have no doubt generated some improvements in total factor productivity. But the main additional element is in the quality of labor. If the additions to the labor force are more productive than the existing force, they will add more to output than they

would under the formula based on labor's share. And the extra contribution from upgrading the quality of labor ends up in the residual.

Adjusting for labor quality makes it easy to identify the residual with technical change—defined very broadly. Technical change includes such obvious innovations as the mechanical picker, the pneumatic tire, the hand-held calculator, the personal computer, the fork-lift truck, and the containerized shipping system.

But technical change also includes numerous ways of reducing real costs. These costs may fall as more discipline is instilled in the work force by a more demanding manager—or as the work force becomes more productive because a too-demanding manager has been fired. An assembly line might be made more productive simply by straightening it out—or a farm by introducing a different fertilizer. Productivity may also be increased by, for example, installing a facsimile machine, closing down unprofitable branches, or buying longer-lasting tires for trucks.

The way to understand more about what makes up the residual is to study the growth of total factor productivity in detail—product by product, industry by industry, sector by sector. Even with close study not every source of cost reduction can be identified, but the most important ones surely can. This identification alone reveals the kaleidoscopic sources of growth encompassed in the residual.

Source: World Bank, *World Development Report 1991, The Challenge of Development* (Oxford: The World Bank and Oxford University Press, 1991), p. 42. Reprinted with permission.

ology, although giving quite a range of results depending on the rate-of-return used, nevertheless was a major contribution because it constituted the first attempt to treat education as a separate production function in a nation's economic growth. Shortly following the publication of Schultz's study, Denison produced a more complete analysis of sources of economic growth, and in 1974 he conducted a follow-up study.[48] Denison indicated that the educational level of the labor force was responsible for increasing input per day by 27.5 percent between 1929 and 1969.[49]

The residual approach continues to be a useful tool in the measurement of education's contribution to real national income growth. Studies using similar methodology have been conducted for other countries, with widely varying results. In a study of South American countries, Correa found that the contribution of education as a percentage of growth in national income ranged from a high of 16 percent in Argentina to a low of 1 percent in Mexico.[50] In 1967, Denison studied nine European countries for the period 1950–1962, finding no country in which education contributed as high a percentage of growth as in the United States. His results varied widely, showing a range in the percentage of growth in national income per employed person of 18 percent in the United Kingdom to a low of 2 percent in Germany, with the United States showing 23 percent.[51]

All of these studies made one overall conclusion quite clear:

> Increased education of the labor force appears to explain a substantial part of the growth of output in both developed and developing countries since about 1950.[52]

The conduct of such studies waned somewhat in the 1970s but renewed interest by the World Bank in determining the contribution that education makes to the economy has prompted more recent analysis. In 1980, the World Development Report[53] of the World Bank relied on the research of Hicks[54] and Wheeler[55] to give further affirmation to education's role in economic growth. Table 3.1, shows the growth percentage

TABLE 3.1   The Contribution of Education to Economic Growth

COUNTRY	PERCENTAGE CONTRIBUTION TO ANNUAL GROWTH RATE
North America	
Canada	25.0
United States	15.0
Europe	
Belgium	14.0
Denmark	4.0
France	6.0
Germany, Fed. Rep.	2.0
Greece	3.0
Israel	4.7
Italy	7.0
Netherlands	5.0
Norway	7.0
United Kingdom	12.0
U.S.S.R.	6.7
Latin America	
Argentina	16.5
Brazil	3.3
Chile	4.5
Colombia	4.1
Ecuador	4.9
Honduras	6.5
Mexico	0.8
Peru	2.5
Venezuela	2.4
Asia	
Korea, Rep. of	15.9
Japan	3.3
Malaysia	14.7
Philippines	10.5
Africa	
Ghana	23.2
Kenya	12.4
Nigeria	16.0

Source: George Psacharopoulos, "The Contribution of Education to Economic Growth: International Comparisons," in *International Productivity and the Causes of the Shutdown,* ed. J. Kendrick (Cambridge, MA: Ballinger, 1984), p. 337. See also Psacharopoulos and Woodhall, op. cit., p. 17. Reprinted with permission.

attributable to education as estimated by Psacharopoulos through the use of the Schultz and Denison methodologies.

Economic analysis fails to explain why the contributions of education vary so greatly among countries. Two countries may have a relatively high growth of national income yet make much different educational contributions to this growth. Several explanations have been advanced. First, it has been pointed out that the aggregate education of the labor force increases as the labor force itself expands, even though the education level of each worker does not increase. Thus, fluctuations in the increased numbers in the labor force can make estimates vary among countries. Second, the type and level of education in the labor force can have an influence on productivity. Third, little is known about the combinations of education, labor, and capital which produce the greatest economic benefits. Overall, the research has failed to produce definitive findings regarding the optimal levels of each of the components of economic growth.

Further study will be required before one can proceed much beyond conjecture in this area.

Cash-Value Approach

Educational benefits can also be measured by relating earnings to the educational level of individuals. On the average, individuals with a high-school education will have higher earnings than those with only a tenth-grade education, and college graduates will earn more than high-school graduates. This pattern has held for many years. In 1939, the average annual earnings of a high-school graduate was 64 percent of the college graduate; in 1949 the figure was 61 percent; in 1957, 60 percent; and in 1968, 69 percent. In 1990, the income of high-school graduates, ages 18–65, was 61 percent of college graduates. Table 3.2 shows how the differential broadens when a graduate-school education of five or more years is compared with a high-school education.

Figure 3.1 shows age–income profiles by levels of education without costs being taken into

TABLE 3.2   1990 Mean Income by Education Level and Age

Education Level	MEAN ANNUAL INCOME (AGE GROUP)*				
	25–34	*35–44*	*45–54*	*55–64*	*18–65*
Elementary 8 yrs or less	$15,887	$18,379	$19,686	$22,379	$18,814
High School dropout (1–3 yrs)	19,453	23,621	24,133	25,280	21,688
graduate	24,038	28,927	32,862	30,779	26,583
College dropout (1–3 yrs)	28,298	36,180	39,953	36,954	32,781
graduate (4 yrs)	35,534	47,401	50,718	55,518	43,823
Graduate (5 yrs or more)	39,833	58,542	62,902	61,647	55,720

Source: U.S. Department of Commerce, Economics and Statistics Administration, Bureau of Census. Current Population Reports, Consumer Income. Series P-60, No. 174. Money Income of Households, Families, and Persons in the United States: 1990. Table 30, p. 157.

*Persons 18 years old and over as of March 1991. All male, year-round, full-time workers.

Annual Income

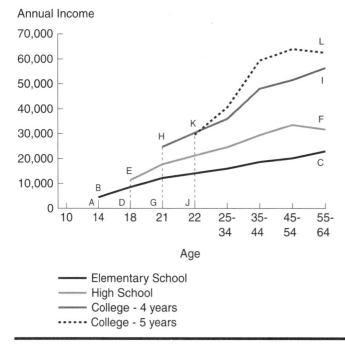

FIGURE 3.1 Mean Year-Round Full-Time Worker's Income by Age and Education, 1990

Source: U.S. Department of Education, National Center for Educational Statistics, *Digest of Educational Statistics, 1992* (Washington, DC: U.S. Government Printing Office, 1993).

account. In other words, this figure shows the cash value of education, by level completed, over the working life of an individual. The line ABC shows the average pattern of income for the elementary-school graduate. Line DEF gives the pattern for the high-school graduate, and line GHI shows that of the college graduate. This income profile can be summarized as follows:

1. Income is highly correlated with levels of schooling.
2. Persons with more schooling consistently earn more than those with less schooling; there is no crossing of profiles.
3. Income rises with age to a peak and then flattens or falls until retirement.
4. Persons with more schooling are more likely to maintain their level of income until retirement.

5. Profiles are steeper for those with more schooling than for those with less schooling.
6. The greater the level of schooling, the later the age at which income reaches its peak.[56]

The continuity of the relationship between more education and higher earnings rebuts earlier warnings by such economists as Seymour Harris of Harvard, who in 1949 erroneously maintained that a persistent increase in college graduates would flood the employment market and make their relative earning power fall. Harris incorrectly predicted that college students within the next twenty years would be doomed to disappointment after graduation, as the number of coveted openings would be substantially less than the numbers seeking them.[57] (See Figure 3.2).

Such conclusions overlook the expansive influence of education on the economy; a better-educated workforce will create economic demand for products which can only be produced by better-educated employees. The demand for highly trained workers has kept pace with the supply, so that they are, by and large, fully employed.[58]

Thus, the monetary benefits to education are well documented and a person progressing through the educational system can be comforted by the knowledge that he or she, on the average, stands a better chance of having a higher income throughout a lifetime. This does not, of course, assure that every individual will earn more with a higher degree than if he or she had only completed, say, the tenth grade. Our history is replete with examples of "self-made" persons who without formal education became economically successful. However, the odds are much better for individuals to become economically successful if they have more education rather than less.

Cost–Benefit Approach

At different school levels, the cash-value approach to measuring the economic desirability of obtaining an education does not give the entire picture. While the cash-value method is accurate, it does not take into account the important element of costs, but focuses exclusively on the benefits. To take costs into consideration requires a more complex analysis of the value of education.

The cost–benefit approach is schematically represented in Figure 3.3. Notice how this differs

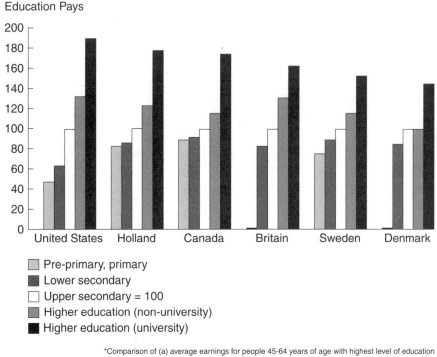

Education Pays

Pre-primary, primary
Lower secondary
Upper secondary = 100
Higher education (non-university)
Higher education (university)

*Comparison of (a) average earnings for people 45-64 years of age with highest level of education completed with (b) those who have an upper secondary education as their highest level

FIGURE 3.2   Relative Earnings of 45–64-year-olds by Level of Education* (latest available year)

Source: OECD as cited in *The Economist*, vol. 325, no. 7786 (November 21, 1992). Reprinted with permission.

from Figure 3.1 in that costs are a negative feature, which must be overcome by income in order for there to be a positive return at retirement age. This schematic is, of course, not drawn to scale. If it were, the costs would possibly show an even more dramatic difference because of foregone income. If we assume that the profile represents individual or private returns on educational investment, and we further assume that the education is taking place in a public school, then the costs to the individual at the elementary level ABC are quite small. Foregone income is very small, since the annual earnings of an illiterate or semiliterate person are relatively small. Additionally, the individual does not incur direct costs in attending a public school since the state pays for the education in its entirety. Thus the benefits of elementary education to the individual can be expected to be quite impressive, since the costs are so low. On the other hand, if one is consider-

ing social benefits, the direct costs of schooling must be taken into account, thereby reducing the benefit–cost ratio (see Figure 3.3).

With a public high-school education, the costs, FGH, are expected to be greater for the individual because of foregone income. The benefit–cost ratio will therefore be reduced somewhat even though income of the high-school graduate (HIJ) is greater.

The individual costs to a college graduate are relatively greater than to either the elementary-school or high-school graduate, since the state does not pay the full cost of a higher education and the student must pay out of pocket for tuition, books, and room and board, in addition to greater foregone earnings. In the schematic, then, KLM is of a greater magnitude and the income, MNO, must be correspondingly higher to offset costs and potential interest thereon over the working life of the individual. Persons com-

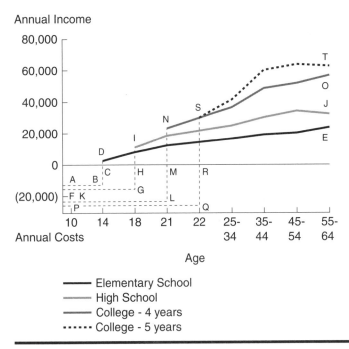

FIGURE 3.3   Mean Year-Round Full-Time Worker's Income and Costs by Age and Education, 1990

Source: U.S. Department of Education, National Center for Educational Statistics, *Digest of Educational Statistics, 1992* (Washington, DC: U.S. Government Printing Office, 1993).

pleting graduate level degrees experience yet higher individual costs (PQR) than individuals completing undergraduate study, and therefore have a correspondingly higher income set (RST), to offset these costs.

Private and Social Costs.   Education has both private and social costs, which may be both direct and indirect. If the student is attending a private school, direct private costs are incurred for tuition, fees, books, and room and board. In a public school, the majority of these costs are subsumed by the public treasury, and thus become social costs. The indirect costs of education are embodied in the earnings which are foregone by all persons of working age; however, foregone earnings are also a cost to society, a reduction in the total productivity of the nation. This may be viewed in macroeconomic terms, but can also be measured in the amount of tax funds which a state forgoes when an individual is unemployed. Of course the state here assumes, as does the individual, that earnings foregone for the sake of education at some early point in the person's career will yield greater returns later. This is the essence of the idea of investment in

education. Table 3.3 shows the major types and categories of costs.

It is within the realm of costs that much of the disenchantment with cost–benefit studies has been generated. Schultz maintained that only about one-half of the total social cost for education should be considered as an investment. It must be acknowledged that all education is not undertaken as an investment. Much of the educational experience of most persons is simply consumed and enjoyed with no thought to what the education will earn them in the future. Does the student make an economically rational choice to invest in education, as he or she would in stocks and bonds?

Private and Social Benefits.   Benefits from education may be either monetary or nonmonetary, and either private (individual) or social. Monetary returns are measurable and are therefore most commonly used in cost–benefit studies. The social externalities of education are difficult to quantify and are therefore seldom relied on for estimating returns to education. Table 3.4 presents a categorization of both the private and social benefits of education.

TABLE 3.3   Types and Categories of Private and Social Educational Costs

	CATEGORIES OF COSTS	
Types of Costs	*Private*	*Social*
Direct Costs	Tuition and fees	Salaries of teachers, administrators, and nonprofessional personnel
	Books, supplies, and equipment (out-of-pocket expenditures)	Books, supplies, and equipment (total)
	Extra travel	Transportation (total)
	Room and board	Room and board (total)
		Scholarship and other subsidies to students
		Capital expenditures
Indirect Costs	Earnings foregone	Earnings foregone

TABLE 3.4   Private and Social Benefits of Education

PRIVATE (INDIVIDUAL) BENEFITS	SOCIAL BENEFITS
Direct Benefits	
Monetary	
Net increase in earnings after taxes	Increase in taxes paid by the educated as a result of education
Additional fringe benefits	
Nonmonetary	
Increased satisfaction derived from exposure to new knowledge and cultural opportunities for both students and parents	
Indirect Benefits	
Monetary	
Work options available at each educational level	Increases in other income
	a) due to increasing productivity of future generations as children become better educated (intergenerational effect)
Increased consumption of goods and services due to extra income	
Nonmonetary	b) due to previously unemployed workers taking jobs vacated by program participants (vacuum effect) (indirect income effect)
Intergenerational effect between parent and child	
Job satisfaction	c) due to reduced tax burden (tax effect)
	d) due to incremental productivity and earnings of workers (indirect income effect)
	Availability to employer of well-trained and skilled labor force
	Improved living conditions of neighbors

Source: Adapted from table by Asefa Gabregiorgis, "Rate of Return on Secondary Education in the Bahamas." (Ph.D. dissertation, 1978, University of Alberta), p. 75.

Direct benefits to the individual are typically measured by increases in earning power after completion of the educational program. The natural ability of the individual, ambition, family connections, family social and economic status, inherited wealth, race, sex, and education of parents may all have a bearing on future earning potential, but cannot be accurately quantified. For example, it has been estimated that anywhere from 5 to 35 percent of income differentials are attributable to differences in ability,[59] while Griliches and Mason have calculated the bias attributable to ability at only about 10 percent.[60] While estimates of the influence of native ability on economic returns

vary widely, the variance in ability contributions does not appear to be a serious source of bias to determination of returns to investment in education.[61]

Three Methods of Calculation.   Cost–benefit analysis requires a determination of costs, benefits, and their distribution over time. Economists have used three basic ways to conduct such an analysis. Psacharopoulos and Woodhall[62] define them as follows:

1. *Cost–benefit ratio.* The *ratio* of the sum of discounted future benefits and the discounted value of costs.

2. *Net present value.* The *value* of the discounted benefits of a project minus the discounted value of its costs.
3. *Internal rate of return.* The *rate of interest* that equates the discounted present value of expected benefits and the present value of costs.[63]

Cost–Benefit Ratio.   The first method, the *cost–benefit ratio*, compares benefits expressed as a *ratio*. If the ratio exceeds unity, then it denotes a positive payoff. When the present value of benefits divided by the present value of costs exceeds 1, the project (or educational undertaking) is worthwhile. For example, if the present value of benefits is $3,000 and the present value of costs in $1,000, then the cost–benefit ratio is 3,000 ÷ 1,000 = 3. Since the benefit is three times as great as the cost, from an economic viewpoint, the investment is a good one.

Net Present Value.   The *net present value (NPV)* is the sum of the benefits minus the sum of the costs, both discounted at an appropriate rate. The result is the net value today of payments in the future.[64] The NPV requires that benefits minus costs be larger than zero.[65] To explain more fully, the values of both benefits and costs may be determined at any point in time. If one is looking into the future, it must be assumed that money invested today in education could have been invested in alternative sources of income. It is therefore necessary to take into account the alternative investment. Studies of this type will usually include two or three or more alternative discount rates of possibly 3, 5, 8, or 12 percent. The NPV approach includes the discount rate in the formula and it is modified until the present value of benefits equals the present value of costs.

Internal Rate of Return.   The other model is the internal rate of return (IROR) which does not use a discount rate as does the NPV approach. Instead, the IROR is concerned only with the relationship of costs to benefits, not the total value of each. In this calculation the rate of return is derived and then compared to a rate of interest which equates the present value of costs and the

present value of benefits. The "internal rate of return figure is obtained simply by finding that rate which makes the estimated future gain in earnings equal to the present cost of obtaining the education; no discount factor enters into this calculation."[66] If the costs of a project are C_t per year and the project is expected to yield benefits of B_t per year over n years, then the rate of return (r) is the rate of interest at which the present value of costs, $C_t/(1+r)^t$, from year 0 to year n.[67]

For example, if a high-school education produces a rate of return of 16 percent and if a realistic alternative investment produces a 10 percent rate of return, the investment in education is more favorable by 6 percent.[68] Those who want to delve more deeply into rate-of-return analysis may wish to refer to formulas given by Psacharopoulos, Cohn, and Alexander and Melcher.[69]

The IROR may be graphically represented as the interest rate which equates the present value of benefits with the present value of costs. Since this rate of return is discovered internal to the calculation in comparing costs to benefits, it is called *internal*, thus the name internal rate of return. The rate (or interest rate), r, at which the curve for benefits intersects the curve for costs, is the internal rate of return (see Figure 3.4).

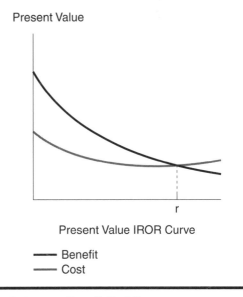

Present Value

Present Value IROR Curve

—— Benefit
—— Cost

FIGURE 3.4   Benefit Cost Curve

RETURNS ON EDUCATION INVESTMENT

The internal rate of return is the most commonly used approach in educational investment studies. Many such studies have been conducted since 1961, the results of which vary somewhat, depending on the particular statistical technique employed by the researcher; but by and large, they show that education is a good investment for both the individual and the state. This holds true internationally as well as within the United States. Psacharopoulos, in synthesizing the findings of 53 studies in 32 countries, found that both private and social rates of return for education were generally higher than returns to investment in physical capital.[70] Psacharopoulos concluded that per capita income differences among countries "can be better explained by differences in the endowments of human rather than physical capital."[71] Averaging rates of return for the 53 studies, he found that private rates of return for primary school were 23.7 percent per year, while for high school and college they were 16.3 and 17.5 per-

cent, respectively. For social rates of return, he found primary education to be 25.1 percent, secondary, 13.5 percent; and college, 11.3 percent.[72] When averages for developed and underdeveloped countries were considered, it was found that overall the returns to investment in human capital were greater in underdeveloped countries. Subsequent analysis by Psacharopoulos in 1981[73] of developing countries confirmed the magnitude of these rates of return (see Figure 3.5).

So many rate-of-return studies have been conducted for various phases of education in the United States that it is virtually impossible to identify them all. Findings of several notable major studies, though, may be identified. Hanoch, in one of the earlier analyses, found that the private IROR for elementary schooling was probably infinite because the elementary-school child has no cost of schooling.[74] Children at such a young age cannot work; therefore, there are no foregone earnings and those who are enrolled in public school obtain their education free. Hansen made similar observations, and Hines, Tweeten,

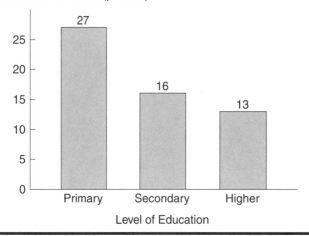

Social Rate of Return (percent)

FIGURE 3.5   The Social Returns to Investment in Education, by School Level in Developing Countries

Source: George Psacharopoulos (1981), p. 333, cited in *Education for Development, An Analysis of Investment Choices* (Oxford University Press, 1985), George Psacharopoulos and Maureen Woodhall, p. 58. Reprinted with permission.

Note: "Developing countries" refers to *22* African, Asian, and Latin American countries.

and Redfern found that the private IROR for elementary-school children was 155 percent.[75]

Primary School

Social returns for elementary schooling are substantially less than for private returns, primarily because the state incurs costs in conducting the public education system and the social benefits only include direct returns to the state obtained through taxation. Hansen found the social IROR for elementary school to be 15 percent, and Hines, Tweeten, and Redfern discovered it to be 17.8 percent. Carnoy and Marenbach, in a 1975 study, found that the social IROR for elementary schooling for white males ranged from a low of 7.2 percent to a high of 13.2 percent, depending upon which year they used.[76] Private rate of return for primary school have been found to be as low as 13 percent per year[77] and as high as 49.1

percent, but studies have generally revealed rates in the 16 to 25 percent range.

Secondary School

Social rates of return for secondary education are generally found to be between 10 and 19 percent per year.[78] Secondary education is therefore an attractive investment for both the individual and the state (see Figure 3.6).

Bachelor's Degree

Several studies have been conducted at the bachelor's degree level, with results usually indicating that a college education is a slightly less attractive investment than either secondary or elementary education. In 1975, Raymond and Sesnowitz, using data for 1970, reported a private IROR for college graduates to be 17.9 percent per year[79]

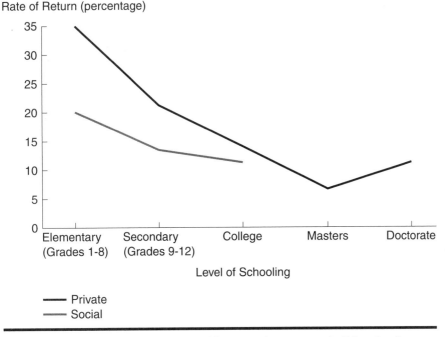

Rate of Return (percentage)

Level of Schooling

— Private
— Social

FIGURE 3.6   Private and Social Rates of Return to Investments in Education by Level of Education

Note: Averages of several major studies conducted for the United States. Note that no good empirical data exist by which to estimate social rate of return for graduate education.

and Carnoy and Marenbach found the IROR for the same year to be 15.4 percent.[80] Several other studies have found lower returns for various years from 1950 to 1973. In another major study, Eckaus found private rates of return for college graduates to be around 12 percent.[81] Such a general figure for all graduates is not of great value because of variations in expected income for graduates in different fields. For example, Eckaus shows that depending on certain assumptions regarding base income, the private IROR for ac-

countants ranges from 12.5 to 16.5 percent, while the private IROR for chemists may range from 13 to 21 percent.[82] Social rates of return for the bachelor's degrees level usually fall into the 10 to 13 percent range (see Figure 3.7).

Graduate Education

Graduate education reveals lower rates of return than any other level of education. Hanoch found that 17 plus years of education had an IROR for

Rate of Return (percent)

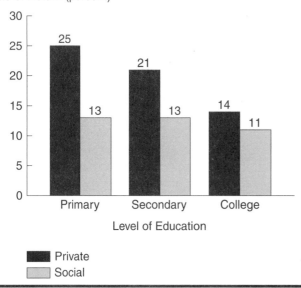

FIGURE 3.7   Returns to Investment in Education, by Level of Schooling in United States

Sources: The rates of return shown in this figure are averages of rates of return in the references below:

W. L. Hansen, "Total and Private Rates of Return to Investment in Schooling," *Journal of Political Economy*, 71 (April 1963), pp. 128–140.

M. Carnoy and D. Marenbach, "The Return to Schooling in the United States, 1939–69," *Journal of Human Resources* 10 (Summer 1975), pp. 312–331.

F. Hines, L. Tweeten, and M. Redfern, "Social and Private Rates of Return to Investment in Schooling, by Race–Sex Groups and Regions," *Journal of Human Resources*, 5 (Summer 1970), pp. 318–340.

G. S. Becker, *Human Capital—A Theoretical and Empirical Analysis with Special Reference to Education* (New York: National Bureau of Economic Research, 1964).

G. Hanoch, "An Economic Analysis of Earnings and Schooling," *Journal of Human Resources*, 2 (Summer 1967), pp. 310–329.

J. Mincer, *Schooling Experience and Earnings* (New York: Columbia University Press, 1974).

the individual of 7.0 percent. Tomaske found it to be 10 percent; Mincer, 7.3 percent, and Bailey and Schotta, interestingly, −1.0 percent.[83] If one proceeds to the doctorate, the returns seem to be improved over completion of a master's degree. The IROR for the Ph.D. has in most studies been found to range between 10.5 and 23.6 percent.[84] Different areas of training of course give various rates of return. For instance, the professor of natural sciences has an IROR of 10.5 percent, if one assumes that without the advanced graduate education the alternative employment would have been secondary-school teaching.[85] Dentists are shown by Eckaus to have an IROR of from 18.5 to 37 percent. Some studies have produced negative private rates-of-return for some graduate fields of study. Thomas, for example, found that graduate training for teachers produced a negative return,[86] and Siegfried in 1971 found a negative private IROR for the Ph.D. in economics.[87] Other disciplines also suffer from declining returns to educational investment, particularly at the graduate level, as documented by Freeman in his book, *The Overeducated American*.[88] Generally, though, the graduate, if he or she uses some economic rationale in selecting a career, can receive a rate of return that makes the investment in college education highly positive. Today, however, it appears that careful selectivity in choosing a career is necessary; no longer is it as likely for those with a liberal education, with no particular career goal in mind, to gain significant economic returns. This of course ignores the rewarding consumption benefits derived from a liberal college education.

Social rates of return to graduate study may be lower than private rates of return for the same level, especially when students attend public institutions. Graduate education is quite expensive to the state because of lower student–teacher ratios and the higher salaries generally paid to graduate professors. Of course, both social and private rates of return are substantially diminished by the higher foregone earnings expected from people of high educational levels who attend schools for a period of time in lieu of working. Of course one should bear in mind that the benefits of social rates of return are calculated using only increased taxes paid by those educated. Researchers have not been able to quantify the effects on the economy of new inventions which have come about as a result of graduate research or the many other externalities which may benefit society from graduate education. Certainly, as far as school teachers are concerned, economists should derive methods of measuring the social value of having trained teachers return to the classroom and spend their lives in the direct production of human capital. Actually, if such values were taken into account, it could well be shown that the social rate of return to investment in teacher education is one of the most productive investments a state can make.

Vocational Education

Studies of vocational education programs have generally shown rates of return to be quite high for both the individual and the state. However, problems related to partitioning benefits between vocational and academic programs have created data difficulties for benefit–cost studies in secondary programs, whereas post-secondary vocational programs are much easier to analyze. At the secondary level, a study by Hu, Lee, Stromsdorfer, and Kaufman compared a vocational education program to the academic programs in three large cities. The private rates of return were found to be extremely high, with an estimated IROR of 56.8 percent.[89] Lower rates were subsequently found in other studies by Corazzini and Taussig.[90] Alexander and Melcher found substantial rates of return to certain post-secondary education courses for licensed practical nursing and heating and air conditioning, but found negative private and social returns for cosmetology.[91] As with both undergraduate and graduate programs, the rates of return vary substantially among the courses and programs in vocational education. While on the whole, vocational education appears to be quite productive, studies which disaggregate both the costs and benefits should be conducted to provide more definitive information.

EXTERNAL BENEFITS TO INVESTMENT IN EDUCATION

Up to this point we have considered only a portion of the benefits to investment in education. The entire value of education must also be viewed in light of its social possibilities and consequences. The monetary benefits considered in rates of return include only the value of increased earnings of the individual and the value of additional taxes collected by the state. Actually, the direct monetary returns are not inclusive of all the economic returns accruable from investment in education. In the broader economic context, benefits include:

1. Anything that increases production
2. Anything that reduces the need to incur costs such as those for law enforcement, thereby releasing resources for alternative uses
3. Anything that increases welfare possibilities directly, such as development of public-spiritedness or social consciousness of one's neighbor[92]

Increased Labor Productivity

The first benefit—anything that increases production—refers to the overall strengthening of the economic system through increased worker productivity. This is not a direct monetary return to education, but a broader economic externality of education.

A World Bank report of 1991 observes that "the single best measure of education or training's economic impact is the additional productivity of workers and farmers with more education and training over those with less."[93] As Denison[94] documents, human capital alone does not determine the optimum productivity of a country, but it is a major contributor. In recent years, the United States has experienced a relative decline in

worker productivity that cannot be attributed to a decrease in educational level, but rather to the inadequacy of capital formation and the obsolescence of the physical assets of many of the major industrial firms in the United States. Further, in some cases, the relative decline may also be attributed to poor planning and questionable management practices.

By and large, though, education can improve the general environment in which production takes place, as well as positively affecting workers who only interact with those who actually received the education. The educated may be better prepared to pass on or receive training than the uneducated and may more adequately enhance productive psychological and motivational factors.

Although the value of education as it relates to work has been drawn into question—as evidenced by the recent all-out attack on credentialism[95]—the value of education for employment is readily apparent. The more educated person in the job market receives preferential treatment from the employer. Whether this is justified is largely irrelevant. Employers appear to recognize that the educated worker has favorable external effects on other workers and on the firm in general. An interdependence exists whereby both the worker and the firm have a financial interest in the education of fellow workers.[96]

Employers believe that the education of the employee improves the financial potential of the firm. There is a definite positive relationship between the amount of formal education of employees and the amount of on-the-job training they received.[97] Firms apparently have found that greater productivity can be achieved with less cost by investing in the more educated employees. Greater benefits can be obtained by grafting job training to the knowledge already acquired from formal schooling.[98] It may also be that the employer responds in part to the worker's own willingness to invest in himself or herself, since employer investment in the worker appears to increase in about the same proportion as the worker's self-investment in schooling. The less-educated experience greater unemployment. (See Figure 3.8.) On the average, "job losers" have almost a year and a half less education than "job keepers."[99] Labor turnover and unemployment are related to consumer demand for goods and services. Although the correlation is rather weak, the more-educated, being more generally employed in service jobs, have greater employment stability.[100] Some evidence also shows that in certain areas of the economy, physical capital is more likely to be substituted for unskilled than for skilled labor. Consequently, the less-educated labor force is more susceptible to layoffs due to advances in technology and fluctuations in types of goods produced and methods of production.[101] *The Economist* notes,

People who leave school early rapidly run out of rungs on the earnings ladder; university graduates not only find plenty of rungs, they also discover that each step upwards is increasingly remunerative. One reason for this is that the well-educated land jobs that provide them with more training, while the uneducated are locked out of opportunities to improve their skills.[102]

Thus, education may be viewed as a type of private (and social) hedge against technological displacement. Weisbrod called this the "hedging option," the value of which is difficult to quantify.[103] Further, inexperienced and uneducated workers who earn less than minimum wage have higher unemployment. Better-educated workers may well have the edge in communication, disci-

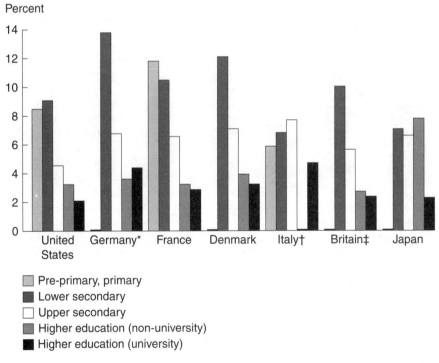

Percent

Pre-primary, primary
Lower secondary
Upper secondary
Higher education (non-university)
Higher education (university)

*People in apprenticeships not considered part of the active population   †Included in universities
‡Women 60-64 years excluded from relevant population

FIGURE 3.8   Unemployment by Level of Education, as Percentage of Labor Force, 25–64-year-olds, 1989

Source: OECD, as cited in *The Economist*, vol. 325, no. 7786, (November 21, 1992). Reprinted with permission.

pline of the mind, flexibility, and adaptability. Also, the more educated the worker, the more likely he or she is to be receptive to new ideas and knowledge.[104]

The Educated Workforce

The production process may be regarded as the transformation of resources into goods and services. Transformation is generally more efficient if the process utilizes educated workers, even though the precise nature of the interaction between education and economic productivity is not known. Bowen lists six ways in which worker productivity is increased by education:

1. *Quantity of product.* Workers with higher levels of education produce more goods and services in a given time period because of their greater skill, dexterity, and knowledge.
2. *Quality of product.* The more-educated produce better goods and render services with greater skill and/or sensitivity to human conditions.

3. *Product mix.* Educated workers may be able to produce goods and services which are more highly prized by society than those produced by workers with less education.
4. *Participation in the labor force.* Educated workers are less susceptible to lost time from unemployment and illness, and are usually characterized by higher aspirations.
5. *Allocative ability.* Workers, through education, may be better able to assess their own talents; to achieve greater skills; and to be more receptive to new technologies, new products, and new ideas.
6. *Job satisfaction.* The educated may have greater job satisfaction because they tend to acquire jobs with greater psychic rewards.[105]

Machlup has summarized the effects of education on increased productivity as follows:

> It is with regard to . . . improvements in the quality of labor, that education can play a really significant role. Positive effects may be expected on five scores: (a) better working habits and discipline, increased labor efforts, and greater reliability; (b) better health through more wholesome and sanitary ways of living; (c) improved skills, better comprehension of working requirements, and increased efficiency; (d) prompter adaptability to momentary changes, especially in jobs which require quick evaluation of new information, and, in general, fast reactions; and (e) increased capability to move into more productive occupations when opportunities arise. All levels of education may contribute to improving the quality of labor.[106]

Education differs in a basic way from most other social or public services in that it constitutes an investment in knowledge and skills that yield economic and social benefits in the future. It differs materially from governmental welfare or health expenditures, which may be characterized as maintenance of human capital rather than development. While it is true that payment of health bills for the needy may help heal and return them to the workforce, or that welfare payments for food or shelter preserve human capital, it is nevertheless important to note that neither of these public programs actually increases the worth of human capital. The same human raw material is maintained but not necessarily enhanced.

Public expenditure for police protection and prison systems is even more nonproductive. While every society expends large sums on these public functions, the benefits cannot be classified as investments in the development of human capital except in a limited sense when rehabilitation of prisoners actually works and the individual is returned to the labor force. Largely, though, penal expenditures must be viewed as economically nonproductive.

While it is true that benefits from these public services cannot be completely self-contained, it is obvious that the provision of public education is quite different from that of other social services. Education, therefore, should not be treated in the same light by legislators. There is a fundamental difference between the mere maintenance of human capital and the development of human capital.

Reduced Need for Other Services

This is not to say, of course, that public expenditures for health and welfare are undesirable and unnecessary, nor that public expenditures for law enforcement should or can be reduced. However, it is important to note that education must be considered in a different context. Education should be viewed as a remedy to the problems and not as a problem itself. Increased investment in education will tend to reduce the necessity of placing more public revenue into health, welfare, and the penal system. An increment of education will show reduced government expenditures for crime prevention, fire protection, public health, and medical care.[107]

Health

Better-educated persons are healthier. In 1989, 37.5 percent of the persons with less than 4 years of education suffered chronic ailments that limited their work and other activities while only 7.7 percent of those with 16 years of education suffered loss of activities.[108] Persons with less than 4 years of education are confined to a bed 17.3 days per year. In contrast, persons with 16 years of education are confined only 3.9 days per year.[109] Additionally, the more highly educated stay in hospitals for shorter periods of time.[110]

Figure 3.9 shows the percentage of persons assessed to be in fair or poor health by years of education and family income. Each chart shows two curved lines, one which is adjusted for age and the other which is unadjusted. The conclusion is obvious, those with more education have better health as do those with greater incomes. Of course, as we have discussed earlier, the better-educated also have higher incomes.

Crime Reduction

It may be argued that education reduces crime primarily because education reduces unemployment, and the employed commit fewer crimes.[111] Some portion of criminal behavior can be attributed to a lack of education.[112] With a rise in family income, a corresponding decrease in delinquency may be found; since more education and greater income are related, a similar relationship exists between education and crime.[113]

Ehrlich found that inequalities in the distribution of schooling may have an effect on the amount of crime, suggesting that equalization of educational opportunity may be a proper governmental goal in crime reduction. According to Ehrlich, whether more education will serve as a deterrent to crime may depend on the extent to which the economic returns of crime are reduced. Thus, education coupled with alternative methods may impair the economic success of criminals.[114]

Certain studies have shown that prisoners have a lower than average educational attainment,[115] and that illiteracy among criminals is much higher than for the population as a whole.[116] Low educational attainment seems to

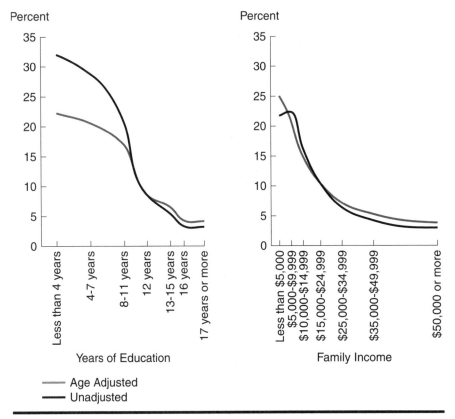

FIGURE 3.9 Unadjusted and Age-adjusted Percentages of Persons Assessed in Fair or Poor Health, by Years of Education and Family Income: United States, 1989

Source: National Center for Health Statistics, *Vital and Health Statistics, Educational Differences in Health Status and Health Care*, Series 10, No. 179 (Washington, DC: U.S. Department of Health and Human Services, 1991), p. 9.

increase the likelihood of one's "turning to illegal means to fulfill his social and economic desires."[117] One national commission found in a survey of riot participants that inadequate education and underemployment were among the top four causes of participation.[118]

Levin estimated the cost of crime against persons and property in the United States to be $1.1 billion per year; the cost of law enforcement and the criminal judiciary to be $4.2 billion; private costs, $1.9 billion; and income foregone by inmates to be $1 billion—a total of $8.2 billion. If one-half of the total costs, an upper limit, can be attributable to lack of education, we find that an astonishing $4.1 billion could have been saved by further education. Even using the lower limit of Levin's estimate, 25 percent attributable to inadequate education, over $2 billion of the costs of crime could have been prevented by more education.[119]

Some contrary assertions have suggested that student riots of the late 1960s were evidence that education does not inculcate a respect for the law,[120] and that compulsory attendance beyond a certain grade level may lead to antagonism and juvenile delinquency. Such assertions, however, are outweighed by the positive relationship between education and crime reduction.

Welfare

Recipients of welfare also generally have lower than average educational attainment. Studies by the U.S. Department of Health, Education, and Welfare have shown that incapacitated and unemployment AFDC fathers have median levels of education far below the average. About 76 percent of the incapacitated fathers and 61.2 percent of the unemployed fathers did not have a high-school education. Since this high percentage did not reflect the 15.9 percent of the incapacitated and 22.8 percent of the unemployed for whom no educational data were available, the percentages of inadequate education may be even higher.[121] Other data show that 84 percent of all AFDC unemployed fathers had less than a high-school education.[122] Over 82 percent of the AFDC mothers lacked a high-school education.[123] AFDC recipients who did become self-supporting generally had more education than those who did not.[124]

In attempting to quantify the impact of welfare costs on the taxpayer, Levin, in another part of the aforementioned study, found that AFDC, medical assistance, and general welfare assistance together cost $5.9 billion in 1970, and unemployment compensation amounted to $4.3 billion. Levin estimated that an upper limit of 50 percent and a lower limit of 25 percent of public assistance, $2.96 billion and $1.48 billion respectively, could be attributed to low levels of education. With an upper limit of 25 percent and a lower limit of 15 percent, he determined the costs of unemployment compensation due to inadequate education to be $1.08 billion and $648 million, respectively.[125] Whether these costs are precisely accurate is probably of little consequence; the importance of the data rests on the establishment of an apparently strong relationship between level of education and public expenditure on welfare.[126] Theoretically, increasing educational levels may enhance the efficiency of the use of public resources, with a corresponding decline in the necessity for welfare.

Social Consciousness and Intergenerational Transfers

Education benefits many people other than the student, including the student's children, who receive positive intergenerational transfers of knowledge, and neighbors who are affected by favorable social values developed by schooling.

Certain nonmonetary returns of education are well known and largely taken for granted. Ignorant people can be more easily misled and propagandized than educated people. As discussed more fully in Chapter 1, the freedom implicit in a democratic society is premised on an educated citizenry.

The Household

If one can assume that the household is a small economic enterprise or multi-product firm which produces many desirables from which members of the family derive satisfaction—such as good health, physical exercise, and nutrition, which are the result of such production activities as convalescing, jogging, and eating—then it is possible to measure the impact of education on the efficiency of the enterprise. In devising this model, Michael theorized that the introduction of additional education into the household's production process would be analogous to the application of new technology to a firm.[127] He concluded that the level of schooling systematically influences consumer behavior independent of the effect of income. His data further suggest that education increases the efficiency of the household's production process.

The general well-being of the family may also be affected by the role of education in increasing the individual's capacity to capitalize on situations to his or her economic benefit. Presumably a more highly educated individual will possess a certain economic concepts which will affect his or her economic choices. Solmon examined the influence of education on saving behavior over and above the ability to earn more on the job, to consume more efficiently, and to generally enjoy life more fully.[128] From reviewing existing saving and consumption-function theories, Solmon concluded that saving propensities tend to rise with the schooling level of the family head. It may be presumed that such tendencies toward frugality will contribute to an ordered growth of the income and wealth of society, and provide for general economic stability. He further found, in studying attitudes, that one could infer that an additional private benefits of schooling may be a greater efficiency in portfolio management.

Worldwide overpopulation will certainly have an important effect not only on the socioeconomic systems of the world, but also on the ecological system of the planet. In recent years, great controversies have surrounded the goal of zero population growth. Population growth usually starts at the micro level of the household. Familial benefits can be maximized by the proper balance of services passed on to children. It may be theorized that the quality of the child's life is greater if the time and goods devoted to him or her are more extensive. For example, family resources may permit the parent to both purchase a musical instrument and provide music instruction for the child. There is little doubt that positive intergenerational transfers are enhanced by limiting the number of children and increasing the parental time devoted to each child. It has been found that the correlation between education and family size is negative. This may be the result of schooling on a couple's preferences, or it may be the result of a realistic economic assessment of the household, reflecting an increase in the cost of raising children as the educational level of the couple increases.

Educated Mothers

A most important aspect of enhanced education is its impact on infant mortality. The better educated the mother, the greater the chances for infant survival (see Figure 3.10). In 1991 the World Bank observed,

The results are quite clear about the importance of educating women. The educational status of adult women is by far the most important variable explaining changes in infant mortality and secondary enrollments. An extra year of education for women is associated with a drop of 2 percentage points in the rate of infant mortality. Household-level studies have reported even larger reductions of 5–10 percentage points.[129]

The level of education has been found to have a consistently high relationship to the use of contraceptives.[130] In 1965 the percentage of women who had used oral contraceptives was over three times as high in the highest educated group as in the lowest. The educated are more aware of, more receptive to, and more effective in their use and selection of contraceptive techniques.[131] Michael found that the relationship between the education of the wife and fertility was negative, indicating that increased education may be an important deterrent to overpopulation.[132]

Women in the Labor Force

The influence of the education of women on the economy of the family and the nation has not gone unnoticed. Although rates of return for investment in women's schooling are lower than for men's, for reasons including job discrimination and home care options,[133] the benefits of education are nevertheless substantial. Women's participation in the labor force is accompanied by a striking relationship with the level of education. Better-educated women are more likely to be in the labor force.[134] The economic explanation for this is that education raises women's productivity in the labor market over and above their productivity at home, making it more costly for highly educated women to remain at home.

However, the positive effect of education on women is expanded by the time they expend at home. As women become more educated and spend a greater amount of time in the labor force, one might assume that they spend a smaller proportion of their time in home production and that a decrease in home production time

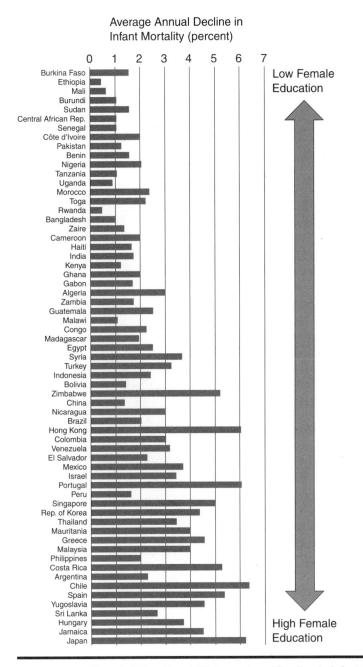

FIGURE 3.10   Female Educational Attainment and Decline in Infant Mortality, Selected Economies, 1960–1987

Source: World Bank, *World Development Report 1991, The Challenge of Development* (Oxford: The World Bank and Oxford University Press, 1991), p. 49. Reprinted with permission.

Note: Economies are listed in ascending order by level of female education, defined as the average years of schooling, excluding postsecondary schooling, of females age 15 to 84.

may indicate a corresponding decrease in child-care activities. These data do not bear out such assumptions. To the contrary, better-educated working mothers generally spend more time with their children in effective and positive transfer of knowledge. The better-educated mothers spend more time in physical care and in activities related to social and educational development of children, including reading to them, helping with lessons, and taking them to social and educational functions.[135]

Intergenerational transfer of knowledge is therefore much more pronounced among educated households. Educational investments in one generation undoubtedly have an important effect on succeeding generations.

SUMMARY AND CONCLUSIONS

The value of investment in education is discussed in this chapter. It is now recognized throughout the world that the wealth of nations is dependent more on human capital than physical capital. This chapter discusses how economists have estimated the value of education in human capital production.

The wealth of nations is highly dependent on the extensiveness of the knowledge of its people. The modern technological state is highly brain intensive as opposed to earlier labor-intensive societies.

Various studies since World War II have shown that sustained economic growth is largely attributable to education.

Today, education reform is at the head of national priorities in virtually all countries, both developed and underdeveloped, in the Americas, Europe, and Asia. In these countries education is no longer treated as a consumer good but rather as a productive asset.

The classical economical view espoused by Adam Smith in 1776 ignored the value of investment in knowledge and assumed that all economic growth resulted from the interaction of the markets. Modern economists maintain that the classical approach of Adam Smith was defi-

cient and limited in its perspective on the actual causes of economic growth.

Investment in physical capital cannot be discounted, but it is now known that the quality of human capital is the active ingredient that enables the efficient use of physical capital.

Nations investing in education must gauge and balance their created systems of elementary, secondary, and higher education as well as give due cognizance to technical training.

The primacy of early or primary education is undisputed and to ignore this sector of education impairs the efficiency of investments in higher levels of education. A country that foregoes investment in early education in favor of higher education will undermine its own economic growth.

The benefits of education may be measured in many different ways, but the most common methods are:

1. *The Relationship analysis approach.* A strong correlation exists between those who are educated and those who have money.
2. *Residual approach.* The reasons for a nation's growth cannot be fully measured without determining the residual contribution of education.
3. *Cash-value approach.* Earnings rise with the level of education.
4. *Cost–benefit approach.* The benefits of education outweigh the costs for both individuals and society.

Returns to investment in education are usually greater to the individual than to society, but both show that investment in education is very lucrative.

Investments in early childhood and elementary education yield greater returns, on the average, than investments in secondary or higher education. On the whole, secondary education yields greater return than higher education.

Education increases worker productivity and is an indirect but real benefit to society. Higher levels of education produce an external benefit of increased opportunities and employment options. The better-educated are more easily employed, are unemployed less, have more continuity and longevity in their jobs, produce a greater quantity and quality of goods and services, and are more satisfied with their employment.

Better-educated persons have less need for health services, commit fewer crimes, are less needful of welfare, have a greater social consciousness, conduct more efficient households, and transfer more beneficial knowledge to their children. Moreover, the better-educated are less likely to overpopulate, while educated women are more active and productive in the labor force. At the same time, better-educated women have proven to be more adept and attentive mothers.

KEY TERMS

Human capital	Relationship analysis approach	Private benefits
Investment in education	Residual approach	Social benefits
Wealth of nations	Cash-value approach	Rate-of-return approach
Human capital approach	Cost–benefit approach	Social externalities
Absorption effect	Private costs	Intergenerational transfers
Skill acquisition	Social costs	

ENDNOTES

1. For an excellent discussion on the history of human capital see Elchanan Cohn and Terry G. Geske, *The Economics of Education*, 3rd ed. (Oxford: Pergamon Press, 1990), pp. 13–24.

2. Barbara W. Tuchman, *A Distant Mirror: The Calamitous 14th Century* (New York: Alfred A. Knopf, 1978), pp. 119–20.

3. Theodore W. Schultz, "Investment in Human Capital," *American Economic Review* 51 (March 1961), pp. 1–17.

4. Sir William Petty, *Political Arithmetick, Or A Discourse Concerning the Extent and Value of Lands, Buildings, Etc.* (London: 1666).

5. World Bank, *World Development Report 1991, The Challenge of Development* (Oxford: The World Bank and Oxford University Press, 1991), p. 42.

6. "Where Tigers Breed, A Survey of Asia's Emerging Economies," *The Economist*, vol. 321, no. 7733 (November 16, 1991), pp. 4–5.

7. Adam Wooldridge, "Education: Trying Harder," *The Economist*, vol. 325, no. 7786 (November 21, 1992), p. 3.

8. Ibid.

9. Ibid.

10. Ibid., p. 5.

11. Ibid.

12. John Stuart Mill, *Principles of Political Economy*, vol. I, rev. ed. (London: Colonial Press, 1900), p. 9.

13. Adam Smith, *The Wealth of Nations*, rev. ed. (New York: Modern Library, 1937), p. 265.

14. R. Blandy, "Marshall on Human Capital: R Note," *Journal of Political Economy* 75 (December 1967), pp. 874–875.

15. Alfred Marshall, *Principles of Economics*, 8th ed. (London: MacMillan, 1930), pp. 787–788.

16. Horace Mann, From the 12th Report (1848), One of twelve *Annual Reports* made by Mann to the State Board of Education, Massachusetts.

17. Ibid.

18. H. Von Thunen, "Costs of Education as Foundation of Productive Capital," in *Readings in the Economics of Education,* eds. M.J. Bowman and others (Paris: UNESCO, 1968).

19. See E. A. Caswell, *The Money Value of Education* (Washington, DC: U.S. Government Printing Office, 1917).

20. Theodore W. Schultz, *Investment in Human Capital* (New York: Free Press, 1971), p. 22.

21. Ibid.

22. Schultz, op. cit., pp. 1–17.

23. Frederick H. Harbison, *Human Resources as the Wealth of Nations* (New York: Oxford University Press, 1973), p. 3.

24. Ibid.

25. W. Arthur Lewis, *The Theory of Economic Growth* (London: George Allen & Unwin, 1977), pp. 183–184.

26. Mark Blaug, ed., *Economics of Education* (New York: Penguin Books, 1972).

27. Jee-Pang Tan and Alain Mingat, *Education in Asia, A Comparative Study of Costs and Financing* (Washington, DC: The World Bank, 1992), p. 78.

28. Ibid., p. 79.

29. Lewis, op. cit., p. 183.

30. Eli Ginsberg, *The Human Economy* (New York: McGraw-Hill, 1976), p. 47.

31. Ibid., pp. 70–71.

32. Pitirim A. Sorokin, *Hunger as a Factor in Human Affairs* (Gainesville, FL: University Presses of Florida, 1975), pp. 156–157.

33. Burton A. Weisbrod, "Education and Investment in Human Capital," *Journal of Political Economy* 70, no. 5 (Pt. 2, 1962 Supp.), pp. 106–123.

34. Ibid.

35. W. G. Bowen, "Assessing the Economic Contribution of Education: An Appraisal of Alternative Approaches," *Higher Education. Report of the Committee under the Chairmanship of Lord Robbins, Report: 961-63* (London: H.M.S.O., 1963), 73–96.

36. Education Department, Chamber of Commerce of the United States, *Education: An Investment in the People* (Washington, DC: U.S. Government Printing Office, 1961), pp. 2–3.

37. "Education: Coming Top," op. cit.

38. Ibid., pp. 4–23.

39. "Targets for Education in Europe" (paper delivered at Washington Conference of O.E.C.D., 1961), p. 75.

40. The simplest form of this production function is a linear model expressed as $y = F(KL)$, where physical capital is K and labor is L. For further information see George Psacharopoulos, "The Contribution of Education to Economic Growth: International Comparisons," in *International Productivity Comparisons and the Causes of the Slowdown*, ed. J. Kendrick (Cambridge, MA: Ballinger, 1984).

41. John W. Kendrick, *Productivity Trends in the United States* (Princeton, NJ: Princeton University Press, 1961), p. 79.

42. B. F. Massell, "Capital Formation and Technological Change in United States Manufacturing," *Review of Economics and Statistics* (May 1960), p. 182–188.

43. Solomon Fabricant, *Prerequisite for Economic Growth* (New York: National Conference Board, 1959).

44. World Bank, *World Development Report 1991, The Challenge of Development* (Oxford: The World Bank and Oxford University Press, 1991), p. 42.

45. Ibid.

46. For an excellent explanation of the aggregate production function, see Cohn, op. cit., pp. 142–145.

47. Theodore W. Schultz, "Education and Economic Growth," in *Social Forces Influencing American Education*, ed. N.B. Henry (Chicago: University of Chicago Press, 1961), pp. 46–88.

48. Edward F. Denison, *The Sources of Economic Growth in the United States* (New York: Committee for Economic Development, 1962).

49. Edward F. Denison, *Accounting for United States Economic Growth, 1929–1969* (Washington, DC: Brookings Institution, 1974).

50. Hector Correa, "Sources of Economic Growth in Latin America," *Southern Economic Journal* 37 (July 1970), pp. 17–31.

51. Edward F. Denison, *Why Growth Rates Differ: Postwar Experiences in Nine Western Countries* (Washington, DC: Brookings Institute, 1967.

52. George Psacharopoulos and Maureen Woodhall, *Education for Development, An Analysis of Investment Choices* (Oxford: Oxford University Press, 1985), pp. 17–19.

53. World Bank, *World Development Report 1980* (New York: Oxford University Press, 1980).

54. Norman Hicks, "Economic Growth and Human Resources," World Bank Staff Working Paper No. 408, Washington, DC.

55. D. Wheeler, "Human Resources Development and Economic Growth in Developing Countries: A Simultaneous Model," World Bank Staff Working Paper No. 407, Washington, DC.

56. See Psacharopoulos and Woodhall, op. cit., p. 40.

57. Seymour E. Harris, *The Market for College Graduates and Related Aspects of Education and Income* (Cambridge, MA: Harvard University Press, 1949), p. 64.

58. Herman P. Miller, *Rich Man, Poor Man* (New York: Thomas Y. Crowell, 1971), p. 168.

59. P. Taubman and Terence Wales, "Education as an Investment and a Screening Device," in *Education, Income and Human Behavior*, ed. F. Thomas Juster (New York: McGraw-Hill, 1975), pp. 95–121; P. Taubman "Personal Characteristics and the Distribution of Earnings," in *The Personal Distribution of Incomes*, ed. A. B. Atkinson (London: George Allen and Unwin, 1976), pp. 193–226.

60. Zwi Griliches and William M. Mason, "Education, Income and Ability," in *Investment in Education*, ed. T. W. Schultz (Chicago: University of Chicago Press, 1971), p. 87.

61. John C. Hause, "Earnings Profile: Ability and Schooling," in T. W. Schultz, ed., op. cit., p. 131.

62. Psacharopoulos and Woodhall, op. cit., p. 30.

63. Ibid.

64. Asefa Gabregiorgis, *Rate of Return on Secondary Education in the Bahamas* (Ph.D. dissertation, University of Alberta), p. 117.

65. See formulas in Appendix.

66. W. G. Bowen, "Assessing the Economic Contribution of Education: An Appraisal of Alternative Approaches," in *Economics of Education* 1, ed. M. Blaug (Hammondsworth, England: Penguin Books, 1971), p. 90.

67. Psacharopoulos and Woodhall, op. cit., p. 31.

68. George Psacharopoulos, *Returns on Education* (San Francisco: Jossey-Bass, 1973); Cohn, op. cit.; Kern Alexander and Thomas Melcher, *A Computerized System for Benefit–Cost Analysis in Vocational Education* (Gainesville, FL: Institute for Educational Finance, University of Florida, 1980).

69. The following explanation of the calculation is taken from Psacharopoulos and Woodhall, op. cit., pp. 68–69.

(1) The *internal rate of return* is the rate of return at which the present value of costs

$$\sum_{t=0}^{t=n} \frac{C_t}{(1 + r)^t}$$

equals the present value of expected benefits

$$\sum_{t=0}^{t=n} \frac{B_t}{(1 + r)^t}$$

or, alternatively, the rate of interest (r), at which the difference between discounted benefits and costs is zero, that is,

$$\sum_{t=0}^{t=n} \frac{B_t - C_t}{(1 + r)^t} = 0.$$

(2) Compound interest and discount factors, for $n = 1$ to $n = 8$, at 10 percent interest are:

Year	Amount to which $1 invested will grow at end of each year	Amount that $1 promised at end of each year is worth today
1	1.100	0.909
2	1.210	0.826
3	1.331	0.751
4	1.464	0.683
5	1.611	0.621
6	1.772	0.564
7	1.949	0.513
8	2.144	0.466

(3) A sum of money (A), invested at a positive rate of compound interest (r) for n years, will grow to $A(1 + r)^n$ by the end of the period. Thus $1 invested for four years at 10 percent grows to $1 $(1 + 0.10)^4$ = 1.464. The present value of a sum of money (A), expected at the end of n years, when the discount rate is r, is $A/(1 + r)^n$. Thus, $1 expected at the end of four years, at a discount rate of 10 percent, is now worth 1(1 + 0.10)^4$ = 0.683.

70. Psacharopoulos, op. cit.

71. Ibid., p. 17.

72. Ibid., p. 65.

73. George Psacharopoulos, "Returns to Education: An Updated International Comparison," *Comparative Education* 17, no. 3 (1981), pp. 321–324.

74. W. Lee Hansen, "Total and Private Rates of Return to Investment in Schooling," *Journal of Political Economy* 71 (April 1963), 128–140.

75. G. Hanoch, "An Economic Analysis of Earnings and Schooling," *Journal of Human Resources* 2 (Summer 1967), pp. 310–29; F. Hines, L. Tweeten, and M. Redfern, "Social and Private Rates of Return to Investment in Schooling, by Race–Sex Groups and Regions," *Journal of Human Resources* 5 (Summer 1970), pp. 318–340.

76. M. Carnoy and D. Marenbach, "The Return to Schooling in the United States, 1939–69," *Journal of Human Resources* 10 (Summer 1975), pp. 312–331.

77. Jacob Mincer, *Schooling, Experience and Earnings* (New York: Columbia University Press, 1974).

78. Carnoy and Marenbach, op. cit.

79. R. D. Raymond and M. L. Sesnowitz, "The Returns to Investments in Higher Education: Some New Evidence," *Journal of Human Resources* 10 (Spring 1975), pp. 139–154.

80. Carnoy and Marenbach, op. cit.

81. Richard S. Eckaus, *Estimating the Returns to Education: A Disaggregated Approach* (Berkeley: Carnegie Commission on Higher Education, 1973), p. 5.

82. Ibid., p. 22.

83. Hanoch, op. cit.; J. A. Tomaske, "Private and Social Rates of Return to Education of Academicians: Note," *American Economic Review* 64 (March 1974), pp. 220–224; Mincer, op. cit.; D. Bailey and C. Schotta, "Private and Social Rates of Return to Education of Academicians," *American Economic Review* 62 (March 1972), pp. 19–31.

84. See O. Ashenfelter and J. D. Mooney, "Graduate Education, Ability, and Earnings," *Review of Econom-*

ics and Statistics 50 (February 1968), pp. 78–86; Y. Weiss, "Investment in Graduate Education," *American Economic Review* 61 (December 1971), pp. 833–852.

85. Eckaus, op. cit., p. 24.

86. S. Thomas, *Development of a Prototype Teacher Salary Schedule for the State of Florida Based on Rates of Return Analysis* (Ph.D. dissertation, University of Florida, 1974).

87. J. J. Siegfried, "Rate of Return to the Ph.D. in Economics," *Industrial and Labor Relations Review* 24 (April 1971), pp. 420–431.

88. Richard B. Freeman, *The Overeducated American* (New York: Academic Press, 1976).

89. T. W. Hu, Mah Lin Lee, Ernst Stromsdorfer, and Jacob Kaufman, *A Cost-Effectiveness Study of Vocational Education* (University Park, PA: Institute for Research on Human Resources, The Pennsylvania State University, 1969).

90. A. J. Corazzini, "The Decision to Invest in Vocational Education: An Analysis of Costs and Benefits," *Journal of Human Resources* 3 (Supp.), pp. 88–120; M. K. Taussig, "An Economic Analysis of Vocational Education in the New York City High Schools," *Journal of Human Resources* 3 (Supp.), pp. 59–87.

91. Alexander and Melcher, op. cit.

92. Burton A. Weisbrod, *External Benefits of Public Education* (Princeton, NJ: Princeton University Industrial Relations Section, Department of Economics, 1964), p. 17.

93. Wadi D. Haddad, Martin Carnoy, Rosemary Rinaldi, and Omporn Regel, *Education and Development, Evidence for New Priorities* (Washington, DC: The World Bank, 1991), p. 4.

94. Denison, *Accounting for United States Economic Growth*, 1974.

95. *Work in America*, Report of a Special Task Force to the Secretary of Health, Education, and Welfare (Cambridge, MA: MIT Press, 1973), pp. 134–152.

96. Burton A. Weisbrod, "Investing in Human Capital," in *Education and the Economics of Human Capital,* ed. Ronald A. Wykstra (New York: Free Press, 1971), pp. 79–81.

97. Jacob Mincer, "On-the-Job Training: Costs, Returns, and Some Implications," *Journal of Political Economy* 70 (October 1962 Supp.), pp. 50–79.

98. Richard Perlman, *The Economics of Education* (New York: McGraw-Hill, 1973), p. 32.

99. John D. Owen, *School Inequality and the Welfare State* (Baltimore: Johns Hopkins University Press, 1974), p. 91.

100. Ibid.

101. Ibid.

102. "Education: Coming Top," op. cit., p. 4.

103. Weisbrod, op. cit.

104. J. Ronnie Davis, "The Social and Economic Externalities of Education," in *Economic Factors Affecting the Financing of Education,* vol. 2, eds. R. L. Johns and others (Gainesville, FL: National Educational Finance Project, 1970), p. 66.

105. H. R. Bowen, *Investment in Learning* (San Francisco: Jossey-Bass, 1977), pp. 159–160.

106. Fritz Machlup, *Education and Economic Growth* (Lincoln, NE: University of Nebraska Press, 1970), pp. 7–8.

107. Carl S. Shoup, *Public Finance* (Chicago: Aldine, 1969), p. 97.

108. National Center for Health Statistics, *Vital and Health Statistics, Educational Differences in Health Status and Health Care* (Washington, DC: U.S. Department of Health and Human Services, 1991), p. 6.

109. Ibid., p. 8.

110. Ibid., p. 11.

111. Weisbrod, op. cit., p. 31.

112. Werner Hirsch, Elbert W. Segalhorst, and Morton J. Marcus, *Spillover of Public Education Costs and Benefits* (Berkeley: University of California Press, 1964), p. 342.

113. Belton Fleisher, "The Effect of Income on Delinquency," *American Economic Review* 56, no. 1 (March 1966), 118–137.

114. Isaac Ehrlich, "On the Relation Between Education and Crime" in *Education, Income and Human Behavior*, op. cit., pp. 313–337.

115. Joseph D. Lohman, Lloyd E. Ohlin, and Dietrich C. Reitzer, *Description of Convicted Felons as Manpower Resources in a National Emergency*, cited in Edwin H. Sutherland and Donald R. Cressey, *Principles of Criminology*, 7th ed. (New York: J. B. Lippincott, 1968), p. 251.

116. Price Chenault, "Education," in *Contemporary Corrections*, ed. Paul W. Tappan (New York: McGraw-Hill, 1951), p. 224.

117. Lillian Dean Webb, *The Development of a Model to Measure Selected Economic Externalities of Education* (Ph.D. dissertation, University of Florida, 1975).

118. National Commission on the Causes and Prevention of Violence, *Crimes of Violence,* vol. 11 (Washington, DC: U.S. Government Printing Office, 1968), p. 394.

119. Henry M. Levin, *The Effects of Dropping Out: A Report to the Select Committee on Equal Opportunity of the United States Senate* (Washington, DC: U.S. Government Printing Office, 1972).

120. Machlup, op. cit., pp. 55–56.

121. David B. Epply, "The AFDC Family in the 1960's," *Welfare in Review* 8, no. 5 (September–October 1970), p. 11–13.

122. Edward Prescott, William Tash, and William Usdane, "Training and Employability: The Effect of MDTA on AFDC Recipients," *Welfare in Review* 9, no. 1 (January–February 1971), p. 2.

123. Perry Levinson, "How Employable Are AFDC Women?" *Welfare in Review* 8, no. 4 (July–August 1970), pp. 12–13.

124. Webb, op. cit., p. 58.

125. Levin, op. cit., p. 58.

126. See Kern Alexander, "The Value of an Education," *Journal of Education Finance,* vol. 1, no. 4 (Spring, 1976), pp. 447-450.

127. Robert T. Michael, "Education and Consumption," in *Education, Income and Human Behavior*, op. cit., pp. 235–252.

128. Lewis C. Solmon, "The Relation between Schooling and Savings Behavior: An Example of Indirect Effects on Education," in *Education, Income and Human Behavior*, op. cit., pp. 253–293.

129. World Bank, *World Development Report 1991, The Challenge of Development* (Oxford: The World Bank and Oxford University Press, 1991), p. 49.

130. Norman B. Ryder and Charles F. Westoff, *Reproduction in the United States, 1965* (Princeton, NJ: Princeton University Press, 1971).

131. Ibid.

132. Robert T. Michael, "Education and Fertility," in *Education, Income and Human Behavior*, op. cit., pp. 339–364.

133. F. U. Edgeworth, "Equal Pay to Men and Women for Equal Work," *Economic Journal* 32 (December 1922), pp. 431–457; see also Gary S. Becker, *The Economics of Discrimination* (Chicago: University of Chicago Press, 1971).

134. Arleen Leibowitz, "Education and the Allocation of Women's Time," in *Education, Income and Human Behavior*, op. cit., pp. 171–172.

135. Ibid., p. 174.

CHAPTER 4

TRENDS IN DEMAND AND SUPPORT FOR THE PUBLIC SCHOOLS

TOPICAL OUTLINE OF CHAPTER

Need and Demand • Population, Enrollment • Average Daily Attendance • School Expenditures • Average Salaries • Increased Expenditures • Income Elasticity • Social and Economic Factors

INTRODUCTION

In the private economy of a free-enterprise nation, the individual votes with dollars for the economic goods he or she chooses to purchase. This economic system stimulates the private economy to quickly produce many types of goods to satisfy the consumer. However, some consumer wants cannot be supplied by the private economy as well as they can be by the public economy. Education is one of the principal goods that must be primarily provided by the public economy.

The machinery for determining what economic goods should be produced and what the quantity and quality of those goods should be differs considerably in the two economies. The machinery of the private economy moves quickly to supply a human want very soon after the want emerges, provided the enterprise for supplying that want can earn a profit. For example, the private economy continues to respond rapidly to demands for increased computer and data processing services. In fact, the continued rapid response made by the private economy in all areas of electronics has hastened the depreciation of most forms of computer-related capital equipment.

It has been apparent to informed observers for many years that the welfare of both individuals and the nation requires a greatly expanded and considerably improved educational program. There have been a series of reports, studies, essays, and books published by various commissions, foundations, and interest groups that have alleged problems with public education, emphasized the importance of education to our society, and recommended myriad solutions.[1] However, it has been extremely difficult to translate the obvious need for improved education into increased public demand for a more adequate investment in education. Several studies have found that the United States has devoted a smaller share of its resources to pre-primary, primary, and secondary education than most industrialized nations.[2]

Concepts of Need and Demand

At this point it is important to note the difference between the concepts of need and demand. What is needed for the welfare of the individual and of society may not always be wanted. For example, people need physical exercise in order to preserve health, but some may not want to make the effort to exercise as needed. A state may need to improve the quality of its school system, but its legislature may not want to levy the additional taxes necessary to meet that need. On the other hand, a demand for a good is always wanted, but it may not be needed. A corpulent individual may want a second piece of cheesecake, and therefore there is a demand for it although it is not needed. In a free society most adults individually and collectively make the decisions which result in demands for goods and services regardless of need.

In the private sector, the policy of some progressive business organizations is to make needers wanters, make wanters buyers, and make buyers satisfied users. This seems to be a reasonable policy for educational leaders to follow. But the public economy moves slowly to meet educational needs, partly because political consensus must be obtained before the decision can be made to provide for a need through the public economy. Such political decisions must be made by some fifteen thousand local school districts, fifty states, and the federal government.

There is another important difference between the two economies. In the private economy, the individual purchases only the economic goods he wants. But in the public economy, once a political decision has been made to provide an economic good, all individuals subject to the taxes levied must purchase the good whether they want it or not. For example, if a decision to provide public kindergartens is made, each taxpayer must participate in the financing of kindergartens regardless of whether he or she wants them. The political decision may be made by popular vote of the electorate concerned, by representatives of the electorate in such bodies as local and state boards of education, or by state legislatures. Usually decisions of this kind are made by majority vote, but in some cases more than a majority is required. The process of obtaining a political decision frequently involves much controversy. For these reasons, the time required to supply a human want is usually much greater in the public economy than in the private economy.

Assuming that the supply of goods is equal to the demand, expenditures in the private economy fairly accurately represent current consumer choices. But the same thing is not true in the public economy, in which consumer wants may go unsatisfied for long periods of time. Also, demands for goods produced in the private economy are stimulated by clever advertising and high-pressure selling. Public funds cannot be expended directly for advertising or promotion by most governments.[3] Therefore, it is not entirely accurate to assume that expenditures for public education for a given year represent consumer demand for public education during that year.

The purpose of this chapter is to explore trends in expenditures for public education since 1930 and to appraise the social and economic forces that will affect demand and expenditures for public education in future years. Trends in expenditures for higher education are not presented here because of the difficulty of obtaining comparable data for this 64-year period.

It is not a simple matter to appraise trends in school expenditures. A comparison of total current dollar expenditures for one year with those of another year reveals only that more or less dollars were expended during one year than during another. Such a comparison becomes more misleading as the time span increases. This is especially true during times of rapid changes in prices, population, and economic growth. Certain years have been selected in order to point out long-range trends during a given period. Depression and war years have been avoided in order to eliminate unusual conditions. The year 1929–30 was selected because it was a predepression year; 1939–40, because it was a late depression, prewar year; the years 1949–50 and 1959–60, because they were fairly normal postwar years; and the years 1969–70, 1979–80, 1989–90, and 1993–94 to show the effects of inflation on educational expenditures during the most recent decades.[4]

Conclusions regarding the amount of change are vitally affected by the base year or years selected for making comparisons. For example, a person attacking an increase in school expenditures may select a depression year with which to compare expenditures for the current year in order to maximize the percentage of increase. Also, someone advocating an increase in educational expenditures may select for comparison the base year that will minimize the percentage of increase. However, the objective student of school finance will avoid, insofar as possible, either extremely high or extremely low years when appraising long-range trends.

Educational expenditures are affected by many factors including the number of pupils educated, the purchasing power of the dollar, economic conditions, the quantity and quality of educational services, and the demand for education. Therefore, trends in educational expenditures will be appraised in this chapter in terms of these factors.

TRENDS IN POPULATION, PUBLIC SCHOOL ENROLLMENT, AND AVERAGE DAILY ATTENDANCE

Please note that average daily attendance (ADA) and enrollment are but two of several units of pupil accounting. Another commonly used pupil accounting unit is average daily membership (ADM). The vast majority of the 50 states use one or more of these three pupil units to distribute state aid to their local school districts.

Shown in Figure 4.1 are the trends in numbers of pupils in ADA from 1929–30 to 1993–94. From 1949–50 through 1969–70,[5] there was an unparalleled growth in the numbers of pupils attending public elementary and secondary schools in the United States, ultimately reaching nearly 42.5 million pupils in ADA. From the early 1970s, the number of pupils in ADA gradually declined to approximately 36.5 million pupils in 1983–84.

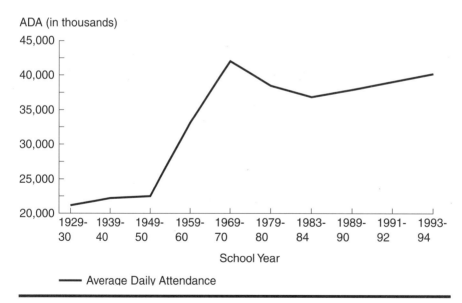

ADA (in thousands)

FIGURE 4.1   Trends In Average Daily Attendance for Public Elementary and Secondary Schools, Selected Years, 1929–30 to 1993–94

Sources: National Education Association, *Estimates of School Statistics* (Washington, DC: NEA, selected years). *Note:* NEA data from 1991–1994; U.S. Department of Education, National Center for Education Statistics, *Digest of Education Statistics, 1993* (Washington, DC: U.S. Government Printing Office, 1993), pp. 51–52. *Note:* NCES data from 1929–1990.

Box 4.1 _____

Enrollment Increase

In the fall of 1985, public elementary and secondary school enrollment increased for the first time since 1971. The increase from 1985 to 1990 was concentrated in the elementary grades, but this pattern is expected to change in the early 1990s. Between fall 1990 and 1995, public elementary enrollment is expected to rise 6 percent, while public secondary enrollment is expected to increase by 12 percent. Overall, enrollment is expected to increase by 3.2 million students, or about 8 percent.

Source: National Center for Education Statistics, *Digest of Education Statistics, 1992* (Washington, DC: U.S. Government Printing Office, 1992), p. 5.

Data presented in Figure 4.2 show that total population and two pupil accounting units, school enrollment and average daily attendance, have had different rates of increase or decrease over the 62-year period of 1930–1994. Note that total population has increased significantly during all decades since 1930, but, as discussed earlier, both public school enrollment and attendance decreased substantially from 1970 to 1984. While both school enrollment and average daily attendance have registered modest increases since 1984, the growth rate for resident population is considerably steeper. It is anticipated that the number of pupils attending public schools will experience a modest annual growth rate of 0.08 percent which is expected to continue until the turn of the century.[6]

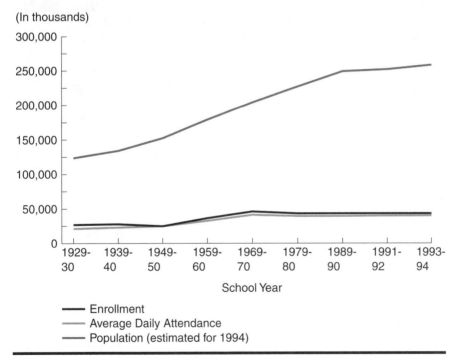

FIGURE 4.2   Trends in Enrollment, Average Daily Attendance, and Resident Population, Selected Years, 1929–30 to 1993–94

Sources: National Education Association, *Estimates of School Statistics* (Washington, DC: NEA, selected years). *Note:* NEA data from 1991–1994; U.S. Department of Education, National Center for Education Statistics, *Digest of Education Statistics, 1993* (Washington, DC: U.S. Government Printing Office, 1993), pp. 51–52. *Note:* NCES data from 1929–1990.

DEFINITIONS

Average Daily Attendance (ADA). The aggregate attendance of pupils during a reporting period divided by the number of days school is in session during the period.

Average Daily Membership (ADM). The aggregate daily membership of pupils during a reporting period divided by the number of days school is in session during the period. States commonly require that pupils miss a specified consecutive number of days in attendance before they are withdrawn from membership rolls.

Enrollment. The total number of pupils registered in a given school unit at a given time, generally in the fall of the year.

Wide fluctuations in numbers of public school pupils create problems in school financing. Rapid increases in school enrollment, such as occurred between 1950 and 1970, required schools to employ additional personnel and created school plant shortages, resulting in considerable fiscal stress. Taxpayers usually resist tax increases, particularly increases that are either large or frequent. A rapid decline in the number of public school pupils is also problematic. As noted earlier, the number of pupils attending public schools began to decline substantially during the 1970s, a trend that continued until the mid-1980s. This decline in the number of public school pupils, among other problems, created a school building surplus and a surplus of teachers in many school districts. This caused many boards of education to close schools and to reduce the number of teachers employed. These actions frequently involved boards of education in political controversies, which did not enhance their chances of obtaining needed school revenue. More recently, increases in school enrollment have once again required additional facilities, and coupled with the need to replace and renovate existing school buildings,[7] have required school boards to seek substantial increases in capital funds. Similarly, the increased numbers of pupils, plus the onslaught of governmental mandates, have required school boards to employ more instructional and support personnel, thereby forcing many school boards to seek approval for significant budget increases.

It is important to recognize that virtually all funding formulas are driven by the numbers of pupils served by the public schools. Thus, when public schools are experiencing a growth in the numbers of pupils served, fiscal resources provided by the federal and state governments usually increase, at least proportionally to the increased numbers of pupils served. Conversely, when the numbers of pupils attending public schools decline, formula-driven revenues likewise tend to decline. Most school finance officers recognize that costs do not decline proportional to the reduction in the numbers of pupils, thereby creating fiscal stress. Those persons responsible for presenting school budgets to the public during periods of declining enrollments are often faced with the unpleasant task of justifying escalating per-pupil costs coupled with reductions in educational services.

As noted earlier, the resident population of the United States has increased much more rapidly since 1930 than has either average daily attendance or school enrollment. In part, this illustrates the effects of a declining birthrate and an aging population. The potential fiscal implications for public schools due to the changing ratio of adults to children are far-reaching indeed. There is little question that adults whose children have graduated from high school, as well as those who have not been patrons of public education, have proven less likely to support funding increases than are current patrons. Other societal funding demands, including accelerating health care costs for the aged and a rapidly increasing prison population, will likely place additional fiscal stress on public elementary and secondary education.

TRENDS IN TOTAL PUBLIC SCHOOL EXPENDITURES

The definitions of total and current expenditures presented below are used by the United States Department of Education, the American Federation of Teachers, and the National Education Association. Payments on the principal of indebtedness are excluded from total expenditures in order to eliminate a meaningless inflation of expenditures. For example, assume that the expenditures of a school system for a 20-year period are being studied, and that a $5 million bond issue for buildings, maturing over a 20-year period, has been floated during the first year of the period. To include principal payments in total expenditures for each of the 20 years would be double reporting; once for capital outlay and once for payments on the principal of indebtedness. Thus, the inflation would total $5 million over a 20-year period.

Students of school finance occasionally use the term *total expenditures* to include all items of current expense plus capital outlay and debt service, even though it includes an unexplained inflation. It would be more precise to define this type of total as gross expenditures. Due to a persistent lack of uniformity in finance terminology, students of school finance should examine carefully the composition of any total of school expenditures before it is compared with a total reported from another source.

Displayed in Figure 4.3 are total expenditures for public elementary and secondary schools, re-

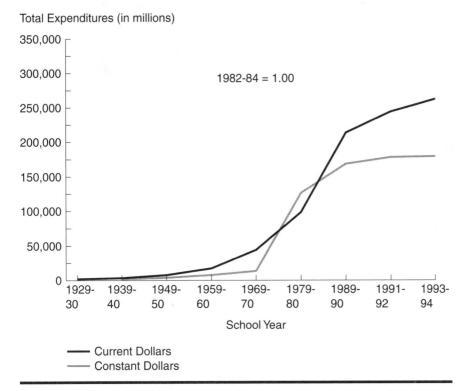

Total Expenditures (in millions)

1982-84 = 1.00

School Year

— Current Dollars
— Constant Dollars

FIGURE 4.3 Trends in Total Expenditures (Current and Constant Dollars) for Public Schools, Selected Years, 1929–30 to 1993–94

Sources: National Education Association, *Estimates of School Statistics* (Washington, DC: NEA, selected years); U.S. Department of Education, National Center for Education Statistics, *Digest of Education Statistics, 1993* (Washington, DC: U.S. Government Printing Office, 1993), p. 43.

DEFINITIONS

Total Expenditures. Expenditures for current expenses, capital outlay, and interest on school indebtedness excluding payments to retire the principal of indebtedness.

Current Expenditures. Expenses for administration, instruction, attendance, health, transportation, net food service, maintenance and operation, and for other net expenditures to cover deficits for extracurricular activities for pupils. Excluded from current expenditures are capital outlay and debt service costs.

ported in both current and constant dollars, for selected years, 1929–30 to 1993–94. It is interesting to note that from 1929–30 to 1959–60, both current and constant total expenditures showed very modest growth. Commencing in 1959–60, in response to the rapid increase in the numbers of pupils entering public schools, total expenditures began to accelerate. Constant dollar total expenditures actually showed a greater rate of increase from 1969–70 to 1979–80 than did current dollar expenditures, reflecting, in part, modest inflationary pressures during this decade. Significant increases in total expenditures have continued to the present, albeit at a more subdued rate in constant dollars. For 1993–94, current dollar total expenditures approached $263 billion.

As can be seen by an examination of Figure 4.4, the growth in total expenditures for pub-

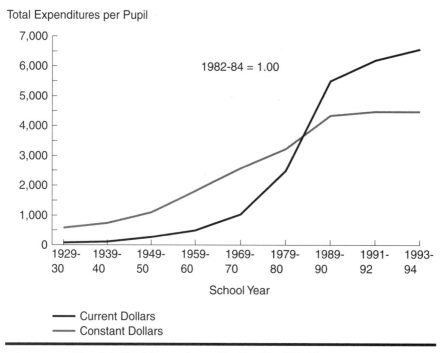

FIGURE 4.4   Trends in Total Expenditures Per Pupil in ADA (Current and Constant Dollars) for Public Schools, Selected Years, 1929–30 to 1993–94

Sources: National Education Association, *Estimates of School Statistics* (Washington, DC: NEA, selected years); U.S. Department of Education, National Center for Education Statistics, *Digest of Education Statistics, 1993* (Washington, DC: U.S. Government Printing Office, 1993), p. 43.

lic schools is paralleled by the growth in total expenditures per pupil in average daily attendance over the same period. From 1929–30 to 1993–94, current dollar total expenditures per pupil in ADA increased from $109 to $6,538 and in constant dollars from $637 to $4,466. Few will disagree that the United States has increased significantly its total expenditures and total expenditures per pupil in ADA from the early years of this century. The question remains, however: is the nation investing sufficiently in its human resources to remain economically competitive in the international market? A related question is: Are we as a people investing in human capital at a rate that is proportional to our fiscal capacity?

TRENDS IN AVERAGE SALARIES PAID TO INSTRUCTIONAL PERSONNEL[8]

The data presented in Figure 4.5 reveal some interesting trends in average salaries paid to instructional personnel. From 1929–30 to 1939–40, there was virtually no change in average salaries paid to instructional personnel, reflecting the economic conditions of the Great Depression. From 1939–40 to 1969–70, salaries of instructional personnel improved gradually, both in current and constant dollars. However, from 1969–70 to 1979–80, despite significant current dollar increases, average instructional salaries, measured in constant dollars, actually declined. Over the 24-year period, 1969–70 to 1993–94, current dol-

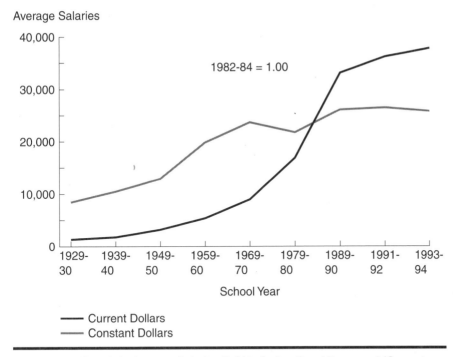

FIGURE 4.5   Trends in Average Salaries Paid to Instructional Personnel (Current and Constant Dollars) Selected Years, 1929–30 to 1993–94

Sources: National Education Association, *Estimates of School Statistics* (Washington, DC: NEA, selected years; U.S. Department of Education, National Center for Education Statistics, *Digest of Education Statistics, 1993* (Washington, DC: U.S. Government Printing Office, 1–93); U.S. Department of Commerce, Bureau of Economic Analysis, *Survey of Current Business* (Washington, DC: U.S. Government Printing Office, April, 1994).

lar average salary increases for instructional personnel again have been significant, although constant dollar increases have been much more modest. From 1969–70 to 1993-94, average instructional salaries, in current dollars, increased from $9,047 to $37,701, or nearly 317 percent. In constant dollars, the average salaries paid to instructional personnel increased from $23,934 to $25,750, or approximately 8 percent.

Further, as can be seen by an examination of Figure 4.6, the instructional staff of public schools has not shared equally with the public in the increased standard of living since 1929–30, a pattern that has continued through the 1990s. For example, from 1970 to 1994, per capita personal income increased from $3,930 to $20,817, an increase of 430 percent. Concurrently, from 1969–70 to 1989–90, average salaries paid in-

structional personnel increased from $9,047 to $37,701, an increase of 317 percent.[9]

Without question, total expenditures and total expenditures per pupil in ADA have increased more rapidly than have average salaries paid to instructional personnel. From 1969–70 to 1993–94, total expenditures and total expenditures per pupil in ADA increased by 546 and 585 percent, respectively. As noted previously, average salaries of instructional personnel increased by 317 percent during the same period. Why have total expenditures per pupil increased more rapidly than instructional staff salaries? The answer is evident when Figure 4.7 is examined. The number of pupils enrolled per instructional staff member has decreased from 29:1 in 1929–30 to 15:1 for 1989–90, before rising slightly to 15:3 for 1993–94. Critics of public education suggest

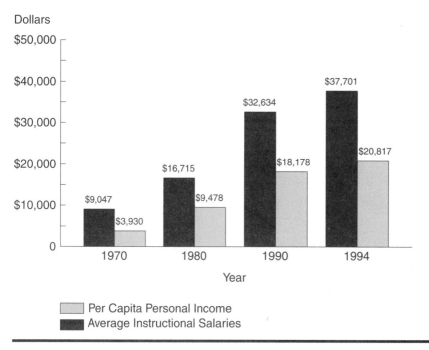

Dollars

FIGURE 4.6   Per-Capita Personal Income and Average Instructional Salaries Paid to Public School Personnel, Selected Years, 1970 to 1994

Sources: National Education Association, *Rankings of the States* (Washington, DC: NEA, selected years); National Education Association, *Estimate of School Statistics, 1993–1994* (Washington, DC: NEA, 1994); U.S. Department of Commerce, Bureau of Economic Analysis, *Survey of Current Business* (Washington, DC: U.S. Government Printing Office, April, 1994).

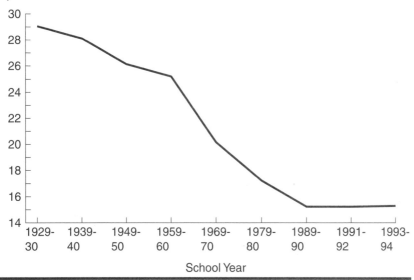

FIGURE 4.7   Trends in Pupil Enrollment Per Instructional Personnel, Public Elementary and Secondary Schools, Selected Years, 1929–30 to 1993–94

Source: National Education Association, *Estimates of School Statistics* (Washington, DC: NEA, selected years).

Box 4.2 _____

Inadequacy of U.S. School Expenditures

Controlled for inflation, public spending on primary and secondary education, per student, has increased since the mid-1970s, but not appreciably faster than it did during the previous fifteen-year period. Between 1959 and the early 1970s, annual spending per student grew at a brisk 4.7 percent in real terms—more than a full percentage point above the increase in the gross national product per person; since 1975, annual spending per pupil has continued to rise about 1 percent faster than the rate of growth of GNP per person. But there are several reasons for believing the more recent increases to be inadequate. . . . By the late 1980s, America's per-pupil expenditures (converted to dollars using 1988 exchange rates) were below per-pupil expenditures in eight other nation, including Sweden, Norway, Japan, Denmark, Austria, West Germany, Canada, and Switzerland. . . . The law of supply and demand is not repealed at the schoolhouse door: If talented people are to be drawn to teaching, teachers must be paid enough to attract such individuals. Yet, average teacher salaries in 1990 (adjusted for inflation) were only 4 percent higher than in 1970, when career choices were far more limited. . . . The average figures on per-pupil expenditures in the United States disguise growing disparities among states and among school districts. During the 1980s, federal support for elementary and secondary education dropped by a third. States and localities picked up the bill, but for some of them the burden has been especially heavy. Although per-pupil expenditures increased in wealthier states and school districts, many poorer states and districts—already coping with the most intractable social problems—have barely been able to fund even a minimum-quality public education.

Source: Robert B. Reich, *The Work of Nations* (New York: Alfred A. Knopf, 1991), p. 255. Reprinted with permission.

that public schools have become less efficient and that the productivity of teachers has declined steadily since 1929–30. Defenders of public schools argue that both quantity and quality of education have expanded since 1930. They point to the great expansion of educational opportunities for children with disabilities, vocational students, children at risk, gifted children, and a host of other educational services targeted to special clients. They also accentuate the need to provide increased educational services to children in isolated and remote areas of the country and the need to reduce further the pupil–teacher ratio in order to meet the needs of individual students.

More recently, the decline in school enrollment during the 1970s and 1980s contributed significantly to the decline in pupil–instructional personnel ratios. While it is simple to increase staff proportional to increased numbers of students, it is often difficult to reduce personnel proportional to incremental student decreases. Reductions in the number of students rarely occur in convenient blocks, thereby prohibiting reductions of personnel without significant changes in pupil attendance zones and/or the consolidation of school facilities. Also, local boards of education often have found it difficult to reduce staff proportional to student decline due to humanitarian reasons, opposition by teacher organizations, parents, and interested citizens.

BENEFITS FROM INCREASED EDUCATIONAL EXPENDITURES

What has the public received from the major increases in educational expenditures from 1930 to 1990? There is indisputable evidence that both the quantity and the quality of public education have increased greatly during that time. An often stated objective is to provide suitable educational opportunities for all pupils, regardless of sex, race, physical or mental characteristics, and place of residence. Extensive arrays of programs have been implemented which are designed specifically to serve special clients. These pro-grams, commonly entitled categorical programs, normally are considerably more expensive than programs for general education students. For example, most senior high school students today have access to extensive programs of vocational education, which was not the case during the early years of this century. Extensive programs of special education for children with disabilities are now required by law.[10] In many school systems over 10 percent of public elementary and secondary pupils are enrolled in special education classes. These special education programs often cost as much as two to five times the cost of programs for students without disabilities. In 1930 very few school systems had established programs for the disabled.

Programs designed to meet the educational needs of the economically disadvantaged are also now being implemented. Until the 1960s, practically nothing was expended for programs designed specifically to compensate children for learning difficulties associated with poverty. Additional educational programs designed and implemented for special clients include at-risk, bilingual, gifted and talented, and a host of others. While not universally available, particularly for low-wealth districts and isolated small rural schools, a broad and enriched curriculum, containing honors and advanced placement courses, is now available to many general education pupils.

The average number of school days attended has increased from 143 in 1930 to 162 in 1990. This increase resulted largely from increasing the average length of the school term from 173 days in 1930 to approximately 180 days in 1990, and increasing the percentage of students transported from 7 percent in 1930 to 60 percent in 1990.

All 50 states now make at least some effort to equalize educational opportunity within the state by allocating state funds through such approaches as the foundation program, the guaranteed tax base, complete state support, or by providing most of the school revenue by flat grants from state sources. In 1930 only a few states made any attempt to equalize educational opportunity. Higher levels of fiscal equalization of educational opportunity was achieved primarily by the assumption of greater financial responsibility by state governments, thereby reducing the influence of disparate local revenue bases. A considerable percentage of the increase in school expenditures since 1970 was used to equalize educational opportunity. Unfortunately, for most states, the gradual movement toward fiscal equalization stalled during the 1980s, and the disparity in fiscal resources and consequential quality of educational services among local school districts began to widen. For many states, grossly disparate systems of public elementary and secondary education now exist, conditions which have spawned a flurry of lawsuits challenging state school finance systems.

Perhaps the greatest single improvement that has been made in public education this century was the abolishment of legal segregation by race in the public schools. Prior to the famous *Brown* v. *Topeka Board of Education*[11] case in 1954, seventeen states legally permitted or required segregation by race in the public schools. In many of those states, the educational provisions for black pupils were inferior to those for white pupils. In some of the southern states in 1930 the average per pupil expenditure for white pupils was more than double the average per pupil expenditure for black pupils. Commonly, average salaries paid white teachers were approximately twice the salaries of black teachers. When the schools were desegregated, school costs were increased significantly in the states that had been maintaining segregated schools, primarily because the per pupil expenditures for black pupils had to be increased to the level provided for white pupils. While the judiciary did not order states to increase expenditures for black pupils, the requirement to end segregation forced the states to level-up rather than reduce the quality of education provided statewide. Currently, the battle in the courts to force states to equalize educational opportunity among their local school districts also rests upon the assumption that states will be coerced to level-up rather than reduce the quality of education presently being provided to pupils in high-wealth school districts.

The percentage of the enrollment in the public schools in grades 9–12 has increased from 17.1 in 1930 to 27.5 in 1990. Figure 4.8 illustrates how the educational profile of persons in the age group 25 to 29 has improved from 1940 to 1990. The median number of school years completed by those 25 years of age and over has increased from 8.6 in 1940 to 12.5 in 1990. Perhaps the most significant single piece of evidence of school improvement during the past 60 years is the fact that in 1930 only 19 percent of the adult population, ages 25 and older, had completed four years of high school. By 1990, this percentage had increased to over 77 percent, a truly remarkable gain. Some critics of the public schools complain about a decline in the standardized test scores of high-school graduates. Sixty years ago most high-school graduates came from the higher socioeconomic strata of society. Today more than 75 percent of all pupils graduate from high school. Because they constitute a much broader band of society it should not be unexpected that average test scores have declined. However, there is no evidence that pupils of high intellectual ability achieve at a lower level than their peers in prior years. As a matter of fact, gifted students in high school today have far more opportunities to be challenged than did their predecessors.

The goal of the public school system of the United States has been to educate all of the children. No other large nation in the history of the world has come as near to achieving that goal as the United States of America, and the attainment of that goal costs money. However, the evidence presented elsewhere in this text shows that education has contributed substantially to the economic growth of the nation. This has made it possible to increase educational resources without depriving other sectors of the economy of needed resources.

Percent of Persons

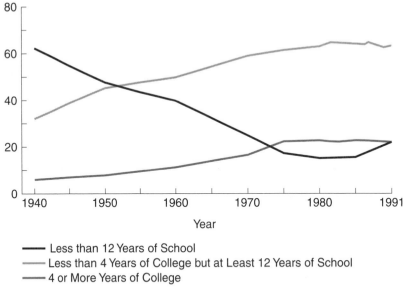

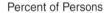

—— Less than 12 Years of School
—— Less than 4 Years of College but at Least 12 Years of School
—— 4 or More Years of College

FIGURE 4.8   Years of School Completed by Persons 25 Years Old and Over:
1940 to 1991

Source: Adapted from U.S. Department of Education, National Center for Education Statistics,
Digest of Education Statistics, 1993 (Washington, DC: U.S. Government Printing Office, 1993),
p. 9.

INCOME ELASTICITY OF DEMAND
FOR EDUCATION

The per capita gross national product has increased rapidly since 1930, excluding the years
of the Great Depression and the occasional extended recessions. Has public school support increased in proportion to the increased economic
productivity of the nation? One way to respond
to this question is to apply the economic concept
of income elasticity of demand. For education,
the income elasticity of demand usually has been
determined by comparing changes in total expenditures per pupil for education with changes
in one of several per-pupil or per-capita measures of national productivity. For example, a coefficient of 1 means that a 1 percent change in
per-pupil national income has been accompanied
by a 1 percent change in per-pupil expenditures.
When the coefficient is more than 1, the demand

is said to have been elastic; and when less than 1,
inelastic. McLoone found that the coefficient of
elasticity was 0.96 between 1929–30 and
1957–58, 1.45 between 1943–44 and 1957–58,
and 1.34 between 1947–48 and 1957–58.[12]
Hirsch found that a 1 percent increase in per-
capita personal income between 1900 and 1958
was associated with only a 1.09 percent increase
in per-pupil expenditures.[13] Both researchers
found that the coefficient of elasticity of income
demand for education in the early part of this

DEFINITION

Income Elasticity of Demand for Education.
The percentage change in quantity (as measured
by educational expenditures) in response to the
percentage change in income.

century was 1 or below. However, each noted that the demand for education has been more elastic since 1950 than in the first half of the twentieth century. What has been the elasticity of demand for education since 1960?

The average annual per-pupil growth rate of national income (NI) in constant dollars between 1959–60 and 1989–90 was 3.6 percent. Concurrently, the average annual increase in total expenditures per pupil in ADA, also measured in constant dollars, was 5.7 percent, yielding an elasticity coefficient of 1.6. Considering the 30-year span as one period, it is evident that the income elasticity of demand for education has been quite elastic. However, the per-pupil NI increased an average of 3.9 percent per year between 1969–70 and 1979–80, whereas total expenditure per pupil for the public schools increased an average of 2.8 percent per year during that period, yielding an elasticity coefficient of 0.7. Therefore, the income elasticity of demand for education was inelastic during the 1970s and elastic during the 1960s and 1980s. There is some indication that the demand for education may be elastic during periods of rapid economic growth when accompanied with modest rates of inflation, and inelastic during inflationary and/or recessionary periods.

FACTORS AFFECTING DEMANDS FOR EDUCATION

As the end of the twentieth century approaches, the United States confronts challenges unlike any that have occurred in the past. The dissolution of the longtime adversary, the Soviet Union, and the emergence of numerous political and ethnic nations has completely altered the international political landscape. Unrest, civil wars, famines, and military confrontations appear commonplace. The Pacific Rim countries, led by Japan, have been acquiring and consolidating economic power and wealth, often at the expense of the United States. Most troubling is the fact that the disparity of wealth and economic power among countries has widened and appears to be accelerating. Animal species are disappearing at an alarming rate, the denuding of the tropical rainforests is likely to significantly alter the world climate. The problems and challenges appear endless.

While public schools have been criticized soundly for their many alleged failures, most people would agree that if the many challenges confronting this country are to be successfully met, a strong and dynamic system of public elementary and secondary education is essential. It is also evident that considerable fiscal resources will be required to upgrade and sustain a system of public schools capable of meeting the challenges of the next several decades. Many social and economic factors will determine whether the public schools will be afforded the necessary financial resources.

Effect of a Stagnant National Economy

During the early 1990s growth of the gross national product was very sluggish in constant dollars. A growing national product makes possible a rise in the standard of living, which creates a consumer demand for more and better goods and services of all kinds, both public and private. As the productivity of our economy increases, consumers will inevitably demand a greater quantity and a better quality of education than is currently available. Is the sluggish growth rate of the GNP a temporary aberration or will it become a long-term pattern of economic activity for this country? If it does become a permanent fixture, will this reduction in the rate of economic growth continue until there is no economic growth in the United States? The economist Rohatyn was asked the following question in 1980: Can we get by on limited or no growth in times ahead? His reply was: "No. The idea of a zero-sum society is baloney. We cannot function as a zero-sum society, because we are not equipped to handle the taking away from some to give to others that a zero-sum society involves."[14] *Zero-sum* is a term used by economists in game theory where the amount one player wins in an economic

Box 4.3

Federal Miscalculation

The fiscal policy in the 1980s accomplished exactly the opposite of almost every key economic promise made by Ronald Reagan early in his presidency. Federal spending, which was supposed to shrink, grew from 21.1 percent of gross national product in the 1970s to 23.4 percent in the 1980s. Investment in factories and machines, which was supposed to blossom, contracted from 3.5 percent of national output to 3 percent. And the federal budget deficit, instead of being reduced as the Reagan administration promised, swelled from 1.8 percent of national output to 3.6 percent.

Source: David Hage, "Dropping off the Charts," *U.S. News and World Report* (June 29, 1992).

game is exactly equal to the amount that the other player loses. It is somewhat similar to the Pareto-optimal concept under which no one can be made better off without making someone else worse off. A fixed quantity of goods and services is implied in both concepts. As discussed earlier, the people of the United States have always sought the better life. In order to have economic growth, we cannot consume all that we produce. In the past we have saved some of our production and invested it in both physical and human capital. The policy of investing in human capital has proven successful and should be continued.

Effect of a Large National Budget Deficit

Historically, the federal government has relied upon deficit financing to meet the needs of the country, particularly during times of national crisis. However, during the 1980s, citizens of the United States witnessed an explosion of the national debt. Bolstered by advocates of supply-side economics, the federal government incurred long-term debt at a frenetic pace. The United States moved from the world's largest lender to the world's largest debtor. The consequences of this ill-advised fiscal policy, or absence thereof,

are now becoming apparent. Unless our economic and fiscal affairs are made sound, this country will lose its preeminent role in the international market, and the standard of living of the public ultimately will decline. Most importantly, the accumulation of this burdensome national debt severely limits the flexibility of policymakers to respond effectively to the needs of society. Resolution of high profile needs, such as national health care and public education, is compromised due to inadequate financial resources. The excessive national debt has implications for state governments as well. Programs previously funded by the federal government have been reduced or transferred to state and local governments, thereby restricting the flexibility of states to respond effectively to the needs of their citizens. Greater competition for fiscal resources among state and local agencies has occurred and likely will increase as the country attempts to address the unacceptable large budget deficits. While many policymakers at both the national and state levels recognize the importance of adequately funding public schools, the extreme pressures to fund other needs will push the country to underinvest in human capital.

Effect of Changes in the Pattern of Skills and Abilities

The pattern of skills and abilities of the working population is changing rapidly. The proportion of the total national income derived from primary production (farming, fishing, and forestry) and manufacturing is decreasing, while the proportion derived from the service sector is increasing. Although the proportion of the total national income derived from agriculture has declined precipitously from the early years of the twentieth century, the agricultural production has increased, indicating the use of more efficient production techniques. However, the decline of the manufacturing sector is much more troublesome and ominous for future generations. Former well-paying blue collar and mid-management white collar jobs are being transferred to other countries where labor costs are a fraction of those in the United States. The inevitable result will be a dramatic restructuring of U.S. society, a society with a much smaller middle class and an expanded lower class. Undoubtedly, the overall standard of living will deteriorate as the demand for skilled labor declines. Unless prompt action is taken through dynamic national and state intervention, these trends evidently will continue in the future. The obvious solution is to prepare a labor force that will effectively compete on the international market. The continued underinvestment in human capital by the United States will guarantee economic and social disaster.

Effect of an Aging Population and Rising Health Care Costs

Due to a declining birth rate and an increase in longevity of life, the median age of our population has been rising, resulting in a larger percentage of the population requiring retirement and social services. Concurrently, health care costs are escalating, driven in part by the increased numbers of citizens requiring expensive services, but also by a grossly inefficient structure. The number of people without access to even the most basic health care services has continued to increase. The demand for a system of national health coverage for all citizens is becoming increasingly likely. The implications for funding public schools are numerous. Certainly, funding national health care will be expensive, taxing an already burdened national budget. Even without the implementation of national health care, the rising costs of the existing system will increase the competition for national and state fiscal resources. As the age of the population increases, political power will likely reflect the interests and demands of older citizens. As noted previously, citizens who are not receiving direct and immediate benefits from the public schools have proven less willing to provide additional resources, making it still more difficult to increase our investment in education.

SUMMARY AND CONCLUSIONS

Despite considerable evidence to justify the need to increase its investment in education, the United States has devoted a smaller share of its resources to pre-primary, primary, and secondary education than have most industrialized countries.

Educational expenditures are affected by many factors, including the number of pupils served, purchasing power of the dollar, economic conditions, quantity and quality of educational services, and the demand for education.

It is projected that public schools will experience a modest annual growth rate in the number of pupils served until the turn of the century.

Funding formulas and the consequential generation of federal and state resources are driven by the number of pupils served in the public schools.

Total expenditures and total expenditures per pupil in average daily attendance, measured in both current and constant dollars, have increased significantly during the past two decades.

While per-pupil total expenditures have increased significantly in recent years, the gains in average salaries paid to instructional personnel have been more modest. Contributing to the differences in the rates of increases between per-pupil total expenditures and average salaries paid to instructional personnel is the fact that the pupil–teacher ratio for the nation as a whole has declined dramatically.

Although average salaries of instructional personnel have improved in recent years, per-capita personal income for the nation has outpaced instructional salary gains during the same time period.

During the past 30 years, the income elasticity of demand for education has been elastic.

The competition for fiscal resources among national and state agencies has increased significantly during the past several years and likely will continue to accelerate during the remainder of the twentieth century. A formidable challenge will face policymakers if they are to adequately invest in human capital.

KEY TERMS

Average daily attendance
Average daily membership
Enrollment
Total expenditures

Current expenditures
Current dollars
Constant dollars

Instructional personnel
Income elasticity of demand
National income

ENDNOTES

1. National Commission on Excellence in Education, *A Nation at Risk* (Washington, DC: U.S. Government Printing Office, 1983); Ernest Boyer, *High School* (New York: Harper and Row, 1983); Theodore Sizer, *Horace's Compromise: The Dilemma of the American High School* (Boston: Houghton-Mifflin, 1984); National Center on Education and the Economy, *America's Choice: High Skills or Low Wages!* (Rochester: National Center on Education and the Economy, 1990); United States Department of Education, *America 2000: An Education Strategy* (Washington, DC: U.S. Government Printing Office, 1991); National Governors' Association, *Time for Results: The Governors' 1991 Report on Education* (Washington, DC: National Governors' Association, 1992).

2. Edith M. Rasell and Lawrence Miskel, "Shortchanging Education" (Washington, DC: Economic Policy Institute Briefing Paper, 1990); F. Howard Nelson, *International Comparison of Public Spending on Education* (Washington, DC: American Federation of Teachers, 1991); Rati Ram, *Public Educational Expenditures in Industrialized Countries: An Analytical Comparison* (Normal, IL: Center for the Study of Educational Finance, Illinois State University, 1991).

3. One notable exception to the expenditure of public funds for advertising is the sophisticated marketing procedures used by state governments to expand public participation in their state lotteries.

4. In some instances, in order to discuss a particular point, additional years were displayed.

5. The largest number of public school pupils was 42,434,720 in ADA for school year 1970–71.

6. United States Department of Education, *Projec-
tions of Education Statistics to 2001, An Update* (Washington, DC: U.S. Government Printing Office, 1990).

7. Education Writers' Association, *Wolves at the Schoolhouse Door* (Washington, DC: Education Writers' Association, 1990).

8. Positions include all public elementary and secondary (junior and senior high) day-school positions (or full-time equivalents) that are in the nature of teaching or in the improvement of the teaching–learning situation. Also included are consultants or supervisors of instruction, principals, teachers, guidance personnel, librarians, psychological personnel, and other instructional staff. Excluded are attendance personnel, clerical personnel, and junior college staff.

9. National Education Association, *Rankings of the States* (Washington, DC: NEA, various years).

10. *Individuals With Disabilities Education Act*, 20 U.S.C. Section 1400–1485.

11. *Brown* v. *Topeka Board of Education*, 347 U.S. 483, 74 S.Ct. 686 (1954).

12. Eugene P. McLoone, *Effects of Tax Elasticities on the Financial Support of Education* (Champaign, IL: University of Illinois, Ph.D. dissertation, 1961).

13. Werner Z. Hirsch, *Analysis of the Rising Costs of Education,* Joint Economic Committee, Eighty-sixth Congress of the United States, Study Paper No. 4 (Washington, DC: U.S. Government Printing Office, 1959).

14. Felix G. Rohatyn, "Bitter Medicine for Ailing U.S. Economy," *U.S. News and World Report* (September 1, 1980), p. 31.

CHAPTER 5

TAXATION FOR PUBLIC SCHOOLS

TOPICAL OUTLINE OF CHAPTER

Types of Taxes • Property Taxes • Property Tax Administration
• Consumption Taxes • Individual Income Taxes • Corporation
Income Taxes • Wealth Tax • Value-added Tax • Expenditure Tax
• Tax Reform Limitations • Homestead Exemptions and Circuit
Breakers • Property Tax Reform • Tax Exemptions

INTRODUCTION

Taxes may be categorized into two groups: (1) those levied on the *flow* of production derived from purchases and sales, and (2) those on a *stock* or wealth. Taxes on the monetary flow in the production process include the major taxes: individual income, corporate income, and retail sales taxes. Property taxes, which are so familiar to the public schools, are taxes on stocks or a portion of the wealth. Taxes within the cycle of monetary flow are those derived from individual or corporate income coming from market activity producing wages, dividends, payrolls, and profits. Household consumption or expenditures of the firm may be taxed through a sales tax on the purchase of consumer or market goods.[1] The second broad type of tax, on wealth, is typified by the property tax but also includes those taxes which are imposed on the transfer of wealth by inheritance or gift.

Another classification of taxes, *in rem* and *in personam*, is commonly used. Taxes *in rem* are levied on "things"; taxes *in personam*, on the person. Property taxes are classified as *in rem* rather than *in personam* because as a "thing" the property has a distinct location, can be assessed, and can be held as security for payment of taxes. The

in rem tax makes no provision for taxing the equity of the property, only the value of the property itself. It makes no difference that the owner's equity is only a small percentage of the full value and a mortgage holds the major value. On the other hand, *in personam* taxes assume the location of the individual being taxed, rather than his possessions, as in the case of income or poll taxes.[2]

Property Taxes

The property tax has always been the mainstay of public school financing in this country. Although general usage of the term *property tax* may refer to tangible personal, intangible personal, or real property, the primary source of revenue for public schools derives from the tax on real property. This tax is sometimes called an *ad valorem* tax, meaning a tax levied on a percentage of the value of the property. *Ad valorem* taxes are different from taxes levied earlier in western states and called "specific acreage taxes"—constituting a set amount per acre regardless of the value of the land.[3]

The tax levied on property may be expressed in terms of mills or as a percentage of a value. A mill is a unit of monetary value amounting to 0.001 of a dollar or one-tenth of a cent. Thus, a tax rate of 5 mills would be equal to 0.5 percent. The formula for determining the exact rate would be:

$$\frac{\text{Amount of tax revenue to be raised}}{\text{Tax base (value of property)}} = \text{Rate}$$

$$\frac{\$125,000}{\$25,000,000} = 0.5 \text{ percent or 5 mills}$$

The property tax has been roundly criticized for many years and reforms have not come easily. Comments about the inequity of the property tax today are not unlike those of Adam Smith in 1776 in his *Wealth of Nations*:

> A land tax . . . necessarily becomes unequal in process of time according to the unequal degrees of improvement or neglect in the cultivation of the different parts of the country. In England the valuation according to which the different countries and parishes were assessed to the land-tax by the 4th William and Mary was very unequal, even at its first establishment.[4]

Taxpayer opposition to property taxes is largely engendered by the fact that property taxes are highly visible with most taxing jurisdictions simply billing taxpayers with one tax notice each year. The property tax thus seems to be psychologically more onerous than other taxes simply because of the method of payment. Sales and income taxes are more easily digested by the taxpayer because the bites taken are smaller.

The reasons for the unpopularity of the property tax are given by Shannon:

1. no other major tax in our public finance system bears down so harshly on low-income households, or is so capriciously related to the flow of cash into the household;
2. when compared to the preferential treatment accorded outlays for shelter under both the income and sales taxes, the property tax stands out clearly as an anti-housing levy. Moreover, as the tax increases steadily, it is viewed by a growing number of families as a threat to homeownership;

3. unlike income and sales taxes, the property tax imposes a levy on unrealized capital gains. . . . (Homeowners unlike economists are inclined to view such gains as mere "paper profit" and beyond the purview of taxation until converted to income.);
4. the administration of the property tax is far more difficult than in the case of either the income or sales tax. At best, the property tax assessment is based on an informed estimate of the market value of property. . . . ;
5. the dramatic increase in taxes (and resultant taxpayer shock) that often follows in the wake of an infrequent mass reappraisal has no parallel in the administration of the income or sales tax. As inflation pushes property values up, the assessment hikes become more pronounced and the taxpayer shocks become more severe; and
6. the property tax is more painful to pay than the 'pay as you go' income and sales taxes. This is especially true for those property taxpayers who are not in a position to pay the tax on a monthly installment basis.[5]

Although all of these criticisms of the property tax are valid, some contribute more to taxpayer resentment than others. Two of them, harshness on low-income households and general administrative problems, bear further consideration.

Regressive or Progressive Taxes. It is often said that the property tax is a regressive tax, and therefore, government should be encouraged to move toward more progressive or proportional revenue sources.

McIntyre, in 1991, observed that the poor pay higher percentages of their income for property taxes than do the rich. This is, of course, the definition of a regressive tax. McIntyre et al. says that "on average, poor families pay four times as large a share of their incomes in property taxes as do the wealthy; middle-income families pay more than twice as large a share."[6] There are, though, differing schools of thought on this issue, each based on a different theory of property tax incidence. One school, the traditional, maintains that the property tax is regressive, particularly in the case of owner-occupied homes where the owner is unable to shift the burden. It is assumed that renters bear the burden of the tax through higher rent payments. Under this theory, the property tax is assumed to be an excise tax on users of commodities and services produced by the taxable real property.[7] Several studies have shown that the lower the income, the higher the percentage of property taxes that is paid. For example, the Advisory Commission on Intergovernmental Relations (ACIR) found that property taxes on owner-occupied, single-family houses were 16.6 percent of family income for the $2,000 and under category and 2.9 percent for the $25,000 and over category.[8]

The opposing view maintains that the property tax is primarily levied on capital and is shared by all owners of capital in proportion to their holdings.[9] Where the owner's effective tax rate is above the national average, it is assumed that the excess burden is distributed among landowners, workers, or consumers in the particular community. This theory asserts that property tax incidence is split between an average national property tax rate of between 1.5 and 2 percent and a second component of incidence, which is the amount that a particular jurisdiction varies from the average. This "new view" argues that owners of capital cannot avoid the average or uniform tax, since the tax is uniform on all capital. If the property is in a school district with higher than average tax, then the owner must bear the excess burden. This theory assumes that reactions of taxpayers will have differing effects in the long run, since in the short run taxpayers may not be able to shift the incidence of a higher than average tax. If this theory is correct, the property tax should be classified as a progressive tax or at least a proportional one. If one assumes that assessment procedures are relatively uniform and capital market conditions are perfect, then a 2 percent tax levied on the valuation of property may be translated into an income tax on the income derived from that piece of property.

Whether the property tax can be classified as regressive or progressive must hinge on assumptions regarding the nature of the market, uniformity of property tax assessments, and, most important, on whether tax burdens are distributed among all owners of capital. All in all, the prevailing view still appears to be that the property tax is regressive and at best proportional. However, with the new view becoming more acceptable among public finance theoreticians, the reputation of the property tax may be enhanced in the future.

The second major issue regarding the property tax has to do with its administration. It is probably the most difficult of all the important taxes to administer equitably and has less justification for use as a major tax on the basis of many of the accepted principles of taxation than any other important tax. Nevertheless, it continues to be a major source of revenue for the local support of schools (and other local governmental agencies) in most states. Inequities and injustices in the procedures utilized to assess property and collect property taxes still exist, although significant improvements have been made in many states during the past few decades.

The concept of tying an expenditure for any single government service (especially a service as extensive as education) to a single source of taxation has been challenged by political scientists and authorities in public administration. A strong case can be made, however, for revenue sources such as gasoline and similar taxes being used primarily for the benefit of those who operate automobiles and utilize the highways. Such a distinction does not exist in relation to education and the property tax. Many persons who benefit from schools do not pay property taxes in the community, and many who pay property taxes receive little direct or easily identifiable benefit from existing public school systems. Moreover, the mobility of the population has given rise to another inequity with reference to the use of the property tax as a major base for the support of education. Many youths educated in one locality may become taxpaying citizens in a locality far removed from the one that contributed to their economic status.[10]

Within the "system" of property tax administration—determining fair property values, carrying out equitable assessment procedures, establishing rates of taxation, and collecting taxes—there are many variations and anomalies throughout the nation. For some years, authorities have been concerned about the defects in existing policies and practices relating to property taxation.

In both theory and law in most states, property is to be assessed at a uniform percentage of full market value. In many localities, local assessors (who in most states are elected officials) determine the value of property. In many states, these officials have no required training for or background in arriving at fair and just property values. Another significant disparity often results from the time span between reappraisals or reassessment years, causing property values to increase or decrease significantly.

The fragmentation of governmental units impairs the equity of the property tax. Many local governmental units are too small to employ full-time, well-trained assessors or to utilize modern assessing techniques. Moreover, dividing the state into a large number of school districts results in great disparities in taxable wealth and extreme variations among different districts in terms of the tax burdens they bear.

The variation among the fifty states regarding property valuation per pupil and its direct influence on educational expenditures per pupil has been well documented by countless studies. Compounding the problem of the effects of wealth on the quality of educational services focuses on the inefficient governance structures maintained by several states. Those states that have continued to operate inordinately large numbers of local school districts generally suffer from both diseconomies of scale and a much greater range in the wealth per pupil among its school districts. Thus, problems relating to financing public schools are made more difficult and complex by the existence of many school districts. Especially difficult is the problem of equalizing educational resources across wide-ranging variations in local wealth as measured by assessed valuation per pupil.

In the process of establishing property tax rates, the usual procedure is that officials of the local governmental body (authorized by state law to establish the rate of taxation) obtain the records giving the aggregate assessed value of properties and the level or amount of expenditures required to meet the anticipated budget for the services needed. The tax rate necessary to meet the budget request is calculated following the aggregation of assessed valuation of property. Unfortunately, this kind of public action gives rise to a very uneven and nonuniform practice of establishing property tax rates from locality to locality, and from year to year within the same locality. Although this brief explanation is an oversimplification of the fiscal operations of local units of government, it should serve to indicate how major disparities and inequities creep into property tax administration procedure.

Problems also arise in equal application of the property tax to all classifications of property and commensurate classifications of families according to age and income. The fact that taxes on residential property (with the exception of farms) are usually shifted to the consumer or renter creates added burdens. The question arises: Given these and other difficulties, should the local property tax be replaced with other forms of local taxation, or should we turn to policies that seek to cope with the major difficulties in property tax administration and bring about reforms? The answer to this question appears to be overwhelmingly the latter course of action. This is partly due to the fact that the property tax plays such a key role in financing the services of local governments, among which public education is of the greatest order of magnitude by far.

Consumption taxes are levies on commodities and transactions, the incidence of which falls upon the consumer through prices paid for goods and services.[11] Consumption taxes are levied on expenditures for consumption and may be classified into six major categories: customs, excise, sales, use, transfer, and gasoline. Of these, the most familiar, as a major revenue producer for general state funds, is the sales tax.

Consumption taxes are justified on the basis that they (1) provide an adequate and immediate flow of revenue, (2) are easily controlled, (3) provide a relatively stable source of revenue, (4) promote tax consciousness, and (5) are economical to collect and convenient to pay.[12] The most glaring deficiency of consumption taxes is their regressive nature.

During the past few decades, the use of sales taxes has increased dramatically as states have sought new revenue sources to offset rising costs of government and to reduce their dependency on the property tax. Sales taxes used by the states are both selective and general. Selective sales taxes are justified on the grounds of the benefit theory. For example, a selective sales tax on motor fuel can be justified as a *quid pro quo* for use of public highways, to which the taxes are usually devoted. If the tax were not levied, the cost of the public highway would be borne not by the user but by the entire community through general taxes. The selective sales tax may also be a consumption tax levied to reduce consumption of certain items. For example, selective sales taxes are levied on liquor, tobacco, and parimutuels. Such taxes, though, traditionally have not been high enough to significantly diminish consumption.

Early state adoption of the general retail sales tax was retarded somewhat by the success of selective sales taxes and by the fear that the levy of such a tax would violate U.S. Supreme Court prohibitions against taxing interstate commerce. This legal interpretation was relaxed during the Great Depression, which saw the dismal response of income taxes and the collapse of property taxes in many jurisdictions. Also, Congress in 1931–32 indicated that a sales tax at the federal level was unacceptable.[13] Mississippi adopted a general sales tax in 1932, followed by thirteen other states in 1933, and by the end of

1938 nine more states had followed suit. By 1944 the general retail sales tax had become the most important state revenue producer and has been so ever since.

The retail sales tax is a single-stage tax which excludes sales to industrial customers either through the ingredient test or the client-use test. The ingredient test removes from the tax base property which is an ingredient in the product to be sold. The direct-use test excludes from the tax base sale of property which is used directly in the production of goods.[14]

In most instances, services are excluded from the retail sales tax. The Tax Foundation has estimated that "discretionary exemptions (i.e., goods and services considered suitable for taxation but exempt in most states) amount to one-half the volume of total taxable sales."[15]

Regressive Nature. The most important objection to the sales tax is its inequity. As a tax on consumption, the sales tax absorbs a higher percentage of the income of the poor than of the wealthy. If equity is measured in terms of a tax to income ratio, then the sales tax is regressive, since the sales tax paid by the poor is a higher percentage of their income than that paid by the rich. Peckman and Okner have shown that "sales and excise taxes are clearly regressive throughout the entire income scale."[16] The richest 1 percent of the people pay 1.3 percent of their incomes in sales and excise taxes while middle-income families pay 4.2 percent.[17] The burden of the poorer families becomes much greater in states that rely on sales and excise taxes for a high percentage of their governmental revenues. Middle-income families may pay 6 percent or more of their income in sales and excise taxes in states that rely heavily on sales taxes. The worst states in the nation in this regard are Louisiana, New Mexico, Washington, Tennessee, West Virginia, and South Dakota where sales and excise taxes consume more than 10 percent of the total income of poor families. The least regressive sales tax now in effect is found in Vermont. There the sales tax exempts food and has a relatively low rate of 5 percent.[18] Sales taxes generally violate the principle of vertical equity (unequal treatment of unequals), and as for horizontal equity (equal treatment of equals), the tax may be even more inequitable. In the absence of definitive studies of this question, one may conclude that horizontal inequity is substantial since the tax does not account for family characteristics and needs.

John Kenneth Galbraith, in his classic work *The Affluent Society*, minimized the importance of conventional wisdom which opposed extension of the sales tax. He maintained that in the affluent society the spending of most persons is so far above the subsistence level that the regressive nature of the sales tax is of little importance.[19]

Seligman probably best characterized the use of the sales tax, after a survey of the tax system of several countries, when he said,

> The conclusion to be drawn from this historical survey is that the general sales tax constitutes the last resort of countries which find themselves in such fiscal difficulty that they must subordinate all other principles of taxation to that of adequacy.[20]

A state sales tax may be made less regressive by relieving low-income persons of the excessive burden of the tax. John Due recommends that this be accomplished by providing a credit against the state income tax representing sales tax paid on a minimum necessary level of expenditures, with a cash refund to those having no income tax liability.[21] A number of states have attempted to reduce the regressivity of sales tax by exempting food and medicine. This policy does not reduce the regressivity of the sales tax nearly as much as the approach recommended by Due. Excise taxes, including state gasoline taxes and cigarette taxes, are even more regressive than general state sales taxes. State gasoline taxes impose 16 times as great a burden, measured as percentage of income, on the poor than on the rich, and cigarette taxes are even worse consuming 27 times as great a percentage of the income of the poor as the rich.[22]

Individual Income Taxes

State individual income taxes find their precedence in the faculty taxes of the colonial days. The faculty taxes were a crude form of taxation which combined specific property taxes with income taxes. In the financial panic of 1836, several states adopted state income taxes, but only Virginia was able to administer the tax efficiently enough to produce income taxes imposed on salaries and specific kinds of personal incomes. These taxes were generally undesirable because they were levied at a flat rate and were based on "estimated" income as measured by a person's "trade" or "calling" rather than actual income. Administration continued to be weak, and eventually all states except Virginia, Louisiana, and North Carolina abandoned such taxes.[23]

A great advance for state income taxes came in 1911 when Wisconsin first imposed an entirely new type of income tax. It introduced a tax on net income at progressive rates which was placed under the control of a powerful state tax commission. The actual administration was conducted by trained civil service employees assigned to districts in the state. The revenues from this tax were so substantial that other states adopted variations of the Wisconsin program.

The federal experience with the income tax had its origins with the financial exigency of the Civil War. From 1789 to 1909 the federal government relied almost exclusively on excise and customs taxes for its revenues. The Civil War income tax was in effect from 1862 through 1871, at which time it lapsed. At its peak, in 1866, it accounted for almost 25 percent of federal internal revenues.[24]

After its expiration, the income tax was not revived until 1894 during the wave of enthusiasm for trust and monopoly reform. The tax applied to both personal and corporate income and levied a low flat 2 percent. This tax was almost immediately challenged under the constitutional restraint that no "direct tax" shall be levied except in proportion to population.[25] In a five-to-four decision, the U.S. Supreme Court held that the income came "from property" and that the tax was tantamount to a direct tax on property itself, and was thus unconstitutional.[26] The effect of this ruling was that no federal income tax could be levied until the Constitution was amended. This was not accomplished until 1913, when the Sixteenth Amendment removed the constitutional barrier. The amendment provided:

> The Congress shall have power to lay and collect taxes on incomes, from whatever source derived, without apportionment among the several states, and without regard to any census of enumeration.

Only seven months after this amendment was adopted a new income tax was imposed on both personal and corporate incomes. This rather low but modestly graduated income tax was upheld as constitutional by the U.S. Supreme Court in 1916.[27]

The income tax has become the major source of revenue for the federal government. Today, the personal income tax produces approximately one-half of the receipts at the federal level.

Despite the apparent virtual preemption of the individual income tax by the federal government, states have found the income tax to be a lucrative source of revenue. Most states have adopted the federal tax base, with some modifications, a move which helps both the state and the taxpayers in determining the tax liability.

State individual income taxes are graduated, but to a more modest level than the federal in-

---

DEFINITION

Direct Taxes. Those taxes levied directly on individuals or firms, including taxes on income, labor earnings, and profits. Direct taxes contrast with *indirect taxes*, which are those levied on goods and services and thus only indirectly on people, and which include sales taxes and taxes on property, alcohol imports, and gasoline.

Source: Paul A. Samuelson and William D. Nordhaus, *Economics.* 14th ed. (New York: McGraw-Hill, 1992), p. 724.

---

come tax. All states except Alaska, Florida, Nevada, South Dakota, Texas, Washington, and Wyoming utilize the personal income tax. New Hampshire and Tennessee have narrowly restricted income taxes, limited to dividend and interest income.[28] State income taxes usually have certain general characteristics that include some form of withholding procedure and they most often use the income determination of the federal income tax as the tax base. Some states simply apply a state tax percentage to the federal income tax liability; this approach assumes for the state the federal income definition.

State personal income taxes are the most progressive of major state taxes, and by their use, most states mitigate the regressive effects of other taxes. Importantly, too, beyond their progressive nature, state personal income taxes are a flexible source of revenue readily generating increased revenue flows as the economy of the state grows.

The fairness of state income taxes has increased in recent years by removing poor families, in the lower fifth of family incomes, from the tax roles completely. The states that do not now levy personal income taxes on the poor are Arizona, Colorado, Kansas, Louisiana, Maine, Maryland, Minnesota, Mississippi, Nebraska, New Mexico, North Carolina, Rhode Island, South Carolina, Vermont, and Wisconsin. Although the trends toward increased tax equity deriving from more progressive use of the income tax are encouraging, the movement is not unanimous. Three states, Alabama, Indiana, and Oregon, have actually increased the income taxes on the poor since 1985. Overall, though, the state's personal income tax is the most equitable of state taxes and generally has been considered a very positive development.[29]

Corporation Income Taxes

The corporation income tax has been used at the federal level since 1909 when, to avoid a constitutional confrontation, Congress levied the tax as an excise on the privilege of doing business as a corporation.[30] Before 1941 this tax was the most effective revenue producer at the federal level, yielding the most revenue in 17 of the 28 years immediately prior to World War II. After 1941 it was the second major revenue producer until it was overtaken by payroll taxes in 1968.[31] The corporation income tax at the state level finds its origins, as did the individual income tax, in the Wisconsin tax of 1911.

The basic method for determining taxable income under this tax is to ascertain the net income by subtracting the costs of doing business from the gross income. One of the major criticisms of the corporation income tax is that it may tend toward "double taxation" of distributed corporate profits. It is argued that since the corporation is a separate legal entity, with its own income, it should be taxed as an independent being. Regardless of views, the governments of the various states have found the tax to be an important source of revenue which should be continued. An attractive feature of the corporate income tax is its progressivity. McIntyre and others found that the corporate income tax was the most progressive of all major taxes "taking six times as large a share of income from the richest families as from the middle- and low-income people."[32]

Another major issue surrounding the state corporation income tax is its apportionment among states so as not to impede interstate commerce. Presently, states use different methods for the division of a net income base for tax purposes. This assumes that business activities can be split into separate pieces based on geography, when in fact most are unitary.[33] Congress has only acted to prohibit state taxation if the corporation only solicits business in the state and does not operate therein.[34] The basic issues of taxation of interstate commerce have not been resolved and the result has been discrimination against certain businesses and excessive costs of administration.

Other Taxes

Aside from the major taxes discussed above, the state and federal governments levy a wide variety of taxes including estate, death, gift, and use taxes. Of particular importance to this discussion though are the payroll taxes which were first introduced at the federal level in 1935 by the Social Security Act.

In 1935 the original programs provided for two social insurance programs: federal old-age benefits, more commonly known as "social security," and a federal-state system of unemployment compensation. The original programs have undergone substantial change, including the addition in 1966 of hospital and medical benefits for persons over 65. The federal unemployment compensation tax rate has increased significantly since its inception. As the benefits rise, the rates of this earmarked tax rise, producing revenues which are a higher percentage of the gross national product each year.

Forms of estate, death, and gift taxes are among the oldest forms of taxation. In fact, the trust as we know it today was developed as a device to subvert the government's efforts in England to tax or take property by death transfer as early as the thirteenth century.[35] Taxes at death were also avoided by making direct transfers of property by gifts *inter vivos* (between living persons). The federal and some state governments have thus tied estate, inheritance, death, and gift taxes together to prevent avoidance by various means. State governments impose inheritance taxes on the privilege of receiving property from the dead, while the federal government imposes an estate tax on the privilege of transfer on the one who dies. Bequests and gifts increase the recipients' ability to pay and could conceivably be taxed as income; however, it would be somewhat unfair to tax a one-time transfer at the fully graduated rates of the personal income tax. The rates of gift taxes are therefore set at lower levels.

Before 1977 estate and gift taxes were separate taxes at the federal level, but were unified in that year. The tax base for the estate tax consists of the gross value of all property at the time of death, including stocks, bonds, real estate, mortgages, and any other quantifiable property. The gross estate encompasses gifts made within three years prior to death, insurance, and the value of any revocable trust. The gift tax is determined by the additional property acquired during the taxable year.

Estate and gift taxes are levied on only a small portion of the privately owned wealth in the United States.[36] Generous exemptions, especially since 1976, when larger exemptions were authorized, prevent encroachment of the tax on the estates of most middle-income taxpayers. For deaths after 1986, an estate tax base of $600,000 has a credit of $192,800.

Possible New Taxes

Three new major taxes have been proposed by various sources in recent years: wealth tax, value-added tax, and expenditure tax.

Wealth Tax.   The wealth tax is a tax on assessed wealth. Wealth is synonymous with capital or "net worth." Its base is determined by the value of the stock of all physical and financial assets, less those liabilities held at a particular time.[37] It differs from the "real property tax," which is a tax on the gross value of only one type of property. The wealth tax is used principally in Europe—Denmark, Germany, The Netherlands, Norway, and Sweden for instance. Tax rates are usually about 1 percent of the annual net worth of an individual: Denmark has a progressive rate of 0.09 to 1.0 percent; Germany, proportional at 2.7 percent; the Netherlands, proportional at 0.8 percent; Norway, progressive at 0.4 to 1.0 percent; Sweden, progressive at 1.0 to 2.5 percent.

Advocates of the wealth tax maintain that it increases horizontal equity because it captures the entire ability to pay of each family, whereas an income tax only identifies one element. This view has been illustrated by the comparable positions of the beggar who has neither income nor property and the Maharajah who has no income but keeps the whole of his wealth in jewels and gold. They both would pay the same income tax, but a much different wealth tax.[38] Another advantage observed by Due is that a wealth tax, "while not taxing increases in capital values as

such, does reach the higher values as they accrue,"[39] whereas a capital gains tax only reaches those values when they are realized. A third argument for the wealth tax is that it is very effective in the redistribution of wealth. Finally, it is argued that such a tax is direct and cannot be readily shifted to the consumer or to lower economic groups.

Those opposing the wealth tax maintain that it poses very difficult administrative problems and that it can have adverse overall economic consequences. Concerning the latter, it almost certainly would reduce the incentive to save which has been the bulwark of personal economic objectives since the founding of this country. Importantly, some maintain the wealth tax is not needed because the diverse system of taxation of both state and federal governments in this country covers those bases—real, personal, and intangible personal property—and is nearly as pervasive as the wealth tax anyway.

Although this tax is not under serious consideration in the United States, in past years it has been seriously discussed in Great Britain. If such a tax were imposed at the state level in this country, the yield would be sufficient to make all residential property tax exempt, with a very substantial surplus.[40]

Value-added Tax.   The value-added tax (VAT), unlike the wealth tax, has been seriously advocated in this country at the federal level. The value-added tax base is the value that a business firm adds in the course of its operations to the goods and services it has previously purchased from other firms.[41] That amount added at each level of production can be measured as the difference between the dollar amounts of the firm's purchases and its sales. The amount of purchases would include costs for merchandise and supplies, advertising, freight, utilities, and so on.

Proponents of the VAT observe that it is economically neutral; it would not distort economic decisions among "products and methods of production or between present and future consumption" and it would not favor labor-intensive industries over those that are capital intensive.[42]

On the other hand, it is a consumption tax and as such is regressive in nature. The tendency would be for business to forward shift the tax to the consumer who is least likely to have the ability to pay.[43] The regressivity could, to some extent, be ameliorated by exemptions or tax credits, but the burden is likely to remain on the poorer segment of society. Further, other critics of a federal VAT say that it would upset the uneasy balance in fiscal federalism by allowing the federal government to encroach on the consumption revenues now largely dominated by the state sales tax. It is, though, maintained by some that the tax would be particularly desirable as a state tax. At the federal level, the ACIR has concluded that the tax has two intergovernmental strikes against it: (1) it is viewed as an intrusion on the state-level use of the sales tax, and (2) it cannot be readily coordinated with the retail sales tax of states and localities.[44] This, coupled with its lack of equity, greatly diminishes its attractiveness as a major new tax.

Expenditure Tax.   A tax which has gained considerable attention of late is the personal expenditure tax. Some experts now believe that this tax is a better alternative than trying to reform the federal individual income tax.[45] Proponents of progressive taxation advance this tax as superior to the value-added tax. The expenditure tax has the theoretical attractiveness of being neither a tax *in personam*, like the income tax, nor an *in rem* tax, like the consumption tax, but constitutes a combination of the two.[46] Unlike the other taxes now in use, this one would use consumption as an index of taxpaying ability. The taxpayer would determine his or her consumption for the year, subtract out exemptions and deductions, and apply a progressive tax rate to the residual amount. Musgrave and Musgrave suggest that the most feasible approach to determining taxable expenditure would be to (1) determine bank balance at the beginning of the year, (2) include all receipts, (3) add net borrowing (borrowing minus debt repayment or lending), (4) subtract net investment (costs of assets purchased minus proceeds from

assets sold), (5) and minus the bank balance at the end of the year.[47]

Proponents of the expenditure tax maintain that it is superior to the income tax because it encourages saving and offers incentive for capital formation. Those who oppose the tax claim that it would not be as progressive as the present federal income tax and that it would lead to excessive accumulation of wealth. The opposition further points out that it would be much more difficult to administer than the present federal income tax. On the other hand, advocates of the expenditure tax say the federal income tax has now become so unwieldy that a completely new tax is the only answer. On balance, the expenditure tax appears to be well worth extensive examination, particularly in an era when the nation's economy is in need of policy to encourage the formation of capital.

TAX REFORM LIMITATIONS
AND EXEMPTIONS

State tax reform measures are generally attempts to make the various taxes more equitable, but in recent years a wave of public sentiment has demanded tax reductions. Inflation and a relative decline in the American standard of living during the past two decades have caused taxpayers to seek shelter from taxation, restricting sources for school districts.

In 1979 the movement to limit local spending intensified and three states passed revenue and expenditure limitations, while two other states placed tax restraint initiatives on the ballot. Oregon, Washington, and Louisiana enacted laws to restrict state appropriations to the annual increase in the states' personal income. Utah passed a state and local appropriations limit which took effect in 1982. Florida, Massachusetts, and New Mexico subsequently placed new limits on local property taxes.[48]

These, and numerous reforms in other states, were largely directed toward limitation of government expenditure through more restrictive tax policy. Tax limitation legislation in 1979 went as follows: 5 states enacted property tax limitation laws, 3 enacted circuit breakers, 19 enacted homestead exemptions, and 10 enacted various credits and rebates. In addition to these changes, 13 states reduced sales taxes, 22 reduced income taxes, and 6 reduced inheritance and gift taxes. In sum, there were 80 acts which in some form reduced taxes in 32 states.[49]

Much of the tax legislation has involved measures to reduce property taxation. Historically, the United States has gone through periods when property taxes were subject to greater taxpayer resentment, as during the Panic of 1870 when many property tax limits were initiated in an effort to stem the proliferation of local government. Another great push for property tax limits came during the depression of the 1930s when property values dropped, resulting in a significant decrease in local school revenues. Indiana, Michigan, Washington, and West Virginia in 1932, and New Mexico, Ohio, and Oklahoma in 1933 responded by revising their tax rate limits.[50] This phenomenon continues today, but nowhere is it more dramatized than in the Proposition 13 struggle that took place in California in 1977.

Proposition 13

The California taxpayer revolt had a resounding effect on public opinion in all states and set in motion what was to become a highly publicized anti-tax and anti-big-government crusade. Proposition 13, approved by the California voters on June 6, 1978, was an amendment to the state constitution limiting local property tax rates and making it difficult for local government to increase other taxes. Specifically, the amendment provided for (1) property taxes to be limited to 1 percent of full cash value plus the rate needed to service bonded indebtedness, approved by the voters before 1978–79; (2) assessed values to be rolled back to 1975–76 levels, with increases of only 2 percent annually, to reflect inflation (newly sold property could be assessed at market value exceeding the 1975–76 level); (3) statutes to increase state taxes to be approved by two-

thirds of each of the two houses of the legislature and no new *ad valorem*, sales, or transaction taxes on real property to be levied; (4) special local taxes, taxes on real property, to be approved by two-thirds of the jurisdiction's voters.

Proposition 13 reduced local governmental revenues by 23 percent, with the greatest portion falling on local school districts, where the loss was estimated to amount to $3.5 billion or 29.2 percent of total revenues.[51] The remainder represented savings to state governments to be paid to local governments to replace local revenues lost because of various homeowner and business exemptions.

To offset the effects of Proposition 13, the state increased appropriations from a state general fund surplus. A total of $4.12 billion was distributed, $2.26 billion of which went to local school districts, reducing the net revenue loss for schools to 10.5 percent.

The action in California increased unemployment in the labor-intensive public sector by about 60,000 jobs, causing some depressive effect on California's economy.[52] The spillover of the California revolt was felt in other states, the most dramatic being in Massachusetts, where in 1980 school revenues were drastically reduced as a result of a constitutional tax limitation amendment, popularly known as Proposition 2½.

The drastic decline in school revenues caused by Proposition 13 had a significant and deleterious effect on many school districts in California. Unfortunately, the ravages of Proposition 13 on school revenues became entangled with the progress toward school funding equalization following *Serrano* v. *Priest*, and many now erroneously attribute the inadequacy of funding in California schools to *Serrano* rather than to the real cause, Proposition 13.

In the aftermath of Proposition 13, McIntyre in 1991 warned,

Lawmakers (and citizens) should beware of property tax relief mechanisms that attempt to provide across-the-board relief, such as property tax "caps" (which typically limit any increases in property tax levies to a predetermined amount each year), or Proposition 13-style initiatives (which place a ceiling on property tax bills at a certain percentage of property value).

These mechanisms fail to distinguish between those who may be in some real need of relief—the middle-class and poor; who are devoting higher shares of their family incomes to property taxes—and rich families who are not. Moreover, they fail to distinguish between residential and nonresidential property.[53]

Tax reform is necessary and highly desirable when well-conceived to increase the equity and efficiency of the tax system, but a "meat ax" approach may well cause unintended side effects that will be harmful to many generations hence. Better options include circuit breakers, homestead exemptions, rate modifications, and administrative improvements all of which can create the desired results without shock to the revenue system or deprivation of educational opportunities.

Property Tax Control Points

State policy makers can control property taxes and local school expenditures by imposing restrictions on rates, levies, assessments, and revenues of expenditures. A common method is to limit the local school property tax rate. Maximum rates, expressed in dollars or mills, may be set for governmental policy boards and levied without the vote of the people. Maximum rates may also be established beyond which the local electorate cannot exceed. This method of control does not limit school-tax revenue if assessed valuation of property continues to rise, as inflation, property improvements, economic growth, or reassessment of property will cause it to do.[54]

Controls may also be placed on the rate of assessment increases, as was done in California under Proposition 13. Assessment-ratio controls may also be used to limit the taxable value to a small percentage of the full market value of the property.

A revenue freeze can also be used to control increases in property taxes. Here the amount of revenue may be restricted to the level of the previous year or may be allowed to increase at a given percentage per year, for example 6 percent per annum. Since property values will increase as a result of economic growth or inflation, this type of control will probably result in local school districts having to reduce property tax rates.

Another device used to control local use of the property tax is the *full disclosure law*, by which the existing political processes are brought more directly into play. Under this method, if a local school board wants to increase its tax rate, or possibly revenues, from the previous year, it must advertise and hold public hearings, and only then can the rate be set. This, it is theorized, will bring about greater public accountability on the part of school boards to more fully justify expenditures.

Homestead Exemptions and Circuit Breakers. The regressivity features of the property tax have been corrected in two major ways. The first of these is homestead exemptions. Exemptions are provisions enacted by the state that exclude a portion of the assessed value of a single-family home from its total assessed value before applying the existing tax rate. Such action helps taxpayers whose income is modest and/or who live in low-valued residences. Under this method, for example, the first $5,000, or some other set amount, of assessed valuation on property is not considered in determining the tax for the resident owner. In a number of states, additional levels of exemption are allowed for senior citizens and veterans.

The second reform, which constitutes a more complex way of achieving some relief from regressivity difficulties, is called a "circuit breaker." This relief is based on the assumption that an excessive tax burden is borne by householders at the low end of the income scale, particularly the elderly. An effort is therefore made to ensure that the property tax bears a reasonable relationship to the flow of cash income into a household. The circuit breaker (the administration of which requires the collection of considerably more information than that of the homestead exemption) may be efficiently administered by a state agency, which rebates to the taxpayer the calculated relief in accordance with provisions of the program. The taxpayer's individual income tax returns and information from property tax administration can usually be used to determine the amount of rebate the state will pay to individuals who qualify.

Two types of circuit breakers are most common: a threshold type and a percentage-of-tax-liability type.[55] The threshold circuit breaker establishes an acceptable amount of tax which a homeowner or a renter in a certain income category should pay. The state will rebate to the taxpayer the amount of money paid for property taxes above the limit. The threshold rate may be held constant (fixed) over the various income groups or it may vary, increasing as income increases. The fixed-threshold approach is used in Connecticut, Nevada, North Dakota, and Oklahoma, while the variable approach is used in Arkansas, the District of Columbia, Illinois, Maryland, Michigan, Missouri, Vermont, and Wisconsin.[56]

The percentage-of-tax-liability formula rebates a part of the actual tax liability, returning higher percentages as the amount of income declines. This approach is demonstrated by the Indiana law which provides that 75 percent of property tax paid be rebated for the $0 to $500 household income category; 70 percent for the $500 to $1,000 category; 50 percent for the $1000 to $1,500 category; and so on down to 10 percent for the $4,000 to $5,000 household income category.[57]

Assessment Reform. One of the more serious problems in property tax programs is that of ensuring fairness and equality in the process of assessing properties. To some extent this may be overcome by requiring property assessors to be professionally trained and to maintain and up-date their competencies to value properties accurately. It also may mean that assessors should become civil-service employees of the state government rather than partisan elected officials. Uniform and standardized procedures for guaranteeing fairness in the assessment process are more easily achieved by state regulation than by attempting to ensure uniform action across many entities of local government. Some states are beginning to effect such measures. In 1973 Maryland enacted a law that required assessors to exhibit competency and skill in valuing property before they can be appointed. Also, the Maryland reform plan specified rigid control by the state in updating and reassessing property values. Competently staffed state boards of equalization also tend to level off discrepancies in property tax assessment procedures and the rate at which properties are taxed.

Nearly all states now have some form of property tax equalization strategy at the state level, including state assessment of utilities and major corporations. The efficiency and effectiveness of these strategies vary considerably from state to state. The ultimate outcome of property tax reform measures targeted at assessment and commensurate administrative difficulties is to make the property tax a state-administered tax. Some states have made considerable progress toward achieving this end. For example, the 1973 Maine legislature enacted a law that made the local school property tax a state tax.

Property Tax Classification. Through the utilization of state-mandated programs of property classification, it is possible to shift the property tax burden from one class of property to another. For example, if state policy makers believe that residential homeowners are overburdened, through a particular classification scheme, they could shift a major portion of the property tax burden from residential homeowners to business properties. Six states have now enacted programs that comprehensively classify property for purposes of property tax administration: Montana, West Virginia, Minnesota, Alabama, Arizona, and Tennessee. Some of the classification schemes are rather complicated. The Minnesota plan, for example, enumerates 25 separate classifications of property. The usual plan, however, is a much simpler one in which property is divided into roughly four classes: transportation and communication property, utility property, commercial and industrial property, and residential and farm properties.

Site-Value Taxation.   One of the newest forms of property tax improvements suggested by theorists is site-value taxation. The concept of site-value taxation is old; the possibility of using it is much more modern. Essentially, site-value taxation provides for a tax on land; it varies in accordance with the value of land and excludes improvements in existence on such land. Those who advocate this reform counter that site-value taxation would remove the financial deterrent to rehabilitation, especially of slum properties in the major cities. Opponents of site-value taxation point out that the existing property tax program takes into account the actual value as the tax base, and if fairly administered would bring about abrupt and dramatic changes in the incidence of the property tax burden. Though this theory is particularly appealing to many who seek to overcome the economic difficulties confronting large cities, the likelihood of its adoption appears remote.

Tax Exemptions

Tax exemptions substantially affect the amount of both state and local revenue available for support of the public schools, as well as other governmental services. The four principal types of tax exemptions are:

1. Exemptions granted for the purpose of adjusting tax liability to taxpaying ability
2. Exemptions granted to attract business and industry
3. Exemptions granted to give preference to certain groups in the population

4. Exemptions granted to governmental, religious, charitable, educational, and other nonprofit institutions

Income Tax Exemptions.   The exemption for dependents allowed by the federal income tax law is a good example of exemptions granted for the purpose of adjusting tax liability to taxpaying ability. This exemption is actually a part of the progressive rate structure, and therefore is fully justified, if one accepts that the progressive income tax is an equitable tax.

Sales Tax Exemptions.   The general sales tax laws enacted by the states vary considerably in the number of items exempted. Some states exempt a great many items, usually on the theory that those items are "necessities." However, what may be necessities for one person may not be for another. The purpose behind this type of exemption is laudable if it is to make tax liability contingent on ability to pay. However, it is an awkward method of accomplishing the purpose. The regressivity of the sales tax can much more readily be reduced by the methods recommended by Due, already discussed in this chapter. Exemptions from the sales tax also contribute to tax avoidance. It is much easier for a retail establishment to conceal its tax liability when it sells both exempted and nonexempted articles than when all its sales are subject to the tax.

Exemptions to Attract Industry.   Exemptions granted to attract industry have been particularly troublesome. Conditions for maximizing the economic progress of the nation are unfavorably affected when artificial barriers or subsidies cause industry to locate at points other than those most favorable for efficient production and distribution.

Despite this fact, states and political subdivisions within states frequently give industry (especially new industry) favored tax treatment. States can do this simply by not having a state corporation income tax or by having very low rates. States also have exempted new industries from property taxes for a given number of years.

The competition for new industries is particularly keen among the political subdivisions of a state. Tax favors usually are granted to industries by entirely exempting them from property taxes for a given number of years or by assessing their properties at a very low rate. Some units of local government have given permanent property tax exemptions to certain industries by actually constructing industrial plants and leasing them to private corporations. Ownership of the property is retained by the local government, and it is completely tax exempt. These types of property tax exemptions seriously affect school financing in many school districts. New industries often bring many additional pupils, but the tax base remains the same. Thus the school district has less taxable wealth per pupil for school support after the new industry is brought to the district than before. Experts on public finance and economics generally agree that if an industry cannot operate in a particular locality without a tax subsidy, the community is better off without it. Furthermore, it is also believed that the influence of tax exemptions or of low tax rates on the location of industries is greatly exaggerated in public thinking. Such factors as access to necessary raw materials; access to markets; and availability of labor, water, power, and community services far more powerfully affect the location of industry than do tax exemptions or low tax rates.

Exemptions for Favored Groups. As discussed earlier in this chapter, tax exemptions are sometimes given to certain groups, such as veterans or homeowners. Exemptions to veterans seem to have little or no justification. This practice certainly cannot be defended by any generally accepted principle or theory of taxation. Its purpose seems to be to establish a group with special privileges, but that practice finds no defense in the principles of American democracy.

The practice of granting exemptions to homeowners emerged during the depression in the thirties. It had great emotional appeal during those times, because many financially distressed persons were in danger of losing their homes. While homestead exemption has a laudable purpose, it is difficult to defend from the standpoint of fiscal policy. The circuit breaker approach discussed before is a far more preferable policy for increasing the equity of the property tax.

Exemptions for Nonprofit Institutions. It is practically universal practice in the United States to exempt from property taxes all property used for governmental, religious, charitable, educational, and philanthropic purposes. Some have questioned the wisdom of this policy, but it has become so firmly established that it is unlikely to be changed.

Property taxes are levied principally on the enterprises where people work and on the homes in which they live. If the principal enterprises at which people work in a school district are exempted from taxes, then the tax base is greatly reduced. Tax-exempt enterprises bring pupils to a community as do other enterprises, and this adds not only to school costs, but also to the costs of other local government services. The federal government has ameliorated this condition in communities receiving a heavy impact from federal activities by providing special grants-in-aid for schools. The federal government also makes payments in lieu of taxes where large areas of national forests are located.

But there are many tax-exempt institutions other than federal properties. For example, state institutions and private colleges may be concentrated at certain locations. States that use the equalization method of apportioning state school funds have taken a step toward solving this problem insofar as school financing is concerned.

SUMMARY AND CONCLUSIONS

This chapter discusses the major types of taxes that are used to fund education and other governmental services. Property taxes receive particular attention because of their attachment and importance to local school districts. The primary points of the chapter are summarized below.

There are two general classifications of taxes, *in rem*, on things, and *in personam*, on the person. Property taxes are taxes on things. Property taxes are sometimes called *ad valorem* taxes.

Tax rates may be expressed in dollars, cents, or mills. A mill is one-tenth of a cent or one-thousandth of a dollar.

Most experts consider property taxes to be regressive, to fall more heavily on the poor than on the rich. Some, though, contend that the property tax is not as regressive as it appears because property owners are unable to readily shift the incidence of the tax to the poor.

The methods of administering the property tax usually make the tax more objectionable. Assessment practices and lump sum billing procedures make the tax both controversial and difficult to pay.

Consumption taxes are levies on commodities and transactions which fall on the consumer. Such taxes include levies on sales, excise, use, transfer, customs, and gasoline. Sales taxes are relatively popular taxes, being more palatable because of their ease of payment. Despite popularity of the sales tax, it imposes a heavier burden on the poor than on the rich. The regressivity of the tax, however, can be mitigated by exemption of necessities such as food and medicine. Excise taxes are more regressive than sales taxes.

Individual income taxes are usually calibrated to be progressive and are the mainstay of the federal tax system. Nearly all states employ the personal income tax with Florida, Texas, and Washington being the largest states to reject the tax.

Other taxes that have been discussed for possible use in the United States include the wealth tax, the value-added tax, and the expenditure tax. The wealth tax and the value-added tax have been commonly used in other countries. The expenditure tax has been proposed in the United States by academics, but have never been seriously considered by Congress or state legislatures.

Tax reform and tax limitation measures in several states have had profound effects on the level and adequacy of public school funding. Proposition 13 in California has produced very severe consequences and Proposition 2½ in Massachusetts has also caused some funding difficulties. Other constitutional restraints such as the Hancock amendment in Missouri and House Bill 920 in Ohio have had important effects on both the levels and adequacy of taxation in those states.

KEY TERMS

Taxes *in rem*	Property tax	Direct taxes
Taxes *in personam*	Real property	Wealth tax
Tax base	Personal property	Value-added tax
Tax rate	Consumption taxes	Expenditure tax
Assessed valuation of property	Excise taxes	

ENDNOTES

1. Richard A. Musgrave and Peggy B. Musgrave, *Public Finance in Theory and Practice,* 2nd ed. (New York: McGraw-Hill, 1976), pp. 224–25.

2. William H. Anderson, *Taxation and the American Economy* (Englewood Cliffs, NJ: Prentice-Hall, 1951), p. 120.

3. Ibid., p. 122.

4. Adam Smith, *Wealth of Nations* (London: Chiswick Press, 1912), p. 394.

5. John Shannon, "The Property Tax: Reform or Relief?" *Property Tax Reform,* ed. George E. Peterson (Washington, DC: Urban Institute, 1973), pp. 26–27.

6. Robert S. McIntyre, Douglas P. Kelly, Michael P. Ettlinger, and Elizabeth A. Fray, *A Far Cry From Fair,*

CTJ's Guide to State Tax Reform (Washington, DC: Citizens for Tax Justice, 1991), p. 12.

7. Abt Associates, Inc., *Property Tax Relief Programs for the Elderly, Final Report* (Washington, DC: U.S. Department of Housing and Urban Development, 1975), p. 38.

8. Advisory Commission on Intergovernmental Relations, *Financing Schools and Property Tax Relief: A State Responsibility* (Washington, DC: ACIR, 1973), p. 36.

9. Henry Aaron, *Who Pays the Property Tax? A New View* (Washington, DC: Brookings Institution, 1975), p. 59.

10. This section was prepared with the collaboration of Harry L. Phillips, formerly of the Office of Legislation, U.S. Department of Education, and formerly executive director, Maryland Commission on the Structure of Governance of Education.

11. Anderson, op. cit., p. 394.

12. Ibid., p. 397.

13. James A. Maxwell and Richard Aronson, *Financing State and Local Governments,* 3rd ed. (Washington, DC: Brookings Institution, 1977), p. 102.

14. Ibid., p. 104.

15. *State and Local Sales Taxes* (New York: Tax Foundation, 1970), p. 63.

16. Joseph A. Peckman and Benjamin A. Okner, *Who Bears the Tax Burden?* (Washington, DC: Brookings Institution, 1974), p. 58.

17. McIntyre, et al., op. cit., p. 11.

18. McIntyre, et al., op. cit., p. 12.

19. John Kenneth Galbraith, *The Affluent Society* (New York: New American Library, 1958), p. 246.

20. Edwin R. A. Seligman, *Studies in Public Finance* (New York: MacMillian, 1925), p. 131–38.

21. John F. Due, "Alternative Tax Sources for Education," *Economic Factors Affecting the Financing of Education*, eds. Roe L. Johns and others, vol. 2 (Gainesville, FL: University of Florida, 1970), p. 310.

22. McIntyre, et al., op. cit., p. 12.

23. Anderson, op. cit., pp. 177–78.

24. Joseph A. Peckman, *Federal Tax Policy* 3rd ed. (Washington, DC: Brookings Institution, 1977), pp. 288–89.

25. Art. I, Sec. 9, Cl. 4.

26. *Pollock* v. *Farmers' Loan and Trust Co.*, 157 U.S. 429 and 158 U.S. 601 (1895).

27. *Brushhaber* v. *Union Pacific R.R. Co.*, 240 U.S. 1 (1916).

28. William H. Hoffman, Jr., Eugene Willis, and James E. Smith, eds., *West's Federal Taxation: Individual Income Taxes* (St. Paul, MN: West Publishing Company, 1990), pp. 1–14.

29. McIntyre, et al., op. cit., pp. 9–11.

30. Peckman, *Federal Tax Policy,* 3rd ed. Brookings Institute, 1987, p. 123.

31. Ibid.

32. McIntyre, et al., op. cit., pp. 14–15.

33. Maxwell and Aronson; op. cit.

34. Public Law 86–272, Sept. 14, 1959.

35. Alexander and Erwin S. Solomon, *College and University Law* (Charlottesville, VA: Michie Company, 1972), p. 266.

36. Peckman, op. cit., *Federal Tax Policy*, p. 225.

37. C. T. Sandford, J. R. M. Willis, and D. J. Ironside, *An Annual Wealth Tax* (New York: Holmes and Meier Publishers, 1975), p. 3.

38. N. Kaldor, *Indian Tax Reform* (New Delhi: Ministry of Finance, Government of India, 1956), p. 20.

39. John F. Due, "Net Worth Taxation," *Public Finance*, vol. XV (1960), p. 316.

40. Kern Alexander, "The Wealth Tax As an Alternative Revenue Source for Public Schools," *Journal of Education Finance* 2, no. 4 (Spring 1977), pp. 451–480.

41. Advisory Commission on Intergovernmental Relations, *The Value-added Tax and Alternative Sources of Federal Revenue* (Washington, DC: ACIR, 1973), p. 18.

42. Ibid.

43. Alan A. Tait, *Value Added Tax* (Maidenhead, England: McGraw-Hill (UK), 1972), pp. 92–93.

44. Ibid., p. 12.

45. Joseph A. Peckman, ed., *What Should Be Taxed: Income or Expenditure?* (Washington, DC: Brookings Institution, 1980), p. 336.

46. Musgrave and Musgrave, op. cit., p. 333.

47. Ibid., p. 334.

48. Kenneth E. Quindry and Niles Schoening, *State and Local Tax Performance 1978* (Atlanta, GA: Southern Regional Education Board, 1980), pp. 13–16.

49. *State Laws Enacted Pertaining to the Interests of the Elderly* (Washington, DC: American Association of Retired Persons, 1979), p. 52.

50. Advisory Commission on Intergovernmental Relations, *State Limitations on Local Taxes and Expenditures* (Washington, DC: U.S. Government Printing Office, 1977), p. 12.

51. California Legislature Conference, *Report on SB 154 Relative to Implementation of Proposition 13 and State Assistance to Local Governments,* June 23, 1978.

52. Congressional Budget Office, *Proposition 13: Its Impact on the Nation's Economy, Federal Revenues and Federal Expenditures* (Washington, DC: U.S. Government Printing Office, 1978), pp. 2–7.

53. McIntyre, et al., op. cit., p. 15.

54. Stephen E. Lile, Don Soule, and James Wead, "Limiting State Taxes and Expenditures," *State Government* (Autumn, 1975), (Lexington, KY: Council of State Governments), p. 205.

55. Abt Associates, op. cit., p. 47.

56. Ibid., p. 132.

57. Ibid., p. 171.

TAX REVENUES AND FAIRNESS OF BURDEN

INTRODUCTION

An analysis of the taxes collected by the different levels of government reveals to some extent the tax-levying capability of each level. Taxes collected by the three levels of government—federal, state, and local—are determined by the types of taxes that are legal or practicable for each to levy. It has been argued that the federal government has no financial ability other than that possessed by the states and that a state has no financial ability other than that possessed by its units of local government. This reasoning is based upon the assumption that the financial ability of the nation is the aggregate ability of the states and that the financial ability of a state is the aggregate ability of its subdivisions. This assumption may appear to be true theoretically, but it does not follow that the states taken together have the same capability to levy and collect taxes as the federal government. Nor does it follow that the subdivisions of a state together have the same capability to levy and collect taxes as the state.

SOURCES OF TAX REVENUES

The amount of taxes collected by the various levels of government in 1990 is shown in Table 6.1. In that year the federal government collected 55.8 percent of all taxes collected, state governments 26.5 percent, and local governments 17.7 percent. Note that this table excludes charges and miscellaneous revenue, utility revenue,

TABLE 6.1 Percentage of Tax Revenue Collected by Level of Government for Fiscal Year 1957, 1979, and 1990

LEVEL OF GOVERNMENT	1957	1979	1990
Federal	70.8%	60.8%	55.8%
State	14.7%	23.8%	26.5%
Local	14.7%	15.4%	17.7%

Source: United States Advisory Commission on Intergovernmental Relations, *Significant Features of Fiscal Federalism 1991*, vol. 2 (Washington, DC: ACIR, September, 1992), p. 124.

liquor store revenue, social security, retirement, and other insurance trust revenue.

The most noticeable feature of these data is the relative decline of the tax collections by the federal government and a corresponding increase in the percentage of taxes collected at the state and local levels. In 1957, combined state and local tax collections constituted 29.4 percent of all taxes and by 1990 this percentage had increased to 44.2 percent. These data may provide information regarding the reasons for the large federal budget deficit that is such a prominent concern in the United States today.

Types of Taxes Collected

The amount of money collected by each level of government—federal, state, and local—from each major tax is shown in Table 6.2, and the percentages are shown in Table 6.3. There are only four major types of tax—individual income, sales and gross receipts, corporation income, and property. These four types provide the vast majority of all tax revenue of all governments combined. Those seeking substantial revenue for the support of the public schools must find it in one or more of these four taxes.

But the different levels of government vary widely in the percentage of tax money derived from different types of taxation. Table 6.3 shows that in fiscal year 1990, the federal government obtained 88.64 percent of its revenue from individual and corporation income taxes, state governments obtained 39.22 percent of their tax revenue from those sources, and local governments obtained only 5.66. State governments obtained 48.94 percent of their revenue from sales and gross receipts taxes, the federal government 8.53 percent, and local governments 15.32 percent. On the other hand, the federal government received no revenue from property taxes and neither did the states, but local governments received 74.46 percent of their revenue from property taxes.

School districts rely almost exclusively on the property tax for local taxation as do local governments. The federal government and the state governments have access to many more types of tax than do local governments. School districts have the fewest taxation options of any division of government.

It also is important to consider the percentage of each major tax collected by different levels of government. Table 6.4 shows that the federal gov-

---

TABLE 6.2   Major Federal, State, and Local Tax Revenue by Source, 1990 (in millions)

TYPE OF TAX	FEDERAL	STATE	LOCAL	TOTAL
Property	—	—	$149,765	$149,765
Individual Income[a]	$466,884	$96,076	11,379	574,339
Corporation Tax	93,507	21,751	—	115,258
Sales and Gross Receipts[b]	53,970	147,069	30,815	231,854
Motor Vehicle and Licenses	—	10,675	—	10,675
Death and Gift	11,500	3,832	—	15,332
All Other	6,406	21,086	9,170	36,662
Total	$632,267	$300,489	$201,130	$1,133,885
Percent of Total	55.8	26.5	17.7	100.0

Source: United States Advisory Commission on Intergovernmental Relations, *Significant Features of Fiscal Federalism 1992*, vol. 2 (Washington, DC: ACIR, September, 1992), pp. 120–121.

[a]Excludes charges and miscellaneous revenue, utility revenue, liquor store revenue, social security, retirement, and other insurance trust revenue. Includes general and selective sales and gross receipts taxes and custom duties.

[b]Includes general and selective sales and gross receipts taxes and custom duties.

TABLE 6.3 Percentage of Tax Revenue Derived from Different Types of Taxes by Level of Government, 1990

TYPE OF TAX	FEDERAL	STATE	LOCAL	ALL
Property	—	—	74.46	13.20
Individual Income	73.84	31.98	5.66	50.66
Corporation Income	14.80	7.24	—	10.16
Sales and Gross Receipts	8.53	48.94	15.32	20.46
Motor Vehicle and Licenses	—	3.55	—	0.94
Death and Gift	1.82	1.27	—	1.35
All Other	1.01	7.02	4.56	3.23
Total	100.0	100.0	100.0	100.0

Source: United States Advisory Commission on Intergovernmental Relations, *Significant Features of Fiscal Federalism 1992*, vol. 2 (Washington, DC: ACIR, September, 1992), pp. 120–121.

ernment collects 81.30 percent of all individual income taxes, 81.13 of corporation income taxes, and 23.28 percent of all sales and excise taxes. The states collect 63.43 percent of all sales and gross receipts taxes, 16.72 percent of individual income taxes, and 18.87 percent of corporation income taxes. The local governments collect 100.00 percent of all property taxes. The federal government, then, has largely preempted the income tax field and is dipping heavily into sales and excise taxes. The heavy use by the federal government of three of the four major types of tax is causing state and local governments to increase demands that the federal government return more of its revenue to them either directly, by a tax-sharing plan, or by increased grants-in-aid.

Recent Trends in Types of Taxes Collected

Table 6.5 shows the percentage of tax revenue derived from different taxes by the various levels of government in 1979 and 1990. The revenue derived by the federal government from the individual income tax increased from 51.0 percent in 1957 to 68.3 percent in 1979 to 73.8 in 1990, and revenue derived from the corporation income tax declined from 30.3 percent of the total in 1957 to 20.6 percentage in 1979 to 14.8 percent in 1990.

TABLE 6.4 Percentage of Each Type of Tax Collected by Different Levels of Government, 1990

TYPE OF TAX	FEDERAL	STATE	LOCAL	TOTAL
Property	—	—	100.0	100.0
Individual Income	81.30	16.72	1.98	100.0
Corporation Income	81.13	18.87	—	100.0
Sales and Gross Receipts	23.28	63.43	13.29	100.0
Motor Vehicle and Licenses	—	100.0	—	100.0
Death and Gift	75.01	24.99	—	100.0
All Other	17.47	57.52	25.01	100.0

Source: United States Advisory Commission on Intergovernmental Relations, *Significant Features of Fiscal Federalism 1992*, vol. 2 (Washington, DC: ACIR, September, 1992), pp. 120–121.

TABLE 6.5   Trends in Percentage of Revenue Derived from Different Types of Taxes by Level of Government

TYPE OF TAX	1957 FEDERAL	STATE	LOCAL	1979 FEDERAL	STATE	LOCAL	1990 FEDERAL	STATE	LOCAL
Property	—	—	86.7	—	2.0	77.5	—	—	74.4
Individual Income	51.0	10.8	1.3	68.3	26.1	5.3	73.8	32.0	5.7
Corporation Income	30.3	6.8	—	20.6	9.7	—	14.8	7.2	—
Sales and Gross Receipts	15.9	58.0	7.2	8.4	51.0	13.1	8.5	48.9	15.3
Motor Vehicle and Licenses	—	9.4	—	—	4.1	0.5	—	3.6	—
Death and Gift	2.0	2.3	—	1.7	1.6	—	1.8	1.3	—
All Other	0.8	12.7	4.8	1.0	5.5	3.6	1.0	7.0	4.6
Total	100.0	100.0	100.0	100.0	100.0	100.0	100.0	100.0	100.0

Source: United States Advisory Commission on Intergovernmental Relations, *Significant Features of Fiscal Federalism 1992*, vol. 2 (Washington, DC: ACIR, September, 1992), pp. 120–121.

The percentage of revenue derived from other federal tax sources changed little.

A dramatic change between 1957 and 1990 occurred in the percentage of revenue derived by state governments from individual income taxes. The states obtained only 10.8 percent of their tax revenue from individual income taxes in 1957, but by 1990 the percentage had increased to 32.0 percent.

The percentage of revenue derived by local governments from different taxes underwent some change between 1957 and 1990. The search by local governments for new kinds of nonproperty taxes resulted in a decrease in percentage of property taxes from 86.7 in 1957 to 74.4 in 1990.

It also is informative to consider changes in the percentage of total tax collections all governments derived from different taxes. Table 6.6 shows that the percentage derived from property taxes declined from 12.6 percent in 1957 to 12.4 percent in 1979, but was back up to 13.2 percent in 1990. Prior to 1957, the percentage of total tax revenue derived from property taxes also declined. In 1942, for example, 21.8 percent of all tax revenue was derived from property taxes. Despite the fact that for fifty years the property tax has been condemned by many tax authorities

for being a regressive tax, it has shown remarkable ability to survive. Perhaps this has been due to the fact that central governments in general have been relatively insensitive to the needs of local governments. Since the needs of local governments have increased rapidly during the past decade, and since the property tax was the only major tax generally available to them that would produce the required revenue, they had no practicable alternative to increasing property taxes.

Recent Trends in Tax Collections by Level of Government

Tax collections for the years 1957, 1979, and 1990 are presented in Table 6.7 by level of government. This table shows that state and local taxes increased at a greater rate between 1957 and 1989 than did federal taxes. The federal government collected 70.8 percent of all tax revenue in 1957 and 55.8 percent in 1990. On the other hand, the percentage of all tax revenue collected by state governments increased from 14.7 percent to 26.5 percent and that by local governments increased from 14.5 percent to 17.7 percent. These data suggest that the federal government has been shifting the tax burden down-

TABLE 6.6 Trends in Tax Revenue for Each Type of Tax for All Governments (in millions)

TYPE OF TAX	1957		1979		1990	
	AMOUNT	% OF TOTAL	AMOUNT	% OF TOTAL	AMOUNT	% OF TOTAL
Property	$12,385	12.6	$64,944	12.4	$149,765	13.2
Individual Income	37,374	37.9	254,773	48.6	574,339	50.7
Corporation Income	22,151	22.4	77,805	14.8	115,258	10.2
Sales and Gross Receipts	20,594	20.9	100,962	19.3	231,854	20.5
Motor Vehicle and Licenses	1,368	1.4	5,539	1.0	10,675	0.9
Death and Gift	1,703	1.7	7,384	1.4	15,332	1.4
All Other	3,058	3.1	13,040	2.5	36,662	3.2
Total	$98,633	100.0	$524,447	100.0	$1,133,885	100.0

Source: United States Advisory Commission on Intergovernmental Relations, *Significant Features of Fiscal Federalism 1992*, vol. 2 (Washington, DC: ACIR, September, 1992), pp. 120–121.

ward to states and localities. Moreover, if we assume that federal activities have remained relatively the same or have expanded, it becomes obvious that the funds must be derived from deficit spending without corresponding revenues to offset them.

DECLINE OF FEDERAL TAX EFFORT FOR PUBLIC SCHOOLS

The predominance of the laissez-faire school of economic thought in the federal fiscal policy during the 1980s led to restraints on public school development in at least two ways. First, as federal tax rates were reduced on the more affluent and the supply of revenues became more constricted, less money was made available to fund federally created education programs. The failure of supply-side economic theory guaranteed a growing federal deficit making adequate funding of education at the federal level highly problematical. Second, an ideological battle was waged by the laissez-faire proponents maintaining that money devoted to the public schools would be wasted unless competition was introduced among all schools, public and private. A stalemate ensued in

TABLE 6.7 Trends in Tax Revenue by Level of Government (in millions)

LEVEL OF GOVERNMENT	1957		1979		1990	
	AMOUNT	% OF TOTAL	AMOUNT	% OF TOTAL	AMOUNT	% OF TOTAL
Federal	$69,816	70.8	$318,932	60.8	$632,267	55.8
State	14,531	14.7	124,907	23.8	300,488	26.5
Local	14,286	14.5	80,605	15.4	201,130	17.7
Total	$98,633	100.0	$524,444	100.0	$1,085,191	100.0

Source: United States Advisory Commission on Intergovernmental Relations, *Significant Features of Fiscal Federalism 1992*, vol. 2 (Washington, DC: ACIR, September, 1992), pp. 120–121.

which liberals opposed competition facilitated by vouchers and tuition tax credits for private schools and conservatives zealously pursued such programs as *quid pro quo* for any substantial increase in federal funding.

According to Friedman and the other laissez-faire economists, the great bulk of the families should finance the schooling of their own children and only children from needy families should be given governmental subsidies.[1] Reflecting the conservative economist's disenchantment with public schools as a noncompetitive and wasteful governmental enterprise, Friedman maintained that "the establishment of the school system in the United States as an island of socialism in a free market sea reflected . . . to a degree the ever present conflict of economic ideology between proponents of conservative and liberal economic systems."[2]

The result was that the federal executive branch, being of the laissez-faire school, exhibited very little commitment to funding public elementary and secondary education during the 1980s. A declining federal fiscal effort to support education was the manifestation of this ideological bent. Table 6.8 shows the relative decline in federal participation in the funding of elementary and secondary school systems between 1969–70 and 1993–94. The federal percentage of all elementary and secondary expenditures rose from 4.4 percent in 1959–60, prior to the enactment of the Elementary and Secondary Education Act of 1965, to 7.2 percent in

1969–70, to a peak of 9.2 percent in 1979–80. From that point onward the percentage rapidly declined as the conservative fiscal policies of the 1980s took hold of federal budget allocations and supply-side economics failed to produce the promised revenues.

FAIRNESS OF THE TAX SYSTEM

Whether a tax system is fair may be measured by the relative burdens borne by rich and poor. If the burden ultimately falls in greater percentage upon the poor, then the tax may be judged unfair. Some may argue that a proportional tax is fair and others may maintain that fairness is not achieved unless a tax is progressive, but most reasonable minded persons will agree that a regressive tax is unfair and is neither socially nor economically desirable. The concept of horizontal equity supports the argument that those in the same income groups should have the same percentage of tax burdens, equal treatment of equals. While vertical equity supports the conclusion that those in higher income brackets should pay a greater proportion of their income in taxes and that the poor should be taxed at a lower rate, fulfilling the standard of unequal treatment of unequals.

State Taxes

Various studies have attempted to show the actual state tax burdens that fall on persons in different income groups. One such study of state

TABLE 6.8   Trends in Sources of School Revenue by Level of Government

	FEDERAL	STATE	LOCAL
	Percent	*Percent*	*Percent*
1959–60	4.4	39.1	56.5
1969–70	7.2	40.9	51.8
1979–80	9.2	48.9	42.0
1989–90	6.3	48.1	45.6
1993–94	7.0	45.7	47.3

Source: National Education Association, *Estimates of School Statistics* (Washington, DC: NEA, various years).

taxes, completed by Lile and Philhours[3] in 1991, shows that all 50 state tax systems produce a combined tax burden from the three major taxes on personal income, retail sales, and property, that is roughly proportional. They found that families with adjusted gross incomes of $15,000 were taxed at 7.1 percent, $30,000 at 7.2 percent, $45,000 at 7.5 percent, $60,000 at 7.8 percent, and $90,000 at 7.6 percent. This study shows state systems in a more favorable light than some other similar analyses. One study conducted by Citizens for Tax Justice that is less than compli-

mentary shows that state tax systems, in totality, are highly inequitable (See Table 6.9). This report found that only four states, California, Delaware, Maine, and Vermont, place a tax burden on the richest families that is equivalent to or greater than that placed on middle-income families.[4] This analysis listed the "terrible ten" states with tax systems that are the most unfair—Nevada, Texas, Florida, Washington, South Dakota, Tennessee, Wyoming, New Hampshire, Pennsylvania, and Illinois. Of these, Washington taxes the poor at the highest rate of 17.4 percent

TABLE 6.9 Fairness of State and Local Taxes

STATE	LOW	MID	RICH	STATE	LOW	MID	RICH
Alabama	11.9	8.5	5.1	Nebraska	16.9	11.5	8.6
Alaska	5.3	3.1	2.5	Nevada	10.0	5.7	1.8
Arizona	14.3	9.6	7.6	New Hampshire	12.7	7.6	3.8
Arkansas	13.2	9.4	7.9	New Jersey	15.2	10.8	9.7
California	14.1	8.8	10.6	New Mexico	13.1	9.4	8.6
Colorado	11.0	9.3	6.4	New York	14.1	13.9	11.3
Connecticut	16.5	9.5	6.7	North Carolina	10.6	9.7	8.4
Delaware	7.4	7.0	8.4	North Dakota	10.3	8.5	6.3
Florida	13.8	7.6	2.7	Ohio	13.4	10.0	9.6
Georgia	13.0	10.1	7.5	Oklahoma	12.2	10.1	7.3
Hawaii	8.7	10.3	9.8	Oregon	9.8	10.5	9.9
Idaho	12.8	9.6	8.8	Pennsylvania	15.9	9.8	5.5
Illinois	16.5	10.8	6.0	Rhode Island	14.2	11.4	9.6
Indiana	4.8	9.9	6.5	South Carolina	10.5	8.8	7.8
Iowa	12.5	9.6	7.9	South Dakota	16.2	8.7	3.5
Kansas	13.2	9.7	6.8	Tennessee	15.2	7.7	3.6
Kentucky	12.5	10.0	8.0	Texas	17.1	8.4	3.1
Louisiana	14.1	9.6	6.5	Utah	13.7	11.2	8.2
Maine	12.4	9.4	10.2	Vermont	7.1	9.2	9.6
Maryland	8.0	10.9	8.1	Virginia	11.8	9.5	7.2
Massachusetts	13.6	11.3	8.9	Washington	17.4	9.5	3.4
Michigan	13.6	11.4	7.6	West Virginia	12.9	9.3	9.2
Minnesota	9.5	10.5	9.6	Wisconsin	12.3	9.3	9.2
Mississippi	12.9	8.6	8.7	Wyoming	9.0	5.3	2.4
Missouri	13.0	9.1	6.0	U.S.	13.8	10.0	7.6
Montana	7.1	7.4	7.0				

Source: Citizens for Tax Justice, April 1991, Washington, DC, as cited in *NEA Today, State Side,* September 1991, p. 8. Reprinted with permission.

Note: "Low" income indicates families in the bottom 20 percent of the income group, averaging $12,700 per year; "Mid" income indicates families in the middle 20 percent income group, averaging $39,100; and "Rich" indicates families in the top 1 percent income group, averaging $875,000 per year.

and Texas is second in imposing an unconscionably high burden on the poor, taxing those families with $27,000 annual income at 17.1 percent. These two states tax the rich at only 3.4 percent and 3.1 percent, respectively.[5]

This report identified "troubling" trends that find the states relying more and more on sales and excise taxes that are highly regressive in nature. In fact, it is observed that on the average this tax tends to be at least three times as burdensome on the middle-income family than on the rich family in the top 1 percent income bracket. In six states, Louisiana, New Mexico, Washington, Tennessee, West Virginia and South Dakota, the sales and excise taxes are so high that they consume over 10 percent of the total income of poor families.[6] As states rely less on the more progressive personal income taxes and more on sales and excise taxes the regressivity of the entire system is exacerbated (see Figure 6.1).

Federal Taxes

Federal revenues have by tradition and law been more dependent on income taxes than have state revenues. The adoption of the principle of equitable taxation, to tax the rich at a higher rate than the poor, was more clearly accepted as national policy after the early American experience with the industrial revolution, the era of the "robber barons," and the adoption of the Sixteenth Amendment in 1913 authorizing Congress to impose an income tax. This amendment was necessary to counter the U.S. Supreme Court's decision in *Pollock v. Farmer's Loan and Trust Company*[7] in 1895 in which Justice Field expounded the famous conservative credo that an income tax was in effect an "assault upon capital" and constituted a war of the "poor against the rich." By 1913, the disparity in wealth in the United States had become so pronounced that the 1873 observance of the Chief Justice of the Wisconsin Supreme Court, when he concluded that "the accumulation of individual wealth seems to be greater than it ever has been since the downfall of the Roman Empire . . . "[8], appeared to have finally come to reality.

Upon enactment, the federal income tax became the most lucrative vehicle for raising revenue and served the valuable purpose of redistribution of income. The progressivity of the federal personal income tax strengthened the social fabric and enhanced the economic productivity of the nation throughout the twentieth century. As shown in Table 6.1, by 1957 the federal personal income tax generated over one-half of all federal revenues and federal revenues constituted 70.6 percent of all taxes collected in the United States.[9] By 1979, however, the total revenue derived from the federal government had declined to 60.8 percent of all tax revenues, a percentage, as noted above, that in turn again declined to 56.76 percent by 1989. Thus, by the 1980s, the government revenues of the United States were less reliant on the progressive federal income tax than in the recent past. Unfortunately, in the 1980s "across the board tax cuts" in reality resulted in middle-income families paying relatively greater shares of the nation's financial burden and the richest families experienced the happy circumstance of having reduced taxation. A May 1991 report, issued by the Congressional Budget Office, found that

> The data show that all but the very richest and very poorest American families now pay a *higher* share of their incomes in overall federal taxes than they did prior to the so-called "supply-side tax cuts" enacted in 1978 and 1981.[10]

Throughout the first half of the 1980s, the taxes for low-income families actually increased, but 1986 corrections produced a slight and favorable reduction for the very poor earning $8,130 or less per year. The greatest benefits of the federal tax policies of the Reagan era benefitted those in the highest income classes. As Figure 6.2 indicates, those families with incomes of over $132,400 had an effective decrease in their taxes of 1.2 percent between 1977 and 1992 and those with incomes of $676,000 had an effective tax decrease of 12.3 percent. These benefits to the wealthy were gained as the lower-, middle-, and upper-middle class paid higher effective rates during the same 1977 to 1992 period.[11] In terms of actual dollars, this

The Most Fair State Tax System: Proportional or Mildly Progressive

Vermont Taxes in 1991

(as shares of income for families of four)

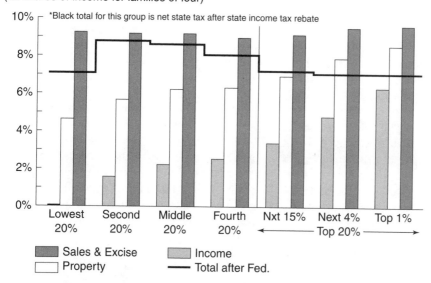

The Least Fair State Tax System: Regressive

Washington Taxes in 1991

(as shares of income for families of four)

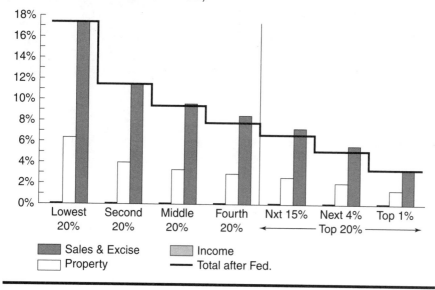

FIGURE 6.1

Source: Robert S. McIntyre, Douglas P. Kelly, Michael P. Ettlinger, and Elizabeth A. Fray, *A Far Cry From Fair, CTJ's Guide to State Tax Reform* (Washington, DC: Citizens for Tax Justice, 1991). Reprinted with permission.

Note: Actually Nevada, Texas, and Florida tax systems are overall more regressive than Washington, but Washington places the greatest burden on the poor.

decrease in taxes on the super-rich, the top 1 per-cent earning $676,000 per year, amounted to a tax cut of $83,457 for each super-rich family or an overall 30 percent reduction compared to what they would have owed by 1977 rates.[12]

These regressive tax changes did not make the impact of the federal income tax system regressive overall, but this enhancement of the coffers of the very rich during the decade of the 1980s did push the progressivity of the federal taxes toward proportional levels. The federal tax system in 1992 is less equitable than it was in 1977.[13]

To illustrate the effect of this change in tax policy, in 1977 the richest 1 percent of the families acquired 8.7 percent of all pre-tax income and by 1992, their pre-tax income had increased to 14.6 percent of total personal income. The average pre-tax income was $314,500 for each

family in the top 1 percent income group in 1977, and this amount had increased 115 per-cent, to $675,900 in 1992.[14] The after-tax income of this same group increased even more dramatically, 136 percent between 1977 and 1992. (See Figure 6.2.) Recent changes, in 1993, by the Congress acting on the proposals of the Clinton administration restored a degree of pro-gressivity to the tax system by raising the in-come tax rates on those earning more than $200,000 a year.

To illustrate the result of the supply-side tax shift in the tax policy of the Reagan-Bush years toward a more inequitable federal tax system, it can be shown that in 1992 the family-income group had $678 billion in income which was more than the entire middle-income group, 20 percent, which had only $664 billion. As the pie in Figure

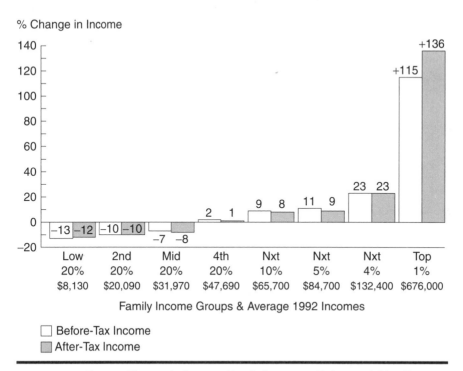

% Change in Income

FIGURE 6.2   Percent Change in Average Family Incomes, Before and After Taxes from 1977 to 1992 (in constant dollars)

Source: Robert S. McIntyre, Douglas P. Kelly, Michael P. Ettlinger, and Elizabeth A. Fray, *A Far Cry From Fair, CTJ's Guide to State Tax Reform* (Washington, DC: Citizens for Tax Justice, 1991). Reprinted with permission.

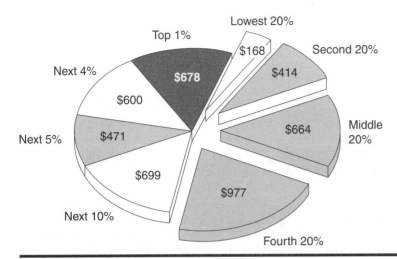

FIGURE 6.3   The Distribution of Pretax Income in 1992 by Family Income Group
(in billions of dollars)
Source: Robert S. McIntyre, *Inequality and the Federal Budget Deficit* (Washington, DC: Citizens
for Tax Justice, September 1991), p. 5. Reprinted with permission.

6.3 shows, the lowest 20 percent had $168 billion of the income in 1992. As can be noted, the top 20 percent of the nation's families had $2.4 trillion in income in 1992, a total greater than the remaining four-fifths of American families.[15]

The tax policies of both state and federal governments working in concert have failed to reduce the wide disparities in income among the income classes of the population, and during the 1980s the problems of disparate incomes, poverty, and disadvantage have become much worse. Increases in both the numbers and percentages of those in poverty and the intensifying of the problems of the disadvantaged evidence the adverse effects of the decline in the redistribution policies of the government. It also indicates the dramatic impact that tax policy can have on equality for all citizens.

**TAX REVENUES AND FAIRNESS
OF THE BURDEN**

Because public school finance operates within the broad spectrum of the nation's economy, the fortunes of educational investment are dependent on the particular political philosophy that governs at any given time. This chapter gives a brief explanation of the two major economic philosophies that have governed the availability of revenues for public schools and then gives specific data regarding the sources of taxation that produce public school revenues.

Within the relatively recent past we have observed polar extremes regarding tax funds for education ranging from the optimism for public investment in education exuded by the "Great Society" of Johnson, to a period of strong reaffirmation of public support for education in the Nixon and Carter years, to a time of intentional and enigmatic neglect in the Reagan and Bush era. Today, the Clinton administration appears to have embarked upon a new reliance on education as a cornerstone of an economic revival.

The events of the 1980s serve as a foil to the earlier era of the 1960s and to the recent turn after the 1992 election, and can probably best be explained in the contrasting forms of two competing economic philosophies, one emanating from the theories of Adam Smith and the other from John Maynard Keynes. Because neither of the theories' validity can be absolutely verified, governments move back and forth between the two seeking economic growth and prosperity.

Adam Smith, an absent-minded professor who once said, "I am a beau in nothing but my books," published in 1776 what is possibly the preeminent economics book of all time. The treatise entitled *The Wealth of Nations* distinguished itself from all previous works by its incisive analysis of the human psychological propensities that self-interest generated on economic systems. His recognition of the "mean and rapacious" ways of the manufacturing class was melded with the reality of the value of competition in creating a productive economy. His primary contribution though was his linking of the "natural history" of humandkind to economic freedom, providing a kind of quasi-moral foundation for the predatory self-interest of humans. It was this self-interest that drove the engines of a viable economic system.[16] He showed how the market was self-regulating and did not need, and indeed could not tolerate, the incursions of government regulation. The market, according to Smith, was its own guardian.[17] The Adam Smith school of thought predominated during the Reagan and Bush presidencies. Building on Smith's ideas, modern conservative economists led by Milton Friedman of the University of Chicago hold that "the market economy works—and that it works best when it is left alone."[18] In his best-known book, *A Monetary History of the United States*, Friedman alleged the failure of John Maynard Keynes's two primary tenets (1) that the market is unstable without the guiding hand of government, and (2) that monetary policy was tried and failed as a cure to the Great Depression.[19] Today the laissez-faire school of economic thought is sometimes loosely referred to as the Chicago school which propounds an unswerving faith in a hands-off policy of government and an abiding conviction that the "invisible hand" of the free competitive market is self-regulating, with a built-in gyroscope that will right itself when it becomes temporarily out of balance. Friedman further

strongly opposes virtually all social mechanisms, such as public schools, as deleterious to the market's invisible hand.

At the beginning of the Reagan administration, an obscure economic idea gained credibility that was to prove ultimately to be an exacerbation of the economic plight of the United States rather than a solution. The idea, an economic retrogression extending back to David Ricardo's 1817 treatise, *Principles of Political Economy and Taxation*, argued that the disincentive effects of high marginal tax rates were responsible for most of the nation's economic ills contributing to low saving, recession, stagnant productivity, and high inflation. It was theorized that if tax rates were lowered, especially on the rich, more productive capital would remain in the private sector the investment of which would produce a stronger overall economy. This stronger economy would, according to the adherents of this theory, produce a much expanded tax base from which lower tax rates would produce greater revenues. Thus proponents contented that by lowering tax rates, governmental revenues would increase. With these greater revenues the nation could balance budget deficits that had begun to develop in earnest in 1980.

The thought of lowering taxes and thereby stimulating the economy was not new to economic dogma, but what was new was the expansion of that theme to the extreme that by solely lowering tax rates and nothing else the economy would blossom forth with such strength and grandeur that the massive budget deficit would be eliminated. This was called supply-side economics. It has always been an article of certitude of the traditional laissez-faire philosophy that the lower the taxes the better, and that any increase in taxes is undesirable from an economic growth perspective.[20] The theory goes that as taxation increases as an instrument of egalitarian governmental policies, the productivity of the economy will inevitably decline. Of course because most citizens feel that they are overtaxed, laissez-faire has the salutary effect of having a credible economic theory to support personal avarice. In his famous treatise on taxation, Ricardo warned that an increase in taxes will ultimately harm a nation's productive capacity. He maintained that, "there are no taxes which have not a tendency to lessen the power to accumulate"[21] wealth and income.

Box 6.1 _____

The Supply-Side Experiment

One of the puzzles about the supply-side revolution is how an obscure idea, which received virtually no support from empirical studies or from mainstream economists, could have achieved such legislative success in a few months. This question is addressed by David Stockman, who was an architect of supply-side policies when he served as director of the Reagan Office of Management and Budget from 1981 to 1984. This is how Stockman describes President Reagan's conversion to the Laffer curve [the following quotation is from David Stockman, _The Triumph of Politics_ (New York, Avon: 1987)]:

> In January 1980, Governor Reagan's campaign managers had sent him to school for a few days to get brushed up on the national issues. There, Jack Kemp, Art Laffer, and Jude Wanniski thoroughly hosed him down with supply-side doctrine.
>
> They told him about the "Laffer curve." It set off a symphony in his ears. He knew instantly that it was true and would never doubt it a moment thereafter.
>
> He had once been on the Laffer curve himself, "I came into the Big Money making pictures during World War II," he would always say. At that time the wartime income surtax hit 90 percent.
>
> "You could only make four pictures and then you were in the top bracket," he would continue. "So we all quit working after four pictures and went off to the country."
>
> High tax rates caused less work. Low tax rates caused more. His experience proved it.

Source: William D. Nordhaus and Paul A. Samuelson, _Economics_, 13th ed. (New York: McGraw-Hill, Inc., 1989), p. 796n.

It has been an implicit tenet of this school that greater economic productivity cannot emanate from public investment. In fact, it is this school of thought that believes that investment and public expenditure are an economic contradiction, that a public expenditure cannot be an investment. Thus, spending for education is not a public investment, but rather a net loss to economic strength generated by the private sector.

This conservative economic philosophy, of course, flies in the face of facts that we know about public investment in human capital through universal education, and it is well documented that economic benefits return to both individuals and society. Nevertheless, until 1993, the federal government followed a neo-Ricardian rationale in its public policy determinations by lowering the relative federal taxation and reducing investment in education. "The Reagan program that eventually passed the Congress increased the return on savings and investment—on corporate profits, on high incomes, on capital gains, and on income set aside as savings."[22] Such tax features all favor the most affluent in society. The faith of the supply-siders that by cutting taxes on the rich all would benefit—that from the largesse of the rich, benefits would "trickle down" to the less fortunate as the entire national economy boomed, of course did not materialize. The federal deficit exploded and the United States economy, relative to other advanced countries of the world, retrogressed at an alarming rate.

In 1993 the short-sightedness of supply-side economics has become painfully apparent. Instead of achieving the Nirvana of productivity and growth promised by supply-side economics, the standard of living in the United States has steadily fallen relative to other industrialized countries. The combined economic force of the European Union and Japan coupled with the internal decline in productive public investment is manifested in poorer living conditions of all upper-middle, middle, and lower income Americans.

Today the citizens of the United States pay among the lowest tax rates of any major industri-

Box 6.2

Investment in Education

Many Americans tend to view all government expenditures, including those on health and education, as forms of collective consumption that periodically must be reduced in order to free resources for productive investment. We fail to appreciate that sums spent by government on health and education are investment in America's future productivity, no less important to that future than private investments. The government deficits that result from productive social investments should cause us no more concern than the debt that private businesses incur in order to invest in productive assets.

Source: Robert B. Reich, *The Next American Frontier* (New York: Times Books, 1983), p. 233.

alized country.[23] In 1993 Congress, acting on the Clinton administration's budget, raised the top rate to 39 percent. The top marginal income tax in several other advanced countries are shown in Table 6.10. The low federal tax rate in the United States is reflective of relatively low taxes that taxpayers pay at the federal, state, and local levels in the United States. When the combined effects of all taxes at all three levels of government

TABLE 6.10   Top Tax Rates in Major Countries

COUNTRY	PERCENT
Netherlands	70
France	57
Germany	53
Japan	50
Sweden	42
Britain	40
United States	31*
Canada	29

Source: Paul A. Samuelson and William D. Nordhaus, *Economics*, 14th ed. (New York: McGraw-Hill, 1992), p. 327.

*Raised by Congress in 1993 to 39.6% for taxable income over $250,000.

are taken into account and expressed as a percentage of the gross domestic product (GDP), compared to the other major developed countries of the world, the tax rate generated by the United States is near the bottom. Table 6.11 show that United States trails all developed countries with the exception of Turkey.

These data have led economists to the Organization for Economic Cooperation and Development (OECD) in Paris to conclude that the United States budget deficit is largely attributable to the simple fact that Americans have been unwilling to tax themselves sufficiently to fund their expensive budgetary appetites.[24] Of course, as we have observed elsewhere, the federal budget deficit cannot be attributed to elementary and secondary education expenditures as tax effort for this purpose steadily fell during the decade of the 1980s.

The Neo-Keynesians.   The failure and discrediting of the supply-siders' theory of economics had a very real effect on the American people in the election of Bill Clinton as president in 1992. Supply-side economics was repudiated by the emergence of a controlled revival of the John Maynard Keynes philosophy of economics that calls for "the deliberate management of expenditures and taxes for economic support or restraint" of the economy.[25] Keynes, in his seminal work of 1936 entitled *The General Theory of Employment, Interest and Money*, argued that market forces were insufficient acting alone to maintain a viable economy. Heilbroner and Thurow have explained Keynes's position very simply, saying, "The revolutionary import of Keynes's theory was that there was no self-correcting property in the market system to keep capitalization growing."[26]

Regarding Keynes's contribution, the Nobel Prize laureate, Paul A. Samuelson of MIT observed in 1992:

Thanks to Keynes and his modern successors, we know that in its choice of macroeconomic policies—those affecting the money supply, taxes, or

TABLE 6.11   Taxes as a Percentage of Gross Domestic Product

Sweden	56.1%	Ireland	37.6%
Denmark	49.9%	United Kingdom	36.5%
Netherlands	46.0%	Canada	35.3%
Norway	45.5%	Portugal	35.1%
Belgium	44.3%	Spain	34.4%
France	43.8%	Iceland	33.8%
Luxembourg	42.4%	Greece	33.2%
Austria	41.0%	Switzerland	31.8%
New Zealand	39.4%	Japan	30.6%
Germany	38.1%	Australia	30.1%
Finland	38.1%	United States	30.1%
Italy	37.8%	Turkey	29.0%

Source: OECD, as cited in *US News and World Report*, "Basic data: Organization for Economic Cooperation and Development," (December 7, 1992), p. 16. Reprinted with permission.

Note: Figures are 1989 data.

government spending—a nation can speed or slow its economic growth, ignite a rapid inflation or slow price increases, produce a trade deficit or generate a trade surplus.[27]

The revival and modern interpretation of the Keynes school of thought has been best enunciated by Robert Reich, the Clinton administration's Secretary of Labor. In his book, *The Work of Nations*, Reich maintained that government has a clear role in the redistribution of wealth through taxation to offset the grave disadvantages of poverty in America, as well as appropriate public expenditure for enterprises that are investments, yield economic returns, and thereby stimulate the economy. Among the areas of productive investment cited by Reich, education and training was high on the list. Reich concluded that "a far greater number of Americans would need a solid grounding in mathematics, basic science, and reading and communication skills."[28] "Integrating the American work force into the new world economy turns out to rest heavily on education and training, as well as nutrition and health care sufficient to allow such learning to occur."[29] In addition, Reich observed that the supply-siders of the 1980s who sought new prosperity by lowering federal taxes on the more affluent did not improve the economy appreciably. In that era, profit-seekers invested in

nonproductive enterprises such as business takeovers while at the same time allowing the nation's productive investments in education, training, and infrastructure to decline. This pattern of profit-taking did not improve the economy and in fact did damage, to the nation's productive capacity.[30]

Thus the neo-Keynesian philosophy which may reemerge in the 1990s maintains that there is no sharp distinction between public and private sectors in the United States or any other advanced industrial economy.[31] Today we live in a complex system of the modern state that intertwines public policies and private decisions so completely that simplistic notions such as that advanced by supply-side economics leave many factors out of the equation. "America's free market has been supplanted by interlocking networks of subsidiaries, conglomerate headquarters, and financial institutions, all of which are dependent upon governmental restraint, subsidy and support."[32] "Even major industry in America is deeply involved with and dependent on government,"[33] by virtue of a hundred different attachments, form tariffs, quotas, export agreements, and bailouts. Thus, it is a complete fallacy to pretend that the private sector can stand alone and prosper if unimpeded by government. It is further hypocrisy for the private sector to maintain that it is not highly dependent on the social and economic infrastructure that government facilitates, the most important of which is education of the people.

SUMMARY AND CONCLUSIONS

An overview of the percentage of all taxes collected by all levels of government shows that the federal government collects more than the other two governmental levels combined. However, since 1951 the federal government percentage has declined from nearly 71 percent to less than 57 percent.

The four major taxes, property, individual income, corporation income, and sales and gas receipts, generate approximately 95 percent of all taxes collected by the three governmental levels.

The federal government's primary taxes, individual and corporation income, have shown dramatic shifts in recent years. The shift has placed an additional burden on individual income and a concomitant reduction on corporation income.

During the 1980s, the effort made by the federal government to support public elementary and secondary education registered a startling decline, reflecting the ideology of the central government at that time.

The fairness of the tax burden depends largely on where a person lives in the United States. Ten states have been labelled the most unfair: Nevada, Texas, Florida, Washington, South Dakota, Tennessee, Wyoming, New Hampshire, Pennsylvania, and Illinois. There is considerable evidence to suggest that, in general, states are increasing their reliance on sales and excise taxes, indicating that tax structures are becoming more regressive.

The across-the-board tax cuts of the federal government in the early 1980s resulted in tax reductions for the very wealthy and very poor, and significant increases for all other income groups.

Conservative economists lately labelled as supply-siders directly contradicts human capital research and its documented economic returns to both the individual and society. The short-sightedness of supply-side economics has become painfully apparent. The tax bill of the average American is among the lowest in the world, but the nation's budget deficit and national debt has grown while our investment in human capital has declined.

A revival of the neo-Keynesian economic philosophy may emerge during the 1990s. This philosophy complemented by human capital investment should lead to a more productive and dynamic economy.

KEY TERMS

Source by taxes	Sales and gross receipts taxes	Tax burden
Property taxes	Laissez-faire	Supply-side economics
Individual income taxes	Tax fairness	Neo-Keynesian economics

ENDNOTES

1. Milton Friedman, *Capitalism and Freedom* (Chicago: The University of Chicago Press, 1962), p. 87.
2. Milton and Rose Friedman, *Free To Choose* (New York: Harcourt Brace Jovanovich, 1980), p. 154.
3. Stephen E. Lile and Joel E. Philhours, *Interstate Comparisons of Family Tax Burdens for 1990* (Bowling Green, KY: Institute for Economic Development and Public School, Western Kentucky University, 1991).
4. Robert S. McIntyre, Douglas P. Kelly, Michael P. Ettlinger, and Elizabeth A. Fray, *A Far Cry From Fair, CTJ's Guide to State Tax Reform* (Washington, DC: Citizens for Tax Justice, 1991), p. 3.
5. Ibid.
6. Ibid., p. 11.

7. 158 U.S. 601 (1895).

8. Samuel Eliot Morison and Henry Steele Commoger, *The Growth of the American Republic*, vol. 2 (New York: Oxford University Press, 1962), p. 448.

9. Roe L. Johns and Edgar L. Morphet, *Financing the Public Schools* (Englewood Cliffs, NJ: Prentice-Hall 1960), p. 110.

10. House Committee on Ways and Means, *1991 Green Book* (Washington, DC, U.S. Government Printing Office, May 1991).

11. Robert S. McIntyre, *Inequality and the Federal Budget Deficit* (Washington, DC, Citizens for Tax Justice, September 1991), p. 5.

12. Ibid., p. 6.

13. Ibid.

14. Ibid.

15. Ibid., p. 9.

16. Robert L. Heilbroner and Lester C. Thurow, *Economics Explained* (New York: Simon & Schuster, 1987), pp. 28–29.

17. Ibid., p. 28.

18. Edwin G. Dolan, *Economics,* 4th ed. (Chicago: The Dryden Press, 1986), p. 339.

19. Ibid.

20. Robert Kuttner, *The Economics Illusion: False Choices Between Prosperity and Social Justice* (Philadelphia, PA: University of Pennsylvania Press, 1991), p. 187.

21. David Ricardo, *The Principles of Political Economy and Taxation* (Guilford, England: J.M. Dent & Sons, 1973).

22. Kuttner, op. cit., pp. 57–58.

23. Paul A. Samuelson and William D. Nordhaus, *Economics*, 14th ed. (New York: McGraw-Hill, 1992), p. 327.

24. *U.S. News and World Report (*December 7, 1992), p. 16.

25. John Kenneth Galbraith, *The Culture of Contentment* (Boston: Houghton Mifflin, 1992), p. 87.

26. Robert L. Heilbroner and Lester C. Thurow, *Economics Explained* (New York: Simon & Schuster, 1987), p. 40.

27. Paul A. Samuelson & William D. Nordhaus, *Economics*, 14th ed. (New York: McGraw-Hill, 1992), p. 397.

28. Robert B. Reich, *The Work of Nations* (New York: Alfred A. Knopf, 1991), p. 249.

29. Ibid.

30. Ibid., p. 261.

31. Robert B. Reich, *The Next American Frontier* (New York: Times Books, Inc., 1983), p. 233.

32. Ibid., p. 232.

33. Ibid., p. 233.

INEQUALITY IN EDUCATIONAL OPPORTUNITY

INTRODUCTION

Practically every U.S. citizen believes in equality of opportunity. However, practical application is a different matter. Vigorous and emotionally charged arguments occur periodically in every community, in every state legislature, and in Congress concerning the desirability of taking additional steps to implement this concept.

Equality of educational opportunity does not mean that every student should have the same program of education. Nor, as the courts have emphasized, does it mean that all students must have the same amount of money expended on them. Instead it means that every person should have the kind of quality education that will best meet his or her needs as an individual and as a member of society. There should be no controversy about implementing a concept such as this in a democracy, yet there frequently is. Apparently it is because many people are complacent about what has been accomplished and are not willing to recognize the serious problems that still exist.

In the future, every citizen must face these problems more realistically than they have in the past. Many studies have shown, and numerous authorities have commented on, the tragedy inherent in wasted human and natural resources. Undoubtedly, this nation has been seriously handicapped by this neglect and it should not continue.

INEQUALITIES IN OPPORTUNITY

It seems impossible to obtain equality of educational opportunity under the present conditions in most areas of the world. However, considerable progress has apparently been made in arousing an awareness and desire for equality. Compared to a generation ago, a larger proportion of the people of the world now realize the importance of at least some education for all. An increasing number of individuals are demanding a fuller life than mere survival. Many have begun to learn that in any nation human beings need not be handicapped by diseases that can be prevented or cured, by malnutrition, by poverty, by inadequate education, or by exploitation. Most people have begun to recognize that education can and should be the key that may make available to them, their children, and their neighbors the better things life has to offer. However, the task of educating people so that each person may make a constructive contribution to society has become vastly larger, more challenging, and much more complex than it was a few years ago. There is more to learn, a greater need for learning, and a greater cost as well.

THE MORALITY OF EQUALITY

Problems of inequality will always be a political question of paramount importance to states and nations. How much of the wealth is to be shared and how much is to be held aside by individuals for their own use is of profound importance to all societies. The issue though is not merely theoretical or philosophical, but is one of the most persistent and pervasive moral questions with which a state or nation must wrestle.

Rousseau best and most succinctly captured the essence of inequality and its origins in his famous first line of *A Discourse on the Origin of Inequality*: "The first man who, having enclosed a piece of ground, bethought himself of saying 'This is mine,' and found people simple enough to believe him, was the real founder of civil society."[1] From this beginning inequality proceeded and has been justified in various ways, by both individual acquiescence and laws of civil society. The economic interests encompassing property and possessions created the conditions of inequality and still persist today. In the vein of Rousseau's *Discourse*, Niebuhr observed that the inequality of privilege that we experience in our society today is due chiefly to disproportion of power, and "the power which creates privilege need not be economic but usually is."[2] As this economic and propertied power influences government, the conditions of inequality have become exacerbated and woven into the fabric of the social, economic, and political systems.

Self-Evident Truth

The concept of equality as a basic tenet of human interaction found little basis in political reality until the philosophers of the new American republic accorded it the status of a "self-evident truth." It was not that the idea was not known, it had been discussed by Aristotle and the Enlightenment philosophers; but any modern notion of practicality or applicability had not been advanced to the level of governmental consideration until the Declaration of Independence, the American Revolution, and later the French Revolution.

Commager, in his classic work *The Empire of Reason*, discusses "how Europe imagined and America realized the Enlightenment,"[3] and he explains how governmental leaders, statesmen, bishops, judges, generals, and admirals in the old world were chosen from the upper one-tenth of the population, a social and economic elite, on the basis of birth, wealth, or religion.[4] The lower classes of Europeans dreamed of rectifying this system of privilege, but only in America was that dream to come to fruition. It was such antecedents of European inequality that caused Jefferson to so stoutly argue for universal public

---

Box 7.1 _____

Equality in America

America differed from Europe: Differences of wealth and rank and social style it did indeed have—but these were not built on laws of privilege. No one claimed that colonial society was composed, like that of Europe, of different 'estates' or upon legally implanted hierarchy of rights. In America, as John Adams remarked, there was 'but one order.'

Source: J. R. Pole, *The Pursuit of Equality in American History* (Berkeley: University of California Press, 1978), p. 36.

education. Jefferson maintained that through education, those individuals possessing talent and merit, not those of birth and social advantage, could rise to govern the new republic. Jefferson most directly related the ideal of equality to the desirability of public education in his education plan for Virginia in 1779 in which he proposed that "By that part of our plan which prescribes the selection of youths of genius from among the classes of poor, we hope to avail the State of those talents which Nature has sown as liberally among the poor as among the rich, but which perish without use."[5]

Public Education: The Bosom of Equality

Jefferson's ideas may have been partially formed by his reading of Rousseau whose 1758 proposal for public education, to bring up children in the "bosom of equality," most directly related the importance of education and equality to a viable civil society.[6] According to Pole, prior to the Declaration in 1776,

> Equality was an intuition rather than a doctrine; and prior to the contributions of the American founders the doctrine of equality had no comparable suggestions to offer to such questions as how civil society was to meet the needs of supply and demand, provide military defence, or organize systems of administration and justice. If ideas of equality were to survive, their proponents had the task of convincing the rest of the world that they were compatible with effective economic and political institutions.[7]

Helping One's Self

Pole also observes that the idea that civil society and government could operate on a basic standard of equality has never been fully accepted in any age. In fact, the political events of the 1980s in the United States and Britain confirm the extent of philosophical opposition to the concept of equality. The laissez-faire school of economic thought that pervaded the governmental policies of the Reagan–Bush and Thatcher years gave

---

DEFINITION

Laissez-faire ("Leave us alone").   The doctrine that government should interfere as little as possible in economic activity and leave decisions to the workings of the market place.

---

scant credence to the importance of equality as a necessary cornerstone of good government.[8] This attitude welded into ideology, coupled with the Soviet Union's demise and economic debacle emanating from its 75-year romance with an incomprehensible combination of communism and totalitarianism, led many to draw the erroneous and often self-serving conclusion that the pursuit of equality was an inappropriate and ultimately impossible goal of U.S. governmental policy.

Actually, few acknowledge that equality and liberty must be delicately balanced in such a way that government fosters equality but does not dampen the competitive spirit of individuals. Equality and economic freedom are ultimately intermingled and highly interdependent. The role of the state in fostering care, protection, and equality as balanced against individual freedom and liberty forms the primary ground on which political philosophy is argued and tested at the polls, in the legislatures, and in the courts of the nation.

Few can argue against man's innate propensities to help himself in preference to others. "What man," said Helvetius, ". . . if with a scrupulous attention he searches all the recesses of his soul, will not perceive that his virtues and vices are wholly owing to different modifications of personal interests?"[9] This natural tendency to self-interest was recognized by Bentham who late in life, after earlier optimism that a broad social interest would prevail, concluded that, "it is the principle of self-preference. Man, from the very constitution of his nature, prefers his own happiness to that of all other sentient beings put together."[10]

Box 7.2 _____

Political Democracy and Market Capitalism

Political Democracy and market capitalism exist in an uneasy marriage. The democratic state proclaims equality. The market generates inequality. The ideological champions of the market *celebrate* inequality. In the *civic realm*, the first democratic freedom is citizenship—membership in a political community, which implies security and an equal voice in governance. In the *market realm*, the first freedom is freedom of exchange—the liberty to achieve personal economic success or failure. Absolute freedom of exchange thus creates extremes of social inequality. By market standards, inequality is not a regrettable necessity, but a virtue. In theory, the dynamism of the market and its unequal outcomes are logically inseparable. And the dynamism supposedly makes up for the social imbalance.

The conflict between polity and market is most acute with respect to the distribution of wealth and income. In a democracy, the rights of citizenship are supposed to be equally distributed and broadly diffused. They necessarily exist in a realm beyond the reach of personal economic differences. But the gross inequality generated by the market, at some point, compromises the ideal of political equality; for citizens cannot enjoy an equal political voice when they live at vastly different standards of material security. At some point unequal wealth purchases unequal influence. (emphasis added)

Source: Robert Kuttner, *The Economic Illusion, False Choices Between Prosperity and Social Justice* (Philadelphia: University of Pennsylvania Press, 1984), pp. 10–11.

DEFINITION

The Invisible Hand. Adam Smith's historic reference to the innate guiding force of man's self-interest that drives economic development. The concept introduced by Adam Smith in *The Wealth of Nations* in 1776 described the paradox that society is made better off economically if government does not interfere with the private pursuit of self-interest because by each person pursuing his own interest the good of all society is enhanced. The whole process is guided by a benevolent invisible hand.

The Invisible Hand

Adam Smith described this self-interest as the "invisible hand" that advanced commerce, economic growth, and man's general betterment. It was Smith's view that an unimpeded pursuit of self-interest would help society, generally. "By pursuing his own interest he frequently promotes that of the society more effectually than when he really intends to promote it. I have never known much good done by those who affected to trade for the public good. It is an affectation."[11]

Smith's great thesis provided a salve and justification for those who wanted to help only themselves, but felt they needed some moral justification. To learn that "in pursuing his own interest, the individual pursues that of the community, and in promoting the interest of the community he promotes his own"[12] was a philosophy that led to the altogether satisfying conclusion that we can, by pursuing our own predatory individual self-interest incidently and, indeed inadvertently, promote the general interests of society.

Harmony of Interests

A "harmony of interests" was thus produced that strengthened all, yet no one needed to be particularly and directly concerned with the common good or the good of the whole. It was contribution enough to be concerned with one's self alone.

By this rationale proponents of unfettered laissez-faire economics claim that their policies of self-interest will ultimately lead to greater equality, as the benefits "trickle down" to the less able. Kuttner, wryly commenting on this conservative economic justification for the lack of governmental attention to inequalities in society, observed: "Thus do the defenders of inequality seek legitimacy for their approach by invoking the egalitarian ideal." Sociologist Philip Green terms this logical twist "the homage that vice self-confidently pays to virtue."[13]

Social Darwinism

This philosophical justification of inequality, advancement of self-interest, naturally found reinforcement in Darwin's *The Origin of Species*, for after Darwin the stronger and more privileged could justify their advantages as predicated on the biological law of nature, the "perpetual struggle for life and the elimination of the unfit."[14] The struggle for existence among organisms leads to a strengthened species. Social organisms that gained strength and trod down the weak were justified in this biological context. This philosophy, of course, had a most attractive and natural appeal to nations that sought hegemony over their less powerful neighbors. At the turn of the century Social Darwinism provided a satisfying justification for European control and colonization of Africa and Asia. "The harmony of interests was established through the sacrifice of 'unfit' Africans and Asians."[15] It later provided much of the philosophical justification for the aggressions that caused the two World Wars.

The rationale was conveniently clear that inequality was a fact of life or even a plan of nature and if it was *ipso facto* natural then it was morally justifiable. Accordingly, not only was inequality justified it was essential if stronger human beings, social systems, and nations were to progress and advance. "The doctrine of progress through elimination of unfit nations seemed a fair corollary of the doctrine of progress through the elimination of unfit individuals."[16]

It is, of course, this kind of reasoning that we too often discover is used to justify inequality of educational opportunity between rich and poor nations, rich and poor states, and rich and poor school districts. Not to mention, of course, that this reasoning also provides the implicit justification for many private schools. Yet even today a strong consciousness of equality lies at the heart of many of our public policy considerations, though the arguments are replayed with each generation.

Moral Man

Several contemporary moral and legal philosophers give cogent arguments against various forms of inequality. It is Niebuhr's thesis that man is basically and innately moral, but his actions are corrupted by society. Niebuhr in his *Moral Man and Immoral Society*[17] observed the fallacies of the many justifications for inequalities by the privileged in society and he identified the "specious proofs" that they used to justify their advantaged positions. Most prominent among the justifications for inequality is faulting of the victim. This has been practiced in different ways, but usually culminates in a rationale that attempts to give moral superiority to the leisured classes and philosophical justification for disparities in opportunity. Thus, the moral justification for inequality may be found in the assertion that advantage is desirable because it emanates from thrift and good habits. It is said that the rich are virtuous because they are diligent and frugal, while the disadvantaged are deserving of their plight because they are lazy and improvident.[18] Niebuhr cites a typical puritanical justification for inequality espoused by Timothy Dwight, president of Yale and a champion and leader of early New England conservatives. Dwight said that the poor and underprivileged had caused their own misfortune because they are ". . . too idle, too talkative, too passionate, to prodigal, and too shiftless to acquire either property or character."[19]

It takes an innate counterbalance of human character to prevent a thesis such as Dwight's to prevail. Equality has its own visceral appeal to most people. The general goal of equality is that each person should have no less than an equal share of the community's resources.[20] Equality of treatment is *prima facie*[21] just as Rawls observes that, "injustice, then, is simply inequalities that are not to the benefit of all."[22] Inequality is only morally justified if it benefits all or if the distribution is made in favor of the least advantaged.[23]

The theory of equality of treatment by government is based on the social contract theories of Plato, Hobbes, and Rousseau. Plato's contract of citizenship between the citizen and the state calls implicitly for equal treatment. Where there are both obligations and responsibilities as well as benefits and detriments under a social contract, the citizen does not contemplate receiving less or inferior treatment from the state; and, in theory, one who does not receive a fair share is justified in withdrawing from the social contract.[24] Both Hobbes and Rousseau recognized this contract, but they differed as to whether the citizen can withdraw if maltreated. Hobbes believed that the citizen is stuck with the relationship and Rousseau argued that everyone had a right to withdraw, even by revolution if necessary.

Of Cakes and Shares

The basic premise of egalitarian philosophy is that similar cases should be accorded similar treatment.[25] Persons should be treated in a uniform way unless there is sufficient reason not to do so.[26] Departure from equality requires reasons and justification. Isaiah Berlin explains it simplest and best:

> A society in which every member holds an equal quantity of property needs no justification; only a society in which property is unequal needs it.[27]

One can see how readily this aphorism applies to public school finance and most notably to the school finance litigation discussed earlier. Legislatures would not be challenged and required to justify allocation of state and local revenues among school districts if fund distributions were equal. Explanation is only required when funds are distributed unequally. What is the reason for the state giving twice as much money to some children for their education as for others?

Box 7.3 _____

Of Cakes and Shares

If I have a cake and there are ten persons among whom I wish to divide it, then if I give exactly one tenth to each, this will not, at any rate automatically, call for justification; whereas if I depart from this principle of equal division I am expected to produce a special reason.

Source: Isaiah Berlin, "Equality," _Concepts and Categories_ (New York: Viking Press, 1978), p. 84.

Equal Shares and Fair Shares

Equal shares may not always be fair shares. Justice may not be done by giving everyone equal amounts. Equity is roughly equivalent to justice, but equality may not necessarily result in equity.[28]

Strict equality requires that equals be treated as equals, but equity, fairness, or justice may require that unequals be treated as unequals. Raphael explains that " 'fair shares' depend on merit, need, and capacity, which of course are not equally distributed."[29] This view emanates originally from Aristotle who pointed out that equity is a matter of proportionate distribution and is not confined to strict equality.[30] "Equity allows, or rather requires, discrimination by reference to morally relevant differences, and forbids discrimination in the absence of such difference."[31] "The rule is to treat like cases alike and unlike cases differently."[32] It is fair to discriminate in favor of the needy, but unfair and inequitable to discriminate in favor of the privileged and advantaged.

Relevant Differences

Only relevant differences should be taken into account in departure from strict equality. Where legislative allocations of funds for public schools often go astray is in providing greater resources for irrelevant differences. Differences in allocations among children based on their economic, social, or family conditions may be relevant to good education. Similarly, natural learning capacities or physical handicaps may be relevant criteria for departure from mathematical equality in the distribution of resources. Property wealth, however, is not relevant to educational needs. The State cannot remain within the bounds of equity and justice while providing more funding to favored children in more affluent school districts.

What is relevant and legitimate becomes the primary issue. Can we give more to the most advantaged, to the intellectually gifted? The school finance cases require that the legislature give reasons as to relevancy. The danger, of course, lies in the justifications of relevancy by those who seek to retain their advantages. As noted earlier, Niebuhr has observed that humankind is very adept in conjuring justifications for inequality and generating specious proofs to justify social and economic privilege. Representatives and residents of affluent communities and school districts have proven both adept and creative in justifying their financial preeminence. Niebuhr says that

> man will always be imaginative enough to enlarge his needs beyond minimum requirements and selfish enough to feel the pressure of his needs more than the needs of others.[33]

Examples of imaginative defenses by affluent school districts in attempting to give relevancy to irrelevant factors supporting discrimination, and to justify and explain their privilege in having greater financial resources include: 1) the sanctity of insularity; we have a separate community and it is our property wealth that produces the advantage and we get to keep it; 2) it is not a state system, it is a local one; 3) the children in rich districts have higher aspirations and thus should have a more enriched curriculum; 4) the costs of living are greater in our district, therefore we need more money than others; 5) ours should be a lighthouse district that will illuminate the way for the others to follow; 6) local control is our right and state efforts toward equality will erode that right; and 7) the poor dis-

tricts in which others live are less efficient and will merely waste additional resources. The inventiveness and ingenuity of those justifying advantage is almost endless.

But possibly the most common response of the privileged is to blame the victim and argue that those in poor school districts do not try hard enough, have little regard for education, and put forth lower tax effort to support their own schools than do persons from the more affluent school districts. Ryan has said that "we cannot comfortably believe that *we* are the cause of that which is problematic to us; therefore, we are almost compelled to believe that *they*—the problematic ones—are the cause" of the problem.[34] Educationally relevant criteria justifying departure from equality thus become difficult to discern. What is relevant to achieve equity and is not merely an excuse to justify inequality? This is a complex dilemma made more difficult by the clouded lenses of self-interest through which we all view the problem.

Helping the Least Advantaged

John Rawls's *A Theory of Justice*[35] is commonly acknowledged as the preeminent work of political and legal theory of this century and may rank him with the great political philosophers of earlier eras. Nozick, an eminent modern conservative political philosopher, has said that Rawls's "*A Theory of Justice* is a powerful, deep, subtle, wide-ranging, systematic work in political and moral philosophy which has not seen its like since the writings of John Stuart Mill, if then. It is a fountain of illuminating ideas, integrated together into a lovely whole. Political philosophers now must either work within Rawls's theory or explain why not."[36] Rawls maintains that natural duties among moral persons require mutual respect and treatment. Accordingly, justice presumes equality. This is to say that among human beings, "none are entitled to preferential treatment in the absence of compelling reasons"[37] to justify inequality. Importantly, Rawls maintains that "the burden of proof favors equality: it defines a procedural presumption that persons are to be treated alike."[38] Where the rationale is not sufficient to support a clear finding that deviation from strict equal division of goods will foster greater equity and justice, then the departure is not justified. Departures from equal treatment must be defended and "judged impartially by the same system of principles that hold for all."[39] The deviation that is permissible may only be for the least advantaged.

It is in this regard that Rawls's "difference principle" is propounded; his general conception is that

> all social primary goods—liberty and opportunity, income and wealth, and the bases of self-respect—are to be distributed equally unless an unequal distribution of any or all of these goods is to the advantage of the least favored.[40]

His principle encompasses education and he rejects the idea that at times the whole society may benefit from certain restrictions on equality

of opportunity.[41] He places a priority on fair opportunity and assumes that all will benefit from particularized attention to the least advantaged. Further, he argues that equality "requires equal life prospects in all sectors of society for those similarly endowed and motivated."[42] While he indicates that fair opportunity may require greater assistance to children of deprived circumstances, if the family is a barrier to equal prospects, he acknowledges that equal outcomes cannot be assured.[43]

INEQUALITY AMONG NATIONS

Brown in *State of the World 1990* summarily concludes that "the poor get poorer."[44] By classifying the world's nations into four groups, poorest, poor, middle, and rich, it is possible to graph the increased divergence in the worldwide economic condition. Figure 7.1 shows that wealthy nations almost tripled their per capita income advantage between 1950 and 1988.

Thousand Dollars (1980 dollars)

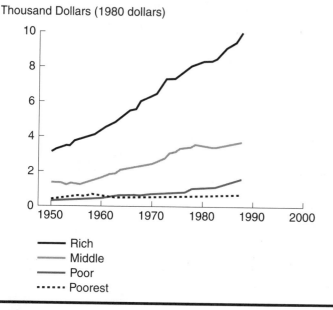

FIGURE 7.1   Income Per Person, Four Economic Classes of Countries, 1950–88

Source: Cited in Lester R. Brown, *State of the World 1990*, A Worldwatch Institute Report on Progress Toward a Sustainable Society (London: Unwin Paperbacks, 1990), p. 137. Reprinted with permission.

While the per capita income of rich countries has continued to increase, those of the poorest and poor have remained approximately level. Brown, however, notes that averages tend to mask even worse conditions, because the internal disparities in the poor countries show even greater inequalities. In virtually all cases, the poorest one-fifth of the people earn less than 10 percent of the income, while the richest one-fifth commonly earn 50 percent of a nation's income.[45] The inequality is both among and within nations. Brown concludes that the world, as a whole, is more disequalized than any one nation.[46]

Inequality in Education Tracks Inequality in Income

Despite a general awareness that education is important to economic development and individual attainment, the underdeveloped countries of the world continue to fall farther behind the developed countries in educational investments. The disparity in educational opportunity between the haves and the have-nots becomes greater yearly and there is apparently no end in sight.

The commitment made to education in underdeveloped countries has fallen in recent years as the economic conditions of the poorer areas of the world have declined relative to the developed countries. In the low-income countries the proportion of central government expenditures allocated for education dropped from 15 percent to 10 percent between 1972 and 1986.[47] In middle-income countries the decline was from 20 to 14 percent.[48] In some countries the actual dollar amount expended on education per pupil declined. For example, in Sub-Saharan Africa the expenditure per pupil for an elementary child was $67 in 1970 and only $52 in 1983, a decline of 23 percent.[49] The average secondary school student received 39 percent less in 1983 than in 1970, a decline in the dollar amount from $362 to $223. Heyneman reports that out of thirty-three developing countries for which comparable expenditure data are available, twenty-one experienced a reduction in elementary expenditure per pupil between 1970 and 1984.[50]

The inequality in educational opportunity worldwide is more apparent if one compares expenditures between underdeveloped and developed countries. In Bolivia, for example, an elementary school child in 1984 had only $0.80 for non-salary support costs, Malawi had $1.24, as contrasted against the developed nation of Sweden that had the equivalent of $300 per pupil.[51]

The gap between underdeveloped and industrialized nations has gotten much worse since 1960. In that year, industrialized countries expended 14 times more per elementary school student than did the world's poorest countries. This gap had increased to 22 times that of the poorest countries by 1970, and by 1980 the gap had grown to 50 times as much per child.[52]

Coombs in his perceptive analysis entitled *The World Crisis in Education* has shown that the great diversity in ability and aspiration for education between the rich and poor nations of the world has manifested itself in a crisis of major proportions.[53] He says that "disparity—taking many forms—between educational systems and their environments is the essence of the worldwide crisis in education.[54]

These disparities are evidenced by inequalities that may be subdivided into four categories. First, there is a great gulf in the level of aspiration for education; those with little education have less aspiration, and a downward spiral of low aspiration feeding poor educational quality drives people toward poverty. Second, there is a scarcity of financial resources and wide variances in fiscal capacity for education. The countries with less education have lower wealth and income and are therefore able to pay for only inferior education. Third, an inherent intellectual momentum exists in countries that have more educated people than in countries with underdeveloped human capital. People in better-developed countries are more efficient as both producers and consumers, and the result is a separation between rich and poor that increases geometrically.

Box 7.4

Inequality of Funding in Underdeveloped Countries

[W]hat does this (inequality) mean in educational terms? If a country is able to spend only one dollar or so per child for non-salary expenditures—chalk, blackboards, furniture, and reading materials—it implies that there is likely to be very little to read. In many parts of rural Africa, Latin America, and South Asia, one finds only one textbook per class. The teacher is expected to copy the content of that single book on the blackboard, and the children, in turn, to copy from the blackboard into their notebooks. The children then try to memorize what they have in their notebooks.

This is referred to as the "copy/copy" situation: an inadequately educated teacher, underpaid (often unpaid for months at a time), copies (often inaccurately) from a book (frequently out-dated and inappropriate to the curriculum), which gets (often inaccurately) copied into a student's notebook. That notebook then substitutes for a textbook. What kind of learning does this yield? It results in the rote memorization of poorly understood information, often with large gaps in logic, of out-of-date facts and interpretations with little or no explanation as to how or why. That is the basic engine of education in many of the least-developed countries, and the typical education millions of children receive.

Source: Stephen Paul Heyneman, "The World Economic Crises and the Quality of Education," *Journal of Education Finance, 15* (Spring, 1990), pp. 461–462.

Disparities and inequalities between underdeveloped and developed countries may be viewed in yet another way. Coombs notes that the disparities are most notably a result of three types of inequalities that must be overcome in order to provide equality of educational opportunity. All three are associated with financial ability and economic circumstance, but each highlights an overlay of inequality that is readily discernible. They are: geographic disparities, sex disparities, and socioeconomic disparities.

The geographic disparities are of course obvious between developed and underdeveloped countries, but within countries the difference may be as great. A common earmark of an underdeveloped country is internal inequality particularly between urban and rural areas. Most urban areas have relatively better education than the usually benighted rural areas.

Second, disparities in the way the sexes are treated create inequalities of opportunity that are often the products of primitive social mores and religious beliefs, both fostering subjugation of women to near or actual abject poverty. The World Bank has shown in an interesting but not firmly conclusive analysis that there is a strong correlation between economic development, civil liberties, and female education. The World Bank says that

> controlling for income growth and regional effects, liberties appear to be strongly and positively associated with measures of welfare improvements such as women's education, overall education, and infant mortality declines.[56]

The actual correlation between female education and the extent of political and civil liberties was 0.63, a statistically significant relationship taken from data in 68 countries. In other words, the greater the equality of educational opportunity for women the more extensive the political and civil liberties. Greater equality relates to greater liberty.[57] (See Figure 7.2.)

Third, disparities associated with socioeconomic conditions emanate from social caste and class of various types, including conditions of

Fourth, the societies themselves have built-in features that either enhance or retard the effects of investment in education. "[T]he heavy weight of traditional attitudes, religious customs, prestige and incentive patterns, and structures—has blocked them from making the optimum use of education and of educated manpower to foster national development."[55] We have all observed how the society of Japan values and enhances educational achievement and how the opposite conditions exist in underdeveloped countries.

Ratio of Female to Male
Educational Attainment

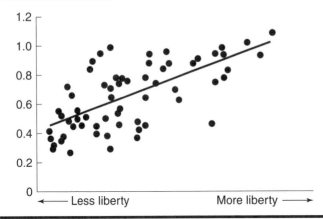

FIGURE 7.2   The Association Between Political and Civil Liberties and Women's
Education, Selected Economies, 1973–86

Source: World Bank, *World Development Report 1991, The Challenge of Development* (Oxford:
The World Bank and Oxford University Press, 1991), p. 50. Reprinted with permission.

Note: Data are period averages for a sample of sixty-seven economies; data for 1974 were unavailable. Educational attainment is defined as the average years of schooling, excluding post-
secondary schooling, of the population age fifteen to sixty-four.

economic incapacity associated with property
wealth and income, and racial and ethnic differences.[58] These, of course, underlie geographic
and sex inequalities discussed above and are pervasive. Advantages of social status and money
are usually associated with better-educated parents who themselves had the advantage of privileged treatment. The more underdeveloped the
country, the greater the likelihood that the inequalities will be pronounced. Coombs notes
that many studies suggest "that children whose
parents are at the bottom of the socioeconomic
hierarchy are not as inclined to seek or gain access to available educational facilities as are children from families located at the middle or top
of the hierarchy."[59]

This is, of course, no great revelation as we
have observed the positive effects of parental advantage on the educational attainment in not only
underdeveloped countries, but in the United
States as well.

INEQUALITIES WITHIN THE UNITED STATES

Arthur M. Schlesinger, Jr. in *The Disuniting of
America* has warned that the decline of commonality and mutuality of interest among Americans
coupled with economic inequality may destroy
America.[60] He quotes James Bryce's *The American Commonwealth* in which Bryce observed
that the genius of America has been its ability to
assimilate many "heterogeneous elements" and
Tocqueville's reference to America's "amazing
solvent powers"[61] to assimilate foreign bodies
that were "poured into her mass."[62] The nature of
this solvent power was identified by Gunnar
Myrdal when he wrote in 1944 that the ideals of
"the American creed" allowed the melting of differences into a compatible whole. This "creed"
explicitly expressed essential dignity for all persons, the equality of all human beings, and the
rights of freedom, justice, and opportunity."[63]

The problem is, however, that this commitment to equality and opportunity in recent years has begun to show signs of fraying at the edges as wealth, income, social, racial, religious, and ethnic difference have become more pronounced. The problem has even been referred to by *The Economist*, as "the coming apart of America."[64]

Coming Apart

Enough evidence has been adduced lately to lead us to be gravely concerned about economic inequality and social immobility among the American people.[65] In a report entitled *State of the World 1990*, the author observed that for the United States in 1979, the "equity of income distribution began to deteriorate rapidly; [and] by 1986, disparities in earnings were the worst on record."[66] Deterioration continued and by 1988

the number of persons in poverty had exceeded 31 million.[67] The *World Development Report 1991* substantiates these disparities indicating an unfavorable state of inequality in the United States compared with other industrialized countries. The relative condition of the poor in this report is shown in Table 7.1. It can be seen that the United States' households in the lowest income quintile had only 4.7 percent of the income in 1985 and the highest quintile had 41.9 percent. An equity ratio, using these figures (dividing the percentage in the lowest quintile into that of the highest quintile for each country), reveals the relatively great inequity now existing in the United States as compared to other countries. By this measure the United States ranks 15th out of 16 countries; only Australia has a more severe separation between rich and poor.

The inequality of incomes is more pronounced today than it has been for many years.

TABLE 7.1   Percentage Share of Household Income by Percentile Group of Households

	YEAR	LOWEST 20%	HIGHEST 20%	EQUITY RATIO
Japan	1979	8.7	37.5	4.31
Belgium	1978–79	7.9	36.0	4.56
Sweden	1981	8.0	36.9	4.61
Netherlands	1983	6.9	38.3	5.55
Germany .	1984	6.8	38.7	5.69
Spain	1980–81	6.9	40.0	5.80
Norway	1979	6.2	36.7	5.92
Finland	1981	6.3	37.6	5.97
Italy	1986	6.8	41.0	6.03
France	1979	6.3	40.8	6.48
United Kingdom	1978	5.8	39.5	6.81
Canada	1987	5.7	40.2	7.05
Denmark	1981	5.4	38.6	7.15
Switzerland	1982	5.2	44.6	8.58
United States	1985	4.7	41.9	8.91
Australia	1985	4.4	42.2	9.59

Source: World Bank, *World Development Report 1991: The Challenge of Development* (Oxford: The World Bank and Oxford University Press, June 1991), p. 263. The data for this table refer to the United Nation's International Comparison Program (ICP) data. The ICP recalculates traditional national account figures through special price collections and disaggregation of GDP by expenditure components. (See page 285 of the *World Development Report* for greater specification of data).

Table 7.2 from Kevin Phillips's book *The Politics of Rich and Poor* indicates that the separation among the economic classes has been on the rise for at least 10 years. Phillips's data show that this inequality in the United States has progressively worsened since 1969 when the lowest quintile had 5.6 percent of the income and the highest quintile had 40.6 percent.[68] According to his statistics, in 1988 the lowest quintile had 4.6 percent and the highest had 44.0 percent of the income. These data show an even more severe inequality in the United States than is indicated by the *World Development Report 1991*. By Phillips's account the disparity ratio between the income of the lowest quintile and the highest was 8.16 (lowest quintile 5.1 and highest 41.6 percent) in 1980. This ratio had increased to 9.57 by 1988 (lowest quintile 4.6 percent and highest 44.0).[69]

This display shows of course that the poor have a lower standard of living today than they did 20 years ago. The lower standard of living experienced by the poor is exacerbated by environmental pollution. This condition has led some concerned parties to conclude that in the United States today, "the poorer the neighborhood, and the darker the skin of its residents, the more likely it is to be near a toxic waste dump. . . . the rich get richer and the poor get poisoned.[70]

The worsening of the problem of income disparity in the United States is further illustrated by a recent article by Sylvia Nasar in the *New York Times* citing Massachusetts Institute of Technology Professor Paul Krugman's synthesis of Congressional Budget Office data which show that 60 percent of the growth in after-tax income of all American families between 1977 and 1989 went to further enrich the wealthiest 1 percent of the population, 660,000 families with an average income of $559,800 per year. The average pre-tax income of this top 1 percent increased by 77 percent during these 12 years, from $315,000 to $560,000 per year. During this same period, pre-tax income of the poorest 20 percent of the U.S. households declined by 9 percent and the lowest 40 percent declined by 1 percent. The gains in after-tax income tracked the pre-tax disparities with the richest 1 percent of the families receiving 60 percent of the after-tax income gain for the entire nation.[71]

Moreover, one of the most important virtues of the American system, social mobility, was diminished during the decade of the 1980s.

TABLE 7.2   Percentage of Family Income Received by Each Quintile in the United States

YEAR	LOWEST	HIGHEST	EQUITY RATIO
1969	5.6	40.6	7.25
1974	5.5	41.0	7.45
1979	5.2	41.7	8.02
1980	5.1	41.6	8.16
1981	5.0	41.9	8.38
1982	4.7	42.7	9.09
1983	4.7	42.8	9.11
1984	4.7	42.9	9.13
1985	4.6	43.5	9.46
1986	4.6	43.7	9.50
1987	4.6	43.7	9.50
1988	4.6	44.0	9.57

Source: Kevin Phillips, *The Politics of Rich and Poor* (New York: Harper Perennial, 1991), p. 13.

Note: Equity ratio calculated separately.

Smeeding and Duncan report that from 1967 to 1980, 35.5 percent of the poor moved into the middle-income group but during the 1980s this movement had been reduced to 30.4 percent.[72] For the same 13-year period ending in 1980, 6.2 percent of the middle-income group dropped to the lower-income category.[73]

In the decade of the 1980s, this decline in economic status of middle-income families reached 7.5 percent.[74] As smaller proportions of Americans moved out of poverty and proportionately more fell into it, the class constituting the poor and near-poor increased by a million persons.[75] At the same time, the 1980s witnessed a 50 percent increase in the proportion of relatively wealthy Americans, a group that grew from 8 to 13 percent.[76]

The deterioration in the relative position of the poor complicated the fiscal burden mounted upon the public schools due in part to increased polarization of economic class. Social and economic fragmentation of society created higher operational costs for the public schools. Because families in poorer economic circumstances have children with greater and more complex educational problems, fiscal resources are required in greater magnitude to redress the deficiencies.

Equality of Educational Opportunity

The economic justification for equality of educational opportunity, although often ignored, is well documented.[77] By addressing educational disadvantage, governments not only increase the absorption power of the labor force, but more directly turn consumers into producers. Beyond economics though, and even more importantly, greater equality of educational opportunity is justified on moral grounds and considerations of social justice.

Most people in this country have assumed that we have been providing reasonably adequate programs of education. In many respects, the record has been impressive. For example, at the turn of the century the most educated fifth of the population received an average of 14 years of schooling,

while the least educated fifth received only 3.7 years. Thus, the most educated person had spent almost four times as much time in school as the least educated.[78] Today this differential had been reduced to the point that the most educated fifth has less than 40 percent more years of schooling, a record of definite progress. Yet the evidence that has been accumulated during recent years clearly shows that the needs of substantial numbers of people have been grossly neglected. African-Americans in the South (many of whom have moved to urban ghettos), Hispanics, Native Americans, Asians, poor whites of Appalachia and in many other parts of the nation have had inadequate opportunities to develop their talents.

A fairly recent phenomenon has been the apparent disenchantment of a number of the more able students. Some have not continued their education after high school graduation, and many have become a part of the nation's youth who drop out at a disturbing rate. Gross inequalities and inadequate opportunities for people of all ages have undoubtedly had a detrimental effect on the development of the nation. The price of indifference and neglect has exceeded the cost that would have been necessary to ensure adequate and equitable opportunities for everyone.

Inequalities among States

Some of the differences in equality of educational opportunity among the 50 states are difficult to demonstrate convincingly, perhaps partly because only limited objective evidence has been available. This may be one reason why many people have not seemed to be seriously disturbed about the existing situation.

One difficulty comes from the fact that state averages disguise the considerable disparities that exist among school districts within each state. The educational opportunities in the best school systems in some of the poorer states may compare reasonably well with those in the best systems in other states. In some of the poorest school systems, however, the deficiencies are striking but are not obvious to those who consider only the averages. State statistics do not create a visual and dramatic impression of the hundreds or thousands of people who are, and will continue to be, seriously disadvantaged because of insufficient opportunities to develop their talents due solely to where they lived during their years of public schooling.

Another difficulty arises from the fact that most of the evidence available deals with factors that, although important, only indirectly reveal variations in educational opportunity. For example, the percentage of adults who have completed four or more years of college work does not give any indication of the number who might have completed college had better educational opportunities been provided by their public schools.

The income of the citizens of a state affects their potential expenditure for education and other governmental services. The expenditures for education on a state-wide basis seem to relate directly to the quality of education provided or at any rate have a positive correlation with selected indicators of quality.

Complicating factors in any interstate analysis arise from (1) the mobility of the population within the United States, (2) migration and concentrations of ethnic and racial groups, and (3) the composition of the population in each of the states—rural and urban dwellers, whites and nonwhites, and so on.

Inequalities within States

The evidence indicates rather clearly that the range in educational opportunities available within most states is considerably greater than the interstate differences indicated by the averages among states. In a few states, a majority of children seem to have reasonably adequate educational opportunities. Generally speaking, the states with the greatest extremes are small-district states in which only limited state support supplements local funds. In some of the small poverty-stricken districts and the urban ghetto areas, educational opportunities are tragically inadequate. The fact that African-American and

other minority children who have attended schools in the South, in the urban ghettos, and in many other impoverished areas have had inadequate educational opportunities has been widely publicized during the past few years and as a result some improvements have been made, but the problem remains unresolved. The opportunities for many other children, regardless of race or similar factors, also continue to be far from satisfactory even in many of the more financially able school districts and states.

Enclaves of Affluence

Economic power and influence are at the root of the problem traditionally faced by state legislatures in providing fiscal resources for education.[79] Initially, in the formation of public schools, legislatures were reticent to accept responsibility for imposing taxes at the state level, and to avert this obligation they delegated substantial taxing authority to localities. The local tax bases included extreme disparities in property wealth, and the revenue yields from the tax bases resulted in great differences in educational funding. By allowing local taxing power, the legislatures created nearly insurmountable problems of inequality.

Many school districts became enclaves of affluence while others were left with little fiscal strength, a pattern that continues to exist in most states. In Ohio, for example, the assessed valuation of property per pupil in the poorest school district is actually less than the annual revenue per pupil available to spend in the wealthiest school district of the state.[80] Ten percent of Ohio's children who are served by the wealthiest school districts have available $953,427,533 in state and local revenue for their education each year and the 10 percent of the children in the poorest school districts have only $596,007,715. The 10 percent from the richest districts have 13.3 percent of state and local revenue while the 10 percent from the poorest districts have only 8.3 percent. The 20 percent of the pupils from the richest districts have 24.5 percent of the revenues and the 20 percent at the poor end of the continuum have 16.8 percent. In terms of total dollars this difference between the richest 20 percent and poorest 20 percent totaled $550,953,847 in the 1990–91 school year (see Figure 7.3). It is this kind of difference in educational opportunity among school districts within states that is so profound as to shock the conscience of most Americans.

While the Ohio disparities are certainly extreme they are not uncommon. The Missouri school finance system, held to be unconstitutional by a lower court in 1993, maintained disparities similar to those of Ohio. Twenty percent of Missouri's children served by the richest school districts captured 23.8 percent of state and local revenues while 20 percent of children from the poorest districts received only 15.3 percent, a difference of $264,653,255 per year (see Figure 7.3).

In Kentucky, at the time of the filing of that state's school finance case, the poorest school district spent only $1,700 per pupil while a small wealthy elementary school district in another part of the state spent $4,800 per pupil. Similar situations are commonplace throughout the country: school districts with great wealth interspersed among inner-city and rural school districts of very low fiscal capacity and generally deficient educational circumstance.

Persons in enclaves of wealth have been adept in convincing legislatures that their advantageous position is in some way justified and indeed necessary for the maintenance of a quality educational system. Such justifications, mostly defensive afterthoughts, have been successful enough to perpetuate wide revenue disparities between rich and poor school districts in many states.

(% of Pupils)

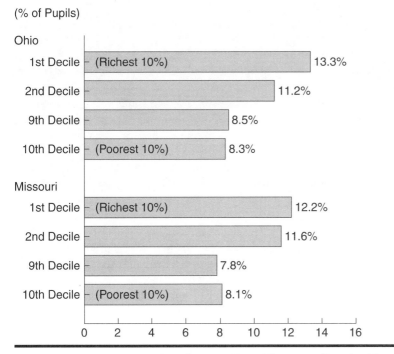

FIGURE 7.3 Percentage of Total State and Local Revenues Received by the 20% of the Pupils in the Richest versus the 20% of the Pupils in the Poorest School Districts in Ohio and Missouri, 1991

These widely disparate conditions have led some to observe that the public school system of the United States is not public at all, but rather a quasi-private or a quasi-public system with a sense of "solidarity and community" based on economic condition and affluence formed around small school districts.[81] The interests of the parents and children in these districts are insular, particularized, and geographically defined. Moreover, their insularity and educational privilege are protected by the state legislatures which continue to enact school funding laws that yield disparate financial results. Parents and neighbors in these advantaged districts are driven by two primary objectives: maintaining the educational advantage for their children, and "a near obsessive concern with maintaining or upgrading property values."[82] State legislatures have in many cases reflected and fortified the insularity of these compounds of wealth through state school financing schemes.

Legislatures influenced by special interests as well as traditional anti-tax forces often stand against educational finance reform. Educational equity falls prey to self-interest, and state legislatures composed of competing political fiefdoms are unable to provide for equality of educational opportunity. The fact that this situation prevails in many states is the reason that advocates of school finance reform have turned to the courts to intervene in an effort to force legislatures toward greater educational equity.

Considerable additional information indicating differences in educational opportunity could readily be presented. Whereas no single set of figures based on one factor should be considered significant, the fact remains that all data tend to show that, in the past, there have been marked differences in the quality of educational services among and within many of the states and that these differences are still sufficient to warrant considerable concern.

With the great mobility of population at the present time, it is evident that inadequate investment in education by a state not only handicap the people in that state but constitute a problem for other states to which some of these people migrate. It is evident that under modern conditions, the United States cannot afford the losses resulting from the presence of substantial numbers in the population who are consumers but because of the lack of educational opportunities have failed to become effective producers.

INEQUALITIES WITHIN LOCAL SCHOOL SYSTEMS

There is usually greater equality of educational services provided by many local school systems than within most states. In each local school system, a uniform tax base is available for support of the educational program, and all schools are operated under the policies established by the local school board. As indicated earlier, the educational opportunities available may be reasonably adequate or quite inadequate, but inequities have not been particularly obvious, except in the poverty or ghetto areas.[83]

Evidence accumulated during the past few years, however, has helped to focus national attention on the fact that the inequalities within many school systems are more serious than most people had realized. The problems are complex and deep-seated, and only the first steps have been taken toward their solution. Not all solutions have been the result of voluntary action on the part of the schools, however. The courts have intervened both in finance and segregation issues. The issue of *de jure segregation* was settled in *Brown*, in 1954, and in 1973 the Supreme Court of the United States in issuing its *de facto segregation* decision in *Keyes* v. *School District No. 1, Denver, Colorado*, settled the legality of affirmative action remedies, but the practical applications of the decisions in remedying the plight of fiscally ill-served urban schools remains a problem of immeasurable national proportion.[84]

REASONS FOR INEQUALITIES IN OPPORTUNITY

Why are serious inequalities in educational opportunity permitted to exist year after year in a country in which a majority of the people seem dedicated to the concept of equality? Some of the background factors involved are:

1. Many people do not realize the extent or implications of inequalities.
2. Some people have become accustomed to the existing situation and accept it as normal.
3. Substantial numbers seem to be more concerned about their own personal problems and the rising costs of living and government than about variations in educational opportunity that do not seem to affect them immediately.
4. Until comparatively recent years, the procedures needed to solve certain aspects of the problem had not been satisfactorily developed or understood.
5. Self-interest many times overcomes common interest and mutuality of concern for others.
6. There are wide differences among local school districts in wealth per pupil.

Inadequate School Districts

Many studies have shown that both small schools and small school districts usually offer less adequate educational programs, are less efficient, and are more expensive to operate than larger schools and districts. Despite the fact that the number of school districts in the United States has been reduced to about 22 percent of the number that existed 40 years ago, there were still over 15,000 in 1994. For school year 1952–53, there were 67,881 school districts in the United States; by 1993–94 the number of school districts had fallen to 15,048, with 14,763 classified as operating. Several states, including Nebraska, Michigan, and Wisconsin, showed dramatic reductions in the number of school districts, all but these three states continue to operate large numbers of local districts.[85]

It is not possible to operate an effective and economical school system in a district having only a few hundred students. Where districts of this size are maintained, the costs per pupil are high, and some of the needed services cannot be provided, except perhaps through intermediate or

area service units. A district having at least five to ten thousand pupils has many potential advantages and has the ability to provide a more adequate program than a small district of similar fiscal capacity.

Any state with a large number of small districts has marked differences in local fiscal capacity to finance its schools. In such states it is difficult if not impossible to develop an equitable finance plan that would make adequate schools possible in all districts. However, as districts are reorganized and larger districts evolve, the problem becomes simpler, and a satisfactory solution is more practicable. In fact, in several states, district reorganization would probably contribute at least as much or more to the equalization of financial support and of educational opportunity than has been accomplished thus far through improvements in state provisions for financial support.

Financial Effect of Reorganization.   If five small districts with wide differences in ability were to combine into one larger district, the extremes in that area would be eliminated. If similar reorganizations were to be effected throughout a state, the range in local ability would be greatly reduced—probably to 10 or 15 to 1. The effect of reorganization on differences in local ability is illustrated in Figure 7.4.

Let us assume that District A, with 2,500 pupils, had $80,000 per pupil in equalized valuation of property; District B, with 1,500 pupils, had $17,000; District C, with 3,500 pupils, had $30,000; District D, with 500 pupils, had $40,000; and District E, with 2,000 pupils, had $4,000. If a new district comprising these five districts were to be organized, the range of 20 to 1 in ability would be eliminated and the valuation per pupil in the new district would be a little under $36,000.

Small Schools

Although few small school districts can be justified under most conditions, some small isolated schools are necessary and probably will continue to be needed. Relatively small high schools are

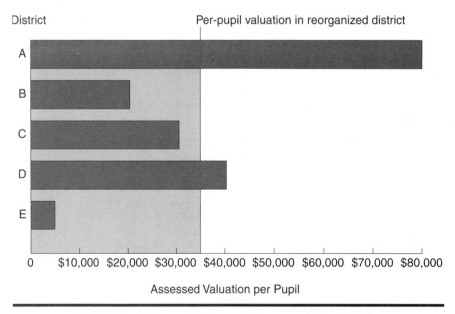

FIGURE 7.4   The Effect of Reorganization on Differences in Local Ability

even more expensive and probably less satisfactory than small elementary schools. The small number of pupils per teacher usually found in such schools is the greatest single factor contributing to high costs, but the limited range of offerings tends to limit the adequacy of educational services. Where small isolated schools are necessary, higher costs can be justified, but not otherwise. Researchers have shown that the per pupil costs of education tend to be higher and the quality of the educational program less satisfactory in elementary schools having fewer than 175 to 200 pupils and in high schools having fewer than 300 pupils, than in larger schools.[86] Whether such a definitive number is accurate in all contexts is doubtful yet it is certain that economies of scale do exist that serve as either enhancements or deterrents to equal educational opportunity.

Effects of Public School Choice Options.   Potentially, implementation of public school choice options could have significant positive effects on the size and structure of local school districts. Small cost-inefficient schools and school districts could be jeopardized and forced to consolidate if public school patrons intellectually select schools that provide more varied and intensive curricula and other educational services. On the other hand, large schools often criticized for this perceived failure to personalize and individualize educational services may face declining enrollments. Hopefully, an equilibrium will develop that provides a balanced level of cost-efficiency and personalized educational services.

It is important to note however that the potential positive effects of public school choice options do not extend to private school participation. School choice options that include state supplemental funding of private schools undoubtedly would prove destructive to public schools, and ultimately to the social fabric of this nation.

Differences in Fiscal Capacity and Fiscal Effort

Some of the variations in fiscal capacity and fiscal effort to support schools among and within the states, together with certain implications for financial support, are discussed in Chapter 8.

However it is important to note that marked differences in fiscal capacity are found among school systems within states and that these are exacerbated by faulty district structure. In small-district states, it is not possible to provide reasonable equity for taxpayers and simultaneously assure anything closely approaching equality of educational opportunity for the children, except perhaps through a system of complete state support. Inadequate and expensive small schools often are perpetuated by the district structure, and as long as such schools exist in nonisolated areas, the problem of equitable and adequate financial support is not likely to be solved.

Inadequate district structure is likewise one of the important reasons for differences in fiscal effort. In districts with extremely limited fiscal capacity, adequate educational opportunities cannot be provided unless the taxpayers make an excessive fiscal effort, assuming of course that the state has implemented an adequate and equitable plan of financial support. Even where substantial state support is provided, marked variations in fiscal effort will be necessary if anything approaching equality of educational opportunity is to be assured.

It must be recognized, however, that even if all districts are properly organized and a sound state plan of financial support developed, there would still be variations in fiscal effort due to differences in the people's interest in their schools, in their attitude toward taxes, and in their willingness to provide the necessary financial support for a satisfactory program of education.

Unsound Legal and Financial Provisions

Legal provisions, in addition to those relating to district organization, have frequently resulted in disparate education opportunities. The intent of these laws probably was not to create or to perpetuate disparities, but certain types of laws have resulted in widely disparate systems of public schools. Many examples are available, but a few should suffice to illustrate the impli-

cations. For instance, when the laws of a state provide that all or practically all state funds for schools are to be apportioned on a flat-grant basis, there are certain to be inequities for taxpayers and inequalities in educational services, even in states in which all districts enroll sufficient numbers of pupils to be cost-efficient. Laws providing variant tax limits for different types of school districts also tend to result in marked inequities. If property valuation on which school taxes may be levied is assessed at a low percentage of full valuation, adequate financial support may be impossible, especially when coupled with restrictive tax limitations. When assessment ratios vary among local school districts, the inequities are likely to be particularly acute, because assessment practices will result in much lower fiscal effort relative to fiscal capacity in some parts of the state than in others. In essence, legal provisions that restrict citizens from establishing and operating a quality system of public education that is needed to permit the nation's youth to reach their maximum potential inevitably will have a negative effect on educational opportunities.

Politics of Inequality

The governmental response of providing better services to low-income families in low-capacity school districts has been very gradual. Per pupil expenditure variations among states and school districts were much greater thirty years ago, but wide differences still persist and have grown worse recently. A theory of redistribution politics in education must recognize that although each person has one vote, the significance and power of each vote is not equal, even after reapportionment. In analyzing the educational power structure, it quickly becomes apparent that redistribution of income through education probably is not the strategic basis on which most voters make fiscal decisions. The people who pay into the system and those who receive the benefits may not be allied on the same economic basis.[87] Families sending their children to parochial schools, or older persons who have very low incomes, may see no benefit to be derived personally from voting for higher taxes to equalize resources among school districts. This will generally result in adversity to both redistribution and equalization of expenditures. Thus, many voters with erroneous perceptions of their own self-interest may join the wealthy at the voting booths and retard a positive reallocation of resources to assist low-income children in poor school districts.

Another condition which tends to inhibit the egalitarian motive of public education is the lack of political power of those who are poor and live in low-capacity school districts. With regard to legislative influence, it is true that the more populous school districts in this country are also the ones with the greatest fiscal capacity.[88] It is to their disadvantage to encourage state governments to fiscally equalize among school districts. Some argue quite rationally that for sheer numbers, more low-income persons are found in high-capacity school districts than in average or below-average-capacity districts, thereby including a low-income voter response which may seek redistribution locally but oppose a similar redistribution effort at the state level. This problem is magnified by unreasonably large numbers of school districts in many states, a variable in the redistribution context which holds important implications for equality.

Even where a majority of low-income voters exercise their franchise in poor school districts, the overall political power structure of the state responds to varying coalitions with divergent goals. In this political content, equality through redistribution becomes a cloudy objective. As Buchanan and Tullock have explained, the taxpayer/voter may respond differently over a series of issues.[89] In one situation, a voter as beneficiary may be in the minority, but with another issue, he or she may derive no benefits and yet stand in the voting majority. Certain individuals may do very well with particular outcomes but badly with others. To this may be added the fact that many voters are deluded into voting against their own self-interest by crafty politicians and demographies of various sorts and hue. It is the phenomenon to which Walter Hines Page addressed his comments in his famous "forgotten man" thesis, discussed in Chapter 1.

The pattern of redistribution cannot therefore be specified under the present democratic method of financing public education. Redistribution through education requires a concerted political effort at even the federal and state levels to form coalitions with mutual interests encompassing the ideal of public education and advancing both the social and economic desirability of greater equality.

SUMMARY AND CONCLUSIONS

In this chapter we sought to give a perspective on inequality in general, as well as more focused attention to inequality of educational opportunity. Much of any discussion of public school finance is devoted to issues pertaining to equality because it is an ever persistent social and economic problem that greatly influences the kind and quality of education that every child receives. We attempted to show that inequality is not simply a political issue, but more importantly it is a philosophical and moral issue that has invoked the great concern of political and moral philosophers since the Age of Enlightenment and even as early as ancient Greece. Further, we sought to tie the philosophical and moral considerations of inequality directly to our immediate concerns for equal and equitable financing of public schools. The following main points were emphasized.

Inequality of privilege was first brought into focus as a primary concern of government during the Enlightenment.

Rousseau is considered to be the fountainhead of philosophical thought who first pointed out the inherent political nature of inequality and the government's responsibility for its alleviation.

Inequality of privilege emanates from disproportionate distribution of economic power.

The concept of equality as a basic concern of human interaction was never realized in Europe until after the American Revolution had established its practical importance to the republican form of government.

Before Jefferson's Declaration in 1776, equality was an intuition without form that allowed practical political application.

The importance of public, mass, universal education as an essential element of freedom and liberty was first and best enunciated by Rousseau's reference in 1758 to public education as the vehicle to nurture children in the "bosom of equality."

Human self-interest is a fact of life that Adam Smith recognized as the driving force of the "invisible hand" that advances society but leaves inequality in its wake.

Laissez-faire economic philosophy eschews equality and perceives great damage to economic growth by governments' efforts to reduce or eliminate inequalities.

The doctrine of "harmony of interest" sought to justify economic inequality by maintaining that unfettered pursuit of one's own self-interest would ultimately raise the economic condition of all in society. This theory has recently been referred to as "trickle-down" economics.

Unfettered pursuit of self-interest was justified on the biological theory of "survival of the fittest" advanced by Darwin, commonly entitled "social Darwinism." The United States followed this philosophy and it pervades the context in which we think about school finance, competition for school fiscal resources, school districts as lighthouses, and so on.

Justifications for maintaining unequal systems of education are many and innovative and all seek to justify inequality on some rational basis.

The basic premise of egalitarian philosophy is that similar cases should be accorded similar treatment, equal treatment of equals.

There is a difference between equality and equity. Equality means all are entitled to equal shares while equity means that all are entitled to fair shares.

Departure from equal shares is not justified unless it can be shown that greater justice is served by unequal shares. Such a departure from equality is only justified for educationally "relevant" reasons intended to elevate the least advantaged. Contrived reasons to give more to the more affluent, advantaged, or privileged cannot be relevant reasons for departure from equal distribution.

Inequality in educational opportunity is particularly evident among nations. Great gulfs of disparity exist between developed and underdeveloped countries and the differences are broadening rather than diminishing.

Inequality in income follows inequality in education and vice versa. Inequality in education among and within nations is always associated with economic and financial disability, but is particularly discernible in geographic disparities, sex disparities, and socioeconomic disparities.

Inequalities within the United States are worse now than a generation ago. Disparity in household incomes is greater today than 20 years ago.

The United States has the greatest disparity between the incomes of rich and poor households of any developed country except perhaps Australia. Japan has the most equitable distribution of household incomes and the largest middle class.

Inequalities in educational opportunity in the United States are particularly severe between rich and poor states, cities and suburbs, rural areas, and among racial and ethnic groups that cluster in these particular geographic areas.

Grave inequalities in educational opportunity exists within states. Many school districts have as much as three times the resources to expend per pupil as other districts. These per-pupil differences amount to differences of many millions of dollar between the rich and poor school districts in most states each year.

Inequalities persist within school districts which are most apparent in many large school districts. This is particularly true in large urban school districts that have enclaves of fiscally advantaged and disadvantaged communities that influences the quality of educational opportunities provided.

KEY TERMS

Laissez-faire school of economic thought	Rawls's difference principle	Wealth inequality among school districts
The invisible hand	Least advantaged	Revenue inequality among school districts
Harmony of interests	Disparity in educational opportunity, among countries	
Social Darwinism		
Egalitarian philosophy	Liberty as connected with equality	
Equal shares	The "disuniting of America"	
Equitable shares	Income disparity	Inadequate school districts
Relevant differences	Inequality of educational opportunity	Fiscal ability
		Fiscal effort

ENDNOTES

1. Jean Jacques Rousseau, "A Discourse on the Origin of Inequality," *The Social Contract and Discourses*, translation and introduction by G. D. H. Cole (London: J. M. Dent and Sons, 1973), p. 84.

2. Reinhold Niebuhr, *Moral Man and Immoral Society* (New York: Charles Scribner's Sons, 1932), p. 114.

3. Henry Steele Commager, *The Empire of Reason* (New York: Anchor Press/Doubleday, 1978).

4. Ibid., p. 135.

5. Thomas Jefferson, *Notes on the State Virginia*, Query XIV, p. 206. (Philadelphia: H. C. Carey and I. Lea, 1825).

6. Jean Jacques Rousseau, "A Discourse on Political Economy," *The Social Contract and Discourses*, translation and introduction by G.D.H. Cole (London: J. M. Dent and Sons, 1973), p. 149.

7. J. R. Pole, *The Pursuit of Equality in American History* (Berkeley: University of California Press, 1978), p. 6.

8. The writings of significant influence on the era were: Freidrich A. Hayek, *Law, Legislation, and Liberty* (Chicago: University of Chicago Press, 1976); Milton Friedman, *Capitalism and Freedom* (Chicago: University of Chicago Press, 1962); Adam Smith, *The Wealth of Nations* (New York: The Modern Library, 1937).

9. Helvetius, *De L'Esprit*, or *Essays on the Mind*, Essay II, (1970) Chap. 2.

10. Jeremy Bentham, *Works of Jeremy Bentham*, vol. X, (New York: Russell an Russell, 1962), p. 80.

11. Adam Smith, *The Wealth of Nations, 1776* (New York: The Modern Library, 1937), p. 423.

12. Edward Hallett Carr, *The Twenty Years' Crisis, 1919–1939* (New York: Harper Torchbooks, 1939), p. 42.

13. Robert Kuttner, *The Economic Illusion* (Philadelphia: University of Pennsylvania Press, 1991), p. 12.

14. Carr, op. cit., p. 47.

15. Ibid., p. 49.

16. Ibid.

17. Niebuhr, op. cit., p. 123.

18. Ibid.

19. Ibid., p. 123.

20. Ronald Dworkin, *A Matter of Principle* (Oxford: Oxford University Press, 1986), p. 206; Brian Barry, *Theories of Justice* (Berkeley: University of California Press, 1989), p. 230.

21. Brian Barry, *Theories of Justice* (Berkeley: University of California Press, 1989), p. 226.

22. John Rawls, *A Theory of Justice* (Cambridge, MA: Harvard University Press, 1971), p. 62.

23. Rawls, op. cit.

24. Plato's Dialogue, *Crito*, discussed in D. D. Raphael, *Problems of Political Philosophy* (London: Macmillan, 1976), p. 86.

25. Isaiah Berlin, *Concepts and Categories* (New York: Viking Press, 1978), p. 82.

26. Ibid.

27. Ibid., p. 84.

28. D. D. Raphael, *Problems of Political Philosophy* (London: Macmillan, 1976), p. 172.

29. Ibid.

30. Ibid., p. 173.

31. Ibid.

32. Ibid.

33. Niebuhr, op. cit., p. 196.

34. William Ryan, *Blaming the Victim* (New York: Vintage Books, 1976), p. 13.

35. Rawls, op. cit.

36. Robert Nozick, *Anarchy, State, and Utopia* (New York: Basic Books, 1974), p. 183.

37. Rawls, op. cit., p. 507.

38. Ibid.

39. Ibid.

40. Ibid., p. 303.

41. Ibid., p. 301.

42. Ibid.

43. Ibid.

44. Lester R. Brown, *State of the World 1990* (London: Unwin Paperbacks, 1990), p.136.

45. Ibid.

46. Ibid.

47. Stephen Paul Heyneman, "The World Economic Crisis and the Quality of Education," *Journal of Education Finance* 15 (Spring 1990), 456–459.

48. Ibid.

49. Ibid.

50. Ibid., p. 460.

51. Ibid., p. 461.

52. Ibid.

53. Philip H. Coombs, *The World Crisis in Education, The View from the Eighties* (New York: Oxford University Press, 1985).

54. Ibid., p. 5.

55. Ibid., p. 5.

56. World Bank, *World Development Report 1991, The Challenge of Development* (Oxford: The World Bank and Oxford University Press, 1991), p. 50.

57. Ibid.

58. Coombs, op. cit., p. 230.

59. Ibid.

60. Arthur M. Schlesinger, Jr., *The Disuniting of America* (Knoxville: Whittle Direct Books, 1991), p. 8.

61. James Bryce, *The American Commonwealth*, vol. II (London, 1988), pp. 709 and 328 as cited by Schlesinger in *The Disuniting of America*, op. cit.

62. Alexis de Tocqueville, *Democracy in America*, vol. I (London: 1835), C. XIV, as cited by Schlesinger in *The Disuniting of America*, op. cit.

63. Gunnar Myrdal, *The American Dilemma* (New York: Harper & Row, 1962), p. 8.

64. "American Survey," *The Economist* (October 26th–November 1st, 1991), p. 23.

65. This section of the inequality discussion is adapted in large part from Kern Alexander, "Financing the Public Schools of the United States: A Perspective on Effort, Need and Equity," *Journal of Education Finance* 17 (Winter 1992), No. 3, pp. 125–128 and 132–136.

66. Brown, op. cit., p. 140.

67. Spencer Rich, "Poverty Level Stabilizes at 31 million", *Washington Post*, October 19, 1989; from Stephen Rose and David Fasenfest, *Family Incomes in the 1980s: New Pressure on Wives, Husbands, and Young Adults* (Washington, D.C.: Economic Policy Institute, 1988); Robert D. Harmrin, "Sorry Americans—You're Still Not 'Better Off.'" *Challenge*, September/October, 1988.

68. Kevin Phillips, *The Politics of Rich and Poor* (New York: Harper Perennial, 1991), p. 13.

69. Ibid.

70. Brown, op. cit., p. 148.

71. Sylvia Nasar, "The 1980s: A Very Good Time for the Very Rich," *New York Times* (March 5, 1992); Paul Krugman, *The Age of Diminished Expectations* (Cambridge, MA: MIT Press, 1990).

72. Timothy Smeeding and Greg Duncan, Study conducted by the University of Michigan's Panel Study of Income Dynamics, 1991; Cited by Richard Morin, "American's Middle-Class Meltdown," *Washington Post* (December 1, 1991), p. C1.

73. Ibid.

74. Ibid.

75. Ibid.

76. Ibid.

77. World Bank, op. cit., pp. 43, 55, and 57.

78. Christopher Jencks, *Inequality: A Reassessment of the Effect of Family and Schooling in America* (New York: Basic Books, 1972), p. 20.

79. Adapted in part from Kern Alexander, "The Common School Ideal and the Limits of Legislative Authority: The Kentucky Case," *Harvard Journal on Legislation* 28, No. 2 (Summer 1991), 348–349.

80. The poorest district in Ohio is Huntington Local School District of Ross County, with an assessed valuation of property of about $14,557 per pupil while the richest is Perry Local School District of Lake County, which has revenues of $17,889 per pupil per year. Kern Alexander and Richard Salmon, *Fiscal Equity of the Ohio System of Public Schools,* (1990), p. 11.

81. Robert Reich, "*Secession of the Successful,*" *New York Times* (January 20, 1991), (Magazine), pp. 16, 42.

82. Ibid.

83. James S. Coleman, *Equality of Educational Opportunity* (Washington, DC: U.S. Government Printing Office, 1966).

84. *Brown et al.* v. *Board of Education of Topeka*, 347 U.S. 483; *Keyes* v. *School District No. 1, Denver, Colo.* 413 U.S. 189 (1973).

85. National Education Association, *Estimates of School Statistics, 1953–54* (Washington, DC: NEA, 1959); National Education Association, *Estimates of School Statistics, 1993–94* (Washington, DC: NEA, 1993).

86. Leslie L. Chisholm and M. L. Cushman, in *Problems and Issues in Public School Finance*, eds. Roe L. Johns and Edgar L. Morphet (New York: Teachers College Press, Teachers College, Columbia University, 1952), p. 103.

87. James D. Rodgers, "Explaining Income Redistribution," *Redistribution Through Public Choice*, eds. Harold Hochman and George Peterson (New York: Columbia University Press, 1974), p. 169.

88. Jack E. Fisher, "A Comparison Between Central Cities and Suburbs on Local Ability to Support Public Education" (Ed.D. dissertation, University of Florida, 1972).

89. J. M. Buchanan and G. Tullock, *The Calculus of Consent* (Ann Arbor, MI: University of Michigan, 1962).

CHAPTER 8

FISCAL CAPACITY AND EFFORT TO SUPPORT PUBLIC SCHOOLS

TOPICAL OUTLINE OF CHAPTER

Fiscal Capacity • Fiscal Capacity of Nations • Measurement of State Fiscal Capacity • Personal Income • Tax Revenues • Representative Tax System • Per-Capita Fiscal Capacity Comparisons among States • Per-Pupil Fiscal Capacity Comparisons among States • Variations in Local Fiscal Capacity • Measurement of Local Fiscal Capacity • Determining Local Fiscal Capacity • Pros and Cons of Economic-Indicator Approach • Equalized Assessment of Property Value • Fiscal Effort to Support Public Schools • Fiscal Effort of the United States • Fiscal Effort of States • Fiscal Effort of Local School Districts

INTRODUCTION

Disparities in physical and human resources of nations, states, and communities result in substantial unevenness in the fiscal ability to support education. As observed earlier in this book, those countries and states that have made investments in human resources have been rewarded with economic growth and higher standards of living. We know that the wealth of a nation or a state lies in the proper mix of physical and human capital and both require appropriate cultivation and investment. If funding for human capital investment is malapportioned and unequal then the nation or state suffers from underinvestment in the deprived sectors. This results in a waste of human capital and becomes a major source of economic inefficiency.

The federal and state governments bear the responsibility of overcoming such inefficiencies and of helping to overcome fiscal disparities that deny equality of educational opportunity. This is accomplished by more equitable and uniform distribution of fiscal resources. In a nation of over 15,000 school systems scattered throughout 50 states, all with different physical and human characteristics, the task of maximizing human capital productivity as well as attending to the moral and ethical responsibility of providing equality of education is not an insignificant undertaking.

FISCAL CAPACITY

At first glance it appears to be a relatively simple matter to use resources from the federal level to even out incapacities at the state level and to use state resources to equalize the revenues of local school districts. The problem though is actually more complex, because there is little agreement

DEFINITIONS

Fiscal Capacity.   The tax base of a governmental entity measured in terms of income, wealth, or other fiscal measures of economic productivity.

Fiscal Position.   Sometimes distinguished from fiscal capacity because capacity alone has nothing to do with need for services. Fiscal position has to do with the ability of a jurisdiction to perform its fiscal tasks taking into account both its capacity relative to the requirements of need for the particular public service. Two school districts may have the same fiscal capacity but have a much different fiscal positions (ability) because the incidence of educational need in one is much greater than in the other.

Source: Richard A. Musgrave and Peggy B. Musgrave, *Public Finance in Theory and Practice* (New York: McGraw-Hill, 1980), pp. 545–546.

as to how fiscal capacity is to be measured and how much is needed for educational services. The matter is further complicated by the myriad social and economic conditions which lead some states or localities to put forth greater financial effort than others to support their educational programs.

This chapter will first provide some insight into the fiscal capacity of the United States relative to that of other nations, then discuss the differences in capacity of states and school districts within the United States. The discussion will then turn to efforts to support education at the national, state, and local levels.

Even though the primary focus of this book is on the funding of public schools in the United States, it is helpful to gain some perspective by briefly viewing the world situation that bears so directly on every aspect of education as a major element in a world economy.

Fiscal Capacity of Nations

The amalgam of physical and human resources producing the economic capacity of a nation, state, or community may be described in terms of various fiscal measures.

For nations, relative fiscal capacity may be measured in terms of gross national product, gross domestic product, or gross national income, and a host of other measures that seek to determine a country's relative economic status such as monetary holdings, manufacturing activity, foreign trade, balance of payments, external debt, and so on.[1]

We have seen in recent years that some countries (e.g., Saudi Arabia, Iran, Iraq, and the United Arab Emirates) may become economically powerful in the short range by merely selling off and depleting their natural resources, but long-term sustained economic growth requires a nation with an educated citizenry. Japan is, of course, the prime example of a country without physical resources, but rich in human resources, and today it, along with the United States, possesses one of the most powerful and viable economies in the world. The United States has been an economic power because it is rich in both human and physical resources. It has developed the human resources primarily through the public schools and universities, while the physical resources were bestowed by nature. It is a phenomenon of modern technological development that the balance between human and physical resources required to make a rich and prosperous nation is becoming increasingly skewed toward the human resources. The importance of physical resources to the wealth of nations will become even less important as we move further into a new information age.

Reich advocates this trend in his book *The Work of Nations.* He foresees a post-national economic system in which we are rapidly progressing to a stage in which the physical resources of a country will become less and less necessary for economic growth. The communication technology on which Japan now prospers has significant implications for the future. The new internationalism will be a non-oil-based industrialization that requires little in the way of

DEFINITIONS

Gross National Product (GNP). The total value at current market prices of all goods and services produced by the economy of a nation during a year.*

Gross Domestic Product (GDP). The total output produced within a country during a year. GDP is different from GNP in that GNP measures the total output produced by all factors owned by the country (private and public) regardless of where the production takes place.

Gross National Income (GNI). The total of the incomes of all individuals in a nation earned in the forms of wages, interest, rents, and profits. It is calculated before deductions are taken for income taxes and excludes transfer payments.

*_Source:_ Richard A. Musgrave and Peggy B. Musgrave, _Public Finance in Theory and Practice_ (New York: McGraw-Hill, 1980), pp. 545–546.

physical assets, but great human intellectual power. Reich says that

> we are living through a transformation that will rearrange the politics and economics of the coming century. There will be no _national_ products or technologies, no national corporations, no national

industries. . . . All that will remain rooted within national borders are the people who comprise a nation. Each nation's primary assets will be its citizens' skills and insights.[2]

The United States is a great and powerful nation with a population of over 250 million people, second only to China and India. It possesses vast fiscal resources that in totality dwarf other individual national economies of the world; consequently no other country approaches the United States in total economic strength when intellectual, physical power, and wealth are taken into account.

Yet the United States, though great in total economic strength, is not the richest country per capita. As recently as 1987, the United States' gross national product per capita still exceeded Japan's, but in 1988 for the first time the GNP per capita of Japan eclipsed that of the United States, $21,400 to $19,700.[3] The Japanese gross national income (GNI) per capita had exceeded that of the United States in 1982; and by 1991, the GNI of Japan was $22,770 per capita and the United States lagged far behind at $19,500.[4]

Table 8.1 shows that in 1989 the United States had ranked sixth, trailing Japan $23,810 to $20,910. But by 1990, as Table 8.2 indicates, the United States had fallen to eighth among the na-

TABLE 8.1 Gross National Product Per Capita, 1989 (ten richest countries)

TEN RICHEST COUNTRIES	1989	RANK
Switzerland	$29,880	1
Japan	$23,810	2
Norway	$22,290	3
Finland	$22,120	4
Sweden	$21,570	5
United States	$20,910	6
Denmark	$20,450	7
Germany	$20,440	8
(formerly West Germany only)		
Canada	$19,030	9
United Arab Emirates	$18,430	10

Source: World Bank, _World Development Report 1991, The Challenge of Development_ (Oxford: Oxford University Press, 1991), Table 1, Basic Indicators, p. 204. Reprinted with permission.

TABLE 8.2   Gross National Product Per Capita, 1990 (ten richest countries)

TEN RICHEST COUNTRIES	1990	RANK
Switzerland	$32,680	1
Finland	$26,040	2
Japan	$25,430	3
Sweden	$23,660	4
Norway	$23,120	5
Germany	$22,320	6
(formerly West Germany only)		
Denmark	$22,080	7
United States	$21,790	8
Canada	$20,470	9
United Arab Emirates	$19,860	10

Source: World Bank, *World Development Report 1992, Development and The Environment* (Oxford: Oxford University Press, 1992), Table 1, Basic Indicators, p. 219. Reprinted with permission.

tions, trailing Japan $25,430 to $21,790 in GNP per capita. Switzerland led all countries in 1990 with the Scandinavian countries and Germany all ranking above the United States.

The preeminence in the financial power of the United States has obviously eroded in recent years. Paul Kennedy in his book *Preparing for the Twenty-First Century* cites 1991 data showing that Germany and Austria have been added to the lists of nations that have overtaken the United States in fiscal capacity, as measured in terms of GDP per capita, 1991 data.[5] By the same measure (GDP) Canada and the United States are in a dead heat.[6] Regardless of the exact measures, however, the fact that the United States is in a relative decline compared to other industrialized nations is not seriously disputed.

These comparisons, while reason for considerable concern, still find the United States far above most industrialized nations. France, for example, in 1990 had a GNP per capita of $19,490 and Australia was even lower with $17,000, as was the United Kingdom with $16,100. The United States and the other technologically sophisticated countries are all, however, in comparatively strong economic conditions when contrasted to the poor and underdeveloped nations of the world. The starkness of the differ-

ences in fiscal capacity between the first and third world countries are nearly beyond comprehension. Ethiopia, for example, in 1990 had a GNP per capita of only $120, Somalia, $120, Zaire, $220, while India with her 832 million people and China with a population of 1.2 billion have only $350 and $370, respectively.

The differences in fiscal capacity worldwide is thus marked by great disparity and vast deprivation. Kennedy observes that the prospects for elevating the poorer countries appear to be bleak if nations are unable to magnify the role of education, control population by decreasing fertility rates, and enhance the quality of political leadership among all the nations.[7] This is a daunting challenge indeed.

The danger is all too apparent. As a nation becomes less capable economically it may err by investing less in education, thereby increasing its downward spiral. As data presented in this chapter show, such a trend is discernible now to some degree in the United States as we lose relative economic strength and invest less in education. Although this country remains the world's most powerful in total productivity, economic strength, and military might, there has been certain decline, particularly during the 1980s, from its earlier position of uncontested preeminence.

Box 8.1

Population and Poverty

If my analysis is roughly correct, the forces for change facing the world could be so far-reaching, complex, and interactive that they call for nothing less than the reeducation of humankind. This is not a new conclusion. Social thinkers from Wells to Toynbee have repeatedly argued that global society is in a race between education and catastrophe; and those stakes are higher at the century's end, simply because population pressures, environmental damage, and human kind's capacity to inflict mass destruction are all far greater.

Source: Paul Kennedy, *Preparing for the Twenty-First Century* (New York: Random House, 1993), pp. 339–340.

MEASUREMENT OF STATE FISCAL CAPACITY

Fiscal capacity is the ability of state and local school systems to obtain revenues from their own sources through taxation.[8] Or fiscal capacity may be broadly defined as a quantitative measure of economic resources within a governmental unit which can be used to support public functions. Relative fiscal capacity among states or localities is determined by dividing the measure of capacity by some unit such as population or pupils.

Traditionally, policy makers have relied on personal income and tax revenues as economic indicators of fiscal capacity. Personal income is most commonly used among states because the data are kept current by the U.S. Department of Commerce, Bureau of Economic Analysis.[9] Data for tax revenues are also collected annually by various departments of the federal government and by several independent agencies.

Personal Income

When the income of the people of each state is known, it is possible to determine the per capita income, the income per child of school age (ages five through seventeen are generally used), or the income per pupil in average daily membership or average daily attendance. The ratio of children to total population varies considerably among states, depending on which pupil measure is used. The personal income per average daily attendance or average daily membership rather than either population or children of school age population are superior measures for determining the state fiscal capacity to support the public schools. The use of school-age population broadens the measure by including children in nonpublic schools, thus inflating the divisor. Thus the relative fiscal capacity of states with large nonpublic school enrollment would be substantially reduced. Similarly the use of population as the divisor does not relate consistently to the numbers of children served by the public schools.

Personal income is the amount of current income received from all sources, including transfer payments from government and business but excluding transfer payments from other sources. The major part of personal income is derived from labor income, proprietors' income, rental income, dividends, interest, and transfer payments.

Personal income, however, does not reflect the total fiscal capacity of the state for two basic reasons. First, personal income represents a measure of the flow of capital and does not capture the stock of wealth that a state might possess. Personal and real property are not included. Income is not wealth; wealth constitutes the total

DEFINITION

Personal Income. The flow of wages or salaries, dividends, interest payments and other revenues accruing to the individual during a specified period of time, usually a year. Personal income may also be simply defined as the total income received by households, including both earnings and transfer payments.

Source: Edwin G. Dolan and David E. Lindsey, *Economics* (Chicago: The Dryden Press, 1986), p. 180.

value of the stock of all assets, physical and financial, held at a particular time.[10] Second, resident personal income does not capture the potential capacity which a state may have from its ability to export its tax burden to other states, such as Florida and Nevada's ability to tax tourists through sales, hotel, and amusement taxes, or the ability of Alaska, Louisiana, West Virginia, Texas, New Mexico, and Wyoming to tax exported oil and mineral deposits.

Tax Revenues

Tax revenues are an inferior measure of fiscal capacity because they reflect taxpayer effort as well as capacity. For example, a poor state could put forth great effort and show a high revenue base, while a rich state could exert little tax effort and show low revenues, thus leading to a misunderstanding of the relative capacities of the two states. Neither measure, personal income or tax revenues, represents a complete and accurate measurement of a state's fiscal capacity.[11]

Representative Tax System

Another measure which largely corrects for the aforementioned deficiencies is the representative or uniform tax system method. This approach, developed by the Advisory Commission on Intergovernmental Relations, derives data by using the following methodology:

1. Determining for each of the various kinds of state and local taxes a national average rate which, if applied throughout the nation, would have produced the same total amount of revenue that state and local governments actually obtained from the particular type of tax in (a base year)
2. Estimating by state the potential yield of each type of tax, if imposed at this uniform nationwide rate
3. Aggregating these potential-yield amounts for each state to arrive at an estimate of its total tax capacity[12]

Box 8.2 _____

The Representative Tax System

The RTS may be "representative" or "typical" of all the taxes actually levied by the state and local governments of a federation. As such, it abstracts from the actual tax policy of individual state and local governments, yet it is representative of those taxing practices in the aggregate.

The purpose of the RTS is to compare the revenue-raising capacities of state governments, including their local governments in the aggregate. This is done by estimating the amount of revenues that each state government, with its local governments, could derive from imposing, at average rates, a *standard tax system* made up of the various taxes and quasi-taxes that are actually levied by states and local governments.

Source: Advisory Commission on Intergovernmental Relations, *1988 State Fiscal Capacity and Effort* (Washington, DC: ACIR, August 1990), m-170, p. 3.

Other researchers have developed additional methods of determining state fiscal capacity. For a number of years Kenneth Quindry annually reported on state fiscal capacity for the Southern Regional Education Board. He computed potential tax collections by using personal income as the representative base measure and supplementing it with alternative bases, such as the value of natural resources severed from land and waters of a state as the measure for severance tax potential. He also used the number of registered motor vehicles as a measure of ability to collect motor fuel and license taxes.[13]

John Akin developed another measure which makes allowances for the interaction among sources of revenue as a result of actual tax impact. He maintains that since all taxes are actually paid from either income or wealth, heavy use of a particular tax prevents full use of another tax. Akin's method involves the use of a regression analysis to estimate tax rates that result in revenues a particular jurisdiction might expect if taxes behaved in a normative manner as in other taxing jurisdictions.[14] Another measure, developed by Charlesworth and Herzel—gross state product—is the state counterpart of gross national product and measures the value of all goods and services produced in a state.[15]

Per-Capita Fiscal Capacity Comparisons among States

The quality of education in the United States to a great extent is dependent on the financial capacity of the sovereign states, but there exists substantial differences in capacity that impede efforts to provide equality of educational opportunity nationwide. Over the years comparisons of fiscal capacity show that there is an ebb and flow of state fiscal fortune, just as there is among countries; by and large the rich remain relatively affluent and the poor tend to cluster near the lower extremes of incapacity.

In 1980 Alaska ranked first among the states in per capita personal income ($12,406), but had dropped to seventh in 1990 ($21,688). Connecticut had ranked second among the 50 states in 1980 ($11,445) but by 1990 had moved to first place ($25,484). During that decade, Connecticut's per capita personal income had increased by 223 percent while Alaska had experienced a 175 percent increase. In 1980 California ranked third ($10,856) and New Jersey ranked fourth ($10,755). By 1990 California had dropped to ninth ($20,677) and New Jersey had progressed upward to second ($24,936). At the other extreme, Arkansas had been last in 1980 ($7,180) but had moved up four places in 1990 ($14,188). Mississippi claimed last place in 1990 ($12,823).

Over the long range, the data indicate that there has been a decrease in the relative per capita personal income differences among the states. In 1948 the per capita personal income in Connecticut was $1,713 and in Mississippi it was $789, or 46 percent of Connecticut. By 1966, Connecticut was $3,678 and Mississippi was $1,651; Mississippi was 47 percent of Connecticut. By 1970 Mississippi's per capita personal income at $2,547 was 52 percent of

Connecticut's and in 1980 Mississippi was $6,508, or 56 percent of Connecticut's $11,445 personal income per capita, a gain of 10 percent between the richest state and the poorest during the 32-year period.

The decade of the 1980s, however, reversed this trend as the nation experienced a renewed separation between the richest and the poorest states as well as among its people. In the ten years from 1980 to 1990, Mississippi's fiscal capacity relative to Connecticut's fell six percentage points from its high point of 56 percent of Connecticut's per capita personal income in 1980 down to 50 percent in 1990. In this brief span Mississippi lost three-fifths of the progress it had made in the previous three decades.

Table 8.3 gives per capita personal income data for 1948, 1966, and 1990 for the highest- and lowest-ranking states in 1966. Notice that the percentage increases for the poorest states are greater than for the richest states and more than the U.S. average, evidencing some decline in the disparities. Yet use of percentages for such comparisons, while of some value, may be somewhat deceptive overall when one considers the actual dollar increases from 1948 to 1990. As can be seen in Table 8.3, Connecticut's dollar increase of $23,771 dwarfed the $12,034 increase of Mississippi even though Mississippi's percentage increase made its gain appear impressive.

If one uses the representative tax system rather than personal income as a measure of fiscal capacity, Mississippi still has the lowest per capita fiscal capacity, only 65 percent of the U.S. average. Arkansas comes next with 74 percent, then Idaho with 76 percent, Alabama with 76 percent, and Utah with 78 percent. Using the RTS measure, Alaska exceeds Connecticut as having the highest capacity, 159 percent of the U.S. average. Alaska's capacity balloons up on this measure because of its high severance tax capacity.[16] Table 8.4 shows the relative capacities of high-, middle-, and low-ranking states. Notice that Mississippi ranks last whether per capita personal income or the representative tax system is used as the measure of fiscal capacity.

TABLE 8.3   Five Highest- and Five Lowest-Ranking States in Income Per Capita, Ranked by 1966 Data; Existing Differences in 1948 and 1990

STATE	PERSONAL INCOME PER CAPITA 1966	PERSONAL INCOME PER CAPITA 1948	PERSONAL INCOME PER CAPITA 1990	PERCENT CHANGE 1948– 1990
High Ranking				
Connecticut	$3,678	$1,713	$25,484	1,488
Delaware	$3,563	$1,721	$20,022	1,163
Illinois	$3,511	$1,815	$20,419	1,125
New York	$3,480	$1,797	$22,086	1,229
California	$3,449	$1,752	$20,677	1,180
Low Ranking				
West Virginia	$2,195	$1,120	$13,755	1,228
Alabama	$2,039	$ 866	$15,021	1,735
South Carolina	$2,027	$ 891	$15,151	1,700
Arkansas	$2,015	$ 875	$14,188	1,621
Mississippi	$1,751	$ 789	$12,823	1,625
U.S. Average	$2,940	$1,430	$18,691	1,307

Source: National Education Association, *Rankings of the States, 1992* (Washington, DC: NEA, 1992), Table D-3, p. 29. Data for 1966 and 1948 are from U.S. Department of Commerce, Office of Business Economics, *Survey of Current Business* (Washington, DC: U.S. Government Printing Office, April 1967), pp. 14–15.

Per-Pupil Fiscal Capacity Comparisons among States.   The relative fiscal capacity of states may vary depending on whether the capacity measures are divided by the total state population (capita) or by the number of pupils in the public schools. Which is more accurate: a per-capita or a per-pupil measure of capacity? Some argue that relative fiscal capacity is best measured if one takes into account the entire population because the tax system must support governmental services for all the people. Further, it is correctly maintained that the income and wealth of all the people constitutes the total fiscal capacity of a state. On the other hand it may be reasonably argued that for education purposes, capacity should be measured in terms of the number of children to be educated. States have varying demographics and a state like Florida has far fewer children ages 5–17, compared to the total state population, than other states. Too, some states have much higher percentages of private school pupils, resulting in differing public school financial burdens. Thus the denominator for calculating fiscal capacity may be either population (capita) or numbers of pupils. As noted previously, pupils attending public schools is preferred. If the number of students is used, it is usually expressed in terms of enrollment, average daily membership, or average daily attendance.

Table 8.5 shows the fiscal capacity per average daily attendance of selected states ranking high, middle, and low. The same states were shown in the per capita capacity in Table 8.4. Notice that when the pupil count of average daily attendance (ADA) is used as a denominator for measuring state fiscal capacity, Connecticut's advantage over Mississippi is substantially expanded. Personal income per capita shows that Connecticut is 136 percent of the U.S. average

TABLE 8.4 Interstate Differentials in Tax Capacity Per Capita (states ranked by per capita personal income, 1990)

STATE	CAPACITY MEASURES	
	PERSONAL INCOME PER CAPITA AS % OF U.S. AVERAGE, 1990	REPRESENTATIVE TAX SYSTEM PER CAPITA, 1988, AS % OF U.S. AVERAGE, 1988
High*		
Connecticut	136%	143%
New Jersey	133	124
Massachusetts	121	129
New York	118	109
Maryland	116	109
Middle		
Ohio	94	91
Wisconsin	94	90
Nebraska	94	90
Vermont	94	105
Missouri	94	90
Low		
New Mexico	76	83
Arkansas	76	74
Utah	75	78
West Virginia	74	78
Mississippi	69	65
United States	100	100

Sources: National Education Association, *Rankings of the States, 1992* (Washington, DC: NEA, 1992), Table D-3, p. 29; Advisory Commission on Intergovernmental Relations, *State Fiscal Capacity and Effort* (Washington, DC: ACIR, August 1990), m-170, Table 501, p. 32.

*Alaska ranks first by RTS method having 159 percent of the U.S. average capacity.

while Mississippi is only 69 percent. But when personal income per ADA is used as the denominator, Connecticut's advantage increases to 154 percent of the U.S. average and Mississippi's is reduced to 56 percent. The pattern is similar if the representative tax system per ADA is used instead of per capita; Connecticut's relative wealth rises from 143 percent of the U.S. average to 159 percent and Mississippi's falls from 65 to 56 percent. These comparisons also show striking differences for Utah which appears relatively much poorer when using ADA as a divisor rather than population. When ADA is used, Utah falls below Mississippi on both personal income and the representative tax system making it by far the poorest state in the country.

Regardless of measure, however, there remains a substantial disparity in tax capacity among the states in the United States. Insofar as financial support relates to educational opportunity, the high-capacity states have a decided advantage. The most fiscally able states can finance a reasonably adequate quality of education with lower tax efforts than can the less able. This means that if schools were to be financed entirely from state and local funds, either the people in the less capable states would have to make a much greater effort to support their schools or

TABLE 8.5 Fiscal Capacity of Selected States as Percent of U.S. Average as Measured by Personal Income and the Representative Tax System by Average Daily Attendance

STATE	PERSONAL INCOME PER PUPIL IN ADA, 1990, AS % OF U.S. AVERAGE	REPRESENTATIVE TAX SYSTEM 1988 PER PUPIL IN ADA, 1990, AS % OF U.S. AVERAGE
High		
Connecticut	154%	159%
New Jersey	156	148
Massachusetts	143	154
New York	141	132
Maryland	131	119
Middle		
Ohio	98%	101%
Wisconsin	100	96
Nebraska	88	87
Vermont	91	103
Missouri	99	98
Low		
New Mexico	70%	77%
Arkansas	66	68
Utah	48	49
West Virginia	66	76
Mississippi	56	56
United States	100%	100%

Source: Advisory Commission on Intergovernmental Relations, *State Fiscal Capacity and Effort* (Washington, DC: ACIR, August, 1990), p. 32.

the children in these states would be relegated to schools that were inadequately financed. Thus the national interest inevitably requires equalizing of funds from federal sources.

Variations in Local Fiscal Capacity.   Each state has its own methods and idiosyncrasies in determining local fiscal capacity; no two are identical. However, the choices made by each state in determining local fiscal capacity have important effects on the extent and effectiveness of the state equalization program. The mathematical weighting of some local capacity factors more than others will inevitably result in substantial shifts in state equalization funds among local school districts.

Variations in the fiscal capacity of school districts are generally much greater than the variation in capacity among the states. As mentioned earlier, the variation of fiscal capacity among districts in states where districts have been reorganized is much less than in states with many small districts. This is inevitably the case because when several small districts with wide differences in wealth per pupil are combined to form one district, differences are eliminated within the combined area.

Recent studies in a number of states have indicated a range in fiscal capacity for county units and other large school district states, from less than 10 to 1 to about 20 or 25 to 1 for small district states. Thus, even when all districts are reasonably adequate in size, it is apparent that a considerable difference exists among the districts in their ability to finance educational programs. If no state aid were provided in these states, the low fiscal capacity districts would have to make from 10 to 25 times the fiscal effort made by their high capacity peers to finance an equitable program of educational opportunity. The situation in the states that maintain large numbers of very small school districts is of course much more serious, with the range often exceeding 100 to 1.

In Ohio, a state with 612 school districts, the highest-capacity district, Perry Local, in 1991 had $894,848 in equalized assessed valuation of property per pupil per ADA and the poorest, Huntington Local, had only $16,050—a fiscal capacity difference of over 55 to 1. In that same state the five percent of the students who attended school in the wealthiest school districts had an average of $171,228 equalized assessed valuation of property supporting their education while five percent of the pupils from the poorest school districts had an average of only $29,179 per pupil.

In Texas, the evidence presented in the *Edgewood* case, 1989, showed that the highest-capacity school district had over $14,000,000 of property wealth per pupil while the poorest district had about $20,000, a wealth disparity ratio of approximately 700 to 1.

In Montana, in 1991, a state with 527 school districts, 90 which enrolled fewer than 40 pupils, the taxable valuation of property per pupil in elementary districts ranged from $911,510 per pupil in Squirrel Creek to $265 in Heart Butte, a fiscal capacity disparity ratio of about 3,440 to 1. Among Montana's high school districts the range was from $365,939 per pupil in Colstrip District to $1,318 per pupil in Hays-Lodge Pole District, a disparity ratio of nearly 278 to 1.

The year before *Serrano I*, 1969–70, legislative reports in California showed a range of assessed valuation per pupil between the highest- and lowest-capacity elementary districts to be $952,156 to only $103 per pupil, while the high school districts exhibited a range of $349,093 to $11,959 per pupil.[17] When the Supreme Court of

Oregon in 1976 rejected plaintiffs' claims for greater equalization funding in the case of *Olsen* v. *State*,[18] the wealth differential in true cash value of property between the wealthiest and poorest unified districts in Oregon ranged from $203,000 to $19,300 per pupil, a 10.5 to 1 disparity ratio.

Thus, the fiscal capacities among school districts in some states vary so much as to be almost incomprehensible while in others the ranges are of more modest proportions. Regardless of magnitude, however, it is easy to understand why local systems of taxation are unable to provide for equality of educational opportunity. Moreover, it is obvious that the current battle to reduce or eliminate the disparities of educational services that exist among school districts in most states will continue as long as states rely extensively upon local non-neutralized tax resources.

The above information, although only shown for a few states, is not uncommon and points to the following conclusions. In no state can the least fiscally able districts finance a reasonably satisfactory program of education from local funds without an unreasonable tax effort. In many districts, the tax effort required would be prohibitive, unless the state neutralizes the variance in fiscal capacity that exists among districts. The differences in wealth in small district states are so great that no program involving state and local support is likely to solve all the financial equality problems until further reorganization occurs. Until further progress is made in many states in district organization and financing of schools, inequalities in educational opportunity are certain to continue. Substantial numbers of students in many states cannot expect to have even reasonably adequate educational opportunities under present conditions.

MEASUREMENT OF LOCAL FISCAL CAPACITY

Equalization of educational opportunity hinges on the appropriate and accurate measurement of local fiscal capacity. The need to equalize the disparities in local fiscal capacity through allocation of state and has long been recognized, and all states have taken steps to ameliorate this situation. In 1906 Cubberley observed that "any attempt at the equalization of opportunities for education, much less any attempt at equalizing burdens, is clearly impossible under a system of exclusively local taxation."[19] The state must take action to overcome the disparities inherent in the diverse economic conditions which characterize different local school districts. This issue has persisted as one of the most complex questions facing states in their attempts to meet the educational needs of all children regardless of where they attend school.

Early analysis showed that equalization could not be accomplished without the states assuming greater responsibility for financing the schools. A recognized function of state government was to provide for a uniform educational program among all local school districts. This can be accomplished utilizing equalization formula that allocates state funds in inverse relationship to local fiscal capacity. (See details on the types of state aid formulas discussed in Chapter 9.) The basic dilemma of course is how best to measure local fiscal capacity in order to bring about optimal equalization. This subject has been much debated in school finance circles in recent years.

Determining Local Fiscal Capacity.   Three basic approaches have been used to address the problem: (1) tax-base, (2) tax-base surrogate, and (3) economic-indicator.

The tax-base approach simply determines taxpaying ability by using the available tax base(s). For example, if real property is the school tax base, then equalized valuation of property is used as the measure of fiscal capacity. If a sales tax or other nonproperty source also is used as a portion of the tax base then it is included as the measure of fiscal capacity.

The second approach, the tax-base surrogate, was used in several states in an earlier era, when property tax assessments were too unevenly administered to be either a reliable or valid measure of fiscal capacity. This method, sometimes called an index of taxpaying ability, utilized selected variables which were predictive of equalized valuation of property at some point in time. The problem of course was to find a time in which property values were reasonably well assessed, in order to set up a predictive equation. This approach served as an interim measure while property tax administration was in the process of being developed and improved.

The economic-indicator approach is a theoretical determination of fiscal capacity utilizing measures of income, wealth, and consumption, regardless of whether they are accessible through local taxation. It is not a proxy or surrogate measure for equalized assessed valuation of property. It departs materially from the other two measures in that it presumes that determination of fiscal capacity does not need to be tied to an accessible local tax base. This approach suggests that since all taxes must be paid out of income or accumulated wealth, it really does not matter what particular tax base is used locally to actually collect the revenues.

Opponents of this approach maintain that local taxing units only have taxpaying capacity relative to their accessibility to legislatively designated tax bases. If inequality of local resources exist, it is created by variation in the capacity of taxpayers to pay the particular available tax. Equalization of funding must therefore, be directed toward erasing disparities created by the revenues from legally levied taxes. If full equalization is to be attained, fiscal capacity must be determined by each and every one of the locally available tax bases.

The tax-base approach addresses this issue by determining the actual ability to pay the schools, rather than using a theoretical measure of fiscal capacity, such as economic indicators. Burrup observed that economic indicators are inappropriate for comparing fiscal capacities of localities unable to tap major wealth bases.[20] Other authorities agree, maintaining that the fiscal capacity of a community is its access to legally permissible taxes.[21]

The quest for better measurement of local fiscal capacity is not new; in 1923 George Strayer and Robert Haig suggested that economic indicators could be used as an alternative to property valuations for purposes of school fund equalization. They recommended that local fiscal capacity be determined in New York by summing taxable income with one-tenth of the full value of real estate, then dividing the result by two. Reasoning that this measure was more comprehensive, since the relative position of localities was much different with each measure, they suggested that the combination would give a more accurate picture of overall economic resources.[22]

Ten years later, Paul Mort criticized economic indicators recommended by Strayer and Haig, observing that they defined theoretical taxing capacity under an ideal system of taxation, not the actual situation. Mort noted that the power to tax rests with state legislatures, not the local taxing units. He said,

> the true criterion of the relative ability of local units to pay for education is the ability-to-pay under the taxing system established by the state rather than the ability-to-pay under an ideal taxing system. . . .
>
> Since we must deal with communities which have no power over their tax systems except through state action, we cannot consider their ability as it would be under an ideal tax system. To build our system of state aid on such a foundation would throw excessive burdens upon actual taxpayers in some communities, simply because there happened to be wealth in those communities that was not taxable under the existing system of taxation.[23]

The theoretical measure of fiscal capacity advocated by Mort is apparently the prevailing view today. Most states use only those measures of ability which relate directly to taxable sources. These states have implicitly followed the philosophy which maintains that local taxpaying capacity should, appropriately, be a measure of accessibility to local tax revenue. The Mort position was reinforced more recently by the National Educational Finance Project:

> The local taxpaying ability of school districts in reality is not their theoretical taxpaying ability, but rather a measure of their accessibility to local tax revenue. If a district only has the authority to levy property taxes then its local taxpaying ability (or effort to support schools) should be measured only in terms of the equalized value of the taxable property of that district. However, if a district has the power to levy local nonproperty taxes, such as payroll taxes, sales taxes, utility taxes, etc., then the yield of such local nonproperty taxes can justly be incorporated in the measure of the taxpaying ability of that district.[24]

Note that school finance authorities do not distinguish fiscal capacity from taxpaying ability, but rather use the terms interchangeably.

A total of 18 states use multiple measures to determine local fiscal capacity other than property valuations alone. Five states, Connecticut, Maryland, New York, Rhode Island, and Vermont, use an index of property and income. For example, Connecticut uses the ratio of district median family income to state median family income as a property valuation adjustment. Maryland combines the assessed valuation of property with net taxable income of the local school district to determine capacity.[25] New York uses full valuation of taxable real property and adjusted gross income per pupil for its measure of local capacity[26] and Rhode Island uses equalized weighted assessed valuation (EWAV) adjusted for median family income. Missouri applies an income adjustment to property valuation.

Five states, Alabama, Illinois, Mississippi, New Hampshire, and Virginia, use indices composed of more than two separate indicators of local fiscal capacity. Alabama still uses an economic index developed in 1939 by Roe L. Johns to respond to inconsistencies and variations in real property assessment practices. The Alabama index includes sales taxes paid, auto licenses paid, public utility valuation, income taxes paid, value of farm products, and value added by manufacturers. These factors are assigned weights and aggregated for a single measure of wealth, an economic index.[27] Mississippi has an economic index similar to that of Alabama that includes weightings for the country's percent of: assessed valuation of public utilities, state motor vehicles license receipts, value of farm products, personal income taxes paid, state total of gainfully employed nonfarm, nongovernmental workers, and retail sales taxes paid in the state.[28] New Hampshire calculates an equalization factor to determine each school district's fiscal capacity by utilizing property wealth, personal income, and a measure of fiscal effort.[29] Local districts in New Hampshire are authorized to levy only the property tax. Virginia presents another interesting example of an index of fiscal capacity. Virginia school districts are fiscally dependent, deriving their local revenues from local governing agencies which have authority to levy taxes other than property taxes, including an optional one-cent sales tax. Local fiscal capacity is determined by a "composite index" made up as follows: (1) true value of real estate and public service corporations, 50 percent, (2) adjusted gross income, 40 percent, and (3) taxable retail sales receipts from a state general sales and use tax, 10 percent.[30]

Seven states, Arkansas, Kansas, Missouri, Nebraska, Nevada, Oklahoma, and Oregon, use multiple deductions as measures of local fiscal capacity for equalization purposes.[31] This category, multiple deductions, is different from the index in that it is simply a series of tax rates applied to different bases and then summed. The bases are not weighted as in an index. Multiple deductions are best illustrated by the Kansas method of determining local fiscal capacity. Kansas equalizes by subtracting each school district's required local effort from the total adopted budget amount set by legislative enactment. The required local effort is determined establishing relative local capacity as the total of five measures:

1. The district's prior year's adjusted valuation of taxable tangible property and taxable income of residents of the school district
2. Federal impact aid (P.L. 874 revenues)

3. Eighty-five percent of the district's share of the state income tax rebate
4. Motor vehicle property tax
5. Motor vehicle dealer's stamp tax
6. Revenue in lieu of taxes on industrial revenue bonds[32]

All of these measures are totalled to become the Kansas measure of local fiscal capacity that is deducted to equalize the fiscal capacities of the several school districts.

A similar approach is found in Oklahoma where local fiscal capacity is determined by aggregating the following.

1. Adjusted valuation of real property of the school district
2. The yield of a 4-mill county property tax levy
3. School land grant earnings
4. Gross production tax
5. Auto license tax
6. REA tax

The total yield from these revenues sources becomes the local required effort that is deducted for charged back to the state formula equalization aid.

Each of these methods endeavors to capture the essence of local fiscal capacity and are generally successful; however, no method is without some degree of inaccuracy. Problems usually emanate from the administration of the property tax and the precision of assessment practices. Some states have much better systems for determining the fair market value of property than do others. Also, the methods used to measure local capacity are not the products of any particular high degree of empiricism; rather, they are all results of political compromise in state legislatures. As with other political questions, the effects that a method may have on a local constituency will always have a bearing on the distribution of state resources. The choice among measures of local fiscal capacity, property valuation, income, sales, or other measures may result in widely varying consequences when the funds are finally distributed. One of the most persistent and authentically perplexing problems of determination of local fiscal capacity is whether income or some other tax base should be used as a measure of local fiscal capacity if the locality does not have the legal authority to levy the particular tax.

Pros and Cons of the Economic-Indicator Approach

Proponents of the economic-indicator approach maintain that it is not necessary for an income tax to be locally accessible for it to be used as a measure of fiscal capacity. They advance three propositions in support of this argument. First, income is generally accepted as the best available indicator of ability to pay, regardless of the tax being levied. Second, several studies have shown that property wealth and income are not similarly distributed among school districts, usually having a low correlation. Third, evidence is increasing that income is a significant factor in the determination of local fiscal effort to support education.

Effect on Fiscal Capacity. It is helpful here to remind ourselves that wealth and income measure two entirely different aspects of fiscal resources. Wealth is a stock, while income is a flow of capital. Real property constitutes only a portion, possibly 35 percent, of the wealth of a state.

School districts with high incomes may be relatively low in property valuation or vice versa. Examples may be found of very high property values in metropolitan areas that have moderate or low per capita income. The Plains states have long experienced the dilemma of property-rich farmers who are barely able to meet their tax obligations because they have such low annual income in relation to their wealth.

Fisher found that in the 28 largest Standard Metropolitan Statistical Areas (SMSAs), several central cities showed substantial differences in relative fiscal capacity when adjusted gross income per pupil was used rather than equalized assessed valuation of property per pupil.[33] Thus, the inclusion of income as an indicator of fiscal capacity could have an important effect on the amount of state funds that flow to some cities.

Correlation between Income and Property. Correlation studies have shown that property values and income may have a rather low relationship. James, Thomas, and Dyck found a low correlation between property valuation and income in Massachusetts (0.20) and New Jersey (0.26). They found somewhat higher correlations in Wisconsin (0.57), New York (0.40), Oregon (0.34), and California (0.34). Kimbrough and Johns also found rather low correlations in Kentucky, Florida, Georgia, and Illinois. Farner and Edmundson similarly found little or no correlation between equalized valuation of property per pupil and income per pupil among counties in eleven western states.[34]

Advocates of the use of an income factor to determine local fiscal capacity maintain that low correlations provide evidence for the need to combine income with property valuations in order to arrive at a more valid measure of fiscal capacity. On the other hand, critics say that income merely measures a different type of tax base than property, and to assume that you should use income as a measure of fiscal capacity without tax accessibility would violate the principle of horizontal equity.

Income and Local Fiscal Effort. Melcher suggested that the most cogent argument yet presented for the use of income as a measure of local fiscal capacity has been given by McMahon.[35] After observing that higher-income school districts usually levy higher property taxes, McMahon recommends broadening the measures of capacity to pay to include income, though the income tax may not be locally tax accessible. His rationale follows:

> Equity on the tax side, is addressed by broadening the measures of wealth and effort for the simple reason that wealth incorporates human capital and

financial assets and (i.e., an income factor) is a better measure of the true ability-to-pay than is a measure of wealth that is limited to real property. All taxes go back to the individual taxpayer's ability-to-pay, which are basic to both the state's and the district's fiscal capacity, irrespective of whether the tax handle used is consumption (for state sales taxes) or real property (for property taxes). Each school district has access to income through the tax handle of real property.[36]

The taxpayer equity issue bears close examination if only property or consumption taxes are accessible and income is used as a measure of fiscal capacity. Horizontal tax equity is the widely accepted principle of taxation which maintains that individuals with equal ability to pay should bear equal tax burdens. For more information on this issue see Chapter 6 of this text discussing principles of taxation. The horizontal inequity of an income factor is seen where two precisely equal low-income families with homes of the same value live in two different local school districts, one high in income, the other low. The family in the high-income school district must put forth greater tax effort to support a similar school program than the family in the low-income school district, because the income factor formulas make the high-income district appear more affluent for state equalization purposes.

Thus, use of income or any other tax-inaccessible measure may unfairly burden individual taxpayers in school districts that show high fiscal capacity when measured by untaxable indicators. Noting this horizontal inequity in 1933, Mort observed that, "A district may be the situs of great wealth, yet if a large part of it cannot be taxed locally, the part that is taxed is penalized heavily."[37]

In a 1979 study of school finance in North Carolina, it was found that the use of a theoretical fiscal capacity measure in local school districts that did not have the legal authority to tax the resources tended to create greater inequity.

Where property is the only locally available tax base, use of theoretical taxpaying ability in a state equalization program requires that districts with a

high ratio of income-to-property levy higher property tax rates than other districts. This disparity in tax rates . . . violates the horizontal equity principle as applied to the individual taxpayer. . . . Those who live in a district whose average incomes are low pay lower property tax rates for a given expenditure guarantee than taxpayers with the same income living in districts where average incomes are high.[38]

On the other hand, a 1990 study of Alabama found that both equalized assessed valuation of property per pupil and personal income per pupil were highly correlated with local revenue per pupil, 0.686 and 0.738 respectively; and when the two were combined, the correlation was improved to 0.770. Such data lend some credence to the argument that income is a significant factor in the local decision to levy more taxes for public schools regardless of whether a local income tax is available or not.[39] It would appear that the income level of the taxpayers is at least as influential in the amount of local funding per pupil as the equalized assessed valuation of property though the local taxpayers have tax access to only the property tax.

Although strong arguments are found on both sides of this issue, it seems that standard practices among the states, coupled with the difficulty of accommodating the principle of horizontal taxpayer equity, weigh against the use of economic indicators. The more appropriate and prevailing view seems to be that if a tax source is not locally tax accessible it should not be used as a measure of local fiscal capacity for state aid purposes. Correspondingly, where the tax source is available it should certainly not be omitted from a determination of local fiscal capacity.

Equalized Assessment of Property Valuation

The aforementioned tax-base approach largely pertains to taxation of real property, since the major portion of local revenues for schools are derived from this source. Because real property is the major resource of local public school funds, the state aid formulas of most states use equalized assessed valuation of property as the sole criterion for equalization of state funds. As noted earlier, difficulty with property tax administration is a traditional problem that continues to be inextricably linked to public school financing.

If all property in every state were assessed at 100 percent of fair market value (i.e., full value, true value), or even at a uniform percentage of full value, the problem of determining local fiscal capacity would be much simpler than it is under present conditions. However, the assessment practices in most states traditionally have been far from uniform. Studies of assessment ratios within states show a range of from less than 2 to 1 percent of value up to more than 8 to 1. Such variations result in many complications, not only in attempts to determine local ability, but also in efforts to devise equitable and satisfactory state plans for financing schools.

One difficulty arises from the wide differences of opinion about the method that should be used to determine the full value of property. It cannot be the original cost because in many areas purchase price or the original cost of construction represents only a small percentage of current value. It cannot in all instances be the sales price, because there may be sales, among relatives or under enforced conditions, at a price far below that for which similar properties are being sold.

The goal in every state undoubtedly should be to attain uniform assessment procedures, but thus far only a few states have made satisfactory progress in that direction. Existing assessed valuations in most states, therefore, do not provide a satisfactory basis either for determining local fiscal capacity or for prescribing local uniform effort.

Four possible measures for accurately determining local property wealth are (1) state equalized valuation based on partial or full value of property, (2) assessed valuation determined largely by local policy, (3) a sales-ratio plan supplemented by appraisals, and (4) an index of tax-paying ability (the aforementioned property tax base surrogate approach).

Many believe that state-equalized property values offer the only satisfactory solution to the problem. However, there is much local resistance in many states for implementation of this concept. When assessors are voted into office by the people of the county where they reside, they are likely to oppose any state effort to equalize or raise assessments in the county, regardless of how low they may be.

Some contend that there should be no effort to establish any sort of foundation program plan for financing schools until assessments are equalized. Many who are seriously concerned about inequalities in educational opportunity insist that improvements in state support need not wait until some uncertain date when assessments can perhaps be equalized. They point out that if this policy were followed, children in many parts of the state would be penalized and denied adequate educational services merely because their elders had not been able to work out a satisfactory political solution to a difficult problem. They insist that as far as school support is concerned, the same objectives that might be attained through equalized assessment can generally be accomplished through a formula. That is the reason many insist that the state adopt and use a sales-ratio plan.

During the past few years, leaders in several states, acting on the assumption that assessments at full value probably will not be politically feasible in the near future, have helped to establish an assessment or sales-ratio plan for use as a basis for determining local fiscal capacity and prescribing uniform local effort.

Unfortunately, in all but a few jurisdictions, sales-ratio studies are sporadic and subject to a high degree of inaccuracy. On the other hand, California is an example of a state in which considerable progress has been made in the proper use of sales-ratio studies. There, computerized assessment of single-family homes has produced differences between assessments and selling prices that are only one-half as much as the most accurate assessors have been able to achieve in other states. However, of sixty jurisdictions nationwide that are considered to have the potential for computerized assessment studies, only eight are using them in assessment administration.

The sales-ratio plan, of course, has some weaknesses. Unless considerable sums are invested in continuing studies of the relationship of sales price to assessed valuation of property and in appraisals of types of property infrequently sold, and unless there is an adequate sampling, the ratio may not be equitable. Critics suggest that sales-ratio studies in several states have been subject to political manipulation. There also may be a tendency for the legislature to pass a law freezing ratios or assessments to those of a certain year. In fact, such laws have already been passed in a few states.

When sales-ratio studies are properly made and supplemented by competent appraisals, especially for commercial and industrial properties, the following procedures can be used, not only in determining local ability, but also in prescribing uniform local effort to finance the schools:

1. The state agency responsible for making the study certifies to the state board of education, at a designated time each year, the ratio for each county.
2. The state board of education uses this ratio as a basis for determining the funds that would be available if a uniform tax levy were made in each county on property assessed at full value or at a designated percentage of full value.
3. The ratio for a county is then applied to the school districts in the county, by finding the percentage of the county's total valuation that the assessed valuation of the district represents and multiplying this by the amount of funds that would be available if equalized valuation and a uniform levy were used.
4. The districts in each county are required to make whatever levy is necessary to provide the funds required, on the basis of a uniform effort (by levying either a higher or a lower

millage than the rate based on uniform assessment practice), until the county brings its assessments in line with state standards.

FISCAL EFFORT TO SUPPORT PUBLIC SCHOOLS

The fiscal effort to support public schools is influenced by many factors: the people's interest in and attitude toward public education, the proportion of pupils in nonpublic schools, the people's "feeling" about government and taxes, the tax structure, the amount of taxes they pay for purposes other than public schools, whether they have children or grandchildren in school, their reaction to the programs offered by the schools, and probably their reaction to the party in power and to the governmental leadership. No one has been able to determine, up to this time, the effects of any one factor, or any combination of factors such as these, upon the fiscal effort made by any state to support its public schools.

Fiscal or tax effort is defined as the extent to which a government utilizes its fiscal or tax capacity to support the public schools and has frequently been characterized as the level of taxpayer exertion made to fund a specific governmental service. Computation of expenditures or revenues per pupil of a nation, state, or locality is insufficient to indicate tax effort accurately. With either of these measures, a richer nation, state, or local district putting forth the same effort as a poorer counterpart will always appear to be making a great effort. Thus, fiscal effort must be expressed in terms of a percentage relationship between expenditures (from state and local sources), or revenues, and the overall fiscal capacity.

DEFINITION

Fiscal Effort is the ratio of revenue (or expenditures) to the tax base. Effort = Revenue (or Expenditure) ÷ Tax Base.

Fiscal Effort of the United States.[40] The overall fiscal effort of the nation for education does not reveal an internal shifting of resources among the federal, state, and local governments. Yet it is important to know how the totality of fiscal effort for education emanating from federal, state, and local sources compares to other nations. Table 8.6 shows the fiscal effort for public schools produced by each level of government.

Between 1980 and 1990, the federal government's fiscal effort for public schools declined from $4.00 per $1,000 of personal income to $2.79. Had the federal government put forth the same level of fiscal effort in 1990 as it did in 1980, the federal funding for elementary and secondary education would have exceeded $18.6 billion, over $5.6 billion beyond the level of actual funding for that year.[41]

For this same period, the fiscal effort of state governments remained virtually the same, $21.26 per $1,000 of personal income in 1980 to $21.42 in 1990. The increase in effort at the local level, $18.05 to $19.75 in 1990, was primarily responsible for the overall maintenance of the nation's total fiscal effort during the decade. For

the same period the total effort of the nation was $43.31 in 1980 per $1,000 of personal income and $43.96 in 1990. In essence, local governments were forced to replace the declining federal funds in order not to further damage the quality of their local public schools.

During the decade of the 1970s, the federal government exhibited a steady rise in fiscal effort from $3.52 per $1,000 of personal income in 1971 to $4.00 per $1,000 in 1980. During the same period the state effort increased from $19.55 per $1,000 of personal income to $21.26, and local fiscal effort fell from $25.82 per $1,000 in 1971 to $18.05 in 1980.

From a macro perspective, this increase in fiscal effort at the federal and state levels during the 1970s had two important positive consequences. First, it tended to shift the tax burden toward more progressive taxes at the federal and state levels and away from the more regressive local property taxes. Second, the movement away from local taxes indicated a reduction in the inequality in funding the state school finance programs. Thus, from a broad perspective, the decline in local fiscal effort represented an equalizing trend from 1970 to 1980.

TABLE 8.6   Revenues for Elementary and Secondary Schools per $1,000 of Personal Income 1980–90

YEAR	FEDERAL	STATE	LOCAL	STATE AND LOCAL	TOTAL
1980	$4.00	$21.26	$18.05	$39.31	$43.31
1981	3.69	20.43	18.25	38.69	42.38
1982	3.16	20.49	19.15	39.64	42.80
1983	3.07	20.27	19.17	39.44	42.51
1984	2.90	19.87	18.79	38.65	41.56
1985	2.87	20.83	18.80	39.63	42.51
1986	2.94	21.58	19.19	40.76	43.70
1987	2.80	21.73	19.09	40.82	43.62
1988	2.78	21.42	19.15	40.57	43.35
1989	2.81	21.50	19.72	41.21	44.03
1990	2.79	21.42	19.75	41.17	43.96
1991	2.86	21.88	21.54	43.42	46.28

Sources: U.S. Department of Education, National Center for Education Statistics, *Digest of Education Statistics* (Washington, DC: U.S. Government Printing Office, various years). National Education Association, *Rankings of the States.* (Washington, DC: NEA, various years).

The decrease in federal fiscal effort during the 1980s and 1990s required a reciprocal response of increased effort at the state and local levels resulting in a slight increase in state effort and a relatively strong rise in local effort. The press for funding in the 1980s caused increased use of fiscally disequalizing local dollars. Local school districts that had little fiscal capacity could not raise the necessary resources, and the educational opportunity of children in poor school districts was eroded or denied.

International Comparisons.   Although international comparisons of fiscal efforts to support elementary and secondary schools are relatively imprecise, and many caveats must be extended, certain impressions may be obtained.[42] In a recent study, Rasell and Mishel said, "The claim that the U.S. spends more than other nations on education is misleading. By most comparisons, the U.S. devotes a smaller share of its resources to pre-primary, primary, and secondary education than do most industrialized countries."[43] Ram in a 1991 report shows that the United States ranked ninth, in 1985 among selected OECD countries in fiscal commitment to support elementary and secondary schools as measured by the ratio of educational expenditures to the GNP. Based on the premise that the U.S. fiscal effort in 1975 was near optimal, he estimated that by 1985 the United States was underspending in the range of 10 to 12 percent.[44] If one assumes that the United States is underfunding by 11 percent in 1989–90, the actual shortfall in total current expenditures for the nation amounts to over $22 billion.

In a similar analysis, the American Federation of Teachers (AFT) shows that the United States ranks 11th among 15 developed countries in public spending on elementary and secondary schools as a percent of the 1987 GDP.[45] Based on these data, if the taxpayers of the United States in 1990 had put forth fiscal effort commensurate with that of Canada, the elementary and secondary school funding for 1990 in the United States would have increased by over $39 billion.[46]

It is important to remember that expenditures or revenues per pupil do not alone measure fiscal effort to support education. Fiscal effort is a ratio of expenditures or revenues to the measure of fiscal capacity. A poor country or state with moderate expenditures per pupil may be putting forth high effort while the same level of expenditures per pupil by a rich country or state would indicate only moderate or low effort. Thus, because the United States, a rich country, has a high expenditure per pupil, it does not necessarily mean that it has a correspondingly high fiscal effort.

A thorough analysis of international effort studies clearly indicates that the United States has in recent years reduced its commitment to public elementary and secondary education. Table 8.7 shows a decline in the effort to fund primary, secondary, and higher education in the United States from 1970 to 1988. In this table, effort is measured as public expenditure for the three levels of education as a percentage of the Gross Domestic Product (GDP).

The question that of course arises is whether the downward slide in fiscal effort to support education is a worldwide phenomenon. If so, the United States may remain at a relatively high level of effort compared to other developed countries. In order to get true comparisons of such data it is necessary to engage in some rather complex calculations to convert the currencies of the various countries allowing for differing exchange rates of the respective currencies and for a standardization of the cost of living among countries. This permits one to assume that the effort figures are comparable and that greater expenditures actually purchase more than lesser expenditures regardless of the country.

The Organization for Economic Cooperation and Development (OECD) has made such corrections and has reported the effort of OECD countries in real values for public educational expenditures.[47] Their calculations of fiscal effort for education based on real educational expenditures as a percent of real Gross Domestic Product (GDP) are shown for 17 OECD countries in Table 8.8.

TABLE 8.7   Effort Measured as Public Expenditure on Primary, Secondary, and Higher Education as a Percentage of Gross Domestic Product (GDP) for the United States, 1970–88

YEAR	PRIMARY EDUCATION %	SECONDARY EDUCATION %	HIGHER EDUCATION %	TOTAL ALL EDUCATION %*
1970	2.8	1.8	1.5	6.1 (6.0)
1971	2.8	1.8	1.5	6.1 (6.0)
1972	2.5	1.8	1.4	5.7
1973	2.4	1.7	1.3	5.4 (5.5)
1974	2.5	1.7	1.3	5.5
1975	2.5	1.8	1.4	5.7
1976	2.5	1.7	1.4	5.6
1977	2.3	1.6	1.3	5.2 (5.3)
1978	2.2	1.6	1.2	5.0
1979	2.1	1.6	1.2	4.9
1980	2.1	1.5	1.2	4.8 (4.9)
1981	2.1	1.5	1.2	4.8
1982	2.1	1.5	1.2	4.8 (4.9)
1983	2.1	1.5	1.2	4.8
1984	2.0	1.4	1.1	4.6
1985	2.0	1.4	1.2	4.6
1986	2.1	1.4	1.2	4.7 (4.8)
1987	2.2	1.4	1.2	4.8

Source: Organization for Economic Cooperation and Development, *Educational Expenditure, Costs and Financing: An Analysis of Trends: 1970–1988* (Paris: OECD, 1992), pp. 80, 122, and 143. Reprinted with permission.

*The percentage in the parentheses in the fifth column is the actual composite effort. The total shown is different because of rounding of numbers.

As can be seen, the real fiscal effort for the United States of 4.50 ranks 15th out of 17; only Germany and Japan are lower. As to why Germany and Japan are lower in effort but yet are world economic powerhouses is open to conjecture. Riddle studied only the United States, West Germany, and Japan and found that, although their fiscal effort varied somewhat, their actual expenditures per pupil for elementary and sec-

ondary education were virtually even; Japan first, $4,806, the United States second, $4,689, and West Germany third, $4,461.[48]

With regard to Germany, the answer for their high productivity and lower effort probably lies partly in that country's use of the renowned "dual system" of education and skill-building through an apprenticeship system wherein the private business sector assumes a major portion of the

TABLE 8.8   Fiscal Effort of OECD Countries Based on Ratio of Real and Nominal Educational Expenditures and Real and Nominal Gross Domestic Product, 1985, for Primary, Secondary, and Higher Education Combined

COUNTRIES	REAL EXP. PER PUPIL IN US $	NOMINAL EXP. PER PUPIL IN US $	REAL EXP. PER PUPIL % REAL GDP PER CAPITA	REAL EXP. % REAL GDP	NOMINAL EXP. % NOMINAL GDP
Australia	3,431	2,693	29.27	6.23	5.4
Austria	3,172	2,746	29.11	5.29	5.8
Canada	4,106	4,013	26.91	6.06	6.9
Finland	3,597	3,173	31.38	6.17	5.7
France	2,651	2,254	23.18	5.58	
Germany	2,230	2,039	18.32	3.76	4.1
Greece	1,425	656	24.22	4.97	4.0
Ireland	2,111	1,166	31.52	8.48	6.0
Italy	3,284	1,783	30.32	6.32	5.0
Japan	2,324	2,344	19.70	4.36	4.7
Netherlands	3,158	2,567	28.05	6.23	6.6
New Zealand	3,684	1,184	36.67	9.56	5.1
Norway	3,751	3,657	26.91	5.81	5.6
Portugal	2,358	393	42.31	9.22	4.0
Sweden	4,358	4,197	34.37	6.93	7.0
United Kingdom	2,463	1,758	22.59	5.10	4.9
United States	3,418	3,520	20.72	4.50	4.6

Source: Organization for Economic Cooperation and Development, *Educational Expenditure, Costs and Financing: An Analysis of Trends: 1970–1988* (Paris, OECD, 1992), p. 28. Reprinted with permission.

expenditure burden.[49] These costs are not included in the OECD public expenditure data.

Japan would appear to be an even greater enigma unless one considers the homogeneity of the population. Japan has the largest middle class of any developed country, requiring less diversion of resources to offset the educational burdens that result from economic disadvantages of a large percentage of persons below the poverty level. Because of these factors less effort presumably buys more education in Japan.

Verstegen says that because the United States has higher poverty rates, more language fluency problems, and substantial cultural and racial differences among its people, it is doubtful the United States could offer comparable education even with greater absolute dollars.[50] Regardless

of the reasons for the varying levels of fiscal effort among countries, the United States finds itself near last among OECD countries and there is a likelihood that the United States' position may erode still further.

Table 8.8 also shows the differences in real dollar expenditures per pupil for all education and nominal dollars. Notice that the United States ranks third in nominal dollars but falls to a rank of seventh when the dollar is converted to "real values" correcting for cost of living and national currency conversion.

The OECD findings with regard to comparative effort figures are corroborated by several other such studies summarized by Verstegen in 1992. She concluded that "the U.S. ranks relatively low for grades pre-K to 12 on expenditures as a percentage of national income and for per-pupil expenditures as a percentage of GDP per capita."[51]

The findings of the various studies are summarized below and in Table 8.9.

1. Economic Policy Institute[52] (EPI)
   a. The United States ranked low on spending for elementary and secondary education as a percent of GDP—The United States tied for 10th through 12th place out of 16 countries, tied with two other countries. (See Table 8.9.)
   b. The United States ranked low—14th out of 16 countries—on grades pre-K to 12 expenditures per pupil as a percentage of per capita income. (Data not shown.)
2. Congressional Research Services[53] (CRS)
   Using expenditures as a percentage of GNP for grades pre-K to 12, the United States tied for third with two other countries. The total countries studied were nine. (See Table 8.9.)
3. National Center for Education Statistics[54] (NCES)
   a. The United States ranked 11th out of 21 countries in effort based on education expenditures as a percentage of GDP. (See Table 8.9.)
   b. The United States ranked 11th out of 22 countries in effort based on education expenditures per pupil as a percentage of GDP per capita. (Data not shown.)
4. American Federation of Teachers[55] (AFT)
   a. The United States ranked 11th out of 15 countries in effort as measured by expenditures for primary and secondary schools as a percentage of GDP.
   b. The United States ranked 12th out of 15 countries on primary and secondary expenditures per pupil as a percentage of GDP per capita. (Data not shown.)

Notice that each of these studies estimates fiscal effort in two ways. The first bases the effort on expenditures for elementary and secondary education as a ratio of total GDP or other fiscal capacity figures. The second esti-mates effort by determining the *per pupil* expenditures for elementary and secondary education as a ratio of GDP or other capacity measure *per capita*. The second method takes into account fluctuations in pupil enrollment as related to the total population. Using the second method, for example, pupil enrollment could decline and total expenditures could decline and the nation's fiscal effort could even rise because the expenditure per pupil could actually increase. Too, if the GDP remains constant and the population declines, the country appears richer. Using the second approach, it is conceivable that a country could shunt children away from public schools, and utterly fail to address attendance and drop-out problems and have its effort for public education rise. Thus there are valid arguments for and against each of the two methods.

These data, however, presented for both calculations tend to show very similar rankings in the four studies presented. Table 8.9 shows fiscal effort of the various countries based only on the aggregate elementary and secondary expenditures as a ratio of aggregate GDP. It does not show effort *per pupil* or *per capita*. The per pupil and per capita ratios, however, are similar for the Economic Policy Institute, the National Center for Educational Statistics, and the American Federation of Teachers studies; the United States ranks 14th, 11th, and 12th respectively. The Congressional Research Services did not make a comparable calculation for fiscal effort based on the per pupil and per capita comparisons.

These international studies of fiscal effort for education provide an interesting picture of how the United States compares with other countries, but one should be admonished again that such studies require substantial caution in their use, particularly for policy purposes. The primary database limitations include the following data differences that tend to draw the data into question:

1. What levels of education are included in the expenditures?

TABLE 8.9 International Effort Comparison of pre-K–12 Current Operating Expenditures as a Percentage of GDP and Rank

COUNTRIES	DATA YEAR, SOURCE AND RANK							
	1985				1987			
	EPI[a]	Rank	CRS[b]	Rank	NCES[c]	Rank	AFT[d]	Rank
United States*	3.8	10	4.1	3	3.50	11	3.4	11
Australia*	3.4	15	3.7	6	2.97	17	3.0	13
Austria*	4.2	8	—		3.77	7	3.8	6
Belgium*	4.7	3	—		3.95	5	3.7	7
Canada	4.4	6	4.6	2	4.14	5	4.1	4
China	—		—		—		—	
Denmark*	4.3	7	—		4.32	3	4.6	1
Finland*	—		—		—		—	
France*	4.8	2	4.1	3	3.70	9	4.0	5
Germany (W)*	3.2	16	3.0	8	2.69	20	2.7	15
Greece*	—		—		—		—	
Iceland*	—		—		—		—	
Ireland*	4.5	5	—		.4.36	2	—	
Italy*	3.8	10	2.6	9	2.91	8	2.8	14
Japan*	3.6	14	4.1	3	—		3.0	12
Luxembourg*	—		—		3.04	14	—	
Mexico	—		—		—		—	
Netherlands*	4.1	9	—		3.43	13	3.5	9
New Zealand*	—		—		3.02	15	—	
Norway*	4.7	3	—		4.32	3	4.3	2
Portugal*	—		—		2.89	19	—	
Spain*	—		—		2.23	21	—	
Sweden*	5.6	1	5.2	1	4.39	1	4.3	3
Switzerland*	3.8	10	—		3.49	12	3.4	10
Turkey*	—		—		1.17	22	—	
United Kingdom*	3.7	13	3.4	7	3.54	10	3.5	8
Total		16		9		22		15

Source: Deborah Verstegen, "International Comparisons of Education Spending: A Review and Analysis of Reports," *Journal of Education Finance* 17, no. 4 (Spring 1992). Reprinted with permission.

*Organization for Economic Cooperation and Development (OECD) countries.

[a]Edith M. Rasell, *Shortchanging Education: How U.S. Spending on Grades K–12 Lags Behind Other Industrial Nations* (Washington, DC: Economic Policy Institute, 1990).

[b]W. C. Riddle, *Comparisons of Elementary and Secondary Education Expenditures in the United States with Those of Other Nations* (Washington, DC: Congressional Research Service, 1990).

[c]National Center for Education Statistics, *The Condition of Education, 1991.* vol. 1 (Washington, DC: U.S. Department of Education, 1991).

[d]F. H. Nelson, *International Comparison of Public Spending on Education* (Washington, DC: American Federation of Teachers, 1991). *See* report for data/method differences.

2. Do the expenditures include or exclude private education?
3. Do the expenditures reflect only current operation or do they include expenditures for capital outlay?
4. How are adjustments made for market currency exchange rates?
5. Are purchase power parties or cost of living differences adjusted?

These issues combined do present some rather formidable problems with data accuracy that have not yet been clearly resolved. Ram, in a thoughtful analysis of these cross-country comparisons, has concluded that these "data on educational expenditures are not good enough for fine comparisons, and . . . even for obtaining broad indication, descriptive comparisons of country ranks do not seem to constitute an appropriate basis for drawing inferences on 'adequacy' of funding. . . ."[56]

Fiscal Effort of States. Fiscal effort may be measured at the state level for any or all governmental services for which revenue or expenditure data are available. A state's effort may be determined for all governmental services or for subparts such as health, welfare, transportation, corrections, and so forth. State fiscal effort for education is reasonably accurate for policy purposes and can provide information about how a state prioritizes its fiscal resources across programs and services. Such information can be helpful in evaluating in an analytical way the results of nonempirical decisions that are made in the state political processes.

As explained earlier, fiscal effort to support a particular governmental function can be measured by determining the ratio of the revenues or expenditures devoted to a particular purpose to a measure of state fiscal capacity. The most accurate and most commonly used fiscal capacity measures are personal income and the ACIR Representative Tax System (RTS).

An analysis of state effort to support the public schools should not include federal receipts in either revenue or expenditure calculations. To include federal revenues falsely inflates state fiscal effort and contaminates precise estimates of a state's real fiscal commitment. For example, in 1993–94, Alaska, Alabama, and Mississippi received, respectively, 12.6, 12.7, and 17.7 percent of their public school revenues from the federal government while New Hampshire, New Jersey, and Wisconsin received only 2.8, 3.4, and 4.6 percent. Failure to remove the federal dollars would have greatly inflated the Alabama, Alaska, and Mississippi fiscal efforts by counting federal tax dollars not gained through state taxation. Thus, interstate comparisons of fiscal effort should be calculated as the ratio of state and local revenues or expenditures to the fiscal capacity measure, with federal funds excluded. The only arguable exception to this general rule would be where federal revenues are in lieu of tax payments provided to the state to offset the loss of real property taken off the tax rolls for federal purposes.

Table 8.10 shows the fiscal effort put forth by selected high-, middle-, and low-capacity states for all government revenues and for state and local public school revenues as a percentage of the U.S. average and reveals several interesting comparisons. First, it is readily apparent that a low-capacity state may frequently put forth more fiscal effort for public schools and for all governmental services than a high-capacity state. For example, Massachusetts, a high-capacity state, is below the U.S. average on all effort measures while the very poor state of Utah, one of the lowest-capacity states, exceeds the national average on all comparisons. Second, some low-capacity states such as Mississippi increase their own difficulties by exerting low effort. To be poor and to exhibit little aspiration as well portends continuing educational difficulties. Third, some states may have high fiscal effort for all governmental functions and show low effort for public schools, as does New York. Conversely, others may exert greater effort for public schools and lower effort for all governmental services, as do New Jersey, Vermont, Arkansas, Utah, and

TABLE 8.10   Interstate Differentials in Tax Effort for All Government and for Public Schools (states grouped by per capita personal income, 1990)

| | EFFORT MEASURES | | | |
| | ALL GOVERNMENT | | PUBLIC SCHOOLS HIGH, MIDDLE, AND LOW | |
State	State and Local Tax Revenues in 1989–90 per $1,000 of Personal Income in 1990 as % of U.S. Average	Tax Effort in 1988 From Representative Tax System as % of U.S. Average	State and Local Public School Revenues in 1989–90 per $1,000 of Personal Income in 1990 as % of U.S. Average	State and Local Public School Revenues in 1991–92 per Representative Tax System Capacity as % of U.S. Average
High				
Connecticut	97%	90%	100%	94%
New Jersey	94	101	105	123
Massachusetts	96	94	86	75
New York	137	152	112	118
Maryland	97	108	93	96
Middle				
Ohio	95	97	102	99
Wisconsin	110	119	112	113
Nebraska	95	98	93	95
Vermont	106	100	133	121
Missouri	82	86	93	94
Low				
New Mexico	109	99	114	103
Arkansas	83	84	98	101
Utah	105	106	124	120
West Virginia	106	88	126	123
Mississippi	91	94	100	95
United States	100	100	100	100

Sources: National Education Association, *Rankings of the States, 1992* (Washington, DC: NEA, 1992), Table E-5 for state and local revenues for all government and Table F-4 for state and local revenue for public schools; Advisory Commission on Intergovernmental Relations, *State Fiscal Capacity and Effort* (Washington, DC: ACIR, August 1990), m-170, Table 501, p. 32.

West Virginia. Fourth, some states evidence a split in fiscal effort based on whether the fiscal capacity measure is personal income or the representative tax system. For example, Massachusetts shows higher effort with personal income than with the RTS. According to the RTS, Massachusetts has substantial unused tax capacity in general sales, selective sales, and property taxes. On the other hand, New York shows greater fiscal effort with RTS and less with personal income because New York has little fiscal capacity beyond its current tax structure.

In this regard Figure 8.1 shows two large states, New York and Florida, with similar fiscal

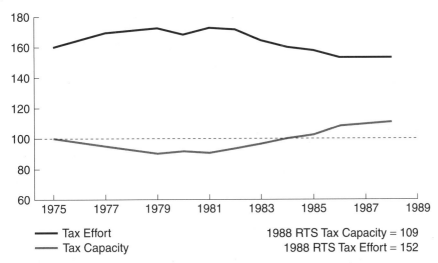

New York

Total RTS Tax Capacity and Tax Effort, 1975-88
(Index Number, U.S. = 100)

1988 RTS Tax Capacity = 109
1988 RTS Tax Effort = 152

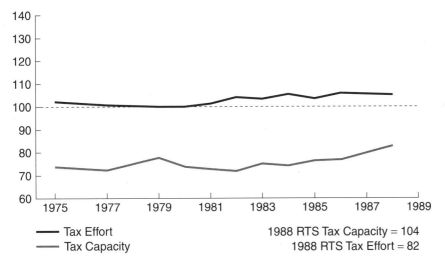

Florida

Total RTS Tax Capacity and Tax Effort, 1975-88
(Index Number, U.S. = 100)

1988 RTS Tax Capacity = 104
1988 RTS Tax Effort = 82

FIGURE 8.1   Fiscal Capacity and Tax Effort as Measured by ACIR RTS
Methodology, 1988

Source: Advisory Commission on International Relations, *State Fiscal Capacity and Effort*
(Washington, DC: ACIR, August 1990), pp. 80 & 103.

capacities but with widely divergent effort patterns. Florida does not tax personal income and has relatively low property taxes while New York greatly exceeds the national average in the use of both its personal income and property tax bases. New York exhibits strong fiscal effort regardless of the fiscal capacity measure and Florida shows weak fiscal effort. Florida also ranks low in effort if personal income is used as the fiscal capacity measure, between 43d and 45th among the 50 states, 1990 data.

Patterns in fiscal effort of states tend to change only very gradually, but exceptions do occur as evidenced by the sharp decline in tax effort experienced by California after Proposition 13 and Massachusetts following the similar Proposition 2½. In California the fiscal effort plummeted from over 120 percent of the U.S. average in 1976 to 94 percent in 1988. The effects of Proposition 2½ in Massachusetts were even more pronounced, dropping fiscal effort in that state from over 140 percent of the U.S. average in 1979 to only 94 percent in 1988.[57] From this one can clearly see how governmental policy can dramatically affect fiscal effort and occasionally does so on a very large scale. Fiscal effort as a measure of governmental activity can therefore be a useful tool for school finance analysis.

LOCAL FISCAL EFFORT OF SCHOOL DISTRICTS

There are several possible measures of local fiscal effort. Expenditures may constitute a very rough indication of effort, but are inaccurate because a district with high capacity may be able, with little effort, to expend a larger amount of funds than a district with low capacity could expend with much higher effort. Expenditures therefore give some indication of the investment in education, but not necessarily of the fiscal effort being made to support the schools.

Local tax levies likewise are often considered an indication of the effort made by a school district. However, a relatively high levy in a district having a low ratio between assessed and full valuation may constitute less fiscal effort than a much lower levy in a district with a relatively high assessment ratio.

Due to variations in assessment practices, relative levels of local effort are difficult if not impossible to determine in many states. A high tax levy in a district may or may not represent high effort, depending upon the assessment ratio in the district as compared with that in other parts of the state. In some states, laws limiting the levy for school purposes may mean that the people in a number of districts are levying far less than they would be willing to make available if the laws permitted.

Despite such factors, it is not uncommon to find districts in a state that are levying from two to four or even six times as much for support of schools as other districts. Undoubtedly, in many cases this represents a major difference in fiscal effort. In addition, districts in states where the laws permit may be receiving funds from other local tax sources, such as payroll or sales taxes. In some cases, however, these other sources of revenue are used in lieu of levies that otherwise would be made on real property. Consequently, property taxes are lower in those districts than in districts which are not permitted or do not choose to use nonproperty taxes as a source of revenue.

If local support is to be utilized, equality of opportunity might theoretically be attained in either of two ways:

1. Limit the effort that may be made by school districts, and perhaps take away and distribute to other districts some of the state funds now received by districts with sufficient revenue to provide a reasonably adequate program
2. Provide sufficient funds from state sources to enable all districts to have as large an amount available per pupil as is now available in the more favored districts

The possibility of limiting local fiscal effort or capturing funds from some of the higher-capacity districts might appeal to a number of people who are concerned about high taxes and believe that too much money is now being devoted to education. People usually want to effect improvements where they are needed instead of limiting opportunities that are now available in the more favored districts and states, although even those people who favor equitable distribution of educational funds might change their opinion if they lived in some of the more favored districts. In states that do not neutralize fiscal capacity and permit unrestrained local effort, the high-capacity districts will always have more local funds available per pupil or per classroom unit than low-capacity districts. Thus, unless limitations are imposed on these high-capacity districts, there will continue to be some inequality in educational opportunity.

Why fiscal effort varies among school districts is a question of great interest to educators and economists alike. Why some populations have higher aspirations for education and are willing exert greater fiscal effort is a more complex issue than was suggested earlier with the argument that variation in income is the determinant.

School districts with less property wealth often put forth greater fiscal effort than their wealthier counterparts. One may assume that people in poor school districts would naturally put forth less effort for education for two very good reasons. First, the poor have less disposable income and the marginal dollar is more valuable to them because they must devote each additional dollar to the immediate needs of food, shelter, and clothing. On the other hand, the more affluent, having their basic needs fulfilled, may look to nonmaterial goods such as education to satisfy their wants and desires. Second, because the affluent are better educated, one could naturally expect them to place more value on education and to want more and better education for their own children. Both of these reasons are quite valid from both an economic and a psychological point of view, yet in fact the more affluent do not always put forth greater effort.

In Missouri, for example, the lowest-capacity school districts put forth greater effort in 1990 than the highest-capacity districts and neither were at the level of the state average. (See Figure 8.2.)

Missouri
County + Local Revenue/Equalized
Assessed Valuation

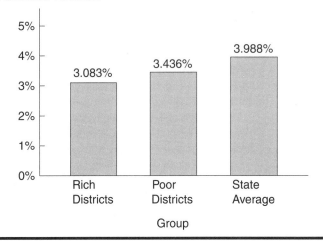

FIGURE 8.2   Local Tax Effort for Education, State of Missouri

Source: Missouri State Department of Education School District Profile File 7—1989–90, State Aid Formula File.

Fiscal effort in this figure is calculated as the ratio of county plus local school district revenues to their respective equalized assessed valuation of property.

In the Texas school finance case *Edgewood* v. *Kirby*,[58] the Supreme Court of Texas noted that: "the lower expenditures in the property-poor districts are not the result of lack of tax effort. Generally, the property-rich districts can tax low and spend high while the property-poor districts must tax high merely to spend low." In Texas, the court found that the 100 poorest school districts had an average tax rate of 74.5 cents and spent only $2,975 per pupil, while the rich districts had an average tax rate of 47 cents and spent an average of $7,233 per pupil.

Other factors, however, can play an important role in a community's level of tax effort to support public schools. Meyers, for example, found that defeat of a millage proposal by Detroit voters in 1963 was attributable in part to opposition of private and parochial school patrons who had no children in public schools. McLoone found that areas with good schools and high taxes tended to have a relatively rapid turnover of young families with children in public schools.[59] Voters over age 50 are less likely to vote for higher tax rates, and professional and white-collar workers are more likely to approve increased school taxes than blue-collar workers and retirees.[60] Too, cyclical economic effects, beyond mere income levels, may affect taxpayers' willingness to pay taxes. In times of rapid inflation, resistance to additional taxes intensifies.[61]

Willingness to provide tax support for public schools is also influenced by the politics and power structure of the community. Districts with competitive power structures tend to make higher local fiscal effort in proportion to their capacity than do districts with noncompetitive or monopolistic power structures. Education appears to benefit from a pluralism of competing power structures, that is, where various power groups are forced to seek allies in order to be politically effective. Educational advocates in such a setting have been found to be effective political allies. Where a school district is dominated by a monolithic, noncompetitive power structure influenced largely by economics, the political effectiveness of educational interests is substantially reduced.[62]

Thus, the nature of local fiscal effort is quite complex, with factors as diverse as the political, educational, social, and economic conditions of each community. Undoubtedly, the wealth and income of the people is an important element, but this alone does not explain why two school districts of the same relative economic level will have greatly different school fiscal efforts. The answer can only be found in the myriad pluralistic conditions of our democratic system of government.

SUMMARY AND CONCLUSIONS

This chapter provided a discussion of fiscal capacity and fiscal effort of nations, states, and local school districts. In various ways this chapter shows how a nation, state, or local school district can measure its fiscal capacity and then gives comparisons of the efforts that these entities in fact make for purposes of public education. The following main points were emphasized.

Fiscal capacity varies greatly among governmental entities creating widely disparate conditions of educational opportunity.

Both physical and human resources combine to produce the economic capacity of a government.

Internationally, measures of gross national product, gross domestic product, and gross national income are commonly utilized to measure fiscal capacity.

Human resources will continue to become increasingly more instrumental in the wealth of nations than physical capacity.

The total economic power of the United States dwarfs all other nations, but in terms of per-capita capacity it falls below several other developed countries. Moreover, the relative position of the United States has declined in recent years and likely will decline still further in the near future.

Worldwide, there is a great chasm between the developed and underdeveloped nations. Although the United States cannot lay claim to being the absolute richest country per capita, both its total and per capita incomes are virtually incomprehensible when compared to the third world countries.

Slippage in economic strength calls for greater attention to education as both an investment and a deterrent to exacerbation of inequalities.

Fiscal capacity of states in the United States vary substantially although there has been a trend toward narrowing of the gap between the richest and the poorest states over the past half-century. Unfortunately during the most recent ten years we have seen the trend reversed, as poorer states have seen their fiscal capacities still further deteriorate.

Two measures of state fiscal capacity are commonly used for comparisons, personal income and the Advisory Commission on Intergovernmental Relations' method called the representative tax system (RTS).

The quality of education among the states is largely dependent on the selective fiscal capacity of the states. States with substantial wealth and income usually have higher expenditures per pupil for public elementary and secondary education.

Per-capita comparisons of fiscal capacity may give a slightly different picture of a state's relative position in financing education than do per-pupil comparisons. Some states educate much higher percentages of children in public schools as compared to the overall population.

Variations in local fiscal capacity create wide differences in financial capability that must be overcome by state government if equality of educational opportunity is to be achieved.

Local fiscal capacity is commonly measured by three approaches, or combinations thereof: tax-base, tax-base surrogate, and/or economic-indicator. The most common method is the tax-base use of the equalized assessed valuation of real property.

Economic indicators, using both property valuation and personal income, are coming into more common usage, but most argue against the inclusion of income unless income is made available as a local optional tax.

Property valuation as a measure of fiscal capacity is often subject to criticism for several reasons, but most often it relates to problems of administration and the taxpayers' perennial aversion to property taxation.

The extent of fiscal effort that citizens are willing to put forth to support their schools is subject to many factors including demographics, education attainment of adults, percentage of children attending private schools, income level, and the political leadership of the state or community.

Fiscal effort for education is not always a manifestation of the affluence of the community. In many instances low-capacity states and school districts exert a greater fiscal effort to support the public schools than their higher capacity counterparts.

Although international comparisons of national fiscal effort to support education must be used with considerable caution, available data indicate that the fiscal effort of the United States is low relative to other developed industrialized nations. The fiscal effort of the federal government to support education declined by 50 percent during the decade of the 1980s.

Fiscal effort for public education may not always be reflective of a state's effort to support all governmental services. Some states have high fiscal effort for public education and low tax effort for general governmental services. Concurrently, this pattern will be reversed in other states.

Fiscal effort to support public education usually changes only gradually, but major taxpayer revolts such as Proposition 13 in California and Proposition 2½ in Massachusetts resulted in immediate reductions in the fiscal effort generated for public schools by the two states.

The fiscal effort of school districts tends to have important effects on local revenues, but fiscal capacity is far more determinative of equality of fiscal resources. In many instances low-capacity school districts put forth substantially more fiscal effort than do more affluent school districts, but high-capacity districts' fiscal effort cannot come near to offsetting their fiscal incapacities.

KEY TERMS

Fiscal capacity
Fiscal position
Gross national product
Gross domestic product
Gross national income
Per capita

Personal income
Tax revenues
Representative tax system (RTS)
Tax base
Tax base surrogate
Sales-ratio

Economic indicator
Multiple deductions
Equalized assessed valuation
  of property
Fiscal effort

ENDNOTES

1. World Bank, *World Tables 1992* (Baltimore: Johns Hopkins University Press, 1992), for an array of national economic measures.

2. Robert B. Reich, *The Work of Nations* (New York: Alfred A. Knopf, 1991), p. 3.

3. World Bank, *World Tables 1992* (Baltimore: Johns Hopkins University Press, 1992), p. 5.

4. Ibid., p. 9.

5. Paul Kennedy, *Preparing for the Twenty-First Century* (New York: Random House, 1993), p. 49.

6. Ibid.,

7. Ibid., p. 339.

8. Advisory Commission on Intergovernmental Relations, *Measures of State and Local Fiscal Capacity and Tax Effort of State and Local Areas* (Washington, DC: U.S. Government Printing Office, 1962), p. 3.

9. U.S. Department of Commerce, Bureau of the Census, *Finances of Public School Systems in 1978–79* (Washington, DC: U.S. Government Printing Office, 1980), p. 9.

10. C. T. Sandford, J. R. M. Willis, and D. J. Ironside, *An Annual Wealth Tax* (New York: Holmes & Meier Publishers, 1975), p. 3.

11. William E. Sparkman, "Tax Effort for Education" in *Educational Need in the Public Economy*, eds. Kern Alexander and K. Forbis Jordan (Gainesville, FL: University of Florida Press, 1976), pp. 299–336.

12. ACIR, op. cit.

13. Kenneth E. Quindry, *State and Local Revenue Potential 1976* (Atlanta: Southern Regional Education Board, 1977), pp. 6–7. See also Kenneth E. Quindry and Niles Schoening, *State and Local Tax Performance 1979* (Atlanta: Southern Regional Education Board, 1980).

14. John Akin, "Fiscal Capacity and the Estimation Method of the Advisory Commission on Intergovernmental Relations," *National Tax Journal*, vol. XXVI, no. 2 (June, 1973).

15. Harold K. Charlesworth and William G. Herzel, *Kentucky Gross State Product, 1969* (Lexington, KY: University of Kentucky, 1972).

16. ACIR, op. cit., p. 72.

17. *Serrano* v. *Priest*, 135 Cal. Rptr. 345, 557 P.2d 929 (1976).

18. *Olsen* v. *State*, 276 Or. 9, 554 P.2d 139 (1976).

19. Ellwood P. Cubberley, *School Funds and Their Apportionment* (New York: Teachers College Press, Columbia University, 1906).

20. Percy E. Burrup, *Financing Education in a Climate of Change* (Boston: Allyn and Bacon, 1974).

21. Roe L. Johns and Edgar L. Morphet, *The Economics and Financing of Education: A Systems Approach*, 3rd ed. (Englewood Cliffs, NJ: Prentice-Hall, 1975).

22. George D. Strayer and Robert Murray Haig, *The Financing of Education in the State of New York* (New York: MacMillan, 1923).

23. Paul R. Mort, *State Support for the Public Schools* (New York: Teachers College Press, Columbia University, 1926), p. 16.

24. Roe L. Johns, "The Development of State Support for Public Schools, in *Financing Education: Fiscal and Legal Alternatives*, eds. Roe L. Johns, Kern Alexander, and K. Forbis Jordan (Columbus, OH: Charles E. Merrill, 1972). See also James A. Hale, "Measuring School Districts Fiscal Capacity," in *Texas Tech Journal of Education* 7, No. 3 (Fall 1980).

25. Richard Salmon, Stephen Lawton, Christina Dawson, and Thomas Johns, *Public School Finance Programs of the United States and Canada* (Blacksburg, VA: American Education Finance Association and Virginia Polytechnic Institute and State University, 1988), p. 151.

26. Ibid., p. 226.

27. Ibid., p. 281.

28. Ibid., p. 180.

29. Ibid., p. 205.

30. Ibid., p. 339.

31. Ibid., p. 7.

32. Ibid., p. 127.

33. Jack E. Fisher, "A Comparison Between Central Cities and Suburbs on Local Ability to Support Public Education," (Ed.D. dissertation, University of Florida, 1972).

34. Thomas H. James, Alan J. Thomas, and Harold J. Dyck, *Wealth Expenditure and Decision Making for Education* (Washington, DC: U.S. Office of Education, Cooperative Research Project #1241, 1963), pp. 7–8; Ralph B. Kimbrough and Roe L. Johns, *The Relationship of Socioeconomic Community Power Structure to Local Fiscal Policy*, Final Report, Office of Education, Cooperative Research Project #1234 (Gainesville, FL: University of Florida, 1968); Frank Farner and John Edmundson, *Relationships of Principal Tax Bases for Public School Support in the Counties of the Eleven Western States* (Eugene, OR: University of Oregon, 1969), p. 11.

35. T. R. Melcher, "The Relationships Between Alternative Local Fiscal Capacity Measures and Selected School Finance Equity Standards" (Ph.D. dissertation, University of Florida, 1978).

36. W. W. McMahon, "A Broader Measure of Wealth and Effort for Educational Equality and Tax Equity," *Journal of Education Finance* 4, No. 1 (Summer 1987), pp. 65–88.

37. P. R. Mort, *State Support for Public Education* (Washington, D.C.: American Council on Education, 1933).

38. Kern Alexander and T. R. Melcher, "Alternative Measures of Local Fiscal Capacity," in *Access to Equal Educational Opportunity in North Carolina*, The Report of the Governor's Commission on Public School Finance (Raleigh, NC: North Carolina Department of Education, 1979), p. 75.

39. Kern Alexander and Richard Salmon, *Testimony* in Alabama school finance case, August, 1992, *Alabama Coalition for Equity, Inc.* v. *Hunt*, Circuit Court of Montgomery County, Alabama, Civil Action No. CV-90-883-R, CV-91-0117-R (1993).

40. Portions of this section are adapted from Kern Alexander, "Financing the Public Schools of the United States: A Perspective on Effort, Need and Equity," *Journal of Education Finance* 17, no. 3 (Winter 1992), pp. 128–132.

41. Actual federal funding for elementary and secondary schools was approximately $9 billion in 1980 and about $13 billion in 1990.

42. Stephen M. Barro, *International Comparisons of Education Spending: Some Conceptual and Methodological Issues* (Washington, DC: SMB Economic Research, 1990) and Deborah Verstegen, *International Comparisons of Education Spending: A Review and Analysis of Reports* (Washington, DC: National Governors' Association, 1992).

43. Edith M. Rasell and Lawrence Mishel, "Shortchanging Education: How U.S. Spending on Grades K-12 Lags Behind Other Industrial Nations" (Washington, DC: Economic Policy Institute Briefing Paper, January 1990).

44. Rati Ram, *Public Educational Expenditures in Industrialized Countries: An Analytical Comparison* (Normal IL: Center for the Study of Educational Finance, Illinois State University, 1991), p. 14.

45. F. Howard Nelson, *International Comparison of Public Spending on Education* (Washington, DC: American Federation of Teachers, February, 1991), p. 11.

46. Ibid.

47. Organization for Economic Cooperation and Development, *Educational Expenditure, Costs and Financing: An Analysis of Trends: 1970–1988* (Paris: OECD, 1992), pp. 24–25.

48. W. C. Riddle, *Comparison of Education Expenditures in the United States, Japan, and Germany* (Washington, DC: Congressional Research Service, June 18, 1991).

49. William E. Nothdurft, *School Works, Reinventing Public Schools to Create the Workforce of the Future* (Washington, DC: The Brookings Institution, 1989), pp. 32–37.

50. Deborah Verstegen, "International Comparisons of Education Spending: A Review and Analysis Reports," *Journal of Education Finance* 16, no. 4 (Spring 1992), p. 272.

51. Verstegen, op. cit., p. 262.

52. Rasell, et al., op. cit.

53. W. C. Riddle, *Comparisons of Elementary and Secondary Education Expenditures in the United States With Those of Other Nations* (Washington, DC: Congressional Research Service, 1990).

54. National Center for Education Statistics, *The Condition of Education, 1991*, vol. 1 (Washington, DC: U.S. Department of Education, 1991).

55. Nelson, op. cit.

56. Ram, op. cit., p. 14.

57. Based on ACIR 1988 TRS Effort calculations, op. cit., pp. 75 and 92.

58. *Edgewood* v. *Kirby*, 777 S.W. 2d 391 (1989).

59. Alfred Victor Meyers, "The Financial Crisis in Urban Schools: Patterns of Support and Nonsupport Among Organized Groups in an Urban Community" (Ed.D. dissertation, Wayne State University, 1964; Eugene McLoone, *Background Paper on State and Local Taxation* (Albany: New York Educational Conference Board, July, 1969).

60. Irving M. Witt and Frank C. Pearce, *A Study of Voter Reaction to a Combination Bond-Tax Election* (San Mateo, CA: San Mateo College, 1968).

61. James M. Buchanan, "Taxpayer Constraints on Financing Education," *Economic Factors Affecting the Financing of Education*, eds. Roe L. Johns, Irving Goffman, Kern Alexander, and Dewey Stollar (Gainesville, FL: University of Florida, 1970), pp. 278–282.

62. Kimbrough and Johns, op. cit., pp. 187–190.

CHAPTER 9

STRUCTURE OF STATE SYSTEMS OF SCHOOL FINANCE

TOPICAL OUTLINE OF CHAPTER

Fiscal Equalization and State Trends • Formula Design Decisions
• Nonequalization Grants • Flat Grants • Equalization Programs
• Full State Funding • Measurement of Equity • Radical
Alternatives • Vouchers • Tuition Tax Credits • Social Cohesion
• Class Orientation • Equity

INTRODUCTION

Although the legal authority for the maintenance and operation of public schools in the United States has always resided with each of the 50 state governments, in most states, local communities initially assumed managerial and fiscal responsibility. As recently as 1929–30, there were over 120,000 school districts serving public elementary and secondary pupils. At that time, local governments contributed 82.7 percent of the revenue, while state governments and the federal government provided the remaining 16.9 percent and 0.4 percent, respectively.[1] Gradually, state governments began to assume greater responsibility for providing the fiscal resources for the public schools. The National Education Association estimated that in 1993–94, state governments provided 45.7 percent of the revenue for public elementary and secondary schools while local governments and the federal government provided 47.3 percent and 7.0 percent, respectively. Figure 9.1 shows the estimated percentages of revenue provided to public elementary and secondary schools by the three levels of government for 1993–94.

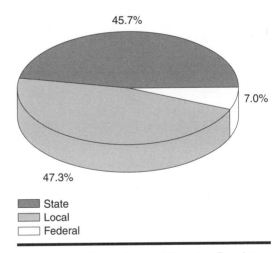

FIGURE 9.1 Percentages of Revenue Receipts Provided Public Elementary and Secondary Education by Source, 1993–94

Source: National Education Association. *Estimates of School Statistics, 1993–94* (Washington, DC: NEA, 1994), p. 38.

However, considerable diversity exists among the 50 states regarding the fiscal support provided by the three levels of government. At one end of the continuum, it is estimated that for

1993–94, Hawaii provided 90.3 percent of the revenue from state sources, 1.8 percent from local sources, and the remaining 7.9 percent from federal sources. At the other end of the continuum, it is estimated that New Hampshire provided 8.5 percent from state sources, 88.9 percent from local sources, and the remaining 2.8 percent from the federal government.[2]

Concurrent with the greater assumption of fiscal responsibility by state governments was a dramatic reduction in the number of local school districts, partially due to state-initiated consolidation and reorganization efforts. The estimated

number of local school districts, both operating and non-operating, in 1993–94 was 15,048.[3]

The evolution of public schools, from systems financed predominantly by local taxation to tripartite fiscal systems in most states, required both the state and federal governments to develop systems for the intergovernmental transfer of revenue. The flowchart in Figure 9.2 illustrates the flow of revenues and expenditures through the budgets of local school districts. As is evident by an examination of this chart, intergovernmental revenue transfer systems have been implemented by both state and federal gov-

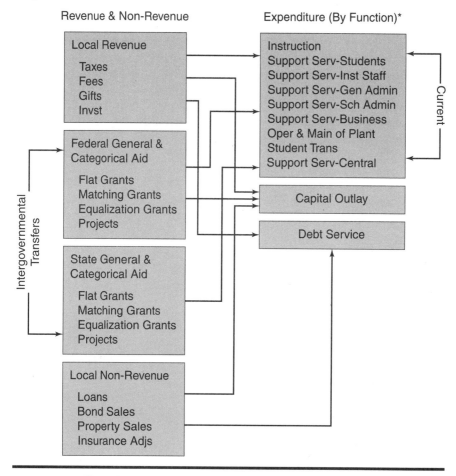

FIGURE 9.2   Flow of Revenue and Expenditures: Local School Districts

*Function titles based upon William J. Fowler, *Financial Accounting for Local and State School Systems* (Washington, DC: U.S. Government Printing Office, 1990).

ernments. While the purpose of this chapter is to discuss the intergovernmental transfer systems, or state-aid programs, that have been developed and implemented by state governments, portions of the discussion concerning the various state systems is applicable also to the several intergovernmental transfer systems currently employed by the federal government.

Undergirding the early development and implementation of state systems for intergovernmental revenue transfer was a recognition by state policymakers that excessive dependence on local communities to fund public schools was problematic, a condition that time has failed to remedy. Historically, wide disparities regarding both fiscal resources and the social resolve to support public schools have existed among local communities within all 50 states. In order to insure at least a rudimentary education throughout its constitutional boundaries, most state governments began to design intergovernmental revenue transfer systems to provide state fiscal assistance to the common schools. In essence, state governments commenced to implement various types of state-aid programs, broadly enti-

tled Grants, that redistributed fiscal resources from areas with high fiscal capacity to those areas with low fiscal capacity. As a consequence, since the resources of the state as a whole are utilized through allocation of state aid to local school districts, nearly all state grants provide some level of fiscal equalization.

FISCAL EQUALIZATION AND STATE GRANTS

Absolute fiscal equalization has proven to be a difficult goal that has been achieved rarely, if at all. Theoretically, a state which has implemented a program fully funded from state resources, such as Hawaii, certainly has the potential of achieving absolute fiscal equalization.[4] Also, a state conceivably could achieve absolute fiscal equalization through judicious allocation of state aid and precise generation of local revenue. The following definition for absolute fiscal equalization addresses the concepts of vertical and horizontal equity discussed in Chapter 10.

While this definition also achieves taxpayer equity, it does not permit the generation of any additional local revenue, regardless of whether the state has neutralized the fiscal capacities of the local school districts. Most scholars of school finance would accept the slightly less rigorous goal of approximate fiscal equalization, which follows. The latter definition would satisfy vertical equity as well as taxpayer equity; however, this definition, since it permits the generation of additional local revenue, albeit a con-

---

Box 9.1 _____

Futility of Equalization Plans: A Criticism

One district will find so ample a sum of taxables behind each child to be schooled that with little effort it can raise abundant school revenue, while another district can support only the most meager schools under a burden of taxation which eventually proves utterly destructive to the tax base. . . . We have a childlike faith in *plans*. When the inevitable disillusionment comes, we conclude that the plan *did not work; and look for another*. In the case of equalization schemes, the disillusionment is prone to come at a time when the original plan has been forgotten and inequality is discovered all over again.

Source: Henry C. Morrison, *School Revenue* (Chicago: University of Chicago Press, 1940), p. 164.

DEFINITION

Absolute Fiscal Equalization is achieved whenever the following three objectives are achieved: (1) Variance in fiscal position among local school districts has been neutralized; (2) Variance in fiscal effort among local school districts has been eliminated; and (3) Variance in educational needs due to incidence of clients has been accommodated.

DEFINITION

Approximate Fiscal Equalization is achieved whenever the following three objectives are achieved: (1) Variance in fiscal position among local school districts has been neutralized; (2) Constrained variance in fiscal effort among local school district is permitted; and (3) Variance in educational needs due to incidence of clients has been accommodated.

---

strained variance, assures neither horizontal equity nor absolute fiscal equalization.

Formula Design Decisions

Whenever a state system of school finance is redesigned or modified substantially, state policymakers are usually faced with four decisions:

Decision I: Determination of the State-Guaranteed Level of Educational Services. For most states, the levels of educational services are determined and prescribed by legislation, accreditation requirements, state board of education regulations and policies, and chief state school officer memoranda and directives. Historically, most state governments mandated minimum levels of educational services which had to be provided by local school districts.

The specification of levels of educational services has to be based on some allocation unit that is uniformly quantifiable for all school districts in the state. Such units traditionally have included counts of census or school-age children, school-attending children, enrollment, average daily attendance (ADA), average daily membership (ADM), and/or some combination or mathematical merger of the above. Fiscal effects, as well as school district policies and procedures, vary according to the allocation vehicle selected by the state. A census of school-age children constitutes the entire population in a particular age group, whether they are attending public schools or not. Cubberley advised against the use of a census measure because, as he said, it "has no educational significance in that it does not place a premium on any effort that makes for better education."[5] School-attending units take into consideration those pupils who attend private as well as public schools, thereby rewarding areas that serve high percentages of children through private education. Enrollment, ADA, and ADM are by far the most commonly used units to measure educational needs and to allocate state revenue to local school districts.[6] Enrollment includes those children who register for school attendance and is a cumulative figure. Average daily attendance is based on the number of days pupils actually attend school. Average daily membership maintains pupil counts on membership rolls until they have missed a specified consecutive number of days of attendance.[7] Several states allocate state funds to their local school districts on the basis of teacher or instructional units. However, the use of such allocation units ultimately are derived from ratios of pupil units, for example, 25 pupils equal 1 teacher unit.

Decision II: Cost Determination of Educational Services. Various methods have been used by state governments to determine the costs that will be required to provide the levels of educational services determined through Decision I. Several states examine prior year(s) costs in order to determine the costs that will be required to guarantee the desired levels of educational services. Such state-conducted studies, referred to as cost analyses, of school district costs range from very simple to extremely tedious and complex. For other states, the establishment of current educational costs is solely a function of the ability of public schools to compete for available revenue. Regardless of the method used to determine the costs of educational services, a combination of economic conditions and the willingness of the public to finance public schools effectively establishes the funding limits.

Additionally, cost determination has much to do with the type of state-aid formula employed by the state and will be discussed later in this chapter. Explained elsewhere in this chapter is the process of establishing costs by weighting full-time equivalent pupils, as is done in Florida; and by weighting classroom or teacher units through varying pupil–classroom or pupil–teacher ratios, as is done in Virginia and several other states. Whatever method is used, each state-aid formula must establish a cost or dollar amount to be applied to the measure of educational need in order to establish the level of educational services to be funded.

Decision III: Fiscal Responsibilities of State and Local Governmental Agencies.

As discussed earlier, on a national basis in 1993–94, local governments contributed the largest percentage of revenue for public schools, followed rather closely by state governments, while the federal government provided limited support.[8] Also, as noted previously, there is considerable diversity among states regarding the percentage of revenue provided public schools from state sources. Shown in Figure 9.3 is a 1993–94 profile of the percentage of state revenue provided public schools by the 50 states. While there is nothing inherently evil in decisions by states to provide low percentages of revenue to public schools from state sources, there is considerable evidence to suggest that those states that have placed primary fiscal responsibility for financing public schools on their local governments often experience considerable difficulty in providing high levels of fiscal equalization.

Decision IV: Fiscal Capacity Determination.

Most state governments have established fiscal equalization programs which provide larger per-unit state allocations to local school districts that are deemed to have less ability to generate local resources than their peers. For this reason, methods that assess the relative abilities of local school districts to generate local revenue have to be developed. Obviously, state governments that allocate state revenue to school districts irrespective of local fiscal capacity or fiscal position, do

not use equalization programs and have no need to make this decision. Alternative measures of local fiscal capacity and local fiscal position are discussed fully in Chapter 8. Suffice it to note that most states use equalized assessed valuation of real property as their measures of fiscal capacity. Consequently, the examples of the several intergovernmental revenue transfer systems presented here will rely on real property valuation to illustrate the generation of local revenues.

DESIGN OF STATE-AID PROGRAMS

There are an infinite number of alternative models of state school financing. No two states have developed and implemented systems of school finance that are precisely identical. Furthermore, each of the 50 state-aid systems are changed, usually subtly, during every legislative session. The state systems of school finance have been developed in political arenas and to a considerable extent reflect the politics of compromise and influence. In more recent years, the judiciary, as a result of fiscal equalization litigation, also has exerted its influence in the design of state-aid programs. It is a sad commentary of U.S. society that the courts have proven more successful in forcing positive reform and greater

---

DEFINITIONS

General Aid Grants are allocated to governmental units without expenditure restrictions, that is, within broad limits. For example, funds may be disbursed for the current operation of public elementary and secondary schools. General aid is relatively free of rigorous accounting and reporting procedures.

Categorical Aid Grants are allocated to governmental units with specific expenditure requirements. Normally, governmental units that accept categorical aid are required to document that these funds were used for the purposes for which they were appropriated.

States

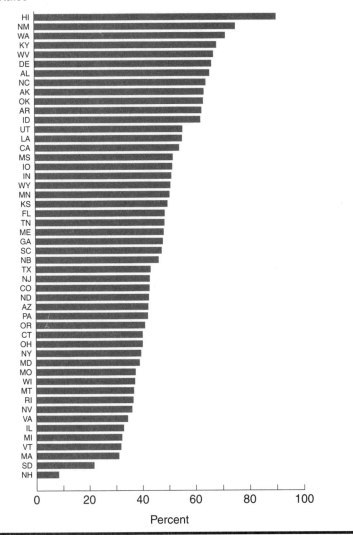

FIGURE 9.3 Percentage of Revenue Receipts Provided from State Sources for Public Elementary and Secondary Education, 1993–94

Source: National Educational Association, *Estimates of School Statistics, 1993–94* (Washington, DC: NEA, 1994), p. 38.

fiscal equalization of state-aid programs than have most state legislatures.

Due to the uniqueness of the 50 state-aid programs, it is difficult to classify them. Acknowledging this difficulty, Figure 9.4 presents a broad conceptual continuum of state-aid programs.

Throughout this chapter, much of the discussion of state-aid programs will be restricted to fiscal equalization of resources among school districts irrespective of the funding difficulties created by variance and incidence of clients. Thus, for the purpose of structuring this discus-

Inequity ⟵⟶ Equity

| Nonequalization Grants | Matching Grants | Flat Grants | Equalization Grants | Full State Funding |

FIGURE 9.4   Fiscal Equalization Continuum: State-Aid Programs

Note: This continuum is intended to array conceptually the levels of equity generally provided by the several types of grants. However, the actual level of equity by a specific state-aid program can be, and often is, dramatically different than is portrayed by the above continuum. For example, a flat grant program, if funded generously, can provide a high level of fiscal equalization. On the other hand, if an equalization program is minimally funded and the state fails to adequately consider the generation of local revenue, the equalization program may fail to achieve equity.

sion, it is assumed that the educational needs of pupils served are identical. As noted previously, the methods used by states to accommodate funding difficulties due to variance and incidence of clients are presented elsewhere in this chapter. It is necessary, however, to distinguish the difference between general and categorical aid grants.

NONEQUALIZATION GRANTS

Nonequalization grants commonly have not been designed to exacerbate the problem created by variance in fiscal capacities among local school districts, but due to unexpected characteristics of the local school districts, high-fiscal-capacity school districts receive more per-pupil state revenue than their low-fiscal-capacity peers. In other instances, subtle legislative changes have been made through political influence so that high-fiscal-capacity school districts are advantaged, thus negating the effectiveness of programs that originally were designed to promote equalization. Until ruled unconstitutional by an Alabama circuit court,[9] the Alabama Foundation Program operated as a nonequalization program. Nonequalization grants can be structured as either general or categorical aid programs, although it is likely that most nonequalization grants will be allocated for a specific purpose, thus qualifying as a categorical program.

Matching grants require low-fiscal-capacity school districts to generate identical per-pupil funds from local resources as high-capacity districts. Since the generation of qualifying matching funds requires the low-capacity school districts to exert several times the tax efforts required of high-capacity districts, matching grants invariably operate in a nonequalization manner. Matching grants, similar to the nonequalization grants described previously can be either general or categorical in design, but most matching grants have been structured as categorical.

FLAT GRANTS

A flat grant is a fixed amount of money allocated per unit of educational need irrespective of the fiscal capacities of the local school districts. The formula for computation and example are displayed below:

Formula: Flat Grant

$$S_i = P_i F$$

Where:

S_i = State flat grant to ith district

P_i = Units of the ith district (pupils, teachers, other measures of educational need)

F = Flat grant unit value

Example

$$S_i = P_i F$$

District A: Number of pupils in ADM = 1,000

Flat grant unit value: $1,000

$$S_i = 1,000 \times \$1,000$$
$$= \$1,000,000$$

As noted earlier, it is inaccurate to infer that flat grants do not provide some level of fiscal equalization. The extent of fiscal equalization provided by a flat grant depends on the size of the total allocation and its ratio to state and local funds combined. If, for example, flat grant allocations represented 60 to 75 percent of total state and local revenue for public elementary and secondary schools, it is likely that the state school finance system would be considered well-equalized. At the extreme, if total funds for public schools consisted of state flat grants, unsubsi-

dized by local resources, the flat grant program would assume the characteristics of full state funding and approach absolute equalization.

The fiscal equalization effects of low- and high-level state-funded flat grants are displayed in Figures 9.5 and 9.6. In Figure 9.5, each of the ten school districts exerted equal tax efforts of 10 mills applied to their respective real property tax bases, yielding $4,000 per pupil for school district A and $400 per pupil for district J. Note that when the flat grant of $1,000 per pupil is allocated to each of the several school districts, the total state and local funds ranged from $5,000 for district A to $1,400 for district J, a difference of $3,600 per pupil.

Figure 9.6 shows a higher level of fiscal equalization when the state flat grant is larger. Each school district exerted a tax effort of 5 mills applied to their respective real property tax bases, yielding $2,000 per pupil for district A and $200 per pupil for district J. When the state flat grant of $3,000 is allocated to each of the several school districts, the total state and local

Fiscal Capacity per Pupil

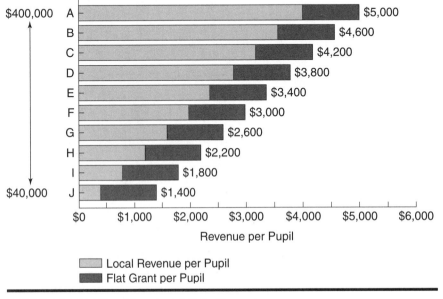

FIGURE 9.5 Flat Grant: Low-Level State Support

Fiscal Capacity per Pupil

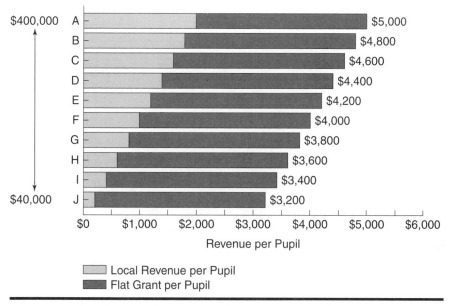

FIGURE 9.6   Flat Grant: High-Level State Support

funds ranged from $5,000 per pupil for district A to $3,200 per pupil for district J, a difference of $1,800 per pupil. Thus, the variance in per-pupil revenue among the 10 school districts was reduced from $3,600, displayed in Figure 9.5, to $1,800 per pupil, displayed in Figure 9.6.

The basic argument against flat grants is that they are inefficient mechanisms of fiscal equalization. It is not efficient for state governments to equalize educational services through the allocation of resources to high-fiscal-capacity areas. Even when equalization grants are used to distribute state aid, states have found it difficult to acquire resources sufficient enough to achieve high levels of fiscal equalization. The economic inefficiency of the flat grant has been sufficient to drive states toward equalization grants as the primary vehicle for the distribution of aid. At the turn of the century, flat grants were used extensively by state governments, using a fixed amount times the census of children of school age in their respective school districts or counties.[10] Despite its inherent inefficiency, several states, including

Delaware, North Carolina, and Nebraska have continued to rely upon the flat grant as their primary program for the distribution of state aid.

Some writers and researchers have erroneously suggested that flat grants are distribution devices that allocate revenue only to education units irrespective of educational need, that is, unweighted for different client groups. However, flat grants by definition merely establish a fixed or constant unit value which is multiplied by the number of educational units, either weighted or unweighted by client group. In the case of North Carolina, a relatively high percentage of revenue receipts for public elementary and secondary schools, 64.3 percent for 1993–94,[11] was provided from state sources, thereby providing some movement toward fiscal equalization. The North Carolina state-aid program, although a flat grant, does take into consideration, albeit limited, the fiscal and educational needs of various client groups and should be classified as a weighted flat-grant program. For the same year, Nebraska provided only 46.3 percent of revenue for their public schools from state resources,[12] but has superimposed an equalization program onto its flat grant, thus achieving a higher level of fixed equalization than North Carolina.[13] The Nebraska flat grant, unlike that of North Carolina, does little to recognize the variance in educational needs among its client groups.

Flat grants are commonly used by states for the distribution of supplementary categorical aid to their primary state school finance program. Such categorical funds are usually either client-centered or pupil-targeted, instructional programs, or pupil support services. Among the former are state-aid programs for disabled, at-risk, or culturally disadvantaged children, as well as vocational education, bilingual education, and remedial education. Categorical flat grants for pupil support services include funds for pupil transportation, textbooks, instructional materials, educational television, and school food services.

If categorical flat grants become numerous and massive, they may detract significantly from the level of equalization provided by the primary state-aid program. During legislative sessions, it is not uncommon for legislators representing high-capacity areas to seek additional funding for flat-grant programs while legislators from low-capacity areas attempt to have new state money allocated through equalization formulas. The result often is a political compromise whereby portions of additional state funds are channeled to both flat and equalization grants. As discussed earlier, while flat grants possess some equalizing tendencies, they are considerably less efficient in achieving a high level of fiscal equalization than equalization formulas. Thus, if large amounts of state aid are distributed through categorical flat grants, the level of fiscal equalization invariably will be less than would have been achieved through the allocation of similar amounts of state aid through equalization programs.

EQUALIZATION PROGRAMS

The conceptual base upon which all fiscal equalization programs rest was designed and developed by several researchers in the early years of the twentieth century. These researchers included Ellwood P. Cubberley, Harlan Undegraff, George D. Strayer, Sr., Robert M. Haig, Paul R. Mort, and Henry C. Morrison. A second generation of scholars who studied under the direction of the original researchers, including Roe L. Johns and Edgar L. Morphet, also substantially contributed to the development, refinement, and implementation of state equalization programs from the 1940s to the early 1980s.

While all fiscal equalization formulas are designed to allocate greater amounts of state aid per unit to low-fiscal-capacity school districts and lesser amounts per unit to their high-capacity peers, there are several distinct types of equalization grants. Even within a specific type of equalization grant, there are both significant and subtle differences in structure and design. Included in this section are in-depth discussions of the following fiscal equalization formulas (1) foundation program; (2) guaranteed tax yield/base program; (3) percentage-equalization program; (4) district-power-equalization program; and (5) tier program.

Foundation Program

George Strayer and Robert Haig, collaborating in 1923, provided the following conceptual model for the foundation program:

1. A local school tax in support of the satisfactory minimum offering would be levied in each district at a rate that would provide the necessary funds for that purpose in the richest district.
2. The richest district then might raise all of its school money by means of the local tax, assuming that a satisfactory tax, capable of being locally administered, could be devised.
3. Every other district could be permitted to levy a local tax at the same rate and apply the proceeds toward the cost of schools.
4. Since the rate is uniform, this tax would be sufficient to meet the costs only in the richest district and the deficiencies would be made up by state subventions.[14]

The foundation program concept embodies the ideal that all pupils throughout each state, regardless of their geographical location, should be entitled to participate and receive a minimum level of educational services. In fact, several states have entitled such programs *minimum foundation programs*. Unfortunately, all too often state legislatures have focused on the term *minimum* which has resulted in minimal programs that have failed to achieve either adequacy or a high level of fiscal equalization.

To be considered a pure foundation program, the following features have to be present:

1. A guaranteed minimum per-unit amount below which no district is permitted to fall
2. Generation of a uniform local tax effort
3. Capability for school districts to generate local leeway funds

The formula for the foundation program can be mathematically stated as:

Formula: Foundation Program

$$S_i = P_i F - rV_i$$

Where:

S_i = State equalization aid to ith district
P_i = Units of the ith district (pupils, teachers, other measures of educational need)
F = Foundation program per unit value
r = Uniform required local effort
V_i = Equalized assessed valuation of property of the ith district

---

Example

$$S_i = P_i F - rV_i$$

District A: Number of pupils in ADM = 1,000
Equalized assessed valuation of property = $400,000,000

Foundation program per unit value = $5,000
Uniform required local effort = 7 mills

S_i = (1,000 × $5,000) − ($400,000,000 × 0.007)

= $5,000,000 − $2,800,000

= $2,200,000

Figure 9.7 shows the potential fiscal equalization effects of a foundation program. Note that the guaranteed level has been set at $5,000 per pupil with a required local effort of 7 mills. For district A, the required local effort generated $2,800 per pupil, which entitled school district A to $2,200 per pupil in state equalization aid. District J generated only $280 per pupil and received $4,720 per pupil in state equalization aid. At this point, or $5,000 per pupil, the foundation program was fiscally equalized. However, the generation of local leeway funds, which reflects both the fiscal capacities and fiscal efforts of local school districts, detracts from the level of fiscal equalization provided by the foundation program guarantee.

Designers of the foundation program, most notably Paul Mort, believed that it was necessary to permit the generation of local leeway funds in order to foster local control and encourage local communities to experiment with innovative educational programs. Mort believed that such communities would become *lighthouse districts* and would encourage all other local communities to follow their leadership.[15] Unfortunately, the lighthouse concept has failed to overcome the problems resulting from extreme variances in the fiscal capacities of local school districts. That is, high-fiscal-capacity school districts are much more likely to provide high quality educational services than the lower-fiscal-capacity school districts. The concept of the lighthouse became more of a justification for fiscal inequality that an earnest attempt to provide innovative educational direction.

The level of fiscal equalization provided by the foundation program is affected primarily by the interaction of two factors:

1. Percentage of state funds provided for the state as a whole
2. Magnitude of the local required effort

As with flat grants, the percentage of the total state and local funds provided from state sources dramatically affects the level of fiscal equalization. If the state share of total state and local rev-

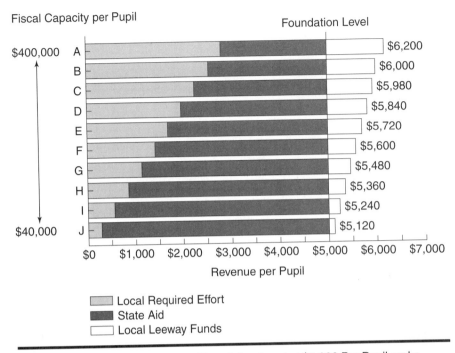

Fiscal Capacity per Pupil

Foundation Level

$400,000   A $6,200
           B $6,000
           C $5,980
           D $5,840
           E $5,720
           F $5,600
           G $5,480
           H $5,360
           I $5,240
$40,000   J $5,120

        $0 $1,000 $2,000 $3,000 $4,000 $5,000 $6,000 $7,000

                          Revenue per Pupil

           Local Required Effort
           State Aid
           Local Leeway Funds

FIGURE 9.7   Foundation Program (Foundation Level at $5,000 Per Pupil and a Required Local Effort of 7 Mills)

enue, including the foundation program, is high, the level of fiscal equalization also will tend to be relatively high. Conversely, if the state share of total state and local revenue is low, it has proven difficult for such states to achieve high levels of fiscal equalization.

Fiscal equalization of the foundation program is also affected by the magnitude of the local required effort. Generally, if the local required effort has been set high, relative to total local effort, the revenue from local leeway will be restricted, thereby reducing the variance in per-pupil revenue among local school districts. However, merely raising the local required effort will not necessarily result in a well-funded system of public schools. On the contrary, if the local required effort is raised without a concurrent increase in the state-guaranteed program, the state will merely reduce its percentage of total funds. This procedure of increasing the required shares of local school districts without increasing the state-

guaranteed level of educational services has been referred to as *leveling-down* in order to achieve greater fiscal equalization. During times of budgetary constraints and/or fiscally conservative administrations, leveling-down policies have been imposed on the public schools in several states. Fortunately, a more politically palatable as well as progressive procedure has been to level-up educational services provided throughout the state. That is, increasing the guaranteed level of services by maintaining or raising the state percentage of total state and local funds while simultaneously increasing the local required effort, can achieve two policy objectives concurrently. A more adequately funded system of public schools is achieved while the variance in state and local revenue among school districts is reduced.

Currently, the most popular fiscal equalization program used by state governments is the foundation program. Approximately 60 percent of the states continue to rely upon the venerable foundation program as their primary vehicle to distribute state aid to local school districts. Much of the popularity of the foundation program can be attributed to Paul Mort and two of his students, Roe L. Johns and Edgar L Morphet. These three individuals served as consultants during numerous state school finance reform initiatives for most of three decades during the mid-twentieth century. There is no question that the foundation program fulfilled an important role in urging state governments to assume a greater fiscal responsibility for funding their public schools. Further, the foundation program replaced flat grants and generally achieved higher levels of fiscal equalization than was provided previously. However, there is growing evidence that the foundation program, as a stand-alone system for the distribution of state aid to local school districts, has been less than effective in achieving and maintaining high levels of fiscal equalization. The series of fiscal litigation lawsuits, which commenced in the late 1960s, have continued to place pressure on state administrations and legislatures to develop and implement state finance systems that provide high levels of fiscal equalization. The failure of stand-alone foundation programs to consistently provide high levels of fiscal equalization has become all too evident. State governments are now searching for replacement funding formulas that will achieve the following three policy objectives: (1) provide a high level of fiscal equalization; (2) provide adequate systems of public schools; and (3) control the growth of state and local revenue for public schools. There is little question that state governments will experience considerable difficulty in achieving these three potentially

contradictory objectives. However, the tier program which is discussed later in this chapter may provide a viable alternative.

Guaranteed Tax Yield/Base Programs

While conceptually identical, guaranteed tax yield and guaranteed tax base programs are technically different. The guaranteed tax yield program promises each local school division a constant unit yield per unit of tax effort while the guaranteed tax base program promises a constant tax base per unit of tax effort. Since the two programs are mathematically equivalent, for the purposes of this discussion and example, the guaranteed tax yield program will be used. Further, since the conceptual base for the guaranteed tax yield/base programs and the district power equalization program are also identical, much of the discussion of the guaranteed tax yield and percentage-equalization programs will overlap. The formula for the guaranteed tax yield is as follows:

Formula: Guaranteed Tax Yield

$$S_i = P_i[(Y - y_i)r_i]$$

Where:

S_i = State equalization aid to i th district

P_i = Units of the i th district (pupils, teachers, other measures of educational need)

Y = Guaranteed yield per unit value

y_i = Yield per unit value of the i th district

r_i = Local fiscal effort (in units)

Example

$$S_i = P_i[(Y - y_i)r_i]$$

District A: Number of pupils in ADM $= 1,000$
Equalized assessed valuation of property $= \$400,000,000$
Yield of 1 mill per pupil $= \$400$
Local fiscal effort $= 10$ mills

Guaranteed yield per unit value $= \$500$

$S_i = 1,000[(\$500 - \$400)10]$
$\quad = 1,000[\$1,000]$
$\quad = \$1,000,000$

Figure 9.8 shows the potential fiscal equalization effects of a guaranteed tax yield program that has been limited to a maximum local levy of 10 mills. Note that the guaranteed level has been set at $500 per pupil per mills levied and a state-required local fiscal effort has not been specified. For district A, the local school district levied 10 mills, which generated $4,000 per pupil (10 × $400 per pupil). School district A qualified for $1,000 per pupil in state equalization aid (10 × $100 per pupil). District J levied 8 rather than 10 mills and generated only $320 per pupil. School district J qualified for $3,680 per pupil in state equalization aid. Note that the state guaranteed tax yield program for district A was $5,000 per pupil and $4,000 per pupil for district J. District A elected to levy 10 mills while district J levied only 8, thus the difference of $1,000 per pupil for the guaranteed programs of the two districts. In effect, districts A, C, and E, by levying the maximum 10 mills, qualified for the

$5,000 per pupil from the guaranteed tax yield program. Districts B and F levied 9 mills and qualified for $4,500 per pupil. All other districts levied 8 mills and qualified for $4,000 per pupil. Districts A, C, and E each levied one additional mill and generated $400, $320, and $240 per pupil local leeway funds, respectively.

The fundamental difference between the guaranteed tax yield and the foundation programs centers on the issue of local fiscal effort. A foundation program requires a minimum local fiscal effort, while the decision to set the level of local fiscal effort of a guaranteed tax yield program has been transferred to the local school district.

The guaranteed tax yield program, in its unrestrained form, provides a state-guaranteed tax yield for unlimited local fiscal efforts (e.g., millage levied). Such guaranteed tax yield programs have the potential of neutralizing the fiscal capacities of local school districts and providing a

Fiscal Capacity per Pupil

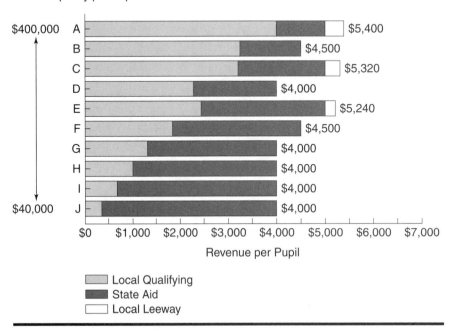

FIGURE 9.8 Guaranteed Tax Yield Program (Guaranteed Level, Set at $500 Per Mill Per Pupil Up to 10 Mills; Local Leeway Permitted)

high level of taxpayer equity. However, most states that have implemented guaranteed tax yield programs have established limitations on the amounts of local effort that may qualify for state equalization aid. The guaranteed tax yield program shown in Figure 9.8 has a state-established limit of 10 mills. Local fiscal efforts generated above 10 mills are ineligible for state equalization funds and any local revenue generated is considered local leeway funds. Typically, states that use guaranteed tax yield/base program target certain school districts, or districts located at certain fiscal capacity percentiles, in order to establish the level of fiscal capacity that will be fiscally equalized. For example, as illustrated in Figure 9.8, if the school district with the highest fiscal capacity generated $400 per pupil per mill, all local school districts would be eligible for state equalization aid. However, if school districts located at the 75th percentile generated $500 per pupil per mill, neither these districts, nor any districts located above the 75th percentile, would be eligible for state equalization aid. The lower the level of fiscal capacity targeted by the states, the lower the number of school districts that may qualify for equalization aid. As a result, a corresponding lower level of fiscal equalization is provided. States often establish levels of guaranteed tax yield or tax base which determine the number of school districts that may qualify for equalization aid. For example, the state may guarantee $500 per pupil per mill up to and including 10 mills, and $400 per pupil per mill for those districts that levy 11 through 15 mills.

Regardless of design distinctions, however, guaranteed tax yield/base programs are structured so that individual local communities have been granted the power by the state to select levels of state and local funding for their schools. As a consequence, while the guaranteed tax yield programs have the potential of providing a high level of taxpayer equity, due to their inherent design they invariably fail to provide high levels of fiscal equalization of educational services among local school districts.

Percentage-Equalization Program

In 1922, Harlan Undegraff presented criteria for state support and a formula for the distribution of state funds that were designed to promote the following: (1) fiscal equalization; (2) efficiency of operation; and (3) the encouragement of local tax effort. The six criteria were:

1. The efficient participation of citizens in the responsibilities of citizenship should be promoted by making the extent of the state's contribution dependent upon local action.
2. The state should neither be timid nor autocratic in withholding state funds because of deficiencies in local action.
3. Special grants should be provided to encourage the introduction of new features in the schools.
4. The districts should receive support in inverse proportion to their true valuation per teacher unit.
5. Efficiency in the conduct of schools should be promoted by increasing the state grant whenever the true tax rate is increased and by lowering it whenever the local tax is decreased.
6. The plan of state aid should be so framed that it will measure precisely the elements involved and will respond promptly and surely to any change in the local district.[16]

The distribution formula proposed by Undegraff became known as the percentage-equalization program and can be mathematically stated as:

Formula: Percentage-Equalization

$$S_i = P_i[1 - ((v_i/V)k)E_i]$$

Where:

S_i = State equalization aid to i th district
P_i = Units of the i th district (pupils, teachers, other measures of educational need)
v_i = Equalized assessed valuation per pupil for the i th district
V = Equalized assessed valuation per pupil for the state

k = Constant established by the state
E_i = Educational expenditure per pupil selected
       by the *i* th district

Example

$$S_i = P_i[1 - ((v_i/V)k)E_i]$$

District A: Number of pupils in ADM = 1,000
            Equalized assessed valuation of
            property = \$400,000,000
            District-established per pupil
            expenditure = \$5,000

            State equalized assessed valuation
            of property = \$200,000
            State-established constant = 0.4

            S_i = 1,000[1 − ((\$400,000/
                    \$200,000)0.4)\$5,000]
               = 1,000[1 − ((2)0.4)\$5,000]
               = 1,000[0.2 × \$5,000]
               = \$1,000,000

Note that in the example, district A has
\$400,000 equalized assessed valuation per pupil
while the state average is \$200,000, yielding a
ratio of 2.0:1.0. When this ratio is multiplied by
the state-established constant (0.4) the resulting
product of 0.8 is subtracted from 1.0, a ratio of
state support of 0.2 is determined. This ratio of
state support, commonly referred to as a state aid
ratio (SAR) is then multiplied by the product of
the district-determined revenue or expenditure
per unit and number of units (i.e., per-pupil expenditure of \$5,000 and 1,000 pupils in ADM),
yielding a state aid amount of \$1,000,000.

As discussed before, the percentage-equalization and guaranteed tax yield/base programs
have identical conceptual bases; therefore,
Figure 9.8, which displays the potential fiscal
equalization effects of the guaranteed tax yield
program is applicable equally for the percentage-
equalization program. The primary difference
between the guaranteed tax yield and percentage-equalization programs is their technical
structures. While the guaranteed tax yield program is focused on units of tax effort (e.g., num-

ber of mills levied) the percentage-equalization
program centers on expenditure per unit. Both
programs promise a certain level of state equalization aid, calculated inverse to the fiscal capacities of the local school districts. In the case of
the guaranteed tax yield program, the state
promises a certain per-unit revenue yield per unit
of tax effort. Similarly, for the percentage-equalization program, the state promises a certain percentage of state support based upon revenue per
unit established by the local school district.

In theory, the percentage-equalization program does not mandate a minimum level of local
fiscal effort, as does the foundation program, but
instead simply equalizes the level of fiscal effort
reflected by each school district's per-unit expenditure level. Identical to the guaranteed tax yield
program, the percentage-equalization formula is
capable of fiscally equalizing all local tax revenues up to the highest-capacity school district
in the state. In contrast, the foundation program
only equalizes up to the state-established funding
level per unit (foundation), and local revenue
generated above the foundation creates per-unit
disparities in relation to the fiscal capacity and
fiscal effort of each school district. If implemented in its unrestrained form, the percentage-
equalization program fully neutralizes
differences in fiscal capacity, while giving incentive for increasing local fiscal effort. However, as
with the guaranteed tax yield program, states
have rarely established unrestrained percentage-
equalization programs, and commonly have limited state equalization aid up to specified
per-unit revenue or expenditure levels, thereby
permitting their school districts to generate local
leeway funds.

Neither the guaranteed tax yield nor the percentage-equalization program have been widely
adopted by state governments. As recently as
1986–87, six states employed guaranteed tax
yield programs and five states used percentage-
equalization programs as their primary fiscal
equalization programs.[17] The reasons for the reluctance of state governments to implement either of these two fiscal equalization programs are

several. First and foremost, the use of these programs places the state in a reactive rather than a proactive mode. State appropriations must respond to local fiscal effort in each district of the state. Such uncertainty makes legislatures uncomfortable in tight budgetary periods. Second, no educational plan is prescribed at the state level and no attempt is made to measure local educational needs or costs. Advocates of local control are comfortable with such a scheme, but legislators tend to want to exercise more authority over the use of funds than either the guaranteed tax yield or the percentage-equalization program provide in their unrestrained form. Third, a system of absolute equalization is extremely difficult to implement because of the massive state revenue which would be required to bring the lowest-capacity district up to the level of the highest-capacity district. Consequently, and as noted with the guaranteed tax yield program, state-imposed limitations that restrict the amount of revenue or expenditure per unit that will qualify for state equalization aid is usually imposed.

These state-imposed limitations thereby alter the conceptual base of both guaranteed tax yield and percentage-equalization programs to an equalization program not unlike the foundation program described previously. For example, a cursory review of the Pennsylvania base payment[18] formula would suggest that the state has adopted a percentage-equalization formula. However, a more in-depth examination would show that the SAR of each school district is applied to a fixed per-unit value, thereby substantially altering the structure of the Pennsylvania formula. Finally, identical to the discussion regarding the guaranteed tax yield program, the percentage-equalization program does not require the local school district to generate a minimum level of local fiscal effort. As a consequence, while both the guaranteed tax yield and percentage-equalization programs have the potential of providing a high level of taxpayer equity, neither program, due to their inherent design, can ensure that all pupils are being equitably served.

Anyone who has studied the politics of education realizes that low fiscal effort for the public schools may result from a myriad of social and economic issues, most of which have little to do with children or education. Also, it is widely believed that the poor and ignorant often have less aspiration for education than their better educated and more affluent peers. More and better education generally breeds a demand for higher quality educational services. Education begets more education. Thus, in many cases it is necessary for the state to intervene and mandate a uniform local fiscal effort for education, in order to bring the poor- and low-aspiration districts upward. Neither guaranteed tax yield nor percentage-equalization formulas, as stand-alone programs, can fulfill this objective.

District-Power Equalization

The district-power equalization (DPE) is a method of equalizing local school district tax bases so that all school children will have access to the same resources. It is a method of distributing state revenue, which is a very close relative to the guaranteed tax yield and percentage-equalization programs described earlier. Either formula, presented previously, will serve for a district-power equalization program and will not be repeated here.

The district-power equalization program was devised by Coons, Clune, and Sugarman in 1970 as an alternative during the early years of fiscal equalization litigation. Coons and his colleagues provided the conceptual basis for the plaintiffs in

---

DEFINITION

A **Recapture Provision**, also entitled **Negative-State Aid**, requires local school districts above a specified level of fiscal capacity to levy a minimum local tax and return a portion of their tax yield to the state for redistribution to less fiscally able school districts.

the famous lawsuit, *Serrano* v. *Priest,*[19] in which the California system of financing its public elementary and secondary education systems was ruled unconstitutional in 1971. In theory, the district-power equalization program contains the following three characteristics:

1. Variance in fiscal capacities among local school districts are neutralized, so that the quality of a pupil's education is not a function of the fiscal capacity of each school district.
2. Local school districts are allowed to determine their own level of fiscal effort which is fully equalized by the state.
3. A recapture provision enables the state to control the amount of state aid that will be required to fiscally equalize statewide.

Thus, the fundamental difference between the guaranteed tax yield and percentage-equalization

programs and the district-power equalization program is the inclusion of the recapture provision for the district-power equalization formula. Figure 9.9 presents the potential fiscal equalization effects of a district-power equalization program.

Note that the total mills levied by the 10 school districts, including both the 10 mills required and the 5 optional mills permitted, are displayed. The state has fiscally neutralized the yield of $350 per pupil per mill, or $3,500 per pupil for the 10 mills required. Two districts, A and B, with $400,000 and $360,000 property valuation per pupil respectively, were not entitled to state equalization support for either the required levy or for the optional local fiscal effort. These two districts, due to their high fiscal capacity, were required to transfer portions of their required local fiscal efforts, $500 and $100 re-

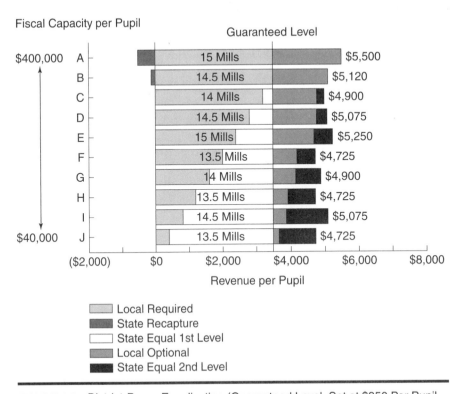

FIGURE 9.9 District-Power Equalization (Guaranteed Level, Set at $350 Per Pupil Per Mill; 10 Mills Required; 5 Mills Optional)

spectively, to the state for redistribution through the recapture provision. Districts A and B exceeded the required local fiscal effort of 10 mills by 5 and 4.5 mills, respectively, and were not required to transfer portions of their optional local fiscal efforts to the state. All other school districts, C through J, qualified for state aid through state equalization levels 1 and 2 since their per pupil per mill yields were less than $350. The district-power equalization program portrayed in this figure does not include a recapture provision for local optional fiscal effort, and as a consequence, some per-pupil revenue disparity due to variance in fiscal capacity is evident. Districts A and B illustrate this point. A state could implement recapture for both the required and optional local fiscal efforts, which would completely neutralize the fiscal capacities of all local school districts. Unfortunately, implementation of a recapture provision applied to all local fiscal effort could chill or reduce the fiscal efforts made by school districts that see portions of their local resources being transferred to the state. Even with the implementation of recapture for both levels 1 and 2 (required and optional local efforts) the inevitable variance in local effort that would occur through level 2 would result in some disparity in per-pupil revenue among local school districts.

Tier Program

The tier program described herein also could be referred to as a stacked program or combination program.[20] The tier program builds on the strength of the foundation program which insures that a minimal, if not minimum, program is provided by all local school districts within a state. The use of a GTY program neutralizes the fiscal capacities of the local school districts that desire to exceed the required local effort mandated by the state for the foundation program. The formulas for the tier program have been provided separately for the foundation and guaranteed tax yield programs and will not be repeated here. Figure 9.10 displays the potential fiscal equalization effects of a two-tier program. Note

that the per-pupil revenue or expenditure ranged from $5,000 per pupil for districts A, B, and F to $3,500 per pupil for district I. However, for the tier program presented here, all school districts are required to provide a $3,500 program for their pupils and are guaranteed a $500 per-pupil per-mill yield for all mills levied above the minimum required 5 mills. As illustrated districts A, B, and F levied 3 mills thus qualifying for an additional $1,500 per pupil. Districts C, D, E, and G levied an additional 2 mills, and qualified for $1,000 per pupil. Districts H and J levied one additional mill qualifying for $500 per pupil while district I did not participate. If the foundation program is established at a high level and the guaranteed tax yield program was unrestrained, a reasonable level of both pupil equity and taxpayer equity could be realized. On the other hand, if the foundation program is inadequately funded from state resources and the guaranteed tax yield program provides the basic state support, it is likely that pupil equity will be sacrificed for the achievement of taxpayer equity.

It is also possible to modify the tier program so that the second tier only guarantees state support up to a specified level of local fiscal effort (not illustrated in Figure 9.10). If school districts are permitted to exert local fiscal effort in excess of the guaranteed level of state support (i.e., local leeway), then neither pupil nor taxpayer equity is assured. When the amount of local leeway exerted is relatively small, then little damage is done to either pupil or taxpayer equity. In contrast, if local leeway becomes a major revenue source for local school districts, the levels of both pupil equity and taxpayer equity will be eroded significantly.

The two-tier program concept has become more popular over the last several years, particularly for states that have had their school finance programs ruled unconstitutional by their state courts. The development and implementation of two-tier programs has permitted states to significantly improve both pupil equity and taxpayer equity without moving to absolute fiscal equalization. While the two-tier program is not a

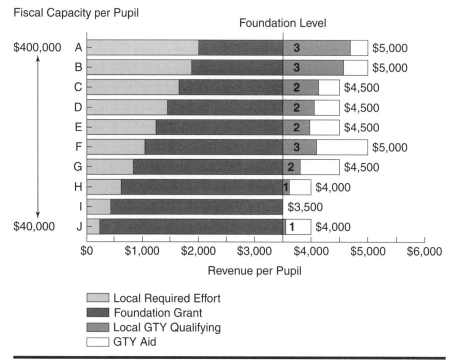

Fiscal Capacity per Pupil

Foundation Level

FIGURE 9.10 Two-Tier Program (Foundation Plus GTY) (Foundation Set at $3,500 Per Pupil; 5 Mills Local Effort; GTY at $500 Per Pupil Per Mill)

panacea for satisfying demands to fiscally equalize state school finance programs, in some instances it does provide a practical alternative, or approximate fiscal equalization.

FULL STATE FUNDING

Full state funding assumes that the state government would be responsible for raising all of the revenue for support of the public elementary and secondary schools. Local school districts would not have taxing authority, and thus could not supplement state funds with locally derived revenues. In the early 1970s, the concept of full state funding was looked upon favorably in some quarters. For example, the Fleischmann Commission in New York State recommended full state funding as an effective means of accomplishing fiscal equalization.[21] The concept of full state funding is credited to Henry Morrison, who

in 1940 proposed that all school funds be collected and distributed from the state level. Morrison reasoned that education is a state and not a local function and therefore local fiscal capacity should not be allowed to affect educational opportunity. Morrison noted that education is different from most other local functions in that the benefits and costs of education programs spill over from one district to another throughout the state. He maintained that if education was viewed as a local function, rich districts would always acquire greater resources than poorer urban slums and underprivileged rural areas. He said, "Our people still largely think of public education as a purely individual and local benefit . . . poor school districts are looked upon as poor relations at best, and perhaps not even that relationship is acknowledged."[22] Over 50 years has transpired since Morrison delivered his eloquent statement regarding the fiscal relationship that invariably exists between high- and low-fiscal-capacity school districts, and his words have proven only too accurate.

State legislatures have been very reluctant to adopt full state funding. Today, only Hawaii can be truly classified as having such a system. Hawaii has a single, unified state school system under the fiscal control of the governor and the legislature. Revenues to support the public schools are appropriated from the state general fund, which in turn is supported by personal income, sales, and excise taxes levied by the state government.[23] Due primarily to successful fiscal equalization litigation, other states, including California, New Mexico, and Washington, have implemented state finance systems that approach full state funding.[24] In its pure sense, the above states do not meet the criteria for full state funding. However, due to the constrained generation of local leeway funds by their local school districts and rigorous control of local required fiscal efforts, these three states marginally approach full state funding. Other states, such as North Carolina, which provide high percentages of revenue from state sources are occasionally classified as approaching full state funding, but unless they substantially restrict the generation of local leeway funds, such states should not be considered fully state funded. The Advisory Commission on Intergovernmental Relations (ACIR) observed that *nearly* full state funding could quickly detract from the concept. Specifically, ACIR stated that, "Failure to circumscribe the amount of local enrichment—by limiting it to 10 percent of the state grant, for example—should undermine [the] . . . objective—[to create] a fiscal environment more conducive to educational opportunity."[25]

Full state funding would not guarantee absolute fiscal equalization, since the vagaries of state politics would still play an extremely important role. Legislators could still advance various rationales for assisting their own local constituencies to the detriment of children attending school elsewhere. While it would remove the per-pupil revenue disparities created by

the variances of local fiscal capacity and fiscal effort (i.e., horizontal equity), it would not necessary recognize the variance in educational needs among client groups (i.e., vertical equity). These two terms, horizontal and vertical equity, are discussed more fully later. The potential mischief that could be created by the manipulation

---

DEFINITIONS

Horizontal Equity. This principle states that students who are alike should receive equal shares. Equity is assessed by measuring the dispersion, or inequality, in the distribution of objects; no dispersion indicates perfect equity. Very often in school finance, for purposes of equity analysis, all students in a state are treated as being equal. When children are so treated, this principle requires (in terms of some of the objects considered above) equal expenditures or revenues per pupil, equal education resources for the basic education program, equal pupil–teacher ratios, equal mastery of basic competency levels, or equal contributions by schooling to long-term outcomes such as income or status in life.

Vertical Equity. While the above principle (horizontal equity) is applicable when children are alike, the second principle (vertical equity) recognizes that students are different and states the positive requirement that unequals receive appropriately unequal treatment. Both the identification of *legitimate* differences among children and the selection of the nature and extent of the appropriate unequal treatment must be made; these choices are based largely on values.

Fiscal Neutrality. Equity is reached when the distribution of the object (educational services) is determined solely by the preferences of the taxpayers for education, and not by their ability to pay, as measured by wealth, income, or some broader variable. This concept of fiscal neutrality (taxpayer equity) also is referred to as *wealth neutrality.*

Source: Robert Berne and Leanna Stiefel, *The Measurement of Equity in School Finance* (Baltimore: Johns Hopkins University Press, 1984), p. 13 & 42.

of factors ostensibly designed to accommodate variances in educational needs of clients attending schools in different geographical areas should not be overlooked. Finally, despite considerable similarities of mission and organization structure, a certain amount of competition exists among local school districts, regarding, for example, instructional programs, educational facilities, and compensation of personnel. To a limited extent, such competition has proven healthy and, due to the need for state governments to address fiscal equalization issues, has forced states to provide comparable services statewide, thereby increasing the level of state-supported funding. This *whipsaw* action that occurs among local school districts would likely be absent in fully state-funded systems.

ACCOMMODATION OF VERTICAL EQUITY

Previously we have discussed how states attempt to obtain a level of horizontal equity, that is, equal treatment of equals. We now need to address vertical equity and how states have attempted to provide unequal treatment for unequals. In order to accommodate vertical equity, or unequal treatment of unequals, three fundamental policy decisions have to be made:

1. Who should be educated? That is, what client population should be served? (For example, prekindergarten, kindergarten, grades 1–12, and special categories such as exceptional or disabled, those with vocational needs, educationally disadvantaged and/or at risk children).
2. What educational goals and objectives should be established for each of these client populations?
3. What kinds of educational programs are needed for these different client populations?

When appropriate decisions have been made concerning these important matters, the next steps would be to:

1. Determine the present number of pupils in the different client populations in the state and to

project for at least a five- to six-year period the estimated number in each category
2. Determine the number and percentage of pupils in each client population that are presently being served by a program designed to meet the needs of those in that category
3. Determine the variation among districts in the percentage of each client population served
4. Determine the extent to which the overall educational goals and the goals and objectives of each client population are being attained

This may seem like a large order indeed, but it is impossible to develop rational fiscal policies for education without first establishing educational policies and goals and determining, insofar as possible, the extent to which those policies and goals are being attained. As pointed out in Chapter 11, decisions on policies and goals must be made through political processes. They are made by direct vote of the people, by local boards of education, by the state board of education, and by the legislature.

Determination of Educational Needs

When an operating consensus has been reached on who should be educated at public expense, what goals and objectives are appropriate for the different clients, and what educational programs are needed for attaining those goals and objectives, it is then possible to determine needs and to make certain evaluations of how well a state is addressing vertical equity. Procedures for statistically evaluating the levels of vertical equity obtained are presented in Chapter 10.

Determining the Number of Potential Pupil Clients

It is essential in long-range fiscal planning to know the present and projected numbers of pupils in different age groups with differing educational needs. For example, what is the present census of children and youth in the following age groups: (1) prekindergarten, ages three and four;

(2) kindergarten, age five; (3) elementary school age; (4) middle school or junior high school age; and (5) senior high school age? How many of these pupils at each age level (1) are physically or mentally disabled; (2) are educationally disadvantaged; (3) are at risk; (4) require bilingual instruction; (5) need vocational training? The numbers of pupils in each of these client populations and in other appropriate groups with special needs should be projected for at least five years into the future. This information should be conducted for each district as well as for the state as a whole.

Determining the Percentage of Clients Served

In order to determine the state's unmet educational needs, it is necessary to ascertain the numbers and percentages of pupils in each pupil population category who are presently served by educational programs appropriate to their needs and the numbers and percentages of pupils who are not so served. This information should be obtained for each district in the state and for the aggregate of the state. For example, what programs for at-risk children are available in each district, and how many pupils are served and how many remain unserved? The same kind of studies should be made of vocational education, education for the educationally disadvantaged, and other special needs programs.

Determining the Extent That Goals and Objectives Are Met

This is probably the most difficult problem of all. It is essentially a measure of the quality and appropriateness of educational programs provided for each category of pupil needs. It is possible to measure the attainment of certain knowledge and skills by appropriate objective tests, but the results of such tests should be used with great caution in inferring satisfactory or unsatisfactory goal attainment for different target groups. Extreme caution should be exercised in comparing the measurable educational attain-

ment of districts that differ widely in socioeconomic and cultural levels of parents.

Frequently, school districts with a low socioeconomic level also have low taxpaying ability and, because of the usual heavy reliance on local property taxes for school support, the districts with the lowest socioeconomic level provide less than adequate educational programs for their children.

Computation of Cost Differentials

Educational programs designed to meet the needs of various categories of pupils vary widely in per-pupil costs. Special programs for exceptional (disabled) children, vocational students, educationally disadvantaged, and at-risk children are "high cost" programs compared with the typical general education elementary and secondary instruction programs.

The Weighted Pupil Method.   One widely used method of comparing the differences in cost is the so-called weighted pupil technique. This procedure is based on the assumption that pupil-teacher ratios are lower, and operating and capital outlay costs are greater, for special education programs. When the weighting procedure is used, the weight of "1" is assigned to general education pupils at certain grade levels that have the lowest cost per pupil. The cost per full-time equivalent (FTE) pupil for the high-cost programs is then computed in relation to the cost per pupil of the lowest cost pupils.

Researchers associated with the National Educational Finance Project studied the per-pupil cost differentials for different types of programs in a number of states.[26] These studies were based primarily on average practice in what was reported to be exemplary programs in each state. It was found that the cost differentials for different types of programs varied considerably from state to state, but that programs for exceptional education, vocational education, and the educationally disadvantaged cost more per pupil in all states than the per-pupil cost of the basic general education program for pupils in grades 1–12. Numerous studies conducted using various cost-accounting techniques have tended to validate the seminal research conducted by the NEFP during the 1970s.

Table 9.1 presents a set of cost differentials used by the state of Florida in 1992–93 for allocating state funds for different types of educational programs.[27] School district boards in Florida utilize program accounting extensively, and the cost differentials in the state school finance program are based largely on the experience of local boards of education.

Note that the weighting is based on full-time equivalency. This means that if a student spends part of the school day in a special highly weighted program and part of the day in the basic program, the weighting for that student is proportionate. For example, if a vocational-agriculture student spends one-half of the school day in the basic program for grades 10, 11, and 12 and half of the day in vocational agriculture, that student is counted as half of an equivalent full-time student in the basic program, with a weight of 1.08 and half of an equivalent full-time student in agriculture, with a weight of 2.26.

It is possible that Florida has gone into more detail than necessary in weighting pupils. However, the concept is sound. The weights presented in Table 9.1 should not be considered either adequate or high-quality weights. The Florida weights represent only average practice in the state of Florida at various points in time. Cost-effective studies may show that different methods of teaching, new technology, or alternative managerial procedures change these cost differentials. In fact, the chief danger of using cost differentials in a school finance program is that they may become a "self-fulfilling prophecy." That is, boards of education may tend to spend in accordance with the cost differentials included in the finance program instead of what is needed to be expended to obtain the goals of the program. Therefore, each state should establish its own cost differentials in terms of what is needed in that state. Ideally, program cost differentials

should be based on cost-effective studies instead of statewide averages or even averages of reported best practice.

In order to plan a state finance program, it is necessary to compute the costs of the state-guaranteed basic program. Historically, the term *foundation program* was most often used to designate the state-guaranteed program financed jointly by the state and local school districts in proportion to their fiscal capacities. As discussed earlier, while the foundation program remains popular, a variety of equalization formulas are now used by the several states.

The current expense costs of the state-guaranteed basic educational program, excluding pupil transportation, school food services, community education, and other small miscellaneous programs can readily be computed from weighted pupils. For example, if the current expense allotment has been established by the state to be $5,500 per Weighted Average Daily Membership (WADM). The total cost of the state-guaranteed program can be computed as follows:

> Multiply the number of equivalent full-time pupils in each program category by the weight assigned to that category. For example, referring to Table 9.1, assume that a school system has 500 full-time pupils in average daily membership in kindergarten and grades 1, 2, and 3. Then, 500 pupils times a weight of 1.014 equals 507 weighted pupils. Follow the same procedure for each program category; find the total of weighted pupils for the district and multiply by $5,500. The product equals the current expense cost of the basic general education program, excluding pupil transportation, school food services and other such programs that are guaranteed by the state.

The basic allotment of $5,500 per pupil can be adjusted for differences among school districts in the cost of living (or better still, differences in the cost of education), and higher costs due to the sparsity of population that forces some boards to maintain small schools at a higher per-pupil cost than large schools. For example, if the cost of living for the same standard of living varies from 5 percent of the average cost to 5 percent above the

TABLE 9.1 Educational Cost Differentials Used by Florida in 1992–93 for Allocating State Foundation Program Funds

	1992–93 COST FACTORS
Basic Programs	
Kindergarten and Grades 1, 2, and 3	1.014
Grades 4, 5, 6, 7, and 8	1.000
Grades 9, 10, 11, and 12	1.225
Mainstream	
Grades K–3	2.028
Grades 4–8	2.000
Grades 9–12	2.450
Programs for At-Risk Students	
Dropout Prevention	1.656
Intensive English/ESOL K–3	1.644
Intensive English/ESOL 4–8	1.679
Intensive English/ESOL 9–12	1.649
Exceptional Student Programs	
Educable Mentally Handicapped	2.184
Trainable Mentally Handicapped	2.922
Physically Handicapped	3.453
Physical and Occupational Therapy, part-time	9.527
Speech, Language, and Hearing Therapy, part-time	5.475
Speech, Language, and Hearing	3.176
Visually Handicapped, part-time	15.145
Visually Handicapped	4.353
Emotionally Handicapped, part-time	3.740
Emotionally Handicapped	2.812
Specific Learning Disability, part-time	2.914
Specific Learning Disability	2.049
Gifted, part-time	1.896
Hospital and Homebound, part-time	11.611
Profoundly Handicapped	4.396
Adult General Education Programs	
Adult Basic Skills	.745
Adult Secondary Education	.763
Lifelong Learning	.700
Adult Disabled	1.337

Vocational-Technical Programs	Job Preparatory 7–12	Adult	Adult Supplemental
Agriculture	1.728	1.537	1.516
Business and Office	1.229	1.292	1.114
Distributive	1.112	1.374	.806
Diversified	1.185	.877	—
Health	1.513	1.506	1.454

(continued)

TABLE 9.1   continued

Vocational-Technical Programs	Job Preparatory 7–12	Adult	Adult Supplemental
Public Service	.930	.959	1.060
Home Economics	1.261	1.433	1.367
Industrial	1.746	1.418	1.332
Exploratory (Grades 6–12)	1.276	—	—
Vocational Mainstream	2.325	—	—

Source: Florida Department of Education, Division of Public Schools, *Florida Education Finance Program, 1992–93* (Tallahassee, FL: Financial Management Section of the Bureau of School Business Services, August, 1992), p. 12.

average cost, the total cost of the state-guaranteed program for a district with the lowest cost of living would be reduced to 95 percent of the computed amount, and the district with the highest cost of living in the state would see its computed amount increased by 105 percent.

The adjustment for sparsity can be computed in a similar manner. In practice, these adjustments may partially cancel each other. For example, a sparsely settled district may have a low cost-of-living factor and a high cost due to sparsity.

The Adjusted Instruction Unit Method.   Another method being used by a number of states to provide for program cost differentials is the adjusted instruction unit method. This method is mathematically identical to the weighted pupil method because it assumes that the necessary pupil-teacher ratio varies for different client groups. If we assume that one instruction unit, supplemented by such instructional service units as librarians, principals, counselors and supervisors is needed for every twenty-four general education pupils, the pupil-teacher ratio for each client population can be computed simply by dividing 24 by the appropriate weight shown in Table 9.1. Note that in Table 9.1, the weight for pupils in grades 4, 5, 6, 7, and 8 in the basic general education program is 1.00. Since one instruction unit is allotted for every 24 full-time equivalent pupils, the total full-time equivalent students in the basic general education program

in grades 4, 5, 6, 7, and 8 is divided by 24 in order to determine the instruction units allotted for those pupils. From Table 9.1 it can be seen that Florida assigns a weight of 2.184 for educable mentally handicapped students. The basic 24-pupil allotment divided by 2.184 equals 10.99. The total full-time equivalent membership of educable mentally retarded students is divided by 10.99 in order to determine the number of instruction units allotted for that particular category. Similar computations are made for all categories.

The state allotment per instruction unit under this plan is equivalent to $5,500 times 24, or $132,000. The total current expense cost of the state-guaranteed program (excluding transportation, school food services, and other small miscellaneous programs) is determined by multiplying the total number of instruction units by $132,000. The cost of the state-guaranteed program under the instruction unit plan is exactly the same as under the weighted pupil plan, provided that the same cost differentials are used.

Choice of Plan.   Which is the better plan for determining the cost of the state-guaranteed program, the weighted pupil or the instruction unit? As discussed above, the two plans are mathematically equivalent, provided the same cost differentials are recognized. It would seem advisable to use the plan that is politically preferred in a state. If a state has been accustomed to using the instruction unit, it may be politically advisable to continue using it. With continued inflation, there may be a psychological political advantage in computing the cost of the basic or foundation program in terms of weighted pupils rather than instruction units. To some legislators, $5,500 per weighted pupil may not seem excessive, whereas $132,000 per instruction unit may seem like a lot of money. The authors have noted that in states where the state teachers' association has come into disfavor because of alleged aggressive tactics, legislatures have urged that the emphasis be placed on children rather than teachers, and they prefer some type of weighted pupil measure. Both the weighted pupil and the adjusted instruction unit methods are sound in principle, and it is good policy on the part of the educational leadership in a state to accept the method preferred by their legislature.

Weighting for Educationally Disadvantaged and At-Risk Children

Cost differentials for the educationally disadvantaged and at-risk children should be included in the program of state support. Studies made by the National Educational Finance Project revealed that school systems with well-developed programs for pupils in this category were spending about twice as much per pupil for educationally disadvantaged as for basic general education pupils. As shown in Table 9.1, Florida currently assigns weights ranging from 1.644 to 1.679 for their at-risk students.[28] This is not to suggest that a weight of 2.0 or the Florida weights should be assigned at-risk pupils for the allocation of state funds. Additional research is needed to determine proper weighting for these pupils. We do know that educationally disadvantaged and at-risk children pose the greatest challenge to public education. Meeting the needs of these client populations undoubtedly will prove extremely costly. However, for this nation to ignore or inadequately serve those children will prove even more costly.

While research has not been precisely definitive as to what cost weightings should be for at-risk or compensatory education programs, it is important that state allocation formulas make some provision for such costs. At-risk and compensatory education programs are provided to redress the problems of educational disadvantage usually found among students from low-income families. Several states now do so and the trend is toward such funding designations. Presently, 29 states include compensatory elements in their state funding schemes. In some instances, limited English speaking programs overlap compensatory education programs as is the case in Hawaii. Hawaii provides full state funding for educational disadvantage caused by factors related to low income as well as limited English language proficiency.

Weightings for at-risk or compensatory education programs may be illustrated by the programs found in the several selected states shown in Table 9.2.

The federal government, through Chapter 1 of ESEA,[29] provided nearly $7 billion in 1990–91[30] for educationally disadvantaged pupils but fell short of the demand for funds. Educationally disadvantaged pupils are not evenly distributed either among states or the school districts of the several states. They tend to be concentrated in most large cities, in some small cities, and in many rural districts. Over 18 percent of central city pupils received Chapter 1 services, 13 percent of rural and small town pupils received such services, and only 10 percent of children attending public schools in urban fringes and large towns received Chapter 1 services.[31] Problems have arisen in state and federal funding of educationally disadvantaged and at-risk pupils because of the difficulty of classification. Many educationally disadvantaged pupils could also be classified as disabled pupils. Additional research is needed for setting the proper weights for the educationally disadvantaged and at-risk pupils.

Weighting of Programs for Disabled Children

State financing of programs for disabled children are now common throughout the 50 states.

TABLE 9.2   Examples of State Pupil Weightings for At-Risk or Compensatory
Education Programs

STATE	PROGRAM WEIGHTS
Connecticut	Weight of 0.5 in general aid formula as determined by low income and low achievement.
Florida	Categorical grant based on number of children scoring in lowest quartile on statewide assessment tests and Dropout Prevention Program (weighted 1.656).
Georgia	Weight of 1.314 for pupils scoring low achievement test scores in reading and math.
Illinois	Federal Title I, Chapter I eligible children are assigned variable weights from 0 to 0.625 depending on the concentration of low-income students relative to the state average concentration of 19.19%. If a district has a concentration of 19.19 percent or more, it received an additional weight of 0.53 per low-income pupil.
Maryland	Weighted 0.25 of foundation amount per Chapter 1 eligible pupil.
Massachusetts	Weighted pupil at 0.20 for Chapter 1 eligible children.
Minnesota	Pupil weighting ranging from 0.5 to 1.1: pupil weight of 0.5 for AFDC pupils. Districts with more than 6% AFDC students receive an additional 0.1 weight per pupil up to an additional 0.6 limit.
Missouri	AFDC and orphans pupil weighting of 0.25.
Nebraska	Culturally deprived students weighted an additional 1.0.
New Jersey	Weight of 0.18 for pupils currently enrolled in at-risk programs.
New York	Pupil weight of 0.25 for students below minimum score on state reading and math tests.
Ohio	Variable weight per pupil based on the percentage of AFDC children in district. Weight increases as percent of AFDC pupils increases.
Oklahoma	Pupil weighting at 0.25 for students who qualify and participate for federal free and reduced-price lunch program.
South Carolina	Pupil weighting: Grades 1–6 compensatory 0.26 Grades 2–6 remediation 0.114 Grades 7–12 remediation 0.114
Texas	0.2 pupil weight determined by number of pupils eligible for federal free or reduced-price lunch program.
Vermont	Pupil weighting of 0.15 for students from families receiving food stamps.

Source: Deborah Verstegen, *School Finance at a Glance*, Denver, CO, Education Commission of the States, 1988; and Richard Salmon, Christina Dawson, Steven Lawton, and Thomas Johns, *Public School Finance Programs of the United States and Canada: 1986–87*, Blacksburg, VA, Virginia Polytechnic Institute and State University, and American Education Finance Association, 1988.

In the early 1970s, the National Education Finance Project conducted several studies of educational programs and costs, of which programs in special education formed an important part. Richard Rossmiller from the University of Wisconsin, in conducting one of the NEFP component studies, examined comprehensive best practice special education programs at several cities in the United States. From this research, cost differentials by special education program area were fashioned that could be used to distribute state funds. Florida used these cost differentials in establishing its foundation program weights in 1973. Rossmiller's program weights are given in Table 9.3.

Following Rossmiller, other researchers established other program and cost categories. In these reports, weights were established that ranged from learning disabilities of minimal excess costs to very high-cost programs for disabling conditions of multihandicapped and the blind.

In addition, changes in special education program services that in recent years call for increased "inclusion" of disabled children in regular classrooms have substantially modified the thinking toward both the delivery of services and the costs associated with them. Thus, the program designed for the delivery of the services has, of course, much to do with the relative costs. Different relative costs may be found in (1) self-contained classrooms, (2) resource rooms, and (3) inclusion in regular classrooms. The dilemma today is to adequately and efficiently address costs that are related to the most effective mode of instruction.

TABLE 9.3 Rossmiller Weights in National Educational Finance Project (NEFP), 1971

Educable Mentally Retarded	2.3
Trainable Mentally Retarded	3.0
Physically Handicapped	3.5
Physical and Occupational Therapy, part-time	6.0
Speech and Hearing Therapy, part-time	10.0
Deaf	4.0
Visually Handicapped, part-time	10.0
Visually Handicapped	3.5
Emotionally Disturbed, part-time	7.5
Emotionally Disturbed	3.7
Socially Maladjusted	2.3
Specific Learning Disability, part-time	7.5
Specific Learning Disability	2.3
Hospital and Homebound, part-time	15.0

Source: Richard Rossmiller, "Resource Configurations and Costs in Educational Programs for Exceptional Children," Chapter 2 in *Planning to Finance Education*, eds. R. L. Jones, Kern Alexander, and K. Forbis Jordan (Gainesville, FL: National Educational Finance Project, 1971).

Weighting for Limited-English-Speaking Children

The enrollment of greater percentages of Hispanic and Asian students in the public schools has necessitated the use of new methods of instruction and additional considerations for financing to bridge the language barrier. Over one-half the states provide a state designation of funding for limited-English-speaking programs. Among these are found allocations determined by flat amounts per pupil, weightings for instructional units and pupil weightings. Colorado and Kansas, for example, distribute funds on a flat per-pupil basis for approved programs. Alaska distributes such funds based on instructional units. At least seven states utilize the weighted pupil approach, as shown in Table 9.4.

As with all special programs, the costs of bilingual education programs are governed by the instructional approach to be used, the number of eligible students, the pace, degree and threshold at which the students are included in the regular school programs, class size, and special instructional equipment. Whether a student is included in such a program will normally depend on an evaluation using some form of an English language proficiency test. The cost of the instructional program is primarily determined by three factors. First, cost will greatly depend on whether there are sufficient numbers of students in need of bilingual instruction to warrant a full-time teaching position. Fewer students may warrant only part-time professional expertise. If intensive instruction may be provided by a few designated teachers, then certain cost considerations may be determined rather easily. A second instructional approach with an alternative cost may be to provide teacher staff development for all teachers. Where teachers are so trained, the ongoing instructional costs differentials may be minimal. Third, programs may be greatly enhanced and costs reduced by the use of additional special instructional materials and technology. Of course, all of these factors may come into play and, to varying degrees, have an impact on costs.

TABLE 9.4   Examples of State Pupil Weightings for Allocating Funds for Limited-English-Speaking Programs

STATE	PROGRAM WEIGHTS	
Arizona	K–8	1.158
	9–12	1.268
Florida	Limited-English-speaking, Intensive English	
	K–3	1.644
	4–8	1.679
	9–12	1.649
Massachusetts	Weight at 1.4	
New Jersey	Additional 0.23 times state average net current expense per pupil for limited-English-speaking students	
New Mexico	FTE limited-English-speaking students weighted an additional 0.3	
New York	Limited-English-speaking students weighted an additional 0.12	
Oklahoma	Additional 0.25 weighting in foundation program.	

Source: Deborah Verstegen, *School Finance at a Glance*, Denver, CO, Education Commission of the States, 1988; and Richard Salmon, Christina Dawson, Steven Lawton, and Thomas Johns, *Public School Finance Programs of the United States and Canada: 1986–87*, Blacksburg, VA, Virginia Polytechnic Institute and State University, and American Education Finance Association, 1988.

Most studies of costs have revealed that add-on costs for bilingual programs range from 15 to 35 percent more than regular instructional programs.

Computing the Cost of Pupil Transportation

The cost of pupil transportation to be included in the state-guaranteed program cannot be computed efficiently in terms of weighted pupils or adjusted instruction units. The costs per pupil transported varies widely among the school districts of a state, due primarily to variations in the density of transported pupils. State formulas for allocating state funds for pupil transportation commonly use density of transported pupils per one-way mile of bus route (referred to as linear density) or density of transported pupils per square mile of the school district (geographical density) as measures of density. While either measure can be used, linear density is invariably more predictive of pupil transportation costs and is preferred.

Before computing the cost of transportation to include in the state aid program, it is necessary for the state to adopt policies with respect to what pupils are entitled to transportation for inclusion in the state finance program. Commonly, pupils living beyond a specified walking distance from the school they attend are eligible for transportation. The states vary in the distance they set, the range being usually from 1.0 to about 2.0 miles, with the average being about 1.5 miles. Several states set shorter distances for elementary pupils than high school pupils. In cases of hazardous walking conditions, the distances for transportation eligibility are often lowered. Disabled pupils living any distance from school are eligible for transportation.

The costs of pupil transportation is usually determined by computing average costs for districts with similar densities of transported pupils. This can be done either graphically or mathematically. The desirable cost differentials due to variations in density of transported pupils should be computed graphically by plotting costs per pupil transported on the X-axis and density per bus mile of transported pupils on the Y-axis of coordinate axes. A smoothed curve should then be drawn which will best fit the plotted data. The relationship between costs per pupil transported and density is curvilinear. The state allotment per pupil transported for different degrees of density can be determined by noting from the curve the allotted cost per pupil at the point where a line drawn vertically from the density measure intersects the curve.

A more precise method of determining an equitable and efficient allotted costs per pupil transported is the employment of a mathematical formula. The following quadratic equation has proved satisfactory for this purpose: The allowable or allotted cost per pupil transported, $Y = A + BX + CX^2$, in which X is the density of transported pupils per bus mile, and A, B, and C are constants determined by a statistical method known as "least squares." Other mathematical formulas can be used for this purpose provided they accurately depict the relationship between the two variables—costs per pupil transported and density. Some states include other factors such as road conditions and topography in their formulas for allocating state funds for pupil transportation, but these two factors normally only modestly predict costs per pupil transported.

The transportation of pupils is an important item in the school budget. For school year 1990–91, more than 57 percent of all public school elementary and secondary pupils were transported to school at a cost of approximately $9 billion.[32] But the percent of local school budgets expended for school transportation varies greatly, due primarily to variations among districts in the scatter of population. Therefore, the state must include financial assistance for pupil transportation in its state financial support program if it is to discharge its responsibility for equalizing the financial support of the public schools. It is all too common for poorer school districts to devote a larger percentage of their current expenditures to pupil transportation services than their wealthier counterparts.

School Food Services

The school food service program, which is funded partially by federal and state governments, has become a major operation in recent years. Approximately 90 percent of public elementary and secondary schools participate in the National School Lunch Act of 1946 and the Child Nutrition Act of 1966.[33] The National School Lunch Act established a program for the distribution of agricultural commodities, grants, and other means to assist and encourage public schools throughout the United States. Later, the Child Nutrition Act amplified and expanded the federal role in school food service. Currently, the following federal programs are administered by the Food and Nutrition Service of the U.S. Department of Agriculture: School Lunch, School Breakfast, USDA Commodities, Special Milk Program, Nutrition Education and Training, Child Care Food, Emergency Food Assistance, and Summer Food Service for Children.

How should the school food service program be funded? The major part of that program is the school lunch program. The amount a pupil is charged for a lunch depends upon the income of his or her parents. Pupils with parents who have an income below a specified level are given free lunches, and pupils with parents who have an income between the lowest level and the next specified level pay a reduced price for their lunches. For 1990–91, 32 percent of public school pupils participated in the reduced and free lunch program funded by the federal government. Pupils with parents who have an income above a specified level pay the highest prices charged pupils. However, pupils charged the highest prices for their lunches do not pay the full costs for their lunches, primarily because of the funding often contributed from tax sources.

Boards of education must ascertain the income of parents of pupils receiving free or reduced price lunches. Furthermore, records must be kept and reports made of expenditures and payments received from pupils in each category. This involves extensive accounting and much paper work. It is obvious that the present system of funding the school lunch program is cumbersome, inequitable, and fiscally inefficient. It is inequitable because it is impossible for local school authorities to ascertain accurately the income level of the pupils' parents. Furthermore, some low-income parents have too much pride to apply for free or reduced-price lunches. It is inefficient because of extensive record keeping required and because full economy of scale cannot be attained in school lunch programs where typically only 60 percent of pupils participate. In order to have an efficient and equitable program for financing school lunches, it should be made a part of the total school program and funded entirely from federal, state, and local tax sources. The school lunch program should certainly be considered as much a part of the total school program as pupil transportation. When school transportation became a major program, it was found to be more efficient to fund it entirely from public funds. It would be relatively simple to integrate state funds with federal and local funds and include the school lunch program as a part of the total state-guaranteed program.

Other Items of Current Expense

A number of other items of current expense relate to accommodation of vertical equity and are often included within a state-guaranteed program. Such items include: (1) Driver Education, (2) Economies of Scale (sparsity factory), (3) Municipal Overburden, (4) Textbooks, Computers, and Instructional Materials, (5) Distance Learning, (6) Sick Leave and Health Care Provisions, (7) Retirement and Social Security Costs, and (8) Extended School Year. All such items of current expense deserve serious consideration for accommodation of vertical equity.

RADICAL SCHOOL FINANCE ALTERNATIVES

The last 20 years has witnessed a wholesale attack on the institution of public elementary and secondary education unlike anything that has transpired previously. As discussed in Chapter 4, a continuous series of national and state commissions have published numerous reports that have alleged and documented the many failures of public schools. Only recently have supporters and researchers begun to present counter-arguments and question the so-called research reports published by many of these blue-ribbon commissions. While there is little question that many of the individuals who served on several of the commissions that have questioned the effectiveness of American public schools were well-intentioned, there is also little question that many published reports castigating public schools were intended to accomplish the following by discrediting public schools:

1. Sharply constrain the growth in federal, state, and local revenue for public elementary and secondary education
2. Shift a larger portion of governmental revenue to private, often sectarian educational institutions
3. Shift the blame for the demise of the United States in international economic competitiveness
4. Reprioritize national and state funding to other agencies of government

The vehicles recommended for replacement or reform of public elementary and secondary education have varied but most of the recent proposed panaceas have marched under the battle flag of *Choice*. Certainly, the decision to use the term *choice* as the battle flag was brilliant. The word *choice* embodies the concept of liberty and democracy, words historically and rightfully precious to most Americans. However, when one examines what the proponents of choice actually mean, we must question its applicability. Further, there is a vast difference between choice if it is applied to private education and choice if it is applied exclusively to public education.

Choice: Private Schools

During the 1980s, the private and public choice movement enjoyed powerful political support, a position articulated by John Chubb and Terry Moe who contended that "the political institutions that govern America's schools function naturally and routinely, despite everyone's best intentions, to burden the schools with excessive bureaucracy, to inhibit effective organization, and to stifle student achievement."[34] Chubb and Moe presented an alternative, a system nearly devoid of state regulations, in which state and private schools are funded equally from the public treasury.

Chubb and Moe cleverly referred to schools that would be eligible for public funds as public schools, but defined public schools as any schools that meet minimal standards, somewhat analogous to standards that states currently use to accredit private schools.[35] While Chubb and Moe gave lip service to the concept of fiscal equalization, they suggest, "The citizens of each district can then determine how important education is to them and how much they are willing to tax themselves for it. This means that children from different districts may have different-sized scholarships."[36] A devastating review of the Chubb and Moe attack on public education recently was made by Marshall and Tucker,[37] who in turn relied extensively on James Liebman.[38] Marshall and Tucker reported that Liebman severely criticized Chubb and Moe's inaccurate if not inane assumptions, as well as their use of incredibly sloppy statistics in order to praise private schools at the expense of public education. For example, Liebman indicated that Chubb and Moe concluded that parents of private school pupils are attracted to private schools because of good organization and less bureaucracy. Liebman indicated that a more plausible explanation is that patrons of private schools are attractive because such schools serve those persons of similar socioeconomic strata and religion and they desire that their children associate with children of similar religious and social values. In regard to Chubb and Moe's statistical methodology, Marshall and Tucker reported,

What is most noteworthy, however, given Chubb and Moe's reliance on the private model of education in their argument for market control of education, is that they do not report any correlation between private control and student achievement. The reason is not hard to find. Over the years, try as they might, no researchers, when adequately controlling for other factors, have *ever* been able to find anything more than a very weak correlation between private control and achievement. Nor is it at all clear that private schools, taken as a whole, produce students with higher achievement, even if other factors, such as student motivation and social class, are not controlled.[39]

The most recent report published by the National Assessment of Educational Progress regarding achievement in mathematics reported that there was no statistical difference between the scores of students enrolled in private and public elementary and secondary schools.[40]

Chubb and Moe also are much enamored with the school reform movement of Great Britain which they believe, due to the parliamentary form of government, has a better chance of succeeding than the choice movement in the United States. According to Chubb and Moe,

The wild card is that a full-blown choice system is most desperately needed by—and bestows disproportionate benefits upon—the poor and minorities in urban areas. . . . This opens up a political opportunity of the first magnitude for the Conservatives: by aggressively pursuing choice-based reforms, they can forge an alliance with a large and enormously important Labour constituency—and Labour can do nothing about it. . . . In our country, it is the Democrats who are the lost causes: wedded to the educational bureaucracy, forced into pitched battles with the poor, incapable of supporting genuine change. It is the Republicans who represent the only real hope—battling the establishment, promoting choice, weighing in on the side of the poor. The progressives have become conservatives, the conservatives progressives.[41]

However, the choice movement in Great Britain is not without its critics. Recently, the education policy of Great Britain has taken a battering. Two issues stimulated the recent battle. The first issue resulted due to a plan to privatize the school inspectorate. In essence, the privatization of the school inspectorate would, in effect, make the regulators clients of the schools they regulate. The government sought to privatize because it was distrustful of the so-called educationists who they believed were responsible for sloppy standards in state schools. They also assumed that they might subvert the 1988 Education Act. The second issue developed over an even more embarrassing issue. The choice movement of Great Britain has been predicated on urging parents to opt out of state schools and

> shift the balance of power in schools away from educationists (supposedly corrupted by trendy educational theories) to parent governors (supposedly instinctive guardians of traditional standards). But in Stratford School, a comprehensive which last year voted to opt out of LEA control and become self-governing, the scheme handed power to quite the wrong sorts of parent-governor—a clique more concerned with rabble rousing than with the three Rs. . . . The clique's leaders have pursued a vendetta against . . . the school's popular and successful head; issued indiscriminate charges of racism and other sins; and demanded postings for themselves and their friends. At times the disruption has been so serious that the police have had to be summoned.[42]

Choice: Public Schools

Partially in response to the private school choice issue, several states have studied, proposed, and enacted versions of public school choice programs. Essentially, there are two types of public school choice programs that have been either proposed or enacted: (1) intra-district choice; and (2) inter-district choice. Options for intra-district choice include, but are not limited to: (1) district-wide open enrollment; (2) enrollment limited to certain client groups (e.g., at-risk, dropouts, etc.); and (3) enrollment for magnet and alternative education schools. Intra-district choice programs are not uncommon in many states, although they are rarely formally so entitled. Policies simply exist which permits parents to transfer their children to other district schools that are not in their atten-

dance zones. Also, children regularly attend magnet schools, alternative education schools, special education centers, and vocational and occupational area schools. However, in some school districts, due to space and transportation limitations, transfers of general education pupils are discouraged. Additionally, pupils seeking intra-district transfers for the purpose of interscholastic athletics are usually forbidden.

Options for inter-district choice programs include, but are not limited to: (1) open enrollment among all state school districts; (2) enrollment limited to specific geographical regions within the state; (3) enrollment limited to contiguous school districts; and (4) enrollment limited to school districts of contiguous states. President Bill Clinton has gone on record as advocating inter-district public choice programs and during his tenure as governor of Arkansas, Arkansas became the second state to implement a statewide open enrollment public choice program.[43] Currently, 21 states have enacted some form of choice legislation, and in 1991, 37 state legislatures considered various choice proposals.[44]

The advantages identified by proponents of public school choice programs center primarily on the alleged instructional improvements that would accrue due to competition among schools. Additionally, parents would be able to select schools that would best fulfill the educational goals of their children, and the freedom to select public schools of their choice would conform more fully with the tenets of a democracy.

Vouchers

Another device to justify public funding for private education was initially popularized by the economist Milton Friedman during the mid-1950s. Friedman's solution has been referred to as the voucher system, when he proposed that the public should finance schools but not administer them.[45] He indicated that the implicit assumption that the government's role is to provide schooling by paying, subsidizing, and administering the schools is not necessarily valid. The two steps, he claims, can be separated, with government financing the schools through vouchers but not actually conducting the educational program. Under such a system, the government would give parents a voucher redeemable at a specified maximum sum per child per year, if spent on approved educational services. Parents could supplement the voucher in any amount they desire, to buy more expensive educational services. The role of government would be limited to ensuring that the schools meet minimum standards similar to the minimum sanitary standards required of restaurants. Presumably, under this scheme, public schools would continue to exist but would enter the marketplace on the same footing with private and parochial schools. In other words, the government would continue to administer certain schools, hire teachers, and conduct programs, but these schools would receive only the resources they could acquire from vouchers or , in the alternative public schools, that could be administered and financed directly by the state. But the state would be required to provide the same financing for students who choose to attend private or parochial approved schools.

According to Friedman, the voucher plan would improve education by

1. Giving parents greater freedom to choose a desirable educational program for their children
2. Doing away with the educational monopoly of public education
3. Increasing competition among schools, so that each would become more effective and efficient

Today, nearly 40 years after Friedman proposed the voucher system, not a single state has adopted the voucher system *in toto*. Several states have implemented pilot programs, mostly restricted to vouchers that could be redeemed only at other public schools. A few pilot programs, including the Milwaukee Parental Choice Program,[46] provided an opportunity for students who fulfilled specific criteria to attend private nonsec-

tarian schools at public expense.[47] The initial success of the Milwaukee Parental Choice Program could best be described as mixed. There was little difference in the achievement test scores between choice and nonchoice pupils, while pupil attendance, parental attitudes toward schools and the choice program, and parental involvement were mostly positive. On the other hand, attrition and return by many choice pupils to their original schools was quite high. It is likely that the Milwaukee Parental Choice Program will continue as a pilot program for some time in order to complete a more thorough evaluation.

Tuition Tax Credits

Still another type of financing scheme to provide public funds for private schools is tuition tax credits. Tuition tax credits have been proposed by Congress and various state legislatures. In essence, tuition tax credits would permit parents who send their children to school to reduce their tax liabilities. Tuition tax credits were first introduced at the federal level by Senators Moynihan of New York and Packwood of Oregon. The original bill, and subsequent legislation, was introduced and received particularly strong support during the Reagan–Bush era but was defeated repeatedly. Should tuition tax credits be enacted by federal legislation, the level of funding of traditional federal general and categorical aids would almost certainly decline, and the impact of such tax credits would undoubtedly tend to restructure the U.S. education system.

Tuition tax credits have fared better at the state level. In the early 1980s, the tuition tax credit plan enacted by Minnesota was challenged in federal court, and in 1983, *Mueller* v. *Allen*[48] was heard by the United States Supreme Court which ruled the Minnesota plan constitutional. The Court reasoned that since the tuition tax credits were available to parents who sent their children to private or public schools, the First Amendment was not violated. Interestingly, the Court was not persuaded that the fiscal benefits accrued nearly exclusively to parents of private school children.

The philosophical basis for tuition tax credits is the same for private school choice and vouchers; proponents allege that they would increase parental choice and strengthen education through competition. Such proposals are attractive to many because they evoke the picture of unfettered liberty in the pursuit of equal opportunity, yet many are convinced that vouchers and tuition tax credits may be much more injurious than beneficial to both public education and the nation.

OBJECTIONS TO PRIVATE CHOICE, VOUCHERS, AND TUITION TAX CREDITS

Private school choice, vouchers, and tuition tax credits represent such extreme changes in the government's role in financing public elementary and secondary education that enactment of such measures could basically restructure the U.S. system of public education. As discussed earlier, the public schools of this country are both free and common. Education should be free because the societal benefits of education are so great that all should pay through general taxation for the education of all youth. Public schools were designed to be common in order to transmit a common language, heritage, set of values, and knowledge, in essence the foundation of a nation. These foundation ingredients are necessary for appropriate political functioning in our democratic society.[49] Public schools were planned to be places where all classes, privileged and underprivileged, rich and poor, regardless of religious or ethnic background, were to learn to work and live together in justice and harmony.[50]

Social Cohesion

Private school choice, vouchers, and tuition tax credits will tend to create educational conditions contrary to the public, common-school purpose of social cohesion, mutual understanding, and socialization. These devices that are intended to transmit public funds to private, often sectarian schools, will likely encourage separation of society through intensification of competition and distrust among individuals grouped by school, religious sect, and social and economic strata. The public will be funding, in part, the schooling of children attending various religious sects, including the schools of television preachers, Jerry Falwell, Pat Robertson, Black Muslims, Jimmy Swaggart and Roman Catholic dioceses. It would appear ill-advised to publicly fund the fragmentation of society along religious lines. The world is replete with examples of hatred, prejudice, and wars fought under the banners of religion. Is there little doubt that the current bloody conflict being waged in Bosnia is motivated by religious differences?

Parental Limitation

Parental choice in all educational matters may not always be in the best interest of the child. The law abounds with hundreds of cases where parents of limited perspective or intelligence have sought to contract the spectrum of knowledge which their own and other children could acquire by seeking to purge the public school libraries of great works of art and literature and to restrain instruction regarding important scientific developments. In a system of private school choice, vouchers, and tuition tax credits, the state would not be in a position to expand and extend the scope of knowledge; in fact, these devices would put state financial assistance in the service of the narrow political, religious, and ideological views of society. What parents do choose, under such systems, is likely to be a direct extension of the beliefs and values they already hold, "with little opportunity for students to experience the diversity of backgrounds, and viewpoints that contribute to the democratic process."[51] According to Henry Levin,

> Vouchers would make this class stratification and socialization even more *efficient* by making it possible for parents to choose particular primary and secondary schooling environments based upon these values. Thus, differences in child socialization among classes in our highly stratified society

would be augmented by a more perfect correspondence between the social class orientations of the parents and the schools they chose. In contrast with the present system, where at least some children find themselves in schools that do not necessarily reflect their parents' social origins, the voucher approach would streamline transmission of status from one generation to the next.[52]

Class Orientation

The choice of lifestyle or education is limited by both fiscal resources and the awareness of available options. A prerequisite to the exercise of liberty to choose is the acquisition, by education, training, or experience, of knowledge of available alternatives. What constitutes success in life to the lower-middle-class, blue-collar parent may be much more limited than that of the upper-middle-class parent. Poorer working-class parents appear to emphasize conformity in their children, while parents in higher-income positions tend to stress independence of thought and expansiveness of thinking.[53] A tendency exists for persons to select experiences which have proven most rewarding; thus, limited experiences produce limited choices.

Under the private choice, voucher, or tuition tax credit system, parental choices would be restricted primarily to class orientations. However, due to the fundamental shift in social strata in the United States, a much smaller section of society enjoy the options that were available to their parents. As suggested previously, the political and vaunted business leadership has failed miserably to maintain the international economic competitiveness of the United States; instead, many corporate chief executive officers (CEOs) and their elected political spokespersons are attempting to use public schools as scapegoats. Additionally, the implementation of the various private choice opportunities would once again expand the opportunities for the children of upper- and upper-middle-class parents to attend publicly-supported private schools with children of similar social strata.

Separation of Church and State

One of the basic and unique tenets of the United States Constitution is that the church and state should be held separate. The burden falls on the state to assure that children receive at least a minimum of secular education, yet have the freedom to acquire sectarian instruction as well. According to the United States Supreme Court, in the 1971 *Lemon* v. *Kurtzman* case,[54] the state cannot inhibit, enhance, or become excessively entangled with religion. Following the *Lemon* decision, the U.S. Supreme Court in the 1973 *Committee for Public Education and Religious Liberty* v. *Nyquist* decision,[55] specifically ruled tuition tax credits of a New York statute unconstitutional. However, as noted earlier, the Supreme Court, primarily due to a change of justices, reversed itself in *Mueller*, and tuition tax credits are now likely to be acceptable to federal courts. It remains to be seen if vouchers and various other private choice plans will also be ruled constitutional by the federal courts. There are many legal scholars that believe that the wall of separation between church and state is crumbling rather rapidly, portending an ominous future for a strong and well-financed system of public elementary and secondary schools. The Supreme Court, in *Wolman* v. *Walter*, said,

> At this point in the 20th century we are quite far removed from the dangers that prompted the Framers [of the United States Constitution] to include the Establishment Clause in the Bill of Rights. The risk of significant religious or denominational control over our democratic processes— or even of deep political division along religious lines—is remote, and when viewed against the positive contributions of sectarian schools, such risk seems entirely tolerable in light of the continuing oversight of this Court.[56]

Within most states, however, the future of publicly supported private schools is much less certain. Due to strong state constitutional provisions prohibiting the expenditure of public funds for private and/or sectarian schools, many state constitutions will have to be amended before public funds can be disbursed to private sectarian elementary and secondary schools.

Equity

Private school choice, vouchers, and tuition tax credits undoubtedly are deficient from the standpoint of both equity and social justice. Recently, Marshall and Tucker, again citing Liebman, said,

> Under any choice plan, schools seeking to do well in the market would be highly motivated to show that students who attended their institution achieved at high levels. Because the biggest contributors to achievement are family income and parents' education, the best way to establish a reputation for high achievement would be to screen clients based on parents' income and education. Those that did the best screening job would experience the fastest rise in achievement, and having done so, would be able to attract the most advantaged student body, in an endless upward cycle of profits, exclusion, and social stratification. If, in addition, prices were permitted to rise to whatever the market would bear, this process would operate with ruthless efficiency. The market, in other words, would do what it has always done best: allocate scarce resources on the basis of wealth. Our schools would be finely segregated, like any other consumer market, on the basis of class. . . . The prospects of the poor would be truly desperate. It would be the end, as a matter of policy, to any aspiration that this country ever had that its schools would serve as the first line of defense in a strategy to provide equal opportunity to all.[57]

The several private school choice devices are inequitable for several reasons, but most obviously because they are given to the rich and poor alike. Although equity of tuition tax credits could be increased by negative tax provisions, whereby parents not paying taxes would be paid directly by the federal government for the amount of the tax credits, the overall effect would still tend to favor the rich. The vast majority of poor people in this country send their children to public schools. Children of the wealthy are often found in private, high-tuition schools where the various choice programs would be most used and valued.

Segregation

While the debate regarding private school choice through vouchers and tuition tax credits commonly centers upon separation of church and state, social stratification, and equity issues, the perpetuation of segregated schools, or perhaps the reinstitution of segregation, deserves discussion. It has been well documented that higher percentages of minorities, particularly African-American, Native-American, and Hispanic pupils reside in the lower economic strata of U.S. society. The various devices used to implement private school choice programs inevitably would segregate schools along racial and ethnic lines.

Private school choice programs would undoubtedly give new impetus and financial leverage to segregation in the educational system. In 1989, African-American and Hispanic children constituted 51.8 percent, 20.0 percent, and 15.3 percent of pupils enrolled in public schools located in central cities, metropolitan, and nonmetropolitan areas, respectively. In contrast, private schools enrolled only 14.1 percent of children classified as African-American and Hispanic.[58] Data presented in *Mueller* v. *Allen*[59] showed conclusively that the fiscal benefits from tuition tax credits flowed disproportionately to parents of private school children. Nationally, only 3.2 percent of low-income families send their children to private schools, compared to 16.5 percent of families at the highest income level.[60] Since a much smaller percentage of African-American and Hispanic children attend private schools than public schools, their parents would receive less financial benefit. Further, parents of African-American and Hispanic children would be less likely, due to fiscal constraints, to participate in the several proposed private school choice programs.

The potential danger that private school choice programs represent to U.S. public schools cannot be overemphasized. If one or more of the private school choice programs are ultimately legislated and funded, it is likely that parallel systems of public schools will emerge. One system, funded exclusively from public funds, would serve the several racial and ethnic minorities from the lower socio-economic strata of society, the disabled, and children rejected from the private system. The other system, funded partially from public funds and supplemented by private tuition and external sources, would serve the children of the middle and upper levels of U.S. society. The battle fought during the latter half of the twentieth century to desegregate public schools would ultimately be lost.

SUMMARY AND CONCLUSIONS

Managerial control of public elementary and secondary schools for most states traditionally rests with local communities; however, legal and fiscal responsibility for the operation of public schools resides with the 50 state governments.

Initially, intergovernmental revenue transfer systems, grants, were designed and implemented by states in order to ensure that common schools were available throughout the respective states. In effect, state grants for public schools use the taxing power of state governments to redistribute the fiscal resources of the state among local school districts.

Whenever a state system of school finance is either developed or modified significantly, a series of four decisions have to be addressed. These four decisions are: (1) determination of state-guaranteed level of educational services; (2) determination of costs; (3) determination of state and local fiscal responsibilities; and (4) determination of local fiscal capacity.

State grants for public schools can be arrayed, albeit crudely, on an equity continuum that ranges from nonequalization to fully state-funded programs.

Flat grants are seldom used by states as their major state-aid program for the public schools. Instead, flat grants are used extensively to distribute categorical aid to the local school districts.

All fiscal equalization grants are designed to allocate, on a per-unit basis, greater amounts of state resources to low-fiscal-capacity school districts than to high-capacity districts.

Although each state has developed fiscal equalization grants that are unique, fiscal equalization programs can be classified broadly into: (1) foundation programs; (2) guaranteed tax yield/base programs; (3) percentage-equalization programs; (4) district-power-equalization programs; and (5) tier programs.

While equalization of educational opportunity has been either explicitly stated or implied during the development of myriad state systems of school finance, absolute fiscal equalization has rarely been achieved.

Radical school finance alternatives, popularly referred to as school choice proposals, pose a significant threat to public elementary and secondary education. These choice proposals are collectively designed to transfer public funds to private or nonpublic schools, and have serious implications regarding social cohesion, parental limitations, class orientation, separation of church and state, equity, and segregation.

KEY TERMS

General aid	Tier programs	Guaranteed tax yield/base
Approximate fiscal	Recapture provisions	programs
equalization	School choice proposals	District-power equalization
Categorical aid	Educational vouchers	programs
Formula design decisions	Absolute fiscal equalization	Percentage-equalization
Matching programs	Nonequalization grants	programs
Foundation programs	Flat grants	Full state funding
Local required effort	Lighthouse concept	Tuition tax credits
Stand-alone programs	Leveling-down vs. leveling up	

ENDNOTES

1. National Center for Education Statistics, United States Department of Education, *Digest of Education Statistics, 1992* (Washington, DC: U.S. Government Printing Office, 1992), p. 49.

2. National Education Association, *Estimates of School Statistics, 1993–94* (Washington, DC: NEA, 1994), p. 38.

3. Ibid., p. 7.

4. There is some question as to whether Hawaii, although classified as fully state-funded has achieved absolute fiscal equalization. See for example John Thompson, "Funding and Spending in Paradise: Notes on the Hawaii Model of Educational Finance," *Journal of Education Finance* 12, no. 2 (Fall 1986), pp. 282–294.

5. Ellwood P. Cubberley, *School Funds and Their Apportionment* (New York: Teachers College, Columbia University, 1906), p. 123.

6. Richard Salmon, Stephen Lawton, Christina Dawson, and Thomas Johns, *Public School Finance Programs of the United States and Canada, 1986–87* (Blacksburg, VA: American Education Finance Association, 1988).

7. See Chapter 4 for precise definitions of enrollment, average daily attendance and average daily membership.

8. The federal government, until the Reagan–Bush Era, was gradually increasing its share of funding for public elementary and secondary education, reaching a high-water mark in 1979–80, when it contributed 9.2 percent. See National Education Association, *Estimates of School Statistics, 1988–89* (Washington, DC: NEA, 1989), p. 21. Throughout the twelve-year Republican administration, from 1980 to 1992, the percentage of revenue receipts provided by the federal government declined, falling to 6.6 percent for 1990–91 before showing a slight upturn to 6.7 percent for 1991–92. See National Education Association, *Estimates of School Statistics, 1993–94* (Washington, DC: NEA, 1993), p. 21.

9. *Alabama Coalition for Equity, Inc.* v. *Hunt*, Circuit Court of Montgomery, Alabama, 1993 WL 204083.

10. Cubberley, op. cit., p. 100.

11. National Education Association, op. cit.

12. Ibid.

13. Education Testing Service, *State of Inequality* (Princeton, NJ: ETS, 1992).

14. George D. Strayer and Robert M. Haig, *The Financing of Education in the State of New York,* Report of the Educational Finance Inquiry Commission, vol. 1 (New York: Macmillan, 1923), pp. 175–176.

15. Roe L. Johns and Edgar L. Morphet, *The Economics and Financing of Education*, 2nd ed. (Englewood Cliffs, NJ: Prentice-Hall, 1969), pp. 198–199.

16. Harlan Undegraff, *Rural School Survey of New York State: Financial Support* (Ithaca, NY: By the author, 1922) pp. 117–118.

17. Salmon, op. cit., p. 4.

18. Commonwealth of Pennsylvania, *Instruction Related Subsidies—Equalized Subsidy for Basic Education (ESBE),* Public School Code of 1949.

19. *Serrano* v. *Priest*, 5 Cal.3d 584, 96 Cal. Rptr. 601, 487 P.2d 1241 (1971), appeal after remanded 18 Cal.3d 728, 135 Cal. Rptr. 345, 557 P.2d 929 (1976), cert. denied 432 U.S. 907, 97 S.Ct. 2951 (1976).

20. The tier program illustrated and discussed is a two-tier program; in some instances, three-tier programs have been developed. At one time Utah utilized a three-tier program and Kentucky currently uses a three-tier program; however, the third tier of the Kentucky program is supported entirely from local resources.

21. Fleischmann Commission, *The Fleischmann Report* (New York: Viking Press, 1973), pp. 61–73.

22. Henry C. Morrison, *School Revenue* (Chicago: University of Chicago Press, 1940), p. 164.

23. Salmon, op. cit., p. 90.

24. Ibid., p. 5.

25. Advisory Commission on Intergovernmental Relations, *Urban America and the Federal System* (Washington, DC: U.S. Government Printing Office, 1969), p. 23.

26. National Education Finance Project, *Planning to Finance Education*, Vol. 3, eds. R. L. Johns, Kern Alexander, and K. F. Jordan (Gainesville, FL: NEFP, 1971).

27. Florida Department of Education, Division of Public Schools, *Florida Education Finance Program, 1992–93* (Tallahassee, FL: Financial Management Section of the Bureau of School Business Services, August, 1992), p. 12.

28. Ibid.

29. 20 U.S.C. 2701.

30. United States Department of Education, National Center for Education Statistics, *Digest of Education Statistics, 1993* (Washington, DC: U.S. Government Printing Office, 1994).

31. Ibid.

32. Ibid.

33. Thelbert L. Drake and William H. Roe, *School Business Management*. (Needham Heights, MA: Allyn & Bacon, 1994), p. 185.

34. John E. Chubb and Terry M. Moe, *Politics, Markets, and America's Schools* (Washington, DC: The Brookings Institution, 1990), p. ix.

35. Historically, most states have enforced loose accreditation standards pursuant to their private schools, partly because of the potential conflict that likely would occur concerning separation of church and state.

36. Chubb and Moe, op. cit., p. 220.

37. Ray Marshall and Marc Tucker, *Thinking for a Living: Education and the Wealth of Nations* (New York: Basic Books, 1992).

38. James Liebman, "Voice, Not Choice," *Yale Law Journal*, vol. 101 (October 1991), pp. 259–314.

39. Marshall and Tucker, op. cit., p. 133.

40. Ina Mullins, John Dossey, Eugene Owen and Gary Phillips, *The State of Mathematics Achievement: NAEP's 1990 Assessment of the Nation and the Trial Assessment of the States* (Washington, DC: National Center for Educational Statistics, U.S. Department of Education, 1991).

41. John E. Chubb and Terry M. Moe, *A Lesson in School Reform from Great Britain* (Washington, DC: The Brookings Institution, 1992).

42. "Embarrassed on Education," *The Economist*, vol. 322, no. 7749 (March 7, 1992), p. 55.

43. Virginia Department of Education, *The Viability of School Choice in Virginia* (Richmond: Virginia Department of Education, 1992), p. 14.

44. Ibid., p. 4.

45. Milton Friedman, "The Role of Government in Education" in *Economics and the Public Interest*, ed. Robert A. Solo (New Brunswick, NJ: Rutgers University Press, 1955), pp. 127–128.

46. John F. Witte, *First Year Report: Milwaukee Parental Choice Program* (Madison: University of Wisconsin, 1991).

47. The administrators of the Milwaukee Parental Choice Program indicated that this program should not be generalized to an unconstrained voucher program—one that would subsidize private school education under much broader circumstances.

48. *Mueller* v. *Allen*, 463 U.S. 388, 103 S.Ct. 3062 (1983).

49. Henry M. Levin, "Educational Vouchers and Social Policy," in *Care and Education of Young Children in America*, eds. Ron Haskins and James J. Callagher (Norwood, NJ: Ablex, 1980), p. 119.

50. Freeman R. Butts, "Educational Vouchers: The Private Pursuit of the Public Purse," *Phi Delta Kappan*, vol. 61, no. 1 (1979), p. 7.

51. Levin, op. cit., p. 17.

52. Henry M. Levin, "Educational Vouchers and Social Policy," in *School Finance Policies and Practices, The 1980's: A Decade of Conflict*, ed. James W. Guthrie (Cambridge: Ballinger, 1980), p. 253.

53. Melvin R. Kohn, *Class and Conformity* (Homewood, IL: Dorsey Press, 1969). See also Levin, op. cit.

54. *Lemon* v. *Kurtzman*, 403 U.S. 602, 91 S.Ct. 2105 (1971).

55. *Committee for Public Education and Religious Liberty* v. *Nyquist*, 413 U.S. 756, 93 S.Ct. 2955 (1973).

56. *Wolman* v. *Walter*, 433 U.S. 229, 97 S.Ct. 2593 (1977) at 2613.

57. Marshall and Tucker, op. cit., p. 135.

58. National Center for Education Statistics, *The Condition of Education, 1992* (Washington, DC: U.S. Government Printing Office, 1992), p. 104.

59. *Mueller* v. *Allen*, op. cit.

60. James S. Catterall, *Tuition Tax Credits: Fact and Fiction* (Bloomington, IN: Phi Delta Kappen Educational Foundation, 1983), p. 33.

CHAPTER 10

THE MEASUREMENT OF EQUITY

TOPICAL OUTLINE OF CHAPTER

Preparation of State Data Base • *Measurement of Horizontal and Vertical Equity* • *Horizontal and Vertical Equity Statistics* • *Measurement of Fiscal Neutrality* • *Fiscal Neutrality Statistics* • *Application of Horizontal and Vertical Equity Statistics* • *Application of Fiscal Neutrality*

INTRODUCTION

The concept of fiscal equalization of educational opportunity has been discussed in Chapter 9, and the subconcepts of vertical and horizontal equity of state systems of school finance have been introduced. Further, the concept of taxpayer equity was discussed during the presentation regarding taxation. Collectively, these concepts and subconcepts provide the philosophical basis for the measurement of equity provided by the 50 state systems of school finance.

The several types of intergovernmental revenue transfer systems, or grants, that are used by states to allocate state resources to local school districts were presented elsewhere in this text. As discussed in Chapter 9, the primary objective of state grants, through shared local and state funds, is to fiscally equalize educational resources among local school districts. Throughout the earlier presentation of grant systems, for purposes of discussion, the measurement of equity was limited primarily to visual evaluations of the several bar charts. Unfortunately, the measurement of equity provided by state systems of school finance is much more complicated and has required the development of more sensitive and

sophisticated statistical measures. The measurement of both horizontal and taxpayer equity pursuant to state systems of school finance lend themselves to statistical treatment of fiscal data. However, as suggested by Berne and Stiefel in their definitions in Chapter 9, the measurement of vertical equity is dependent, at least partially, upon the values and educational priorities of those who conduct equity analyses. Following the discussion of horizontal and taxpayer equity measurement, recommendations concerning the measurement of vertical equity are provided. Prior to the statistical measurement of equity, it is necessary to establish and refine the state data base, a process that requires several key research decisions. The following recommendations for preparation of the state data base, while not universally accepted, are based upon best practice.

PREPARATION OF STATE DATA BASE

Ideally, the application of the several equity statistics to a state data base would be conducted precisely the same by all school finance researchers. The data from the 50 states would be configured identically, including similarity of school district organization, fiscal capacity measure, accounting terminology, fund structure, pupil unit, and other factors. Unfortunately, while some commonality does exist among states, significant differences exist and will continue to exist for the foreseeable future. While adherence to the following nine procedural steps for preparation of the state data bases will not completely satisfy the problems created by the dissimilarity of state systems of school finance, such adherence should make interstate comparisons of fiscal equity analyses more reliable.

1. While either revenue or current expenditure may be used as the input cost measure, *current expenditure per pupil (adjusted by deducting federal revenue) is likely the more reliable measure*. There is an argument to use state and local revenue since it is a measure of total fiscal resources available to local school districts. However, the revenue input reported by states often contains nonrevenue for capital outlay, making revenue a volatile input measure.[1]

2. The *unit of analysis* should be based upon pupils and not the local school district. Some researchers inappropriately use local school districts as the unit of analysis, thus disregarding the differences in numbers of pupils served by local school districts. To achieve horizontal equity analysis the focus should be on pupils served throughout the state and not on the administrative structure that serves only as a vehicle for delivery of educational services. In the case of Virginia, by treating school districts as the unit of analysis, Highland County Public Schools, serving approximately 350 pupils, would exert an identical statistical influence as Fairfax County, serving approximately 135,000 pupils. While current school accounting does not provide individual per-pupil revenue or expenditure data, an acceptable alternative is to assume a common per-pupil expenditure for a single school district and weight the school district proportionally to the number of pupils served.

3. Local school districts should be *segregated according to district type* before the application of equity statistics. It is inappropriate to statistically treat elementary, secondary, and K–12 school districts together. Even if identical educational programs were being provided among all local school districts, the differences in per-pupil revenue or expenditure that inherently exist among elementary, secondary, and K–12 districts would likely distort horizontal equity analyses.

4. *Specially configured local school districts should be excluded* from the equity analysis. Intermediate, cooperative, and regional districts, as well as special education service centers, vocational area districts, and other specially configured districts (schools) are often funded uniquely and complicate the interpretation of equity analyses. While the exclusion of specially configured districts is necessary prior to statistical analysis, their services and concurrent costs to local school districts need to be assigned only to benefitted local school districts.

5. *Local school districts that are structural anomalies should be excluded* from the equity analysis. Due to geographical constraints, states occasionally experience exceptionally high per-pupil costs to provide educational services for limited numbers of pupils. For example, Ohio maintains three island districts, each district enrolling no more than six pupils.

6. *Federal funds should be excluded* from the equity analysis. Federal grants contain provisions that require that states not supplant federal funds.[2] The nonsupplanting provisions make a powerful argument for excluding all federal funds, with the possible exception of federal impact aid. Federal impact aid specifically authorizes states to take into consideration a portion of federal impact aid allocated to their local school districts if the state can meet certain equity requirements.[3]

7. *Categorical funds, whether contained within the basic state grant or separately funded, should be included* in the equity analysis. This procedure does not enjoy universal acceptance among school finance researchers. Some researchers argue that horizontal and vertical equity analyses should be conducted separately; and as a consequence, they argue that the horizontal equity criterion should be applied only to client groups where equality can be agreed upon.

Those opposed to the exclusion of categorical funds from the equity analysis suggest that high-capacity school districts often are able to compete more effectively for competitive grants than other districts. Further, due to a lack of accounting uniformity and grant structures among states, interstate comparisons of equity statistics is complicated by attempting to exclude categoricals from equity analyses. Finally, if differences among client groups, school district characteristics, and educational programs are accommodated properly prior to the application of the several equity statistics, the evaluation of horizontal and vertical equity can be conducted simultaneously. Further discussion of this procedure is presented later in this chapter.

8. The differences that exist among school districts due to client needs, school district characteristics, and educational programs should be identified and per-unit weights should be applied, resulting in a weighted pupil count for each school district included in the equity analyses.

9. In longitudinal studies, either appropriate inflators or deflators should be applied to current expenditures in order to convert to constant dollars. While most equity statistics are unaffected by constant-dollar adjustments, the range, restricted range, and measures of central tendency are subject to distortion due to inflationary pressures and should be converted to constant dollars for cross-time comparisons.

MEASUREMENT OF HORIZONTAL AND VERTICAL EQUITY

As defined earlier, horizontal equity requires that equal resources are provided to pupils who have similar needs. If all pupils required identical educational services, the measurement of horizontal equity could be achieved by simply

applying a series of dispersion statistics to a properly prepared state data base. Unfortunately, each state, local school district, school, and classroom serve diverse clients who require varying amounts and forms of educational services. As a consequence, the different amounts and forms of educational services result in considerable variance in per-pupil costs. If the objective is to measure horizontal equity without consideration of vertical equity, one could exclude all pupils who require unequal services and their concomitant costs from the data, that is, categorical funds and eligible pupils. Application of dispersion statistics to the remaining pupils and costs would provide an analysis of horizontal equity. While the nine-step procedure will effectively measure horizontal equity, it does not yield an analysis of vertical equity, and does, in fact, greatly complicate such an analysis. Due to limitations of fiscal accounting practices employed by most public schools, precise identification and assignment of the full costs required to provide services for unequal pupils has proven extremely difficult.

According to Berne and Stiefel, the measurement of vertical equity is value-laden, certainly an understatement for researchers who have struggled with this difficult problem.[4] While most school finance authorities agree that unequal pupils require unequal treatment, there is little agreement regarding either client identification or the costs required to provide educational services to identified clients. Even among client programs universally accepted as requiring unequal or extraordinary costs, such as disabled children, there is little agreement regarding what constitutes either appropriate educational services or their respective costs. Each of the 50 states have established unique systems for providing and funding educational services to a varied array of client groups. How then should the level of vertical equity by a state system of school finance be measured?

Perhaps the most defensible procedure is to conduct the analysis of horizontal and vertical equity simultaneously as suggested by procedural step 7. In order to conduct a simultaneous evaluation of horizontal and vertical equity, all current costs, excluding federal funds, should remain in the analysis. A series of state-specific pupils weights should be developed based upon a cost-accounting analysis of statewide historical data.[5] These state-specific weights should be developed relative to pupils who are not eligible for unequal costs. For example, a cost-accounting analysis might show that disabled children identified as learning disabled who receive educational services through self-contained classrooms require twice the per-pupil expenditure than normal children, resulting in a weight of 2:1. The weights thus developed would be applied to the identified clients for each local school district, yielding a weighted pupil count. Current costs, excluding federal funds, for each school district would be divided by its respective weighted pupil count, resulting in costs per weighted pupil for all local school districts in the state data base.

Following is a series of dispersion statistics commonly used to measure horizontal and vertical equity, each including its definition, strengths, weaknesses, and interpretation. Since this book is not intended to be used as a statistical manual, it does not include discussions of formula derivation and its theoretical basis. However, for the convenience of researchers, equity statistics formulas are contained in Appendix A.

Range

Among local school districts that are ranked from high to low per-pupil inputs, either revenue or expenditure, within a state, the range is the difference between the highest and lowest per-pupil inputs.

Strengths and Weaknesses.   The range is calculated simply and easily explained; however, its utility is limited since it focuses exclusively on extremes rather than the entire distribution. For example, due to circumstances unique to a particular state, high per-pupil inputs for very small, isolated school districts many be necessary and

are justified. Reliance solely upon the range as a measure of horizontal and vertical equity may suggest erroneously that considerable disparities exist although the vast majority of pupils are provided equitable educational services.

Interpretation.   As the range increases, the levels of horizontal and vertical equity decrease.

Restricted Range

Among local school districts that are ranked from high to low per-pupil inputs within a state, the restricted range is the difference between the per-pupil inputs at selected percentiles, that is, the 95th and 5th percentiles. The per-pupil inputs for local school districts in which the 95th and 5th percentiles of all pupils in the state fell are used as proxies for the per-pupil inputs for the 95th and 5th percentiles of pupils.

Strengths and Weaknesses.   Conceptually, the restricted range ignores the upper and lower ends of the continuum, thus correcting some of the weaknesses of the range measure. The restricted range is calculated simply and is easily explained, but it provides little information concerning the entire distribution of per-pupil inputs.

Interpretation.   As the restricted range increases, the levels of horizontal and vertical equity decrease.

Restricted Range Ratio

The restricted range ratio is calculated by dividing the per-pupil inputs at the 5th percentile by the per-pupil inputs at the 95th percentile.

Strengths and Weaknesses.   Again, calculation of the restricted range ratio, like the range and restricted range, is calculated simply and is easily explained. The use of a ratio, rather than actual dollars, provides a statistic that can be used, albeit roughly, for longitudinal and interstate comparisons. However, identical to the range and restricted range statistics, the restricted range ratio focuses on the extremes and provides little information concerning the entire distribution of per-pupil inputs.

Interpretation. As the restricted range ratio increases, the levels of horizontal and vertical equity decrease.

Federal Range Ratio

The federal range ratio is a statistic used by the federal government to determine eligibility for states to take into consideration federal impact aid payments to local school districts.[6] The federal range ratio is calculated by subtracting the per-pupil inputs at the 5th percentile from the per-pupil inputs at the 95th percentile and dividing the result by the per-pupil inputs at the 5th percentile.

Strengths and Weaknesses. The federal range ratio is mathematically equivalent to the restricted range ratio and possesses identical strengths and weaknesses. However, since it is a standard codified into federal law that establishes a specific equity standard, the federal range ratio enjoys a certain amount of governmental prestige.

Interpretation. As the federal range ratio increases, the levels of horizontal and vertical equity decrease.

Coefficient of Variation

The coefficient of variation is the standard deviation of a distribution of per-pupil inputs divided by the mean, expressed as a percentage.

Strengths and Weaknesses. The coefficient of variation is designed to measure the variability of the distribution of per-pupil inputs relative to the mean. The CV is easily calculated and can be explained simply to those who have a basic understanding of elementary statistics. Further, the

CV utilizes the entire distribution of per-pupil inputs to measure the dispersion of per-pupil inputs.

Interpretation. As the coefficient of variation increases, the levels of horizontal and vertical equity decrease.

Lorenz Curve and Gini Coefficient

The Lorenz Curve is developed by plotting data for cumulative proportions of pupils and cumulative proportions of per-pupil inputs on coordinate axes. Local school districts are sorted by ascending order of per-pupil inputs (i.e., revenues or expenditures). The cumulative proportions of pupils are represented by the horizontal axis and the cumulative proportions of total inputs accounted for by these districts are represented by the vertical axis. The curve thus plotted would be a 45-degree straight line if the per-pupil inputs were identical for all school districts. The Gini Coefficient is defined as the area between the plotted curve and the 45-degree line, expressed as a fraction of the total area below the 45-degree line. A graphic portrayal of the Lorenz Curve is presented in Figure 10.1. Thus, the measure of inequality as defined by the Gini Coefficient (G) is given by the formula in Figure 10.1.

Strengths and Weaknesses. The Lorenz Curve provides a visual measure of the level of horizontal and vertical equity provided by a state system of school finance and can be explained simply. However, calculation of the Gini Coefficient is more difficult to explain and interstate comparisons are somewhat problematic.

Interpretation. As suggested, if the plotted curve conforms precisely to the 45-degree straight line, per-pupil inputs would be identical for all school districts, representing absolute equity. The further the plotted curve falls, or sags, below the 45-degree line, the more inequitable is the state system of school finance. In regard to

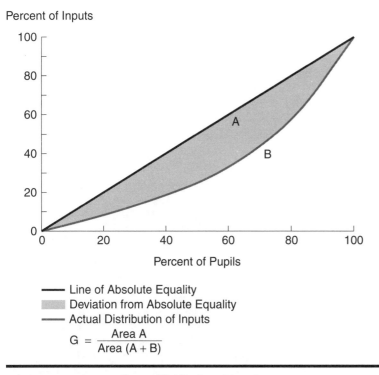

Percent of Inputs

Percent of Pupils

Line of Absolute Equality
Deviation from Absolute Equality
Actual Distribution of Inputs

$$G = \frac{\text{Area A}}{\text{Area (A + B)}}$$

FIGURE 10.1   Lorenz Curve: Distribution of Inputs

the Gini Coefficient, the coefficient may vary from 0.0 to 1.0; when the coefficient falls to 0.0, absolute equity is presumed to exist, and as the coefficient increases, the levels of horizontal and vertical equity decrease.

McLoone Index

The McLoone Index is the ratio of the actual inputs for all pupils below the median per-pupil inputs relative to the total inputs these pupils would receive if they were posited at the median per-pupil input level for the entire distribution.

Strengths and Weaknesses.   It is calculated simply and is easily explained to those with a basic understanding of statistics. The primary weakness of the McLoone Index is that it measures equity provided pupils located below the median per-pupil inputs for the state, thus ignor-

ing pupils served above the median. Implicit in the conceptual base of the McLoone Index is the assumption that horizontal and vertical equity is necessary only up to the median per-pupil inputs.

Interpretation.   The McLoone Index ranges from 0.0 to 1.0, and as the McLoone Index increases, the levels of horizontal and vertical equity also increase.

Theil Index

The Theil Index, an equity measure based on information theory, was originally designed to measure the inequality of income distribution. In place of income, per-pupil inputs are used to assess the horizontal and vertical equity of state systems of school finance. Additionally, the Theil Index can be used to gain insight into the subsets of the distribution.[7]

Strengths and Weaknesses. The Theil Index is a powerful econometric measure designed to measure the dispersion of income within societies and has been adapted to measure the level of horizontal and vertical equity provided by state systems of school finance. Unfortunately, while calculation of the Theil Index is not particularly difficult, explanation of its conceptual and theoretical base has proved problematic.

Interpretation. The Theil Index ranges from 0.0 to 1.0, and as the Theil Index increases, the levels of horizontal and vertical equity decrease.

Atkinson Index

The Atkinson Index is based upon a function that converts a distribution of per-pupil inputs into a single number that theoretically measures the social welfare (desirability) of the distribution. The welfare function simultaneously considers the magnitude of per-pupil inputs and the horizontal and vertical equity provided pupils. Parameters, referred to as E, can vary from 0.0 to ∞ and are incorporated into the welfare function. The larger value assigned to the parameter, the more concern provided the lower end of the distribution, as measured by per-pupil inputs.

Strengths and Weaknesses. Similar to the Theil Index, the Atkinson Index is a powerful econometric measure, adapted for application to the measurement of horizontal and vertical equity. Also, similar to the Theil Index, explanation of its conceptual base and theoretical base has proved problematic.

Interpretation. The Atkinson Index ranges from 0.0 to 1.0, and as the Atkinson Index increases, the levels of horizontal and vertical equity also increase.

MEASUREMENT OF FISCAL NEUTRALITY (TAXPAYER EQUITY)

Several commonly used statistics have been used to measure the relationship of the fiscal capacities of local school districts to their respective per-pupil inputs. That is, statistics are employed to assess the strength of the relationship that exists between fiscal capacity and the quality of education provided by a state system of school finance. Following are definitions, strengths, weaknesses, and interpretations for the following commonly used statistics: correlations, regressions, slopes, and elasticities.

Correlation

The Pearson Product-Moment Correlation is commonly used to measure the relationship between per-pupil inputs of local school districts and their respective fiscal capacities.

Strengths and Weaknesses. The correlation statistic has been used widely by researchers of all professions. It is calculated simply and is easily explained to those with a basic understanding of statistics. The often-cited weakness of the correlation statistic is that it fails to show causality and measures only the strength of a relationship between variables. Further, the correlation statistic by itself does not measure the magnitude of the variance of per-pupil inputs among local school districts. Finally, and most serious, the conduct of a simple correlation does not control for the variance in per-pupil inputs created by varying levels of fiscal effort.

Interpretation. The correlation coefficient may vary from 0.0 to ± 1.0. A correlation coefficient of 0.0 would indicate that there was no relationship between fiscal capacities of local school districts and their per-pupil inputs, and as the correlation coefficient increases, the level of fiscal neutrality decreases.

Regression

The square of the simple correlation is the fraction of variation in the dependent variable that is explained by the regression line.

Strengths and Weaknesses. Instead of discussing a coefficient of correlation, the relationship between variables is explained on the basis of a fraction, or percentage of the variance. Since the regression statistic is a function of the simple correlation, it possesses similar qualities.

Interpretation. The regression percentage may vary from 0.0 to 100.0. A regression equation that explains 0.0 percent would indicate that there was no relationship between fiscal capacities of the local school districts and their per-pupil inputs, and as the percentage of variance explained increases, the level of fiscal neutrality decreases.

Slope

The *slope* shows the size of the change in the dependent variable (per-pupil inputs) associated with a one-unit change in the independent variable (fiscal capacities of the local school districts) in absolute terms.

Strengths and Weaknesses. Unlike the correlation and regression statistics the slope measures the magnitude, rather than the strength, of the relationship that exists between fiscal capacity and per-pupil inputs. It is calculated simply and is easily explained to those with a basic understanding of statistics. However, similar to the correlation and regression statistics, the slope neither shows causality nor does it control for other factors, including varying levels of fiscal effort generated by local school districts. Due to its dependence on absolute values, interstate and longitudinal comparisons of slope values are problematic.

Interpretation. The slope may vary from 0.0 to any amount. A slope of 0.0 would indicate that there was no relationship between fiscal capacity and per-pupil inputs, and as the slope increases, the level of fiscal neutrality decreases.

Elasticity

The *elasticity*, identical to the slope, measures the magnitude of the relationship that exists between fiscal capacity and per-pupil inputs. Unlike the slope, elasticity is reported in terms of percentage changes rather that absolute values.

Strengths and Weaknesses. Elasticities are derived from the same equations that yield correlations, regressions, and slopes and have similar deficiencies regarding their inability to show causality or control for other factors. Elasticities are calculated simply and are easily explained to those with a basic understanding of statistics. Since elasticities are reported as percentage changes rather than absolute values for slopes, some of the problems of interstate and longitudinal comparisons are eliminated.

Interpretation. The elasticities may vary from 0.0 to any amount. An elasticity of 0.0 would indicate that there was not a relationship between fiscal capacity and per-pupil inputs, and as the elasticity increases, the level of fiscal neutrality decreases.

APPLICATION OF HORIZONTAL AND VERTICAL EQUITY STATISTICS TO THE OHIO SYSTEM OF SCHOOL FINANCE

Table 10.1 presents the results of the application of several horizontal and vertical equity statistics to an actual state data base. These data were obtained from evidence presented in the Ohio school disparity lawsuit, *DeRolph* v. *State of Ohio*[8] and provide an excellent example of a cross-time equity analysis of a state system of school finance. The equity statistics package applied to the Ohio data base was developed by Deborah Verstegen of the University of Virginia and Nancy Stevens of the Texas Education Agency. The Verstegen–Stevens statistics package has been designed for computer mainframe application and was adopted from Statistical Analyses Systems, Inc. software. The Verstegen–Stevens package provides the school finance researcher with an excellent and convenient means of measuring fiscal equity.

Generally, from 1980–81 to 1990–91, Ohio saw the level of equity provided by its system of school finance deteriorate, although there

TABLE 10.1   Selected Equity Statistics Applies to Current Expenditures Minus Federal Revenue, State of Ohio[a], Cross-Time Comparisons, Selected Years, 1980–81 to 1990–91

STATISTIC	SCHOOL YEAR					
	1980–81	1982–83	1984–85	1986–87	1988–89	1990–91
Mean[b]	$3,245	$3,165	$3,597	$3,884	$4,073	$4,237
Range[b]	$6,626	$6,926	$9,314	$9,865	$9,406	$8,739
Restricted range[b]	$1,951	$1,785	$1,894	$2,054	$2,310	$2,320
Federal range ratio	0.7959	0.7404	0.6739	0.6713	0.7376	0.7346
McLoone Index	0.8903	0.8954	0.9068	0.8937	0.9005	0.8794
Coefficient of variation	19.81	21.04	19.52	19.16	20.51	21.25
Gini Coefficient	0.1078	0.1096	0.1006	0.0993	0.1074	0.1148
Theil Index	0.0187	0.0204	0.0174	0.0168	0.0194	0.0213

Note: Equity statistics were determined through the use of Verstegen–Stevens software.

[a]Four small island school districts, North Bass, Middle Bass, Put-In-Bay, and Kelley's Island, were excluded from the analysis.

[b]Adjusted to school year 1990–91, constant dollars.

was not universal agreement among the statistics applied. Also, the overall decline in the level of equity did not fall steadily throughout the decade; instead, most of the statistics pointed to modest improvement from 1982–83 through 1986–87. After 1986–87, equity declined and most of the statistics indicated that fiscal equity was a more distant goal for Ohio in 1990–91 than in 1980–81. The selected statistics are as follows:

1. *Mean.* The mean was presented only for descriptive purposes and is not an equity statistic. It is, however, a rough indicator of adequacy and suggests that improvement was made over the decade, increasing from $3,245 to $4,237 per pupil. Note that the mean, range, and restricted range statistics are reported in constant dollars.

2. *Range.* The range grew from $6,626 in 1980–81 to $8,739 in 1990–91, an increase of $2,113 per pupil. The largest difference, $3,239, was registered in 1986–87 when the range reached $9,865 per pupil. (Equity declined.)

3. *Restricted range.* The restricted range grew from $1,951 in 1980–81 to $2,320 in 1990–91, an increase of $369 per pupil. (Equity declined.)

4. *Federal range ratio.* The federal range ratio declined from 0.7959 in 1980–81 to 0.7346 in 1990–91. The lowest federal range ratio was achieved in 1986–87, yielding a score of 0.6713. However, it is important to note that the minimum acceptable score of the federal range ratio is set at 0.2500 by federal regulations. (Equity increased.)

5. *McLoone Index.* The McLoone Index fell from 0.8903 in 1980–81 to 0.8794 in 1990–91. The highest score was achieved in 1984–85, showing a score of 0.9068. (Equity declined.)

6. *Coefficient of variation.* The coefficient of variation grew from 19.81 in 1980–81 to 21.25 in 1990–91, the highest CV registered during the decade. (Equity declined.)

7. *Gini coefficient.* The Gini coefficient grew from 0.1078 in 1980–81 to 0.1148 in 1990–91, the highest Gini coefficient registered during the decade. The lowest Gini co-

efficient, or highest level of equity, was 0.0993 for 1986–87. (Equity declined.)

8. *Theil Index.* The Theil Index grew from 0.0187 in 1980–81 to 0.0213 in 1990–91, the highest Theil Index registered during the decade. The lowest Theil Index, or highest level of equity, was 0.0168 for 1986–87. (Equity declined.)

APPLICATION OF FISCAL NEUTRALITY STATISTICS TO THE OHIO SYSTEM OF SCHOOL FINANCE

Several fiscal neutrality statistics, including correlations, regressions, slopes, and elasticities were also obtained from evidence presented in the Ohio fiscal disparity lawsuit. Table 10.2 presents the results of these several statistics for selected school years, 1982–83 to 1990–91.

From 1982–83 to 1990–91, the relationship between the fiscal capacities of Ohio's school districts and their respective current expenditures minus federal revenue per pupil, reflected by all four statistics, showed a slight decline. However, even with the modest relaxation in the relationship between fiscal capacity and per-pupil inputs, the relationship remained very strong. Results for each of the statistics followed an identical pattern. From 1982–83 to 1984–85 all statistics showed slight increases; thereafter, a gradual decline occurred, resulting in a 0.5285 correlation

coefficient, a 0.2793 regression, a 0.0119 slope, and a 0.1957 elasticity for 1990–91. In essence, although a strong relationship between fiscal capacity and per-pupil inputs continue to exist, modest movement toward greater fiscal neutrality occurred for the Ohio system of school finance from 1982–83 to 1990–91.

Students and researchers interested in applying the equity statistics to an actual state data base are referred to Appendix B. Contained in this appendix are the results of the application of the several equity statistics and the appropriate data base obtained from Rhode Island for school year 1990–91.

INTRASTATE COMPARISONS OF HORIZONTAL EQUITY, 1980–1990

Table 10.3 displays intrastate comparisons of horizontal equity as measured by the coefficient of variation for several years during the 1980s. It is important to note that it is inadvisable to rely solely on a single measure to evaluate the relative equity provided by a state system of school finance. Each of the equity statistics previously discussed collectively provide the researcher with the proper basis to make a valid evaluation. Further, as discussed elsewhere in this text, intrastate comparisons are difficult due to inconsistent data reported by the states. Adding to already difficult problems, longitudinal comparisons are often

TABLE 10.2 Selected Equity Statistics Applied to Current Expenditures Minus Federal Revenue, State of Ohio[a], Cross-Time Comparisons, Selected Years, 1980–81 to 1990–91

	SCHOOL YEAR				
STATISTIC	1982–83	1984–85	1986–87	1988–89	1990–91
Correlation	0.6439	0.6483	0.6196	0.5752	0.5285
Regression	0.4146	0.4203	0.3839	0.3309	0.2793
Slope	0.0156	0.0160	0.0153	0.0129	0.0119
Elasticity	0.3293	0.2991	0.2699	0.2228	0.1957

Note: Equity statistics were determined through the use of Verstegen–Stevens software.

[a]Four small island school districts, North Bass, Middle Bass, Put-In Bay, and Kelley's Island, were excluded from the analysis.

TABLE 10.3 Intrastate Comparisons of Horizontal Equity Among States as Measured by the Coefficient of Variation, 1980–1990

	COEFFICIENT OF VARIATION							
STATE	1979–80	RANK	1984–85	RANK	1986–87	RANK	1989–80	RANK
Alabama	10.5	7	11.0	7	9.1	5	10.6	9
Alaska	45.9	49	52.0	48	34.3	47	43.4	49
Arizona	16.0	24	17.0	26	12.7	17	16.2	32
Arkansas	16.1	25	13.0	13	10.9	11	12.9	16
California	13.2	14	13.0	12	9.5	6	16.1	31
Colorado	19.6	38	12.0	9	15.8	30	11.4	12
Connecticut	17.7	31	21.0	36	13.8	22	12.7	15
Delaware	17.9	32	13.0	11	13.7	21	10.0	4[a]
Florida	11.3	10	9.0	4	10.1	8	10.3	7
Georgia	16.4	27	18.0	31	17.8	35	18.7	41
Hawaii	—	—	—	—	—	—	—	—
Idaho	14.3	19	17.0	25	17.1	33	15.5	26
Illinois	17.4	29	25.0	44	14.8	25	16.4	33
Indiana	19.0	36	15.0	16	16.4	31	14.0	22
Iowa	9.8	5	7.0	2	9.6	7	7.8	3
Kansas	14.0	16	16.0	21	15.3	28	13.7	21
Kentucky	18.2	33	17.0	24	19.0	38	16.0	30
Louisiana	11.9	11	13.0	10	11.8	15	11.2	11
Maine	14.3	18	18.0	30	14.2	23	12.4	14
Maryland	14.2	17	15.0	17	16.8	32	15.5	27
Massachusetts	18.5	35	24.0	42	21.0	44	23.0	45
Michigan	17.6	30	20.0	35	19.1	41	21.6	44
Minnesota	28.2	46	16.0	20	13.6	19	13.2	19
Mississippi	12.3	12	17.0	23	11.2	13	12.0	13
Missouri	32.9	47	22.0	37	42.4	49	27.3	48
Montana	41.1	48	74.0	49	35.6	48	16.6	36
Nebraska	16.0	23	23.0	40	18.0	36	17.3	38
Nevada	4.6	1	10.0	6	8.0	3	10.0	4[a]
New Hampshire	18.4	34	27.0	45	14.5	24	14.6	24
New Jersey	15.1	20	18.0	29	17.2	34	14.8	25
New Mexico	9.5	4	16.0	18	10.7	10	16.0	29
New York	20.2	40	22.0	38	20.4	43	23.0	46
North Carolina	9.1	2	9.0	3	7.9	2	10.2	6
North Dakota	13.4	15	28.0	46	14.9	27	18.6	40
Ohio	22.8	44	24.0	41	20.0	42	24.3	47
Oklahoma	21.1	42	19.0	33	13.6	20	13.1	17
Oregon	9.9	6	13.0	14	10.6	9	17.1	37
Pennsylvania	20.4	41	19.0	34	19.0	39	20.9	42
Rhode Island	10.7	8	11.0	8	11.7	14	7.7	2
South Carolina	19.8	39	10.0	5	7.8	1	10.9	10
South Dakota	15.3	21	18.0	32	15.5	29	18.2	39
Tennessee	19.4	37	18.0	27	18.4	37	16.4	34
Texas	17.3	28	18.0	28	14.9	26	14.0	23
Utah	10.8	9	16.0	22	10.9	12	13.1	18
Vermont	25.2	45	31.0	47	32.2	46	16.5	35
Virginia	21.5	43	22.0	39	19.1	40	21.3	43
Washington	15.4	22	16.0	19	13.2	18	10.5	8
West Virginia	9.2	3	7.0	1	8.1	4	6.8	1
Wisconsin	16.2	26	14.0	15	12.7	16	13.6	20
Wyoming	12.8	13	24.0	43	21.5	45	15.7	28

Sources: 1979–80 and 1986–87 data obtained from J. H. Wykoff, "The Intrastate Equality of Public Primary and Secondary Education Resources in the U.S., 1980–87." *Economics of Education Review,* vol. 11, no. 1, 1992, pp. 19–20; 1984–85 data obtained from Jay Moskowitz, *Fiscal Equity in United States, 1984–85* (ERIC 315 852, Feb., 1988), p. 12; 1989–90 data obtained from Wayne Riddle, *Variations in Expenditures Per Pupil Among Local Education Agencies* (Washington, DC: Congressional Research Service, July 26, 1993).

drawn from the works of several researchers, as is the case in Table 10.3. The methodology used by the different researchers also may vary somewhat, further complicating the comparison.

However, with these caveats in mind, the data reported in Table 10.3 generally provide a consistent pattern. Specifically, Iowa, Nevada, North Carolina, and West Virginia consistently ranked high throughout the decade of the 1980s. At the other end of the continuum, Alaska, Missouri, Ohio, and Vermont consistently ranked near the bottom of the 49 states. Hawaii, due to its unique governance structure of a single school district was not included in the analysis.

It is interesting to note that regardless of the equity score, there does not appear to be a discernible pattern relating to whether litigation has occurred. Even states that rank relatively high have not been exempt from fiscal equalization lawsuits.

The evidence suggests that absolute fiscal equalization has rarely occurred, and even approximate fiscal equalization has remained an elusive goal.

SUMMARY AND CONCLUSIONS

A technical discussion of the statistical measurement of horizontal equity, vertical equity, and fiscal neutrality was presented. Contained within the discussion, a step-by-step procedure for the preparation of a state data base prior to the application of equity statistics was outlined.

A series of horizontal equity, vertical equity, and fiscal neutrality statistics were reviewed. The review included definitions, strengths, weaknesses, and interpretations for each statistic.

From fiscal evidence presented in a fiscal disparity lawsuit, *DeRolph* v. *State of Ohio*,[9] equity statistics were discussed.

KEY TERMS

Horizontal equity	Theil Index	Federal range ratio
Fiscal neutrality	Correlation	Lorenz curve
Range	Slope	McLoone Index
Restricted range ratio	Vertical equity	Atkinson Index
Coefficient of variation	Unit of analysis	Regression
Gini coefficient	Restricted range	Elasticity

ENDNOTES

1. See explanation of why revenues usually exceed expenditures in National Education Association, *Estimates of School Statistics, 1991–92* (Washington, DC: NEA, 1992), p. 26.

2. 45 C.F.R Subsection 116.17(h) (1974) as cited in *Bennett* v. *Kentucky*, 470 U.S. 656, 105 S.Ct. 1544 (1985).

3. 34 C.F.R. Ch. 11 (11-1-89 Edition) Section 222.61(a).

4. Robert Berne and Leanna Stiefel, *The Measurement of Equity in School Finance* (Baltimore: Johns Hopkins University Press, 1984), pp. 33–40.

5. A case could be made to develop a set of national weights required to service the traditional client groups. If national rather than state-specific weights were used, interstate equity analyses would become more reliable and meaningful. See Robert Berne and Leanna Stiefel, "Equity Standards for State School Finance Programs: Philosophies and Standards Relevant to Section 5(d)(2) of the Federal Impact Aid Program," *Journal of Education Finance* 18, no. 1 (Summer 1992), pp. 89–112.

6. 34 C.F.R. Ch.11 (11-1-89 Edition) Section 222.61 (a).

7. Berne and Stiefel, *The Measurement of Equity in School Finance,* op. cit., p. 21.

8. *DeRolph, et al.* v. *State of Ohio, et al.*, Case No. 22043 (1994).

9. Ibid.

APPENDIX A

The Measurement of Equity in School Finance Formulas for Revenue-Disparity
Measures (Pupil Unit of Analysis)

MEASURE	FORMULA
1. The range	Highest χ_i − lowest χ_i
2. The restricted range	χ_i at or above which 5 percent of the pupils lie − χ_i at or below which 5 percent of the pupils lie.
3. The federal range ratio	(restricted range)/(χ_i at or below which 5 percent of the pupils lie).
4. The relative mean deviation	$\left(\sum\limits_{i=1}^{N} P_i \mid \bar{X}_p - \chi_i \mid \right) \Big/ \left(\bar{X}_p \sum\limits_{i=1}^{N} P_i \right)$
5. The McLoone index	$\left(\sum\limits_{i=1}^{J} P_i \chi_i \right) \Big/ \left(M_p \sum\limits_{i=1}^{J} P_i \right)$ where districts 1 through J are below M_p
6. The variance	$\left(\sum\limits_{i=1}^{N} P_i (\bar{X}_p - \chi_i)^2 \right) \Big/ \left(\sum\limits_{i=1}^{N} P_i \right)$
7. The coefficient of variation	$\sqrt{VAR}/\bar{X}_p$
8. The standard deviation of logarithms	$\left[\left(\sum\limits_{i=1}^{N} P_i (Z - \log_e \chi_i)^2 \right) \Big/ \left(\sum\limits_{i=1}^{N} P_i \right) \right]^{1/2}$ where $Z = \left(\sum\limits_{i=1}^{N} P_i (\log_e \chi_i) \right) \Big/ \left(\sum\limits_{i=1}^{N} P_i \right)$
9. The Gini coefficient	$\left(\sum\limits_{i=1}^{N} \sum\limits_{j=1}^{N} P_i P_j \mid \chi_i - \chi_j \mid \right) \Big/ \left[2 \left(\sum\limits_{i=1}^{N} P_i \right)^2 \bar{X}_p \right]$
10. Theil's measure	$\left(\sum\limits_{i=1}^{N} P_i (\chi_i \log_e \chi_i - \bar{X}_p \log_e \bar{X}_p) \right) \Big/ \left(\bar{X}_p \sum\limits_{i=1}^{N} P_i \right)$ or $\dfrac{1}{N} \sum\limits_{i=1}^{N} \left(P_i \left(\dfrac{\chi_i}{\bar{X}_p} \right) \left(\log_e \dfrac{\chi_i}{\bar{X}_p} \right) \right)$
11. Atkinson's index (E) 0; $E \neq 1$)	$\left[\left(\sum\limits_{i=1}^{N} P_i (\chi_i \mid \bar{X}_p)^{1-E} \right) \Big/ \left(\sum\limits_{i=1}^{N} P_i \right) \right]^{1/(1-E)}$

Source: Robert Berne and Leanna Stiefel, *The Measure of Equity in School Finance* (Baltimore: The Johns Hopkins University Press, 1984), p. 20. Reprinted with permission.

Note: The following symbols are used in the formulas above: P_i equals number of pupils in district i; N equals number of districts; X_i equals average revenues (expenditures) per pupil in the district i; X_p equals means revenues per pupil for all pupils; M_p equals median revenues per pupil for all pupils.

APPENDIX B

Rhode Island Data Set

SCHOOL DISTRICT	WADM	WEALTH PER WADM	CUR EXP PER WADM
New Shoreham	109	2,840,347	11,089
Narragansett	1,796	616,930	6,613
Barrington	2,440	471,498	5,810
East Greenwich	2,025	463,581	6,468
Westerly	3,126	423,256	5,649
Newport	3,204	420,420	6,525
Smithfield	2,361	336,703	5,348
Portsmouth	2,622	334,688	5,739
South Kingstown	3,309	320,587	5,883
Scituate	1,535	314,020	5,354
Lincoln	2,667	305,990	5,641
North Kingstown	4,019	304,134	5,843
Tiverton	2,005	296,791	5,752
Warwick	11,649	291,846	6,064
Chariho	3,310	287,590	6,254
Johnston	3,173	286,245	5,385
North Smithfield	1,669	282,229	5,240
Cranston	9,410	278,674	5,629
Bristol-Warren	3,860	276,527	6,062
North Providence	3,362	274,050	5,730
East Providence	6,178	268,505	5,496
Cumberland	4,293	262,653	5,545
Middletown	2,900	243,465	5,210
Exeter-West Greenwich	1,621	209,239	5,227
West Warwick	3,950	196,607	5,258
Coventry	5,113	182,943	5,045
Pawtucket	8,283	172,328	5,473
Burrillville	2,870	149,813	5,322
Providence	20,431	143,309	5,314
Woonsocket	6,260	113,520	4,572
Central Falls	2,573	53,929	4,842

Application of Horizontal and Vertical Equity Statistics to Rhode Island Data Base

STATISTIC	SCORE (APPLIED TO CURRENT EXPENDITURES MINUS FEDERAL REVENUE)
Range	$6,517
Restricted range	1,414
Restricted range ratio	1.2920
Federal range ratio	0.2920
Coefficient of variation	8.31
Gini Coefficient	0.0439
McLoone Index	0.9514
Theil Index	0.0034
Atkinson Index	
I8	0.9774
I10	0.9709

Application of Fiscal Neutrality Statistics to Rhode Island Data Base

STATISTIC	SCORE (APPLIED TO CURRENT EXPENDITURES MINUS FEDERAL REVENUE)
Correlation (r)	0.7122
Regression (r^2)	0.5072
Slope	0.0024
Elasticity	0.1144
F-Ratio	34.99
Probability	0.0001

CHAPTER 11

THE POLITICS OF SCHOOL FINANCE

TOPICAL OUTLINE OF CHAPTER

The Political Pendulum • Coloration of Politics • Nature of Politics
• Purposes of Politics • Politics of Security • Politics of Stability
• Politics of Change • Political Reality • Condition of the Economy
• Shaping of Attitudes • Politics of Religion • Urban–Suburban
Politics • Politics of Race • Politics of the School System
• Politics at the State Level

INTRODUCTION

Public schools are an integral part of the politics of the United States. The formation of public schools was originally a political consideration and its subsequent governance and financing is entirely political in nature. As public democratic institutions, the schools are conducted by political processes to obtain the ends assigned by society. The reliance on political considerations in the conduct of the schools is in keeping with the U.S. tradition of republican government. Politics thus permeates all aspects of public school finance. By definition politics has to do with public affairs and education is at the heart of virtually all considerations of public policy. Every chapter in this book, in fact, encompasses some aspect of politics.

Tocqueville in the 1830s observed that politics was "the only pleasure an American knows,"[1] and Bryce half a century later noted that political parties were "organized far more elaborately in the United States than anywhere else in the world."[2] Smith, the American historian, cites the watershed of the maturation of modern U.S. politics to be the election of An-

drew Jackson, after which democratic politics and a kind of people's capitalism merged to form the basis of a laissez-faire economic individualism that still prevails.[3] It was about this time that the germination and growth of public schools began.

The Political Pendulum

Since the presidency of Jackson, U.S. politics has emerged as action and reaction, an ebb and flow of governmental policy as it is shaped and molded by the interplay between public and private interests. Periodically, throughout U.S. history, swings in public opinion between the conservative self-interest and the public common interest result in a divergence of governmental policies that produce a political pendulum effect. Schlesinger referred to these swings in public opinion as cycles of political history.[4] In documenting these cycles he comments:

> In short, the conservatism formed in the 1980s among intellectuals, religious zealots and the

young does not necessarily prove a fundamental transformation in the national mood. It is exactly what the historian would expect during the private-interest swing of the political cycle.[5]

The emergence of any swing toward self-interest and away from common public interest, finds its philosophical justification in Adam Smith's *Wealth of Nations*, in which he states that as the individual promotes his own interests he effectively promotes the public interest as well. During the 1980s this ethos of private self-interest was the dominant political philosophy.[6] The arc of the pendulum had banked in the 1980s to the opposite extreme from the "New Society" programs of the 1960s. In 1992, the pendulum began to move back as voters expressed another political vision as reflected in the election of President Clinton. These political phenomena, of course, have a direct effect on policies of public school financing. The implicit reliance of public schools on political processes makes equality of educational opportunity much more problematic in some eras than in others.

Box 11.1 _____

Politics in America

America has given the world its most modern and efficient economic organizations. It has pioneered social benefits for the masses: mass production, mass education, mass culture....

The distinctive American contributions to politics are in the organization of popular participation. The one major political institution invented in America is, of course, the political party. Americans created the caucus before the Revolution and committees of correspondence during the revolutionary crisis. Upon these beginnings at the end of the eighteenth century they organized the first political parties.

Source: Samuel P. Huntington, *Political Order in Changing Societies* (New Haven and London: Yale University Press, 1968), pp. 130–131.

DEFINITION

Politics. The science of government; the art or practice of administering public affairs. Pertaining to, or incidental to, the exercise of the functions vested in those charged with the conduct of government; relating to the management of affairs of state; as political theories; of or pertaining to exercise of rights and privileges or the influence by which individuals of a state seek to determine or control its public policy.

Source: Black's Law Dictionary, 4th ed. (St. Paul, MN: West Publishing Company, 1968), p. 1319.

Coloration of Politics

Politics itself is value free; it may be moral or immoral, beneficial or harmful. Politics as we know it has at its foundation the social obligations presumptive in a liberal democratic state. Politics taken out of a democratic or other ideological context is Plato's *techne*, merely an art or a craft similar to any other ordinary social interaction. It is technique, simply steering the ship of state while not deciding course or direction. In a democratic state the course is supposedly set by ideological standards broadly enunciated in constitutional law. The politician, as helmsman, is to steer the ship in the constitutionally prescribed direction. In fact, the word *governor* derives from the Latin translation of the Greek for *helmsman*.[7]

For the public schools, the governors, legislators, and judges are the helmsmen who both steer and interpret direction set by the people through constitutions and political processes. The primary problems experienced in funding education derive from not knowing which ideological bent of politics should steer the public schools.

Politics may of course misguide so as to subvert the people's intent. When this happens democratic government may falter and its purposes become obscure. Lately, Americans have experienced a disenchantment with politics to the extent that the term *politics* itself has taken on a broadly pejorative connotation. For example, Bork, in his widely read book *The Tempting of America*, has little good to say about politics and refers to it only in a negative context. He contends that public policy has lost its "identity" and "integrity" and that "logic," "objectivity" and "intellectual honesty" are ignored in favor of a politically motivated undesirable end.[8] His theme is that the objectivity of the law has been subverted to an inappropriate political agenda. According to Bork, law has integrity but politics does not. He says, "In the clash of law and politics, the integrity of the law has already been seriously undermined." However, it is not actually the insertion of politics into the interprocesses of the law to which he objects but rather the direction that law has taken as a result of political interposition. It is the port toward which the ship is headed that bothers Bork and shapes his opinion of the worth and danger of politics. To Bork, the conservative direction is desirable and the liberal direction is, by definition, destructive of U.S. law and democratic processes.

Thus, most criticisms of politics have little to do with politics per se, but rather are remonstrances against a particular ideological direction toward which politics is thought to lead. It is the coloration of politics that is objectionable to most persons and not politics itself.

Nature of Politics

"Politics," according to Raphael, "concerns the behavior of groups and individuals in matters that are likely to affect the course of government."[9] Politics in a democratic state is the means by which the sovereign power of the state is enforced.[10] Politics in a democracy is the peaceful process by which certain persons are acknowledged and authorized to exercise power and authority over others.[11] Subjugation by war or force cannot be construed to be "politics" because there is not acknowledgment of, or acquiescence to, authority without compulsion.[12]

Volition.   According to Locke, "Politic societies all began from a voluntary union, and the mutual agreement of men freely acting in the choice of their governors, and forms of government,"[13] and "that the beginning of politic society depends upon the consent of individuals, to join into, and make one society."[14] Without consent and volition on the part of the governed, the system of government cannot acquire unity and hold together. As a part of this volitional arrangement in a democracy, the public schools are dependent upon the free will of the people to contribute in common through their taxation for the general educational benefits of all. When voters withhold their support of public schools at the local, state, or federal levels they are exercising their Lockean political prerogatives to withdraw their private consent from the whole. Of course, once the majority decides to tax itself for the benefit of education, all, dissenters included, must join in payment of taxes regardless of whether or not they individually believe in the purposes of public schools.

Obligation.   Republican politics authorizes some persons to act as the representatives of the people to protect, restrict, enable, or constrain, for the common good of all. In education we vote for school board members and give them the authority to impose taxes on us and to expend our money for our public schools. By politics we elect legislators and governors to make and enforce laws that both enhance and restrict us. A democratic society cannot function as a viable institution without the means of authorizing power to be vested in a few persons for the conduct of government. Politics in a democratic state can only function if it is grounded in a political obligation of those governed.[15] The citizen is obliged to obey the rules established by those individuals who by election are given the authority to act. Political authority implies, (1) an obligation to obey the commands issued by the person or body vested with authority; and (2) implies the person or body (representative) has a right to issue the commands and possesses a right to be obeyed.[16]

This means of course that in the conduct of public schools, failure to abide by the laws and regulations of school authorities may result in the punishments as specified by society. Failure to pay properly levied taxes, refusal to abide by compulsory attendance laws, or failure to stop behind school buses all have consequences that flow from the obligations implicit in the politics of public education in a democratic society.

Moral Ends.   Although politics itself is value free, a reciprocal obligation between the governors and the governed can only be justified in a democratic state if the objectives are moral ones. The ends of politics must be moral, to promote social justice for the common good.[17] If an obligation is merely a legal one without moral underpinnings, no political obligation exists to acquiesce to the authority. Simply having power without a moral foundation is insufficient.

The particular moral ends that support our democratic government are couched in a basic belief in liberty and equality. "Liberty and equality are distinctive aims of democracy,"[18] and the direction of U.S. politics properly prescribed will be in keeping with these goals. According to Raphael "Liberty and equality are what distinguish the democratic ideals from the other political ideals."[19]

Interestingly, the U.S. public may value liberty more than equality. A 1987–88 Gallup poll (Table 11.1) showed that when persons in the United States were asked what was more important, equality or freedom, 72 percent chose freedom and 20 percent chose equality. Supposedly freedom implicitly implied a strong belief in several types of liberty including political, religious, economic, and liberty of expression.[20] Both Europeans and Japanese viewed equality and freedom more evenly. In keeping with their leanings toward liberty, U.S. citizens feel less compelled to reduce income differences. The vast income differences in the United States, discussed in Chapters 6 and 7, therefore appear to be more by design than by happenstance. Also, the poll referred to does reflect the especially conservative Reagan era in which Americans were more interested in their own economic self-interest than in helping others. It should be kept in mind, however, that the poll shown in Table 11.1 does not indicate that Americans do not believe in equality; it merely shows that between the two choices of equality and freedom, they value freedom relatively more than citizens of other leading countries.

Educated Voters.   A well-educated and governmentally active citizenry is more capable of governing itself than a poorly educated one. As our founders observed, it is difficult to constrain and

TABLE 11.1   An Odd Place, America

WHICH IS MORE IMPORTANT: EQUALITY OR FREEDOM?			IS IT GOVERNMENT'S RESPONSIBILITY TO REDUCE INCOME DIFFERENCES?	
	% choosing			
	Equality	*Freedom*		*% Yes*
United States	20	72	Italy	81
Britain	23	69	Hungary	77
France	32	54	Holland	64
Italy	45	43	Britain	63
West Germany	39	37	West Germany	56
Japan	32	37	Australia	42
Spain	39	36	United States	28

Source: Gallup International Research Institute, 1987–88 as cited in *The Economist Yearbook*, 1993 Edition, "American Values" (London: The Economist Newspaper), p. 59. © 1993 The Economist Newspaper Group, Inc. Reprinted with permission.

deny liberty and equality to a well-educated and governmentally active electorate. Security of democracy is enhanced by education. An indication of the effect of education on voting behavior in Congressional elections is shown in Figure 11.1.

1. There is a strong positive relationship between voting and schooling. Voter participation increases with educational attainment.
2. Among persons in the 25–44 age group in 1990, college graduates were 67 percent more likely and high school dropouts were 52 percent less likely to vote than high school graduates.
3. Differences in voting behavior have widened over time.[21]
4. Overall there was a slight decline in voting rates for all groups during the period.

Whether this decline is significant in estimating a general voter disenchantment with politics is not known, but if it is a definitive trend, it is an unhealthy one. A trend away from voter participation by all groups could mean that in the long run the strength of liberal democracy could be diminished. If participation by voters should continue to fall and politics of special interests increases whereby various groups intervene to sway the actions of elected officials, then we could have what social scientists call "a crisis of the regime." If this transpires, the system of government is undermined and can even disintegrate.[22]

In this regard, there has been substantial concern of late about the disuniting of America, the erosion of the ideal of commonality, and an absence of unity of purpose as a nation. Schlesinger has probably best enunciated the evidence in his potent book *The Disuniting of America*[23] in

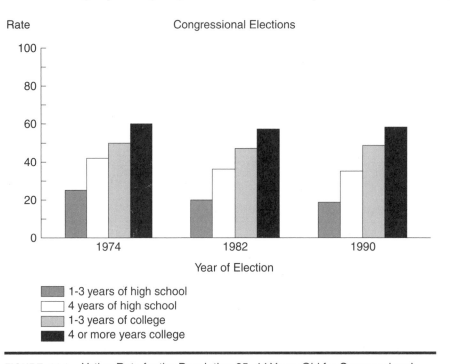

FIGURE 11.1   Voting Rate for the Population 25–44 Years Old for Congressional Elections and Educational Attainment, Selected Years, 1974–90

Source: U.S. Department of Commerce, Bureau of the Census, *Current Population Reports,* "Voting and Registration in the Election of November . . . ," Series P-20, nos. 143, 293, 322, 383, 440, 453.

which he maintains that the central values on which the United States was founded are now becoming lost in ethnic, cultural, linguistic, and nationalistic divisions. Assertions, for various reasons, of group identities and interests over and above the ultimate bond of unity is an ominous experiment. Schlesinger says,

> The genius of America lies in its capacity to forge a single nation from peoples of remarkably diverse racial, religious, and ethnic origins. It has done so because democratic principles provide both the philosophical bond of union and practical experience in civic participation.[24]

Importantly, Schlesinger points out that the protections of the U.S. Constitution are focused on individual rights, not group rights.[25] The current strife created by various groups wanting special and separate status in society are tending to dissipate the central unity around which the nation was founded.

The political problems are further magnified by the "decline of middle-class prosperity," widening the economic separation between rich and poor families in the United States. Kevin Phillips, in his book *Boiling Point,*[26] states that the disparity in advantage among economic groups is of crisis proportions. Phillips says,

> Public dissatisfaction with Washington policy favoritism to the rich and well connected showed little likelihood of subsiding, and the too softly named 'middle-class squeeze'... was coming into focus as something potentially ominous.[27]

Thus, politics in a democracy is not value free but reflects those ideals that are value-laden in the conduct of a virtuous government. Authority is vested through politics, and the obligations of the governed will be assured so long as the democratic ends are maintained. However, if imbalances toward inequality or repression become too great, the government will either adjust or possibly even fall as individual obligations to sustain it become tenuous and subverted to group or self-interest which is detrimental to the whole of society.

PURPOSES OF POLITICS

The basic purposes of politics in society are:

1. Insuring security by settlement of disputes and prevention of conflicts
2. Prevention of harm to existing rights and maintenance of stability
3. Promotion of welfare and social justice

Politics of Security

In settling disputes, politics keeps order and maintains security both domestic and foreign. In this regard, politics and education are mutually reinforcing, as education contributes to security. An educated citizenry is more knowledgeable, more law abiding, more tolerant, and more economically productive than an uneducated one. The attributes of the educated usually contribute to domestic peace and social accord.

External security is greatly enhanced by a better-educated electorate. Historically, the nations with high percentages of uneducated people have been more easily controlled and economically exploited.[28] Fukuyama observes that the most powerful argument linking economic development and the politics of liberal democracy is that liberal democracy demands the participation of an educated citizenry, without which it cannot function successfully.

Moreover, where liberal democracy exists there must be a political demand for an equality of rights that produces the economic elevation that results in an increase in the size of the middle class, thus reducing the disparity between rich and poor. The equality of rights in a liberal democracy that enhances internal accord and external political and economic strength emanates from the bedrock of education. Equal educational opportunity for self-development directly translates into internal and external security and economic productivity.

Politics of Stability

The second function, preservation and maintenance of existing rights, is negative but useful politics. This function has as its guiding objective the maintenance of the status quo. This was the dominant governmental theory of the seventeenth and eighteenth centuries that held that present rights were to be protected and that the role of government was to preserve the current privileges, rights, and liberties, and had no reason to upset the inertia of the status quo. The politics of stability, then, was calculated to prevent encroachments on already established privately determined social and economic conditions.

> The business of the State was to leave to each individual as large an area of liberty as possible. Its interventions should therefore be minimal, limited to the negative function of preventing one individual or group from encroaching on the liberty of another.[29]

This objective of politics of course has a deleterious effect on progress and positive reform. The reality though is that reactionary resistance to change is an important aspect of the human need for stability and certainty. It will therefore always be a potent force in the politics of education.

The Peacekeeper.   This minimalist conservative view of politics, the "peacekeeper doctrine," seeks to preserve rather than change and is thereby an important aspect of stability. As may be expected, this particular political philosophy is most favored by the affluent. The more advantaged and better-educated usually want to keep things as they are and the "have-nots" agitate for change. This minimalist function was the only aspect of politics with which Bentham's utilitarianism was concerned. To Bentham the role of politics was to preserve and reflect the objectives of the majority.[30] E. H. Carr best summarizes the politics of stability in this way:

> The political arena is the scene of a more or less constant struggle between conservatives who in a general way desire to maintain the existing legal situation, and radicals, who desire to change it in important respects; and conservatives, national and international, have the habit of posing as defenders of the law and of decrying the opponents

as assailants of it. In democracies, this struggle between conservatives and radicals is carried on openly in accordance with legal rules. But these rules are themselves the product of a pre-legal political agreement. Every system of law presupposes an initial political decision, whether explicit or implied, whether achieved by voting or by bargaining or by force, as to the authority entitled to make and unmake law. Behind all law there is this necessary political background. The ultimate authority of law derives from politics.[31]

One can easily find many examples of this political conflict between stability and change in school finance. Those that have quality schools for their children seek to defend them and ensure their preferential status. The more affluent attempt through political processes to defend their local fiscal advantage of greater income and property wealth. Attempts to equalize educational opportunity by introducing more equalization into state school finance programs often meet with intense political lobbying on the part of the rich school districts who are seeking stability or maintenance of their present elevated position. Parents in property-poor school districts are typically advocates for changing funding schemes in the cause of greater equalization. Such changes tend to upset political stability and are therefore confronted with great opposition.

Political Equilibrium.   Thus the politics of public school finance has commonly been a two-tier struggle in destabilizing the political equilibrium. First, public school advocates have sought to acquire a shift of private fiscal resources to the public sector, and, second, to rearrange the fiscal resources, once shifted to the public by way of taxation, in such a way as to equalize opportunity.

The former is sometimes called the adequacy issue, whereby overall adequate funding is sought, based on the educational needs of the children and the ability of the private sector of the state or nation to bear the tax burden. Chapter 7 documents this condition and shows how the politics of school financing has produced widely varying levels of expenditure and fiscal effort among localities, states, and nations.

Exclusion. Reich observes that in the United States there is a growing philosophy that reveres the politics of exclusion. He says that "generosity and solidarity end at the border of similarly valued properties."[32] The result, according to Reich, is that the more affluent congregate in enclaves of affluence and do not exercise their political strength for the betterment of the whole community, state, or nation beyond the narrow boundaries of their own advantaged neighborhoods.

He notes that the wealthy exercise political muscle to protect and defend their position resulting in a "secession" of the wealthy citizens who have effectively "withdrawn their dollars from the support of public spaces and institutions shared by all and dedicated the savings to their own private services.[33] This political phenomenon accurately describes the plight of U.S. city schools and their loss of political strength in garnering support for more local or state funding.

As a result of this secession phenomenon the public schools in certain areas of the various states are deprived of the political leadership that could ensure adequacy of funding. The status quo as established by private economic conditions is upheld. The secession phenomenon described by Reich also affects equalization of resources among school districts. The enclaves of political strength that have tended to cluster in the suburbs of U.S. cities have sapped the core cities and rural areas of political and economic strength resulting in a skewing of influence in favor of the more affluent. William Schneider has said that "the third century of American history is shaping up as the suburban century," and the "word that best describes the political identity of the middle class is 'taxpayers'."[34]

The taxpayers in suburban enclaves see their economic advantage of residing in an affluent, property-rich suburb as an existing right and through political processes will resist redeployment of state and local school funds for the pur-

pose of equalizing educational opportunity. State equalization programs are interpreted as an encroachment on the integrity of their favorable economic circumstance. The politics of the affluent school district, usually suburban, tends to be employed to preserve the existing wealth advantage, to maintain stability, and to resist change, because change can only reduce their relative advantages.

Politics of Change

The third purpose of politics in society is the promotion of welfare and justice and it tends to run counter to the politics of stability. This is a newer, largely nineteenth and twentieth century view of politics in the modern state. This philosophy asserts that a vital role of politics is to improve the condition and well-being of all members of society, and is couched in the moral imperative of social justice. The social justice philosophy supports the use of taxation as a governmental mechanism for the redistribution of wealth and income, maintaining that government has a positive role in correcting income and wealth disparities caused by the interactions of the private marketplace. This same perspective led to the adoption of the Sixteenth Amendment to the U.S. Constitution in 1913 permitting Congress to enact a graduated income tax, one of the purposes of which was to redistribute wealth.

This positive role of politics reflects the philosophy of the enlightenment that assigns to government the role of correcting the abuses of the economic marketplace. Found herein is the grand design of the United States, the essence of enlightened humanity, to implement a political system that elevates social and economic conditions through an enlightened intellect. It was thought that "if political rulers were men of merit and talent and governed only in the public interest, they would naturally command affection and respect of the people."[35] Wood has said in reviewing the radical nature of the new political system established in early America, that "the first steps in constructing a new republican society were to enlighten the people and to change the nature of authority."[36]

The foundation of this political philosophy is in universal public education. Conversely, the stability or minimalist view of politics advanced by Bentham and Adam Smith supports private schools, asserting that those who are most capable and possess the economic wherewithal are entitled to education, and government has no definitive role in expanding educational opportunity to the less able. On the other hand, the social justice or change view of politics calls for the governmental creation of public schools to advance the condition of individuals who are not able to finance their own education.

The latter view of politics supports initiatives to increase the relative level of public school funding and to increase the equitable allocation of school resources. Also, this political view moves a society to attempt to remediate educational disadvantages caused by natural, economic, or environmental conditions. The politics of social justice argues for governmental action to address differing educational needs as well as to mitigate the educational disadvantages of children in low-income and property-poor school districts.

POLITICAL REALITY

The adequacy of financing public schools is dependent on certain political realities. These realities bear strongly on the global question of the willingness of the private sector to release fiscal resources for the public enterprise of education. The extent of receptivity to taxation and funding of public schools has much to do with the economy, demography, and attitudes of the public toward education, all of which interplay in various ways to complicate the politics of public schools.

Condition of the Economy

The condition of the national or state economy may have much to do with the level of tax effort devoted to public schools. In a period of high inflation and relatively low economic growth, the public's expenditure for public schools tends to diminish. Or one may find that a slowdown in economic productivity restricts the revenues gained from taxation and a nation or state is without the necessary resources to invest in education. A good case in point was California in 1992. The state faced a $11 billion budget deficit that was largely fed by welfare needs that were growing at four times the rate of the increase in the state's population. In the preceding two years approximately 600,000 jobs had been lost to the state and unemployment reached 9.5 percent.[37] As a result, the plight of education was to contend with a reduction in revenues and experience a concomitant decline in quality.

The explosion of the federal budget deficit in the 1980s was accompanied by a dramatic drop in federal tax effort to support public elementary and secondary education. Of course public attitudes and federal leadership had much to do with the level of education expenditure, and the economy was not the only issue, but, the overall economic problems resulting from a massive federal budget deficit was not an unimportant factor.

Box 11.2 _____

Politics and Education

The effect of education on political attitudes is complicated, but there are reasons for thinking it at least creates the conditions for democratic society. The self-professed aim to modern education is to "liberate" people from prejudices and traditional forms of authority. Educated people are said not to obey authority blindly, but rather learn to think for themselves. Even if this doesn't happen on a mass basis, people can be taught to see their own self-interest more clearly, and over a longer time horizon. Education also makes people demand more of themselves and for themselves; in other words, they acquire a certain sense of dignity which they want to have respected by their fellow citizens and by the state.

Source: Francis Fukuyama, _The End of History and The Last Man_ (New York: Avon Books, 1992), p. 116.

There is of course a very real danger that government in a time of economic downturn will make inappropriate expenditure choices and will restrict its outlays for economically productive investments. Also, a danger exists that it will continue to expend money for governmental activities that have little or no continuing stimulus effect on the economy. This was the federal response in the United States in the 1980s, during which period the response to economic decline was to invest less in education and thereby to exercise a false economy, exacerbating economic problems and reducing the nation's long-term competitive position relative to other countries.

Shaping of Attitudes

The better-educated are less susceptible to propaganda and political delusion. One of the most important attributes of a highly educated citizenry is that it is less susceptible to being propagandized and led in directions that are contrary to its own best interest. Barbara Tuchman in her bestseller *The March of Folly* marvels how at times entire societies may be influenced to pursue directions that are opposed to their own interest.[38] She cites the Trojan horse, the Renaissance Pope's provocation of Protestant secession, Britian's political intransigence in the loss of her colonies, and the American debacle in Vietnam as persuasive cases in point. People's attitudes, and sometimes deceptions, may emanate from some stimulus of government leadership, or at times may simply develop unaided as a cycle of political history. While the well-educated and highly literate are more fortified against deceptions and provocations of leadership, all are to some degree susceptible.

Cultivation of Negative Attitudes.   During the 1980s conservative political elements made a concerted effort to draw into question the viability and value of U.S. public schools. Whatever the motivation, President Bush, while bestowing upon himself the title of "Education President" maintained a relentless effort to downgrade the

effectiveness and efficiency of public schools. This calculated neglect was orchestrated with a synchronized effort to deconstruct public education by means of vouchers and tuition tax credit initiatives to aid private schools. The publicity blitz that accompanied this effort highlighted the shortcomings of public schools and ignored their accomplishments. As a result, a public attitudinal shift was fostered that has undoubtedly undermined the public's confidence in public schools.

Alternatives to Public Schools.   The severity of the public's disenchantment with public schools has led major national journals and magazines to seriously discuss the alternatives to public common schools. For example, one major national magazine in December 1991, in an article entitled "The Exodus From Public Schools," gave the impression of wholesale flight from the public schools. The author cited "drugs, violence, bureaucratic bloat and ill-educated students"[39] as eroding "public confidence in the American tradition of 'common' schooling."[40] The article referenced a *Houston Post* September 1991 survey that found that 85 percent of the parents polled felt their children were unsafe in the public schools.[41] The "Exodus" article acknowledged that there had actually not been a flight yet, but it assumed that a mass migration from public to provide schools was imminent.[42] This particular magazine, in fueling opposition to public schools, identified the following five leading alternatives to public schools:

1. Parochial schools
2. Independent "prep" schools
3. Home schools
4. Afrocentric academies
5. For-profit schools[43]

The article then proceeded to paint portraits of failures in public schools and educational successes in the five alternatives. For example, the article attributed the successes of preparatory schools in large part to the fact that they have little bureaucracy and no unions. One headmaster is quoted as saying, " 'There's no school board, no superintendent. Teachers are handpicked at prep schools, not assigned from union seniority rolls, and the emphasis is on liberal-arts degrees rather than education-school training.' "[44]

A similar portrait is painted in contrasting homeschools and public schools. The article observes that in homeschools, children recite the "Pledge of Allegiance and a prayer," and that being largely conservative Christians they are able to "stress the Bible."[45] The impression is given that homeschooling has a vast moral superiority over public schools, an obvious political asset. As a result of such widely conveyed impressions implying that public schools are devoid of "family values," the politics of homeschooling has worked to reduce the effectiveness of compulsory attendance laws in many states. The article observes,

> Spurred by an aggressive home-school lobby, no fewer than 34 states have passed measures since 1982 that have eased the way for home schooling, primarily by relaxing teacher-training and curriculum requirements.[46]

Of course, education for-profit has become a motivating factor in the private sector and has gained substantial support in recent years, leading some entrepreneurs to create grand designs to build networks of schools that will yield substantial profits to their investors. Perhaps the most elaborate of such schemes is that of Chris Whittle, the head of Whittle Communications, a Knoxville-based media company, who sought to create a national system of private for-profit schools by 1996. The thought of such entrepreneurs is that the "invisible hand" of the marketplace can improve the quality of schools while showing a profitable investment. Unfortunately, advocates of this position have felt compelled to deride the value and contributions of public schools in order to establish the political climate in which to cultivate their own for-profit schemes. Within the push and pull between advocates of private, parochial, and for-profit schools and those who believe in the concept of common public schools, a powerful political debate is taking place. This

debate was of such importance that it became a major issue in the presidential debates of 1992. With the election of President Clinton, the people implicitly rejected the movement toward privatization of education although the disenchantment with public schools remains in the forefront of political consideration.

Politics of Religion

The politics of religion is too obvious and too complex to discuss in any detail here, yet it would be remiss to not mention its pervasive political force and its interconnection with the financing of public schools. The intensity of the issue and the historical strife resulting from it caused Thomas Jefferson, James Madison, and other forefathers to attempt to separate the politics of the church from that of the state. With such a separation they sought to strengthen both church and state. Here they were paradoxically not at odds with the laissez-faire political economy of Adam Smith who voiced in *The Wealth of Nations* in 1776 a strong opposition to the use of public money for religious purposes. Adam Smith, the *paterfamilias* of the conservative politicians, said,

> It may be laid down as a certain maxim, that, all other things being supposed equal, the richer the church, the poorer must necessarily be, either the sovereign on the one hand, or the people on the other; and in all cases, the less able must the state be to defend itself.[47]

Smith gained his insights from observations of the religious conflicts that had transpired in Europe and their resulting negative economic effects on the state and the people.

American Religiosity. Jefferson and Madison, contemporaries of Smith in viewing the same religious strife in Europe, believed that separation of church and state would make religion more viable while at the same time strengthening the functioning of a democratic government. The result has been much as Jefferson and Madison had anticipated, not only is the U.S. government strong and viable, but religion in the United States has thrived. A 1988 Gallup poll showed that the U.S. public was far more likely to be affiliated with a church or religious organization than persons in other advanced countries (Table 11.2). As the table shows, in the United States where separation of church and state has been a basic tenet of politics, religious affiliation was 57 percent, while in Britain, a nation with an established church, the Church of England, religious affiliation was only 22 percent of those persons polled. In Holland where the state provides government funding of religious schools, the percentage was 35 percent. Other countries that provided government-financed assistance to church schools had far lower percentages of religious education than the United States.

Not only are the people of the United States more religious, but their government leaders are more avowedly religious as well. A recent editorial in *The Economist* observed, "It remains inconceivable that an American could become president without a highly visible commitment to the church. . . . Between 40% and 50% of all Americans are in church on a typical Sunday. . . . Nearly two-thirds of Americans say a strong religious commitment is 'absolutely essential' or 'very important' (for a president)."[48]

TABLE 11.2   Religious Affiliation

ARE YOU AFFILIATED WITH A CHURCH OR RELIGIOUS ORGANIZATION?

	% Yes
United States	57
Holland	35
Britain	22
Spain	15
West Germany	13
Italy	7
France	4

Source: Gallup International Research Institute, 1987–88 as cited in *The Economist Yearbook*, 1993 Edition, "American Values" (London: The Economist Newspaper), p. 59. © 1993 The Economist Newspaper Group, Inc. Reprinted with permission.

The U.S. Congress is an overwhelmingly religious body with only 10 members reporting no religious affiliation in 1992. Table 11.3 shows that Catholics make up about one-fourth of the membership with 141 members, followed by Methodists with 65 members and Baptists with 62. Between the 1990 and 1992 congressional elections, the Methodists' and Episcopalians' numbers fell by 10 and 9 respectively, while Baptists, Presbyterians, and others gained.

By any measure, the citizenry of the United States and its governmental representatives must be presumed to be overwhelmingly formally religious. It matters little what the motivation for this religiosity happens to be. The fact is that the United States, relative to other countries, is very religious. Apparently, Jefferson and Madison were correct; by separating church and state, both religion and the state have prospered.

The irony is of course that by having strong churches and a high percentage of religious persons, the maintenance of the separation between church and state becomes even more difficult. The politics of religion drives many religious groups to use their substantial political power to gain financial assistance from the government, although it may not be in their long-term best interest.

Taxes for Churches.   Concerted political efforts by the Catholic Church, fundamentalist Protestant churches, and certain other denominations have resulted in the shaping of a federal judiciary that is more receptive than ever before to reducing the strength of the Establishment clause of the First Amendment in order to allow governmental funding of religious schools. With the Reagan-Bush appointees of Justices Thomas, Scalia, and Kennedy to the U.S. Supreme Court, the votes are apparently in place to override earlier precedents that prohibited the use of public tax funds for church schools. In 1983, the U.S. Supreme Court in *Mueller* v. *Allen*[49] had already partially opened the door by approving tax benefits for parents of private and parochial school children. As now constituted, the U.S. Supreme

TABLE 11.3 Congressional Religious Affiliation 1992 (House and Senate Are Combined)

	ELECTION 1992	ELECTION 1990	CHANGE
Catholic	141	142	− 1
Methodist	65	75	−10
Baptist	62	59	+ 3
Presbyterian	54	51	+ 3
Episcopalian	50	59	− 9
Jewish	42	41	+ 1
Protestant	29	30	− 1
Lutheran	21	22	− 1
United Church of Christ	14	12	+ 2
Mormon	12	13	− 1
Unaffiliated	10	5	+ 5
Unitarian–Universalist	7	10	− 3
All Others	26	16	+10

Source: Voice of Reason, The Newsletter of Americans for Religious Liberty, no. 43 (Fall 1992), p. 7.

Court will probably expand on this opinion and extend the opening for the state and federal governments to subsidize parochial schools.

Because of the leanings of the Supreme Court and the corresponding possibility of government assistance to church schools, the Catholic Church has redoubled its political efforts to influence legislation in state legislatures. A major national public-relations campaign in 1992 with the theme of "Discover Catholic Schools 1992" was used to gain additional credence as a governmentally funded alternative to public schools. The president of the National Catholic Education Association told *U.S. News and World Report*, "Instead of people throwing all this money at public schools, they should throw a little money at private schools that work."[50]

Moreover, the Catholic-education political lobby initiated even more aggressive efforts to influence legislation and to acquire vouchers and tuition tax credits for parochial schools. "In 1990, the Catholic bishops voted overwhelmingly to earmark $2 million to establish a national office to help parent groups push state legislatures and the U.S. Congress to support private schooling."[51]

Political campaigning for religious advantage is probably even more pronounced among fundamentalist Protestant groups. In 1992 the Internal Revenue Service found the Jimmy Swaggart Ministries guilty of engaging in partisan politics in violation of IRS tax-exemption regulations. Under IRS rules, "religious and educational organizations that claim 501(c)(3) tax-exempt status may not intervene in partisan politics by endorsing candidates for public office."[52] The IRS ruling was provoked by Swaggart's endorsement of T.V. preacher Pat Robertson's candidacy for president in October 1986.

Because of vague and rather ambiguous questions several polls have been of little help in determining how the people are disposed toward state aid to religious schools. However, one of the most precise and properly enunciated questions was posed in a poll for the Carnegie Foundation for the Advancement of Teaching released on October 26, 1992. The Carnegie poll asked the direct question:

Some people think that parents should be given a voucher which they could use toward enrolling their child in a private school at public expenses. Do you support or oppose that idea?

The response was 62 percent opposed and 32 percent in favor of vouchers.[53] The response to the question of vouchers as stated by the Carnegie Foundation was similar to actual voter response in Oregon in 1990, Colorado in 1992, and California in 1993, in which vouchers were rejected 2 to 1. This issue is discussed further in Chapter 2.

Creationism.   Religious political influences have even invaded the curriculum of U.S. schools. Protestant fundamentalists have launched intensive political efforts to instill creationism in the public schools and exclude the idea of evolution and natural selection. Such limitations on legitimate knowledge may have deleterious effects on scientific development. The London *Times Higher Education Supplement* reported that a quarter of the biology teachers in the United States rejected the idea of evolution and as many as 45 percent of the local school board presidents in Ohio and 20 percent of the nation's public school and college students rejected evolution.[54] The American Association for the Advancement of Science has pointed out the changes implicit in political incursions by the religious right into the educational curriculum, not the least of which is lower economic development in a scientific and technological age.[55] The London *Times Higher Education Supplement* says,

> creationist beliefs like these are alarming. What chance has the U.S. of defeating Japan in science-based industry when 47 percent of its people think that humans were created in their present form in the past few thousand years, as recent Gallup polls show?[56]

Thus the political ramifications of religion become important not merely to public school finance per se, but more broadly to the entire educational process and to the flow of valid research and scientific information. Moreover, as the above *Times* editorial suggests, the scientific, and thus economic, progress of the country could be deleteriously affected although such effects are subtle and virtually imperceptible to normal observation.

The politics of religion is probably even more devisive today than it has been for over a century in the United States. The possibility of both judicial and legislative breakthroughs by religious groups to gain state support for their schools and churches will undoubtedly keep this issue at the forefront of the education political agenda in the foreseeable future.

Urban-Suburban Politics

The politics of cities and suburbs is today one of the most potent forces affecting the financing of the public schools. The lure of the city has long been a reality of humankind. The social nature of the human being in concert with prospects for better economic circumstance has inexorably drawn people into larger groups with more complex interactions. Munro has written, "The city of today is responsible for most of what is good, and for most of what is bad, in our national life and ideals."[57]

The reasons for the movement of people to urban areas are exceedingly complex, but at least two phenomena are most noticeably basic. First, urban life often offers economic options that are not apparent in the rural areas. This is particularly true in countries where people are poorly educated and the fertility of the soil has been depleted or never existed. Mexico City, Cairo, and Istanbul provide excellent examples of ballooning movement to cities that has been caused by the poverty of rural areas and the search for perceived, but seldom delivered prosperity in the urban areas. The second reason, related to the first, is that as more people are freed from the search for food directly from the soil, they are free to acquire food from secondary sources in urban areas.

The "lure of the city" as Arthur Schlesinger called it, has to do with social and psychological reasons as well as economic ones. As Degler has observed, the people, the noise, the lights, the gaiety, the cultural opportunities, and the variety and mystery of the cities generally prove compelling for humankind.[58] Dunlap, in surveying hundreds of novels concerned with the newcomer to the city, concluded that people come to cities for the eminently reasonable objective of finding "more favorable surroundings and enlarged opportunities."[59]

Thus as agriculture has become more efficient and more persons have been released from the soil, more have moved to the cities. In 1945 eight urban families were fed by a single farm family, and by the decade of the 1980s this figure was up to 33 families being fed by one farm family.[60] Cities have therefore grown as the efficiency of food production has increased and more persons have been released from the soil to move to urban areas to assume other lifestyles and means of employing themselves.

The New Urban Reality in the United States. The urban reality in the United States today is a bifurcation between cities and suburbs. The core cities are growing less rapidly than the suburbs and are generally inhabited by minorities. Urban decline has been accompanied by a massive "secession" of whites to enclaves in the suburbs. This emigration from cities to suburbs by whites has left the cities populated primarily by lower-income African-Americans and Hispanics. Moreover, within the boundaries of the cities themselves there exist large bands or sectors of segregated living.[61]

It may of course be argued that the plight of the cities, their poverty and economic impotence, is a function of political decision. At least political decisions have been a factor in exacerbation rather than remediation of the problem. Welfare requirements by the federal government have actually given incentives to the neediest groups to remain isolated and segregated within the nation's central cities.[62] Also, the plight of cities was caused to a great extent by the racial discrimination and poverty of poor states, primarily

in the South, from which the poor persons left to seek better economic circumstances in the northern cities.

The resulting condition of the central city in the 1990s is one of relatively lowering economic condition relative to the rise of affluent suburbs. The problem is worsened by the fact that those who populate the cities have vastly greater educational needs emanating from deprivations caused primarily by poverty. Yet while educational burdens are heavier and the costs of educational programs are greater, the cities have correspondingly fewer fiscal resources than do suburbs and many other school districts with fewer educational problems.

Suburban Political Power. The political dilemma faced by cities is ironically made worse by the dilution of political power. As a result of *Baker* v. *Carr*[63], the one-person, one-vote case, fundamental shifts in the political strength has occurred throughout the nation. One result has been that political power has flowed from central cities and rural areas to the suburbs that have generally gained in both population and wealth.

The net effect has been for suburbs to become economically insular, racially and economically segregated and more politically powerful. For example, the area encompassing northern Virginia and the Maryland suburbs of Washington, DC has been referred to by the Greater Washington Board of Trade as the 51st state, or the "State of Potomac," an economic powerhouse.[64] This area has 16 central business districts, "edge cities" as defined by Joel Garreau in his book *Edge City.*[65] These huge suburban or "outer-urban core" areas such as Tyson's Corner in northern Virginia, which is twice as large as downtown Miami and San Diego in terms of office rental space and employment, are able to translate economic strength and population size into political power. This "edge city" phenomenon in the United States is having a direct effect on the way state legislatures view the allocations of state and local revenues among core cities, suburban communities, and rural areas.

In many states, suburban communities have banded together to resist more equal distribution of school funds. For example, strong suburban education lobbies now exist in Missouri, Ohio, New Jersey, New York, Massachusetts, and Michigan that seek to maintain the present state systems of school funding that create substantial revenue disparities favorable to the suburbs.

Buying Your Government. The political reality of the suburb is accurately depicted to a substantial degree by Schneider when he says,

> A major reason people move out to the suburbs is simply to be able to buy their own government. These people resent it when politicians take their money and use it to solve other people's problems, especially when they don't believe that government can actually solve those problems.[66]

There is considerable resistance to state taxation for the purpose of equalizing educational opportunity through state-aid formulas, and it is strongest among suburban voters.[67] The urban poor, on the other hand, are cynical about the prospects for economic and educational change, as are the poorly educated.[68] Suburban voters are primarily property owners and are highly tax-sensitive.[69] In 1990, the congressional representation of suburban areas was about 50 percent republican, but the urban city areas were over 80 percent democrat.[70]

Eighty-five percent of the richest families in the Philadelphia area live outside the city limits and 80 percent of the area's poorest live inside.[71] The city has far greater educational burdens yet the suburbs spend more on schools and have better programs. The city has by far the highest tax rate.[72]

Some commentators believe that the middle-class suburban voters will support public works expenditures like good schools, highways, and a clean environment, things that they directly benefit from, but will not support social-welfare type programs that may assist the poor in core cities or rural areas.[73]

The polls indicate that people of the suburbs want more to be done about public education, but generally object to improvements being made in other school districts if they must share their tax money. Such political orientation emanates from a belief in specified benefits as well as special-purpose taxes. "Special-purpose taxes are the suburban ideal—not just private government but private taxes."[74] Such a mindset militates against state measures to alleviate the educational funding problems of core cities and poor rural school districts. To a great extent, this political situation has fueled the recent series of judicial actions challenging state school finance programs.

Politics of Race

Before the desegregation cases and the civil rights litigation of the 1950s and 1960s, racial discrimination was direct, obvious, and unambiguous. School buildings for African-American children were markedly inferior, and their teachers were paid less. Simply because these schools served minority children, funds for the maintenance and operation of schools for black children were minimal. African-American children had limited access to public transportation and their classes in schools often were merged to permit the use of fewer teachers.[75] Schools serving these children had shorter terms and regular attendance was discouraged. Some states even sought to keep attendance low among black children by rescinding compulsory attendance laws. This discrimination was justified on purely racial

---

Box 11.3

Politics of Race

When the official subject is presidential politics, taxes, welfare, crime, rights, or values ... the real subject is race.

Source: Thomas Byrne Edsall with Mary E. Edsall, "Race," *Atlantic Monthly* 267, no. 5 (May 1991), p. 53.

grounds, but when pressed by politics and the courts for better defenses for the continuing discrimination, the segregationists sought refuge in simplistic economic explanations, or in raw assertions to the effect that "blacks simply did not need and could not benefit from increased schooling."[76]

Such blatant direct discrimination has today given way to more subtle political justifications for discrimination. Edsall points out that "race is no longer a straightforward morally unambiguous force in American politics; instead, considerations of race are now deeply embedded in the strategy and tactics of politics."[77]

In fact, race and ethnic origins in the United States permeate national political considerations, "shape presidential coalitions of both Democrats and Republicans," create alliances, establish social and geographical boundaries, and reflect economic disparities between rich and poor.[78] The presidential elections of the 1980s defined the reality of race and politics. Working and middle-class persons in white urban and suburban neighborhoods defected from the Democratic to the Republican party because they felt that

> The Democratic Party had not stood with them as they moved from the working to the middle class. They have a whole set of middle-class economic problems today, and their party is not helping them. Instead it is helping blacks, Hispanics and the poor.[79]

The lower-income and middle-class whites blamed school, housing, and employment desegregation "for almost everything that had gone wrong with their lives."[80] Court decisions[81] of the 1960s and 1970s that required the integration of previously segregated neighborhood schools fueled the fears of whites who were in economically precarious positions and therefore felt threatened by the progress toward equality that was being achieved by minorities. Unfortunately the crime rates of the cities, showing much higher offenders among some minorities than whites, simply magnified the prejudice and fears. Edsall observes, "Social dysfunction, and

crime in particular, have tragically served over the past two and a half decades to reinforce racial prejudice."[82] All this has created a defection of whites to more conservative political preserves, which has tended to produce an equal and opposite reaction among African-Americans who feel deserted and ill-served by an unresponsive political system.

Lipset has pointed out that groups or individuals "regard a political system as legitimate or illegitimate according to the way in which its values fit with theirs."[83] The problem of racial prejudice in the United States has engendered a disenchantment in the political system from much of both the white and the African-American communities. "The American Dilemma," as described by Myrdal, remains an intractable problem.[84] This dilemma has even taken on new and recent dimensions with the immigration of Hispanics and Asians who are perceived by African-Americans as encroaching on the limited employment opportunities that were previously staked out for themselves and low-income whites.

Figure 11.2 shows that African-American and Hispanic students tend to be concentrated in public schools in the central cities. In 1972, public schools in central cities enrolled 32.5 percent African-American and 10.8 percent Hispanic students, but by 1989, the percentage of African-Americans had increased to only 32.8 while the percentage of Hispanics had nearly doubled to 20.8 percent. Throughout the 1980s African-American and Hispanic students together constituted a majority of public school students in central cities.[85] Of all the African-American and Hispanic students enrolled in schools in the United States in 1989, 85.9 percent attended public schools and 14.1 percent attended private schools.

Employment statistics show that the job market is far less promising to African-Americans than to whites. In 1990, 75 percent of recent white high-school graduates were employed compared to only 45 percent of African-American graduates. Of those who dropped out of high school, 56 percent of the whites found jobs to

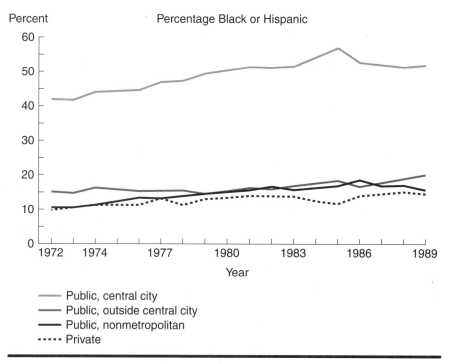

FIGURE 11.2 Race and Ethnicity of Students in Grades 1 to 12, Residence and Control of Schools, 1972–1989

Source: U.S. Department of Commerce, Bureau of the Census, *Current Population Reports*, Series P-20, "School Enrollment . . . ," various years; October Current Population Surveys. As compiled in *The Condition of Education 1992* (Washington, DC: U.S. Department of Education, 1992), p. 105.

only 31 percent of the African-Americans. Such statistics document the reasons for disenchantment with the present political system and how it deploys opportunities.[86] (See Figure 11.3).

It is said in southern California that "if [Hispanics] were not around . . . , nonblack employers would be forced to hire blacks."[87] However, whether continued immigration of Hispanics and Asians will further absorb low-level jobs that may have been the domain of African-Americans may be questionable.[88] Fallows notes that substantial evidence exists that suggests there is no relation between the rate of self-employment among Koreans and unemployment among African-Americans. Asians don't soak up opportunities that African-Americans would otherwise have had.[89] Nevertheless, the jobs in contest are

those of lower pay and less desirable circumstances, and they are contested for among the poorest quintile of workers.

The problems manifested by race, poverty, and foreclosure of opportunity were specifically and dramatically highlighted by the Rodney King affair and the anarchy of the Los Angeles riots of 1992. More generally, the unsafe conditions that now pervade U.S. cities each day at sunset is also an unfortunate but omnipresent testimony to the political incapacity of those cities.

Problems of race are pervasive in U.S. politics today, and public schools reflect this condition. Undoubtedly, the "exodus from public schools,"[90] when examined beyond the surface, is to a great degree a matter of race. School choice, home-

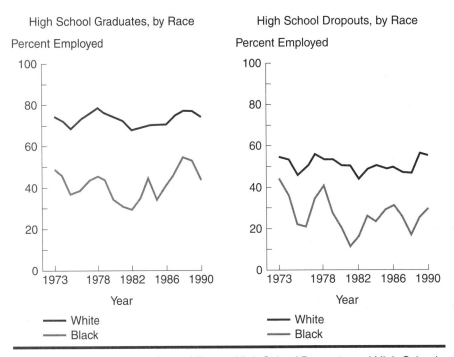

High School Graduates, by Race

Percent Employed

High School Dropouts, by Race

Percent Employed

FIGURE 11.3 Employment Rate of Recent High-School Dropouts and High-School Graduates Not Enrolling in College, by Race, 1973–1990.

Source: U.S. Department of Labor, Bureau of Labor Statistics, *Labor Force Statistics Derived from the Current Population Survey: 1940–1987*, and tabulations based on the October Current Population Surveys. As compiled in *The Condition of Education 1992* (Washington, DC: U.S. Department of Education, 1992), p. 81.

schools, private schools, and suburban flight are some of the manifestations of this racial conflict. Moreover, the public school ideal of commonality and social interaction is greatly weakened in the public's eye by this underlying problem of race. In responding to this racial prejudice and other forces of separation, some politicians have vigorously advanced the subterfuge of choice and public funding of private and parochial schools. Effectively, the advocates of private school choice, and to some degree, possibly, public school choice, have as an underlying motivation racial separation.

All this bears greatly on issues of public school funding. Public schools become less adequately funded as private schools become a more economically realistic option. Concurrently, equity in funding among public schools becomes more politically difficult as the more affluent whites flee to suburban enclaves that are both racially segregated and economically self-sufficient.

Politics at the Local Level

The levy of any type of local tax involves political decision making. Local taxes for schools are levied either by direct vote of the electorate or by vote of the boards of education in districts that are fiscally independent. In districts that are fiscally dependent, the tax must be approved by other local governing bodies. The levy of a tax, either for current expenses or to service a bond issue, gives the public an opportunity to express its approval or disapproval of the allocation of its resources to support the services requesting the tax levy.

Part of the opposition to local school taxes is no doubt due to the unpopularity of the property tax. However, variations in tax effort for public schools may not be directly related to the nature of the tax per se, but rather to the particular type of local political leadership.

Numerous studies have shown that each community contains groups of people who possess more than average influence in affecting public policy.[91] Johns and Kimbrough found that school districts had different types of power structures but that all districts had some type of power structure.[92] In that study, six school districts of above 20,000 population were selected from each of four states. Three of the districts in each state had been districts of high local financial effort for a period of years, and three had low financial effort. Four types of power structures were found among these 24 districts.

1. Monopolistic elite—districts in which a few powerful influentials cooperate to control decision making
2. Multigroup, noncompetitive structure—districts in which two or more groups of powerful influentials exist but have approximately the same values, goals, and beliefs and usually agree on most issues
3. Competitive elite—districts in which two or more elite groups compete for power
4. Segmented pluralism—districts in which many groups compete and there is wide citizen participation in decision making

Johns and Kimbrough found that among the 24 districts studied, 6 had monopolistic elite structures; 9 multigroup, noncompetitive; 6, competitive elite; and 3, segmented pluralism. They found that 10 of 15 monopolistic elite and multigroup, noncompetitive districts combined had made a low local financial effort over a period of years and 5 had made a high effort. Of the 9 districts with competitive elite or segmented pluralism structures, 7 were high local financial effort districts and 2 made low effort.

The study showed that although most districts with noncompetitive power structures were low-effort districts and most districts with competitive power structures were high-effort districts, districts with any type of power structure could be either a low-effort a or high-effort district. Therefore it would seem advisable for local school administrators who desire to be politically effective in presenting the needs of the school to do the following:

1. Become aware of the community power structure and identify the values, goals, and beliefs of the different groups within it.
2. Communicate with the influentials in the power structure—parent groups, teacher organizations, taxpayer groups, chambers of commerce, labor unions, lay advisory committees, and other community groups—to give all of them the opportunity to communicate with the board of education and its administrators.

Communication is a two-way process and the public cannot gain an understanding of the financial needs of the schools unless there is effective two-way communication. The school administrator is no longer the philosopher king of Plato's *Republic*. The public needs the leadership, advice, and counsel of the professionally trained school administrator. As the educational level of the public rises, the school administrator who attempts to rule will become less and less politically effective. If the modern school administrator is a leader, he or she must be politically effective.

Politics at the State Level

Whenever there is a shift in school support from local taxes to state taxes, it has been accompanied by political controversy. Wealthy areas of states often object to a policy that results in their contributing more in state taxes than is received in state grants. State legislators from wealthy school districts have frequently opposed state equalization formulas that apportion state school aid in an inverse relationship to local taxpaying capacity. Such legislators in many states have either opposed increases in state support of the public schools or insisted that if state aid were provided, it should be apportioned on a flat grant basis without consideration of variations in local tax-paying capacity. An examination of methods used by the states for allocating state funds[93] shows that political compromises have been reached in many states by allocating part of state funds on a flat grant basis or by guaranteeing a minimum of state funds to wealthy school districts, to secure passage of a state equalization appropriation.

Another political factor involved in increasing the percentage of school revenue from state sources is fear of the erosion of local control of education if state financing is increased. The virtues of local control are continually extolled by politicians seeking office. They also inveigh against the dangers of central controls, despite the fact that public school education is a state responsibility. It has become folklore to believe that "he who pays the fiddler will call the tune." While there is some truth to this assumption; the state can constitutionally establish state controls over education without providing any state financing. It can also allocate state funds for the schools with few or no controls, or it can attach many controls. State school legislation in the 1980s and continuing into the 1990s greatly increased state control over localities without commensurate increases in funding. In fact, the innovations of this era that included a manyfold increase in student testing, increases in graduation requirements, and curriculum content changes were seldom accompanied by adequate funding.

The politics of school financing at the state level deals with many issues, but the principal one is the extent and adequacy of school funding. The principal actors in the politics of state school financing include teachers' organizations, parent–teacher associations, school administrators' organizations, school board organizations, the chief state school officers, state boards of education, and governors and legislators. Other groups such as chambers of commerce, the Farm Bureau, labor unions, associations of industries, and antitax groups also participate in the politics

of school financing from time to time, especially when issues of taxation arise.

Educational Interest Groups.   The education power structure in most states is rather complex, involving many groups and individuals with special interests. Some years in the past, administrators' associations, school board associations, teachers' associations, parent–teacher associations, and state education agencies commonly worked together on state school financing proposals. This is no longer true. Teachers' associations for many years have insisted that administrators have had too much influence on educational policy. As discussed earlier, adversarial relationships have developed among teachers, school administrators, and boards of education in many states. Consequently, these different interest groups have frequently advocated conflicting fiscal policies. This conflict has no doubt retarded progress in school financing in a number of states. In some states, the primary legislative goal of school finance reform has not been to improve school financing, but rather to reform taxation. This conflict between the goals of state legislatures and the goals of education interest groups makes it all the more politically desirable that education interest groups compromise their differences and form coalitions that speak to the governors and the legislatures with one voice.

The Governor.   The governor has a powerful influence on school financing in all states. He or she can initiate fiscal policy and veto legislative bills. Campbell and Mazzoni found that "governors were crucial in the formulation and initiation of fiscal legislation affecting school finance and tax reform."[94]

Governors, as well as state legislators, are influenced by education interest groups and other special-interest groups. In some states, education associations have become politically active in supporting or opposing candidates for the governorship or seats in the legislature. When they happen to support successful candidates, their influence is augmented, but if their candidates do not win, their influence is diminished.

In more recent years the National Governors Association and the Education Commission of the States have encouraged governors to exercise a more proactive role in education. This has been accomplished primarily through governors' budgeting prerogatives, which if exercised fully can give the chief executive almost limitless control over education. Such extensive control while viewed by some as highly desirable has been viewed with a cautious eye by others.

It is particularly important that the state education agencies and education interest groups work cooperatively with their governors in developing the fiscal program they present to their legislatures. Competing state services will certainly present their needs to the governor and the legislature. It is highly important that each governor have a full understanding of the fiscal needs of public education before presenting their proposed budget to the legislature.

The State Legislature. The legislature plays the most important role in determining state school fiscal policy. It first must pass a bill before the governor can either approve or veto it. The legislature deals with school fiscal matters through a committee structure. Usually there is an education committee in both houses of the legislature. There will also usually be a finance committee, a ways and means committee, or a committee on taxation, as well as an appropriations committee in one or both houses. Those interested in educational finance, if they are to be politically effective, must lobby all of these committees as well as individual legislators. The term *lobby* should not be considered derogatory. It is the constitutional right of all groups and individuals to present their needs and interests to the legislature. In order for the democratic process to be successful, it is essential that lobbyists be ethical in their activities. If all lobbying were prohibited by law, the legislature would have insufficient information with which to make intelligent decisions.

Box 11.4

Politics Is Not a Game

It exists to resolve the largest questions of the society—the agreed-upon terms by which everyone can live peaceably with one another. At its best, politics creates and sustains social relationships—the human conversation and engagement that draw people together and allow them to discover their mutuality. Democracy promises to do this through an inclusive process of conflict and deliberation, debate and compromise. Not every citizen expects to speak personally in the governing dialogue, but every citizen is entitled to feel authentically represented.

Source: William Greider, *Who Will Tell the People* (New York: Simon and Schuster, 1992), pp. 13–14.

Politics of Federal Aid. Federal control of education is opposed by practically everyone. However, the appropriation of federal funds through categorical grants is a powerful federal control. Furthermore, court decisions and certain federal laws establish federal controls that affect school financing.[95] As a matter of fact, establishment of a federal requirement sometimes results in political pressure being brought on Congress to provide additional federal funds to meet the new requirement. Examples are court-ordered busing, resulting in emergency school aid appropriations to assist in racial integration; and federal requirements with respect to the education of the disabled, resulting in large federal and state increases in appropriations for the disabled.

Increasing the amount of federal aid for the public schools is opposed by many lay interest groups and political conservatives. Such powerful organizations as the National Association of Manufacturers, the U.S. Chamber of Commerce, and the Farm Bureau Federation have generally opposed federal aid for the public schools. Certain religious sects also oppose federal aid for education unless they can share in it.

Political conservatives generally support a reduction in federal expenditures for any function of government that can be provided for by the state or local units of government. During the Reagan and Bush administrations this conservative philosophy prevailed and federal effort to support elementary and secondary education declined by about 50 percent between 1980 and 1990. It will require strong and effective leadership in support of federal aid for the public schools if that aid is to be increased substantially in future years.

Academic Politics.   Academic political activists have had a major influence on school finance reform almost from the beginning of this century.[96] Teachers College at Columbia University produced George D. Strayer, Paul R. Mort, and Ellwood P. Cubberley. Strayer and Mort became professors at Teachers College, and Cubberley became a professor at Stanford University. These men were the pioneer developers of school finance theory. They trained students of school finance who became professors at various universities throughout the nation, and they in turn also produced students of school finance. This process has continued to the present time. Strayer, Mort, Cubberley and many of their successors, including R. L. Johns of the University of Florida, Edgar L. Morphet of the University of California, Berkeley, and Monfort Barr of Indiana University have been political activists, seeking through their efforts to improve the quality of public school education in the United States. Much evidence exists that through their consultancies, surveys, research, and writing they have had a major impact on the betterment of education. The academic political activists will no doubt continue to have a significant influence on the improvement of school financing at the federal, state, and local levels.

SUMMARY AND CONCLUSIONS

In this chapter we attempted to define the nature of politics as it affects school finance. We observed the historical cyclical movement of attitudes between the liberal and conservative philosophies of government. Importantly, the overall purposes of politics were related to public school finance. Four potent areas of political concern—the economy, religion, the urban–suburban cleavage, and the problems of race relations—were discussed specifically. The following main points were emphasized.

Public schools are by nature an integral part of the politics of the United States. Public schools are creatures of the political system of a liberal democracy and are in fact a foundational element of liberal democracy.

The public schools are reflective of the historical interest that Americans have for politics. Public education has contributed to the strength of the nation, and both the nation and public schools have benefitted from the political involvement of the citizenry. Political populism and equality merge with the ideals of capitalism and laissez-faire economics to form the unique brand of U.S. politics. In this regard, Hofstadter, the American historian, has said, "It has been our fate as a nation, not to have ideologies but to be one."[97]

The political fortune of public schools is dependent on the interplay between public and private interests and the acquisition of fiscal resources. When conservative political forces unnecessarily restrain the distribution of the wealth of a state or nation by way of taxation for education, public schools are diminished.

Politics in and of itself is value free and it is only its application that creates desirable or objectionable results. U.S. democracy sets a positive direction for politics through fundamental, constitutional laws that basically call for liberty and equality. Departure from these ends misshapes politics and deters human advancement.

The political system of a republic requires a political reciprocity between the governed and the governors, while each has an obligation. The citizen must obey reasonable laws, and the representatives of the people must make reasonable laws, carrying out the general will of the people.

Educated voters are more capable of governing themselves than uneducated voters. The better-educated tend to vote in higher percentages and their preferences are usually more in keeping with the moral objectives of a liberal democracy. Today there is some worrisome evidence that the center may not hold and that various political interest groups will tend to "disunite" America.

The theoretical purposes of politics may be seen as falling into three categories: security, stability, and change. All three may be related to the politics of school finance. The security and stability of government is premised on the quality and adequacy of its educational system. Yet, stability that freezes in inequality may be detrimental, maintaining differences in class that are created by the economic environment of the private sector. Change, if equitably implemented, would result in governmental action to compensate for the vagaries and disparities created by the marketplace. An educated citizenry is more inclined to stimulate equitable change than an uneducated one. Equitable change in school finance would result in more adequate and equal funding of public schools. More advanced societies put forth greater fiscal effort to fund education than do underdeveloped societies. Equality of funding is also an indicator of a better-educated and more enlightened citizenry.

Political reality warns that the adequacy and equity of educational funding may be affected by the economic conditions of a state or nation as well as by other conditions that may create political discord. The recent federal budget deficit has undoubtedly had an adverse effect on public school financing. Not all deterrent effects though emanate from economic conditions, but may emerge from social or group differences. For example, negative attitudes toward public school financing may be fostered by a government that has philosophical beliefs that are contrarily pre-

disposed. Various ideologies may assert strong political energies to use public resources to fund alternatives to public schools such as parochial or religious schools, private preparatory schools, homeschools, race- or ethnic-oriented schools, or for-profit schools. Political philosophies supporting these alternatives call for reduced funding of public schools and increased funding for alternative types of education.

The politics of religion tends to become a powerful force in shaping governmental education policy. During the past decade the political importance of the religious school lobby has increased substantially. Under the rubric of choice and liberty, church school groups have influenced educational funding at both federal and state levels. Moreover, these groups have attempted to convey negative images of public schools in an attempt to enhance the attractiveness of their respective educational interests.

The demography and the urban nature of U.S. society has had a profound effect on the way schools are funded. The decline of the central city and the corresponding rise of suburban communities have important implications on the equity of educational financing. Also, racial overtones attendant upon political decisions permeate the governments at both state and federal levels. The new urban reality in combination with problems of race cast a daunting shadow over the politics of school finance in the country at large, and in virtually all the large populous states of the United States.

Reason for optimism is to be found in the strength of the philosophical conceptualization of public common schools and the viability of that concept as a cornerstone of a liberal democracy.

KEY TERMS

Politics	Obligation of the governed	Decline of middle-class
Cycle of history	Moral ends of politics	Politics of security
Political pendulum	Issue politics	Politics of stability
Coloration of politics	Crisis of regime	Politics of change
Volition in political society	Disuniting of America	Peacekeeper doctrine

Political equilibrium	Creationism	Political alliances
Politics of exclusion	Lure of the city	Suburban flight
Politics of secession	New urban reality	Power structures
Self-interest	Edge city	Interest groups
Politics of religion	Politics of race	

ENDNOTES

1. Alexis de Tocqueville, *Democracy in America*, I, Ch. XIV (NY: Colonial Press, 1899).
2. James Bryce, *The American Commonwealth* (New York: Macmillan, 1888), p. 506.
3. Page Smith, *The Rise of Industrial America*, vol. 6 (New York: McGraw-Hill, 1984), p. 455.
4. Arthur M. Schlesinger, Jr. *The Cycles of American History* (Boston: Houghton Mifflin, 1986), p. 40.
5. Ibid.
6. Ibid., p. 41.
7. Michael Walzer, *Spheres of Justice* (New York: Basic Books, 1983), p. 286.
8. Robert H. Bork, *The Tempting of America, The Political Seduction of the Law* (New York: Free Press, 1990), p. 1.
9. D. D. Raphael, *Problems of Political Philosophy* (Houndsmills, England: Macmillan, 1976), p. 27.
10. Ibid., p. 55.
11. Ibid., p. 69.
12. Hobbes would disagree that acquiescence of the governed by force is not politically legitimate. He maintains that choice of governments is based on fear. Hobbes says that fear is the basis on which political society is formed; each person seeks protection and is willing to concede certain rights and liberties to acquire the protection of common, concerted power of an absolute monarch, democracy, or any other form of government. Thomas Hobbes, *Leviathan*, first published in 1651 (New York: Macmillan, 1962), p. 151.
13. John Locke, *Second Treatise of Government,* originally published in 1690 (Indianapolis: Hackett Publishing Company, 1980), p. 55.
14. Ibid., p. 56.
15. Ibid., p. 108.
16. Ibid., p. 81.
17. Ibid.
18. Ibid., p. 142.
19. Ibid.
20. Herbert McClosky and John Zaller, *The American Ethos* (Cambridge, MA: Harvard University Press, 1984), p. 18.

21. Nabeel Alsalam, Lawrence T. Ogle, Gayle Thompson Rogers, and Thomas M. Smith, *The Condition of Education 1992* (Washington, DC: U.S. Government Printing Office, 1992), pp. 86–87.
22. David McKay, *American Politics and Society* (Oxford: Basic Blackwell, 1985), p. 78.
23. Arthur M. Schlesinger, Jr., *The Disuniting of America* (Knoxville: Whittle Direct Books, 1991), p. 80.
24. Ibid.
25. Kevin Phillips, *Boiling Point, Republicans, Democrats, and the Decline of Middle-Class Prosperity* (New York: Random House, 1993).
26. Ibid.
27. Ibid., p. 81.
28. Raphael, op. cit., p. 46.
29. Raphael, op. cit., p. 47.
30. John Stuart Mill, *Utilitarianism on Liberty: Essay on Bentham*, ed. Mary Warnock (New York: Meridian/Penguin Books, 1974), pp. 115–116.
31. E. H. Carr, *The Twenty Years'Crisis 1919–1939* (New York: Harper Torchbooks, 1939), pp. 180–181.
32. Robert B. Reich, "Succession of the Successful," *New York Times Magazine (*January 20, 1991), Section 6, p. 42.
33. Ibid.
34. William Schneider, "The Suburban Century Begins," *Atlantic Monthly* 270, no. 1 (July 1992), p. 33.
35. Gordon S. Wood, *The Radicalism of the American Revolution* (New York: Alfred A. Knopf, 1992), p. 189.
36. Ibid.
37. *The Economist,* "1992 in Review" (London: The Economist Newspaper, 1993), p. 51.
38. Barbara W. Tuchman, *The March of Folly, From Troy to Vietnam* (New York: Alfred A. Knopf, 1984).
39. *U.S. News and World Report*, "The Exodus From Public Schools" (December 9, 1991), p. 66.
40. Ibid.
41. Ibid.
42. Ibid., p. 67.
43. Ibid.
44. Ibid., p. 73.

45. Ibid., p. 73.

46. Ibid., p. 73.

47. Adam Smith, *The Wealth of Nations*, published in 1776 (New York: Modern Library, 1937), p. 765.

48. *The Economist*, vol. 325, no. 7791 (December 26, 1992–January 8, 1993), p. 80.

49. *Mueller* v. *Allen*, 463 U.S. 388, 103 S.Ct. 3062 (1983).

50. *U.S News and World Report* (December 9, 1991), p. 71.

51. Ibid.

52. "IRS Tells Sweigart Ministry to Stay Out of Elections," *Church and State*, vol. 45, no. 2 (February 1992), p. 3(27).

53. *Voice of Reason*, quarterly newsletter of Americans for Religious Liberty, Silver Spring, Maryland, no. 43 (Fall 1992), p. 2.

54. *Times Higher Education Supplement* (London: Times Supplements, April 9, 1993), p. 17.

55. Ibid.

56. Ibid.

57. Carl N. Degler, *Out of Our Past*, 3rd ed. (New York: Harper Torchbooks, 1984), p. 332.

58. Ibid., p. 334.

59. Ibid.

60. Degler, op. cit., p. 333.

61. Paul E. Peterson, *The New Urban Reality* (Washington, DC: The Brookings Institution, 1985), p. 15.

62. Ibid., p. 25.

63. *Baker* v. *Carr*, 369 U.S. 186, 82 S.Ct. 691 (1962).

64. Stephen Soltis, "A Power Plant on the Potomac," *Washington Flyer Magazine* (March/April, 1993), p. 16.

65. Ibid.

66. Schneider, op. cit., p. 37.

67. Ibid.

68. Ibid.

69. Ibid., p. 37.

70. Ibid., p. 37.

71. Robert Reich, op. cit., *New York Times Magazine*, p. 44.

72. Ibid.

73. *Atlantic Monthly*, op. cit., p. 38.

74. Ibid.

75. Richard Kluger, *Simple Justice* (New York: Vintage Books, 1977), p. 459.

76. Ibid.

77. Ibid.

78. Ibid.

79. Ibid., p. 55.

80. Ibid., p. 56.

81. *Alexander* v. *Holmes* 396 U.S. 19, 90 S.Ct. 29 (1969); *Keyes* v. *School District No. 1*, Denver, 413 U.S. 189, 93 S.Ct. 2686 (1973); *Pasadena City Board of Education* v. *Spangler*, 427 U.S. 424, 96 S.Ct. 2697 (1976).

82. Ibid., p. 56.

83. Seymour Martin Lipset, *Political Man: The Social Bases of Politics* (New York: Doubleday, 1963), p. 64.

84. Gunnar Myrdal, *American Dilemma: The Negro Problem and Modern Democracy* (New York: Harper and Row, 1962).

85. U.S. Department of Education, *The Condition of Education 1992* (Washington, DC: U.S. Government Printing Office, 1992), p. 104.

86. Ibid.

87. Jack Miles, "Immigration and the New American Dilemma," *Atlantic Monthly* 270, no. 4 (October 1992), p. 53.

88. James Fallows, *More Like Us* (Boston: Houghton Mifflin, 1990), p. 203.

89. Ibid.

90. "The Exodus From Public Schools," *U.S. News & World Report* (December 9, 1991), p. 71.

91. Two of the most important of these early studies were made by Floyd Hunter, *Community Power Structure* (Chapel Hill, NC: University of North Carolina, 1953); and Robert H. Dahl, *Who Governs?* (New Haven: Yale University Press, 1961).

92. Roe L. Johns and Ralph B. Kimbrough, *The Relationship of Socioeconomic Factors, Educational Leadership Patterns and Elements of Community Power Structure to Local School Fiscal Policy*, Final Report, Office of Education, Cooperative Research Project No. 1324 (Gainesville, FL: University of Florida, 1968).

93. *Public School Finance Programs*, periodically compiled by the Department of Education, U.S. Office of Education (Washington, DC: U.S. Government Printing Office).

94. Roald F. Campbell and Tim L. Mazzoni, Jr., *State Policy Making for the Public Schools* (Berkeley: McCutchan, 1976), pp. 169–171.

95. Kern Alexander and M. David Alexander, *American Public School Law*, 3rd ed. (St. Paul, MN: West Publishing Company, 1992).

96. R. Freeman and Lawrence A. Cremin, *A History of Education in American Culture* (New York: Henry Holt, 1953).

97. Richard Hofstadter, 1956, as cited in David McKay, *American Politics & Society* (London: Basil Blackwell, 1985), p. 8.

CHAPTER 12

THE FEDERAL ROLE
IN FINANCING EDUCATION

TOPICAL OUTLINE OF CHAPTER

Federal Aid Criteria • Political Realities • Governmental Powers
• U.S. Constitution • Limitations on Congress • Limitations on
States • Early Land Grants • Federal Grants • Elementary and
Secondary Education Act • Individuals with Disabilities Education
Act • Trends in Federal Funding • Equalization Tendencies
• Status of Federal Funding • The Future

INTRODUCTION

The role of the federal government in the financing of education will always be a subject of much controversy. Many believe that the federal government has a special responsibility for education that emanates from a national interest in the general welfare, and that this responsibility requires substantial federal financial commitment. Others maintain that the nature of U.S. federalism places little financial responsibility for education on the central government. Still others are of the opinion that the federal government should provide funding only as a stimulus for change and innovation or to deal with educational needs that are of particular national interest. The issue of federal aid is further complicated by strong lobbies representing other interests that historically have had difficulty in accepting the political philosophy of public schools. A full discussion of the several interest groups that for various reasons are opposed to public schools is contained in Chapter 11. To this unstable state of affairs can be added the marketplace enthusiasts who believe that all good in society derives from competition and that it is not necessary for the federal government to fund elementary and secondary education in any appreciable magnitude, so long as the federal government creates schemes of organization and finance that enhance competition among schools, parents, and students. Any consideration of federal aid to public elementary and secondary schools must recognize and fashion political accommodations for these varied interests.

Those who have advocated reduced governmental involvement, less taxation, and smaller governmental expenditures controlled the federal political agenda throughout the 1980s. During that period, the response of most politicians regardless of party was to exhibit a new sense of fiscal conservatism that negatively influenced the nation's investment in education. Today, presumably, we are entering into a new era in which the concept of education as a vital and elemental aspect of human capital development will reemerge. Recent pronouncements of the Clinton administration indicate that there will be a substantial national reliance on educational investment as an essential force in renewing the nation's economic vitality and resolve.

FEDERAL AID CRITERIA

Twenty years ago, the National Educational Finance Project[1] recommended a substantially greater involvement of the federal government in the financing of elementary and secondary schools. To this end certain criteria for federal funding were set forth

1. The purpose of the program must be worthy of and appropriate for the federal government.
2. The administrative arrangements must be conducive to sound federal–state relationships.
3. The combined federal programs should promote the development of adequate public school programs in all states.
4. The federal programs should equalize financial resources among states.

Each of these criteria remain applicable today. Regarding the first, the federal government should give first consideration to those educational needs that transcend state lines. Due in part to our mobile society, educational deficiencies cannot be quarantined within state boundaries. The spillovers of poor quality education in one state threaten all states. The federal interest must therefore be broad and pervasive. Thus it is within the realm of federal concern to make general purpose grants to states to supplement state and local funds and to provide incentives for states to expend the necessary tax effort to maintain an adequate system of education. Regarding the second, the federal–state partnership must be so conceived as to capture the special strengths of each level of government. Historically and legally the states occupy the central role in the formation and maintenance of public education. The legal relationship between federal and state government has been described in terms of a contract, with the states agreeing to certain conditions in exchange for federal aid. The federal government acts under the general welfare clause of the U.S. Constitution and the states respond with fiscal cooperation and mutual interest to that concern. This is as it should be and should continue. The localities do not stand alone, but are of the states, and as such form subsidiary units whose purpose is to bring the prescribed educational initiatives to the people. Historically, these roles have been found to be workable and should continue. Regarding the third criterion, the combined federal programs should be viewed as to their effects on state educational policy. Federal categorical grants that disregard considerations of educational needs in the national interest should be supplemented with other more far-reaching and comprehensive programs.

The last criterion, the need to equalize financial resources for education, is a vital one. All federal programs regardless of their substantive purpose should be so designed as to equalize the fiscal capacities of the states. Federal programs

---

Box 12.1 _____

Politics of "A Nation At Risk"

In 1983, when (Michael) Deaver wanted to tackle Reagan's do-nothing public image on education, (Craig) Fuller brought him information about a largely ignored presidential commission on excellence in education. "Nobody had paid any attention to it," Deaver recalls, "but I was looking for a way to reverse the president's negatives on education, and we took it around the country for six weeks." In speech after speech, Reagan cited the commission as evidence of his commitment to educational issues. At the end of that period, 59 percent of the public gave him a favorable rating on education issues, whereas before 65 percent had viewed him negatively on the issue.

"It was a great lesson in presidential communication," Deaver says—though the exercise did nothing to change the quality of American schools.

Source: Steven Mufson, "The Privatization of Craig Fuller," _Washington Post Magazine_ (August 2, 1992), p. 19.

should also be fashioned with a cognizance of inequalities internal to the states. This concern for equality should be a broad one with due consideration for the needs of pupils.

It is this last criterion that has unique importance today as we view the role of the federal government. Inequalities of funding both among and within states stand as possibly the most insidious threat to the provision of equal educational opportunity in the United States.

Current Political Realities of General Federal Aid

Serious considerations of substantial general federal subventions for the elementary and secondary schools have been attempted on numerous occasions and have failed because of a complexity of political issues that pervade education.

Throughout the years, general federal aid for education has been discussed and on occasion seriously pursued by its various advocates. During the 1920s and 1930s the predominate position of both Democrats and Republicans was that education was not a federal function and except for certain special circumstances should be left to the states and localities. This viewpoint has been unerringly adhered to by the Republican party over the years with notable reaffirmation during the 1980s. The Democratic party, while earlier in the century was officially opposed, later assumed a positive stance toward major subventions for education. The Democratic party did not mention federal aid to education in its platform of 1932, but indicated limited advocacy in the 1936 platform.[2] The Democrats finally reversed their position on the issue and in the platforms of 1944, 1948, and 1952 advocated federal aid to education with the proviso that it be without federal control. President Truman actively supported federal aid to public schools accompanied by higher education scholarships.[3] Truman had even included funds in his budgets in the late 1940s and early 1950s that went undistributed for lack of authorizing legislation.

During these years, at frequent intervals, major national education groups and organizations proposed general federal aid to education with variously stated caveats concerning federal control. Butts and Cremin describe the view of these groups by the mid 1950s.

> Prevailing control of education should be at local and state levels, but the federal government should aid the states to achieve a minimum level of quality of education and aid should be granted according to wealth, ability to tax, and need of the several states to help.[4]

A flurry of legislative proposals in the early 1950s circumscribed the issues and defined the boundaries of the political conflicts that had to be resolved before general federal aid could be achieved. The contentious issues can be summarized into four categories each having substantial political support. Combined they constituted a formidable obstacle to substantial federal subventions particularly in the form of general aid.

1. Fear of federal control
2. Fiscal conservatism
3. Religious opposition
4. Reluctance to provide funds to racially segregated schools

Each of these issues came to light in the late 1940s and early 1950s as general education aid was widely debated. In 1952 three types of bills were proposed in Congress that highlighted these issues. One was the Taft–Thomas bill (Senate Bill 246) that proposed an expenditure of $300 million per year for a federal foundation program that would bring public school expenditures up to a minimum of $55 per pupil in all states. Under the formula some states would have received $5 per pupil while others could have received up to $25 per pupil.[5] Two controversial limitations were written into the bill that contributed to its defeat. One required that states maintaining segregated schools must allocate a just and equitable portion to African-American schools. The other provision allowed states general use of the funds for school transportation of parochial school children. This bill passed the Senate in both 1948 and 1949, but failed in the House.[6]

The second bill, the Barden bill, sponsored by Representative Graham A. Barden of North Carolina (House Bill 4643) proposed a similar foundation program concept, with funding levels comparable to the Taft–Thomas bill, but the Barden bill specifically provided that the funds could be used only for the support of public schools, not private and parochial schools. The clarity of this bill's provision for African-American schools was less certain.[7] This bill also failed after much political wrangling.

A third bill, called the Murray–McMahon bill (Senate Bill 947) and Fogarty bill (House Bill 915) included a provision that required states to allocate funds to parochial schools for auxiliary services. Representatives of church organizations testified for this legislation and against the Taft–Thomas and Barden bills. A clear line of political demarcation developed that formed well-organized opposition to federal aid to education unless it provided considerable amounts of funding for nonpublic schools.[8] The controversy over aid to nonpublic schools was therefore instrumental in killing all three of the bills.

The Johnson administration in 1965 compromised in the issue of aid to nonpublic schools by providing for dual enrollment and shared time arrangements allowing parochial school children to participate in Title I, ESEA, Title II library books and materials, and Title III consortium arrangements. The provisions moderated the dispute to a sufficient degree that the large Democratic majority in the Congress could enact the Elementary and Secondary Education Act of 1965. Comparable conditions for compromise coupled with the budgetary wherewithal have not existed since the 1960s.

Today the path may be clearer for larger federal subventions for several reasons. Fear of federal control does not appear to be as great today as in earlier years. In many aspects state governments have become stronger and apparently more confident of their roles in the federal system. Fiscal conservatism reached an extreme state in the early 1980s and will presumably be more limited in the near future. Also, there seems to be a continuing working solution to the problem of aid to nonpublic schools by virtue of the precedents of the ESEA agreements of the Johnson era. Last, even though the racial problem is still one that stridently haunts education, the political dimensions of race have changed so that the forces involved tend to be more proactive toward increased federal aid for education. The political problems associated with race today have become more economic, demographic, and geographic with problems of education funding being most notably concerned with the allocation of funds to core cities and poor rural areas and less concerned with segregated schools per se.

Division of Power among Governments

The Tenth Amendment to the Constitution of the United States provides: "The powers not delegated to the United States by the Constitution, nor prohibited by it to the States, are reserved to the states respectively or to the people." Since the Constitution makes no specific reference to education, it has been assumed that education is the legal responsibility of the states. The governmental powers of the states are plenary except for the powers that have been delegated to the federal government or withheld from the states by some provision of the Constitution. On the other hand, the federal government is a limited government with no powers except those specifically conferred upon it by the Constitution or those that can reasonably be implied as necessary to exercise the powers and responsibilities specifically granted.[9]

The Constitution, in addition to being a broad statement of principles, also provides specific delegations of power to the central government. Since the federal government has no specific grant of power to finance, regulate, control, or operate schools, colleges, institutions, or educational programs, its authority to do so must be found in its implied powers. It is in the area of implied powers that the controversy centers.

As will be shown later in this chapter, it is an historical fact that the federal government has assisted in financing many types of public educational institutions, including the public schools; it has regulated and controlled public education to some extent, and it has operated practically every type of educational institution and numerous special programs. In fact it is still doing so. Interestingly, this exercise of implied powers has never been successfully challenged in the courts. The issue is not whether the federal government has any implied powers with respect to education, but rather the extent to which those powers should be exercised. Realistically, it would appear to be impractical or impossible to define neatly by Constitution or statute the limits of the exercise of the implied or discretionary powers of government, the times when they should be exercised, or the objects for which they should be exercised.

The issue of the implied powers of the federal government has caused bitter controversy between the states and the federal government itself. It was one of the fundamental issues of the Civil War and a basic issue in the current controversy over desegregation in the public schools and institutions of higher learning and over civil rights. It was a controversial issue of the past and remains a live issue today.

One of the earliest issues causing the formation of political parties arose over differences of opinion concerning the relative roles of the federal and state governments. The term *states' rights* means many things to many people. But in general it emphasizes the powers of the states and de-emphasizes the powers of the federal government. It was inevitable that the issue of federal aid to education should become associated in the minds of many people with these same issues. Therefore the position that many people take with respect to federal aid to education is not determined by the virtues of the proposals or the reality of the need for federal aid, but by their thinking concerning the centralization of governmental powers.

The point of view of many modern thinkers is that the trend toward increasing governmental expenditures in today's technological civilization is necessary and desirable because (1) only government (especially central government) can provide many of the services essential to a modern civilization, and (2) the expenditures of government are necessary for maximizing employment. The fiscally conservative view is that government taxing and spending should be limited to providing the minimum of necessary government services, because

1. continued increase in government spending eventually will result in socialism and a welfare state; and
2. socialism will destroy the free-enterprise system and eventually result in the loss of other liberties.

These two sharply contrasting views are often found to be at the heart of much of the present-day political controversy over federal funding of education.

Those not fearing the effects of government spending generally support increased revenue for education from all three levels of government and especially at the state and federal levels. Those fearing the effects of government spending generally oppose increased spending for education at all levels, especially by the federal government. Conservatives generally oppose increased spending for public education, not because they are opposed to public education, but rather because of their opposition to increases in government spending in general.

The goal of the fiscal conservative is to maximize the market economy and to minimize governmental activity. In times of inflation the fiscal conservative advocates the reduction of government expenditures and taxes on the basis that government expenditures add to inflation. In times of deflation and depression, this same conservative still advocates the reduction of government expenditures and taxes contending that "one more penny of taxes may well break the back of the overburdened taxpayer."

Experts on school financing generally insist that expenditures for education should not be determined by whether they inflate or deflate the economy, but by the educational needs of the nation. Such a policy tends to stabilize the economy rather than contributing to either inflation or deflation. Furthermore, as pointed out in Chapter 3, investment in people more so than investment in physical capital increases the total volume of goods and services available for consumption.

The General Welfare Clauses of the Constitution

Article I, Section 8 of the Constitution deals with the powers granted to Congress. Clause 1 reads as follows: "The Congress shall have Power To lay and collect Taxes, Duties, Imposts, and Excises, to pay the Debts and provide for the common Defense and general Welfare of the United States; but all Duties, Imposts and Excises shall be uniform throughout the United States." Although this clause deals with such important matters as levying and collecting taxes, the payment of debts, and providing for the common defense, it is commonly called the General Welfare clause because of the great controversies over the meaning of the phrase *General Welfare of the United States.* At the time the Constitution was adopted, probably only a few people realized the significance of those words.

The eighteenth clause of Section 8 grants Congress the final power "to make all Laws which shall be necessary and proper for carrying into Execution the foregoing Powers, and all other Powers vested by this Constitution in the Government of the United States, or in any Department or Officer thereof." This clause gives to Congress a broad grant of implied powers. The meaning of clauses 1 and 18 became a matter of bitter controversy very early in our history. James Madison and Alexander Hamilton took the lead in presenting the opposing points of view. Madison argued that the phrase *General Welfare of the United States* conferred on Congress no additional powers to tax and spend and that the power of Congress to tax and spend therefore was limited to the purposes specifically enumerated by the Constitution. Hamilton held that those words did confer additional power on Congress to tax and spend for purposes other than those specifically enumerated in the Constitution and the Congress thereby had the power to tax and spend for any purpose that it deemed to be for the general welfare.

Hamilton and Madison did not resolve their differences. In fact, controversy over this issue still continues, but the details have changed somewhat. The Supreme Court has supported some of Hamilton's contentions. In a ruling on the Agricultural Adjustment Act, the Court held that "the power of Congress to authorize expenditures of public moneys for the public purposes is not limited by the direct grants of legislative power found in the Constitution."[10] The Supreme Court, in ruling on the Social Security Act, held that the decision as to whether an expenditure was for the general welfare had to be made by Congress, provided that it was not a display of arbitrary power. The Court also held in this decision: "Nor is the concept of general welfare static. Needs that were narrow or parochial a century ago may be interwoven in our day with the well-being of the nation. What is critical or urgent changes with the times."[11]

The authority of Congress to tax and spend for public education has been assumed to be valid relying on these and other judicial opinions for support. Actually, the legal power of Congress to appropriate and spend money for public education has never been challenged in the Supreme Court. But the rulings of the Court have not settled the controversy between the "liberal constructionists" and the "strict constructionists" of the Constitution. The battle still continues, but the major issue has changed from the legal power of Congress to tax and spend for the general welfare to the wisdom of the policy of doing so. What laws are "necessary and proper" (Article I, Section 18) to provide for the "general Welfare of the United States" (Article I,

Section 8, Clause 1)? That issue never will be finally resolved, because what is necessary and proper for the general welfare "changes with the times."

The General Welfare clause has been used extensively during the past 40 years to justify the expansion of old federal activities and the addition of new ones. The advocates for the extension of federal educational involvement now contend that Congress has not only the power to promote the general welfare but also the duty to do so. This point of view is vigorously opposed by the conservatives who bitterly contest virtually all expansion of federal spending except for national defense. Therefore, the issue of federal aid to education remains at its core an ideological controversy of no small proportions.

Limitations on Congress

Various constitutional provisions are specifications of limitations on Congressional or state power. Foremost among such limitations are the provisions in the Bill of Rights, but there are others.

Article I, Section 9 of the Constitution sets forth certain powers denied to Congress. Two of its subsections have some relationship to financing education. Subsection 4 reads as follows: "No Capitation, or other direct, Tax shall be laid, unless in Proportion to the Census or Enumeration herein before directed to be taken." This provision of the Constitution has effectively prevented Congress from levying a property tax.[12] It is obviously impracticable to levy a property tax in proportion to the census. The last time Congress attempted to levy such a tax was during the Civil War. Had it not been for this provision of the Constitution, Congress probably would have levied property taxes very early in our history.

This subsection also prevented Congress from levying income taxes until it was removed by the Sixteenth Amendment, ratified in 1913. It reads: "The Congress shall have power to lay and collect taxes on income, from whatever sources derived, without apportionment among the several States, and without regard to any census or enumeration." This amendment greatly increased the taxing powers of Congress.

The federal government obtains far greater tax revenues from the income tax than any other tax source. This broadening of the taxing powers of Congress has made it possible for the federal government to greatly extend federal services and to increase equity through the redistribution of wealth and income among the people.

Subsection 5 prohibits Congress from laying taxes or duties on articles exported from any state. This provision and the provisions of Subsection 4 as amended by the Sixteenth Amendment are the only specific limitations upon the taxing powers of Congress, except for the provision of Article I, Section 8, Clause 1, requiring that "all Duties, Imposts and Excises shall be uniform throughout the United States." Therefore, the Constitution vests Congress with very broad taxing powers. The enormous amount of revenue collected annually by the federal government is evidence of that fact.

The federal government has another important advantage in obtaining revenues. When taxes are levied nationwide, the difficulties of competition among states and local governments are avoided. The income tax, both personal and corporate, is levied nationwide. A person or corporation cannot escape the federal income tax by moving to another political jurisdiction within the nation. But the income taxes and certain other taxes of state and local governments can be avoided by moving into jurisdictions not levying the tax. Tax competition therefore limits the potential tax revenues of state and local governments.

Limitations on the State

Article I, Section 10 of the United States Constitution sets forth the powers denied the states. There are only a few provisions of this section that are related to the financing of education. Subsection 1 includes the provision that no state shall pass any law impairing the obligation of contracts. Subsection 2 provides: "No State shall, without the Consent of the Congress, lay any Imposts or Duties on Imports or Exports, except what may be absolutely necessary for executing its inspection Laws; and the net Produce of all Duties and Imposts, laid by any State on Imports or Exports, shall be for the Use of the Treasury of the United States; and all such Laws shall be subject to the Revision and Control of the Congress." Subsection 3 provides: "No State shall, without consent of Congress, lay any Duty of Tonnage . . ." These are the only limitations placed upon the taxing powers of the states by the Constitution. They are relatively minor and therefore place no serious restrictions on the states with respect to levying and collecting taxes.

But it should not be assumed that Article I, Section 10 of the Constitution contains the only federal limitations upon the states in the operation of systems of public education. The Constitution as interpreted by the United States Supreme Court is the supreme law of the land. Any law of any state on any matter, including education, that is in conflict with any provision of the Constitution is null and void if so declared by the U.S. Supreme Court. People who argue that the federal government should have no control whatsoever over public education seem to have overlooked this fact. It would be impossible to have a federal government of the United States if the states could nullify the Constitution. Therefore, some measure of federal control of public education is inescapable.

Equal Protection of the Law. The Fourteenth Amendment, Section 1, provides in part: "No State shall make or enforce any law which shall abridge the privileges or immunities of citizens of the United States; nor shall any State deprive any person of life, liberty, or property, without due process of law; nor deny to any person within its jurisdiction the equal protection of the laws." It was this amendment as interpreted by subsequent rulings of the Supreme Court that

firmly established the inviolability of equal rights under the law.

One of the Court's most dramatic rulings was made on May 17, 1954 in *Brown* v. *Board of Education*. The Court had before it five cases dealing with segregation in the public schools. Segregation by race in the public schools was declared unconstitutional when the Court stated: "We conclude that in the field of public education the doctrine of 'separate but equal' has no place. Separate educational facilities are inherently unequal. Therefore, we hold that the plaintiffs and others similarly situated for whom the actions are brought are, by reason of the segregation complained of, deprived of the equal protection of the laws guaranteed by the Fourteenth Amendment."[13]

Interestingly the 1954 *Brown* decision reversed a ruling the U.S. Supreme Court had made in 1896 that had given legal sanction to the separate but equal concept that was subsequently used to justify segregation of public facilities. The Court ruled in that case that separate but equal facilities were constitutional.[14] In reversing this precedent, the 1954 *Brown* ruling prohibited policies of states that created segregation, whether they emanated from policies of legislatures or boards of education. This decision overthrew the "states' rights" theory insofar as certain aspects of public education were concerned.

The Civil Rights Act of 1964 greatly increased the power of the federal government to enforce the 1954 decision of the Supreme Court. Title VI of this act states: "No person in the United States shall on the ground of race, color or national origin, be excluded from participation in, be denied the benefits of, or be subject to discrimination, under any program or activity receiving federal financial assistance." Under the provisions of this act, any federal agency disbursing federal funds is given the power to withhold such funds if the recipient agency or institution violates this act. The federal agencies in recent years have frequently used their power to withhold funds to enforce the provisions of the Civil Rights Act and the 1954 decision of the Supreme Court. As the level of federal funds for education has increased, it has become a more powerful force in bringing about desegregation.

Separation of Church and State.   The relationship of the schools to religion is regulated by the federal government under authority of the First and Fourteenth Amendments to the Constitution. The First Amendment provides: "Congress shall make no law respecting an establishment of religion, or prohibiting the free exercise thereof." The Supreme Court has held that the provisions of the First Amendment also apply to the states because of the following provision in the Fourteenth Amendment: "No State shall make or enforce any laws which shall abridge the privileges or immunities of citizens of the United States." Therefore any privilege or immunity granted a citizen of the United States by the Constitution cannot be denied by the states. A more extensive discussion of this topic is contained in Chapter 2.

Impairment of Contracts.   As has been pointed out, Article I, Section 10 of the Constitution contains a provision prohibiting a state from passing a law impairing the obligation of contracts. School financing involves many different types of contracts. School boards, for instance, issue bonds that are important financial contracts. The U.S. Constitution's prohibition against the impairment of contracts undoubtedly has improved the credit of boards of education as well as the credit of all state and local governments. This type of federal control seems to be applauded by almost everyone. Actually, it is not generally recognized as a control, but the fact that it is a control makes it a valuable asset in school financing.

One ruling of the Supreme Court has significance in relation to teacher retirement. The Court has held that "a legislative enactment may contain provisions which, when accepted as a basis of action of individuals, become contracts between them and the state or its subdivision."[15] Teacher retirement laws should be so drafted as to make it clear that provisions for retirement constitute a contract between the teacher and the state.

HISTORICAL DEVELOPMENT OF FEDERAL AID

There is no complete historical record of all the federal funds that have been expended for education. Actually, no office or agency of the federal government can give an accurate statement of federal funds being expended directly or indirectly for education. Even objective investigators working independently cannot arrive at the same total of federal funds expended for education during any given fiscal year. Therefore it would not be possible to present an accurate history of federal aid even if space permitted. However, it is possible to present certain examples that cast some light on its development.

Early Land Grants

A national interest in education was revealed even before the adoption of the Constitution. It all started when the Congress, operating under the Articles of Confederation, set aside lands from the national domain for public schools in each new state upon entry into the Union. The Ordinance of 1785 provided the manner in which western territory would be surveyed and further specified a portion of each section for creation of public schools.[16] The Ordinance of 1785, however, did not actually carry out the transfer and sale of the lands, postponing such procedures to later legislation, in the Ordinance of 1787. Titled "An Ordinance for the Government of the Territory of the United States, North West of the River Ohio," this ordinance, also sometimes referred to as the Northwest Ordinance, was adopted on July 13, 1787. The document itself made no stipulation for the reservation of lands for public schools even though the Ordinance of 1785 had specified land for that purpose. The only reference in the Ordinance of 1787 to education was found in the third article, the oft-quoted section that enunciated the belief that education was necessary for good government and the happiness of the people. Thirteen days after passing of the second ordinance, a third ordinance was passed on July 27, 1787 for the sale of over 5 million acres to the Ohio Company. This geographical area encompassed what became in 1803 the state of Ohio. These were the origins of the federal government's involvement in the financing of public schools in the United States.[17]

Two characteristics of these early land grants were of great significance. First, the grants were for general public school purposes. Second, the federal government exercised no control over education as a condition for receiving the grants. Despite this early precedent establishing a pattern of nondirective federal aid, practically all federal grants-in-aid to the public schools after 1862 have been special-purpose grants.

National Domain. One may ask, however, how the central government acquired land to grant to the states in the first place. What were land grants and where did the land come from that was being granted? The answer is that these were lands that were known as the "national domain," and was constituted of the western territory beyond the agreed upon boundaries of the original 13 colonies. Harvey explains that seven of the colonies, Massachusetts, Connecticut, New York, Virginia, North Carolina, South Carolina, and Georgia, had laid claim to all the westward territory to the Mississippi river,[18] but the boundaries were unsurveyed and indefinite and the six remaining colonies feared that probable annexation of this land would make the other seven colonies too powerful. A compromise was struck in the Articles of Confederation by which the seven colonies claiming dominion over these territories would relinquish their claims. These promises were fulfilled between 1781 and 1802 thus placing these lands in the national domain under the control of Congress. Cubberley clarifies:

While the treaty of 1783 had recognized the boundary of the new Nation as extending westward to the Mississippi, there were many conflicting claims to the land west of the Alleghenies. By way of settling the matter, the Continental Congress, in 1780, proposed that the different States cede their claims to the National Government and thus create a national domain. New York, in 1781, was the first to do so, followed by Virginia (1784), Massachusetts (1785), Connecticut (1786), South Carolina (1787), North Carolina (1790), and Georgia (1802). The "common estate" thus created served as a real bond of union between the States during the critical period in the life of the new Nation.[19]

Illustrated in Figure 12.1 is a map of the United States as it existed in 1783.

Ordinance of 1785 (First Ordinance). The Congress operating under the Articles of Confederation had promised lands to Revolutionary War soldiers, beginning in August 1776, ranging from 500 acres for a colonel to 100 acres for each noncommissioned officer.[20] In 1780, additional grants were made of 1,100 acres to a major general and 850 acres to a brigadier general. Granting of western lands was also stimulated by Congress's need for money to pay other war debts. The selling of western lands was the most immediate solution to the problem. The western lands were therefore considered valuable currency for the new government. Before sales could be consummated, however, the land had to be surveyed.[21] In response to a petition by 200 Revolutionary War officers in 1783 who sought to claim their lands, Congress appointed a committee headed by Thomas Jefferson to ascertain a method of locating and disposing of public lands.[22] This committee recommended an ordinance requiring lands to be divided into "hundreds" or townships of ten geographical miles square, and these hundreds were to be divided into "lots" of one mile square (640 acres) and numbered from 1 to 100. "These numbers were to commence in the northwestern corner, continue from west to east, and then from east to west."[23]

The recommendation of the Jefferson committee was carried over to the Continental Congress of 1785 where it was referred to a new

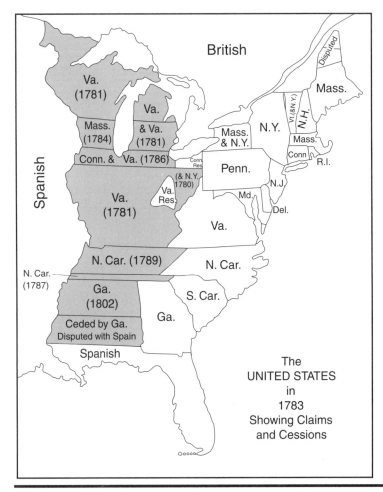

FIGURE 12.1 The United States in 1783 Showing Conflicting Claims to Western Lands

Source: Ellwood P. Cubberley, *Public Education in the United States.* Copyright © 1934 by Houghton Mifflin Company. Reprinted with permission.

committee and debated. It was argued that practicality required smaller tracts of less than the recommended ten square miles. Ultimately the Continental Congress decided that a township should be six miles square and the Ordinance of 1785 was finally passed on May 20.[24] The idea of "Congressional townships" was maintained as were the basic dimensions of one square mile or 640 acres.[25] (See Figure 12.2) The ordinance, officially entitled "An ordinance for ascertaining the mode of disposing of lands in the Western

Territory," set out the method for the survey and sale of the land of the Northwest Territory.[26]

The pertinent provision for public schools in the Ordinance of 1785 was as follows:

The surveyors . . . shall proceed to divide the said territory into townships of six miles square, by lines running due north and south, and others crossing these at right angles, as near as may be . . .

The plots of the townships respectively, shall be marked by subdivisions into lots of one mile square, or 640 acres, in the same direction as the external lines and numbered from 1 to 36.

There shall be reserved for the United States out of every township, the four lots being numbered 8, 11, 16, 19 . . . for future sale. There shall be reserved a lot No. 16, of every township, for the maintenance of public schools, within the said township. . . . [27]

This was the origin of the sixteenth-section land grant for public schools that was carried throughout the subsequent Congressional legislation admitting new states into the Union.[28] Swift points out that the ideas behind public land policy ultimately benefitting public schools emanated from several sources including the following: 1) Connecticut, Massachusetts, and other colonies had reserved sections for schools in newly surveyed townships; 2) an abiding interest in education by enlightened legislators (not the least of whom was Thomas Jefferson who had chaired the committee in 1784); 3) the urgent need for revenues and the inability of the Continental Congress to raise funds from other sources; and 4) the desire to make westward expansion attractive.[29]

Ordinance of 1787 (Second Ordinance). As indicated earlier, the Ordinance of 1787, passed on July 13, 1787, did not actually reserve or convey lands for education, but the Continental

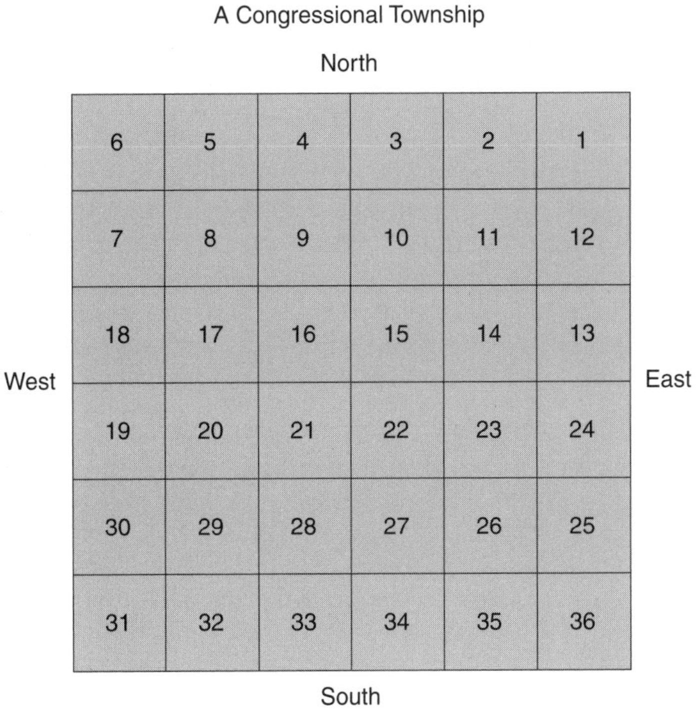

A Congressional Township

North

6	5	4	3	2	1
7	8	9	10	11	12
18	17	16	15	14	13
19	20	21	22	23	24
30	29	28	27	26	25
31	32	33	34	35	36

West   East

South

FIGURE 12.2   A Congressional Township

Source: Ira W. Harvey, *A History of Educational Finance in Alabama, 1819–1986* (Auburn, AL: The Truman Pierce Institute for the Advancement of Teacher Education, Auburn University, 1989), p. 17. Reprinted with permission.

Note: Showing sections, quarter sections, plan of numbering, and the location of section 16 required for public schools. The township is six miles on a side, containing 36 square miles. It is subdivided into 36 sections containing one square mile or 640 acres.

Congress, meeting in New York in July 1787, simultaneous with the Constitutional Convention meeting in Philadelphia, forged the often quoted statement of education's value to a new nation, to wit: "Religion, morality and knowledge, being necessary to good government and the happiness of mankind, schools and the means of education shall forever be encouraged."[30] However, there was no specification as to how these lands would be used to advance education. This was to come later in a third ordinance and ultimately with the enabling act that admitted Ohio as the first state of the Northwest Territory in 1803.

Ordinance of 1787 (Third Ordinance).   Shortly on the heels of the second ordinance of July 13, 1787 followed a third ordinance on July 27, 1787. As may have been expected, both ordinances had been accompanied by intense lobbying by land speculators who saw a huge profit from real estate transactions in the new territories. Land speculation was a well-regarded profession of the day with impressive and respectable British forerunners such as Parliament's creation of the Muscovy Company (1553), the Levant Company (1592), the East India Company (1600), and the Hudson Bay Company (1669). All had been highly successful ventures for both economic development and commerce. Reputable speculators in the new colonies included George Washington who had been a principal promoter of the Mississippi Company in 1763 and had lobbied vigorously for his continental army officers to obtain land grants as payment for their services.[31]

Following the precedents of the British Parliament, Congress sitting in New York established the Ohio company and conveyed 1.5 million acres of choice land at nine cents per acre at the juncture of the Ohio and Muskingum rivers[32] to Manassah Cutler, founder of the Ohio Company. The remaining 3.5 million acres were reserved for private speculation. A quorum of only eight states was present in New York when the ordinance was passed and it was widely known that the United States' biggest contract was vividly marked by widespread corruption

and graft as congressmen, speculators, and squatters reaped huge profits.[33]

Cutler himself jubilantly wrote,

> We obtained the grant of near five million acres . . . one million and a half of the Ohio Company and the remainder for a private speculation, in which many of the principal characters of America are concerned. Without connecting this speculation, similar terms and advantages could not have been obtained for the Ohio Company.[34]

It was these "principal characters of America," including congressmen, who were the beneficiaries of the speculation.[35] Even though self-interest, laissez-faire capitalism and avarice were principal motivations of those persons in power, the common person did eventually become a beneficiary of the transaction through the education policy enunciations of 1785 and 1787 and the ultimate westward expansion and economic development. However, it remained for a fourth stage of the land grant policy to more clearly determine how the land could be used for the educational benefit of the people.

Ohio and the Land Grant.   Clarification and implementation of the educational intent of the Ordinances of 1785 and 1787 were not achieved until negotiations began between the new state of Ohio and the U.S. Congress of 1802. Ohio agreed not to tax the public lands of the United States if the United States would in turn give to the new state of Ohio the sixteenth section of land in every township for the maintenance of schools within the township.[36] The enabling act for the admission of Ohio as a state thus became the precedent that formally reserved the sixteenth section lands for public schools and other designated lands for public use.[37] The act for Ohio stated in part:

> First. That the section numbered sixteen in every township, and where such section has been sold, granted, or disposed of, other lands equivalent thereto, and most contiguous to the same shall be granted to the inhabitants of the township for the use of schools.[38]

The enabling act fashioned for Ohio was used by all new states except Texas, which owned its own land, and West Virginia and Maine, which were carved from original states.[39] With the admission of California in 1850, and for new states thereafter, the grant was increased to two sections in each township, the sixteenth and thirty-sixth sections. Later when Utah (1896), Arizona (1912), and New Mexico (1912) were admitted due to sparsity and the low value of land, an additional two sections, totalling four were set aside for public schools. For all the 48 contiguous states, the federal government granted for schools and other public purposes, approximately 145 million acres or about 226,562 square miles of public lands.[40] This constituted an area larger than France and nearly four times the size of New England.[41]

Alaska and Hawaii came into the Union in 1959 under the two-section provision that designated sections 16 and 36 for the benefit of public schools. In Hawaii the enabling act of admission did not designate a section (or sections) of land for public schools, but rather stated,

> The lands granted to the State of Hawaii (by the United States) . . . shall be held by said State (Hawaii) as a public trust for the support of the public schools and other public educational institutions. . . . The schools and other educational institutions supported, in whole or in part, out of such public trust shall forever remain under the exclusive control of the State; and no part of the proceeds or income from the lands granted under this Act shall be used for the support of any sectarian or denominational school, college, or university.[42]

Although Hawaii's admission did not designate specific surveyed sections of land, it did set aside public lands in trust for the support of public schools.

Thus it may be accurately concluded that the federal government through its land grant policy, emanating from 1785, was a substantial force in the creation of public schools in the United States. Though it cannot be maintained that the policy was the sole motivating force for public schools,

or the motivation at all in some of the states, remembering that the 13 original colonies, as well as Vermont, Kentucky, West Virginia, Maine, and Texas established their systems without the land-grant impetus. The federal land grant policy nevertheless must certainly be counted as one of the most potent forces in the establishment and financing of public schools in the United States.

The Morrill Act

The first Morrill Act was passed by Congress in 1862 providing for a grant of 30,000 acres to each state for each representative and senator then in Congress. This same grant of land was made available to states thereafter admitted to the Union. The act provided for the giving of scrip to the states in which the public lands were insufficient to make up the allotment. It was provided that the land be sold and the proceeds used for the "endowment, maintenance and support of at least one college where the leading object shall be, without excluding other scientific and classical studies and including military tactics, to teach such branches of learning as are related to agriculture and the mechanic arts in such manner as the legislatures of the state may respectively prescribe." Another stated purpose of the act was "to promote the liberal and practical education of the industrial classes in the several pursuits and professions of life."[43]

This original Morrill Act is the first instance of the federal government providing a grant for specific educational purposes. It should be noted that federal requirements were limited to specifying that agriculture, mechanic arts, and military tactics be taught in those institutions. No limitation was placed on other subjects that might be taught. Also, the act specifically placed the determination of the educational policies of the land-grant institutions in the hands of the respective state legislatures.

This act is of great significance because it again demonstrated the national interest in education and it also showed that, when existing educational institutions did not provide adequately for the general welfare, the federal government could and would take action.

At the time the Morrill Act was passed, the institutions of higher learning were largely classical and academic in character. They catered primarily to the select few. The land-grant colleges have been called people's colleges. Their curricula included subjects that were not "academically respectable" in 1862, but their educational programs grew in popularity. The influence of these land-grant colleges has been so great that they have contributed substantially to liberalizing the educational programs of many non-land-grant colleges. But more importantly these land-grant universities have served as models of practical research throughout the world and have been in the forefront of technological and agricultural advancement. In 32 states, a land-grant college is also the principal state university.

The Smith–Lever Act

The Smith–Lever Act was approved by Congress in 1914. It provided for extension services by county agricultural and home demonstration agents, 4-H leaders, and specialists in agriculture and homemaking, and for the professional training of teachers in those subjects. This act was far more specific in detailing the purposes for which the grant funds could be spent than was the Morrill Act. Actually, the services provided under the Smith–Lever Act were practically nonexistent prior to its passage. This act is additional evidence that Congress, when it deems it desirable to do so, will provide or stimulate the creation of educational services that are not being furnished by the educational organizations.

The extension services provided under the Smith–Lever Act are not an integral part of the system of public education. The service at the local level is usually allocated to the control of the county governing body. Boards of education, especially county boards, have sometimes subsidized the extension service, but they have no authority over it. The state director of the extension service is usually associated with a land-grant college, but this is about the only direct relationship with the system of public education.

The extension services made a major contribution to the dissemination of the results of the research conducted on agricultural experiment farms. The extension services brought the people's colleges to the people. It should be remembered that the extension services were inaugurated before the days of radio and television. In that era the extension agents were the major communicators of new and improved practices in agriculture and homemaking. The success of the federally subsidized extension services undoubtedly influenced the state and institutions of higher learning to establish additional extension services and adult education programs.

The Smith–Hughes Act

Between 1862 and 1917 the federal government seemed to be concerned primarily with inadequacies in the programs of institutions of higher learning. No new federal act of any major significance to the public schools was passed by Congress during this period. In 1917 Congress passed the Smith–Hughes Act, which provided funds for vocational education below the college level. Appropriation was provided for vocational education in agriculture, trades and industry, and homemaking. A provision was also made for teacher training in these fields. The original Smith–Hughes Act required dollar-for-dollar matching by the states and local units. Some states provided all the matching funds required from state revenues. Other states required local units to match the state funds dollar for dollar and thereby provide one-half the matching funds required by the federal government. This retarded the development of vocational education in some of the least wealthy districts because of their inability to provide the required matching funds. Some other acts that supplemented and broadened the Smith–Hughes Act were the George–Reed Act of 1929, the George–Ellzey Act of 1935, the George–Deen Act of 1937, the George–Barden Act of 1946, the Vocational Education Act of 1963 as amended in 1968, and subsequent amendments.

The Smith–Hughes Act provided the first special-purpose grants to the public schools by Congress. Vocational education was not a new educational idea. A number of school systems had established some type of vocational education programs prior to 1917. For example, some 500 agricultural high schools had been established by 1909. Some schools in 44 of the 47 states in 1911 offered training in homemaking. A number of city systems had developed trade schools or trade courses in regular high schools. However, most high-school students did not have access to suitable kinds of vocational programs.

At the beginning of the twentieth century, most lay people—and also most educators—believed that the high-school program should be largely academic in character. The prevailing belief was that if a high-school student was not interested in college preparatory work, he or she should not go to high school. High schools did not become mass education institutions until after World War I. Following that war, however, there was a remarkable increase in the demand for secondary education. The development of vocational education, which was stimulated by the Smith–Hughes Act, provided opportunities for large numbers of pupils whose needs could not have been served by the high-school programs that existed prior to 1917.

Grants-in-aid for vocational education have been criticized on the grounds that such grants tend to turn the educational programs in the direction of the subsidized purpose. The more generously financed programs often become the centerpiece of the several programs regardless of whether they meet the needs of the students or the community. This was no doubt true in the years immediately following 1917. But that was probably one of the purposes of the Smith–Hughes Act. Any special-purpose grant influences the direction of the educational program. Therefore, a special-purpose grant of any kind, state or federal, contains an element of control.

Defense-Related Educational Activities. A long-term federal program that was designed primarily to assist states and local communities support defense-related activities was enacted in 1941. This law, known as the Lanham Act, or federal impact aid, provided for the construction, maintenance, and operation of community facilities in areas where defense and war activities created unusual burdens for local governments. Schools received considerable federal aid for building construction and for current expenses under the provisions of this act. The Lanham Act was superseded in 1950 by Public Law 815 and 874, which continued approximately the same types of benefits.

Other Important Federal Legislation Affecting Education

The year 1958 marked a turning point in the relationship of the federal government to education. The launching by the Russians of the first satellite in 1957 caused great alarm in the United States. It was a popular myth that the Russians could not possibly develop advanced science and produce high-tech goods under their socialist system. When pundits are found to be wrong, they seldom admit error, but blame others. Therefore, the first reaction of many people to the success of the Russians was to blame the public schools for alleged inefficiency. Fortunately this state of public opinion did not last very long and, beginning in 1958, successive sessions of Congress enacted a long series of laws designed to improve education in the United States, extending from the preschool training through college and university education and continuing throughout adult life.

The National Defense Education Act of 1958—Public Law 85-864—authorized the expenditure of substantial sums for the following purposes:

1. Providing loans to students in institutions of higher learning
2. Providing equipment for and remodeling of facilities for science, mathematics, and foreign language teaching

3. Providing graduate fellowships for those interested in teaching in institutions of higher learning
4. Providing assistance for guidance, counseling, and testing services and for identification and encouragement of able students
5. Providing centers for teaching modern foreign languages
6. Providing assistance for research and experimentation in the more effective use of television and other related audio–visual media
7. Providing assistance for certain area vocational programs

Manpower Development and Training Act of 1962—Public Law 84-415. The basic purpose of this act was to reduce unemployment by retraining workers whose skills had become obsolete. Although it was directed primarily toward the relief of unemployed adult workers, it also provided for testing, counseling, and selection of youth, 16 years of age and older for occupational and other schooling. This act was amended in 1966 to provide these same services for persons 45 years of age and older.

Vocational Education Act of 1963—Public Law 88-210. This act more than quadrupled federal appropriations for vocational education, and it greatly broadened the purposes of the original Smith–Hughes Act. The major purpose of the act of 1963 was to provide occupational training for persons of all ages and achievement levels in any occupational field that does not require a baccalaureate degree, and to provide for related services that will help to ensure programs of quality. It also provided financial assistance for the construction of area vocational facilities, work–study programs, and residential schools.

The Elementary and Secondary Education Act of 1965—Public Law 89-10. This law is by far the most important measure affecting the financing of the public schools that has been enacted by Congress up to the present time. It originally contained a broad program of categorical aids

under five titles designed to strengthen public education at what was considered by Congress to be its weakest points.

Title I provided financial assistance for education programs specifically designed to benefit children from families with incomes of less than a specified amount or who were receiving welfare aid to dependent children. Title II provided funds for libraries, textbooks, and audio–visual materials. Title III provided funds for supplementary education centers for students in both public and private schools. Title IV provided funds for regional educational research and training laboratories. Title V provided funds for strengthening state departments of education. This act was amended and reorganized in 1981, as explained in more detail later in this chapter.

Education of the Disabled Act—Public Law 94-142. Enacted in 1975 as the Education for All Handicapped Children Act, the purpose of this act was to assist in the initiation, expansion, and improvement of programs and projects for the disabled children at pre-school, elementary, and secondary levels through grants to states and outlying territories. This act has been of great assistance to the states and local boards of education in meeting the needs of disabled pupils through the provision of appropriate educational programs.

This act was amended and subsumed under the Individuals with Disabilities Education Act effective in October 1990, which is discussed in more detail below.

ESEA AND IDEA

Of the aforementioned federal education acts, applying to all states and all school districts, the two most potent are the Elementary and Secondary Education Act of 1965 (reconstituted into a block grant in 1981) and the Individuals with Disabilities Education Act. With the possible exception of vocational education laws, these laws constitute the weightiest federal assistance to elementary and secondary education, both in terms of money and regulation. For this reason we will discuss the main provisions of both acts. ESEA's primary purpose is to help states provide meaningful instruction for educationally deprived children. The ten titles of the 1981 blocked version of ESEA also include several other categorical grants designed to provide other educational thrusts as well.

Elementary and Secondary Education Act (ESEA)

The concern over the proliferation of the number of federal categorical programs and the burden of extensive reporting requirements that had fallen on states and localities had created a desire to consolidate funding sources and the attendant procedures and processes. As a result of this preceived problem, Congress passed the Education Consolidation and Improvement Act (ECIA) which became effective in July 1982. Under the new act, the old Elementary and Secondary Education Act was replaced by block grants that eliminated several categorical programs. The enunciated intent of the new legislation was to allow state education agencies to administer the funds "with a minimum of paperwork."[44] The block grant consolidation was designated and defined in three chapters.

Chapter 1, Title I, ESEA.   This part authorized the continuation of Title I, ESEA and rewrote several administrative provisions to reduce reporting requirements. The statement of purpose of Chapter 1 in the act states:

> The purpose of assistance under this chapter is to improve the educational opportunities of educationally deprived children by helping such children succeed in the regular program of the local educational agency, attain grade-level proficiency, and improve achievement in basic and more advanced skills. These purposes shall be accomplished through such means as supplemental education programs, schoolwide programs, and the increased involvement of parents in their children's education.[45]

The actual declaration of policy for Chapter 1 states,

> In recognition of—
> (1) the special educational needs of children of low-income families and the impact of concentrations of low-income families on the ability of local educational agencies to provide educational programs which meet such needs, and
> (2) the special educational needs of children of migrant parents, of Indian children, and of handicapped, neglected, and delinquent children, the Congress declares it to be the policy of the United States to—
> (A) provide financial assistance to State and local educational agencies to meet the special needs of such educationally deprived children at the preschool, elementary, and secondary levels;
> (B) expand the program authorized by this chapter over the next 5 years . . . with the intent of serving all eligible children by fiscal year 1993; and
> (C) provide such assistance in a way which eliminates unnecessary administrative burden and paperwork and overly prescriptive regulations and provides flexibility to State and local educational agencies in making educational decisions.[46]

Chapter 1 funds are allocated under two basic types of grants, basic and concentration grants. Basic grants distribute the large majority of Chapter 1 funds; 89 percent of Chapter 1 funds in 1992 were basic grants. This portion of the distribution has not been changed to any significant degree since the early 1970s. Basic grants are allocated annually to counties according to a formula that uses two factors: the number of formula-eligible children in each county and the average expenditure per pupil in each state.[47]

Concentration grants allocate supplemental funds to local education agencies with high numbers or high percentages of poor children. Counties receive these funds if their formula-eligible children exceed 6,500 or the number of such children constitutes 15 percent or more of all school-age children (ages 5–17) in the county.[48]

The basic grants allocation formula determines the formula-eligible children by totalling the number of children ages 5–17 with family incomes below the poverty level *plus* the number of children ages 5–17 in families receiving Aid to Families with Dependent Children (AFDC) when these payments are above the current census poverty level, plus the number of children ages 5–17 in institutions for neglected and delinquent children that are not state-operated, plus the number of children ages 5–17 in foster homes supported with public funds.[49]

This number of formula-eligible children is then multiplied by 40 percent of the per-pupil expenditures for the respective state, and is not to be less than 80 percent nor more than 120 percent of the national average per-pupil expenditure. Further, provisions guarantee that a county will not receive less than 85 percent of its previous year's allocation and a small state assurance program.

In the 1993 fiscal year, basic grants for local education agencies totalled $5.4 billion dollars of Chapter 1 funds while concentration grants amounted to $676 million.[50]

Chapter 1 funding during the 1980s failed to incease and in fact in 1990 the inflation-adjusted amount per eligible-pupil amount remained below the 1980 level. In 1980, Chapter 1 funding per participant was $916 in constant 1991–92 dollars while in 1990–91, the corresponding amount was $884. In 1979–80 there were 5.162 million participating children and in 1990–91 there were 5.546 million.[51] As shown in Table 12.1, the actual inflation-adjusted appropriation had increased from $4.733 billion to $4.905 billion in

TABLE 12.1   Chapter 1 Funding

YEAR	APPROPRIATIONS CURRENT $ IN BILLIONS	ANNUAL CHANGE	APPROPRIATIONS (INFLATION-ADJUSTED) CONSTANT 1991–92 $ IN BILLIONS	ANNUAL CHANGE
1979–80	$ 2.777		$ 4.733	
1980–81	$ 2.732	−1.6%	$ 4.191	−11.4%
1981–82	$ 2.611	−4.4%	$ 3.738	−10.8%
1982–83	$ 2.563	−1.9%	$ 3.547	−5.1%
1983–84	$ 2.758	7.6%	$ 3.696	4.2%
1984–85	$ 3.004	8.9%	$ 3.887	5.2%
1985–86	$ 3.200	6.5%	$ 4.053	4.3%
1986–87	$ 3.062	−4.3%	$ 3.777	-6.8%
1987–88	$ 3.454	12.8%	$ 4.094	8.4%
1988–89	$ 3.830	10.9%	$ 4.335	5.9%
1989–90	$ 4.026	5.1%	$ 4.349	0.3%
1990–91	$ 4.768	18.4%	$ 4.905	12.8%
1991–92	$ 5.558	16.6%	$ 5.558	13.3%
1992–93	$ 6.134	10.4%	$ 5.944	7.1%
1993–94	$ 6.126	−0.1%	$ 5.745	−3.5%

Source: U.S. Department of Education, *Targeting, Formula, and Resource Allocation Issues: Focusing Federal Funds Where the Needs Are Greatest* (Washington, DC: U.S. Department of Education, 1993), p. 9; U. S. Department of Education, Budget Service (appropriations); U.S. Office of Management and Budget (CPI-W inflation index); Westat, Inc., *Summary of Chapter I Participation and Achievement Information, 1990–91*, unpublished manuscript (participation); National Center for Education Statistics, *Digest of Education Statistics, 1992* (total current education expenditures per pupil). Inflation-adjusted figures differ from the Interim Report for the National Assessment of Chapter 1 because the inflation index has been updated.

1990–91 to $5.745 billion in 1993–94. The appropriation increases from 1992 to 1994 will presumably push the per-pupil Chapter 1 funding levels, in constant dollars, back above the 1980 level.[52]

Under this act a local education agency may use funds only for programs and projects which are designed to meet the particular needs of educationally deprived children. Educationally deprived children are defined as those between the ages of 5 and 17, inclusive, those from families below the poverty level, and those eligible for aid to dependent families. Also included are those under approved state plans pursuant to Title IV of the Social Security Act and for those neglected and delinquent children living in foster homes supported by public funds.[53]

The programs and projects under Chapter 1 may include preschool through secondary programs, including the acquisition of equipment, instructional materials, books, and school library resources. Salaries and wages may be paid for personnel including teachers, librarians, education aides, and other personnel, as appropriate. Payment for construction of school facilities may also be made where necessary. Further, state and local education agencies are encouraged to develop year-round programs and services for educationally deprived children.[54] Other provisions of Chapter 1, Title I, include:

- *Part B, Chapter 1, Title I, ESEA* is a program entitled "Even Start" operating at the local level for the purpose of integrating early childhood education and adult education for parents in a unified program.
- *Part C, Chapter 1, Title I, ESEA* is designed to improve basic skills and assist in preventing dropouts.[55]
- *Part D, Chapter 1, Title I, ESEA* funds programs directly operated by state education agencies for the development of special programs for migrating children, disabled children, and neglected and delinquent children.

Chapter 2, Title I, ESEA.   Under this part of the law, funds are provided for federal, state, and local partnerships for educational improvement. The purpose is to enable State and local educational agencies to implement promising or innovative programs that can be demonstrated to be effective in improving student achievement, student behavior, teaching, learning, and school management. Further, these funds are to provide a continuing source of innovation, educational improvement, and support for library and instructional materials.[56]

This chapter consolidated 29 federal categorical programs that before 1981 had been authorized under six different education acts.[57]

Title II, ESEA.   This portion of the ESEA is for critical skills improvement. For fear that U.S. students were falling behind students of other nations in the critical skill areas of mathematics, science, and foreign languages, Congress moved to encourage and give incentives to states to improve the quality of mathematics and science educational programs. The statement of purpose of Part A of Title II, entitled the Dwight D. Eisenhower Mathematics and Science Education Act,[58] says,

> The purpose of this part is to strengthen the economic competitiveness and national security of the United States by improving the skills of teachers and the quality of instruction in mathematics and science in the Nation's public and private elementary and secondary schools through assistance to State educational agencies, local educational agencies, and institutions of higher education.[59]

The act authorized the U.S. Secretary of Education to make grants to states for the purpose of strengthening the skills of teachers and improving instruction in mathematics and science.

Part B of Title II, ESEA resulted from conclusions drawn by Congress that "the economic and security interests of the Nation require significant improvement in the quantity and quality of foreign language instruction."[60] This part responds to that concern by creating the Foreign Language Assistance Act of 1988.[61]

Part C of Title II, ESEA provides for presidential awards for teaching excellence in mathematics, science, and foreign languages.[62]

Title III, ESEA is for assistance to magnet schools[63] with the purpose of preventing minority group isolation while strengthening the students' knowledge of academic subjects and improving their grasp of "tangible and marketable vocational skills."[64]

Title IV, ESEA is a catch-all provision that provides some funding for women's educational equity; gifted and talented educational programs; fellowship programs for students, teachers, older Americans, and recent immigrants; territorial assistance; and an innovation program to be directly administered by the U.S. Secretary of Education.[65]

Title V, ESEA is entitled the Drug-Free Schools and Community Act of 1986. The law provides for a variety of grants for local and intermediate educational agencies, consortia, and community-based organizations to create programs for drug abuse prevention, rehabilitation referral, and the education of dropouts and other high-risk youth. Portions of this funding are designated for institutions of higher education.[66]

Title VI, ESEA is for projects and programs designed to address school dropout problems and to strengthen basic skills instruction.

Title VII, ESEA is the Bilingual Education Act.[67] This act recognizes that the "Federal Government has a special and continuing obligation to assist language minority students to acquire English language proficiency. . . ." In addressing that obligation, this act declares it to be the policy of the United States "to establish equal educational opportunity by encouraging the establishment and operation of bilingual educational programs and to encourage special alternative programs for children with limited English proficiency."[68]

Title X, ESEA contains general administrative provisions. These ten titles make up the ESEA as it now stands, eight are briefly discussed herein. Originally, in 1965, there were five titles with much different and more limited

purposes. The ESEA today constitutes a large block of several separate categorical grants that have been merged for the purpose of reducing paperwork. Taken in totality, however, the act exhibits little coherence and only limited overall policy purpose and direction.

Individuals with Disabilities Education Act

Perhaps the second most important federal initiative after the ESEA is federal assistance for the education of disabled children. This is the successor law to the Education for All Handicapped Children Act of 1975, Public Law 94-142 enacted November 29, 1975 and amended October 30, 1990, Public Law 101-476. The purpose of this act is to assure that all children with disabilities have available to them "a free appropriate public education" which emphasizes special education and related services designed to meet the children's unique needs.

The need for the Act was set out by Congress as:

1. There are more than eight million disabled children in the United States today.
2. The special educational needs of such children are not being fully met.
3. More than half of the disabled children in the United States do not receive the appropriate educational services that would enable them to have full equality of opportunity.
4. One million of the disabled children in the United States are excluded entirely from the public school system and will not go through the educational process with their peers.
5. There are many disabled children throughout the United States participating in regular school programs whose disabilities prevent them from having a successful educational experience because their disabilities are undetected.[69]

The allocation formula for funds distributed to the states under this act contemplates a specified percentage of the public elementary and secondary schools' average per-pupil expenditure. Unfortunately the actual appropriations have not kept pace with the more lofty funding goals to which the authorizing legislation aspires. The allocation is based upon the number of children with disabilities for programs not to exceed 12 percent of the number of all children 3 to 17 years of age. The law actually provides a special contract provision to assist states in the education of children with disabilities from birth to eight years of age and for post-secondary education.[70]

TRENDS IN FEDERAL FUNDING

Political pressure to reduce governmental expenditures was most directly manifested at the federal level of government during the late 1970s and throughout the 1980s. As the federal government became more parsimonious toward education and other social programs, greater costs were shifted to the state and local levels. The decade of the 1980s saw a decline in the federal effort to support elementary and secondary education. From 1965 to the late 1970s federal funds for elementary and secondary education rose steadily and then in the 1980s fell dramatically once again only to crawl back upward in the early 1990s. Figure 12.3 shows the rise and fall in constant dollars since 1965 for on-budget federal funds, that is, funds derived from Congressional appropriations. In 1975 the federal government appropriated support in current dollars of $10.6 billion for elementary and secondary schools; the amount rose to $16.0 billion in 1980, then fell to $14.5 billion in 1983, finally to rise to $21.9 billion in 1990 and an estimated $28.3 billion in 1992.

In constant dollars, however, as shown in Figure 12.3, the picture is much different. Adjusted to 1992 constant dollars, the 1975 appropriated amount was equivalent to $27.1 billion, the 1980 amount to $27.4 billion, the 1983 amount to $20.1 billion, the 1990 amount to $23.7 billion and in 1992 the constant dollar

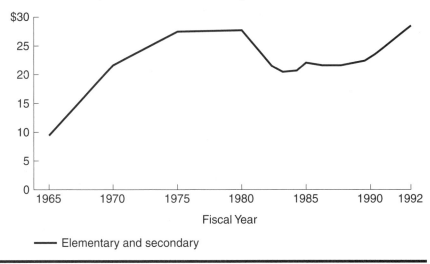

In Billions of Dollars (in constant FY 1992 dollars)

Fiscal Year

⎯⎯ Elementary and secondary

FIGURE 12.3   Federal On-Budget Funds for Elementary and Secondary Education, by Level: 1965 to 1992

Source: U.S. Office of Management and Budget, *Budget of the U.S. Government,* fiscal years 1967 to 1993; National Science Foundation, *Federal Funds for Research and Development,* fiscal years 1965 to 1992 and unpublished data.

amount was $28.3 billion. As the comparison of constant dollars indicates, the severity of the decline in the mid-1980s was far greater than a comparison of current dollars reveals. In current dollars the dip from 1980 to 1983 was only about $1.5 billion, but in 1992 dollars, there was a decline of $7.3 billion. By 1990 the federal funding of $23.7 billion still fell significantly below the 1980 $27.4 billion constant dollar figure. Only in 1992 had the funding of elementary and secondary education returned to its 1980 constant dollar level.

The trend toward greater reliance on local taxation for the support of elementary and secondary schools is shown in Figure 12.4. In

1980–81 local taxation provided 42.7 percent of school revenues and the federal and state governments contributed 8.5 percent and 48.8 percent, respectively. By 1993–94 state revenue had declined by nearly 3 percentage points and federal revenue had declined by about 1.5 percentage points. Concurrently, local school districts were forced to increase their revenue by nearly 5 percentage points. This trend is not a positive one for public education. The local revenue disparities found in most states contribute materially to inequalities in educational opportunity. The school financing inequalities that are the subject of the school equity cases nationwide emanate from unequalized local taxation. Fed-

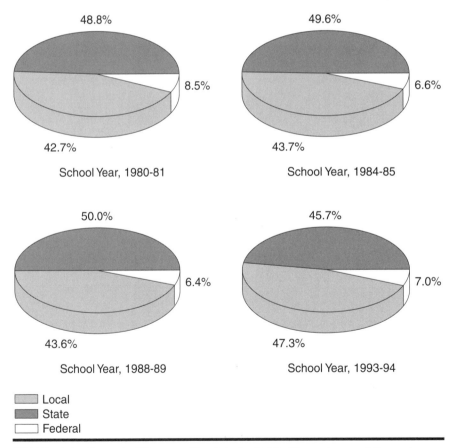

48.8%

8.5%

42.7%

School Year, 1980-81

49.6%

6.6%

43.7%

School Year, 1984-85

50.0%

6.4%

43.6%

School Year, 1988-89

45.7%

7.0%

47.3%

School Year, 1993-94

☐ Local
■ State
☐ Federal

FIGURE 12.4 Percent of Revenue Receipts for Public Elementary and Secondary Education, by Source, Selected School Years, 1980–81 to 1992–93

Source: National Education Association, *Estimates of School Statistics,* various years.

Box 12.2 _____

Expanded Federal Role

An expanded federal role is desired by many who believe that only by the infusion of federal funds can equalization among states be achieved. A federal effort to achieve a national level of financial support for all students is deemed consistent with intrastate equalization obtained through minimum foundation programs. The national interest in both a healthy economy and a strong defense would be served by a program of general education support that could only be achieved through the taxing power of the federal government. Anything less than interstate equalization leaves students in some sections of the country at a disadvantage.

Source: National Education Association, *What Everyone Should Know About Financing Our Schools* (Washington, DC: NEA, 1993), p. 30.

EQUALIZING TENDENCIES OF FEDERAL FUNDS

That federal subventions should be designed to contribute to equality and to serve to some extent as redistributional mechanisms in advancing a specified national purpose is commonly avowed as a national interest.

Today the flow of federal funds for all programs, including education, to the states has a net equalizing effect. Table 12.2 shows the per-capita net flow of all federal funds from 1988 to 1990 for the top 10 states in per-capita personal income and the 10 lowest. This table shows the federal expenditure for all purposes minus federal tax collections. If we simply take the unweighted average, we see that the per-capita flow of all federal funds to the poorest states is substantial. Factors influencing this flow include the progressivity of federal tax collections coupled with the equalization features of the federal allocation formulas. Of course tax structure and distribution formulas do not account for all the differences. Categorical grants of various sorts for special purposes, such as national installations for research, military, and other national in-

eral policy inadvertently contributes to inequality when the federal and state funding levels decline and more fiscal pressure is relegated downward to local governments.

TABLE 12.2   Per Capita Federal Funds, 1988–1990, Ranked According to 1990 Per Capita Personal Income (parenthesis indicate net loss)

INCOME RANK	TEN RICHEST STATES	FEDERAL	INCOME RANK	TEN POOREST STATES	FEDERAL
1	Connecticut	(1,161)	41	North Dakota	1,533
2	New Jersey	(1,989)	42	South Carolina	816
3	Massachusetts	(39)	43	Alabama	1,100
4	New York	(831)	44	Kentucky	611
5	Maryland	1,002	45	Louisiana	525
6	Alaska	971	46	New Mexico	2,929
7	New Hampshire	(1,216)	47	Arkansas	754
8	California	(253)	48	Utah	1,131
9	Illinois	(1,154)	49	West Virginia	853
10	Hawaii	1,270	50	Mississippi	1,613
Unweighted Average		(340)			1,187

Source: ACIR, *Significant Features of Fiscal Federalism, Revenues and Expenditures*, vol. 2 (Washington, DC: U.S. Advisory Commission on Intergovernmental Relations, October 1991), M-176-11, Map 1, p. 9.

terests make a substantial difference in the continuity of the pattern.

Elementary and Secondary School Equalization

With regard to federal funds for public schools alone, the data are less dramatically egalitarian, but nevertheless create a positive movement toward equality. In 1971 the National Educational Finance Project, in analyzing the equalization aspects of federal funds to public schools, found that all federal funds for public schools combined to produce an equalizing effect.[71]

Later, studying the equalizing effects of federal funds in 1972, Berke and others concluded that federal funds had only a mild equalizing effect among school districts within states. He identified interdistrict negative correlations between per-pupil revenues from major federal programs and median family income in metropolitan areas as follows: California –0.27, New York –0.31, Texas –0.67, Michigan –0.17 and Massachusetts –0.30. That is, there were nega-

tive relationships between the amounts of federal revenue allocations and median family income, thereby providing some fiscal equalization. However, among these states, only in Texas did federal funds show a particularly strong equalizing correlation.[72] The pattern of moderate equalization was not, however, consistent. Some districts with low median family income actually received less federal funding per pupil than some more affluent districts. Also, Berke found that when ESEA, Title I funds were removed, the remaining federal funds were either random or displayed a slight disequalizing tendency.[73]

Several measures today suggest that current federal distributions have equalizing effects. We know that the poorer states receive a substantially greater percentage of their public school revenues from the federal government than do the richest states. Table 12.3 shows that in 1991–92 the estimated percentage of revenue that came from federal sources ranged from 16.9 percent in Mississippi, the poorest state, to 2.5 percent in New Hampshire, one of the richest states. As this table indicates, there is a definite pattern of a greater

TABLE 12.3   Estimated Percent of Revenue for Public Elementary and Secondary Schools from the Federal Government, 1993–94

INCOME RANK	TEN RICHEST STATES	% FEDERAL	INCOME RANK	TEN POOREST STATES	% FEDERAL
1	Connecticut	4.6	41	North Dakota	11.8
2	New Jersey	3.4	42	South Carolina	9.3
3	Massachusetts	6.1	43	Alabama	12.7
4	New York	5.9	44	Kentucky	9.9
5	Maryland	5.6	45	Louisiana	11.7
6	Alaska	12.6	46	New Mexico	12.8
7	New Hampshire	2.8	47	Arkansas	9.4
8	California	8.8	48	Utah	6.8
9	Illinois	8.2	49	West Virginia	7.9
10	Hawaii	7.9	50	Mississippi	17.7
Unweighted Average		6.1			11.0
Without Alaska		5.9			
U.S. Average		7.0			7.0

Source: National Education Association, *Rankings of the States, 1993* (Washington, DC: NEA, 1993), Table F–10, p. 47.

percentage of federal funds flowing to poorer states. If Utah and Alaska are excluded from their respective groups, all states in the poor group in Table 12.3 receive higher percentages of funding from the federal government than the states in the richest group. From this evidence alone it may be concluded that even though the federal funding levels are generally quite low relative to state and local funding, the federal funds do appear to have an equalizing effect.

Another and perhaps more accurate view of the equalizing tendencies of federal funds can be obtained by comparing the actual dollar amounts per pupil that flow to the various states. Table 12.4 shows the federal funds for elementary and secondary education per pupil in average daily attendance. Using per-capita personal income as the criterion to determine rich and poor states, we see that the poor states generally receive greater per-pupil federal funding. For example, the poorest state, Mississippi, receives $648 per pupil and the richest state, Connecticut, $385. West Virginia is allocated more per pupil than New Jersey, New Mexico is provided more than New York, Louisiana gets more than Massachusetts, and so on. If Alaska is excluded from the comparison, due to its high cost of living and extensive federal presence then the unweighted average allocation for the groups is $90 per pupil more for the poor states than for the rich. Even when Alaska is included, the rich group receives less than the U.S. average of $420 and the poor group $81 more than the U.S. average.

A simple correlation between federal public school revenues per pupil in ADA in 1992–93 and personal income per pupil in ADA shows a slightly negative correlation of –0.1024, a small equalizing tendency. The federal funds, however, are shown to have stronger equalizing aspects if the criterion for equality is effective buying income per household, rather than personal income per pupil. The correlation between federal aid per pupil and effective buying income per household is –0.4754, indicating that federal funds do have a relatively strong equalizing tendency. Thus these simple tests do indicate that current

TABLE 12.4 Federal Revenue for Elementary and Secondary Education Per Pupil in Average Daily Attendance, 1993–94

INCOME RANK	TEN RICHEST STATES	FEDERAL REVENUE PER ADA	INCOME RANK	TEN POOREST STATES	FEDERAL REVENUE PER ADA
1	Connecticut	$415	41	Oklahoma	$348
2	New Jersey	364	42	Alabama	519
3	Massachusetts	453	43	South Carolina	480
4	New York	563	44	Idaho	362
5	Maryland	393	45	Louisiana	602
6	New Hampshire	197	46	New Mexico	682
7	Hawaii	540	47	Arkansas	428
8	Alaska	1226	48	Utah	273
9	California	473	49	West Virginia	508
10	Delaware	589	50	Mississippi	690
Unweighted Average		$521			$513
Without Alaska		$443			
U.S. Average		$446			$446

Source: National Education Association, *1993–94 Estimates of School Statistics* (Washington, DC: NEA, 1994), pp. 33 and 38.

Note: Unweighted average means that we simply added the amounts and divided by ten.

federal funds have beneficial redistributional tendencies.

All of this of course assumes that these income measures are appropriate equalization criteria. This type of analysis has the very obvious limitation that it refers merely to fiscal equalization, dollar per scholar horizontal equity, and does not take into account the varying educational needs among the states. Because a high percentage of the federal funding is influenced by the Chapter 1, Title I, ESEA counting of educationally deprived children, the actual dollar amounts among states can be expected to vary substantially from a simple linear relationship.

Status of Federal Funding

Table 12.5 shows the major areas of emphasis of federal funds for elementary and secondary education. The generic area of grants for the disadvantaged is the predominant area of funding, rising from $3.2 billion in 1980 to nearly $6.6 billion in 1992. Funds for school improvement and education of the disabled also consume a substantial portion of federal education re-

sources and have had the greatest percentage increase since 1980 of any of the major areas of federal funding. In 1980 the federal contribution for the education of the disabled student was only $409. By 1992 this amount had increased to $1,169. One should bear in mind, though, that this amount still remains only a small portion, of what it actually costs a typical local school district to educate the disabled child.

The policy of Congress in providing categorical aid for the public schools has been to designate federal appropriations to provide for certain educational needs that its members believed were not being met adequately by the public schools. Categorical aid obviously creates much more control over the public schools than does general aid. Advocates of categorical grants believe the controls are benign for the following reasons:

1. States and boards of education can refuse to accept a categorical grant if the grantee objects to the federal controls accompanying the grant.
2. Federal interest requires that certain unmet educational needs be specifically provided for by categorical grants.

TABLE 12.5   Summary of Federal Funds for Elementary and Secondary Education Administered by U.S. Department of Education

	1980	1985	1992
Grants for Disadvantaged	3,204,664	3,745,855	6,560,500
School Improvement Programs	788,918	748,000	1,910,890
Bilingual Education	169,540	171,605	225,407
Native-American Education*	75,900	67,404	76,710
School Assistance in Federally Affected Areas	812,873	695,746	807,375
Education of the Disabled (IDEA)	1,555,253	2,666,056	5,332,672
Vocational Education and Adult Programs	1,153,743	856,271	1,893,377

Source: National Center for Education Statistics, *Digest of Education Statistics 1992* (U.S. Department of Education, 1992), Table 349, p. 371.

Note: This table shows funds (in current dollars) distributed by the U.S. Department of Education only and does not include other federal agency funds such as those for Native-American education distributed through the U.S. Department of Interior.

These categorical grants to the public schools undoubtedly cause a great deal of paperwork by the agencies receiving them. However, the educational opportunities of the culturally and economically deprived and the disabled have been greatly expanded by these grants.

What are the prospects for federal funds for education in the 1990s? Currently, there is great political pressure to reduce federal expenditures for all purposes because of the federal deficit, yet the Clinton budget recommendations for 1994 called for relatively substantial increases in federal categorical funds, especially for disadvantaged children where the proposed increase was about 10 percent.

THE FUTURE OF FEDERAL FUNDING

What the Clinton years will hold for public elementary and secondary education is as yet uncertain. To project the emerging federal role in education under a new administration would be hazardous indeed, but we also know that changes will occur due to substantial philosophical shifts. Regardless of political philosophy, however, we do know that the massive federal budget deficit introduces a realism that will work to the detriment of any substantial federal outlays for education in the near future.

Choice: Vouchers and Tuition Tax Credits

Philosophically, the Clinton administration will have a more communitarian orientation, stressing the values of community interest rather than individualistic self-interest. The communitarian values are in keeping with the public common school ideals emphasizing cooperation rather than competition. In this regard it has already become evident that the Clinton administration will eschew the voucher and tuition tax credit funding options that would feed federal tax dollars into private and parochial schools. Upon assuming his new position of Secretary of Education in the Clinton cabinet, Richard Riley, former Governor of South Carolina made it clear that the

Clinton administration was in favor of parental choice of schools, but such choice should be limited to the public sector. The Progressive Policy Institute, an organization that repeatedly has the ear of the Clinton administration, in what may be an accurate reflection of the current Democratic philosophy toward choice, has said,

> The purpose of choice is to create a new form of public education, not to finance private schools or to transform public education into private education. . . . It is possible to introduce the dynamics necessary for change and improvement into the public education system while still retaining its essential principle, and the values of opportunity, diversity, and community that are so important to this democracy. Private education should remain and will remain; but as private education, privately financed.[74]

With regard to choice and tuition tax credits as a means to obtain public support of private schools, Robert Reich, Clinton's Secretary of Labor, has written, "Proposed tax credits for parents who send their children to private schools would further erode middle-class support for public education."[75] This presumably will be the position of the Clinton administration.

Youth Apprenticeship

Much has been said about the "forgotten half" of U.S. youth who do not go on to college.[76] Any type of comprehensive view of educational change must accommodate this large and essentially underdeveloped well of human resources. In seeking viable options for education and training, Clinton administration planners have looked with interest upon the highly regarded German, Swiss, and Austrian apprenticeship programs. These plans provide for a more direct transition from school into the workforce. In the German system apprentices normally spend one day a week at a *Berufsaschule* (state vocational school) that specializes in the chosen trade of the student, and four days a week in a structured program at the employer's work site under the guidance of a master of the trade.[77] During the period of training, the apprentices are paid a training wage, that increases during the course of the apprenticeship.[78] This system was formalized in the German Vocational Training Act of 1969. Today most German secondary school graduates who do not go on to college become apprentices in one of the 480 trades and occupations at the age of 15 or 16.[79] In this regard, Marshall and Tucker have said,

> The superb preparation of the German front-line worker is a key factor in German economic success. It provides workers who are not only well trained for specific occupations, but, because of the quality of the basic school system, creates a pool of workers with the flexibility to learn new skills quickly, contributing heavily to the capacity of the German industrial system to respond quickly to changes in consumer taste.[80]

While it would be unrealistic to attempt to transplant another national system of education and training into the United States, it is certain that many valuable lessons can and will be learned from carefully examining foreign successes. It seems likely that the Clinton administration and Congress will support some type of modified apprenticeship program, perhaps grafted on to the present system of vocational and community college education in the United States. At least there appears to be a new vitality in the federal government's interest in such efforts.

Goals for 2000

One may also expect a continuing federal advocacy of the six goals adopted by the state governors in working with the Bush administration. The goals, as enunciated in the state governors response to Bush's America 2000, An Education Strategy,[81] stated:

1. By the year 2000, all children in the United States will start school ready to learn.
2. By the year 2000, the high-school graduation rate will increase to at least 90 percent.

3. By the year 2000, U.S. students will leave grades four, eight, and twelve having demonstrated competency in challenging subject matter including English, mathematics, science, history, and geography, and every school in the United States will ensure that all students learn to use their minds well, so they may be prepared for responsible citizenship, further learning, and productive employment in our modern economy.
4. By the year 2000, every adult in the United States will be literate and will possess the knowledge and skills necessary to compete in a global economy and exercise the rights and responsibilities of citizenship.
5. By the year 2000, every school in the United States will be free of drugs and violence and will offer a disciplined environment conducive to learning.

These goals, though laudable, were largely rhetorical and their actual realization given the federal budget deficit was highly problematical. It was to be largely a state effort without federal funding. The Clinton administration has vowed to pursue these goals for the year 2000, but it may be anticipated that there will be a more assertive federal role in the funding of education despite the federal budget deficit. In addition it is reasonable to expect some type of a system of national testing, as well as an attempt to create minimal volitional national curriculum standards. Recent legislation has already established various commissions to move toward that end. Whether such efforts will materialize into a federal initiative is uncertain, but more accuracy and sophistication in comparative test analysis as well as improvements in data processing make such efforts more politically feasible.

Children at Risk

Almost certainly the 1990s will see a reassertion of the federal interest in helping the underprivileged and at-risk children. The initiatives begun in 1965 under the Elementary and Secondary

Education Act will presumably be given new life in the 1990s. The plight of at-risk children in benighted rural areas and the worsening of the core city educational problems are clarion indicators of the necessity of a major federal financial commitment to the education of underprivileged children. As observed in Chapters 6 and 7 of this book, the expansion of income inequality in the United States since 1980 dramatizes the urgency of this dilemma. Reich has noted,

> Most poorer towns and regions in the United States have grown relatively poorer; most wealthier towns and regions, relatively wealthier. American cities and counties with the lowest per-person incomes in 1979 had dropped even further below the nation's average by the 1980s; cities and counties with the highest incomes headed in the opposite direction.[82]

As a result the underprivileged are in relatively worse circumstances today than in 1980 and the corresponding educational burdens on the schools are even greater. Thus the costs of dealing with at-risk children are of greater magnitude today and the need for major initiatives at the federal level to address the problem has become more pronounced.

In response, the U.S. House of Representatives, prior to the retirement of Augustus Hawkins, produced a 1990 report that advocated not only increased equity in funding at the state level but a more affirmative federal response to the problems of at-risk children.[83]

Levin has estimated that there are at least 13 million at-risk students and that funding a meaningful educational program would cost an additional $2,000 per student, a total bill of about $26 billion.[84] The federal Chapter 1 program now devoted to at-risk children funds only about one-fifth of this amount. Assuming that the states and the federal government shared the necessary additional costs for the education of at-risk children, the federal share would of course be substantially less than the $26 billion total that is needed. While the appropriate amount to be derived from federal resources is

uncertain, one could logically maintain, as did the National Educational Finance Project in 1971, that the federal government should fund at least 30 percent of the burden. Thirty percent of $26 billion would find the federal government increasing its contribution for the education of at-risk children by about $3 billion. Levin has suggested an even greater federal sharing of 60 percent based on the fact that the federal government collects about 60 percent of all taxes in the United States.[85] Regardless of the amount, it is reasonable to expect a renewed federal interest in the resolution of the educational problems of underprivileged children. This will likely transpire as a supplement to the current Chapter 1, ESEA program.

Fiscal Equity

Increasingly, Congress has become more concerned about the wide revenue disparities in state school funding. In 1990, Representative Hawkins, Chairman of the House Education Committee, proposed legislation that would stimulate corrective action by state legislatures. According to Hawkins, at-risk children were doubly shortchanged because the state school finance formulas usually provided less funding to students with the greatest needs. Hawkins's bill entitled The Fair Chance Act was designed to motivate the states to take action toward greater equalization of funding among school districts. The purpose of the proposed legislation as described by Wise was to encourage states "to do the right thing."[86] Wise said, "The Fair Chance Act would create additional incentives for states to provide what they morally, legally and prudentially should— equal educational opportunity."[87]

In this regard the former Governor of Arkansas, President Clinton, said that a greater federal role in education should be calculated to "coax and embarrass states and schools into meeting higher standards of educational equity and attainments."[88] In commenting on the proposed Hawkins legislation, Christopher P. Lu observed, "A more active federal role can spur school finance reform in the 1990s, but federal action will be effective only with greater federal spending for education."[89]

With regard to the federal role in stimulating equity, Alexander[90] in testimony before the U.S. House Education and Labor Committee said that a federal initiative for elementary and secondary education should recognize and take into account several factors.

1. A federal plan should acknowledge the importance of investment in education in "nation building" and confirm that adequate funding of elementary and secondary schools is in the national interest and is a national priority. Such a plan should advance the value of elementary and secondary education as a public investment and call for the fashioning of investment strategies in keeping with that objective.

2. A federal plan should provide incentives for states to create and fund more uniform and equitable state systems of education. Attention should be explicitly given to the problems of fiscal disparities among school districts and to the effects of unequal education on the lower economic and working classes of Americans. Measures should be taken to accelerate efforts taken by state courts and legislatures to reduce these problems of disparate and inadequate funding.

3. The plan should be funded by the federal government at a level sufficient to maintain a competitive standard of federal fiscal effort and to provide an incentive and impetus for states to more adequately and equitably fund their elementary and secondary schools.

4. The plan should, importantly, take into account the fluid and changing mix of educational needs of children and the corresponding educational burdens confronting state school systems.

While these guidelines may generally apply to nearly all federal programs for education, they are particularly appropriate for federal plans that would promote equity in state school funding formulas.

SUMMARY AND CONCLUSIONS

In this chapter we saw how the federal role in the financing of education evolved from the original system of land grants to the specific categorical financial grants of today. An historical, political, and constitutional perspective was presented, all of which had important implications for the forming of the present structure of federal and state relations in education today.

U.S. federalism is the foundational concept on which the federal role is premised. Education is primarily a function reserved to the states by the U.S. Constitution. The federal role is indirect, but may be pervasive depending on the nature of the federal interest.

Criteria for federal aid are set out as having been formed by both law and convention. These criteria call for an appropriate federal role, administrative arrangements conducive to sound federal–state relationships, adequacy of provision of education, and the fostering of equality of educational opportunity.

Political realities have fashioned federal involvement in education. Both Democratic and Republican positions toward federal aid have changed over the years.

Fear of control, fiscal conservatism, religious opposition, and racial segregation have all played important parts in the extent of federal activity in education.

Constitutional provisions, the General Welfare clause and the Commerce clause have been the specific legal vehicles that empower the Congress to provide funding for education.

State governments are also constitutionally limited by the federal Bill of Rights and the Fourteenth Amendment in the governance and control of education.

The federal impetus for the founding of the public school system was grounded in the early ordinances and land grants, of the late eighteenth century. The Congressional requirements for the conversion from national domain to statehood compelled new states to make provisions for public schools. Beyond the 13 original colonies, enabling legislation for the entry of new states into the Union was fashioned to form and encourage public instruction.

The Morrill Act of 1862 continued the land-grant stimulus of forming comprehensive education systems by originating the great land-grant universities of the United States.

Through other acts of the early twentieth century, including the Smith–Lever Act of 1914 and the Smith–Hughes Act of 1917, the federal government began to provide grants in the form of money rather than land. From that point on, Congressional appropriations resulted in a more obvious and aggressive federal role in education.

The Elementary and Secondary Education Act of 1965 was a watershed event in federal aid to education. At this point the federal government recognized that greater federal funding was in the national interest. Thirty years later this act remains the main vehicle for federal aid to elementary and secondary schools.

More recently, funding for educationally disabled children became a prominent part of federal involvement in financial assistance to education. This legislation has been given renewed emphasis by the enactment of the Individuals with Disabilities Education Act (IDEA).

Trends in federal funding showed a retreat from a federal financial commitment to elementary and secondary education during the decade of the 1980s, but more recent trends suggest a recovery to earlier levels of federal effort. The retrogression of federal effort in the 1980s had the consequence of forcing a greater burden on state and local levels.

The federal formulas in totality, especially those of the ESEA, tend to equalize funds among local school districts. Because the funds flow to children from poor families, those districts with more poor children tend to get a greater proportion of financial aid.

The future of federal funding will of course hinge on the economic condition of the country, the extent of the continuing federal deficit, and the prevailing political philosophy. The philosophy of the current administration will also have much to do with the future strength and viability of the public schools and whether radical mechanisms such as vouchers and tuition tax credits will turn tax money toward nonpublic schools and away from public schools.

KEY TERMS

Division of power
General Welfare clause
Contract clause
Land grants
Ordinance of 1785
Ordinances of 1787
National domain
Congressional township

Sixteenth section
Morrill Act
Smith–Lever Act
Smith–Hughes Act
Defense-related federal acts
Elementary and Secondary
    Education Act (ESEA)

Individuals with Disabilities
    Education Act (IDEA)
Vouchers and tuition tax credits
Youth apprenticeship
Goals for 2000
Children at risk

ENDNOTES

1. National Education Finance Project, *Alternative Programs for Financing Education* (Gainesville, FL: NEFP, 1971), pp. 198–202.
2. R. Freeman Butts and Lawrence A. Cremin, *A History of Education in American Culture* (New York: Henry Holt and Company, 1953), p. 534.

3. Ibid., p. 535.
4. Ibid.
5. Ibid.
6. Ibid., p. 536.
7. Ibid.
8. Ibid., p. 537

9. Newton Edwards, *The Courts and the Public Schools,* 3rd ed. (Chicago: University of Chicago Press, 1971), p. 1.

10. *United States v. Butler*, 297 U.S. 1, 56 S.Ct. 312 (1936).

11. *Helvering v. Davis*, 301 Cr. S 619, 57 S.Ct. 904 (1937).

12. John E. Novak, Ronald D. Rotunda, and J. Nelson Young, *Constitutional Law*, 3rd ed. (St. Paul, MN: West Publishing Company, 1980), p. 181.

13. *Brown v. Board of Education*, 347 U.S. 483, 74 S.Ct. 686 (1954).

14. *Plessey v. Ferguson*, 163 U.S. 537, 16 S.Ct. 138 (1896).

15. *Indiana ex rel. Anderson v. Brand*, 303 U.S. 95, 58 S.Ct. 443 (1938).

16. Ira Harvey, *A History of Educational Finance in Alabama, 1819–1986* (Auburn, AL: The Truman Pierce Institute for Advancement of Teacher Education, Auburn University, 1989), p. 11.

17. Harvey, ibid., p. 12, citing *Journals of the American Congress, From 1774–1788*, vol. IV (Washington, DC: Way and Gideon, 1823).

18. Harvey, op. cit.

19. Ellwood P. Cubberley, *Public Education in the United States* (Boston: Houghton Mifflin, 1934), p. 91.

20. Ibid.

21. Benjamin Horace Hibbard, *A History of the Public Land Policies* (New York: Macmillan, 1924), pp. 32–33.

22. Harvey, op. cit.

23. J. M. Faircloth, "Land Surveying in Alabama," (Montgomery, AL: The Board of Registration for Professional Engineers and Land Surveyors, 1916).

24. Ibid.

25. Harvey, op. cit., p. 12.

26. Ibid.

27. United States Congress, *Journals of the American Congress Vol. IV*, (Washington, DC: Way and Gideon, 1823), pp. 520–521,

28. Willis G. Clark, *History of Education in Alabama* (Washington, DC: U.S. Government Printing Office, 1889), p. 217.

29. Fletcher Harper Swift, *A History of Public Permanent Common School Funds in the United States, 1785–1905* (New York: Henry Holt, 1911), p. 217.

30. See Harvey, op. cit., p. 12, citing *Journals of the American Congress, From 1744–1788*, vol. IX (Washington, DC: Way and Gideon, 1823), p. 753.

31. Catherine Drinker Bowen, *Miracle at Philadelphia* (Boston: Little, Brown, 1966), p. 172.

32. Ibid., p. 173.

33. Harvey, op. cit., p. 13.

34. Bowen, op. cit., p. 173.

35. Ibid.

36. Cubberley, op. cit., p. 92.

37. Harvey, op. cit., p. 13.

38. Ibid., p. 13, citing *Land Laws of the United States,* vol. I, p. 88.

39. Cubberley, op. cit., p. 92.

40. Ibid., p. 93.

41. Ibid.

42. *Hawaii—Admission Into Union*, Public Law 86-3; 73 Stat. 4, March 18, 1959, Laws of 86th Congress—1st Session, Sec. 5(f).

43. U.S.C.A. Title 20, Education 81 to 1686.

44. Federal Register 47, no. 22 (November 19, 1982), *Rules and Regulations* (Washington, DC: U.S. Government Printing Office, 1982), p. 1.

45. 20 U.S.C. 2701.

46. Ibid.

47. Jay Moskowitz, *Targeting, Formula, and Resource Allocation Issues: Focusing Federal Funds Where The Needs Are Greatest*, (Washington, DC: U.S. Department of Education, 1993), pp. 12–17.

48. Ibid.

49. Ibid.

50. Ibid.

51. Ibid.

52. Ibid.

53. *A Compilation of Federal Education Laws, Volume II—Elementary and Secondary Education, Individuals With Disabilities and Related Programs*, prepared for the use of the Committee on Education and Labor, U.S. House of Representatives (Washington, DC: July 1991), serial no. 102-K, Sec. 1005, p. 11.

54. Ibid., Sec. 1012, p. 17.

55. 20 U.S.C. 2761.

56. Ibid., Section 1511, pp. 80–81.

57. Percy E. Burrup, Vern Brimley, Jr., and Rulon R. Garfield, *Financing Education in a Climate of Change*, 4th ed. (Boston: Allyn and Bacon, 1988), p. 205.

58. 20 U.S.C. 2981.

59. 20 U.S.C. 2982, Section 2002.

60. 20 U.S.C. 3002.

61. Ibid.

62. 20 U.S.C. 3011.

63. 20 U.S.C. 3021.

64. 20 U.S.C. 3023.

65. 20 U.S.C,. Subsec. 3041–3151.

66. 20 U.S.C. 3172.

67. 20 U.S.C. 3281.

68. 20 U.S.C. 3282.

69. "Part II—Education and Training of Individuals With Disabilities, Individuals With Disabilities Education Act," *A Compilation of Federal Education Laws,* op. cit., pp. 267–268.

70. Ibid., p. 308.

71. Roe L. Johns, Kern Alexander, and Dewey H. Stollar, eds., *Status and Impact of Educational Finance Programs* (Gainesville, FL: National Educational Finance Project, 1971), p. 261.

72. Joel S. Berke, Stephen K. Bailey, Alan K. Campbell, and Seymour Sacks, "Federal Aid to Public Education: Who Benefits?" *Issues in School Finance,* Select Committee on Equal Educational Opportunity, United States Senate, September, 1972, p. 39.

73. Ibid., p. 41.

74. Will Marshall and Martin Schram, eds., *Mandate for Change* (New York: Berkeley Books, 1993), pp. 135–136.

75. Robert B. Reich, *The Next American Frontier* (New York: Times Books, 1983), p. 214.

76. Marshall and Schram, op. cit., p. 129.

77. Ray Marshall and Marc Tucker, *Thinking for a Living, Education and The Wealth of Nations* (New York: Basic Books, 1992), p. 45.

78. Ibid., p. 44.

79. Ibid., pp. 44–45.

80. Ibid.

81. *Educating America: State Strategies for Achieving the National Education Goals*, Report of the Task Force on Education (Washington, DC: The National Governors' Association, 1990), p. 12.

82. Robert B. Reich, *The Work of Nations* (New York: Alfred A. Knopf, 1991), p. 273.

83. William Taylor and Dianne Peche, *A Report on Shortchanging Children: The Impact of Fiscal Inequity on the Education of Students at Risk*, prepared for the Committee on Education and Labor, U.S. House of Representatives, 101st Congress (Washington, DC: U.S. Government Printing Office, 1990).

84. Henry Levin, "Economics of Investing in the Educationally Disadvantaged," *American Economic Review* 79 (May 1989), pp. 52–56; "Financing the Education of At-Risk Students," *Educational Evaluation and Policy Analysis* 11, no. 1 (Spring 1990), pp. 47–60.

85. Levin, op. cit.

86. Arthur Wise, *The Fair Chance Act*, Testimony before the Subcommittee on Elementary, Secondary, and Vocational Education of the House Committee on Education and Labor, 101st Congress, 2d Session, 1990, p. 61.

87. Ibid.

88. "Governors and Experts are Divided on Setting Nation's Education Goals," *New York Times*, (December 6, 1989), sec. B14, col. 4.

89. Christopher P. Lu, "Liberator or Captor: Defining the Role of the Federal Government in School Finance Reform," *Harvard Journal on Legislation* 28, no. 2 (Summer 1991), p. 564.

90. Kern Alexander, "Financing the Public Schools of the United States: A Perspective on Effort, Need, and Equity," *Journal of Education Finance* 17, no. 3 (Winter 1992), pp. 142–43.

CHAPTER 13

PERSONNEL POLICIES AND TEACHER SALARIES

TOPICAL OUTLINE OF CHAPTER

Policies • Collective Bargaining • Supply and Demand • Zero-Sum Economy • Taxes and Salaries • Economic Status of Teachers • Interprofessional Salary Comparisons • International Teachers' Salaries • Purchasing Power • State Provisions • State Salary Schedules • Salaries of Administrators • Merit Pay • Career Ladders • Cost-of-Living Index • Noncertified Personnel

INTRODUCTION

Financial support as it relates to personnel has traditionally attracted more of the attention of citizens, board members, and school officials than most other problems relating to the public schools. This attention is understandable, primarily because the quality of educational programs provided in any well-managed school system is largely determined by the qualifications and distributions of the personnel employed.

Even the best personnel policies, however, will not necessarily resolve the problems of education in many school systems without due attention to personnel planning and financing. An essential but often neglected first step is the systematic and thoughtful planning for the improvement of all aspects of education. Identification and agreement on appropriate goals, determination of needs and priorities, development and implementation of relevant programs and procedures, and other similar steps are necessary to establish a sound basis for developing defensible personnel and salary policies. This chapter discusses several of the per-

sonnel policy considerations that have fiscal implications and seeks to provide a perspective on the relative financial position of teachers within the nation's economy as compared with teachers in other industrialized countries.

Although plans and policies for improving education are essential, they have little meaning until they are implemented—that is, utilized intelligently as guides for the decisions and actions of everyone concerned or involved. All factors and conditions in the external, as well as internal, environment of education should be reasonably favorable if significant progress is to be made. These include the attitudes and expectations of the school staff, the community, the local school board, and the administration; the policies established by law and regulations of the state board of education; the quality of leadership provided; and many others. Also, sufficient funds must be made available to provide adequate and appropriate compensation for all members of the professional, supporting, and managerial staff, as well as for facilities, equipment, and supplies.

306

Expenditures for personnel (certified and noncertified) in school systems currently constitute from 80 to 85 percent of the funds expended for the current operation of the schools. Policies relating to provisions for personnel and the expenditure of these funds significantly influence the quality of education in a school system. It is important therefore that not only boards of education and school officials but also the citizens in each community make every effort to ensure that all conditions are favorable and conducive to providing a high-quality program of education.

From time to time, various school systems have found themselves confronted with an especially difficult problem. If financial support has been so limited or if personnel policies have been so inadequate that the schools have not been performing satisfactory many people become dissatisfied and critical. This tends to make it difficult or impossible to either maintain or obtain additional local support. When inadequate funds are responsible for the difficulty, only exceptionally competent leadership on the part of the board, the citizens of the community, and the administrative staff, or the provision of additional funds from state sources, can establish a basis for resolving the dilemma. If, however, the difficulty has arisen primarily because of unsatisfactory of inadequate personnel policies, it seems apparent that prompt and effective attention to the improvement of those policies should provide a sound basis for effecting improvements.

POLICIES RELATING TO PERSONNEL AND FINANCE

The development of appropriate personnel policies is of crucial importance in every state and local school system. In fact, policy planning is a major aspect of comprehensive long-range planning, which is essential for the continuous improvement of education in any school system. These plans and policies should include careful consideration of the following:

1. Aims (the establishment and maintenance of instructional and instructional-support programs)
2. Organizational structure (concerned especially with positions generated by the aims structure)
3. Personnel processes (those designed to attract, develop, and retain personnel needed to maintain and improve the system generated by the aims structure)

Each of these important personnel processes must, of course, be further subdivided into sequential tasks that are essential to achieving the purposes and goals of the system.[1] All of the major policies established through this process have important implications for the financial support that is essential if the system is to function effectively.

Policies relating to personnel may be stated in law, in state and local board regulations, and in administrative directives, or they may be unwritten and consequently somewhat intangible. Both written and unwritten policies are important in every community. Written policies serve as guidance and are expected to be observed until they are repealed or revised. Unwritten policies are often the most difficult to successfully manage and monitor. They are expressed through the attitude of the people of the community, the local school board, and the administrative staff toward teachers and other employees. This attitude determines the climate or conditions under which school personnel have to work. It may indirectly affect, and in some cases determine, what is included and what is not included in written policy. If the attitude is favorable to schools and to school personnel, working conditions are likely to be better and morale much higher than if the attitude is one of distrust, suspicion, and criticism. In fact, the attitude of the people of a state or community may determine whether the funds provided for salaries and the salaries paid are adequate or inadequate, and it may even have a decided effect on whether these funds are used wisely or unwisely in terms of the personnel services provided.

Factors Affecting Personnel and Financial Policies

As a result of recent developments, personnel administration in education has moved from a somewhat peripheral and largely managerial position, to one more concerned with the human condition as well as organizational goals. Studies by psychologists, sociologists, and economists, and the resulting modifications in management theory, have contributed significantly to this development, which has had a considerable influence in industry as well as in education. Modern concern both for employees and for students has directly contributed to the maximum development and utilization of the potential of individuals, and to efforts to encourage greater self-direction and responsibility.

Many factors today interplay with modern management theory, having important implications for the financing of school personnel. Problems associated with urbanization as well as the unique problems of the large cities have been and continue to be of paramount importance. Demographic trends, the ebb and flow of teacher supply and demand, and employment and salary considerations in the collective bargaining context also have strong effects on management personnel policies.

Collective Bargaining.   The demand for collective bargaining on salary as well as other policies has spread rapidly during the past few years. The adversarial process of collective bargaining has on the one hand expanded the power of teacher organization's to affect policy processes, while on the other hand it has introduced a new fervor on the part of administrators to preserve and enlarge management's rights and prerogatives.

Presently, over 30 states have some type of state public employee labor-relations legislation affecting education.[2] Some legislation is in the form of meet-and-confer statutes, but most pertain to collective bargaining. Most public collective-bargaining laws generally follow the private sector's requirements under the Taft–Hartley Act to bargain wages, hours, and other terms and conditions of employment. The overall scope of the area of bargaining, though, is difficult to define and is always fluctuating. Wages, we know, cover regular pay, overtime, and cost of living, while hours and conditions include fringe benefits, holidays, vacations, sick leave, pregnancy leave, and so forth. Teachers, though, are different from most other private and public sector employees since they often expand the scope of bargaining to include curriculum planning, textbook selection, and other issues of educational policy.[3]

The precise impact of collective bargaining on the financing of public schools is not fully understood. Whether it ultimately leads to an improved quality of education or even to better wages and working conditions for teachers is a subject of much needed objective research.

A few studies, that cannot be considered conclusive, found that salaries increased in bargaining districts over nonbargaining districts from about 0 to 4 percent for the year in which the studies were conducted.[4] Yet other studies have found either no effect or an adverse effect of collective bargaining on teachers' salaries. Teacher militancy in Florida during a 1968 teacher walkout had serious detrimental effects on the political potency of the Florida Education Association, which was reflected in the legislative attitude toward teacher salary increases for several years thereafter. In an interstate study, Kasper found that "there is no statistically significant positive effect of teacher organizations on salaries, once other variables such as income and urbanization are taken into account." In another study, Balfour found a negative association between salaries and collective negotiations. Similarly, Zuelke, and Frohreich found that collective bargaining had a significant negative effect on teacher salaries in small- and intermediate-sized districts in Wisconsin.[5] It is important to note that this latter study was conducted in school districts in which collective bargaining had been in effect for many years. Several studies that did show increased salaries as a result of collective bargaining measured only the short-term positive effects of bargaining.

The array of research suggests the inconclusiveness of this line of research. The research does not measure the other effects that bargaining may have on working conditions or the general quality of education. Even more difficult to measure is the psychological effect of bargaining on teachers and the community. Presumably, the quality of the educational program is positively affected by high teacher morale, and bargaining may well be good for teacher morale in that it provides them with a formal structure through which their voices can be heard at policy levels. Of course, little evidence exists to show that long-range improvements are achieved in this manner. Some maintain, to the contrary, that the adversarial roles implicit in collective bargaining may have an overall detrimental effect.

The educational efficacy of collective bargaining cannot be reduced to a mathematical formula. It must suffice to conclude that teachers generally must feel that the benefits to the teaching profession and to education outweigh the detriments, as evidenced by the spread of collective bargaining in education during the past decade.

Supply and Demand

Teachers who complain that their salaries are too low may take some solace in the fact that their situation has not changed significantly over the last 200 years. In 1776, Adam Smith attributed the low compensation of teachers to oversupply, which was caused by the education of vast numbers of clergy, who, unable to find positions in churches, overflowed into the teaching profession. The education of these clergy was paid at "public expense" in England. Smith observed:

> The usual reward of the eminent teachers bears no proportion to that of the lawyer or physician; because of the trade of one (the teacher) is crowded with indigent people who have been brought up to it at public expense; whereas those of the other two (lawyers and physicians) are encumbered with very few who have not been educated at their own expense.[6]

The parallels between Smith's world and today's are tenuous at best, but the supply-and-demand analogy may well be appropriate for even the twenty-first century.

During the Smith era, greater numbers of people went into the clergy and into teaching because they could not afford to pay for the more expensive education required to become lawyers or physicians. Thus the numbers of teachers swelled and, according to Smith, their wages declined.

The supply-and-demand phenomenon explains why prices rise and fall in a free-market economy. The theory of supply and demand was adequately explained early by John Locke as he sought to describe the market phenomenon:

> All things that are bought and sold, raise and fall their price in proportion, as there are more buyers or sellers. Where there are a great many sellers to a few buyers, they use what art you will, the thing to be sold will be cheap. On the other side, turn the tables, and raise up a great many buyers for a few sellers, and the same things will immediately grow dear.[7]

Whether teachers are held dear depends to a degree on their supply. Teachers' salaries may then be at least partially determined by the student population as representative of demand and the quantity of teachers as indicative of supply.

In its simplest form, the supply-and-demand principle may be applied to teacher salary determination as depicted in Figure 13.1. Demand, D_T, represents both the private demand for public education and the spillover demand of society in general. Private demand is the want of families with school-age children who desire education for individual benefit. At the same time, there are social or spillover benefits to society in that everyone gains from having an educated citizenry. The curve indicates that at very high salaries, fewer persons will buy education and fewer teachers will be demanded. The supply curve, S_T, suggests that as teacher salaries rise, assuming other salaries remain constant, more persons will enter the teaching profession.

Teacher Salaries

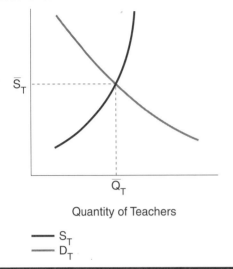

FIGURE 13.1   Supply of and Demand for
Teachers

Source: James A. Richardson and J. Trent Williams, "Determining an Appropriate Teacher Salary," paper delivered at American Education Finance Association Conference, New Orleans, 1981.

On the other hand, as Adam Smith observed, as the supply of teachers dramatically increases, salaries will fall.

The simplicity of the marketplace model, however, may be deceiving where public education is concerned. The demand for teachers is greatly affected by the numbers of students to be educated, but beyond this, as Richardson and Williams observe, the value and significance that the public places on education must be taken into account if one is to relate salaries to demand.[8] In other words, the level of salaries or price may not relate directly to demand in public education as it does in Adam Smith's marketplace. In public education, salary levels are largely controlled by the legislature, particularly in states where various types of caps and limitations have been placed on local school districts to enhance overall statewide equalization. Also, the state legislature establishes certification standards, and regardless of the numbers of students,

can effectively regulate the supply of teachers by raising or lowering the requirements necessary for entering the teaching profession. Minimum accreditation standards for schools are also governed by the state, which may greatly influence the demand for teachers. Many other factors contribute to the state's influence on both the supply of teachers and the demand for their services. For example, the state may choose to expand services to certain types of students, such as the disabled, and thereby create a substantial new demand for teachers trained in that area.

Thus public school teachers' salaries are not established in the conventional sense of the marketplace. Hale suggests that the economic pattern has aspects of both an oligopoly and an oligopsony.[9] An oligopoly is a market structure in which a small number of firms control a major portion of an industry's output. In education, the state legislature is in a position to control both the certification of teachers and the accreditation of schools, both of which can significantly affect supply. An oligopsony is a market structure in which there are relatively few buyers with a high degree of concentration or interdependence.[10] When a state greatly influences the demand for teachers through the creation or deletion of programs, alteration of required pupil–teacher ratios, or other policy determinations, the result is a "kinked" demand curve deviating substantially from the curve which would be expected under unregulated market conditions.[11] States with greater numbers of local school districts and lower levels of state regulation could be expected to evidence greater adherence to the supply-and-demand characteristics of the marketplace than states with few school districts and more centralized control.

Regardless of how one classifies the teacher market, it is certain that it does not function and probably should not function in the traditional sense of the laissez-faire market. No one will deny, however, that the forces of the marketplace are present and undoubtedly influence teachers' salaries. As to whether they actually control them, remains highly debatable.

Box 13.1

Teachers Bear Public Burden

In the purchase of what we eat and wear and in rent we pay the increased cost, but not for education, as the teachers there help pay the increased cost of producing an output—teaching—which the public enjoys at lower relative cost than it does almost any other thing it buys. This is not because our people believe that the social worth of the teacher is less than that of the plumber or painter, but because teaching has always been on a competitive basis, since the tax rate is always concerned, and because we have . . . no proper standards for computing what teachers' salaries should be.

Source: Ellwood P. Cubberley, *State School Administration* (Boston: Houghton Mifflin, 1927), p. 652.

The Complexity of Measuring Teacher Supply and Demand. Proper planning for teacher personnel administration requires the collection and analysis of data that accurately depicts the true nature of the supply and demand for teachers. Supply of teachers is determined by two major components, the number of continuing teachers and new entrants. The number of teachers continuing in the teaching profession is governed by several factors, including the average age of the teachers and the power of the profession in retaining teachers who may move to other employment. To illustrate, in projecting the supply of teachers from 1961 to 1976, the percentage of teachers with fewer than 5 years of full-time teaching experience was fairly stable, ranging between 27.3 percent and 32.8 percent. This percentage, though, showed a decline to 13.5 percent in 1981 and 9.4 percent in 1986. By 1991 this percentage rose again back to 13.7 percent. Similar fluctuations are found within the ranks of more experienced teachers. The percentage of teachers with 20 years or more of full-time teaching experience decreased from 27.6 percent in 1961 to 14.1 percent in 1976, and then rose to 21.9 percent in 1981, 27.7 percent in 1986, and 34.7 percent in 1991.

Moreover, such fluctuations are related to gender. The percentage of male teachers having 20 or more years of full-time teaching experience increased substantially from 10 to 13 percent during the 1961–1976 era to a high of 44.9 percent in 1991. The percentage of female teachers having 20 years or more of full-time teaching experience declined during the 1961–1976 era, from 34.3 to 15.2 percent, and then rose to 31.0 percent in 1991.[12] Such volatile statistics make supply and demand projections very tentative.

Career breaks in the continuity of service also further complicate estimates. In 1966, 26.7 percent of the teachers had had one break in service, in 1976, 18.7 percent had had one break, and by 1991, 23.1 percent had experienced one break in their teaching career. Secondary teachers had fewer breaks in service than did elementary teachers, and the percentage of male teachers with no breaks in service has always been higher than females.[13]

Projections for teacher demand are nearly as complex as those for supply. Demand must take into account the relationship between teachers and pupil enrollment, the disposable income of teachers, and the availability of school revenues.[14] Assuming all these caveats, the best available demand estimates by the U.S. Department of Education, Table 13.1, indicate that by the year 2002, 2.8 million public school teachers will be employed as compared to 2.4 million in 1990.[15]

The Zero-Sum Economy. Since the oil crisis of 1973, we have seen dramatic shifts in the fortunes of the U.S. economy. Americans have been forced to make choices that were not necessary prior to the oil embargo. As Thurow has observed, "Our political and economic structure simply isn't able to cope with an economy that has a substantial zero-sum element."[16]

Zero-sum is an economic condition in which the losses exactly equal the gains. If you aid poor people, you are taking the money from the richer ones. If you increase teachers' salaries, you are drawing greater tax resources from taxpayers

TABLE 13.1   Estimates of Demand for Public School Classroom Teachers, 50 States and Washington, DC, 1991 to 2002* (in thousands)

	K–12	ELEMENTARY	SECONDARY
1991	2,465	1,378	1,087
1992	2,433	1,389	1,043
1993	2,482	1,414	1,067
1994	2,530	1,439	1,090
1995	2,579	1,467	1,112
1996	2,628	1,495	1,133
1997	2,673	1,520	1,153
1998	2,709	1,541	1,167
1999	2,742	1,559	1,182
2000	2,774	1,576	1,198
2001	2,805	1,592	1,213
2002	2,838	1,608	1,230

Source: National Center for Education Statistics, *Projecting of Education Statistics to 2002* (Washington, DC: U.S. Department of Education, NCES 91–490, December 1991), p. 75.

*These data are the middle alternative estimates of the National Center for Education Statistics (NCES). NCES provides no data on supply.

who may be unable to bear the burden. Whether they can afford it or not, they believe that they have other priorities which are more important to their well-being than increasing the standard of living of the teaching force. Hard political decisions thus arise which require voters to evaluate their needs for education relative to other pressing priorities. The public has not found teachers' salaries to be a high priority in a zero-sum economy. Teachers have incurred economic losses because they have lacked the political strength to maintain at least a stable economic condition. However, these losses cannot be entirely attributed to a diminution of teacher political power, but are probably more accurately attributed to the decline in the relative value that the public places on educational attainment. Also, a downward slide in the relative economic condition of teachers may well be attributed to a general belief that the public schools are not directly benefitting those who bear the brunt of the taxes. Economic choices are more difficult to make in a distressed economy, and the tendency is for voters to forget or lay aside the long-range social benefits of education in favor of more immediate short-range in-

dividual demands. Zero-sum, discussed in Chapter 4, does not merely exist in a declining or a static economy, but in a growing one as well. In an expanding economy, however, the choices are easier to make, since the total pie gets larger and more benefits can be acquired by a greater percentage of the population.

Balancing Taxes and Salaries.   Education and other governmental services are in a much different position than those in business and industry. If salaries of public employees are increased, the cost must be met through the proceeds of taxes levied on and paid by the citizens. Almost everyone watches taxes carefully. Many assume that the more money they expend for taxes, the less they have for private use. However, as pointed out in Chapter 3, certain governmental services, and especially education, may contribute to the productivity and to the taxpaying ability of the people—a fact not commonly recognized. If salaries paid by business and industry are raised, the increases must come either from increased production per worker-hour or from profits passed on to the consumer in price increases.

There is very little the consumers can do directly about price increases for products they want. Yet from one point of view, these increases may be similar to indirect taxes. The consumers have to pay these costs if they purchase the goods, but they may have other means directly at hand to keep down or limit tax levies and price increases for public services.

For some reason, many citizens fail to realize that in a capitalistic society the values people hold are reflected in part by the prices they are willing to pay for products and services. Thus the salaries paid teachers and other educational personnel in the various states and communities are always partly a reflection of economic conditions and partly an indication of the importance attached by the citizens to education and teaching.

The question the people of the United States are attempting to resolve in this respect is: How much should teachers and other school employees be paid in order to attract to education sufficient people with adequate competence and qualifications to provide the kind of schools and education needed in this country? It is apparent that this question has not been satisfactorily answered. Salaries of teachers in particular have tended traditionally to lag behind those of equally well-prepared people in business and industry. As one result, insufficient numbers of highly competent people have been attracted to education, the schools have not accomplished as much as the people seem to expect, and many people have been critical. Criticisms of salary policies and other matters will be beneficial if they result in a reorientation of people's thinking and the development of better perspectives regarding the significance of public education, but will be harmful if they result in decreased support and lowered morale.

Economic Status of Teachers

The dictum of Adam Smith, mentioned in the discussion of supply and demand, indicates that a more favorable social attitude toward the value of teaching must be present before the public will be willing to pay teachers more competitive salaries. The relative economic position of teachers over time can be estimated by a comparison of teachers' salaries adjusted for inflation over several years and by determining the ratio of teachers' salaries to the per-capita personal income of a state or the nation.

Salaries in Constant Dollars. Constant dollars differ from current dollars in that constant dollars have been corrected for inflation over time. The correction is usually made using the Consumer Price Index (CPI), a definition of which follows.

During the 20 years from 1973 to 1993, teachers' salaries, in current dollars, increased from \$10,174 to \$35,334, an increase of \$25,160.[17] Yet when the effects of inflation are taken into account, the average salary of teachers grew by only \$1,466, or 6.4 percent, over this period of 20 years. Figure 13.2 represents the actual marginal gain in the standard of living for public school teachers.

TRENDS IN TEACHER SALARIES

That teacher salaries have slightly exceeded inflation can be shown by comparing the mean annual contract salary for all teachers in 1960–61 through 1990–91. Table 13.2 shows both the contract salaries and the Consumer Price Index (CPI) for the 30-year period. In 1990–91 the mean annual contract salary of \$31,790 was 6.04 times the 1960–61 figure of \$4,264, but the CPI for 1990–91 was only 4.52 times the CPI for 1960–61. In 1990–91 the mean salary was 3.43 times the 1970–71 figure and the 1990–91 CPI was 3.37 times that of 1970–71. Salaries have therefore exceeded inflation, though increases in some years are relatively less than others depending on the range of years used in the analysis. The end result is that the average teacher in 1991 was in a better financial condition than the average teacher of 30 years earlier. The average teacher's salary had risen by 503.7 percent and the CPI had increased by 352.0 percent.

(In Thousands)

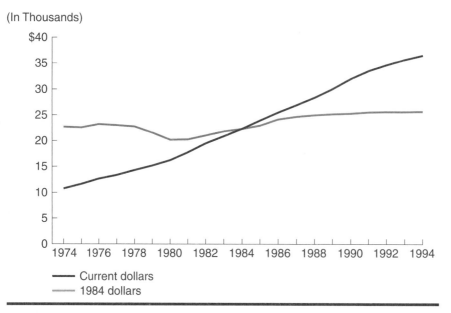

FIGURE 13.2 Trend in Average Salary Paid Teachers, in Current and Constant Dollars, 1974 to 1994

Source: National Education Association, *1993–94 Estimates of School Statistics* (Washington, DC: NEA, 1994), p. 17. Reprinted with permission.

Interprofessional Salary Comparisons

Some perspective can be gained by comparing teachers' salaries with other comparable professional employment in the United States and by comparing U.S. teachers' salaries with teachers'

TABLE 13.2 Mean Annual Contract Salary for All Teachers and the Consumer Price Index (CPI), School Years 1960–61 through 1990–91

SCHOOL YEAR	SALARY	CPI-U[a]
1960–61	$ 5,264[b]	89.3
1965–66	6,253	96.2
1970–71	9,261	119.8
1975–76	12,005	167.7
1980–81	17,209	263.9
1985–86	24,504	326.8
1990–91	31,790	403.6

Source: National Education Association, *Status of the American Public School Teacher 1990–91* (Washington, DC: NEA, 1992), p. 70.

[a]CPI indexed to 1967 (1967 CPI = 100.0)

[b]1961 figures include extra pay for extra duties.

DEFINITION

Consumer Price Index (CPI). A statistical measure of the changes in prices of goods and services purchased by a typical urban household. It indicates pricing patterns that have a direct bearing on the cost of living.

Source: U.S. Department of Commerce, *Statistical Abstract of the United States* (Washington, DC: U.S. Government Printing Office, 1991).

---

salaries in other countries. Only persons in the armed forces and computer operators make less than teachers according to a comparison of accountants, auditors, scientists, architects, surveyors, engineers, lawyers, medical doctors, armed forces personnel, computer operators and teachers (See Figure 13.3).

Nelson shows that the economic position of teachers relative to other white-collar professions has gained during the last two and a half decades. His data indicate that from 1964 to 1989, teach-

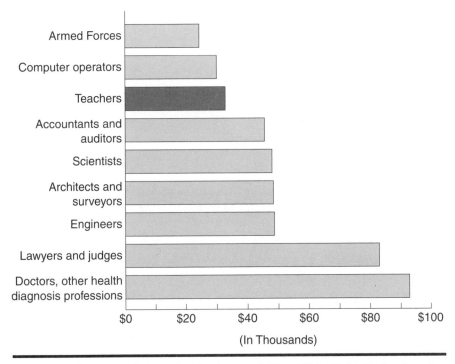

FIGURE 13.3   Average Salaries for Teachers and Other White-Collar Professions in the United States, 1991

Source: F. Howard Nelson, *Survey and Analysis of Salary Trends 1990*, Research Report (Washington, DC: American Federation of Teachers, July 1990), Table II–3. Reprinted with permission.

ers' salaries increased relative to accountants, auditors, attorneys, chemists, engineers and college professors. Table 13.3 shows for example that in 1964 accountants, on the average, made salaries 32 percent higher than teachers. Teachers' salaries have also shown gains against full professors in public doctoral institutions and against assistant professors in public comprehensive universities. Assistant professors in 1990 exceeded teachers by only 5 percent, $32,730 to $31,315, virtual parity. Yet despite the rather steady improvement, teachers' salaries still remain behind other white-collar professions.

International Teachers' Salaries

Salaries of school teachers in the United States in 1992 were roughly comparable to salaries in England, and were considerably less than in the Netherlands, Germany, Canada, and Switzerland

(see Figure 13.4). The top salaries for U.S. high-school teachers averaged $38,000 a year as against $43,000 in Germany, $45,000 in Japan, $47,000 in Canada, and $70,000 in Switzerland. Both European and Asian countries tend to have longer school years than the United States, so U.S. teachers on the average work fewer days. Training of teachers in Europe and Japan is usually longer than the four year bachelor's degree minimum teaching requirement in the United States. The question is, of course, whether the increased education and training of teachers and shorter school years abroad justify the difference in pay. Evidence cannot confirm whether additional teacher training would be met with greater public enthusiasm for paying higher teacher salaries. Too, whether increasing the length of the school year would ultimately result in increased wages of U.S. teachers as compared to teachers in other countries is unknown. Of

TABLE 13.3   Ratio of Salaries in Other Occupations to Teacher Salaries

	TEACHERS	ACCOUNTANT III	AUDITOR III	ATTORNEY III	CHEMIST IV	ENGINEER IV	FULL PROF. PUBLIC DOCTORAL	ASSISTANT PROF. PUBLIC COMPREHEN.
1990	1.00						1.84	1.05
1989	1.00	1.15	1.21	1.93	1.59	1.60	1.83	1.04
1985	1.00	1.27	1.33	2.03	1.67	1.74	1.81	1.04
1980	1.00	1.32	1.37	2.05	1.72	1.77	1.87	1.11
1975	1.00	1.24	1.31	1.93	1.64	1.66	1.94	1.19
1970	1.00	1.24	1.33	1.96	1.65	1.70	2.10	1.25
1964	1.00	1.32	1.42	2.14	1.77	1.84	2.09	1.28

Source: F. Howard Nelson, *Survey and Analysis of Salary Trends 1990*, Research Report (Washington, DC: American Federation of Teachers, July 1990), Table II–3. Reprinted with permission.

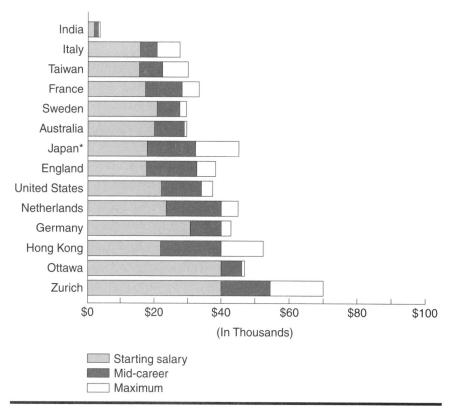

FIGURE 13.4   Salaries of Teachers in the United States Compared to Teachers' Salaries in Other Countries*

Source: William Celis, "Teachers in U.S. Trail More Elsewhere in Pay," *New York Times,* August 18, 1992, Education section, p. A.17.

*Average 1992 salaries of upper secondary school teachers. Countries are shown in order of mid-career salaries.

course if the school year increased from the current approximate average of 180 days to 185 days, legislative appropriations would presumably be made to cover the expanded work year. There is little evidence, however, to indicate that state legislatures would continue to provide funds for salaries at a comparable effort, as a percentage of the state's personal income or of the state's gross domestic product. Whether additional training and working hours would elicit increased fiscal effort is uncertain.

The relative pay of teachers compared to the general economic conditions of a country is perhaps more important to consider than the absolute wages received. A teacher receiving what would be an average or lower salary on an international scale may be well paid compared to other workers in an underdeveloped or low-income country. Undoubtedly, a teacher at the lowest of the pay scales in the United States would be well paid if he or she made the same salary in a poor country. On the other hand, a teacher of average pay on an international scale may be considered to be poorly paid if employed in a high-income nation such as the United States.

The quality of the teaching force is materially affected by such relative wage conditions. When teacher salaries are in a relatively low ratio to the per-capita personal income of a nation, or are low relative to some other measure of national wealth such as gross domestic product per capita or private consumption per capita, less able people will enter the teaching profession. Prospective teachers will, all other things being equal, choose alternative white-collar employments that require comparable education and training.

Lawton has observed that the quality of the teaching force is almost certainly affected by "the portion of the national wealth paid to 'typical teachers' . . . , their share of the national pie."[18] In 1985 he found that primary school teachers' salaries in the United States as a percentage of the gross domestic product (GDP) was less than the average of developed countries. As Table 13.4 shows, the U.S. percentage was 160 while the average for all the selected coun-

tries was 173; the United States trailed Canada, Spain and the United Kingdom. This table also shows U.S. primary teachers' salaries as a percentage of private consumption per capita. By this measure, U.S. salaries lag behind Canada, Japan, Denmark, Germany, Greece, Ireland, Italy, Luxembourg, Netherlands, Norway, Portugal, Spain, and the United Kingdom. These data suggest that the poor relative position of U.S. teachers' salaries relative to the economy in the United States will likely have an important bearing on the quality of the supply of teachers.

Yet such an analysis of the relative economic conditions of teachers in the various countries, while of much value, has certain limitations that must be recognized. Specifically, this analysis does not take into account the working conditions of the teachers, such as class size, length of school year, and types of responsibilities.[19] Further, it is assumed that the reported salaries are taken from reliable and competent data sources, an assumption that is not necessarily true. Many countries have suspect reporting mechanisms making salary comparisons tentative at best.

Box 13.2 _____

Comparing Teachers' Salaries in Canada to Those in the United States

The lesson to be learned from the international data is that levels of pay that attract well-qualified people to teaching, even in areas of relatively short supply, are possible. Sights should not be set too low. At the same time, it is necessary to understand the social, political and economic contexts that make such levels of pay possible if useful plans to alter teacher pay levels are to be made. My only concern, I must admit, in suggesting such an agenda is that Canadians might learn from Americans how to pay their teachers less, rather than Americans learn how to pay their teachers more.

Source: Stephen B. Lawton, "Teachers' Salaries: An International Perspective," in *Attracting and Compensating America's Teachers*, eds. Kern Alexander and David H. Monk (Cambridge, MA: Ballinger, Harper & Row, 1988), p. 79.

TABLE 13.4 Primary Schoolteachers' Salaries as a Percentage of Gross Domestic Product per Head and Percentage of Private Consumption per Head, 1985

COUNTRY	SALARY AS PERCENTAGE OF GDP PER HEAD	SALARY AS PERCENTAGE OF PRIVATE CONSUMPTION PER HEAD
United States	160%	241%
Canada	199	357
Japan	187	339
Austria	120	210
Belgium	148	236
Denmark	149	293
Finland	119	231
France	109	172
Germany	158	288
Greece	230	355
Ireland	258	464
Italy	161	258
Luxembourg	204	345
Netherlands	155	250
Norway	119	276
Portugal	240	392
Spain	239	362
United Kingdom	165	279
Average	173	297

Source: "Teacher's Salaries" by Stephen B. Lawton from *Attracting and Compensating America's Teachers,* edited by Kern Alexander and David H. Monk. Copyright © 1988 by American Education Finance Association, pp. 79–81. Reprinted by permission of HarperCollins Publishers, Inc.

Note: GDP and private consumption per head were calculated in U.S. dollars using current PPPs for 1982 and 1984 are from OECD (1986).

Purchasing Power Parity

Purchasing power parity theorizes that the exchange rates between or among countries will adjust to reflect the differences in price levels.[20] Paul Samuelson defines purchasing power parity as "what incomes will buy."[21] Lawton further explains that the "PPP for a given country is the amount of national currency needed to purchase the same amount of goods and services (usually termed a "market basket") that one U.S. dollar will purchase in the U.S. domestic market."[22] Any currency may be used for a comparative basis, but by general practice, for purposes of inter-national economics, the U.S. dollar is used. An interesting explanation of purchasing power statistics was furnished by *The Economist,* in terms of a purchasing power parity based on the cost of McDonald's Big Mac hamburger, which is now sold in at least 41 countries. *The Economist* explained:

> In Washington, Big Mac costs $1.60 (U.S.); in Tokyo, our Makundonarudo correspondent had to fork out 370 yen ($2.40). Dividing the yen price by the U.S. dollar price yields a Mac-PPP of $1 equals 231 year; but on September 1 the dollar's actual exchange rate stood at 154 yen. The same

method gives a Mac-PPP against the German mark of 2.66 marks, compared with a current rate of 2.02 marks. Conclusion: on Mac-PPP grounds, the dollar looks undervalued against the yen and mark.[23]

Normally, however, purchasing power parity is calculated by means of a market basket broader than a Big Mac (although the Big Mac may be a good proxy) typified by methodology and by the Organization for Economic Cooperation and Development (OECD) in Paris.[24] By applying the OECD method to salaries, a substantial and more accurate picture of the relative value of teachers' salaries can be determined. Comparing salaries of teachers in Canada to those in the United States, Lawton observes that a primary school teacher in the United States would need to be paid about 23 percent more to have the same purchasing power as a primary school teacher in Canada. Yet in terms of purchasing power parity, only teachers in Luxembourg, Australia, and Switzerland join Canadian teachers in enjoying greater purchasing power than U.S. teachers. Teacher purchasing power in Japan, Denmark, France, Germany, and the United Kingdom was markedly below that in the United States.[25]

From this analysis one can draw two basic conclusions. First, the relative economic position of U.S. teachers within the U.S. economy is lower than teachers in other countries relative to their own economic system. That is, salaries of teachers in the United States are less competitive compared to other U.S. white-collar professions. Further, salaries of teachers in most other countries are relatively higher than salaries of U.S.

teachers when compared with comparable white-collar professions in those respective countries. Put another way, teachers in the United States are not as well off; relative to teachers in other countries, their standard of living is not as high as that of other persons of similar education and training within the United States.

On the other hand, teachers in the United States tend to have greater purchasing power than do teachers in most other advanced countries. This means that despite the fact that U.S. teachers find themselves in a poorer relative position internal to this country, the higher standard of living provided by the U.S. economy gives U.S. teachers greater purchasing power than teachers in other advanced industrialized nations except for those in Australia, Canada, Luxembourg, and Switzerland. In summary, the U.S. teacher's standard of living is generally higher relative to teachers in other countries, but is relatively low compared to other white-collar professions within the United States.

INTERSTATE COMPARISONS OF TEACHERS' SALARIES

As previously discussed, state laws and regulations may directly affect salary provisions in the local school districts. If only limited funds for schools are provided from state sources, the salary level in each school system will be determined chiefly by the willingness and the ability of the citizens in the district to provide funds for schools. When state funds are meager, salaries in the least wealthy districts generally may be expected to be much lower than salaries in the most wealthy. However, when an adequate and realistic state funding program has been established, all districts, regardless of their wealth, should be placed in a satisfactory position to provide the necessary funding for teacher salaries.

Many states, because of concern about this problem, have taken one step or another relating directly to salaries. Several have established state minimum salary schedules. West Virginia apparently established the first state minimum salary

---

DEFINITION

Purchasing Power Parity. Notice that in Table 13.4, Lawton used purchasing power parities (PPPs) for international comparisons. What is the definition of PPP? The purchasing power of any given amount of money is the volume of goods and services it will buy.

law in 1882. By 1937, 20 states had some kind of minimum salary legislation.[26] There are three major types of state minimum salary laws relating to teachers.

1. Those that provide a state minimum salary schedule recognizing both training and experience
2. Those that fix a minimum salary on the basis of two or more flat rates but with no recognition of experience
3. Those that fix a minimum salary as a single flat amount

The interest of states in minimum salary schedules first developed largely because salaries paid in some districts were obviously inadequate. Those who were concerned with the problem apparently assumed that if a state minimum salary schedule could be established by law, the problem would be solved. Cubberley, in his book *State School Administration* written in 1927, discusses the origin and rationale for state salary schedules.[27] He points out that the Pennsylvania state salary schedule legislation adopted in 1921 was a prototype that was designed to advance teacher preparation and encourage entrants to the teaching profession by paying "at least a living wage."[28]

As with the early salary schedules, however, the modern ones still have difficulty in establishing salaries that are scientifically based. Those states that have utilized salary schedules have generally identified teacher training and experience as the primary criteria for salary schedule differentials. Other considerations such as teacher locale, teaching results, and merit factors have been used, but only infrequently.

Principles that should ideally be used to create salary schedules have been occasionally borrowed from collective bargaining agreements and other education and teacher welfare guidelines. A partial list of these principles include:

1. The *comparability principle*. Teachers should have a wage comparable to other white-collar employment.

2. The *education and training principle*. The schedule should provide incentive for higher levels of knowledge and pedagogical expertise.
3. The *improvement principle*. Teachers should be given incentive to refurbish their knowledge of their particular field of learning.
4. The *experience principle*. Experience is preferable to inexperience and retention of professional teachers is desirable.[29]
5. The *teaching load principle*. Some measure of work load should be considered (e.g., number of pupils per teacher).
6. The *efficiency principle*. The schedule should be so designed so as not to encourage the retention of poorer quality teachers. In this regard some form of merit factor accompanied by periodic evaluations of professional growth should be included.[30]

It is safe to say that no state to date has successfully merged all or even a majority of these principles in a state salary schedule.

One of the problems with state salary schedules is of course that of uneven fiscal capacity of local school districts. Many poor districts cannot maintain a desirable pupil–teacher ratio, provide a satisfactory length employment, and conform to the minimum salaries required for all teachers. Since state laws in many cases require a certain minimum length of term, the only alternatives for these districts has often been to maintain the minimum school term, increase the number of pupils per teacher, employ only teachers with minimal training and experience, and/or to levy onerous local taxes. Thus, the state salary schedule must be fiscally equalized if it is to work effectively, compensating for the fiscal incapacities of poorer school districts.

The tendency in most states during recent years seems to be to attempt to develop an adequate and realistic plan for financing schools from state and local revenues. Progress in this direction facilitates provisions for reasonably adequate salaries, rather than emphasizing minimum salaries as the basic salary policy.

DETERMINATION OF LOCAL SCHOOL DISTRICT SALARY POLICY

Salary policies constitute one important aspect of general personnel policies. There has been a decided tendency during the past quarter of a century for districts to develop written statements relating to salary policy. These are usually developed with the cooperation of the staff or through the joint efforts of representatives from the staff and citizens of the community. These groups, however, can only recommend salary policy, since the local school boards may or may not approve their recommendations. However, when committees have done a good job of developing sound policies, the recommendations usually have been approved by the boards without major altercation. The purposes of salary policies are to give assurance to the community that sound procedures will be observed in compensating employees, to give assurance to the staff that recognized policies rather than haphazard procedures will be followed, and to provide guidance to administrators and their staffs in developing satisfactory procedures for obtaining and retaining the services of competent personnel.

Suggestions for salary policies or schedules have been made in a number of studies. The following suggestions from a 1958 study may still be used as a guide for policy considerations.

1. Meet reasonable competition for good beginning teachers without attempting to offer the highest starting salary.
2. Assure dignified living standards for maturing personnel.
3. Assure relief from hardship for heads of households.
4. Contribute an uplifting influence to the dignity and prestige of teaching in the United States.
5. Help to attract and hold teachers and principals of the highest quality.
6. Stimulate increased graduate study through the master's degree.
7. Encourage study, research, and travel beyond the master's degree.
8. Provide adequate and dignified maximum salaries for teachers for whom teaching is only a part of their career.
9. Provide markedly distinguished salaries for teachers who, in the tradition of the community, make substantial and measurable contributions to education in the district and in the United States.
10. Provide a relatively long period for salary improvement before reaching maximum, but with safeguards against automatic advancement if a teacher's work is unsatisfactory.
11. Provide annual increments of sufficient amount to be "felt."
12. Contrary to long-established tradition, provide an opportunity for teachers to achieve professional distinction and corresponding salary recognition without having to leave teaching for administrative or supervisory positions.
13. Recognize any special economic factors in the community.
14. Serve the long-term needs of the district, the board of education, and the faculty, and not be merely a temporizing, stopgap measure.[31]

It is also desirable for policies to include adequate leaves for study, conferences, travel, and generous fringe benefits for all personnel. The importance of adequate provisions for in-service education is likewise indicated as necessary board policy in addition to the salary policies proposed.

TRENDS IN DEVELOPING LOCAL SALARY SCHEDULES

A salary schedule is simply a plan for compensating individual members of any group of employees, such as principals, teachers, secretaries, or custodians. This plan may be good or bad, satisfactory or unsatisfactory, in whole or in part. Givens noted some years ago, "Salary schedules for teachers are social inventions that have been developed by insight and ingenuity to meet the problems of personnel administration in the schools."[32]

As previously indicated, there has been a distinct movement toward the development of salary schedules for all groups of school employees. Some additional trends are discussed briefly below.

1. For some years, there has been a marked trend toward the establishment of single-salary schedules for teachers. In the single-salary schedule, the plan for paying salaries is based on the training and experience of the persons employed. However, there now seems to be some tendency for this policy to be modified.

2. For certain types of employees, there has been increased consideration of job evaluation as one basis for salary schedules and placement on schedules. This has been particularly evident in the development of schedules for noncertified employees and to some extent has been considered in connection with schedules for administrative, supervisory, and certain other types of positions.

3. Cost and standard-of-living factors have been increasingly emphasized. It is generally accepted that school employees must be able to maintain an adequate standard of living if they are to work effectively.

4. For a number of years, minimum salaries provided in schedules were increased more rapidly than maximum salaries. However, there is some indication that maximum salaries are tending to be increased as much as, or at a somewhat higher rate than, minimum salaries, thus tending to restore the balance that was upset by special cost-of-living and other adjustments resulting from postwar and other economic developments.

5. In a number of school systems, an effort has been made to provide maximum salaries, especially in the higher ranks, that are at least twice as high as those established as minimums. Only a few systems have been able to attain this goal. We do know that in 1966, of all teachers under the age of 30, 80 percent earned salaries that were 80 percent of the salaries of teachers age 50 and over, and by 1991 the percent had fallen to 60 percent.[33]

6. The fact that proper preparation is essential for satisfactory teaching in modern society differential salary schedules have come to be increasingly recognized as a means of encouraging professional personnel to complete their college training before accepting full-time positions. Also differential salary schedules have been used as a means of providing an incentive for teachers who have not completed their college degrees and the differential in salaries for the two groups has gradually been increased by a number of school systems. Many systems also recognize that there are places with needs for experienced teachers who have completed preparation beyond the master's degree; consequently, there has been a tendency to add another column to the schedule.

7. Numerous districts have adopted index salary schedules. Instead of stating a dollar amount for each rank and step in the schedule, only a base amount is stated in dollars—for example, $24,000–$28,000 for a beginning teacher who is a college graduate. An index number (such as 1.1) is then assigned to teachers who hold a master's degree, and the salary can readily be determined in relationship to the basic amount, whatever it may be. Similarly, salary amounts for each step of experience can be determined by applying an appropriate index number.

8. There has been some tendency to consider factors other than training and experience for teachers as well as for other groups of employees. For instance, some systems have adopted, or are experimenting with, a plan for relating salaries, to some extent, to the level of responsibility for certain kinds of positions. Others are attempting to evaluate and recognize merit and to provide special increments for merit. Still others have made some provisions for dependency allowances, and so on.

9. The length of service during the year for various school employees has been increased in many systems. Sometimes this has been accomplished by increasing the length of the term, and often by providing for needed educational and other services during the summer. Schedules in many systems thus provide for adjustments for length of service beyond the traditional school year.

OTHER ECONOMIC BENEFITS

Although salaries are important in establishing the basic economic position of each group of employees, other benefits should be as carefully considered as part of the total personnel compensation plan. A policy that attempts to provide reasonably adequate salaries without considering other economic benefits or working conditions is not as satisfactory as a similar policy that places considerable emphasis on the other benefits. For this reason, most groups devote considerable attention to this problem. For example, a school district may consider a supplementary retirement plan (beyond the state plan), provisions for group life insurance, a comprehensive medical insurance program, and/or disability insurance.

Although all states now have retirement plans, either for teachers or including teachers and other employees, some of these are unrealistic or inadequate in the context of recent economic developments. Some still limit the salaries that may be used in computing retirement benefits, others fail to provide for survivors, and some are not on a sound actuarial basis. Adequate retirement provisions, perhaps supplemented by state provisions including or comparable to those for Social Security, are essential for every state.

The provisions of worker's compensation laws are applicable to teachers and other school employees in most states. Although most appear to be performing satisfactorily, improvements are needed in several states, and existing provisions probably should be supplemented by plans for group life, accident, and even liability insurance.

Practically all the larger school systems have reasonably adequate provisions for certain kinds of leaves of absence. In some cases, these provisions are statewide. Usually sick leave may be taken without loss of compensation up to a designated number of days per year, cumulative up to several months over a period of years. Many small school systems, however, either have inadequate or no provisions for the accumulation of sick leave. For example, in some instances, teachers who have to be absent due to illness must pay the salaries of their substitutes. Provisions for sabbatical leave are found in some of the larger and more efficient school systems but in practically none of the smaller, poorer systems. The implementation of statewide leave and sabbatical plans would help to resolve this problem.

Assurance of reasonable security in employment has significant economic implications. Some states in their attempt to provide security for their teachers have enacted legislation that makes it unduly difficult and expensive to discharge incompetent teachers. Other states still do not have satisfactory provisions for tenure and continuity of service for teachers, especially among their smaller districts. Reasonable assurance that employees who are rendering effective service not be subject to loss of position at the whim of local school boards or administrators should be expected in all states.

Salaries of Administrative and Supervisory Staff

In some school systems, administrators and supervisors are considered to be paid for their administrative competence and leadership qualities and their salaries have no relationship to the salaries of teachers. However, authorities point out that principals and others are leaders of teachers as well as administrators. Many hold that there should be some defensible relationship between the salaries of teachers and those of administrators and supervisors. On the assumption that some relationship should exist, attempts have been made to devise a formula that can be used in developing a schedule for salaries of administrators and supervisors.[34] Should the salaries of administrators and supervisors be based on a ratio to teachers' salaries and automatically increased as teachers' salaries are increased? Should administrators represent the board of education in collective bargaining with teachers if their salaries are tied to the teacher salary schedule? Should school administrators represent the board in the collective bargaining process?

In more than two-thirds of the larger school systems, the salary schedules for administrative and supervisory personnel have been related rather directly to the salary schedules for teachers. More than half of these were based on an index or ratio adjusted to the schedule for teachers.[35]

For some time, many school systems that provide summer or extended-year programs for some students and teachers have recognized that a time factor should be utilized in determining the additional compensation for teachers who serve beyond the regular school term. Thus, one-ninth or some other specified salary supplement would be added to the salary of a teacher who served for a month beyond the regular term of nine months. This factor is also utilized for administrators and supervisors who serve beyond the customary term.

The other factor commonly utilized in the index is a responsibility ratio that can be utilized for all professional personnel who have assignments requiring special competencies and extra responsibilities. For example, if the responsibility ratio for a regular teacher is 1.0, the ratio for the head of a teaching team might be 1.15, and for a principal of a larger school the ratio might be 1.75 to 2.00. Such ratios need to be developed on the basis of detailed studies and analyses made with the concurrence of the entire professional staff.

The gap between superintendents' and teachers' salaries is somewhat less today than in 1976. In 1976 the average teacher's salary was 38 percent of the average superintendent's salary and in 1990 it was 41 percent. Similarly, the average teacher's salary was closer to the average high school principal's salary in 1990 than fifteen years earlier. In the 1975–76 school year the average teacher's salary was 53 percent of the average high school principal's salary, and by 1990 the average teacher's salary was 60 percent of the average for principals (see Table 13.5).

This slight narrowing of the differential between salaries of teachers and administrators may be the result of several factors. Among such factors may be (1) a greater public concern for quality instruction, and (2) a growing public concern that too few financial resources of the school districts are actually directed to the classroom. Whatever the cause, the trend would appear to be positive. Measures taken to make classroom teaching positions more attractive to prospective teachers will undoubtedly serve to enhance the quality of the public schools by attracting and retaining better qualified teachers.

MERIT PAY

Many citizens contend that salaries for teachers should be related in some way to competency. Whenever salary increases are proposed, there are those who indicate that they would support higher salaries for the most competent teachers, but they are opposed to salary increases for all teachers. They insist that industry has had merit pay plans for a number of years and has used them successfully, and that these plans could readily be adapted for use by the public schools.

Many teachers, administrators, and teacher organizations have opposed merit pay. They call attention to the difficulty of establishing an objective and effective plan for determining merit and point to the danger that subjective factors cause in any merit rating plan. Davis early stated this view:

> A merit wage system is primarily a procedure for one person to make subjective judgments about another, which means that it is fraught with human relation problems and is one of the most difficult of all personnel practices to administer. Its human problems cluster around the merit-increase philosophy, the rating process, and the use of rating for merit increases.[36]

Others, Urban,[37] Cohen, and Murmane,[38] Lipsky and Bacharack[39] have documented the failures of merit pay schemes. The factors have

TABLE 13.5 Salaries or Earnings of Teachers and Administrators, 1975–76 to 1989–90 (in 1990 constant dollars and percentages)

	1975–76	1979–80	1981–82	1983–84	1985–86	1987–88	1988–89	1989–90	1975–76 TO 1989–90
1990 Dollars									
Teachers-Average	$28,165	$24,303	$26,029	$27,585	$30,148	$30,877	$30,946	$31,276	3,999
Superintendents	73,661	60,087	63,016	65,691	72,409	74,538	74,408	75,425	3,390
H.S. Principals	52,779	44,606	46,962	49,233	52,235	55,249	55,382	55,722	1,452
Annual Percentage Increase									
Teachers-Average	8.1%	6.8%	9.0%	5.9%	7.2%	5.6%	4.9%	5.6%	171.8%
Teacher Beginning	6.9	5.9	7.9	5.5	7.8	5.6	4.9	5.4	156.0
Superintendents	7.0	6.6	8.5	4.4	6.6	5.5	4.5	5.9	148.2
H.S. Principals	1.8	6.5	7.9	4.6	4.0	5.5	4.9	5.2	143.4

Source: Educational Research Service, *Salaries Paid Professional Personnel in Public Schools and Wages and Salaries Paid Support Personnel in Public Schools* (Reston, VA: ERS, 1991).

been attributed primarily to a lack of clear measures of performance.

Proponents of merit pay, on the other hand, argue that the disreputa of merit pay plans are contrived by teacher unions who feel that their ranks are weakened when teachers are forced to compete for salary increases. Proponents further maintain that rewards or incentives for teachers would elicit desirable competitive responses as are found in other occupations where money is the incentive for greater productivity. Merit pay proposals are therefore most often justified on two basic assumptions.

1. Teachers are motivated primarily by monetary incentives.
2. The opportunity for extra compensation can be effectively used to motivate teacher behavior throughout their teaching careers.[40]

Some argue that these two assumptions are not necessarily valid. Regarding money as the primary motivator, some research has shown that the monetary incentive lacks uniformity among teachers. For example, money is more important to young teachers while working conditions and an agreeable teaching atmosphere are of greater importance to more experienced teachers.[41] For example, Greenberg and McCall[42] found that career teachers are more likely to seek transfer or reassignment to schools in higher socioeconomic neighborhoods not so much for pay increases but for nonpecuniary rewards. Sewell[43] found similar propensities in experienced teachers who were willing to remain in inner-city schools if their class sizes were reduced, they were given paraprofessional support, and their working conditions were generally improved.

Thus, merit pay alone may well fail to fully provide the motivation and incentive suggested by its proponents. At the very least, research suggests that what drives some teachers to greater performance may not produce the same effects on others. In this regard Johnson notes,

> While teachers unquestionably deserve higher salaries and will not remain in teaching without financial security, . . . incentive strategies for keeping our best teachers in schools should center on the workplace rather than on the pay envelope.[44]

Career Ladders

Some maintain that career ladders and other systems of differentiated staffing are superior to merit pay as motivators. The Holmes Group, made up of the deans of education of several major universities, has expressed the view that the flat career pattern of the typical teacher is itself a deterrent to self-improvement and professional ambition.[45] This group argued that educational productivity of the schools would be greatly enhanced by ending the present "careerlessness" of the teaching profession. The Holmes Group has called for both career levels and/or a differentiated or tiered system of professional advancement. This group recommended a three-tiered system of teacher licensing that prescribes career phases—an entry phase, a professional phase, and a career professional phase.

Other forums have expressed similar views. The Carnegie Foundation recommended that teacher salaries be differentiated on the basis of job function, seniority, and productivity, and also, called for differing levels of teacher certification.

In contrast to merit pay schemes that are supposed to increase productivity through competition, these alternative methods, career ladders and differentiated staffing, contemplate cooperation. Apparently it has been assumed that cooperation among teachers within a school would enhance student performance more readily than would merit pay, thereby avoiding disruption of school productivity by overly intensifying teacher competitiveness. Research, though, is not conclusive as to which is the more desirable of the approaches.

Salary Adjustments Based on a Cost-of-Living Index

Cost-of-living escalators have become commonplace in collective bargaining agreements in the private sector in recent years, and have been increasingly built into government wages and programs.[46] Many school systems have related salaries to the Consumer Price Index. The idea has been proposed in several other school systems and has even been considered by some states as a basis for determining the amount of the apportionment for salaries from the state-aid program.

Some of the arguments in favor of using a cost-of-living index to adjust amounts in a salary schedule are:

1. Many discussions and controversies regarding salary adjustments could be avoided.
2. The use of an index would provide an automatic plan for adjustments and would eliminate subjective factors.
3. Salaries would automatically increase or decrease as the cost of living increased or decreased.

The primary objective to a cost-of-living index is that it constitutes a political assumption that inflation is inevitable and has to be accommodated. Unfortunately, cost-of-living factors help to drive inflation and reduce the effectiveness of government in dealing with inflation. One must ask if indexing is an appropriate policy of government, for if teachers are allowed to index, then shouldn't everyone else in all parts of the economy do the same? On the other hand, teachers will not want to be excluded from the indexing game if everyone else is participating. Thurow characterizes the dilemma in this way: "Each of us organizes to avoid being subject to falling prices. But if we all succeed, we have an economy where inflation is endemic. To stop inflation, someone's income must go down."[47] The question is: Should teachers make the personal sacrifice for the national economy? This is an issue which has not been resolved for any other working group in either the public or private sector.

Another valid objection to such an index, from the teacher's perspective, is that salaries for teachers and other school employees are much less than the salaries paid many other kinds of workers. Consequently, if cost-of-living index were tied to present salaries, it would merely result in an adjustment upward or downward of salaries that are already inadequate and would not provide for desirable improvements. Many teachers believe that before there is any attempt to use a cost-of-living index to adjust salaries, there should be more realistic and comprehensive studies of standards of living and of budget requirements for various standards of living.

Salaries of Noncertified Personnel

Most of the attention in the laws and in the literature seems to have been given to the problem of assuring adequate salaries for teachers and other members of the instructional staff. In many cases, there is no legal requirement that salary schedules be established for noncertified personnel. Many believe that the relation between salaries of teachers and those of other school employees should be governed by the laws of supply and demand. Thus, if secretaries are in short supply, a school system should expect to pay as much or more for a competent secretary as for a competent teacher. Others oppose this point of view and insist that the nature of the work and the preparation required by various kinds of employees should be the major factors in determining salary policy.

Data for the period from 1976 to 1990 indicate that salaries of secretaries in central school district offices have maintained about the same relative position when compared to average teacher salaries, increasing 173.8 percent while salaries of teachers increased 171.8 percent. Salaries of other noncertified personnel in school districts over this same period have been somewhat less than salaries of teachers. See Table 13.6 for a comparison of salaries of teachers and noncertified personnel.

As a practical matter, most school systems will have to pay secretaries, custodians, and other personnel roughly the "going" wage in the community. Some are required to do so by civil service provisions. If the salaries authorized are too low, the schools cannot employ or retain competent people. Moreover, some of the employees in many communities belong to unions,

TABLE 13.6 Salaries or Earnings of Nonteaching School Personnel, 1975–76 to 1989–90 (in 1990 constant dollars and percentages)

	1975–76	1979–80	1981–82	1983–84	1985–86	1987–88	1988–89	1989–90	1975–76 TO 1989–90
1990 Dollars									
Teachers–Average	$28,165	$24,303	$26,029	$27,585	$30,148	$30,877	$30,946	$31,276	3,999
Secretaries									
Central Office	17,956	15,778	17,175	17,981	19,541	19,929	19,906	20,038	2,691
School Building	14,767	12,749	13,911	14,536	15,784	16,132	16,058	16,184	1,852
Hourly Workers									
Instructional Aides	$6.61	$5.94	$6.59	$6.86	$7.40	$7.35	$7.37	$7.43	$0.53
Custodians	8.56	7.45	8.03	8.12	8.68	8.55	8.56	8.54	0.15
Cafeteria Workers	6.41	5.77	6.17	6.37	6.87	6.81	6.86	6.77	0.58
Bus Drivers	9.15	7.96	8.45	8.62	9.21	9.09	9.18	9.21	0.32
Annual Percent Increase									
Teachers–Average	8.1%	6.8%	9.0%	5.9%	7.2%	5.6%	4.9%	5.6%	171.8%
Secretaries									
Central Office	8.3	8.1	9.9	5.3	6.8	6.0	4.5	5.2	173.8
School Building	7.9	7.4	10.1	5.5	5.8	5.8	4.2	5.3	167.7
Hourly Workers									
Instructional Aides	0.3	9.0	8.9	3.8	5.3	4.5	4.9	5.4	155.3
Custodians	6.8	7.7	11.2	4.2	5.5	4.1	4.7	4.3	141.2
Cafeteria Workers	8.4	8.6	9.6	4.5	6.3	5.2	5.3	3.2	159.4
Bus Drivers	7.7	5.7	8.9	5.0	6.2	3.1	5.7	4.9	145.6

Source: Educational Research Service, *Salaries Paid Professional Personnel in Public Schools,* *and Wages and Salaries Paid Support Personnel in Public Schools* (Reston, VA: ERS, 1991).

and there would be difficulties with the unions if salaries were too low.

Since principals, teachers, and noncertified employees must work in close cooperation, many believe that special steps should be taken in every school system to assure that each group understands the basis for, and supports the general idea behind the salary schedules for other groups. For this reason, provisions are made in many salary studies for representatives of non-certified employees to serve on teacher salary schedule committees and for teachers to serve on committees to study schedules for other groups.

SUMMARY AND CONCLUSIONS

This chapter gives selected attention to certain personnel policies that bear on school financing and provides specific detail and discussion of teachers' salaries. Of concern is the relative financial condition of teachers in the U.S. economy.

Personnel policies that address both the needs of the children and the welfare of the teachers are necessary for a productive educational system. Such personnel policies are affected by the supply of a quality teaching force as well as by the economic and demographic conditions of the school district.

Collective bargaining plays an important role in the welfare of teachers in over half of the states; but, the evidence is inconclusive as to whether over the long term, teachers' salaries are higher in states and school districts where collective bargaining is practiced.

Teachers have historically been subjected to low levels of compensation. As early as 1776, Adam Smith attributed the low wages of teachers to the plentiful supply. The fact that public school teaching is not subject to conventional market forces with regard to both supply and demand prevents teachers' salaries from being competitive with other white-collar employments. Rather than having the characteristics of an open marketplace the public school teaching profession exists as an oligopoly wherein the

state legislature can if it chooses control supply and demand.

The measurement of both the supply and demand of teachers is extremely complex. The supply is generally dependent on the number of teachers continuing in the profession and the number of new entrants. Both variables are dependent on factors such as age of teachers, retention power of the profession, opportunities for other employment, and the like. Further complication is added by the length and number of career breaks and the gender of teachers.

Investment in public schools and the economic conditions of teachers is influenced by the general condition of the economy. In periods of revenue shortfalls, teachers tend to personally absorb or cushion the effects of the economy.

An objective measurement of how much teachers should be paid to provide a quality education is not likely to be found; but, by comparative statistics, the condition of the teaching profession can be broadly determined. If teachers' salaries exceed the rise of inflation it is thought to be good. Also, if teachers' salaries in the United States are relatively better than in other countries, there may be reason to assume some relative elevation of teaching status in the economic system.

Today, teachers' salaries fall short of most other white-collar professions in the United States, but appear to provide greater purchasing power for U.S. teachers than teachers' salaries in other advanced nations.

State school finance programs may or may not contain salary schedules that force local school districts to pay specified minimums. State salary schedules are, however, frequently employed to assure that state funds flow to teachers or that local school districts will not be permitted to pay below a specified level.

At the local level, teacher salary schedules should be calibrated to attract and retain the highest quality teaching staff available. Considerations that should come into play when fashioning local salary schedules include: comparability to other professions, education level and training desired, incentive for improvement, reward for experience, workload measures, and an efficiency criterion that seeks to attract highly competent teachers and free the school districts of less productive teachers.

Administrators and supervisory staff should be paid in a measured relationship with teachers. Time factors and responsibility ratios may be legitimately employed to provide administrative personnel wages beyond that of teachers. The gap between superintendents' and teachers' salaries today is less than it was in prior decades indicating that teachers' status has improved somewhat. This may be attributable to greater public concern for quality instruction or to a decline in the status of administrators in the eyes of the public in a period of fiscal parsimony.

Merit pay has been employed in some states and/or school districts with the purpose of giving an incentive to teachers to be more productive. Merit pay has a long and controversial history and has been generally opposed by teacher organizations. Critics of merit pay maintain that such selective incentive devices are merely gadgets with no proof of success and, in fact, are a detriment to overall school productivity. Merit pay schemes may be more notable for their failures than for their successes. Such failures have been largely attributed to a lack of clear and measurable performance standards. Yet most agree that teachers need and desire some incentives to be more productive and rewards for those who are more effective.

Career ladders are another alternative that have been experimented with in several instances. Career ladders are premised on the idea that teachers need more structure in their careers permitting them to be elevated at certain points. Several such methods have been implemented.

Cost-of-living escalators have been included in many salary arrangements, in particular many of those that have been negotiated in a bargaining process. Such indices have been used in other public and private employment. Yet legislatures and school boards remain reluctant to tie their fiscal fortunes to such provisions.

KEY TERMS

Collective bargaining	Constant dollars	State salary schedules
Supply and demand	Consumer price index	Merit pay
Oligopoly	Gross domestic product	Career ladders
Oligopsony	Purchasing power parity	Cost-of-living index
Zero-sum economy		

ENDNOTES

1. For a more extensive discussion of this important area see Edgar L. Morphet, Roe L. Johns, and Theodore L. Reller, *Educational Organization and Administration: Concepts, Practices and Issues*, 4th ed. (Englewood Cliffs, NJ: Prentice-Hall, 1982), Ch. 18 and references.

2. Doris Ross and Patricia Flakus-Mosqueda, *State Education Collective Bargaining Laws* (Denver: Education Commission of the States, 1980), pp. 12–14.

3. Benjamin Werne, *The Law and Practice of Public Employment Labor Relations*, vol. 1 (Charlottesville, VA: Michie Company, 1974), pp. 393–455.

4. National Education Association, *Estimates of School Statistics 1979–80* (Washington, DC: NEA, 1980), p. 16.

5. Robert Thornton, "The Effects of Collective Negotiations on Teachers' Salaries," *Quarterly Review of Economics and Business 2* (Winter 1971), pp. 37–46; Robert N. Baird and John H. Landon, "The Effects of Collective Bargaining on Public School Teachers' Salaries: Comment," *Industrial and Labor Relations Review*, vol. 27 (October 1973), pp. 18–35; W. Clayton Hall and Norman E. Carroll, "The Effects of Teacher's Organizations on Salaries and Class Size," *Industrial and Labor Relations Review*, vol. 26 (January 1973), pp. 834–41; David Lipsky and John Drot-

ning, "The Influence of Collective Bargaining on Teachers' Salaries in New York State," *Industrial and Labor Relations Review* 27 (October 1973), pp. 18–35; Donald E. Frey, "Wage Determination in Public Schools and the Effects of Unionization," Working Paper 42E, Princeton University, Industrial Relations Section, 1973; H. Kasper, "The Effects of Collective Bargaining on Public School Teachers' Salaries," *Industrial and Labor Relations Review*, vol. 24 (October 1970), pp. 57–72; A.G. Balfour, "More Evidence That Unions Do Not Achieve Higher Salaries for Teachers'," *Journal of Collective Negotiations in the Public Sector* 3 (Fall 1974), pp. 289–303; and D.C. Zuelke and L.E. Forhreich, "The Impact of Comprehensive Collective Negotiations on Teachers' Salaries: Some Evidence from Wisconsin," *Journal of Collective Negotiations* 6, no. 1 (1977), pp. 81–88.

6. Adam Smith, *The Wealth of Nations*, rev. ed. (New York: Modern Library, 1937).

7. Locke, who lived from 1632 to 1704, was best known for his famous philosophical and political investigations, but he also wrote in pure economics. The quotation comes from his book *Some Considerations of the Consequences of the Lowering of Interest and Raising the Value of Money* (1691), published as *Essay on Interest and Value of Money* (London: Alex Murray & Son, 1870), p. 245.

8. James A. Richardson and J. Trent Williams, "Determining an Appropriate Teacher Salary," *Journal of Education Finance* 7, no. 2 (Fall 1981), pp. 193–194.

9. James A. Hale, "The Supply and Demand For Public Elementary and Secondary School Teachers," in *Educational Need in the Public Economy*, eds. Kern Alexander and K. Forbis Jordan (Gainesville, FL: University Presses of Florida, 1976), pp. 125–26.

10. Douglas Greenwald and Associates, *Dictionary of Modern Economics* (New York: McGraw-Hill, 1973), p. 409.

11. Hale, op. cit., p. 126.

12. National Education Association, *Status of the American Public School Teacher 1990–1991* (Washington, DC: NEA, 1992), p. 27.

13. Ibid., p. 29.

14. National Center for Education Statistics, *Projections of Education Statistics to 2002* (Washington, DC: U.S. Department of Education, NCES 91-490, December 1991), p. 70.

15. For the aforementioned reasons, supply and demand estimates are relatively unreliable. Projections by the National Center for Education Statistics, U.S. Department of Education, have been critiqued by a National Academy of Sciences (NAS) study that concluded that while the NCES was overall "fairly accurate," the supply estimates were limited to only new teacher graduates and not the total supply. Presently, the NCES is preparing new models based on alternative assumptions. See National Center for Education Statistics, *Projections of Education Statistics to 2002*, ibid., p. 69.

16. Lester C. Thurow, *The Zero-Sum Society* (New York: Penguin Books, 1980), p. 11.

17. National Education Association, *1992–93 Estimates of School Statistics* (Washington, DC: NEA, 1993), p. 17.

18. Stephen B. Lawton, "Teachers' Salaries: An International Perspective," in *Attracting and Compensating America's Teachers,* eds. Kern Alexander and David H. Monk (Cambridge, MA: Ballinger, Harper & Row, 1988), p. 79.

19. Ibid., p. 85.

20. William J. Baumol and Alan S. Blinder, *Economics, Principles and Policies*, 4th ed. (San Diego and New York: Harcourt Brace Jovanovich, 1988), p. 411.

21. Paul A. Samuelson and William D. Nordhaus, *Economics*, 14th ed. (New York: McGraw-Hill, 1992), p. 693.

22. Lawton, op. cit., pp. 70–71.

23. Ibid.

24. Organization for Economic Cooperation and Development, *Educational Expenditure, Costs and Financing: An Analysis on Trends: 1970–1988* (Paris: OECD, 1992).

25. Lawton, op. cit., pp. 72–73.

26. National Education Association, Research Division, *State Minimum Salary Laws for Teachers, 1950–51* (Washington, DC: NEA, 1950).

27. Ellwood P. Cubberley, *State School Administration* (Boston, MA: Houghton Mifflin, 1927), p. 655.

28. Ibid., p. 654.

29. "Musical Chairs," *The Economist*, July 17–23, 1993, p. 67. The Economist reports that among the advanced industrial nations Japan has the least labor-market turnover for all employment with workers having an average of 10.9 years of tenure, Germany is second with 10.4 years, and France is third with 10.1 years. The United States has the greatest rate of labor-market turnover, next to Holland with average job tenure of only 6.7 years. Moreover, *The Economist* observes that only 10 percent of young recruits into the U.S. labor force have any type of formal training from

their employer, while in both Japan and Germany employer training of young recruits is about 70 percent.

30. Cubberley, op. cit., p. 656.

31. *Report of the Winnetka Citizens Advisory Committee on Teacher Salaries* (Winnetka, IL: The Committee, 1958), pp. 12–13.

32. Willard E. Givens, "Analysis of Single Salary Schedules," *NEA Research Bulletin* 25, no. 3 (October 1947), p. 76.

33. National Education Association, *Status of the American Public School Teacher 1990–91* (Washington, DC: NEA, 1992), Table 55, p. 71.

34. Robert B. Howsam, Edgar L. Morphet, and John G. Ross, "Proposed Salary Schedule for the Professional Staff of the Anchorage Independent School District," mimeographed (Anchorage, AK: Board of Education, 1959), p. 39.

35. Margaret Stevenson, "What Is the Need? Not Merit Rating but Sound Personnel Policies," *NEA Journal* 46, no. 6 (September 1957), p. 13.

36. Keith Davis, *Human Relations in Business* (New York: McGraw-Hill, 1957), p. 309.

37. Wayne J. Urban, "Old Wine, New Bottles? Merit Pay and Organized Teachers," in *Merit, Money and Teachers' Careers*, ed. Henry C. Johnson, Jr. (Lanham, MD: University Press of America, 1985), pp. 25–38.

38. David K. Cohen and Richard J. Murmane, "The Merits of Merit Pay," *Project Report No. 85-A12* (Palo Alto, CA: Standard Education Policy Institute, 1985).

39. David B. Lipsky and Samuel B. Bacharack, "The Single Salary Schedule vs. Merit Pay: An Examination of the Debate," NEA Research Memo (Washington, DC: NEA, 1983).

40. Stephen L. Jacobson, "Merit Pay and Teaching as a Career," in *Attracting and Compensating America's Teachers*, eds. Kern Alexander and David H. Monk (Cambridge: Ballinger, Harper & Row, 1988), p. 162.

41. Ibid., p. 168.

42. David Greenberg and J. McCall, "Teacher Mobility and Allocation," *Journal of Human Resources* 9 (Fall), pp. 480–502.

43. O. Sewell, "Incentives for Inner City School Teachers," *Phi Delta Kappen* (October), p. 129.

44. Suzan Moore Johnson, "Merit Pay for Teachers: A Poor Prescription for Reform," *Harvard Educational Review* 54 (May), pp. 175–85.

45. The Holmes Group, *Tomorrow's Teachers: A Report of the Holmes Group* (East Lansing, MI: The Holmes Group, 1986).

46. Thurow, op. cit., p. 59.

47. Ibid., p. 61.

CHAPTER 14

FINANCING CAPITAL OUTLAY

TOPICAL OUTLINE OF CHAPTER

Financing Capital Facilities • Local Options • Current Revenues
• Building Reserve Funds • General Obligation Bonds
• State Options • Complete State Support • Equalization Grants
• Percentage-Matching Grants • Flat Grants • Loans
• Building Authorities • Fiscal Problems
• Characteristics of Equitable Programs

INTRODUCTION

The costs required to provide adequate capital facilities for public elementary and secondary education have often been overlooked during comparative assessments of state systems of school finance. However, neither the need for new and renovated school buildings nor the costs required to provide adequate facilities are insignificant. In 1989, the Education Writers Association estimated that the education infrastructure of the nation needed an investment of $84 billion for new and retrofitted construction and an additional $41 billion for deferred maintenance and repairs to existing facilities.[1] While most states provide modest financial assistance to their local school districts for capital construction, the preponderance of capital funding traditionally has been provided from local resources. As a consequence, the quality of public school facilities commonly is a function of local community fiscal capacity and aspiration. Only recently, partially due to judicial intervention, has this doctrine of local fiscal responsibility for the provision of capital facilities been questioned.[2]

The proportions of total expenditures allocated to capital outlay and interest on indebtedness for capital outlay in the public schools has varied greatly in different decades. Arrayed in Figure 14.1 is a graphic display of the percentages of

---

DEFINITIONS

Capital Outlay. An expenditure that results in the acquisition of fixed assets or additions to fixed assets, which are presumed to have benefits for more than one year. It is an expenditure for land or existing buildings, improvements of ground, construction of buildings, additions to buildings, remodeling of buildings, or initial, additional, and replacement equipment.

Debt Service. An expenditure for the retirement of school district indebtedness, including bond and loan principal, interest, and service charges.

Source: National Education Association, *Estimates of School Statistics, 1991–92* (Washington, DC: NEA, 1992), p. 47.

Percent

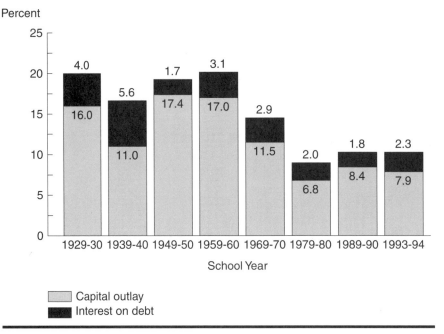

FIGURE 14.1 Percent Capital Outlay and Interest on Debt of Total Expenditures, Selected School Years, 1929–30 to 1993–94

Source: National Center for Education Statistics, *Digest of Education Statistics, 1992.* National Education Association, *Estimates of School Statistics, 1991–92 and 1993–94.*

total expenditures allocated for capital outlay and interest on indebtedness for selected school years, 1929–30 to 1993–94. Expenditures for capital outlay and interest on indebtedness ranged from a high of 20.1 percent of total expenditures in 1959–60 to a low of 8.8 percent in 1979–80. Note that expenditures for capital outlay plus interest have constituted the highest percentages of total expenditures in years when the school enrollment was increasing, and the lowest when the enrollment became static or was decreasing. Enrollment increased rapidly in the 1950s and 1960s, became static in 1970, and started declining in 1975. The decline continued until the mid-1980s; since 1984–85, a modest but sustained growth in public school enrollment has occurred.[3]

The construction of new buildings is a major financial undertaking for most boards of education. It is impossible for most of them to finance major capital outlays solely from current revenue

receipts. Local boards of education commonly issue serial bonds that mature annually, usually over a period of 20 to 25 years. Therefore, the annual interest on school debt for capital outlay plus the capital outlays made from current revenue receipts is the best national measure of the annual tax burden for capital outlay.

Since only a small part of capital outlay comes from current revenue,[4] the proportion of revenue receipts expended for indebtedness annually is a better measure of the annual tax burden than either expenditures for capital outlay or capital outlay and interest on debt combined. During the school years arrayed in Figure 14.1, the interest on school debt ranged from a low of 1.7 percent for school years 1949–50 and 1989–90 to a high of 5.6 percent for 1939–40. These data suggest that the annual tax burden for capital outlay, as measured by the percentage of expenditures allocated to interest on school debt, has not fluctuated significantly. The smoothing of the annual tax burden for capital outlay is sound fiscal and sound educational policy.

It is not possible to provide the school facilities needed from current revenue during periods of rapid growth in school enrollment. Even during periods of static or slow growth most school districts find it difficult if not impossible to finance their capital needs solely through the use of current revenue. However, many boards of education do not have the bonding capacity to provide for their capital outlay needs by issuing bonds. Unfortunately, far less progress has been made in school finance reform for capital outlay than in school finance reform for current expenditures. There are many indications that the tradition of relying almost entirely on the current and anticipated (through bond issues) revenues from local property taxes to finance school plant construction and other major capital outlay costs is no longer equitable. Even when districts are reorganized in rural and suburban areas, there will be many school systems that will not have the local resources needed to provide adequate school housing in addition to helping to support modern programs of education. The problems of providing modern school plants, not only in the ghetto areas of cities but also in many rural and metropolitan area school districts, cannot be resolved until appropriate new designs, provisions, and procedures for financial support are developed and implemented.

The tradition of local responsibility for financing school sites, buildings, equipment, and other capital costs still is strongly entrenched in many states. Many people believe that if the state assists in financing the current costs of operating schools, local school districts should be expected to provide their own buildings and meet other capital-outlay needs. In many parts of the nation, however, there are serious shortages and inadequacies, and many school systems cannot provide suitable facilities from local resources.

Even in the large-district states there will continue to be problems in providing satisfactory facilities in all communities if the construction has

---

Box 14.1 _____

Glory Days Are Over

Should a state underwrite the costs of school construction in order to equalize facilities? In 1971, Maryland began what one legislator called "a glorious effort" to assume the new construction burden of school districts. For fiscal year 1972 to 1988, the Public School Construction Program received $3.3 billion in requests from local school districts and authorized $1.6 billion for new construction. It also paid off almost all of the $755.6 million outstanding on debts incurred by the school districts for construction. . . .

The state effort enabled Baltimore City, for example, to replace or renovate about 70 buildings, including some built in the 1880s and still with their original cast iron furnaces. Through fiscal year 1987, the city schools had received about $358 million from the state for new construction and debt service. Montgomery County, an affluent suburb of Washington, D.C., received $230 million in state aid during the same period.

However, the glory days are over. The state's Board of Public Works has shifted the burden of school construction more squarely onto the shoulders of local school districts. . . . Its 1987 report noted that, "Given the basic constraints on state debt, the growing needs of the state itself, the expanded aid to local governments for capital projects in several unrelated categories, and the continued growth in school construction requests, it is apparent that school construction costs will have to be shared by local governments to a much greater degree than is now the case."

Source: Education Writers Association, *Wolves at the Schoolhouse Door* (Washington, DC: Education Writers Association, 1989), p. 30.

---

to be financed entirely from local funds. In county-unit states, the range of fiscal capacity is much less than in small-district states, but the variance in fiscal capacity is still at least ten to one in most of these states. If little state support is provided for current operating programs, the problem of financing school buildings will be more acute both in small- and large-district states than would be the case if satisfactory and adequate state support programs had been developed and fully financed in those states.

Thus, the tradition of local responsibility for financing school plant construction is neither sound nor realistic in any state. The high-capacity school systems may have ample resources to provide excellent facilities for all their pupils. The districts of average capacity may be able to provide reasonably satisfactory facilities if they are willing to exert high tax efforts. However, those districts with low capacity will not be able to afford satisfactory facilities unless funds from state and perhaps federal sources are provided to assist in meeting the costs.

The federal government provides only a negligible amount of aid for capital outlay. Therefore most boards of education have only two sources of revenue available for financing capital outlay—local and state. In some states, boards of education have only local revenue available.

FINANCING CAPITAL FACILITIES: LOCAL OPTIONS

Prior to the twentieth century, financing public school facilities was the responsibility of local governments in the United States. The schools were an integral part of American frontier life, and the actual construction of buildings often proved to be one of the year's biggest social events.[5] Initially, public school facilities were financed by private donations of sites and materials and erected by volunteer workers. Later, special local property taxes were levied in order to finance the construction of needed facilities. By the latter part of the nineteenth century, local communities found it necessary to borrow funds, and state legislatures enacted laws which permitted the issuance of bonds for school construction by specific school districts or municipalities.[6] Although the population of the country was burgeoning and the costs of providing public school facilities were increasing rapidly, most states were reluctant to have their state government assume more responsibility

for financing the construction of local public school facilities. An examination of current public school support programs will show a myriad of state capital-outlay and debt-service-assistance programs; however, the tradition of financing public school facilities primarily by local governments continues to exist in most states today.

With the exception of the limited funds available from state-supported capital-outlay and debt-service programs, local school districts in most states have relatively few options available for obtaining the funds necessary to finance the construction of their school facilities. In essence, local school districts are faced with one, or a combination, of the following three choices.

Current Revenues

Often referred to as "pay-as-you-go" financing, the ability to finance the construction of school facilities from current revenues is an alternative available only to the large and/or very affluent school districts. Thus, the entire cost of a project or projects is accrued from the proceeds of one fiscal year's local tax levy, which usually results in sharp increases in the local tax rate. According to Burrup, for those districts with the available resources, financing the construction of school facilities through current revenue "is an ideal way to finance capital outlays. It is the quickest perhaps the easiest way to getting the necessary resources from the private sector of the economy. It eliminates expenditure of large sums of money for interest, the costs of bond attorney fees, and election costs."[7]

In opposition, there are those who argue that the use of current revenue for financing capital facilities results in:

1. Creation of tax friction among both taxpayers and governmental agencies because of increased school taxes
2. Failure to distribute capital costs among the generations who benefit from the school facilities

3. Failure to realize the economic advantages of borrowing in periods of inflation.

Primarily due to the inability of most school districts to finance capital construction through current revenue, the latter argument has prevailed. The use of current revenue to finance the costs of constructing public school facilities has been minor when compared with the total funds generated for capital purposes in the United States.[8]

Building Reserve Funds

Some states permit school districts to accumulate tax funds for the purpose of funding the construction of future school facilities. Such funds, referred to as building reserve funds, are kept separate from the school districts' current operating funds and are commonly financed by special tax levies. Generally, state laws stipulate that building reserve funds can only be invested under very controlled conditions, and as a consequence, the interest yield normally does not keep pace with inflation.

Critics of the building reserve fund option claim that changes in school district leadership often result in diversion of reserve funds to purposes other than those intended when the funds were collected. Also, critics contend that many of the taxpayers who contribute to the reserve funds will not realize any benefits. Most importantly, although reserve funds and current operating funds are usually financed and maintained separately, the taxpayer is only concerned with the total costs of the school district's budget. The higher tax rates required to finance reserved building funds often create taxpayer resistance and result in a reduction of the current operating budget.[9]

On the other hand, there are several advantages to the use of the building reserve fund option. After sufficient funds have been accumulated, the project can be constructed without the delays and expenses associated with gaining voter approval for the issuance of bonds. Debt service charges are avoided and local restrictions on taxing or debt limitations will not interfere

with the project.[10] Building reserve funds are used by several states but currently provide only a small amount of the total funds used for the construction of public school facilities.

General Obligation Bonds

The vast majority of public school facilities are constructed through the sale of general obligation bonds by local school districts. School bonds, generically referred to as municipal bonds, are legal papers issued by the borrower as evidence of debt, which specify interest rates, payment periods, and security.[11] Municipal bonds enjoy tax-exempt status from the federal income tax and from state income taxes in most states. The tax-exempt status makes the purchase of municipal bonds particularly desirable for investors with high incomes.

Probably one of the most desirable features of municipal bonds from the vantage point of the investor is the relative safety of principal. According to the New York Stock Exchange,

> [municipal bonds] They are considered second only to obligations of Federal Government. During their severest test—The Great Depression—only about 1/2 of 1% suffered any loss of principal on time. In most of these cases, bondholders eventually received their interest and principal.[12]

One variety of municipal bonds, general obligation bonds, is secured by the full faith, the credit, and generally the unlimited taxing power of the issuer. In effect, the borrower promises to use every available means to meet interest payments when due and to return the full face value of the bond to the investors at maturity. General obligation bonds are usually recognized as the most secure of the municipal bonds.

Municipal bonds, including general obligation bonds, are normally rated by one of the national rating companies for the purpose of alerting potential purchasers of the relative security of the issue.[13] The rating awarded the school district by the rating company significantly influences the interest charged the issuer.[14]

Most general obligation bonds issued by school districts are in the form of serial bonds chronologically arranged so that the bonds comprising the issue mature at regular intervals, usually annually or semiannually. Therefore, balanced debt service can be arranged over the life of the total issue. In contrast, the *term bond* is rarely used and actually prohibited in some states, due to a history of poor management practices. A term bond is used in conjunction with a sinking fund and is designed to meet interest payments at regular intervals, but there is a delay in the repayment of the principal until the end of the indebtedness period.

The constraints that school districts operate under regarding the issuance of general obligation bonds vary considerably among states and even among school districts in some states. Most states have enacted school district debt limitations in the form of a percentage of locally assessed valuation of real property which cannot be exceeded. Restrictive debt limitations have proved particularly troublesome for those states or school districts with limited local tax bases. There is also considerable variation among the states regarding the approval process required prior to the sale of general obligation bonds by the school districts. Some states require a simple majority of those voting at referendum, while other states require considerably more than a simple majority. The lack of uniform property assessment practices resulting in inequitable tax rates plagues some states, while voter-initiated property tax limitations confront other states. Voter-initiated property tax limitations, such as the infamous Proposition 13 of California, have also severely restricted the sale of school bonds. Nevertheless, despite the many problems inherent in the sale of general obligation bonds, this method remains the primary option for many, and the only option for some school districts for financing public school facilities in the United States.

During the inflationary periods of the 1970s and early 1980s, municipal bonds, including school bonds, were sold at the highest interest rates in this century. It was not sound fiscal policy for boards of education to bind themselves to taxpayers with high interest rate for 20 to 25 years. Prudent school boards sold their bonds during that period so that they could refinance them when interest rates abated. Thus, local boards were able to call their long-term bonds bearing the highest interest rates and refund their bonded debts at lower interest rates. Bonds issued for a period of 20 to 25 years usually carry a sliding scale of interest rates, the earlier-maturing bonds bearing a lower interest rate than the longer-maturing bonds. Most municipal bonds are now subject to call, with a small premium, ten years after the date of issuance. Bonds with this provision are usually sold at nearly the same price as noncallable bonds. However, if bonds are issued callable at any time after issuance, the issuing body will have to pay a higher interest rate than on noncallable bonds or bonds subject to deferred call at a premium.

The number of years over which a bond issue matures should not exceed the life of the facility for which the bond was issued. This is not a problem for a school building, which usually has a life of from 40 to 50 years. School bonds are usually issued to mature over a period of 20 to 25 years, because it would be difficult to market 40- to 50-year bonds without paying excessive interest rates. However, certain types of equipment such as school buses have a life of only approximately 10–12 years. Some boards of education finance school buses by separate bond issues, and such bonds should mature in not more than 10 years.

As indicated, it is good fiscal policy to have a school bond rated by a national rating company such as Moody's Investor Service or Fitch's Investor Service. However, these rating agencies often will not rate a small bond issue that is issued by a small district or will give it a low rating. A marketed bond issue or one with a low rating will be sold at a higher interest rate than a highly rated issue. A board of education issuing a bond which might otherwise be unrated or rated low can obtain a high rating if the issue is insured with a municipal bond insurance company such as the Municipal Bond Insurance Association or the American Municipal Bond Assurance Corporation. Such insurance will guarantee the payment of principal and interest on an insured bond issue. This insurance will costs the board of education a fee, but the lower interest rate obtained by the board often will make it a good investment.

FINANCING CAPITAL FACILITIES: STATE OPTIONS

As discussed previously, prior to the twentieth century capital facilities for public elementary and secondary education were financed almost exclusively from local resources. Undoubtedly, some school districts experienced difficulty in providing adequate school facilities before 1900, but no state had seen fit to develop a continuing capital facilities assistance program until Alabama took the initiative in 1901 and established an aid plan for rural schools. Two years later in 1903, Louisiana, by constitutional amendment, enacted a state plan in which bonds could be issued for the construction of school facilities in impoverished areas of the state. By 1909 South Carolina was providing state assistance for financing capital facilities serving African-American rural school children, while Virginia and North Carolina established modest state loan funds.[15] The following 20 years saw several states implementing matching grants for the purpose of assisting and encouraging school consolidation, and in 1927 Delaware took the first major step toward a comprehensive state capital facilities financing program. The Delaware plan required that primary support for the financing of local public school facilities be borne by the state government, with only a small contribution required of the local school district.

During the years of the Great Depression and World War II, a shortage of both local and state resources virtually prohibited local school districts from engaging in extensive building programs. Burdened with the problems of aging facilities, inadequate and insufficient buildings,

and a growing desire for more and better school facilities, the limited number of state assistance programs were either woefully inadequate, inequitable, or both. A report by Webber in 1941 indicated that of the 12 states that had established various forms of state-aid programs for helping local school districts finance their public school facilities, none had programs that could be regarded as equitable.[16] Such programs were either crude and inequitable distribution systems, in which the principles of equalization were neither recognized nor applied, or else were simple devices for easy-term loans to districts by the state.

Shortly after World War II, attention once again focused on the problem of providing necessary funds for financing the construction of capital facilities for public school children. In 1947 Florida became the first state to develop and adopt a comprehensive plan. The Florida program was based on the concept of determining annually the financial resources needed for each school district to replace buildings that were at the end of their normal life expectancies. The Florida plan, once considered as fully state funded, is now a shared-cost program. Stimulated primarily by the increased demand for school facilities due to the postwar baby boom, many more states enacted various forms of state capital facilities assistance plans. By 1950 approximately 20 states had enacted some form of state-aid program for assisting at least some of their local districts in funding their school construction programs.

After 1950 a still greater effort was made to encourage state participation in financing the construction of local public school facilities. For many years, school finance experts had been urging state legislatures to enact a wide assortment of state capital-outlay programs.[17] Additional impetus was given to the drive for increased state funding of public school facilities when the United States Office of Education and the University of California at Berkeley cooperated in a national study of state public school capital-outlay programs. After analysis of the various state programs, the researchers recommended in part that the states should provide additional leadership and financial resources for comprehensive and efficient public school capital-outlay programs.[18]

According to Barr and Wilkerson, 40 states had developed various forms of assistance programs for financing local public school facilities by 1965.[19] By 1978–79, Webb indicated that 37 states provided financial support through five primary mechanisms for aiding local school districts with capital expenditures.[20] Updated results of a somewhat similar classification of state-assisted capital-outlay and debt-service programs as used by Webb are displayed in Table 14.1. This classification places each of the 50 states into the following categories:

1. Complete state support
2. Grants-in-aid (that is, subcategories of equalization grants, percentage-matching grants, and flat grants)
3. Loans
4. Building authorities
5. No state assistance

Each of these categories with the exception of "no state assistance" are discussed along with the relative advantages and disadvantages of each.

Complete State Support

As its name suggests, a complete-state-support program requires that the funding of capital and debt-service expenditures of the public schools be borne by the state. It is apparent from an examination of Table 14.1 that only the three states of Alaska, California, and Hawaii are classified as having implemented complete-state-support programs by 1986–87.

Advantages cited by proponents of complete state support usually include the following:

1. A higher degree of fiscal equalization is achieved within the state because the quality of facilities is not a function of the taxpaying abilities of local education agencies.
2. State governments normally have access to a greater variety and quantity of resources than

do local governments and can avoid the overutilization of a single resource.
3. A state government can develop an allotment mechanism based upon needs, which will provide a higher level of efficiency.
4. If it were necessary for the state governments to acquire the necessary funds from the issuance of bonds, it is likely that the larger issue would result in overall savings in interest and services charges.

Disadvantages cited by opponents of the complete-state-support program usually include the following:

1. Additional concentrations of power and control of the public schools will become focused at the state level, thereby further alienating local citizens from public schools.
2. The centralization of power would result in uniformity of public school facilities throughout the state, and such facilities would not recognize the unique needs of varying localities. In addition, it is likely that the centralization of power would result in less experimentation and innovation in school facilities and in a high level of mediocrity.
3. Due to a high level of competition for resources at the state level, the construction of urgently needed public school facilities could be unnecessarily delayed.

Equalization Grants

The primary purpose of the equalization grant is to provide increased taxpayer equity within the state. In the absence of state support for the construction of public school facilities, taxpayers in school districts with low capacity are required to make a significantly greater fiscal effort to construct capital facilities than taxpayers in districts with high capacity. Consequently, equalization grants are designed to allocate revenues per unit of need inversely to the fiscal abilities of the local school districts. As can be determined by an examination of Table 14.1, approximately 16 states in 1986–87

TABLE 14.1 Classification of State-Aid Programs for Capital Outlay and Debt Service, 1986–87

GRANTS: CAPITAL OUTLAY			GRANTS: DEBT SERVICE			CAPITAL LOAN PROGRAMS	FULL-STATE FUNDED
Equalized	*Matching*	*Flat*	*Equalized*	*Flat*	*Matching*		
Arizona	Delaware	Alabama	New Jersey	Connecticut	Delaware	Arkansas	Alaska
Connecticut		Mississippi	New York	Mississippi		Indiana	California
Florida		South Carolina	Rhode Island	New Jersey		Minnesota	Hawaii
Georgia		Tennessee	Utah	South Carolina		North Dakota	
Illinois			Vermont			Virginia	
Maryland			Wyoming			Wisconsin	
Massachusetts						Wyoming	
New Jersey							
New Mexico							
New York							
Pennsylvania							
Rhode Island							
Utah							
Vermont							
Washington							
West Virginia[1]							
Wyoming							
Total: 17	Total: 1	Total: 4	Total: 6	Total: 4	Total: 1	Total: 7	Total: 3

Source: Reprinted by permission, Richard G. Salmon, Stephen Lawson, Christina Dawson, and Thomas Johns, *Public School Finance Programs of the United States and Canada, 1986–87* (Blacksburg, VA.: American Education Finance Association, 1988), p. 9.

[1]Modified to reflect implementation of state capital support program by West Virginia in 1988.

had enacted some form of equalization grant-in-aid for the allocation of state capital-outlay assistance to local school districts. Six states had implemented equalization grants designed to assist local school districts to retire debt service obligations. Note that some states had implemented both capital-outlay and debt-service equalization grants. The variety of equalization grants in use was very extensive, ranging from an annual allocation in the manner of the Strayer-Haig equalization model for current expenses, to a varying percentage of state support based on the local school districts' relative fiscal capacity standard.

Advantages cited by proponents of equalization grants usually include the following:

1. Comparable public school facilities can be provided throughout the state without the imposition of an excessive local tax burden on districts with low ability to pay.
2. Since some local contribution is required for participation in most equalization grants-in-aid, the frivolous use of state funds would be curtailed.
3. Reduced dependency on the local property tax for the construction of school facilities would provide local governments with additional resources for other governmental services and/or tax relief. In addition, the economic health of local governments would be strengthened and the marketability of municipal bonds for purposes other than education would be enhanced.

Disadvantages cited by opponents of equalization grants usually include the following:

1. In order to guarantee funds for all school districts in the state, a substantial amount of state resources would have to be dedicated to this purpose, while inadequate appropriations would render the program ineffective
2. A statewide system would not necessarily be responsive to the variety of local needs, and local schools initially might experience difficulty in responding to immediate construction needs.

Percentage-Matching

The percentage-matching grant is designed to provide a fixed percentage of state support for each local (usually state-approved) public school capital-facilities project. The fiscal capacity of the local school district is not taken into consideration, and the total amount of state assistance varies in accordance with the cost of the project. For the school year 1986–87 only one state, Delaware, had either enacted or was using a percentage-matching grant to fund local capital facilities grant program. Delaware also used a percentage-matching grant to assist local school districts in retiring debt service obligations.

Advantages usually cited by proponents of percentage-matching grants include the following:

1. Initiation of school construction projects remains the prerogative of local school districts, and the building programs can be tailored to meet the needs and desires of local citizens.
2. The state, through the use of its approval process, can encourage cost-effective construction practices and influence the design and location of school buildings.
3. State assistance would reduce the dependency of local school districts on the property tax, thereby freeing local resources for other governmental purposes. In addition, the economic health and the marketability of municipal bonds for purposes other than education would be enhanced.

Disadvantages usually cited by opponents of percentage-matching grants include the following:

1. A percentage-matching grant invariably penalizes local school districts with limited fiscal capacity to support school building programs. Local school districts with high fiscal capacity can obtain sufficient funds to qualify for state matching funds with relative ease, while districts with less capacity can only obtain the required matching funds through an extraordinary tax effort by their citizens. Of course, if the state's matching

percentage were quite high (for instance, 90 percent state to 10 percent local), the disequalization effect of the percentage-matching grant would be neutralized, and the percentage-matching would take on the characteristics of an equalization grant-in-aid.

2. In order to guarantee funds for all local school districts with qualifying building projects, it would be necessary for the state to appropriate substantial resources. Insufficient appropriations would render the program ineffective.

3. School districts with sufficient capital facilities would not be eligible for state assistance, and citizens would see little direct benefit from their state taxes.

Flat Grants

As its title implies, the flat grant is designed as a fixed amount of funds per unit allocated by the state to the local school district, to be used to finance local capital construction. Some states annually allocate a fixed amount of funds per ADA or ADM, while other states allocate a fixed amount per state-approved project. Regardless of the unit of need used by the state, the flat grant ignores the variation in fiscal capacity among the state's school districts. For the school year 1986–87 four states were classified as either using or having enacted a flat grant for the distribution of state funds for construction of local capital facilities. Four states also used flat grants to assist local school districts in retiring their debt-service obligations. Two states, Mississippi and South Carolina, used flat grants to distribute capital outlay and debt-service funds.

Advantages cited by proponents of the flat grant usually include the following:

1. Control of the local school building program generally remains with the local school district, thus the building program can be tailored to meet local needs or desires.

2. While usually viewed as nonequalizing, the flat grant does provide some measure of eq-

uity, since statewide resources are used for funding the flat-grant program. Obviously, the greater the amount of the flat grant provided by the state (in other words, as the flat grant approaches complete state aid), the greater will be the equity provided to taxpayers.

3. State assistance in the form of a flat grant would reduce dependency of the local school districts on the property tax, thereby freeing local resources for other governmental purposes. In addition, the economic health of local governments would be strengthened and the marketability of municipal bonds for purposes other than education would be enhanced.

4. The flat-grant program can be easily administered, due to its simple allocation technique and the ability to accurately anticipate required funds.

Disadvantages cited by opponents of the flat-grant program usually include the following:

1. Most state flat grants only supplement the local funds required to finance the school building program. Consequently, variation in the quality of school facilities among the states' school districts is considerable, coupled with an inequitable tax effort.

2. In those states that annually allocate funds on a percentage basis without consideration of building needs, some school districts receive unneeded funds while others have unfunded capital needs.

Loans

State capital-assistance loan funds have been established to provide direct financial assistance to local school districts. Commonly, states have established a permanent fund, or funds, often through the use of dedicated revenues, for the purpose of providing low-interest loans to local school districts. Unlike the previous state assistance plans, loans provided by the states contain the provision that the funds be repaid at some future date. With some exceptions, loans do not take into consideration the relative fiscal capacities of the local school districts, and as a consequence, do not provide for a high degree of fiscal equalization.[21] Funds available from state loan funds are usually modest, and states have either had to restrict all school districts to a certain amount per approved project or to control the number of eligible school districts by implementing certain qualifying criteria. For example, a school district may have to tax or bond itself at a certain level or fall below a specified measure of fiscal capacity in order to qualify for a state loan. For the school year 1986–87 seven states either had enacted or were using loan funds as a means of helping local school districts finance their capital facilities.

Advantages cited by proponents of state loan funds usually include the following:

1. The loan funds provide local school districts with an economical mechanism for borrowing necessary funds, due to the modest interest charged by the state.
2. Generally, state loans to local school districts are not charged against the local school district's debt limitation, thereby giving them access to additional resources.
3. The time required to acquire funds from state loan funds is usually considerably less than the time required to acquire funds through the sale of bonds.
4. The state, through the use of its approval process, can encourage cost-efficient construction practices and influence the design and location of school buildings.

Disadvantages usually cited by opponents of state loan funds include the following:

1. Normally, state loan funds are extremely limited and serve only as a minor resource in the local school district's total building program.
2. Due to limited funds in most state loan funds, plus the common practice of permitting all school districts equal access to state loans, fiscal equalization is not enhanced.
3. The establishment of modest state loan funds often diverts the attention of the legislature

from adequately funding the construction of public school capital facilities.
4. Local control of school construction may be diluted through use of the state approval process required for those school districts seeking state loans.

Building Authorities

A unique device designed to help local school districts finance the construction of their school facilities is the school building authority. Building authorities can be designed to function at either the local or state levels of government. In essence, a building authority is an agency established by the state for the purposes of circumventing the restrictive taxing or debt limitations of local governments and/or facilitating the construction of essential local school facilities. According to Jordan and others,

> The public school building authorities, local and state, and state bond banks are state-established public corporations that provide alternatives for funding local school facilities. School building authorities were first developed for the purpose of circumventing restrictive debt limitation imposed by state constitutional provisions. Originally, state authorities were designed so that loan purchase agreements were made with school districts for the acquisition of school facilities; however, recent state authorities have evolved into mechanisms designed to achieve greater efficiency in financing and fiscally equalizing the quality of school facilities among school districts.[22]

Since the building authorities are separate agencies of government and do not operate schools, the taxing or debt limitations of the local school district need not apply. All states do not permit the use of building authorities to construct school facilities. In several states, state court decisions have ruled against legislation which attempted to establish building authorities. Camp has pointed out that, as recently as 1983, 11 states used local or state building authorities and bond banks to assist local school districts with their capital outlay needs.[23]

Advantages cited by proponents of building authorities usually include the following:

1. Many of the debt and taxing restrictions on local school districts are imposed by state constitutions, which often are difficult to amend. The use of building authorities permits the state to assist local school districts in financing the construction of needed facilities without constitutional amendment.
2. Unless prohibited by the state or federal governments, a combination of state, local, and federal current revenues may be used by the school district to pay the costs of lease-rental or lease-purchase agreements with the building authorities.
3. Often, building authorities can be used by the local school districts without acquiring voter approval, thereby avoiding building delays and added expense.

Disadvantages usually cited by opponents of building authorities include the following:

1. The enactment of building authorities only ignores the more pressing problem of adequately financing the construction of public school facilities, by evading taxing and debt limitations.
2. Revenue bonds are generally used to finance building authorities, which results in higher interest costs than the interest costs of the more secure general-obligation bonds.
3. The right of taxpayers and citizens to express their approval or disapproval is circumvented by the use of building authorities.

Persistent Fiscal Problems in Financing Capital Facilities

The National Educational Finance Project made a national survey of the problems of financing school facilities in 1971. Twenty-two years later in 1993, the problems identified then still exist. The following is a summary of the findings of the study of school facilities made by that project.[24]

In any general discussion of aid for public school construction throughout the nation, two paramount problems emerge:

1. Many state-aid plans are only token in nature, and several states do not provide local school districts with any financial assistance for school construction.
2. The federal government has not provided financial support for any general programs for school construction. Even though title for school buildings may legally reside with the state and education has historically and legally been considered a state function, the entire, or a major portion of, the financial burden for providing housing for educational programs and students has been placed upon the shoulders of the local school district in a great number of states.

This general pattern throughout the nation has resulted in a heavy drain upon local fiscal resources as a source of financial support for school construction. Various constitutional limitations and statutory provisions restrict the latitude available to the local school district by imposing constraints such as the following:

1. Unduly restrictive debt and tax-rate limitations in some states, and wide variations among the states in these matters
2. Assessment practices in local districts which do not coincide with statutory or constitutional prescriptions, and wide variations in assessment levels among local districts, which result in property tax bases unrelated to the real fiscal capacity (as measured by property value) of the several districts
3. A property tax base which is heavily relied upon for school construction funds, is not immediately responsive to changes in the economy as a whole, does not necessarily coincide with taxpaying capacity, and is regressive in terms of assumption of the burden
4. Voter reactions to property tax rates which suggest that psychological limits may have been reached and that rates may have reached confiscatory levels in many states
5. Unduly rigid voter qualifications and provisions which require more than a majority vote for passage, thereby making it extremely difficult to obtain approval in some states
6. An extremely rapid increase in school construction costs, without a uniformly corresponding increase in revenue potential from property taxes

7. Overdependence on the property tax, which is also heavily relied upon to support other local governmental functions
8. School district geographical boundaries which result in the isolation of commercial and industrial taxable wealth, thereby creating residential areas with low revenue-generating capacity
9. Variations in local district facility needs and fiscal abilities which are so extreme that many districts could not meet their needs even if all legal restrictions on local debt and tax rates were removed.[25]

It is obvious that an equitable plan of financing school plant facilities cannot be based exclusively on local school district financing, even if all legal obstacles were eliminated, because of the wide variance among local school districts in wealth and taxpaying ability. School districts often vary in equalized valuation as much as 10 to 1 in states with large school districts such as county unit states, and variations are much greater in states with many small districts. Therefore, an equitable plan for financing school facilities must involve either full-state financing or an equitable combination of local and state financing. A case can be made for the federal government to also contribute to the financing of public school facilities. Unfortunately, the likelihood of significant federal support for capital outlay is improbable at best.

CHARACTERISTICS OF EQUITABLE STATE CAPITAL-OUTLAY PROGRAMS

Characteristics of an equitable capital-outlay program should contain the following:

1. The quality of school facilities available to the pupils of a school district should not be determined by the fiscal capacity of the district. Either the state must fully finance the facilities needed or it must provide equalization grants which substantially equalize the financial resources of the school districts that are available for financing needed facilities. This is one of the principal criteria used for evaluating the

equity of a state's plan for financial current expenses.

2. An equitable measure of need for school facilities should be utilized. The measure of need for school facilities should be based primarily upon the educational program needed. The measure of need should give consideration to at least the following factors:

a. The school buildings of all school districts depreciate at a rate of about 2 percent per year. Therefore all districts have a depreciation need of at least 2 percent of present replacement cost. The depreciation of equipment is still greater. Therefore the depreciation of buildings and equipment combined is probably about 2½ percent per year. Unit depreciation costs can readily be computed on a pupil- or teacher-unit basis.

b. The measure of need should include pupil growth, projected pupil growth, and capital-outlay needs resulting from a shift in the residence of the pupil population within a district.

c. Different types of educational programs costs varying amounts per unit. Furthermore school plants may cost more in some school districts than the state average, due to differences in site costs and other factors. These cost variations should be included in the measure of need.

d. Some districts may have issued bonds and provided the needed facilities without waiting for the state to develop an equitable plan of school financing. The debt service on such bonds should be included in the measure of need for such districts.

3. The finance plan should provide for financing school facilities by borrowing and by current revenue. Boards of education should have ample authority to issue bonds for school facilities and utilize annual state grants to pay all or part of the debt service on such bonds. If a district does not have the bonding capacity needed to finance the facilities needed, a state authority should be given the power to issue state bonds on behalf of the district and should utilize all or part of the annual state capital-outlay allotment to the district to pay the debt service on the bonds. School

districts should also have the authority to use current annual state allotments for capital outlay and current local revenue, in order to reduce the interest costs of excessive borrowing.

4. The school plant program should be carefully planned and projected over a period of years. The state departments of education should provide technical assistance to their local boards of education for this planning process.

5. The state should not exercise unnecessary controls over the plant program of a school district. It is recognized that the state should enforce minimum standards with respect to health and safety, but the state should not establish state plans for school buildings or require a uniform number of square feet per elementary or high-school pupil. The need for the school plant originates in the educational program, and local boards of education should be given a large measure of authority in determining the educational program needed in the district. Educational needs vary among the districts of a state and the same program in every district would not be equitable to the pupils. The school plant should facilitate the educational program needed, not control it.

6. The plan for financing the school plant should be an annual, continuing plan as contrasted with ad hoc, emergency plans.

SUMMARY AND CONCLUSIONS

The doctrine of local fiscal responsibility for capital facilities has resulted in a backlog of unmet needs and considerable variance in the quality of school facilities throughout the nation.

The proportion of total expenditures for public elementary and secondary education allocated for capital outlay and interest on school indebtedness tends to follow the growth or decline in pupil enrollment.

Local options for funding capital construction commonly include: pay-as-you-go using current revenue; the use of building reserve funds; and the sale of general obligation bonds.

For those states that provide fiscal support for local capital construction, funding options commonly include: complete state support; equalization grants; percentage-matching grants; flat grants; loans; and building authorities.

Persistent problems encountered by local school boards seeking to construct or renovate their capital facilities include: restrictive debt limitations; overburdened property tax bases; high costs of construction; and lack of public support.

Characteristics of equitable state capital-outlay programs include the neutralization of the fiscal capacities of local school districts in order to break the link between fiscal capacity and quality of school facilities, and the development and use of accurate measures of capital needs.

Resources for capital construction should include a mix of current and nonrevenue funding sources.

Unduly restrictive state controls pursuant to the design of local school facilities should be avoided in order to tailor school buildings to the needs of the local communities.

KEY TERMS

Capital outlay	Percentage-matching grants	Term bonds
Pay-as-you-go financing	Complete state support	Credit rating
General obligation bonds	Debt service	Equalization grants
Sinking funds	Building reserve funds	Flat grants
Serial bonds	Municipal bonds	Bond referendums
Callable bonds		

ENDNOTES

1. Education Writers Association, *Wolves at the Schoolhouse Door* (Washington, DC: Education Writers Association, 1989), p. 4.

2. See for example *Pauley* v. *Bailey*, 324 S.E. 2d 128 (1984).

3. National Center for Education Statistics, *Digest of Education Statistics, 1993–94* (Washington, DC: 1992); National Education Association, *Estimates of School Statistics, 1992* (Washington, DC: NEA, 1993–94).

4. The vast majority of capital outlay is financed through the sale of bonds, loans, and other nonrevenue sources.

5. W. Monfort Barr and William Wilkerson, *Financing Public Elementary and Secondary School Facilities in the United States*, Special Study Number Seven, National Education Finance Project (Bloomington, IN: Indiana University, 1970), p. 25.

6. Ibid.

7. Percy Burrup, *Financing Education in a Climate of Change* (Boston: Allyn and Bacon, 1993), p. 292.

8. Glen Earthman, *Planning Educational Facilities for the Next Century* (Reston, VA: Association of School Business Officials International, 1992), pp. 78 & 88.

9. K. Forbis Jordan, Mary McKeown, Richard Salmon, and Dean Webb, *School Business Administration* (Newbury Park, CA: Corwin Press, 1985), p. 272.

10. Ibid.

11. Ibid., pp. 272–278.

12. New York Stock Exchange, *Understanding Bonds and Preferred Stocks* (New York: New York Stock Exchange, August 1978).

13. One of the most widely used of the rating companies is Moody's Investor Service, which rates each issue on an eight-point scale continuum for Aaa to C.

14. Earthman, op. cit., p. 93.

15. M. David Alexander, "Financing Capital Outlay," in *Critical Issues in Educational Finance*, eds. Stephen B. Thomas and Koy M. Floyd (Harrisonburg, VA: Institute for Educational Finance, 1975), p. 109.

16. Gerald D. Webber, *State Equalization of Capital Outlays for Public School Buildings* (Los Angeles: University of Southern California Press, 1941), p. 5.

17. Barr, et al., op. cit., p. 137.

18. A total of 16 specific recommendations were made by the researchers. See Lindman, et al., *State Provisions for Financing Public School Capital Outlay Programs* (Washington, DC: U.S. Government Printing Office, 1951), p. 136.

19. W. Monfort Barr and William R. Wilkerson, "State Participation in Financing Local School Facilities," in *Trends in Financing Public Education,* Eighth National Conference on School Finance (Washington, DC: National Education Association, 1965), pp. 224–232.

20. L. Dean Webb, *Financing Capital Outlay* (Tucson: Joint Select Committee on Tax Reform and School Finance of the Arizona Legislature, 1979), pp. 11–17 to 11–19.

21. Some states have combined the techniques of loan funds and grants by implementing loan-grants which are designed to assist school districts that cannot make full repayment in a reasonable time period without enacting a burdensome tax effort. In such cases, the state is authorized to cancel the unpaid portion after a certain number of years.

22. Jordan, et al., op. cit., pp. 273–274.

23 William E. Camp, *Public School Building Corporations Financing Public Elementary and Secondary School Facilities* (Blacksburg, VA: Virginia Tech, 1983), unpublished dissertation.

24. Adapted from W. Monfort Barr and K. Forbis Jordan, "Financing Public Education and Secondary School Facilities," in *Planning to Finance Education,* eds. Roe L. Johns, Kern Alexander, and K. Forbis Jordan (Gainesville, FL: National Educational Finance Project, 1971), pp. 251–252.

25. Ibid., p. 252.

CHAPTER 15

EDUCATION PRODUCTION FUNCTIONS AND WHETHER MONEY MATTERS

TOPICAL OUTLINE OF CHAPTER

Production Functions • Coleman Report • Does Money Matter?
• The Industrial Model • The Education Model • The Cost Side
• Time as a Variable • Teacher Differences • Sequence of Inputs
• Variations in Variables • Statistical Problems • Causality
• Experimental Conditions • Model Specification • Coleman
Report Flaws • Needed Improvements

INTRODUCTION

Much has been said about the limits of investment in education. Many governmental leaders at both the federal and state levels have vigorously argued that more money for education is simply throwing "good money after bad." The supporting rationale for this position has emanated largely from several studies that have attempted to relate inputs of dollars to outputs as measured by pupil achievement test scores. The majority of these studies have shown that there is no consistent relationship. These analyses, called production-function studies, have been widely misinterpreted to argue that such a lack of co-linearity is good evidence to support either reductions in public school funding or no further increases.

Proponents of this position maintain that until public schools can show that there exists a systematic relationship between money inputs and achievement outputs no additional funds should be forthcoming. Moreover, this argument has been widely used by states in defending inequities in fiscal distributions to local school districts. The argument goes this way: if additional resources do not result in measurable additional cognitive learning then there is no justification to equalize funding or provide more funds for poor districts.

This school of thought is advocated and articulated by Hanushek who has written,

> There is no systematic relationship between school expenditures and student performance. This implies significant inefficiency in the operation of schools and has obvious and profound implications for the discussion about altering school finance arrangements. . . . Evidence about spending variations is generally irrelevant for either an equal protection or an educational disparity challenge in court. Such evidence about differential expenditures simply does not indicate differential quality of education.[1]

This chapter was adapted from Aubrey Price, *Education Production Functions in Policy Making: A Critical Analysis* (Doctoral dissertation, Virginia Tech, 1994).

The conclusion that money and educational quality are unrelated finds its research foundation in production-function studies. Production-function studies in education have a 30-year history. The production-function or input–output analysis is a model of relationships based on the economic theory of U.S. industry. It requires the measurement of precise increments of resource inputs that yield specific increments of production outputs. The model is a valuable tool for planning industrial production. The unity of theoretical design, empirical analysis, and practical result has been basic to the development of the production-function model. In education, however, wide variations in the use of the model in empirical studies under very diverse conditions have resulted in confusing and contradictory results. Unfortunately, premature claims about the efficacy of this analytical tool for policy making can result in counterproductive decisions that reduce the efficiency and productiveness of schools.[2] Yet policymakers cannot ignore the opportunity to develop a more precise understanding of the links between resource investment and achievement in education.

Box 15.1 _____

Productivity, A Moving Target

To create the productivity that can justify high wages, American K–12 education will have to improve. Numerous studies have sharply defined the problem. The performance of American high school graduates may have declined, it depends upon exactly how performance is measured, but the real problem is not deterioration. The rest of the world is simply reaching levels of performance far above those ever reached in the United States. This is especially true if one looks at performance standards for the bottom half of the distribution. Even in the good old days, America wasn't very good at the bottom. Blacks that are today left uneducated in America's central cities were yesterday left uneducated in its rural South.

Source: Lester Thurow, _Head to Head_ (New York: William Morrow, 1992), pp. 273–274.

Education production-function analysis began with the Equal Educational Opportunity Report often cited as the Coleman Report for its principal author. The project, funded by Section 402 of the Civil Rights Act of 1964 represented a major comprehensive effort to collect and analyze data on a national scale. The researchers sought to determine the extent to which differing expenditures affected the quality of education with a particular focus on school segregation. The four major questions examined by the study were:

1. The extent to which racial groups were segregated in the public schools
2. The presence of equal educational opportunities by criteria regarded as indicators of quality: tangible characteristics of schools in physical facilities; curriculum areas such as high school tracking; characteristics of teachers including salary, verbal ability, experience, and attitudes; student body characteristics including self-attitudes and academic goals, socioeconomic status (SES), and parent education levels
3. How much students learn as measured by standardized tests
4. The relationship between what students learn and the kinds of schools they attend[3]

These objectives covered most of the areas investigated by the education production-function analysis. Since many readers interpreted the study to indicate that schools had little influence on student achievement independent of family background and general social context, it provided great impetus for further research.[4] This report and the debate it initiated have been the catalysts for much of the research into education cost–quality issues that have employed production-function analyses.[5]

The questions about the influence of financial resources on the achievement of students that emerged from the Coleman Report lie at the heart of two dramas now playing on state education stages: one is the national reform effort that began with _A Nation at Risk_; the other is the wave of state litigation that seeks to reshape education finance and distribute resources more equally among all students.[6] In both dramas in education the use of production-function analysis has provided information to justify the perspectives and decisions of policymakers. For example, during his tenure as U.S. Secretary of Education, William Bennett often referred to research that proved that there was no relationship between school expenditures and student achievement. According to Baker,[7] Bennett was referring to Eric Hanushek's 1986 education production-function study.[8] Also, recent equity suits have involved the litigants in arguments about the importance of financial resources based on education production-function analyses.[9] These examples show the important role such studies have played, and continue to play, in federal and state education finance policies.

Implications for School Finance Policy

The Coleman Report and its genre tend to perpetuate misconceptions about public education, providing ammunition to those who oppose investment in public education on philosophical grounds. The formulation of policy on the basis of a half-formed conceptual methodology can result in faulty policy decisions and undermine support for social science research. Using the findings from education production-function studies to determine important policy issues merely multiplies the errors. More importantly,

though, such research has been used to launch anti-public school attacks that have been deleterious to the adequate funding of education, generally. Premature advocacy of production-function conclusions that are based on poorly specified research models can lead to diversions as expressed by Christopher Edley, Jr.:[10]

> However imperialistic lawyers can be in offering their services and habits of mind in the solution of all problems, economists are even more dangerous with implicit claims that their grossly simplified models should displace the instincts and experiences of professionals, such as educators, who have worked for decades to understand the ingredients of progress. Crucial research must focus not on the empirical analysis of aggregated input–output models, but on the more conventional, less tidy, applied problem of program evaluation and replication. That is how social science can best serve struggling educators and advocates, who ought not to be diverted to rebutting and perfecting flawed economic models.[11]

Does Money Matter?

The fundamental proposition that the quality of a child's education should not be determined by the wealth of the community in which the child lives, translates of course into a quest for equal per-pupil funding. Because most state legislatures failed to resolve the issue, the drive to reform disparate systems entered the state courts.

The erratic findings of production-function studies have been used as a political weapon for those who would perpetuate the inequities that exist in school funding. Hanushek (1991) and others, by showing that there is no systematic relationship between expenditures and achievement, lay the foundation for the bold assertion that "money does not matter." Kozol (1991) in quoting the *Wall Street Journal* that "money doesn't buy better education," notes that "the *Journal* does not tell its readers that the current average figure masks disparities between the schools that spend above $12,000 . . . and the ones that spend less than $3,000 (per pupil).

Many of the poorest schools today spend less than the average district spent ten years ago."[12] Those who read Kozol's book are likely to conclude that the production-function model misses some very important details and of course such a conclusion would be correct. Some production-function studies, however, do document ways in which money makes a difference in the education of children. A study by Ferguson provides an excellent example.[13] The quantity and quality of his data make his findings far more credible than those of most earlier studies.

The desire of the courts for information with which to make informed decisions is understandable. The opportunity for researchers to influence policy is compelling. However, decisions based on the production-function model in its current state can be accurate only by chance. Its explanatory power is problematic, and its predictive ability is without validation.

THE CONCEPT OF PRODUCTION FUNCTIONS

The concept of the production-function model was developed and applied first to industry where it achieved reasonable success. When later applied to education, the production-function model has proven to be both flawed and controversial.

The Industrial Model

The production-function or input–out analysis is a model of the economic relationship between the maximum amount of output that can be produced and the inputs required to make that output. The model is defined for given technological levels that are subject to change differentially. When linked with cost analyses, the production-function model can be used to measure increments of resource inputs that yield specific increments of production outputs at precise cost estimates. The model is a valuable tool for efficiently planning industrial production based on least cost input estimates. "There are thousands of different production functions in the American economy: at least one for each firm and product."[14]

In the early development of the production model, Cobb and Douglas tried to measure changes in the amount of labor and capital used to create a given amount of goods and to determine the relationships between the product, labor, and capital.[15] They quantified the components for a given time and estimated the relationship between factors using regression analysis. Although data collection in the late nineteenth and early twentieth centuries was imperfect, Cobb and Douglas compared the results of their analytical model with information provided from federal government sources enabling the concept to be validated. Today of course, cost and quantity data are abundant for measuring the physical factors in production.

The Education Model

The goal of the education model is to explain the relationships between inputs and outputs that would permit the maximization of student achievement from a given combination of input factors. This approach employs the use of regression analysis for explanatory purposes. Such a use of regression analysis requires the specification of a conceptual model from which the data can be meaningfully interpreted.[16] Variables in the education equation may include some measures of the individual's ability, family, peer, financial, and school inputs with a measure of student achievement as the output factor.

Since precise measures for the inputs do not exist, proxies developed and collected for other purposes must be entered into the regression equation. Proxies are measurable variables that are assumed to correlate highly with a latent, unmeasurable variable identified in the model. The true variables cannot be identified from proxies, only estimated. The qualities and interactions considered in the true variables are not normally purchased in the marketplace.[17] The marginal products identified in the conceptual model refer to the true variables—those which yield output changes when altered, not to proxy variables. Therefore, a true education production function is not available and under present circumstances cannot be known. Any policy decision based on an estimated production function is clearly speculative.

The proxies for each variable in most education models represent a broad range of demographic and economic data.

1. *Family background.* "Income level, SES, parents' education, number of people in the family, the family structure, languages spoken in the home, size of home, indices of parent interest in education, and so forth."[18]
2. *Peer influence.* "Appropriately aggregated vectors of the attitudes, backgrounds, and performances of other students and children which the individual comes into contact with. Empirically this implies using aggregates of proxy measures of home environment."[19]
3. *Initial endowments.* "In empirical work, no measure of initial endowments is available."[20]
4. *School factors.* "Teacher characteristics and attitudes, physical characteristics of the school, curriculum, etc. . . . School inputs to the individual should be analyzed."[21]
5. *Achievement measures.* Mean verbal and mathematics scores on standardized tests were used for separate analyses.

Comparison of the Models

Several features of the industrial model deserve attention because of differences from the education model. Foremost among the differences is the measurement of the marginal product. The marginal product of an input is the additional output produced by a unit of that input when all other inputs are held constant. It is a function of the law of diminishing returns. "The law of diminishing returns holds that the marginal product of each unit of input will decline as the amount of that input increases, holding all other inputs constant."[22] Monk says that the dependency on teachers (hired inputs) epitomizes a reliance on one factor of production that economists would find alarming.[23] Without alternative instructional inputs being available, the theoretical probability is that the marginal product will decline. The education model, however, assumes a linear relationship between inputs and outputs in which there is a constant and unchanging marginal product. In the industrial economic analysis model, the marginal product displays a curvilinear relationship to the input. It is important to identify these fundamental differences between the industrial and the education models so that policymakers do not assume a false equality between them.[24]

Returns to Scale

Another problem in relating the two models lies in the economic concept of "returns to scale." Returns to scale refers to the "responsiveness of total product when *all* the inputs are increased *proportionately*."[25] Economists usually seek to identify increasing, decreasing, or constant returns to scale. Constant returns to scale are assumed to be attainable in most production activities.[26]

One method of addressing returns to scale in education has been through the consolidation of smaller districts into larger ones.[27] The research suggests that larger districts produce lower achievement than smaller districts.[28] The per-pupil expenditures in large cities, however, must address dysfunctional socioeconomic conditions that smaller localities may not have. This comparison of larger and smaller school districts therefore may too often ignore conditions within the districts that work against achievement. For example, the Fairfax County system in Virginia (135,000 ADM in 1993–94) is the largest in the state and

DEFINITION

Returns to Scale. The amount that output will expand if all inputs are increased simultaneously by the same percentage. Returns to scale can be contrasted with *returns to a single input* which is the amount that the output will expand with the increase of just one input, holding all other input quantities unchanged.

Source: William J. Baumol and Alan S. Blinder, *Economics: Principles and Policy*, 4th ed. (San Diego: Harcourt Brace Jovanovich, 1988), p. 521.

produces an enviable record of achievement.[29] Socioeconomic factors in the Fairfax district strongly favor high investment in education and equally high student achievement. Throughout the country, however, per-student costs in the range of district size from 500 to 5000 students tend to differ very little.[30] These results suggest that constant or increasing returns to scale are not the norm in education and illustrate yet another area in which the industrial and the education production-functions models diverge in substantive ways.

Substitutability

The substitutability of elements (input substitution) in the production-function model is a rationale for its use in manufacturing and industry. If the price of one factor falls while other factor prices remain the same, substituting the lower-priced input for another could allow for a reduction in costs without any loss of quantity or quality.[31] To do this, it is necessary to identify inputs that contribute to outcomes, determine how much difference each input makes and its costs, and substitute effective resources for less effective ones.[32] The opportunity to evaluate the substitution of elements in the education model is severely limited. Children require human supervision and guidance, restricting the possibilities of the substitution of capital for labor. Beyond this condition, however, it is a consequence of

the limitations imposed on experimental research within the school setting. From another perspective, it represents the inflexibility of the education model. If classroom level analyses were developed to the point that teacher effects could be assessed, then alternative classroom level inputs might be evaluated.

Moreover, problems with substitutability among education inputs is a consequence of the interpretation of analytical results. "If we find that two variables—an input and an outcome—are unrelated statistically it may be because (a) the data are accurate and in fact the two variables are unrelated; (b) the variables are related but one (or both) of the measures is insensitive (not detecting variance that actually exists) or is producing random values; or (c) the variables are unrelated as the data show, but we have failed to measure a relevant outcome that the input does contribute to in some significant manner."[33]

Teachers remain the most important schooling input. The addition of electronic teaching aids, such as computers, has not reduced the need for professional instruction. The use of paraprofessionals to replace teachers is as close to the concept of substitutability as education has come. The substitution of longer hours in the school day or the extension of the school year into the summer to more efficiently use facilities represent efforts to substitute resources—traditional downtime for building use substituted for the cost of additional facility construction. Un-

DEFINITION

Input Substitution or Substitutability. As any one input becomes more costly relative to other competing units, the firm is likely to substitute one input for another; that is, to reduce its use of the input that has become more expensive and to increase its use of competing inputs.

Source: William J. Baumol and Alan S. Blinder, *Economics: Principles and Policy*, 4th ed. (San Diego: Harcourt Brace Jovanovich, 1988), p. 518.

fortunately, the inability to provide information on resource arrangements within the educational model limits the value of the production-function study to meet the needs of decision makers.

Technological change is the "invention of new products, improvements in old products, or changes in the processes for producing goods and services."[34] In education, technology encompasses the methodology of instruction (processes) as well as the hardware of computers and other media. Education has remained labor intensive as other industries have replaced people with machines. The inability to substitute capital for labor in education makes teacher training a primary means to transform the process. Teacher behaviors, however, lie outside the ability of the production-function analysis to evaluate. Therefore, crucial policy information that could transform the education system also lies outside the purview of the production-function study.[35]

Since the education model lacks direct measures of the variables identified in the conceptual design, and proxies must be selected from available data to serve as substitutes in a regression equation, there is no opportunity to validate the model against data supplied from other sources. A comparison of the estimated production-function model cannot be made with the true inputs since only proxy data are available. Using this kind of comparison with true data enabled Cobb and Douglas to validate and refine the industrial model.[36] The education model, however it may be defined, remains unverified by any objective methodology.

The Cost Side of the Equation

Costing-out variables is a relatively simple task for calculations using the industrial model. The costing-out of variables for the education model remains in a primitive condition, partially because inputs and outputs are not exclusively physical. Efforts such as those of Rossmiller and Ferguson[37] remain promising but relatively unmatched examples of the possibilities of costing-out variables for U.S. schools.

Human Variables

Human variables play a significantly different role in the industrial and education models. Cobb and Douglas recognized that neither the quality of labor nor the intensity of work could be measured quantitatively in their initial application of the industrial model. This is a reasonable certainty for the education model as well. Nevertheless, labor inputs in the industrial model could be quantified and held as a measurable factor to determine the relative input value since other factors were easily quantifiable. Teacher and student inputs remain less easy to quantify. The student is both an input and an output factor. In the industrial model the output commodity is inert and is not an active participant on the input side. The child in school is both an active input and the output commodity in the education model. This dual role of the student in the model adds a confounding characteristic to education production. If one could assume along with the economists that student acquisitiveness was maximized (for knowledge, in the education model, as the equivalent to wealth in the economic model), the problem of student behavior would be less of a conundrum. Such an assumption is difficult to sustain for production functions in the K–12 school environment.

Time as a Cumulative Variable

The use of time in the industrial model is recognized as a continuum on which certain measurable material conditions exist.[38] It is not an independent factor in production. Time affects the definition of an input as fixed or variable (changeable) based on the length of the production planning period.[39] In education, time is a contributor to the product of student achievement. "Time inputs are important determinants of cognitive achievement."[40] Quantitative proxies for specific time inputs may be determined, but the estimate of cumulative effect is unspecified for the short time period or cross-section of time analyzed by most education studies.

The relationship of initial student abilities to achievement in an academic year, for example, can be measured and this may offer a means to evade the problem of cumulative effect, yet since important time factors remain in the control of students (homework time for specific subjects and television time), reliable measures remain elusive. Unfortunately, measures of initial endowments are often excluded from equations. IQ may be challenged as a baseline, because it is demonstrably a changeable measure and time may have a significant unmeasured cumulative effect upon it.[41] Thus, the dynamism and the evolving nature of the human intellectual condition presents a variable that remains unspecified to a degree of reliability.

Teacher Differences

The inability to measure skill differences between teachers who share similar quantifiable attributes such as level of education, years of experience, or certification credentials, is a deficiency in education research and thus in production-function analysis. Differences in teaching styles, strategies, attitudes, and behavior of teachers are likely to be important factors in student achievement. Significantly different amounts of learning do occur in different classrooms in the same school and between different schools. Clearly, teachers and schools can have significant effects on student achievement. Production-function studies are simply unable to capture the behaviors that produce achievement.[42]

Murnane and Nelson argue against the use of production-function analysis in education because of teacher differences.[43] Production-function analysis is based on a standardized process derived from fully articulated and detailed production inputs and techniques that allow very little variation. Teaching is characterized by techniques that are essentially situation-specific and idiosyncratic. Teachers are constantly making production decisions in the classroom about methods, procedures, and materials. This pro-

---

Box 15.3 _____

Methodological Problems

Since the United States' "Coleman Report," a large number of studies have addressed this issue in both developed and developing countries. The results of these "educational production functions" vary widely and are fraught with methodological problems, not least of which are that it is unclear what unit of production to use (individual pupil, classroom, school, school district) and whether the relevant unit of production is maximizing academic achievement or some other output. Neither do any of the studies specify an underlying theory of learning that would define the nature of the school inputs–academic achievement relationship: they all assume that teacher inputs can be measured by teacher characteristics (education, experience, and aptitude), ignoring the way or the degree to which those characteristics are engaged in the teaching–learning process.

Source: Wadi D. Haddad, Martin Carnoy, Rosemary Rinaldi, and Omporn Regel, _Education and Development, Evidence for New Priorities_ (Washington, DC: The World Bank, 1990), p. 50.

---

duces considerable variation in the teaching process. Teaching inherently involves constant experimentation to identify those techniques that will increase student performance in the classroom. Education inputs and techniques gradually evolve as teachers reshape and modify instruction. Research is normally conducted away from the setting of schools and does not capture the realities of the process of constant adjustment and modification necessary to meet the needs of individuals and classroom groups. The problems contained herein are thus obvious and their solutions for production-function model specification are extremely cloudy.

Attenuated Data

Production-function analyses have not generally addressed several other critical problems.[44] While outputs of individuals vary widely, school inputs (i.e., expenditures per pupil) often may not vary greatly at all. When there are small input differences, the effect of the input may not be statistically significant because of the attenuation of variance in the measurement of samples. An example provided by the measurement of the effects of facilities illustrates this point. Hanushek[45] found statistically significant effects of facilities on student achievement in a study of Brazilian education, but he found no such relationship in his earlier studies in the United States. The differences in the resources available in the two settings provide statistical evidence that money does matter in facilities investment when there is a significant variance in the measures compared. When the variance in facilities is reduced (attenuated) by limited measurable differences between the samples, no statistical significance is found. Production-function analyses have rarely addressed attenuated variance, although it is normally present in district-level analyses within states that provide moderate equalization in funding, especially among expenditures per pupil that cluster closer to the mean. Pass/fail measurements of student achievement are particularly vulnerable to the problem of attenuated variance.[46]

Sequence of Inputs

The interaction between inputs can have an effect on output measures. Bronfenbrenner demonstrated that pre-school intervention involving parents and schools can have measurable effects on IQ scores, but interventions that did not involve parents failed to produce measurable effects.[47]

According to Piaget, the sequence of inputs can be important in the acquisition of knowledge. Attempts to teach reading before the child is "ready" will fail. Accordingly, failure to provide learning experiences at the suitable time can limit a child's development. Ethologists and psychologists provide evidence that suggests "windows of opportunity," "readiness," and "critical periods" in the development of individuals. Pro-

duction-function studies have been much too limited in scope to examine such issues. The results of a production-function analysis can fail to assess the presence or absence of important time-related learning inputs that have significant effects on achievement.

Threshold Effect

The need for the application of a certain amount of an input before it produces measurable results is called the threshold effect.[48] The analogy to the "take-off" period in Walt Rostow's *The Stages of Economic Growth* [49] is a useful comparable construct. Certain material preconditions must develop before a society can move into a sustained growth economy. Before these conditions are met, a ceiling exists on the attainable output.[50] Phillips and Marble surveyed 1,548 farmers in Guatemala.[51] The empirical results suggested that a threshold effect of four or more years of education is necessary to produce a measurable effect on agricultural production. Recent analyses by Fortune[52] suggest that a threshold of $600 to $700 per pupil may be linked to measurable achievement differences in otherwise homogeneous school districts in several states where average expenditures per pupil for the state are in the range of $3,500 to $4,500. The threshold would presumably change with the average level of expenditure for the state. While he is careful to explain that such findings are frequently lost in the analysis of very diverse systems, and the amount of money is likely to vary from state to state, the evidence of a threshold effect that relates student achievement to financial resources is a new and interesting perspective. Previous studies have not examined these possibilities.

Variations in Variables

Most education production-function analyses select from a common set of variables. Studies include some or all of the following on the input side of the model formula: characteristics of the home or family, the community, peers, individual students, and the school or district. Such examples indicate the current dilemma in selecting appropriate measures that have impact on student achievement. Variable selection contributes to the discrepancies that exist in the results of empirical studies, although it is by no means the sole explanatory element.

Selecting variables for a production-function model is a decision complicated by the need to measure the variables. No one simple, direct, and complete measurement exits for family characteristics or any of the other variables. Consequently, a variety of existing measures or proxies are used to operationalize the constructs. The following lists taken primarily from Lau[53] is reasonably thorough.

Home background (family characteristics) may include: IQ, age, education, income, occupation, race, religion, attitudes, expectations, preferences, or values of either or both parents; the structure and stability of the family; the number of siblings; and locational stability. Indicators of the home learning environment may include: possession of books, radios, and televisions; frequency of travel; and knowledge of foreign languages. Direct home inputs to the learning process could include the time that either or both parents, an older sibling, or even a tutor devoted to the instruction of the students being assessed.

School characteristics include the type of school (public, parochial, private), type of curriculum, level (K–12), size, ethnic composition of enrollment, class size, per-pupil expenditure, or method of instruction. Direct inputs may include facilities or specific features such a science laboratories or libraries; administrators—quantity, quality (degree, experience, or other accomplishments), attitudes, and other attributes (including IQ or verbal ability, knowledge of subject, ability to communicate, responsiveness to questions); and teacher time inputs to preparation, lecturing, student consultation, and grading. Instructional methodology emphasized in the school must be measured and may include: traditional forms, instructional television, computer-assisted instruction, or variations and combinations of these or other technical processes.

Community characteristics are intended to measure the degree of support for education. The type of neighborhood; size of the city; degree of community interest; attitudes, average age, education, income, and socioeconomic status (SES) (described by some measure of community wealth) of the community; and property value are among the measures selected. In some studies the peer group variable is incorporated into community characteristics.

Student characteristics include: measures of ability (IQ), age, aptitudes, race, sex, birth order, number of siblings, and previous educational achievements on standardized tests. Measures of subjective conditions that may affect achievement such as attitudes, interests, motivation, self-concept, self-expectations, and values have been used. Student time inputs to homework, class attendance, laboratory work, or self-study have been used.

Peer group characteristics are selected from the proxies for student and community characteristics. The influence of peers is included because of the effect on individual student achievement. These characteristics also influence teacher classroom behavior. These proxies may shift from one category to another in different studies. SES is determined by another measure such as personal income or percent of free lunch depending on whether the SES of the student body (peers) or the community is the variable. Without belaboring the obvious, studies on the proxies selected for variables may produce results that are significantly influenced by the proxies selected rather than the actual variables.

Statistical Procedures and Problems

Nearly all education production-function studies use a variation of regression analysis.[54] Linear model equations (ordinary least squares) have been the predominant tools of analysis. Stepwise regression, variance-partitioning, commonality analysis, and path analysis have also been used. Simultaneous equations (two-stage least squares) procedures have been employed with greater frequency recently. Ferguson[55] used this procedure in his analysis of Texas data. Thompson and Correa[56] tested for significant differences between groups before utilizing regression procedures. Subhypotheses were tested using four-way analysis of variance.

Regression analysis may be used for prediction or explanation. In education, the purpose has been to explain the variation in student achievement on the basis of the inputs selected for the model. The ultimate goal is to be able to predict the effect of inputs, to calculate the cost of changes to these inputs, and to maximize student achievement for the lowest cost. The percent of the variance in the dependent variable explained by the regression model, and the amount of change in the dependent variable (student achievement) for a unit change in each independent variable, however, do not represent causal relationships in education.[57] The researcher is forced to recognize the speculative and uncertain nature of the findings from such an analysis.

Experimental Conditions

Aside from the lack of hard data from measurable material relationships, education research is plagued by a basic problem: lack of experimental conditions. Experimental conditions allow the researcher to randomly select treatment and control groups to test hypotheses. A random sample is one that is selected by chance from a larger population. When this principle is followed, the assumption can be made that the presence of any characteristic or subgroup will be as large or small in the sample as it is in the population at large. This principle is the foundation for any conclusions the research can form about the larger population from the sample selected and analyzed.[58] The education researcher must work with students, classrooms, schools, or districts that cannot be altered to meet the needs of the researcher. Even a project as huge as that conducted for the Coleman Report could not avoid the claim of systematic bias in the final result.[59] Without the opportunity to randomize the samples with which a research study is conducted, the findings are diminished in power and reliability.[60]

Model Specifications

"The general term for the description of the variables and the model is *model specification*. . . . The true model is the starting point in all of our developments and the frame of reference by which to judge results. But the exact and correct formulation is not always known. The theories of the social scientist are usually not developed to the point of giving a complete model specification. . . . Nor can one always expect to have the required data. . . . Both of these situations, incomplete theories and incomplete data, can lead to specification errors."[61] Specifically, an important variable may be left out of the model, or it may be included in the model, but no satisfactory measure may exist for it. In his study, Coleman did not include a measure of the innate ability of students. He thus conducted his empirical analysis without an important variable. Therefore, a specification bias exists in the estimated regression coefficients for this analysis. Such a specification error will tend to bias the results.

THE COLEMAN REPORT'S FLAWED DATA AND ANALYSIS

The Coleman Report has been a major influence on governmental policy. The influence of this study, however, goes beyond its effect on policy. The report has had a pervasive influence on production-function studies as a data source. Because the report was interpreted to mean that schools have little or no independent effect on the education of children beyond the influence of family and peers, it has been subjected to considerable analysis.

Hanushek and Kain[62] provided a substantive critique of the Coleman report in which they described problems that undermined the reliability of the report's data and analytical procedures. While the plan for data collection was enormous, many difficulties plagued the project. The student sample size of 900,000 was reduced by non-response to 569,000. The failure to link students to specific schools limited the accuracy of the analysis. Further, reductions in usable data resulted in stratification by grade, race, region, and rural/urban divisions. Nonresponse was a major problem since 41 percent of 1170 schools were not included in the study. The issue of systematic nonresponse was not addressed in the study, so the conclusions may be misleading. Since many sensitive questions were not answered, many questionnaire items relating to qualitative conditions were unusable. Cross-checking showed many miscoded responses. The frequency of such errors raises doubt about the reliability of the Coleman survey data in general.[63] Other concerns involved the failure to ask questions about the quality of facilities, to collect information on per-pupil expenditures, and to collect data on school organization.

Employment of analysis of variance as the statistical methodology, as the Coleman researchers did, is a useful analytical procedure if no relationship exists between independent variables, and if they are indisputably independent without any correlations between them. Unfortunately, when the variables have high correlations, as they do in social research, multi-colinearity makes interpretations of analysis of variance exceedingly difficult. Frequently, interaction terms become the most significant source of variance between samples and must be explained if the research is to provide meaningful information. The method of analysis of interaction variables was highly questionable in the Coleman Report, however. The order of variable entries in the equation was a major factor in the results since interaction variance was added to the first term entered into the equation, weighing its explanatory power unjustifiably and inaccurately. Family

background was entered first and school inputs last. Thus, family background consumed explanatory powers that may have belonged to schooling. The temporal order by which a student experiences the variables may not have a necessary relationship to the way interaction terms are distributed. Indeed, the main issue is how interaction effects should be partitioned among explanatory variables. In fact, since interaction effects could not be partitioned, the Coleman Report assigned all the interactions to family background. They could as easily have been assigned to school inputs. Hanushek and Kain[64] also found that there was not enough independent variations in the school factors, which resulted in attenuated variance. The absence of any measure of student ability undermined the conclusion. Since within-school variance is much greater than between-school variance, school inputs may vary more significantly within schools than between them. The authors of the report suggested this possibility, but the issue was not researched.

Teachers were not considered a school input in the report. Systematic departures of variables actually used in the analysis from those in the conceptual design were greatest for school inputs. For example, a 12th grade student is likely to have attended many schools and experienced wide differences in educational experiences to a much greater extent than in peer and family experiences. The heterogeneity of student experiences in schools represented by vocational and college preparatory tracking obscures the variability of school experiences as reflected in mean standardized test results and school-level input aggregations.

According to Hanushek and Kain, the finding by Coleman of little school effect is a result of the method of analysis and not the "underlying behavioral reality." Such a conclusion is "dangerous and destructive" as policy. "The extent to which minority groups are systematically discriminated against in the provision of educational inputs is still unknown. This is a serious matter since the correction of input inequalities is a logical and necessary first step in insuring equality of opportunity for minorities."[65]

In summary, the sample size of the study was reduced by a 41 percent nonresponse rate. Systematic nonresponse appeared to occur, particularly on sensitive issues. Many responses were miscoded and the frequency of such errors raised doubt about the reliability of the data in general. Information was collected about per-pupil expenditures, school organization, and the quality of facilities. In fact, the report found little difference between schools that were predominantly black or white. The data did not provide information on students by school, so that the value of a large sample was significantly reduced. Finally, the researchers stated no theoretical model with which to interpret the data.

OTHER PRODUCTION-FUNCTION STUDIES

Burkhead compared small-community high-school achievement to that of Chicago and Atlanta.[66] He described the education formula as an exploration, not a true production function. Unlike the industrial model, he recommended changing factor combinations to find the best configuration for increasing education output. This study included a value-added approach in the Chicago and Atlanta studies. He described three levels of resource use: acceleration, perpetuation, and amelioration. Acceleration referred to the practice in Atlanta in the early 1960s of investing more money in wealthier, higher-achieving white schools. The perpetuation design involved equal expenditure across all students. This maintained the existing condition in achievement reflected in the Chicago schools of the period. Amelioration required greater investment in schools for lower-income and lower-achieving students. His study demonstrated the importance of family income in student achievement. To improve student performance, he found it necessary to break the linkage of educational inputs to community income levels. If family income could not be changed, improvement in school outputs required dramatic increases in inputs or significant changes in re-

source combinations. This proposition could lead to the assumption of an unidentified threshold effect for breaking the link between family income and student success, as well as leading to experimentation with resource combinations in educational production.

Hanushek[67] emphasized the importance of production-function studies in policy decisions. His central concern was the education of minorities and the ability of education to cure the conditions of minorities in income, jobs, and life expectancy. Hanushek was careful to identify the problematic nature of conclusions from his analyses.

Because of the complexity of high-school production functions and the difficulty of assessing cumulative factors in student performance, Hanushek examined elementary schools. He collected data at the individual school level in one of his three analyses. The other two studies were based on data from the Coleman Report.

Hanushek assumed that a public institution is inefficient because it does not operate in an openly competitive market. Incentives do not exist for the efficient maximization of resource use or educator performance. The production-function study could identify, with greater precision than existing methods, where efficiencies could be achieved. Hanushek defined efficiency as consisting of two elements: knowledge of the relationship between inputs of the educational process, and a research decision that connects costs of various inputs of the educational process to their educational outputs. Armed with this knowledge, policymakers could mix resources in ways that would be efficient and productive for student achievement. He conducted three studies that suggested areas of inefficiency in the purchase of teacher experience and additional education. Schools were incapable of curing the condition of minorities without changing the pattern of expenditures.

Rossmiller[68] evaluated public elementary school classrooms in relation to equity and efficiency. Analyzing data at the classroom level enabled Rossmiller to examine the achievement of students who directly received specific resources at precise costs. Time utilization, school expenditures, home environment, and teacher characteristics and attitudes were all carefully studied. Money and time correlated negatively with achievement because of the greater application of these resources to assist lower-achieving students. This suggested a trade-off between economic efficiency and efforts to ameliorate student achievement deficits.

Thompson and Correa[69] researched a specific cohort of students in a private elementary school setting. They rated the cumulative effect (over three years) of certain input variables on student achievement. Using Glasman and Biniaminov (1983) as a reference, they found differential effects of these variables on private and public school students. As in public school analyses, teacher and school variables played a minor role in the prediction of variance in student achievement. Student academic ability was more important than school inputs. Teacher fluency, academic degree, and annual salary correlated with higher math achievement in contrast with achievements of public school students in both reading and math. Class and school size correlated negatively with private school achievement, but positively in some public school studies. The authors concluded that "caution should be used when applying the results of effective school research conducted in the public school directly to the private schools."[70] The results of this private school study, where there is a competitive market, did not differ in any significant way from the results of public school analyses.

Ferguson[71] used an unusually large and complete data set from 900 districts in Texas that provided information on a student population five times that of the Coleman Report. Using a district-level analysis, Ferguson examined the determinants of student test scores, factors that influence which districts attract the most effective teachers, and how and why money matters in student achievement.

According to Ferguson, money is important in producing higher student test scores when it

Box 15.4 _____

Indefensible Use

In my view, it is simply indefensible to use the results of quantitative studies of the relationship between school resources and student achievement as a basis for concluding that additional funds cannot help public school districts.

Source: Richard J. Murnane, "Interpreting the Evidence 'Does Money Matter'?" _Harvard Journal on Legislation_ 28, no. 2 (Summer 1991), p. 457.

purchases teachers with strong literacy skills, reduces class size to eighteen students per teacher, retains experienced teachers, and increases the number of teachers with advanced degrees. In addition to equalizing funding per pupil, ameliorative programs for low SES districts could include state-subsidized higher pay for teachers in lower SES districts. Good teachers are attracted to higher SES districts and the salaries they pay. Offering salary subsidies is a market decision that would encourage higher quality teachers to accept the challenge of teaching in difficult conditions. Possibly this could begin to break the link Burkhead found between family income and student achievement. This study uses other recent research to undermine the basic conclusion of the Coleman Report and the findings of less data-rich studies about the impact of teacher quality on student achievement.

IMPROVEMENT OF PRODUCTION-FUNCTION STUDIES

At the very least, an education production-function model requires that variables be manipulable and predictable. The questionable validity of the model remains the overriding concern for the usefulness of the production-function analysis in education. A means must be found to fashion a valid model before production-function studies can be taken seriously as policy instruments. Subsequently, a particular model must be designed for each specified educational setting.

There may be a different production function for every individual, school, or district.[72] Quality variations in inputs refer in part to differences of type. Some inputs are fixed for long periods of time, such as basic facilities and type of school (elementary, middle, or high, and public or private); some are variable in the long run but fixed in the short run, such as teacher characteristics; some are variable in the short run, such as teacher and student time. No one manager controls all these inputs, yet every actor influences their effect on the production function. For production-function studies to be of any value for policy purposes a means must be found to validate the model in a given setting. To do so requires much greater attention to overcoming difficulties in the identification and quantification of inputs.

The findings of empirical studies have been challenged for mixing levels of analysis between district, school, classroom, and student. Model adequacy requires uniformity of level. The important question to address, however, is the appropriate level for an accurate, policy-useful model. Some researchers have concluded that "there probably aren't many policy manipulable predictors of academic achievement much above the level of the individual classroom."[73] Since this is the locus of direct school inputs to each student's education, it is not a surprising conclusion. It would, however, render most research in the area invalid for policy purposes.

The collection of data at the classroom level is the direction research activities must take in order to develop a useable production-function model. That is not to say that other levels of analysis cannot be valid. It only appears that the sequence of development is best pursued inductively.

Determining the contribution of school factors to student achievement became an important research objective in the wake of the Coleman Report. The recognition of the need for a measure of ability or achievement as a pretest score is also a vital concern in the development of an adequate model of education production. Lau[74]

and others have acknowledged the "uninformative" nature of cross-sectional studies that lack such measures. Bowles described achievement scores as measures of gross output. The goal was "to estimate the relationship between school inputs and *net* output, or value added."[75] Measures that allow the assessment of value-added performance are generally regarded as important components of an adequate model. The lack of such data seriously impairs the usefulness of empirical studies.

The development of an adequate model requires the purposeful collection of data that have a direct relevance to a conceptual production-function design. A national testing program could provide the impetus for such a collection process. Yet a strong movement among educators challenges the adequacy of quantitative measures of student achievement. The development of a broad-based qualitative methodology for student evaluation through portfolio building has begun to spread across the country. This approach is partially based on dissatisfaction with purely statistical appraisals. For this reason alone, any effort to collect national data for production-function analyses would probably face vigorous political opposition.

SUMMARY AND CONCLUSIONS

In this chapter we sought to present the concept of production functions and to identify some of the shortcomings of such studies in their application to education. The discussion explained how poorly conceived model specifications and research design have led to baseless conclusions about both adequacy and equity of funding for public schools. The production function's use in industry as compared to education helps to clarify some of the problems of directly applying a rather simple industrial concept to a complex social phenomenon like education. The production-function model is an industrial model and its application to education requires a specification and precision of measurement that is difficult to quantify.

The use of poorly specified production-function analyses in education have led some researchers to erroneously conclude that money has little bearing on the quality of education.

Foremost among the production-function studies was the famous Coleman Report that was widely quoted as evidence that more funds for education would not increase the educational achievement of students. While the Coleman Report was often misquoted, it was nevertheless a poorly designed and carelessly analyzed project that has very little continuing educational research value.

The education production-function process is of such a complex nature that it is safe to say that no production-function study has yet been designed to accurately capture the value of increments of fiscal inputs. The elusiveness of both inputs and outputs in education prevents the researcher from measuring direct inputs and outputs. Instead the researcher is forced to use proxy variables that introduce varying degrees of invalidity.

Education productivity does not track the industrial model in several ways, but two of the most troublesome areas are the failure of measurement for returns to scale, and the issue of substitutability. Neither apply as readily to education as to the industrial situation.

A primary difficulty in most education production-function studies is the inability to relate costs directly to the educational process. Most such studies have aggregated data by school district or school rather than by classroom. Also, such cost data have often included expenditures for aspects of education that are not applicable to the particular educational function being analyzed. Such studies have also been unable to capture the changes over time. Most have constituted mere cross-sectional views of the educational process.

One major shortcoming of production functions when applied to education is the inability to capture the essence of the teaching process itself. So little is known about what constitutes effectiveness in teaching that measurement is problematic at best.

The characteristics of the home backgrounds, the students themselves, the schools, and the community all bear on the educational process, but their relative magnitude and importance is virtually impossible to discern.

Production-function studies in education could be useful if models of measurement were so specified as to reveal reliable and valid results. To date however most such studies have major flaws that greatly limit their value. Unfortunately, such studies regardless of their accuracy have been misconstrued and sometimes misappropriated in an attempt to influence public policy choices in education. Having poorly conceived models accepted as the basis for important educational investment decisions or as a deterrent to school finance reform are the chief dangers presented by the present crop of production-function studies.

KEY TERMS

Production function

The Coleman Report

Socioeconomic status (SES)

The industrial model

The education model

Returns to scale

Substitutability

Model specification

Causality

ENDNOTES

1. E. A. Hanushek, "When School Finance 'Reform' May Not Be Good Policy," *Harvard Journal on Legislation* 28, no. 2 (Summer 1991), pp. 425 and 442.

2. D. H. Monk, *Educational Finance: An Economic Approach* (New York: McGraw-Hill, 1990); D. C. Berliner, "Educational Reform in an Era of Disinfor-

mation," *Education Policy Archives: An Electronic Journal,* vol. 1, no. 2 (1993).

3. J. S. Coleman, Ernest Campbell, Carol Hobson, James McPactland, Alexander Good, Frederick Weinfeld, and Robert York, *Equality of Educational Opportunity* (Washington, DC: Government Printing Office, 1966).

4. E. A. Hanushek and J. F. Kain, "On The Value of Equality of Educational Opportunity as a Guide to Public Policy," in F. Mosteller and D. P. Moyniham, eds., *On Equality of Educational Opportunity* (New York: Vintage Books, 1972).

5. J. Coons, W. Clune, and S. Sugarman, *Private Wealth and Public Education* (Cambridge, MA: Howard Belknap, 1972); and E. A. Hanushek, op. cit., pp. 423–456.

6. National Commission on Excellence in Education, *A Nation at Risk* (Washington, DC: U.S. Government Printing Office, 1983); Educational Testing Service, *The State of Inequality* (Princeton, NJ: ETS, Policy Information Center, 1991).

7. K. Baker, "Yes, Throw Money at Schools," *Phi Delta Kappan* 72, no. 8 (April 1991), 628–631.

8. E. A. Hanushek, "The Economics of Schooling: Production and Efficiency in Public Schools," *Journal of Economic Literature* 24 (1966), pp. 1141–1177.

9. Testimony of H. J. Walberg, "In the Matter of *Raymond A. Abbott, et al.* vs. *Fred G. Burke, et al.*, 100 N.J. 269, 499 A.2d 376," State of New Jersey Office of Administrative Law, EDU-5581-85 (Roseland, NJ: Essex-Union Reporting Services, April 27, 1987); J. C. Fortune, *Rebuttal to the Deposition of Eric A. Hanushek,* unpublished document (Blacksburg, VA: Virginia Tech, 1992).

10. C. F. Edley, Jr., "Lawyers and Education Reform," *Harvard Journal on Legislation* 28, no. 2 (Summer 1991), pp. 293–305.

11. Ibid., p. 296.

12. J. Kozol, *Savage Inequalities: Children in America's Schools* (New York: Crown, 1991), p. 133.

13. R. F. Ferguson, "Paying for Public Education: New Evidence On How and Why Money Matters," *Harvard Journal on Legislation* 28, no. 2 (Summer 1991), pp. 465–498.

14. P. A. Samuelson and W. D. Nordhaus, *Economics,* 13th ed. (New York: McGraw-Hill, 1989), p. 499.

15. C. W. Cobb and P. H. Douglas, "A Theory of Production," *American Economic Review Supplement (*1928), pp. 139–165.

16. E. J. Pedhazur, *Multiple Regression in Behavioral Research: Explanation and Prediction*, 2nd ed. (New York: CBS College Publishing, 1982).

17. E. A. Hanushek, *Education and Race: An Analysis of the Education Production Process* (Lexington, MA: D.C. Heath, 1972).

18. Ibid., p. 27.

19. Ibid., p. 27.

20. Ibid., p. 30.

21. Ibid., p. 31.

22. P. A. Samuelson and W. D. Nordhaus, op. cit., p. 501.

23. D. H. Monk, op. cit.

24. S. Bowles, "Towards an Educational Production Function," in W. L. Hansen, ed., *Education, Income, and Human Capital* (New York: National Bureau of Economic Research, 1970); G. R. Bridge, C. M. Judd, and P. R. Moock, *The Determinants of Educational Outcomes: The Impact of Families, Peers, Teachers, and Schools* (Cambridge, MA: Ballinger, 1979).

25. P. A. Samuelson and W. D. Nordhaus, op. cit., p. 503.

26. Ibid.

27. D.A. Verstegen, "Efficiency and Economies-of-Scale Revisited: Implications for Financing Rural School Districts," *Journal of Education Finance* 16, no. 2 (Fall 1990), pp. 159–179; H. J. Walberg and W. J. Fowler, Jr., "Expenditure and Size Efficiencies of Public School Districts," *Educational Researcher* 16, no. 7 (1987), pp. 5–13.

28. Ibid.

29. *Outcome Accountability Project: 1992 Virginia Summary Report* (Richmond, VA: Virginia Department of Education).

30. H. J. Walberg, "The Knowledge Base of Educational Productivity," *International Journal of Educational Reform* 1, No. 1 (January 1992), pp. 5–15.

31. P. A. Samuelson and W. D. Nordhaus, op. cit.

32. G. R. Bridge, C. M. Judd, and P. R. Moock, op. cit.

33. Ibid.

34. P. A. Samuelson and W. D. Nordhaus, op. cit.*,* p. 506.

35. H. J. Walberg, op. cit.

36. C. W. Cobb and P. H. Douglas, op. cit.

37. R. Rossmiller, *Resource Utilization in Schools and Classrooms: Final Report* (Madison, WI: Wisconsin Center for Educational Research, University of Wisconsin), (ERIC Document Reproduction Service No. ED 272 490), 1986; R. F. Ferguson, op. cit.

38. C. W. Cobb and P. H. Douglas, op. cit.

39. J. M. Henderson and R. E. Quandt, *Microeconomic Theory: A Mathematical Approach* (New York: McGraw-Hill, 1971).

40. L. J. Lau, "Educational Production Functions," in *Economic Dimensions of Education* (Washington, DC: The National Academy of Education, 1979), p. 42.

41. D.C. Berliner, op. cit.

42. E. A. Hanushek, op. cit.; R. J. Murnane, *The Impact of School Resources on the Learning of Inner City Children* (Cambridge, MA: Ballinger, 1975).

43. R. J. Murnane and R. R. Nelson, "Production and Innovation When Techniques Are Tacit," *Journal of Economic Behavior and Organization* 5 (1984), pp. 353–373.

44. G. R. Bridge, C. M. Judd, and P. R. Moock, op. cit.

45. E. A. Hanushek, *Education and Race*, op. cit.

46. J. C. Fortune, D. C. Strickland, and A. H. Price, "Methodological Differences in the Use of Educational Productivity Function Analyses," in *Proceedings of the 11th Annual Conference of the Association of Management* 11, no. 1 (1993), pp. 53–58; A. H. Price, D. C. Strickland, and J. C. Fortune, "A Critical Review of Walberg and Hanushek's Contribution to School Equity Issues," in *Proceedings of the 11th Annual Conference of the Association of Management* 11, no. 1 (1993), pp. 80–85.

47. Urie Bronfenbrenner, *Ecology of Human Development: Experiments by Nature and Design* (Cambridge, MA; Harvard University Press, 1979).

48. G. R. Bridge, C. M. Judd, and P. R. Moock, op. cit.

49. Walt Rostow, *The Stages of Economic Growth* (Cambridge, MA; Cambridge University Press, 1971).

50. G. R. Bridge, C. M. Judd, and P. R. Moock, op. cit.

51. J. M. Phillips and R. P. Marble, "Farmer Education and Efficiency: A Frontier Production Function Approach," *Economics of Education Review* 5, no. 3 (1966), pp. 257–264.

52. J. C. Fortune, D. C. Strickland, and A. H. Price, op. cit.

53. L. J. Lau, op. cit.

54. J. A. Thompson and L. H. Correa, "A Study of School and Teacher Inputs on Student Achievement Outputs," *Journal of Education Finance* 14 (Winter 1989), pp. 390–406; F. MacPhail-Wilcox and R. A. King, "Production-Functions in the Context of Educational Reform," *Journal of Education Finance* 12 (Fall 1986), pp. 191–222; F. MacPhail-Wilcox and R. A. King, "Resource Allocation Students: Implications for School Improvement and School Finance Research," *Journal of Education Finance* 11 (Spring 1986), pp. 416–432; N. S. Glasman and I. Biniaminov, "Input-Output Analyses of Schools," *Review of Educational Research* 51, no. 4 (Winter 1981), pp. 509–539; G. R. Bridge, C. M. Judd, and P. R. Moock, op. cit.

55. R. F. Ferguson, op. cit.

56. J. A. Thompson and L. H. Correa, op. cit.

57. E. J. Pedazur, op. cit.; L. J. Cronbach, G. C. Gleser, H. Nanda, and N. Rajaratnam, *The Dependability of Behavioral Measurements: Theory of Generalizability for Scores and Profiles* (New York: John Wiley & Sons, 1972).

58. D. C. Howell, *Statistical Methods for Psychology*, 2nd ed. (Boston: PWS-Kent, 1987).

59. E. A. Hanushek and J. F. Kain, op. cit.

60. D. C. Howell, op. cit.; Pedhazur, op. cit.

61. E. A. Hanushek and J. E. Jackson, *Statistical Methods for Social Scientists* (New York: Academic Press, 1977).

62. E. A. Hanushek and J. F. Kain, op. cit.

63. Ibid., p. 121.

64. Ibid.

65. Ibid., p. 131.

66. J. Burkhead, *Input and Output in Large-City High Schools* (Syracuse: Syracuse University Press, 1967).

67. E. A. Hanushek, *Education and Race*, op. cit.

68. R. Rossmiller, op. cit.

69. J. A. Thompson and L. H. Correa, op. cit.

70. Ibid., p. 406.

71. R. F. Ferguson, op. cit.

72. D. H. Monk, op. cit.

73. K. T. Hereford and T. Z. Keith, *Effects of Local Financial Effort on School District Achievement* (Blacksburg, VA: Virginia Tech, 1991), p. 27.

74. L. J. Lau, op. cit.

75. S. Bowles, op. cit., p. 26.

INDEX